THE BURNING BUSH

RUDOLF STEINER, ANTHROPOSOPHY AND THE HOLY SCRIPTURES

An Anthroposophical Commentary on the Bible

TERMS AND PHRASES : VOLUME I

THE
BURNING BUSH

EDWARD REAUGH SMITH

ANTHROPOSOPHIC PRESS

Published by Anthroposophic Press
3390 Route 9 Hudson, NY 12534

Library of Congress Cataloguing-in-Publication Data

Smith, Edward Reaugh, 1932–
    The burning bush / Edward Reaugh Smith.
        p. cm. — (Rudolf Steiner, anthroposophy, and the Holy Scriptures.
Terms and Phrases ; v. 1)
    Includes bibliographical references and indexes.
    ISBN 0-88010-449-X (hardcover). — ISBN 0-88010-447-3 (pbk.)
    1. Anthroposophy.   I. Title.   II. Series: Smith, Edward Reaugh, 1932–
Rudolf Steiner, anthroposophy, and the Holy Scriptures.
Terms and phrases ; v. 1.
BP595.S895S57 1997
299'.935—dc21   97–18340
                                                              CIP

10 9 8 7 6 5 4 3 2 1

Printed in the United States of America

CONTENTS

Acknowledgments

Foremost of my enablers is Jo Anne, the bride of my youth, who makes all things possible.

To Mary at the Press, who steered me in early readings, became a cherished advisor and friend, and contributed her expertise in the final steps of bookmaking, my debt is inestimable.

To Press editor Chris Bamford, who first seriously encouraged me, led me step by step in this my initial book-length publication, orchestrated the many necessary helping hands, and stood by through a time of great personal loss, words alone fall short.

To special editor, Will Marsh, Thoreau-like in simplicity and devotion, for countless suggestions and corrections, always modestly advanced even from his depth of professionalism, and for his unselfish personal commitment to the cause of this work, my admiration and thanks are great.

To Beth at the Rudolf Steiner Library, I am beholden, for without her tireless and cheerful assistance in shipping, box by box, unpublished or out-of-print English translations of Steiner's works to me, I would not have had access to a substantial portion of Steiner's work.

To René Querido who alerted me to the existence of the late Karl Koenig's study on the two disciples John (unpublished in English), and then to Christof-Andreas Lindenberg who chanced me worthy to inspect a copy of its typescript, goes the credit for many of the incredible scriptural insights in the essay "Peter, James and John'" building upon Steiner's own legacy, that would otherwise have escaped my attention.

To the talented young professional reader, Gene Talbott, to my friend, Norton Baker, who is far more to me than my longtime law partner, and to my busy but ever so diligent and talented friend, W. Frank Newton, Dean of the Texas Tech University School of Law and current President of the State Bar of Texas, my thanks for their invaluable criticisms of the manuscript.

Finally, to those new and old friends of the cloth from a spectrum of main line Christian confessions whose professional lives would be most affected by the theological adjustments this work suggests, my sincere thanks for time sacrificially squeezed from heavy clerical demands and for comments and insights of great value.

The art work on the cover is by Julia Tucker Franklin, the author's niece. It portrays the following image of the burning bush given by Philo in his On the Life of Moses, I:

THERE WAS A BUSH OR BRIAR, A VERY THORNY PLANT, AND VERY WEAK AND SUPPLE ... ENTIRELY ENVELOPED ... BY THE ABUNDANT FLAME, ... IT NEVERTHELESS REMAINED WHOLE WITHOUT BEING CONSUMED, LIKE SOME IMPASSIBLE ESSENCE, AND NOT AS IF IT WERE ITSELF THE NATURAL FUEL FOR FIRE, BUT RATHER AS IF IT WERE TAKING THE FIRE FOR ITS OWN FUEL.

PREFACE

THIS IS THE FIRST VOLUME of a series envisioned as a complete Bible commentary based upon the "anthroposophical" understanding given to humanity by Rudolf Steiner during the first quarter of the twentieth century. Bible commentaries have always reflected the general line of thinking of their authors. However, the dramatic newness of anthroposophical thought means that perhaps the usual method of using a Bible commentary will not be appropriate here. A large part of the present work must necessarily be devoted to laying an anthroposophical groundwork. This is necessary since a major assumption indulged in other commentaries—that one can go directly to portions dealing with given passages of scripture and understand what is being said about them—does not fit.

Anthroposophy was founded, and is essentially based, upon Rudolf Steiner's prophetic intuition of the spiritual world. That world's character as Steiner explains it, so foreign to worldly thinking, is profoundly and pervasively reflected in the Bible when its words of spiritual art are given their deeper occult meaning. Anthroposophy shows that the reading of the Bible in its common understanding, as wonderful as that can be, does not reveal its deeper message—one that gives its perplexingly difficult sections and passages deep spiritual meaning as part of a uniform theme consistent from Genesis to Revelation. Consequently, this work undertakes in its first several volumes to examine key terms and phrases that in themselves, when anthroposophically understood, cast the Bible in an entirely new light, one that can stir the soul with indescribable joy and lift it to a new level of understanding and eventually to a higher consciousness.

An inspection of the list of terms and phrases in this volume reveals that about two-thirds are recognized as part of our conventional Christian theology. The rest are different. They show that the Bible says things that powerfully build a beautiful integrity of the whole account. The whole array here is substantially different from non-anthroposophical approaches that have been advanced previously.

The second volume goes more deeply into a smaller number of terms and phrases. It deals at the outset with the related Alpha and Omega, creation and apocalypse, Genesis and Revelation; then with the intensely critical mystery of the "Blood." It also addresses such vital Biblical concepts as Fire, Light and Darkness, and the deep significance of the classical Four Elements. It presents the unity between these spiritual concepts and true science, ending with the relationship between the heavenly bodies and the human being longingly sought in the Biblical cry, "What is Man?"

As an interlude in the "Terms & Phrases" series, Vol. 3, *Companions Along The Way*, presents a number of writings, both anthroposophical and non-anthroposophical, classical and contemporary, significantly cognate to Steiner's own works. It also gives a substantial condensation of the "basic books" of anthroposophy.

The present volume, *The Burning Bush*, is probably the best place for the normal beginner to start a study of this larger work. However, more or less concurrently with reading the first essays, the reader will probably find it essential to go through about the first twelve or thirteen items in the Charts & Tabulations section, giving heaviest consideration to the first one. References to the Charts & Tabulations are in bold print, e.g., **I-1, I-33**, etc. It is most important that one be able to hold concepts tentatively in mind as individual building blocks until a sufficient structure can be seen to take shape.

As a practical matter, this approach required an initial decision about how the extensive cross-referencing in the final work should be handled in serially published volumes. While it is intended that each volume will be, to the maximum extent possible, a stand-alone book, it is also intended that each will fit into a final set as originally envisioned.

This first volume includes the comprehensive Bibliography in which I have endeavored to list all Steiner's works that have been translated to English, whether or not published, but undoubtedly there are many I have not listed. Other relevant works are also included.

The student of anthroposophy soon comes to realize that Steiner's works, either individual lectures or lecture cycles, are often cited not by title but by date and location (city). The complete Steiner works are to be found only in archives in Dornach, Switzerland, at the headquarters of the international Anthroposophical Society. They are in German and are catalogued according to a "GA" number. Often only this reference is given, but it is of less use to those readers in the English language, and no attempt is made in this work to reference the GA number. Another caveat about titles remains. Frequently more than one English translation of a given Steiner work exists, and it is not unusual for these to be given different titles. The Bibliography, in such cases, will include only one, which will be identified (other translations will not generally be identified).

These are some of the reasons why an alphabetical arrangement of the bibliography, insofar as it lists Steiner's works, would be less useful than a chronological one, and why the latter has been chosen. There are five categories of bibliographical references following the chronological Steiner list, all of which are arranged alphabetically. The first of these are anthologies of Steiner's works. This is followed by a section on Steiner biographies, which are also found in the alphabetical section that follows it. Other anthroposophical writers, non-anthroposophical writers, and treatises and other reference materials compose the final three.

All references are assigned an abbreviation. With the exception of treatises and other reference materials (the last category above), the first time a work is referred to in an essay in the Terms & Phrases section, its title is given followed by its abbreviation. Thereafter, within the essay only its abbreviation is used. A cross-reference table is given at the first of the Bibliography. In it the abbreviations for all Steiner titles are arranged alphabetically. Opposite each abbreviation is the date to be used in locating the full citation in the chronological list.

Generally when a term or phrase is put in quotation marks with initial capital letter(s), it refers to that term or phrase as elaborated in the "Terms & Phrases" volumes. The serial method of publication means that many terms and phrases will be referenced before the volume where are to be found has been published. This can alert the reader to a special significance pending ultimate publication. The extensive cross-references may be jumped over in an initial reading, except where the student feels compelled to stop to examine them, and left for more thorough study on a later reading. Their purpose is to assist in eventually tying things together rather than to confound or disrupt at the beginning.

Finally, a word about the avoidance of sexist writing. This appropriate modern policy had not evolved at the time of Steiner's works or of some of the writings in the *Companions* volume. In these and elsewhere, when quoting directly from another source, we do not modify the quote. It is in the nature of the topic that the English words "man" and "mankind" recur constantly in the generic sense in Steiner's works. Their appropriate counterparts must be carried forward herein, but in so doing they are converted to "human being" and "humanity," respectively. The neuter "it" is used in reference to the human being.

GENERAL INTRODUCTION

A SIGNIFICANT PREMISE OF THIS WORK is that the "parable"[1] of the Prodigal Son (Lk 15,11-32) is an allegory in which Christ crystallizes the full Bible message. This vivid story is a microcosmic presentation of what is macrocosmically expressed by the full Bible account. Both speak eloquently of the human condition. But it was only after discovering the anthroposophical understanding of Rudolf Steiner that I came to see both accounts of outgoing and return as expressions of the human being's own evolutionary journey, itself macrocosmic. In both we see the theme of two sons, one of whom leaves home, loses the original inheritance, comes to self-knowledge, and returns home transformed. One account consists of seventeen verses, the other of an entire canon.

The origin of the human being was in the spiritual world untold expanses of time and timelessness ago. Leaving home, it descended farther and farther into matter in a long process of solidification or densification. This descent, if left alone, would have doomed human beings, but at the right time it was arrested and reversed by the Christ, whose descent and incarnation on Earth made human beings' reascent possible. The Bible, when seen in anthroposophical light, tells us of this journey. All of its parts then fit together beautifully, seeming contradictions are resolved, and otherwise perplexing passages radiate new splendor— as does the larger whole, now connected, closed into an effulgent orb like the Sun.

The following are but a sampling of the dramatic new understandings of scripture that come with anthroposophical insight:

---

1. Modern theology has often taken the position that this scripture is a parable, as distinguished from an allegory, and that as a parable it can have only one meaning. In such cases, that meaning is normally taken to be an illustration of the nature of the Heavenly Father's divine love. That is certainly not here denied, but such love is seen as being simply part of the meaning the much larger allegorical picture presents.

1. The essential structure of the human being, and how it is disclosed in scripture over and over again;

2. The meaning and enormous significance of Isaiah 6, especially of Isaiah's mandate, quoted in all Gospels, the conclusion of Acts, and in Romans, to tell the people that they would see but not see, hear but not hear, and not understand;

3. The disappearance of the many apparent discrepancies between the birth narratives of Matthew and Luke, and the relationship of these birth stories to each other;

4. The meaning and significance of the genealogies in Matthew and Luke, which have otherwise thus far been unexplained and, by apparent consensus, generally ignored by theology;

5. The meaning and significance of the virgin birth, the immaculate conception, and the perpetual virginity of Mary;

6. The meaning and significance of the passage about the twelve-year old Jesus in the temple, and of the Simeon and Anna passages that precede it;

7. The distinction between Jesus of Nazareth and Jesus Christ, and when the former became the latter;

8. The unity of Gen 1-3, which is a single, sequential account of the human being's creation, not two separate accounts from different sources (normally called the "Yahwist," or "Y," and "Elohist," or "E"); and the meaning of the numerous seeming instances, there and later, of dual stories in an amazingly different light;

9. Why the documentary hypothesis of the synoptic Gospels is also without a significant basis in truth;

10. The reason for the superior status of the Gospel of John, and the identity of its author;

11. Why the apparent discrepancies between the four Gospel accounts, and especially between the synoptics and John, are not in fact such;

12. The difference between "the law" that Christ spoke of fulfilling in Mt 5,17 and what is pointed to as "the law" in the Old Testament, and how the latter is merely a passing shadow image of the former;

13. A portrait of the three New Testament John beings (exclusive of John Mark and Peter's father), namely, the Apostle John (son of Zebedee),

the disciple whom Jesus loved, and the Baptist, and their relationship to each other and to the authorship of the Johannine corpus;

14. For the first time in theological history, a rational and consistent explanation of the Apocalypse of John and its authorship, showing not a book reflecting persecution, but one reflecting past and future human evolution;

15. The nature and consequence of the forgiveness of one's sins by Christ and/or by his disciples (then or now);

16. The higher meaning of the "parable" of the "Prodigal Son";

17. The meaning of Paul's "first and second Adam," and how they are reflected in Luke's Nativity account;

18. The scope and meaning of Paul's foreseen redemption of all creation spoken of in Rom 8,19-23;

19. The meaning of the "fading splendor" of Moses' face and the shortcomings and ultimate end of all written scripture (2 Cor 3);

20. For the first time, the true meaning of the Mystery of Golgotha and how it has worked for the salvation of the human being and of the other kingdoms;

21. The nature of the resurrection, and of the second coming of Christ, and when and under what circumstances each occurs;

22. The human being's relationship to the stars and other heavenly bodies, and how this is disclosed in scripture.

23. The extensive scriptural manifestation of the truth that each person has lived and will live many times before attaining the necessary perfection, and where and how the truth of karma and reincarnation is reflected, and why it was not to be taught by the church until present times;

24. The distinctly different meaning, in such areas as function, term and effect, of the important but heretofore theologically baffling and generally avoided topics "judgment of the Father" and "judgment of the Son";

25. The significance of the ancient "four elements," their relationship to the "four ethers," why some characteristic of "fire" is generally present in the Bible whenever a spiritual being is directly perceived by a human being, and why Christ came to cast fire upon the Earth;

26. The course of the human being's spiritual journey between one life and the next incarnation, and how it is reflected in scripture;

27. The true nature of the relationship between male and female, and how it changes;

28. The true nature of the reality of evolution, and of the fact that animals are a by-product of humanity's evolutionary descent and that the human being is not evolved from any animal;

29. The nature and significance of such misunderstood works as the Song of Solomon, Jonah and Job;

30. A better understanding of the unity of the apparently bipartite or tripartite book of Isaiah.

31. The higher meaning of the phrase "born again," and its relationship to the path that "few find;"

32. The identification, nature and function of the various levels of the spiritual Hierarchies between the human being and the Trinity, of which the Angels are the lowest and the Seraphim the highest, and how these are reflected in the human being and in all creation;

33. Profuse evidence, not heretofore generally recognized, that Paul is indeed the author of the book of Hebrews; and

34. An understanding of why, even though individual acceptance of Christ is essential, there is no such thing as individual salvation apart from that of the rest of humanity and eventually of all the kingdoms of creation.

To repeat, this list is only a sampling. The revelations go far beyond these examples, but they will suffice for now.

From the perspective of human development, a thousand years from now Rudolf Steiner will be looked upon as the evolutionary equivalent of Abraham.[2] Such, at least, is my belief. These two led humanity, so to speak, at times respectively equidistant from the incarnation of the Christ, the former during the human being's parabolic descent from the spirit world, the latter during its struggle to reascend thereto. Each served as the faithful agent of the Christ. The essential work of each was a

---

2. See fn 3 and related texts in "Second Coming."

remarkable departure, primarily of a spiritual nature, from his "homeland" (Gen 12,1-3, Mt 19,27-29, Mk 10,28-30, Lk 18,28-30), without large entourage or notable fanfare.

No thinking reader will accept the above uncritically, nor should such be done. It is only presented here to suggest the scope of newness and magnitude represented by the works of Rudolf Steiner. But how can this be, when even to this date, the name of Steiner hardly sparks any recognition, at least in the English-speaking world? There are at least four reasons for the lack of recognition: 1. His teachings do not fit neatly with much ecclesiastical dogma; 2. His works are so extensive and interrelated that great commitment of time and effort is necessary to comprehend them; 3. The world conditions were not conducive to the spread of a German's spiritual teachings beyond the borders of Europe—two world wars involving his country separated by the direst economic conditions in his native land in the twenties and then worldwide in the thirties, followed after World War II by the greatest explosion of materialism the world has ever known; and 4. Not until 1965 were even small volume printings of any of his works available in English, and even now perhaps less than a third of the number of his total works can be purchased in the English language, and only if one knows where.[3]

While to a very large degree Rudolf Steiner's powerful revelations carry within themselves the unique conviction of authority, particularly for those highly conversant with both scripture and phenomena, sooner or later the serious student must look intensely into his life story to evaluate the sources of his insight. Extensive biographical resources for that search are available. The following paragraphs taken from the Introduction by Christopher Bamford to the recent *Anthroposophy in Everyday Life* (AEL) will serve as a brief sketch of Steiner and the milieu into which he was placed:

A major task facing humanity as it moves into the new millennium is that of uniting spiritual and practical life.

---

3. The diminutive exposure of the United States to Steiner's works is disclosed by the figures. According to a recent pamphlet by Christopher Bamford and Michael Dobson, the roots of the Anthroposophic Press (the principal source of Steiner's works in the United States) go back to 1916. But by 1965, the cumulative sales of the Press from inception were only $1,500. By 1981 sales had increased to a level of $200,000 annually, still a pittance considering the volume of Steiner's work and the relatively small number of books which such volume could represent. While larger now, our groaning times demand far more.

In the Middle Ages—the time of Christendom—science, art, religion, and society were still to a great extent united. Untold monks and nuns labored and loved mightily for the sake of God and the world. Their lives of prayer and devotion, centered around the Eucharist, kept the interior flame of worship burning brightly. Radiating outward, the spiritual consequences of their steadfastness resonated throughout the landscape, impregnating villages, towns, and cities with a sense of the divine presence in the world.

At this time, too, great Cathedrals and humble churches alike filled ordinary people with the understanding that every aspect of life participated in God's purpose. Scholars, philosophers, scientists, and crafts people—all of whom contributed to the creation of a sacramental vision of the world in which each thing and every human act were imbued with spiritual significance—gathered around these Houses of the Spirit, amplifying its effectiveness.

This pervasive sense of the sacred also existed in earlier, pre-Christian times, when the priests and hierophants of the ancient Mystery Centers and Temples coordinated human culture in a way that permitted the spirit to realize itself in the manner appropriate to the moment. But, with the rise of the Modern Age, a powerful cleft was driven between human beings, nature, and the divine. We may call the process "secularization." Religion and spiritual life became increasingly marginalized. Instead of spiritual realities, human beings pursued this-worldly ends, such as comfort and wealth. Thus, gradually, the thread connecting saints and esoteric masters with the general life of humanity was broken; meaning fragmented; and the sacramental relation of human beings to each other and the cosmos ceased to function. Materialism in its many guises—positivism, Darwinism, Marxism etc.—now became the guiding principle in science and society. Religion and culture—religion and the state—were separated and spiritual, religious life became a question of individual responsibility.

This was a heavy burden to bear for individuals who had not only to create a spiritual life for themselves, but increasingly had to do so in opposition to the very quarters from which help might have been expected. For, as society plunged into materialism, the Churches, not wishing to be left out, joined willingly in the descent. There were, of course, exceptions to this tendency, but such generally was the situation at the beginning of the twentieth century when Rudolf Steiner (1861-1925) began to teach, initially under the auspices of the Theosophical Society.

As a natural clairvoyant, of great spiritual gifts, Steiner began his journey by assimilating the best of what the culture of his time had to offer. He chose for himself a scientific-technical education. At the same time, realizing the need to transform our present consciousness so that it might become a vehicle of spiritual knowledge, he undertook a phenomenological study of the processes by which we come to know—what is called "epistemology." Up against the pervasive influence of the philosopher Kant, who maintained that we could never truly know anything in itself but only our own forms of thought, Steiner knew from his own experience as a free spiritual being that the possibility of brain-free thinking lay within the capacity of human beings who thus could know truly and fully the world's actual spiritual reality. In two central early works—*Truth and Knowledge* [TK] and *Intuitive Thinking as a Spiritual Path* [originally, *The Philosophy of Freedom*, and then in America, *The Philosophy of Spiritual Activity* (PSA)]—he laid the ground for what he would accomplish in the future. He was greatly helped in this work of preparation by prolonged study and meditation on the scientific works of Goethe, which he was asked to edit for a new edition of the Complete Works—the Kurschner "*Deutschen Nationaalliterature*" edition. From this, too, a series of fundamental, ground-breaking texts resulted [*Goethean Science* (GS), *Goethe's World View* (GWV) and *The Science of Knowing* (SK)].

During this period, though already initiated into his spiritual task, Steiner was still very much a free thinker of his time. Then, as he wrote in his *Autobiography* [*The Course of My Life* (CML)], "shortly before the turn of the century," a profound experience was given to him: an experience that "culminated in my standing in the spiritual presence of the Mystery of Golgotha in a most profound and solemn festival of knowledge." This experience marked a call. Shortly thereafter, he left the literary and philosophical world of letters and joined his destiny to the movement for the renewal of spiritual knowledge in our time.

The tasks lying before him were manifold. In order to undertake them, he realized that, acting wholly and freely out of the spirit, he would also have to connect himself horizontally with the various traditions flowing together to herald the possibility of a "new age of light."

He linked himself first to the Theosophical Society founded by H. P. Blavatsky, becoming the Secretary of the German Section. From the very beginning, he made complete independence and autonomy the condition of his taking on this task. Thus, as an independent spiritual teacher, working within the Theosophical Society, Steiner began to lecture freely from his own experience on spiritual matters. At the same time, he began to work more esoterically—transforming the legacy of masonic, hermetic, and esoteric Christian streams and taking on esoteric students. From this period (1904-1910) date what would become the basic texts of Anthroposophy [*Christianity as Mystical Fact* (CMF) in 1902, *Knowledge of the Higher Worlds and its Attainment* (KHW), *Theosophy* (THSY) and *Occult Science, An Outline* (OS) and the previously published PSA (1894)]. But Anthroposophy itself, under that name, would not arise as a separate, independent spiritual movement until 1913 when, as a result of the controversy surrounding the young Krishnamurti—whether he was, or was not, the reincarnation of Christ [Steiner himself denying such]—Steiner split permanently from the Adyar theosophists.

From the beginning, Steiner saw his task as the rescue of humanity from materialism and secularism. He knew that for evolution—the divine work of the Gods—to continue in an organic, healthy direction, the world and human beings—which are essentially not two, but one—must once again be seen and lived as the profound spiritual reality they are. The task of Anthroposophy, he recognized, could not proceed piecemeal, but called for a renewal of culture as a whole—a bringing together of science, religion, and art in a sacred unity. It was in this sense that Steiner described the work of Anthroposophy as the renewal of the ancient Mysteries. But renewal here does not mean repetition. The old must die away for the new to come into being. But it cannot simply be replaced by something already known, no matter how illustrious or well tested. Rather, something new must be created. But such a new revelation can no longer be received passively from the Gods, as was the case in previous epochs. It must now be created by, in, and through human beings.

Two basic ideas pervade Steiner's work, namely, the essential nature of the human being, and the evolution of consciousness. Subsumed particularly under the second is the reality, indeed the absolute necessity, of karma and reincarnation. That the reality of karma and reincarnation is sensed by such a large segment of Western humanity today is merely evidence of the spiritual stirrings of our time. But what is generally said about it must be extensively modified and expanded to come into harmony with anthroposophical understanding. When this is done, it shall be seen to be not only in complete harmony with the Bible story but expressed in and inexorably demanded thereby. Indeed, both "basic ideas" are profusely manifested by the scriptural account as radically new insight into its meaning takes shape. One who comprehends such insight can take new hope for humanity and for the universal power of the essential Christian message.

In anthroposophical understanding, the human being, in its most condensed portrayal, is threefold, made up of body, soul and spirit. The "body" is then seen to be made up of three interpenetrating elements or "sheaths"—in fact to be "Three Bodies"—namely, physical, etheric (also called life) and astral (manifesting as sense, passion and the like). Only the physical can be seen by the sensual eye, and this only because the spiritual physical form has been filled out by mineral substance. (Implicit in this statement is the first hint of what is theologically known as "the resurrection body," the spiritually physical form emptied of its mineral substance). The other two "bodies" can be known from their manifestations, but are actually more real than the physical. We humans have physical bodies in common with the mineral kingdom, etheric (life) bodies in common with the plant kingdom, and astral bodies in common with the animal kingdom. Thus, insofar as their earthly presence is concerned, the animal is comprised also of three "bodies," the plant of two, and the mineral of only one. It is only through coming to a fuller understanding of these three "bodies" that many scriptural mysteries can be understood.

There is, however, a fourth element that makes the human being unique as the crown of creation. It is the Ego, or the "I Am," the self-consciousness that enables each human being to say "I" and to have a sense of continuity of that "I." The Ego here is not the Jungian ego, which is the personality; the Jungian term for the individuality is the Self. In anthroposophy, the Ego or "I Am" is the eternal *individuality*, the "burning bush" as we shall see, while the *personality* is its embodiment in a particular incarnation. A personality is unique in the sense of never having lived before nor ever living again after this life, but the individuality manifests again and again in appropriate personality-form during the course of its own evolutionary perfection.

The human Ego is the "soul" in the body-soul-spirit makeup. The soul is the mediator between body and spirit, receiving impressions from the outer world through the body and reshaping them through the three human activities of thinking, feeling and willing. Actually, each element is itself again threefold so that, in its largest presentation, the human being is ninefold. The eternal soul, being central, is enabled by taking into itself the Christ to work from life to life in the evolutionary task of perfecting, one by one, its lower three bodies into its higher three components that compose the perfected human spirit. At this eventual point, one has attained to the resurrection in the ultimate sense, having returned full cycle to the point from which the human journey began in the spiritual world. We said at the outset that Christ condensed the sixty-six or so books of the Bible into seventeen verses in the account of the Prodigal Son. He then condenses the human journey from seventeen to a single verse in Mt 13,33, "The kingdom of heaven is like leaven which a woman took and hid in three measures of flour, till it was all leavened."

The development of the higher human components requires many lifetimes on Earth. After death, the physical body dissolves into the mineral world, the etheric body into the etheric world, and, after a period of purification (sometimes described as "judgment," "burning," "refiner's fire" or terms of similar import), the astral body into the astral world. But an extract is saved from the etheric and astral bodies, the transformed fruit of the experiences of the immediate past life. This unites with the immortal Ego. Together they become a "Seed" that now begins a sojourn in the world of spirit, where its spiritual elements will be built up. There, in accordance with the extract or fruit of the past life the Ego, with the help of spiritual beings, creates an archetype of a new human being, the personality it can become in its next earthly life. Thus the destiny or karma of the next life is determined by the accumulated fruits of an Ego's past lives on Earth. And through its deeds on Earth, a human being can evolve more and more into a spiritual being. Because an individual's actions also have an outer effect on other human beings and on the life of the Earth, these deeds also contribute to the spiritual evolution of humanity as a whole.

As indicated, inherent in this whole out-and-back journey of the Prodigal Son is a changing human consciousness. In its earliest condition of consciousness, the human being dwelled in the spiritual world with, was interpenetrated by, and felt itself at one with the Hierarchies (the "Heavenly Host"). What is described by Moses as the "fall" from the "garden" was infection of the human astral body, before the entry of the Ego and moral responsibility, with the Luciferic urge for sensual experience and knowledge. From this point, ever so slowly over vast eras the human being descended into materiality, and the spiritual world "hid its face" more and more. At the outset, memory was near perfect but individual intellect did not exist. As the human Ego approached the three bodies, conscious communion with the Hierarchies faded and human beings began to associate, first in families, then in tribes or groups. Individual identification did not exist separate from these. Memories and loving relationships were carried by the blood lines. Only gradually did tribal consciousness give way to individual consciousness. Its announcement was most dramatic to Moses on Mt. Sinai: "I Am the I Am." But Moses scarcely comprehended what was happening. He still represented the fading light of ancient clairvoyance, or, as Paul said, his was a "Fading Splendor." The seraphim painfully revealed to Isaiah that the ancient ability to "see, hear and understand" was disappearing, to return only after long ages of torment. Still, he, along with Jeremiah, the Gospel writers and Paul, realized that the day would come when a new insight would be given directly to each human being. This could not happen unless the descent of humanity were arrested and reversed, a deed that could only be accomplished by the incarnation of the Christ on Earth and the shedding of his blood before humanity had hardened beyond redemption.

The loss of consciousness is additionally expressed by the end of ancient prophecy—vision was darkened, and awareness of the eternal nature of the individual Ego was lost. It was essential that for two millennia humanity forget the reality of its nature in order to concentrate on the importance of each individual life on Earth. But those who gave us the scriptures were themselves aware of the recurring lives of the individual Ego, and buried this knowledge within the scriptures themselves in such a way that it would be uncovered and recognized when the time was right. For humanity was not, at the time of Christ, ready for all that would be later revealed.

Commensurate with the fading of ancient clairvoyance and memory capacity, human intelligence increased. But it was an intelligence associated with the material world, shut off from the direct revelation of spiritual consciousness. This change of consciousness was accompanied by the development of individual identity in place of fading group identity. Egoism was born and flowered, and will be the cause of much tragedy still. Recognition of the true nature of the Christ and of human salvation is imperative for those who would escape its clutches. The purpose of anthroposophy is to enable that recognition and to encourage the pursuit of its demands. As yet, that goal is still in the distance, but there is evidence of spiritual readiness among much of humanity.

Far from being a book from minds crazed by persecution, and likely having no direct relation thereto, St. John's Apocalypse is shown by anthroposophy to be not only a recapitulation of the creation, but a picture of what lies ahead in the evolution of humanity on the return leg of its journey. Those who understand and follow the Christ in his crucifixion of the flesh will again gain clairvoyance, but this time with individuality infused by the Christ so that once again it will become possible to unite not only with all of humanity, but indeed with all of creation and eventually in full consciousness with the Hierarchies. The redeemed of humanity will then become the "gods" spoken of by the prophets and by the Christ.

Overview

RUDOLF STEINER ASSERTS that his writings and lectures do not in any way depend upon the content of the Bible, but upon his own perceptions in the spiritual world. While his unusual biography suggests a most unique and exalted personality, the vast domain, prodigious output and authoritative character of his life work, in the form of writings, lecture cycles and sacrificial service, demonstrate the autonomy of his source and the verity of his assertion. And so, Steiner says, it was only after his own investigations into the spiritual world that, taking up the Bible, he found it to be true in the fullest sense of the word as a matter of direct personal knowledge. One who is intimately familiar with the Bible and delves deeply into Steiner's works can hardly fail to see, cloaked in ordinary language not in any way apologetic of the Bible, the most marvelous insights into scripture. From 1908 through 1914, Steiner gave considerable attention in his lectures directly to portions of the Bible, most notably the Gospels, Genesis 1-3, and the Apocalypse. But in truth, from the breadth of his works, the entirety of the Bible comes into focus with ever more breathtaking clarity. One feels the truth because the revelations concur with and explain the phenomena while striking rich chords within the soul.

Unfortunately, the immensity of Steiner's output has constituted an impregnable bastion against intrusion by any other than the most committed seekers. Traditional Christians have either passed by the fortress walls unaware, or gone on their way after but brief encounter, while anthroposophists have seldom shown extensive independent familiarity with the Bible and the traditions of its interpretation. It is as though soul mates sit divided by a wall, oblivious of each other, yet desperately in need of one another. The goal of the present undertaking, as grossly limited and imperfect as it must be, is to bring back to the traditional Christian side of the wall, whence I came, knowledge of that deeply Christian soul mate on the other side. The reader who is willing to take a fresh and unprejudiced look at the Bible may find, as I have, a new source of radiant life and hope, not only for self but for humanity and indeed for all creation.

Much terrain lies ahead. Let us oversimplify for now.

Simple research, e.g., 12 Brit 555, "Week," shows, as does Steiner, that the names of the days of our week represent the long ages, i.e., "days," of creation, and that this ancient knowledge antedated Moses but was perceived by him and related to some extent in the Biblical account. Three ages have preceded our present Earth stage:

Old Saturn	Saturn's Day	Saturday
Old Sun	Sun's Day	Sunday
Old Moon	Moon's Day	Monday

These were "Conditions of Consciousness," prior to any materialization such as could have been detected by a present-day human being. Each Condition passed into a state of rest, in effect dying to be reborn in a condition of enhanced newness. The fourth such stage, or Condition of Consciousness, is that of Earth. The part of Earth evolution prior to the Incarnation of Christ is represented by Mars, the part since by Mercury, appropriately called "the morning star" in Rev 2,28. Our simple research confirms that Tuesday is Mars' Day and Wednesday is Mercury's Day. Earth (i.e., our solar system) will die or pass away and be reborn in the ennobled Jupiter Condition of Consciousness—this is Jupiter's (Thor's) Day, or Thursday. Today's senses will be of no use there, just as they were of no use in those Conditions prior to Earth, but consciousness will greatly increase. The Jupiter Condition will then expire phoenix-like into the Venus Condition, represented by Venus' Day, Friday. The seventh and final Condition, within the scope of spiritual investigation, is that called Vulcan, the octave, for it is the mirror image of the first stage in humanity's creation and descent, when its perfection will be attained and all the lower kingdoms redeemed. These Conditions of Consciousness are what the largest available spiritual lens shows to constitute the seven pillars (Prov 9,1). But each Condition is again and again divided into seven, so that enormous eons of time interspersed by timelessness are involved in the marvel that humanity, with all its entanglement, represents.

All of this emanated from the "Word" of God, which is recognized as the Christ. We are told that it was "with God in the beginning" (Jn 1,1), and if we visualize Christ as "the Son" of God, the Eternal Masculine, then there was also from the beginning (Prov 8,22) the fruitful Eternal Feminine, the highest and holiest "Virgin" aspect of the Spirit.

Between this Trinity (here, at this stage, considering the Eternal Masculine and Feminine as still divinely One) and Humanity were the Hierarchies, a major part, at least, of the Heavenly Host. The Hierarchies are ninefold, being in three ranks of three. The highest rank comprises, in descending order, and using their names as reflected in scripture, the Seraphim, Cherubim and Thrones; the second rank (though variously ordered by different Christian authorities) comprises the Dominions, Powers and Authorities; and the third rank the Principalities, Archangels and Angels. Steiner gave each of these a name in keeping with its character in the creative process. The Greek terminology corresponded with the English terms, but it is noteworthy that the Hebrew term for "Authorities," or for the "Exusiai" in Greek, was "Elohim," the plural term used for God in Gen 1. Yahweh was one of the seven Elohim, the one who sacrificially took up abode on the Moon while the others served from the Sun. Careful attention to the Genesis account will clearly reveal this. Notably the Elohim were, according to Steiner, called "Spirits of Form," and thus in the final materialization of the Earth Condition they were the gods who served most directly as the divine agents, and in the case of Yahweh, of the particular "Form" of the Hebrew Folk. St. Paul can be considered the source of the high knowledge of these Hierarchies. It is he who used their Christian names, and he was the high teacher of Dionysius the Areopagite (Acts 17,34), who formed the School of Athens. In keeping with the ancient occult tradition, its teachings were oral, but they were finally reduced to writing by "Pseudo-Dionysius" around the early sixth century. Dante's divine vision also gave the Hierarchies, and they were well known among eminent Christians, including Aquinas, until the sixteenth century when materialistic Christianity lost this spiritual view of the universe.

The earliest creation of humanity, which was during Old Saturn, began with the sacrifice by the Thrones, and thereafter through all the stages humanity and its lower kingdoms came into being through progressive sacrifice by the descending orders in the Hierarchies, it being a sacred law that not only human beings but beings at even such high levels advance only by sacrificing themselves, that is, dying to be reborn at higher spiritual levels.

The makeup of the human being is threefold, fourfold, sevenfold or ninefold, depending upon how it is viewed. These are demonstrated by the following tabulation from Chart **I-9**:

Threefold	Fourfold	Sevenfold	Ninefold
	Physical	Physical	Physical
Body	Etheric	Etheric	Etheric
	Astral	Astral	Astral
			Sentient Soul
			Intellectual
Soul		Ego	(Mind) Soul
			Consciousness
			(Spiritual)
			Soul
	Ego		
		Spirit Self	Spirit Self
		(Manas)	(Manas)
Spirit		Life Spirit	Life Spirit
		(Budhi)	(Budhi)
		Spirit Man	Spirit Man
		(Atma)	(Atma)

The essential nature of the body and soul components is as follows:

Component of Human Being	Essential Nature of Component
Ego	Lasting or eternal Individuality
Astral body	Seat of consciousness, passions & desires
Etheric (Life) body	Seat of life
Physical body	Seat of, or pattern for, mineral accumulation

The ninefold division corresponds with the nine Hierarchies and is reflected in the nine Beatitudes as well as in the nine characteristics of the "one like a son of man" (Rev 1,13-16). The sevenfold corresponds with the seven "Conditions" represented by the days of the week. The fourfold corresponds with the "Four Elements" and with the four Conditions that have existed thus far, namely, Old Saturn, Old Sun, Old Moon, and Earth. Finally, the threefold represents the threefold division expressed by Paul in 1 Thess 5,23, "body, soul and spirit." In fact, all such multifold divisions are merely different ways of referring to the same entity.

The fourfold human of Earth evolution is composed of three bodies (physical, etheric or life, and astral or sense) plus an Ego. The physical body is not synonymous with the mineral body, for the latter is an attribute of the physical only during Earth evolution. A comprehension of this distinction is essential if one is to understand the physical body as the "resurrection body." The physical body had its origin on Old Saturn, the etheric or life body on Old Sun, and the astral or sense body on Old Moon. Not until Earth evolution were these joined by the Ego—the "I Am." The existence of these bodies is represented profusely in hidden language in scripture. The physical is the oldest and most perfected, the Ego the youngest and most immature, the etheric and the astral fall progressively in between. The Animal Kingdom has the three bodies on Earth, the Plant Kingdom the older two, and the Mineral Kingdom only the oldest, the physical. Each lower kingdom has the other bodies, as well as the Ego, but only in the higher worlds (to be more fully explained in due course). Human beings did not evolve from the lower kingdoms; the latter evolved as by-products, so to speak, of human evolution. Human beings came first, but descended into mineral materiality last. Thus, the skeletons, fossils and remains of the lower three kingdoms, in succession, demonstrate themselves to archaeology, whereas the skeletal remains of humanity are of but recent origin without any connecting link to its origin existing in mineral form.

Earth evolution, or the Earth Condition of Consciousness, is itself progressively divided and subdivided again and again into seven stages, as shown in different ways in **I-1**, **I-2** and **I-3** in Charts & Tabulations in this volume. Each level, at its outset, recapitulates what has gone before but on a higher plane. It is important for us to see, for instance, particularly as we approach the conditions revealed in Gen 1,2, that this phenomenon applies to the first three "Evolutionary Epochs" of the Mineral Physical Conditions of the earthly Condition of Consciousness. The Polarian, Hyperborean and Lemurian Epochs respectively recapitulate the Old Saturn, Sun and Moon Conditions of Consciousness. These three Conditions represent the following stages of "descent" of the human being into materiality:

Body Formed	Related Element
Physical	Earth (i.e., solids)
Etheric	Water (i.e., tangible fluids)
Astral	Air (i.e., gas)

However, each element moved a notch further toward materiality, "densification," with each progressive Condition. Thus, not until the fourth stage was there any "Earth" or solid matter. What was Water in the third stage became Earth in the fourth, and so on. So, in the third Epoch of Earth evolution only Water, Air and the fourth element, Fire (i.e., heat), existed, the Fire having been created first.

It is these three elements that we find in the Elohistic account in Gen 1,2. There is water, air ("wind" or "spirit") and fire (heat, represented by the concept of "brooding," like a hen "brooding" over the eggs in her nest). This "heat" is related to what mysteriously causes the human body, for instance, to regulate its own temperature; it is not the "heat" spoken of by the so-called physical sciences, which include mineralization in all the elements so that "heat" is merely more active solids. At the time of Gen 1,2 in the third Epoch of Earth evolution, "Form" did not yet exist, for the Elohim were only recapitulating the prior stages. But Earth evolution came under the special province of this order of the second rank of Hierarchies, the Authorities, Exusiai or Elohim, appropriately "named" by Steiner the "Spirits of Form." At all levels the Hierarchies truly reflected what came from above so that the highest levels were indeed involved through the agency of the respective lower levels. In the same manner, the Yahweh-Eloha, from the Moon, truly reflected the spiritual light of the Christ from the Sun. The material reality of moonlight is merely the earthly reflection of the higher spiritual reality.

In the earliest stage of Earth evolution, the Polarian, the Earth was of an enormous size, made up only of fire or heat but containing all that became our present solar system. The second stage, the Hyperborean, was a period of densification and shrinking, and the Sun separated out from the rest to provide the higher spirits an abode, leaving the lower beings a denser home. In the third stage, the Lemurian, the Moon also separated out, taking the lowest beings and the densest materialization with it, along with Yahweh-Eloha, the primary guiding Spirit in the Formation of the Earth. The formation of the other planets from the original fireball is beyond the scope of this overview. Only after the separation of both the Sun and the Moon could human beings descend to the Earth, but their form was grotesque and comprised as yet nothing solid. Not until Gen 3,17 was there an "Adam," which means "hard human being." The progressive densification prior to that time had resulted in no bones and thus no ability to rise upright.

The physical, etheric and astral bodies of human beings were progressively bestowed during Earth evolution in the first three Epochs (but nothing solid). Thus, in the third, that of Lemuria, human beings were huge in dimension (not unrelated to the "giants" or "mighty men of old" in Gen 6,4). Through the passions and desires of their astral bodies, and the fluidity of their denser etheric and physical bodies, they were able to control the Elements, and their uncontrolled passions brought about mighty catastrophes of fire that eventually destroyed ancient Lemuria. The account of the fall of the human astral body is given in Gen 3, where we witness the transition, after the "deep sleep" period (Gen 2,21) intervening between Lemuria and Atlantis, from the fluid to the earliest solid condition of humanity in "Adam." The human being was originally both male and female (Gen 1,27 and 5,2).

The separation of the androgynous human being into different sexes (Gen 2,18-25) came toward the end of Lemuria, corresponding with the "Fall." As yet, the human being had no indwelling Ego, hence, like an animal, no consciousness of sin. But from what would have been the rank of an Archangel, Lucifer, meaning "light," disobedient to the higher spirits, desired to bring the "light" of the "tree of knowledge" to the human being. The account of this Fall of the human being and the Archangel Lucifer is given in Gen 3. By virtue of this, the human being's astral body was no longer pure but rather infected by "original sin," a sin invested in it through the Luciferic spirits before it even became a responsible being conscious of sin.

Prior to this time, the human being dwelt in the bosom of the gods and rather fully perceived their presence and divine guidance. Death was unknown for consciousness was uninterrupted. But by virtue of this fall, the human being was severed from the "tree of life" (Gen 3,24), and began to experience pain, suffering, toil and death (i.e., returning to dust, Gen 3,16-19). Only at this point, did a human being's consciousness leave it periodically in the phenomena of both sleep and death. Its continuity did not cease, but rather only its consciousness. It was here, through the infection of the astral body and consequential infections of the etheric and physical bodies in turn, that karma and reincarnation began. Through the divine Virginal Wisdom, however, the governing spiritual powers, had anticipated the infection of the human astral body and consequently also of its etheric body, and had held back from the incarnating human being the higher element of its etheric body. Thus the higher etheric body of the original Adam did not descend until the Virginal Wisdom caused it to descend as the pure and unspoiled, primal etheric body of the Nathan-Jesus child in Luke's Gospel. When Luke's teacher, Paul, spoke of the "First and Second Adam," it is this of which he spoke.

By this time the Sun, Moon and other planets had separated from the Earth, leaving it far smaller than at the outset of the Polarian Epoch of Earth evolution. However, it was still larger than at present, and much of its water content was still in the form of vapor. Mists largely enshrouded the Earth during the Atlantean epoch. The "Nephilim" (Gen 6,4) were still large (i.e., giants), though not very solid; their name derives from the Greek "nephos" meaning "cloud or mist."

Progressively from the time of the Fall until the coming of Christ (and even until the present for the bulk of humanity, which continues to misapprehend and miss the fullness of Christ), the consciousness of the human being darkened. The gods (God) "hid their face" more and more through the Atlantean epoch even until now. This was experienced by Moses as the "Fading Splendor," by the prophets as typified by the echo of Isaiah lamenting the loss of spiritual seeing, hearing and understanding (Is 6,9-13), and by the people of Israel first as the encroaching shades of "Sheol" and ultimately as the "end of prophecy."

The separation from the gods in the form of loss of divine consciousness brought about an increase in "wickedness" (Gen 6,5). The fifth of the seven Atlantean eras (or ages) is called that of the Shemites, the ancestors of the Semitic race of the post-Atlantean Epoch. The exalted leader of those who came to be called Shemites was head of the Sun Oracle, or Sun Mysteries. He was known as "Manu," who is called "Noah" in the Bible, and he brought it about that certain advanced individuals, seven in number (Gen 6,10,18 and 7,7), should be fashioned to lead Atlantean civilization into the next epoch. Atlantis was eventually brought to an end by violent earthquake and volcanic activity, causing it to subside and become the floor of the ocean named for it. Plato speaks of the unnavigable mud from this subsidence west of the "pillars of Hercules" (Gibraltar). Prior to the final cataclysms, however, the floods were increasingly menacing, brought about by the condensation of the ancient "mists" as the earth condensed, along with massive glacial melt caused by the increasing sunlight through the decreasing mists. Eventually, the mists were so thin that the Sun became visible to the human being's eyes and it was even possible for a rainbow to be seen (Gen 9,13).

The human being, in its evolution, had expelled, one by one, the various animal natures that hardened into the animal kingdom. However, some residue of the astral nature of each animal remained within the human being, so that when Noah took into the ark the animals of all kinds, he was taking into the post-Atlantean Epoch the human being filled with animal nature of all kinds, which would have to be purified over time. The dimensions of the ark, 300 by 50 by 30 cubits (Gen 6,15), are essentially proportional to the mineral-physical body the human being would carry over from Atlantean to post-Atlantean times. This was the original "ark of the covenant."

The disappearance of Atlantis actually covered a long period of time, but the final events were approximately ten to twelve thousand years ago, coinciding with the end of the last great ice age and the first archaeologically established appearance of humanity in the areas of the Biblical account. The migrations from Atlantis were much more extensive and complex than can presently be indicated, but it was the Noah migration that established the principal lines of the human passage into the post-Atlantean Epoch.

Human etheric and astral bodies extended far beyond the physical body in Atlantean times. Being without an indwelling Ego, and thus not yet possessed of any degree of intellect, the human being was endowed, instead, with incredible memory. That memory was a function of the etheric body and included the experiences of one's ancestors for long periods of time through the blood connection. The Biblical reckoning of generations prior to Abraham was different from subsequent times in that it counted as a single generation all those generations through which the memory was carried by the blood connection—being thus known by the name of the first of the line.

Gradually over time the etheric and astral bodies condensed ever further into the physical body so that today they are nearly coterminous. Because it was through the portion of these less dense bodies not yet integrated into the physical that perception of spiritual beings was possible, this capability dwindled away with the passage of time, but the myths of old are real experiences of the human being of Atlantean times, given of course in allegorical form. Today's disinclination toward these myths corresponds to the inclination to interpret the Biblical allegorical myths according to their vulgar meaning, but the deeper truths will not be attained in this manner, however much historical fact may be conveniently woven within them. It is the deeper truth and not the few surface facts that the purveyors intended.

So complete were the memories of ancient times that there was no need to write anything down. Only as this capacity faded did the necessity for writing arise around 3,000 B.C. But as the human etheric body drew ever more within the physical, thus losing memory and perception within the spiritual world, the intellect correspondingly grew, albeit still in a most primitive state. All the time, hardening was proceeding as the material world came more and more into the human being's focus and interest in the spiritual faded away.

The advanced Atlanteans led by Noah (Manu) went first to an area near Ireland and then overland to settle in a secluded portion of Asia. Post-Atlantean evolution also comprises seven divisions known as "Cultural Eras," of which we are now in the fifth. The first two were prehistoric, being the Ancient Indian (emanating from Manu) and then, "from the east" (Gen 11,2), the Ancient Persian led by one prehistoric Zarathustra. These were followed by the Chaldo-Egyptian, Greco-Roman and the present Germanic. Still in the future will be the Slavic and finally the Anglo-American. Each era lasts 2,160 years, and is known from the predominant evolutionary impulse of its time. These seven Cultural Eras are reflected in the "churches" whose "angels" are addressed in the seven "letters" of the Apocalypse. The characteristics of each Era can be readily detected in the light of anthroposophical insight.

The Ancient Indians under Manu and his "seven holy rishis" were a people who looked backward at the spiritual world, seeing reality there and "maya" in the tangible world. But they still understood the universal word expressed in the letters of the ancient alphabet, the representatives of the heavenly bodies. With the transition to the times of Ancient Persia, the human being turned its attention to the outer world. Under the leadership of Zarathustra, it was able to see there the manifestation of the spirit. Zarathustra ("shining star") could see the Spirit of the descending Christ in the Sun's aura, which he called Ahura Mazda, or Ormuzd ("great aura"). As its antithesis, he spoke of Ahriman, the evil being who hides the reality of the spirit existing in all creation and leads human beings to think of materiality as the ultimate reality. This Zarathustra lived many earthly lives between then and the Incarnation, including one as the great Babylonian teacher of the Hebrew prophets known as Zarathas or Zoroaster (or Zarathustra). The Matthew Gospel, via the Essenes, reflects what Zarathustra taught.

Approximately 1900 B.C. we come to Abraham. Because of the nature of his brain, he became the ancestor of, among others and most significantly, the Hebrew people. If he were able to "number the stars" his descendants would be like them (Gen 15,5). It is a perversion of the original meaning handed down by Moses that our Bibles now say, most particularly in passages subsequent to Gen 15,5, that Abraham's descendants were to be as numerous as the stars of the sky or the sands of the sea. What was meant was that his descendants would be molded by the heavenly spirits reflected in the twelve zodiacal signs. It was in accordance with this that he became the father of the twelve tribes of Israel, not to mention the twelve of Ishmael, and that Jesus later patterned his own followers in terms of twelve, and that St. John's vision sees the return to the Holy City in terms of twelve. The Biblical account from beginning to end reflects this truth. But the knowledge of it was hidden, along with much else, until revealed by Steiner. Significantly, this revelation came 1,900 years after Christ's Incarnation, equaling the period between Abraham and Christ, the significance of which will become more apparent as one meditates on the higher meaning of the parable of the Prodigal Son. The Genesis account takes us through the patriarchal era and into Egyptian slavery.

The account of Moses' birth and training is an account of his Initiation into the higher Mysteries, first those of Egypt and later of the Chaldeans through his father-in-law, Reuel or Jethro. Of paramount importance is what we read in Ex 3, the account of the burning bush. We are here dealing with the descent of the Ego, the "I Am," to its dwelling place within the earthly human being. For now, it can be said that the Ego of each of the lower three kingdoms (Animal, Plant and Mineral) dwells in higher worlds and not on Earth. Further, the Ego that belongs to those kingdoms is not an individual one but collective. The human's Ego has dwelt on Earth at least from Atlantean times, but only as a highly immature creation and even then not as an individual Ego. Rather, it commenced as a Group Ego, so that human beings thought of themselves not as individuals but only as members of a tribe or clan united by blood kinship with some common ancestor, for the blood was the only entry port for the Ego into the human being. The Hebrews' ascription of themselves as children of Abraham, Isaac and Jacob is a reflection of this tribal unity, which of course, was broken down further into individual tribes and clans. Ever so gradually over time the Ego approached the individual human being. But it was Moses to whom the essential revelation of this development was given by Yahweh-Eloha. Moses was first shown that the Ego, though purified between lives from its impure astral body by the fire of what has been otherwise characterized as "purgatory," is not consumed thereby. The Ego is the "burning bush which is not consumed." Later, upon asking the "Name" of Yahweh, Moses is told, "I Am the I Am." One has to search to find any two translations of the Bible that connect the two "I Am's" with the same word, and will probably not find any that uses the simple "the." But the translations are usually footnoted with an indication of uncertainty. Steiner assures us, and the overall account verifies, that "the" is the ancient and true meaning.

We are told that the people were fed by "Manna" in the wilderness. "Manna" is essentially an Oriental term, but it is also the term applicable to the stage of spirituality that the human being will attain when its Ego has become the complete master of its astral body—a development still far in the future for all but those very few who are able to attain to a state of Initiation and developed clairvoyance (as contrasted with atavistic clairvoyance, which is a remnant of old consciousness to be either overcome or converted). The "manas" state is the state next above the Ego in the sevenfold and ninefold characterizations of the human being. It represented a special form of spiritual leadership (i.e., spiritual food; 1 Cor 10,3) given to the people in the wilderness. Moses lived in the Third Cultural Era, the Chaldo-Egyptian, and thus this "Manna" is described in the letter to the angel of the third church, as is the "new name... which no one knows except him who receives it" (Rev 2,17). As Steiner points out, the only name that meets that criterion is the name "I" or "I Am," for no one can speak that except in reference to oneself.

The "I Am" thus introduced for the first time to Moses runs through the prophets, then through the heights of John's Gospel, and finally in this and other passages of his Apocalypse.

We shall see how abundantly the truth of the three bodies is also disclosed. And we shall hardly ever come to understand Job without seeing that his three friends represent these progressive bodies, while the "youngest" (Job 32,4) represents the Ego, and the two monsters at the end represent the Lesser and Greater Guardians of the Threshold (terms extensively discussed by Steiner in other contexts). When Job has passed these, he is restored to all that he had before he was tempted—a clear allegorical reference to the Fall and eventual ascension of the human being.

Paul says that Christ died at "the right time," and the Baptist proclaimed that "the time is fulfilled." These proclamations are full of meaning. From the time of the Fall until the Mystery of Golgotha, the human being had been in uninterrupted descent into materiality and mineralization. This had progressed to the point of no return. Had humanity hardened further, salvation from its hardened state would have been irretrievable. The Divine Powers had foreseen this, and the descent of the Christ from highest heaven to the Sun and then downward to Incarnation had been prepared over the millennia. A special people had to be set apart to prepare the inherited bodies for that event. They were indeed set apart, a "chosen race." As a race, their function was fulfilled with the Incarnation, though Paul recognized and agonized over the fact that they would be among the last to come to this realization. In fact, all racial, national and other such prideful distinctions must fade away commensurate with the degree to which humanity takes the Christ into itself.

"The Nativity" itself is too magnificent and complex for summary, but follows in some detail immediately after this Overview. The two apparently conflicting Gospel accounts must be addressed as a unity because neither is adequate standing alone, inasmuch as they tell of the births of two different children, one descended from David's son Solomon (Mt 1,6) and the other from David's son Nathan (Lk 3,31). This astounding and, Steiner alone (almost, as we shall see) excepted, universally overlooked or ignored fact, takes on unbelievable force when the full picture of the Incarnation, heretofore "hidden," is seen to be so perfectly and literally revealed by scripture.

In spite of their seeming "synopticity," the first three Gospels cannot be understood as giving historical facts for the sake of giving an historical account; they are rather spiritual accounts from the perspective of three different Mystery traditions. Facts are not always used to establish historical chronology but rather to establish spiritual development. Thus one version cannot safely be used to interpret the meaning in another, aside from the latter's own mission. Similarities in mission explain the use of similar language, but different nuances in mission mean that seemingly conflicting factual statements are not so at all.

For the first time it becomes clear that "the disciple whom Jesus loved" was Lazarus who, having been initiated into the highest Mysteries by Christ himself in the ancient manner of the 3 1/2 day "temple sleep," was brought forth from a deathlike state as described in Jn 11. As in the case of so many others whose names were changed to reflect the impact of a significant spiritual event (e.g., Abraham, Sarah, Jacob, Peter and Paul), Lazarus was thereafter called John. After the prologue of his Gospel, Lazarus/John gives us the testimony of John the Baptist up through Chapter 10. The architectural middle or peak of the Gospel is the account of the Evangelist's own Initiation. What follows is the testimony of Lazarus/John himself, and it is he who is the author of the Epistles and the Apocalypse. His Gospel is said by Steiner to be the highest spiritual writing ever given to humanity. We will explore why that is so.

No book of the Bible has thrown humanity into such a state of obfuscation as has John's Apocalypse. It is almost universally thought to have been a book emanating from persecution, perhaps even from a mind virtually crazed by it. Now it can be seen that persecution must surely have had little, probably nothing, to do with the vision or its recordation. Lazarus/John was an old man, presumably alone on Patmos. His immense spiritual insight opened the windows of heaven to him, and the risen Christ came again to him in signs and symbols that he set down. It will be seen that the book sets out four series of seven (letters, seals, trumpets and bowls of wrath) followed by a trend from sevens to twelves culminating in the "new heaven and new earth," the Holy City, and the restoration of the "tree of life" with its "twelve kinds of fruit." We have moved from the sevens of the solar system to the twelves of the zodiac. But what is so startling in its authenticity, when realized, is how Lazarus/John is giving us the picture, starting with the seven Cultural Eras of the post-Atlantean Epoch and carrying us then ever higher in the cycles of seven, portrayed by Steiner in his principal lecture cycle on the Apocalypse (see **I-1**). When we get to the end of the seven trumpets, the last of which Paul also spoke of (1 Cor 15,52), we are told of a "beast" whose "human number" is 666. That represents the human being who has come to the end of the third cycle of seven, namely, the end of the "Physical Condition of Form," without having sufficiently taken the Christ into his or her being.

The degree to which a careful examination of the entire Bible confirms the above becomes increasingly amazing. And as it does so, the uncertainties about the reality of karma and reincarnation fade away, for the entire scenario is meaningless without it. Careful reflection upon this divine scheme will bring the realization that each human being has been, and will continue to be, a part of it from the time of Old Saturn until that of Vulcan (Job 38,21). The usual objections to the concept will be seen to be incompatible with the divine scheme; scriptural passages so often quoted as negating reincarnation will be seen to actually confirm it; and authentic new understanding of countless passages will demand nothing less. Further reflection upon the life-changing implications of karma and reincarnation, when Christians understand and take it seriously, offers the power of a glorious new Hope for addressing the awesome demonic evils that so grip our agonizing world today.

This Overview is necessarily fragmentary and skeletal. It does, however, point to a beginning, a critical midpoint, and an ending. In doing so it shows how humanity fell, how Christ incarnated at precisely the "Right Time," and how the human being must make its way back, by evolutionary stages, to the point beyond which death is no more.

Aside from the obvious elementary relevance of the "parable" of the Prodigal Son in illustrating the parental love of the Father, we see in it the deeper "allegory" of the outgoing and return of humanity itself, the reenactment, if you will, of the prodigal "son of God" (Adam, Lk 3,38) who "left home," and of the divine "Son of God" who stayed with the Father save only to go after the Prodigal. The Father sacrificed what belonged to the "Son" to celebrate the salvation of the "son."

Terms and Phrases

Caveat

AMONG THE THROES of this volume's nine-year birth process, the ordering of the essays has been one of the most difficult, but all pale compared to the final pang, the ultimate decision about where to place "The Nativity." It is by far the most difficult and complex of the essays in this introductory volume. At both the outset and conclusion of the publisher's editing and review procedures, the suggestion was made that putting it first would bewilder, if not offend, the reader, perhaps even blocking entry into the more apprehensible portions beyond.

But throughout that process, and in spite of its difficulties, I have obstinately maintained that there is only one place it can go, at the beginning. For this, I bear sole responsibility. The two Evangelists who even undertook to tell us of the birth of Christ placed it first. Their divine accounts are brilliant, collectively complete, and without conflict in the finest detail. While they are probably the most widely known portions of the Bible, they are also among the least understood and most problematical. Yet they are the foundation for understanding the entire Biblical message.

The preeminent Evangelist John says simply "And the Word became flesh and dwelt among us" (Jn 1,14). Etched deeply in my mind are words of Steiner, beyond my present retrieval, to the effect, "If we are to understand the most magnificent event in all creation, how can we expect it to be simple or to demand less than the greatest effort that we can put forth?" The opening paragraph of Lect. 5 in *From Jesus to Christ* (JTC), though not the one I have in mind, is similar:

> If you recall that in the course of our lectures we have come to look upon the Christ-Impulse as the most profound event in human evolution, you will doubtless agree that some exertion of our powers of mind and spirit is needed to understand its full range of influence. Certainly in the widest circles we find the bad habit of saying that

that the highest things in the world must be comprehensible in the simplest terms. If what someone is constrained to say about the sources of existence appears complicated, people turn away from it because "the truth must be simple." In the last resort it certainly is simple. But if at a certain stage we wish to learn to know the highest things, it is not hard to see that we must first clear the way to understanding them. And in order to enter into the full greatness, the full significance, of the Christ-Impulse ... we must bring together many different matters.

One who meditates upon how the Creator (Jn 1,3) could become also the Created (Jn 1,14) must surely recognize the majesty of the powers and scope of actions involved. We cannot expect that understanding them should demand less than our most exacting spiritual and intellectual efforts.

My indebtedness to, and gratitude for the skill of, both the special editor and the final reader of this volume is immense. The latter, a highly talented young person, appended the following note to the essentially final draft of "The Nativity":

It can be initially observed that there are many—perhaps too many—threads weaving in and out of this essay, making it difficult to apprehend the whole.

The severest test came from my own dear life companion, Jo Anne, whose instinctive beliefs unwittingly led me to Steiner in the first place. More simply disposed, she readily accepted the essay's conclusions but found its detail frustrating and burdensome in the extreme.

For many, a simpler and more linear presentation may have sufficed. Yet what has held me on the original course is the conviction that over time all the essential elements of the story must, to the extent possible with my limited capacities, be included. For the fact that these could not be more skillfully presented, I can only apologize. But I must ask the indulgence of all who venture beyond this point to realize that the difficulties they encounter are not placed there for the sake of erudition and that they should not expect to fully grasp all in the first reading.

Much could be said for placing the essay at the end rather than the beginning, and some may actually benefit from reading the contents in that order. An understanding of the "Three Bodies" is possibly the most critical element of all. It is touched upon in the latter part of the General Introduction and then again in the Overview. Its threads permeate all essays, but it might be well at the outset to study at least the portions of the essay about the "Three Bodies" that precede their scriptural indications. One who expends some initial effort on the Charts & Tabulations will also gain understanding. But let there be no mistake. While this fundamental principle of the human being, the three bodies (physical, etheric and astral), is met at the beginning, it runs through the highest levels of anthroposophical study. Just as the child struggles to learn its ABCs, yet remains challenged in their use for life, so it is with this critical knowledge.

Even beyond the first essay only a rare reader will initially grasp the whole with ease. Not only is the subject matter in some instances demanding, but the mode of my presentation may often seem obscure or concentrated, particularly in spots where I have perceived thorny theological issues to be involved on the basis of otherwise existing understanding. Here I may dwell in greater detail or even engage in what, in Biblical polemic, is pejoratively termed "proof texting." The circumstance inheres in the goal I have undertaken, which is, considering the newness of approach to Biblical understanding, to meet the needs of two diverse groups. One comprises Biblical scholars, the other all those less focused who nevertheless sincerely seek, with some diligence, to understand the Bible's theme and message in anthroposophical light. Both groups fall within the larger category of persons who recognize that the core of the Gospel (good news), the kerygma as we know it, is skeletal, and that vast portions of our "theology" are man-made doctrines or interpretations added after the passage of the Evangelists and those who saw the risen Christ in apostolic time. While I exclude no part of the Bible from consideration, both groups must exclude all who are too wedded to any particular doctrinal persuasion within Christendom to objectively and conscientiously consider what anthroposophy has to offer. Finally, the greatest understanding will come from reading when one has both alertness of mind and time for contemplation, as well as the patience of allowing some things to be taken tentatively and matured by accreting knowledge.

THE NATIVITY

NOWHERE MORE THAN in the two Biblical Nativity accounts is the result of Steiner's intuition more penetrating or astonishing, nowhere more nobly prophetic in rending the ages-long veil of darkness to reveal mighty truths hidden in holy scripture from the first. In the Biblical account of humanity's Fall from the spiritual world to gain self-knowledge and its return journey to that world, the Nativity is the central point, representing both the nadir, the farthest descent of the Prodigal humanity, and the zenith, the entry of Spirit into the material world in human form so that humanity would fall no farther and could now begin the reascent. Thus the Nativity can be seen imaginatively as both the bottom point and the top point of the Star of David, with the two left-hand points representing the Creation (Gen 1-3) and the right-hand points representing the Revelation (Apocalypse of St. John). (See **I-87** for the esoteric significance of the Star of David.)

For the first time humanity can witness the holy wedding between the masculine Matthew and the feminine Luke accounts, long recognized not to be the same, but only now seen in their foreordained sacred union. Gone now are the conflicts, the seeming inconsistencies; essential now the long disdained and ignored genealogical components and other elements heretofore seen as mere appendages. The two interdependent and "non-synoptic" versions of the Incarnation, and indeed of all the Biblical account, are shown to have a deep integrity.

The casual reader should be cautioned, however, that judgment should be put on hold until the account can be seen in the context of a broader understanding of anthroposophy. Otherwise, it may appear bizarre in the extreme.

The primary Steiner reference sources for the nativity are *The Gospel of St. Luke* (GSL), Lects. 2-7; *The Gospel of St. Matthew* (GSMt), Lects. 1-7; and *The Gospels* (GOSP). We will consider the Nativity to comprise the following scripture: Mt 1-2 and Lk 1-2 and 3,23-38.

NATIVITY OVERVIEW

I start with the assumption that the Incarnation is part of a divine plan, orchestrated from the highest ramparts of heaven. The earthly births of which we are told are brought about by the action of the Divine Wisdom, Sophia, the procreative Holy Virgin, acting as an original creation by the Father (Prov 8,22; cf. fn 23 of "Three Bodies" and related text)), in union with the Holy Spirit as the creative activity of the descending Christ. All the Hierarchies were involved in this agency. The Bible can be seen to be literally true throughout if one comes to understand that it is not all to be taken in the mundane vernacular of ordinary prose, and that allegory, metaphor, poetry, all the literary arsenal, are equally tools to be employed. The important thing in the writing is not whether its account was literally true in the vulgar mode, as mere earthly phenomena, but rather whether it was true in its ultimately more real and lasting spiritual meaning. Ideally, and often, it was true in both, at least in the sense that its earthly connection was clear. But seldom will the deepest meaning be attained through a strictly earthly understanding of the words, for the Evangelists wrote of what they saw with eyes of spirit.

From the very first of its development, humanity has been involved in a materialization process whereby it has descended from intimate communion with its spiritual creators to an ever denser form. At the beginning the human being had no sense of Individuality, of separateness, but over long periods of evolution took on increasing density and personality at the expense of its primeval spiritual perception which faded in the passage downward. Only late in the process did the human being become "Adam," that is, hard or solid. Only at about that time did the human being begin to divide into sexes and, as spiritual perception and memory faded, to enter into the process of reincarnation. But still, the human being was a tribal creature, who functioned as part of a group Ego, and whose incredible memory was effected by blood relationship. Over time, the Ego, or the "I Am," entered more and more into separate human beings, and was ultimately expressed to Moses on Sinai: "I Am the I Am" (see "I AM"). Yet the Ego (I Am) was the youngest member of the human being, immature, with many struggles ahead of it, and gripped by the Luciferic influence from having eaten of the "tree of knowledge." As its knowledge or intellect increased, the human being's connection with the spiritual world diminished to the point where such connection existed no longer, so that between lives human beings languished in the gloom of "Sheol" instead of in the bosom of the Father and his Hosts. Isaiah perceived the encroaching loss, crying out, "How long, O Lord?" (Is 6,9-13; see also "Fading Splendor"). But later he saw and prophesied of the One who was descending and would one day incarnate as the Savior of all humanity. Without this, humanity would sink on endlessly downward into the abyss of hardness and bestiality (Rev 13,11-18). The prophets (and finally Evangelist John) could see that the Christ was the truest form of "I Am," and that only by taking that form into oneself could the human being and all creation reascend to the spirit by a transformed retracing of the descent. The Christ Spirit, having descended from the highest heavens to the Sun, was in the process of descending to incarnate. And it was the divine plan that by the spilling of his Blood in sacrifice, the Earth would then become a Sun, growing in its heavenly brilliance as not only humanity, but all creation, was gradually infused by the power of that Blood.

To bring this about, special people were called upon throughout time. In the transition from prehistoric Atlantis to prehistoric Aryan time, Noah and his son Shem were involved. Later, Abraham and the patriarchs, then Moses and David. It was necessary that this people be kept pure for the development of the appropriate human sheaths (the three "bodies," physical, etheric and astral) to receive the Christ Spirit. Unsullied blood descent was vital to this goal. The people of Israel were chosen for the spiritual task, then more particularly those of David.

And here we come to one of Steiner's truly unique understandings, probably the most difficult one for modern Christians to comprehend. Traditional scholarship has had great difficulty in reconciling the two Nativity accounts because it has assumed that they were two accounts of the same birth. But they were not. There were two Jesus boys born to two different sets of parents.

It is with David, one millennium before the Incarnation, that the division that brought this about occurred. The masculine, kingly line of the Matthew child came through the Davidic blood of Solomon (Mt 1,6), while the feminine, priestly line of the Luke child came through Nathan (Lk 3,31). Earthly history is simply a mirror of what had already occurred in the spiritual world, and it is important to know that while the blood line was being thus developed in Israel, other spiritual forces were working simultaneously in other nationalities to develop the sheaths. In particular, Steiner tells of the role of the Individualities of the prehistoric Zarathustra in Ancient Persia and of the historic Buddha (Siddhartha Gautama) in India. The former figures powerfully into the Solomon Jesus child of Matthew's Gospel and the latter into the Nathan Jesus child of Luke's Gospel.

The names given to the father, mother and child are identical in both accounts. We may take these names as implying the spiritual roles being filled, but probably they were actually such, particularly the infants'. The tendency still existed in that day to take a name indicative of one's inner nature. Thus, just as Simon became Peter, Saul became Paul and Lazarus became John, so too would the mother of Jesus become Mary and the father Joseph, whatever their earlier names might have been.[1] It should be noted that Steiner made no suggestion other than that Joseph, Mary and Jesus were the names of the persons in both accounts, but he obviously could not delve into everything. Here note must be taken, however, of something that will mean more to the reader as the remainder of this volume is considered. In the preeminent Gospel of John no mention is anywhere made of the name of two very important persons, Zebedee John and the Mother of Jesus. The reason for the former will become clear in "Peter, James and John" herein. And the reasons for the latter may include the fact that, as Steiner said, the surviving Mother of Jesus, the Solomon Mary of Matthew's Gospel, according to John's Gospel (Jn 19,25) had a sister named "Mary"; see GSJ, Lect. 9, p. 149 and also 1 ABD 1066, "Clopas," saying, "Although the phrases 'the sister of his mother' and 'the Mary of Clopas,' seem to refer to separate individuals, the ambiguity of the Gk makes it quite possible that only 3 women are present." The literal ambiguity of vs 25 is also recognized by 9 NIB 831; 29A AB 904-906 (Raymond E. Brown); and INTPN, John, p. 211. In each of the last two references (AB and INTPN), the possibility of there having been two, three or four women is recognized. Perhaps when the soul of the Nathan Mary entered the surviving Solomon

---

1. According to WNWD, "Mary" derives ultimately from the Hebrew "Miryam," which means literally, "rebellion." And according to 3 ABD 976, "Joseph, Son of Jacob," "Joseph" comes from the Hebrew verb form *ysp*, meaning, "He adds," and "the popular etymology" is "May the Lord add (to me another son)." Considering that Jesus was the end of the line for the incarnating heritage, and was "*the* Son," both the "adding of another Son" and "rebellion" (against such line) tend to fit the names as thus given, whether prophetically by their parents or as a new name by virtue of their mission—which would apply to both sets of Nativity parents.

Mary at the Baptism of Jesus, as discussed later in this essay, the latter was then called Mary, just as the Beloved Disciple, Lazarus, was called John after his initiation by Jesus. Thus Mary may have taken, like John, a new "Name" indicative of character though the name was also held by another.

The different lineages from David to Jesus are shown in **I-39**. The two lineages from Abraham to David comprise an identical fourteen generations if the Arni-Admin twosome in Luke is really one as scholarship seems to suggest.[2]

	Mt 1,2-6	Lk 3,31-34[3]
1.	Abraham	Abraham
2.	Isaac	Isaac
3.	Jacob	Jacob
4.	Judah	Judah
5.	Perez	Perez
6.	Hezron	Hezron
7.	Ram	Arni
		Admin
8.	Amminadab	Amminadab
9.	Nahshon	Nahshon
10.	Salmon	Sala
11.	Boaz	Boaz
12.	Obed	Obed
13.	Jesse	Jesse
14.	David	David

Let us look then at the two births.

2. See 1 ABD 73, "Admin," and 399, "Arni," and 5 ABD 613, "Ram." Note that both Ruth 4,18-22 and 1 Ch 2,9-15 are in accord with the Matthew list. But we shall soon see that there is a reason for this which "scholarship" has missed.

3. In GSMt, Lect. 6, Steiner deals with the question of how time was reckoned in generations. We consider a generation now to be about 33 years, while for the period covered in Mt 1,1-17 from Abraham to Jesus, the number works out to be about 75-80 years. For the period in Luke 3,34-38, from Adam to Abraham, "generation" referred not to an individual life but to the period within the scope of the blood-enabled memory of one's ancestry, which would be a large number of what we call generations today.

The Solomon Jesus Child

The lineage of the Matthew child is traced through forty-two generations from Abraham to Jesus. Mt 1,1-17 carefully divides these into three
groups of fourteen generations each. In GSMt, Lect. 3, we are told that
the deep wisdom involved in this arrangement came from Zarathustra of
Ancient Persia who had seen the descending Christ in the Sun's aura and
that this wisdom was preserved in the Mystery schools. Finally it came
through the esoteric instruction of the Essenes' "True Teacher," Jeschu
ben Pandira, about 100 B.C., who taught how it was necessary to perfect
what had been given to Abraham in its first rudiments so that a threefold
human body would be able to receive the highly advanced human Ego of
Zarathustra, who would later sacrifice himself to the entry of the great Sun
Spirit, the Christ. To receive Zarathustra, it was necessary that there be
three successive cycles of fourteen generations to perfect through heredity
first the physical, then the etheric and finally the astral body.

In Lect. 3, Steiner tells us that "heredity works in such a way that the
qualities transmitted do not pass from one human being to his nearest
descendant in the immediately following generation; the salient qualities
and attributes cannot be transmitted directly from father to son, from
mother to daughter, but only from father to grandson—thus to the second
generation, then the fourth, and so on." Thus, fourteen generations were
necessary to have seven hereditary steps for the perfection of each of the
three bodies or "sheaths." The physical body was perfected in the first
fourteen generations, the etheric in the second, and the astral in the third.

The Individuality of the great Zarathustra, who had given the impulse
to post-Atlantean evolution in ancient Iranian culture, was intimately
involved in the preparation of the Solomon Jesus child. In Ancient Persia,
Zarathustra had given a precious gift to humanity. "This most precious
gift was knowledge of the outer world, of the mysteries of the Cosmos
received into the human astral body in thinking, feeling and willing"
(GSL, Lect. 5). "Zarathustra had imparted this mighty truth to his pupils,
particularly to the two among them who can be said to have been his most
intimate disciples and were incarnated later on as Hermes [founder of the
Egyptian culture] and Moses" (GSMt, Lect. 3; see also GSL, Lect. 5).[4]

---

4. Further insights into the significance of these two, insofar as the Nathan Jesus child is
concerned, can be gathered from the essay "Spiritual Economy" later in this volume.

The Zarathustra Individuality continued to develop through successive incarnations, and it could be said that he was "the individuality who above all others had seen most clearly and deeply into the spirituality of the Macrocosm" (JTC, Lect. 8). And with the birth of the Matthew Jesus child, it was time for Zarathustra's great gift to be given again to humanity, in a rejuvenated form. To this end, the Zarathustra Individuality reincarnated, for a time, in the prepared physical body of the Solomon Jesus child of the kingly line, such line being significant because it has to do with knowledge of the outer world.

The name Zarathustra, later also known as Zoroaster (or Nazarathos), means the great lustrous or shining star. Not only is the etheric body, reflecting the human head and four limbs, shaped like a star, but in Zarathustra's case, he was the one who had seen the Ahura Mazdao (the Great Aura), or Christ, sojourning in the Sun, had predicted his future Incarnation on Earth, and was thus himself, as the ultimate vehicle of the Christ, also known by a similar name. The knowledge of all of this existed in those initiated from the time of Zarathustra, and these were known as Magi, or kings by virtue of the magical nature of their abilities in regard to ruling humanity (recalling that the authorities in all fields were the initiated priests in ancient times).[5] These initiates were able to see in the etheric world the descent of their Master, Zarathustra, into Incarnation in Bethlehem, and this is the "star" that brought them there (see GSMt, Lect. 6).[6]

And so we see the immense significance of Matthew's genealogy as an essential part of the Nativity account. But one further point seems critical for adequate appreciation of the provenance of Matthew's Gospel. In GSMt, Lect. 6 (see also *The Wisdom Contained in the Ancient Documents and in the Gospels/The Event of Christ* [WCAD]), Steiner speaks again of Jeschu ben Pandira as the great Teacher of the Essenes. This Teacher "had five pupils ... each of whom took over a special branch of his general teaching.... The names of these five pupils were: Mathai, Nakai ... Netzer ... Boni and Thona." Jeschu himself "suffered martyrdom on account of alleged blasphemy and heresy, a hundred years B.C.," but these

---

5. Mt 2,1. Such knowledge was also brought directly into the Abraham stream "by Melchizedek, the bearer of the Sun-Mystery," constituting a subsidiary stream (GSMt, Lect. 4).

6. Mt 2,2. It should not be taken as negating actual signs in the heavens (see "As Above, So Below," Vol. 2, "*What Is Man?*"), but for the nature of these see the works of Robert Powell cited in fn 17.

five "propagated his teachings in five different sections." The teaching
reflected in Mt 1,1-17 "was propagated especially by Mathai," and it is
from his name that the title of this Gospel derives. On the other hand,
"the special concern of the pupil Netzer" was the founding of a little colony "which led a secluded existence and which then, in the Bible,
received the name 'Nazareth'. There, in Nazareth—Netzereth—an Essene colony was established ... [for] those whose lives were dedicated to
the ancient Nazirite order [who] lived here in fairly strict seclusion.
Hence after ... the flight to Egypt and the return, nothing was more natural than that the Jesus of St. Matthew's Gospel should be brought into
the atmosphere of Netzerism." It was for this reason that Mt 2,23 spoke
of the prophecy being fulfilled to the effect that "He shall be called a Nazarene." Recall that the Nazirite order was a part of the promulgation of
Moses (Num 6), who had both the teaching passed on by Zarathustra
and the Abrahamic instruction from Melchizedek.[7]

This then, briefly speaking, is the background for understanding the
significance of the three appearances of the angel to Joseph to announce,
first, the marvelous spiritual happenings that he was to implement by
fathering Zarathustra's Incarnation of the Solomon Jesus child, whose
conception was thus by virtue of the Holy Virgin (Sophia, Divine Wisdom) in the spiritual world; *second*, the flight into Egypt; and *third*, the
return to Nazareth. We will return later to the matter of the virginity of
the two Marys and the puzzlement (Mt 1,19) of the Solomon Joseph.

The Nathan Jesus Child

Steiner has told us that the Incarnation of Christ represented the fulfillment (up to that point) of all true religions. But the process was
reflected in the three main streams he identifies (GOSP) as having come
to a point in the Incarnation, namely, those of Zarathustra, Abraham and
Buddha. Traditional Biblical scholarship generally has recognized only
Abraham, but Steiner shows us that these other streams were involved, as
subsequent discoveries in this century of ancient documents (Qumran
and Nag Hammadi)[8] providentially hidden for millennia, have extensively corroborated. We have seen the Zarathustra stream in the Solomon

7. More will be said of the significance of Melchizedek under "Spiritual Economy."
8. See, for instance, *The Essene Odyssey* (TEO) as well as the works by Andrew Welburn.

Jesus child. Let us now look at the Buddha stream in the Nathan Jesus child.

In his descent from the highest heaven, the Christ Spirit became the leader of those spiritual beings (on the Sun) who previously had caused the Sun to separate from the Earth in the Hyperborean Epoch (see **I-2**). In the first post-Atlantean Cultural Era, that of (prehistoric) Ancient India, the seven holy rishis, as initiates, knew of this Spirit but he was beyond their earthly wisdom; they called him Vishva Karman.[9] Zarathustra, as we have seen, saw him in the Sun's aura, calling him the Great Aura, or Ahura Mazdao, or Ormuzd. As time went on and he approached ever nearer the Earth, Moses saw him in the Burning Bush and called him Yahweh-Eloha (a god dwelling on the Moon; see **I-6**) as a reflection of the sunlight. Even later the Christ Spirit brought the Bodhisattva Siddhartha Gautama to enlightenment under the bodhi tree (see "Under the Tree").

Let us digress to look at who the Bodhisattvas are. A Bodhisattva is one whose Individuality never fully incarnates, a part remaining in the spiritual world (GSL, Lect. 6). Only when such Individuality fully incarnates into physical earthly life can it attain to Buddhahood. That stage was attained by Gautama in his twenty-ninth year, as a result of which he was no longer required to incarnate. He had moved from the Bodhisattva state to the Buddha state (see Nirmanakayas, **I-23**). In GSL, Lect. 7, at the end of the Nativity discussion, Steiner asks, "What is the relationship of Christ, of Vishva Karman, to Beings such as the Bodhisattvas … ?" And then, "This question brings us to the threshold of one of the greatest mysteries of Earth evolution," one difficult for people today to have any inkling of. Here Steiner says, "the mission of the Bodhisattva who became Buddha was to incorporate into humanity the principle of compassion and love"; elsewhere he pointed out that nowhere prior to this did it exist in humanity. Love prior to that time was related to the blood. Even later on, Christ had to illustrate that the Levitical commandment to "love one's neighbor as oneself" included persons of mixed Jewish blood, leaving aside for then those wholly Gentile (Lk 10,25-37; Lev 19,18). Conscience sprang from this very Buddhistic insight, and we find this

---

9. Which presumably is also now called "Vishnu." Interestingly, 12 Brit 397, shows a statue of Vishnu holding in his right hand what appears to be a cross with a sun covering its intersection. WNWD says that Vishnu is the second member of the trinity Brahma, Vishnu and Siva.

corroborated by its Biblical usage also (see "Conscience"). Buddha's
Eightfold Path endowed humanity with something completely new in
human relationships—but it was totally Christ inspired. Until then,
morality was introduced through revelations given from without, as in
the Ten Commandments. Such inwardness as the Buddha revealed had
to be withheld from the Hebrew people until the right time (see "Right
Time"). Until then, the external "law" had to prevail.

We are told in Lect. 7 that twelve Bodhisattvas are connected with the
cosmos to which the Earth belongs, and that the Bodhisattva who
became Buddha is one of these twelve, all of whom have specific missions.
There is thus a Lodge of twelve great teachers who serve the Christ Spirit
according to their own special missions in Earth evolution. In the midst
of the twelve is a thirteenth, he who has been called Vishva Karman,
Ahura Mazdao, and now Christ.

"The Baptism by John in the Jordan marked the point of time ...."
when this heavenly 'Thirteenth' ... appeared on the Earth," as all four
Gospels relate. Here Steiner asks, "Why was the union of this Being with
the evolution of humanity on the Earth so long postponed?" In the Fall
(Gen 3), humanity commenced ever deeper entanglement in earthly matter. Had nothing else intervened, "the Luciferic forces anchored in the
human astral body would have taken effect in the etheric body as well."
Realizing that humanity had to be protected against the effect of these
forces upon its etheric body, the cosmic powers took special measures
making it impossible for humanity to use the whole of its etheric body;
part of it was removed from its arbitrary control to be preserved for later
times. This is described in Gen 3,22-24 as the expulsion from Eden. Having tasted, with the astral body, of the "tree of knowledge," a part of the
etheric (life) body, called the "tree of life," was withheld.

To explain this, Steiner reverts to a discussion of the four elements
(fire, air, water and earth) and their related four ethers (fire, light, sound
and life), taking fire and fire ether as the point of conjunction.[10] He tells
us that the human functions of thinking, feeling and willing (and the
higher "meaning") relate to the elements and the ethers as follows:

---

10. A much more extensive look at the four ethers and their relationship to the classical
four elements, as well as the involvement of both in the journey of the Prodigal Son, is to
be found in the second terms and phrases volume, *"What is Man?"*.

Meaning   Life ether
Thinking   Sound ether

Feeling   Light ether
Willing   Fire ether
                           Air
                           Water
                           Earth

The line dividing the upper two functions from the lower two represents the action taken by the cosmic powers in Gen 3,22-24. How so?

Fire ether and light ether are perceived by the human being as fire and light. But sound ether is not revealed to the human in its original form; the sound a human being hears is only a reflection or shadow of sound ether, and the life a human being experiences is also only a reflection of life ether. Human willing expresses itself and so does human feeling. But thinking, and words, which serve as thinking's mode of expression, are shadows of the sound ether. "Whereas each man's feeling and willing are personal, we immediately come into something *universal* when we rise into the realm of words and the realm of thoughts.... Thought and "meaning" were withheld from the power of arbitrary human will and preserved for the time being in the world of the Gods, in order not to be given to man until a later time."[11] Thus, sound and life (the "tree of life," Gen 3,24) were withheld.

This relates, of course, to the "First and Second Adam," which we will come to, but here another point is made. To quote Steiner, "Hence Zarathustra said: 'Look upwards to Ahura Mazdao; see how he reveals Himself in the physical raiment of light and warmth. But behind all that is the Divine, Creative Word—and it is approaching the Earth!'" And then we are told (Jn 1,14), "The Word became flesh." "The Divine-Spiritual Word which had been preserved since the Lemurian epoch came forth from ethereal heights at the Baptism by John and entered into the etheric body of the Nathan Jesus." And Luke, recognizing that Zarathustra and those attuned to his knowledge had been seers ("eyewitnesses") and "servants of the *Word*" (Lk 1,2), recorded what those "seers" and "servants" had proclaimed. He knew, as had his mentor, Paul, of the "First and Second Adam."[12]

---

11. The time of the development of the Intellectual Soul; see **I-24**, **I-25** and **I-26**.
12. See "Novalis" in Vol. 3, *Companions Along The Way.*

The Buddha, though no longer required to incarnate, continued to work with humanity from the spiritual world. He continued to work down as far as the astral and etheric worlds. Steiner tells us (GSL, Lect. 2) that it was the image of the glorified astral body (the Nirmanakaya) of Buddha, he who had first brought into humanity's evolution the principle of peace and goodwill, that appeared, along with the angel, as the Heavenly Host, to the shepherds (Lk 2,13-14); likewise in the radiance that surrounded the Nathan Jesus child before the shepherds in the manger. But the Buddha played a far larger role in the Nativity of this child.

Only reverently can we now approach the event of the birth of the Nathan Jesus child to the very young Mary, barely into childbearing age. In *Occult Science* (OS) we are told that the division of the human being into two sexes (Gen 1,27; 2,18-25; 5,2; Mt 19,4; Mk 10,6) was approximately contemporaneous with the infusion of the Luciferic influence into the human astral body (Gen 3); prior thereto reproduction by division did not involve the same physical process as thereafter, and it was not until after such perverting influence that humanity became conscious of the act of procreation.[13] The soul of the Nathan Mary, which received the portion of Eve's etheric body held back by the divine powers and not affected by the Fall, had not gone through prior incarnations, and was thus unspoiled, virginal. It had not built up any instinctive consciousness or even awareness of the normal human procreative function. So the Nathan Mary could not have perceived its

---

13. The last paragraph of **I-23** shows us the Biblical development of consciousness through the traditional five human senses as follows:

Smell	Gen 2,7	Relates to "breathing"
Taste	Gen 3,6	"Ate" the fruit
Sight	Gen 3,7	"Eyes … were opened"
Touch	Gen 3,7	"Knew" their nakedness
Hearing	Gen 3,8	"Heard the sound … of God walking"

Throughout the Bible, the verb "know" is used to indicate sexual intercourse. Immediately after this passage, it occurs three times in Gen 4,1,17,25: successively with Adam and Eve, Cain and his wife, and Adam again with his wife after Cain killed Able. It seems particularly true that this type of consciousness was within the meaning of Gen 3,7, for it is used in connection with "nakedness." Only souls whose astral and etheric bodies were affected by the event of the Fall in Gen 3 could consciously experience the act of sexual intercourse.

occurrence in the same manner as a normal person whose etheric and physical bodies bear the full effect of the Fall, and her soul would have remained virginal thereafter. She knew not any relationship with her husband in the normal sense—whether or not any had occurred. Therefore, her etheric body could not carry the impress of such knowledge and so, the etheric body being what molds the physical, her physical body remained (or resumed its status as) virginal also. She remained pure after conception of the Nathan Jesus child to the time of her death. The six siblings of Jesus (four brothers and two sisters; Mk 6,3) were born to the Solomon Mary, as we shall presently see. Steiner could thus properly refer to the Nathan Mary as the true virgin of the two Marys, though the physical blood of her Son was of the line of David.

It is essential to carry this somewhat further, and to bring into it the activity of the (Nirmanakaya of) Buddha. Of necessity we must bring in some things Steiner said in *Rosicrucian Esotericism* (RE), Lect. 5, beginning with the passage below:

> Now, before earthly fertilization, before the physical act of love, there is reflected in this play of astral forces, the individuality, the being who is coming down again to the earth. That is the essential reality in the procreative act. So one can say that before physical fertilization, what is descending from the spiritual world is also instrumental in bringing about the meeting of the man and woman. A wonderfully intimate play of forces from the spiritual world is taking place here. The being who is descending is, generally speaking, connected from the beginning with the product of fertilization. It is emphatically *not* the case that an individuality connects with it only after a certain time. From the moment of conception this individuality is in touch with the outcome of physical procreation. There are exceptions, of course, there, too. During the first days after conception, this spiritual individuality who is descending does not yet actually affect the development of the physical human being, but it is close by, as it were, is already in contact with the developing embryo. The actual attachment takes place from about the eighteenth, nineteenth, twentieth and twenty-first days after conception; what is descending from a higher world is then already working together with the being who is in process of coming into existence.

He then tells what is introduced into the child by the female and male elements. Essentially, "The principle of generality, homogeneity, originates from the female element.... The male element provides *individuality*. Hence, not until bi-sexuality had been established on the earth were successive embodiments or reincarnations possible." Prior thereto the primal female element (Prov 8,22-31) caused the reproduction of totally homogeneous (prospectively human) beings without any real Ego (Individuality) presence. "It is essentially the etheric body that is worked upon by the female element." But without the male, these would be "copies only." (As we know from Steiner elsewhere, each of us comprises both male and female elements today. Whatever our physical body is, the etheric is the reverse. The female element tends toward the security of the past, the male toward the thrust into the future.) We leap forward:

> We said that from the eighteenth to the twenty-first day after conception onwards the Ego is already working on the embryo; but not until much later, after six months, do other forces also work on the embryo, forces that determine the karma of the human being. This can be expressed by saying that the web woven out of karma there takes hold; gradually these forces come into play.[14] Now exceptions occur here, too, so that later on an exchange of the Ego may take place. We will speak of that later. The Ego is the first factor to intervene for the purpose of development.
>
> ... it is the individual who is in the process of incarnating who brings together those who love one another....The astral passion surging hither and thither on the earth below, mirrors the astral substances of the descending entity.... When we think through this thought to its conclusion, we must say that the reincarnating individual definitely participates in the choice of his parents.... The parents' love is therefore the answer to the child's love, it is the responsive love.

We can now begin to appreciate what Luke was saying in 1,41-44, when he describes the Nathan Mary's visit to Elizabeth:

------

14. This in no way conflicts with Steiner's teaching that the zodiacal and planetary forces are working during the entire gestation period. See Powell's *Hermetic Astrology I* (HA1), Chap. 10, dealing with the embryo.—ERS.

And when Elizabeth heard the greeting of Mary, the babe leaped in her womb; and Elizabeth was filled with the Holy Spirit and she exclaimed with a loud cry, "Blessed are you among women, and blessed is the fruit of your womb! And why is this granted me, that the mother of my Lord should come to me? For behold, when the voice of your greeting came to my ears, the babe in my womb leaped for joy."

What was here being told was that the fallen soul of Adam caused the embryo, during its last trimester in Elizabeth's womb, to react to the proximity of not only its unfallen sister-soul, the Nathan Soul, but also of the unfallen sister-soul of Eve, the Eternal Feminine, in Mary, *both* of whom Elizabeth calls "Blessed."

Only now can we begin to appreciate what Luke's master, Paul, was flashing with his references (Rom 5,12-14; 1 Cor 15,45-49) to the "First and Second Adam." Luke's Nativity account gives them both, the first was in Elizabeth's womb and the second in Mary's.

This brings us then to the point of Steiner's remarks in GSL, Lect. 5, about the Lk 1,41-44 passage above:

But the same Ego that was withheld from the Jesus of the Gospel of St. Luke [i.e., the "First Adam"] was bestowed upon the body of John the Baptist; thus the soul-being in Jesus of the Gospel of St. Luke [i.e., the "Second Adam"] and the Ego-being in John the Baptist were inwardly related from the beginning. Now when the human embryo develops in the body of the mother, the Ego unites with the other members of the human organism in the third week, but does not come into operation until the last months before birth and then only gradually. Not until then does the Ego become active as an inner force; in a normal case, when an Ego quickens an embryo, we have to do with an Ego that has come from earlier incarnations. In the case of John, however, the Ego in question was inwardly related to the soul-being of the Nathan Jesus. Hence according to the Gospel of St. Luke, the mother of Jesus went to the mother of John the Baptist when the latter was in the sixth month of her pregnancy [Lk 1,26,36,39], and the embryo that in other cases is quickened by its own Ego was here quickened through the medium of the *other* embryo.

To understand what is going on here, we need to look at Lect. 6, where we are told that Elijah was "inspired," "impelled by the Spirit," because he, like the Bodhisattvas, was one of those special Individualities "who were not wholly contained in the human personality; one part of their being was in the earthly personality and the other in the spiritual world."

When this Individuality was born again he was to unite with the body of the child born to Zacharias and Elizabeth. We know from the Gospel itself that John the Baptist is to be regarded as the reborn Elijah. But in him we have to do with an Individuality who in his earlier incarnations had not habitually developed or brought fully into operation all the forces present in the normal course of life. In the normal course of life the inner power or force of the Ego becomes active while the physical body of the human being is developing in the mother's womb. The Elijah-Individuality in earlier times had not descended deeply enough to be involved in the inner processes operating here. The Ego had not, as in normal circumstances, been stirred into activity by its own forces, but from outside. This was now to happen again. But the Ego was now farther from the spiritual world and nearer to the Earth, much more closely connected with the Earth than the Beings who had formerly guided Elijah. The transition leading to the amalgamation of the Buddha-stream with the Zarathustra-stream was now to be brought about.

Everything was to be rejuvenated. It was now the Buddha who had to work from outside—the Being who had linked himself with the Earth and its affairs and now, in his Nirmanakaya, was united with the Nathan Jesus. This Being who on the one side was united with the Earth but on the other withdrawn from it because he was working only in his Nirmanakaya which had soared to realms "beyond" the Earth and hovered above the head of the Nathan Jesus— this Being had now to work from outside and stimulate the Ego-force of John the Baptist.

Thus it was the Nirmanakaya of Buddha which now stirred the Ego-force of John into activity, having the same effect as spiritual forces that had formerly worked upon Elijah.... But being nearer to the Earth this force [which had worked upon Elijah[15]] now worked as more than an inspiration; it had an actual formative effect upon the Ego of John....

What may we now expect?

Even as the words of power once spoken by Elijah in the ninth century before our era were in truth "God's words," and the actions performed by his hand "God's actions," it was now to be the same in the case of John the Baptist, inasmuch as what had been present in Elijah had come to life again. The Nirmanakaya of Buddha worked as an inspiration into the Ego of John the Baptist. That which manifested itself to the shepherds and hovered above the head of the Nathan Jesus extended its power into John the Baptist, whose preaching was primarily the re-awakened preaching of Buddha. This fact is in the highest degree noteworthy and cannot fail to make a deep impression upon us when we recall the sermon at Benares wherein Buddha spoke of the suffering in life and the release from it through the Eightfold Path. He often expanded a sermon by saying in effect: "Hitherto you have had the teaching of the Brahmans; they ascribe their origin to Brahma himself and claim to be superior to other men because of this noble descent. These Brahmans claim that a man's worth is determined by his descent, but I say to you: Man's worth is determined by what he makes of himself, *not* by what is in him by virtue of his descent. Judged by the great wisdom of the world, man's worth lies in whatever he makes of himself as an

---

15. Here we note the similarity between the Elijah Individuality and that of a Bodhisattva, namely, that it is not fully incarnated, and does not become so until the incarnation when it fully descends in order to complete its work on Earth, thus ending its physical incarnation cycle. We are not, to my knowledge, explicitly told by Steiner that the Elijah Individuality is one of the twelve Bodhisattvas, but we might well consider that possibility. Steiner does not say that it fully incarnated in John the Baptist, but simply that it was "nearer." And if we look at the later incarnations as Raphael and Novalis (see "Novalis" in Vol. 3) we are impressed by the powerful, yet incomplete, nature of their work. The reader is referred to the marvelous work *Eternal Individuality* (EI) by Prokofieff, in particular the last four chapters, dealing with the work of this Individuality since Novalis and on into the future. It cogently presents the scenario that the Individuality of the First Adam, having led humanity in its Fall, will lead it in its "reascent" (its "ascension") in which it is still in its nascent stages.

It should also be noted that, as we shall see later, especially in John's Gospel, the spirit of John the Baptist, after his beheading, entered into the souls of the twelve, and particularly into Lazarus/John. How similar this is to the Elijah/Naboth account and to the prevalence of the Spirit of Elijah at times throughout the land. It has all the appearance of the workings of a Bodhisattva, whether or not it is one.

individual!"—Buddha aroused the wrath of the Brahmans because
he emphasized the individual quality in men, saying: "Verily it is of
no avail to call yourselves Brahmans; what matters is that each one
of you, through his own personal qualities and efforts should make
of himself a purified individual." Although not word for word, such
was the gist of many of Buddha's sermons. And he would often expand this teaching by showing how, when a man understands the
world of suffering, he can feel compassion, can become a comforter
and a helper, how he shares the lot of others because he knows that
he is feeling the same suffering and the same pain.

Thus far we have seen that it was the Nirmanakaya of Buddha which
appeared to the shepherds in the field (Lk 2,13-14) and which, in conjunction with the embryonic sister soul of Adam in Mary's womb,
quickened the Ego of John the Baptist in Elizabeth's womb (Lk 1,41-
44). Having seen above how the cosmic Powers withheld a portion of
the first human being's etheric body from the consequences of the
Luciferic influence at the time of humanity's Fall (Gen 3), we are now
told by Steiner (GSL, Lect. 4), "In the Nathan Jesus-child there was
present the Adam-soul as it was before the Fall." The "soul" of Adam
at that time consisted only of what had then evolved in humanity. The
Ego was present only as a seed from Lemurian times. The etheric body
existed in pure form, not having been infected by any perverse influences from the younger astral (sense and passion) body. What is meant
then by Steiner's saying the "Adam-soul, as it was before the Fall, was
present in the Nathan-Jesus child"? It meant that we were dealing with
a soul which had had none of the earthly experiences of humanity, no
sophistication whatsoever, no developed aptitude for anything that the
culture of humanity had developed over the millennia, no inclination
to learning of the type taught to children in schools—the ultimate
innocent and naive creature, but with bottomless understanding, compassion and love for all of God's creatures, an openness to all, an inscru-
table "power for distinguishing between good and evil," and a primeval
understanding of "the tree of life" withdrawn from the rest of humanity
(Gen 3,24).

Because that "soul" had not gone through the Ego development of
humanity subsequent to the Fall, Steiner refers to it as "a provisional
Ego" (Lect. 4). And he tells us that the astral body of the Nathan Jesus

child was the Nirmanakaya of Buddha (GSMt, Lect. 5; GOSP). The reader will recall that the definition of "Nirmanakaya" from *Foundations of Esotericism* (FE) was a perfected astral body, and elsewhere it is referred to as a body of "transformation" (cf. Mt 17,2; Mk 9,2-3; Lk 9,29). When one has attained perfection of the astral body, one has attained to the manas ("Manna") state (see **I-9**). Thus, the constitution of the Nathan Jesus child at birth was as follows:

Physical — From blood of David through Joseph (Lk 1,27)
Etheric — Pre-Fall etheric body of Adam
Astral — Nirmanakaya of Buddha
Ego — Pre-Fall Ego-germ of Adam as a "provisional Ego"[16]

Luke reflects the ages of the souls of the "two Adams" through the ages of their parents, it being necessary that the "old soul" of the "first Adam" should be born of the old parents, Zechariah and Elizabeth (Lk 1,18), and that the "young soul" (Lk 1,27; the term for "virgin" also meaning "young woman"), kept so through the ages, of the "second Adam" should be born of the youngest possible parents at the threshold of reproductive maturity.

Luke reveals the presence of the Nirmanakaya of Buddha as the astral body of the Nathan Jesus child in the account of Simeon (Lk 2,22-35). Its nature is revealed by Steiner in his GOSP lecture:

At the birth of the Nazareth Jesus-Boy there descended into his astral body what we might call the later embodiment of Buddha. Buddha, in his etheric body, was now in this re-embodiment united at birth with the Nazareth Jesus-Boy, so that in the aura of this boy we see Buddha in the astral body. This is very profoundly hinted at in St. Luke's Gospel. The Indian legend related that at the time when Prince Gautama was born, who was to become the Buddha, there lived a wonderful Wise Man, whose name was

---

16. Near the end of the GOSP lecture, in discussing the event of the twelve-year old, Steiner says that, "a separate Ego, such as was born in man in the Lemurian epoch, did not exist in the Nazareth Jesus-Boy," and that he could not have gone on developing without the entrance of an Ego. Probably this is not in conflict with the above statement that he had only the "Ego-germ," since such a germ only, while appropriate in that far remote time, would be equivalent to none in the present Epoch. His "soul," would appear to include only the earliest beginnings of the "sentient soul" (see **I-9**) related to the astral body.

Asita. Through his clairvoyant faculties he knew that the Bodhisattva had been born. He saw the child in the King's palace, and was filled with enthusiasm. He began to weep. "Why weepest thou," asked the King, "I see no misfortune." "Oh, King, on the contrary, the child now born is the Bodhisattva, and will become the Buddha. I weep because I am an old man and cannot hope to live to see this Buddha." Then Asita died, and the Bodhisattva became the Buddha. Now the Buddha descends from on high and unites himself with the aura of the Nazareth-Jesus-Boy, in order to contribute his mite to the Great Event of Palestine. Through a karmic connection the old Asita was reborn at about the same time, and became Simeon, who now saw the Buddha who from a Bodhisattva had become what he now was. The Bodhisattva as Buddha, whom 600 years before he had not been able to see, he saw now; for, as he held the Nazareth Jesus-child in his arms, he saw the Buddha soaring above in the child's aura, and he then uttered the beautiful words: "Lord, now lettest thou thy servant depart in peace, for I have seen my Master."

In 1986 my wife and I traveled to Singapore, Hong Kong and China. In one of those locations, I acquired two books on Buddhism, one of which was given to me free of charge by Bukkyo Dendo Kyokai (Buddhist Promoting Foundation), of Tokyo, Japan, the English title of which (it contains also a French translation) is *The Teaching of Buddha*, 14th Ed., Tokyo, 1981. The following paragraph about the newborn infant Siddhartha Gautama is found in its introductory biographical sketch:

> A hermit, called Asita, who lived in the mountains not far away, noticed a radiance about the castle and, interpreting it as a good omen, came down to the palace and was shown the child. He predicted: "This Prince, if he remains in the palace, when grown up, will become a great king and subjugate the whole world. But if he forsakes the court life to embrace a religious life, he will become a Buddha, the Savior of the world.

That a wise man saw his destiny at birth is confirmed also by 15 Brit 263 at 265, "The Buddha and Buddhism." Speaking of Siddhartha's early travels in search of truth, it says

He was joined there by a group of five ascetics, among whom was Kondanna, the Brahman who had predicted at the name-giving ceremony that the child Siddhartha would definitely become a buddha one day.

While neither account reports the sadness of Asita, Steiner's version seems most plausible given the age difference and the wise man's clairvoyance, both apparent from the account. Nor would a book promoting Buddhism judge the seer's sadness a fact worth telling, particularly if not known to be connected with the birth of the Christ.

How the Solomon Jesus and Nathan Jesus Became One:

The "Nathan" family was from Nazareth all along, and we have seen how the "Solomon" family, originally from Bethlehem, went to Egypt and then returned to reside in Nazareth, all clearly in accordance with the scriptural account (hitherto deemed one of the many Nativity "inconsistencies"). Steiner says (GSL, Lect. 5), "The parents were in friendly relationship and the children grew up as near neighbors until they were about twelve years old."[17] Although no precise difference in age of the two boys is established, in GSL, Lect. 5, immediately after stating that the two births "were separated by a period of a few months," Steiner says, "Has the thought never struck you that those who read about the Bethlehem massacre must ask themselves: How could there have been a John?"[18] Had there not been two Jesus children, with both John and the Nathan child born after the slaughter, John could not have survived unless something took him out of "the region," a very significant fact which presumably would not have been omitted from the account. And is not the very existence of this (ignored) circumstance evidence of both *1.* the truth of the birth of *two* Jesus children rather than only one, and *2.* the intention

---

17. While it is probably not terribly important, the comparative age between the two boys is not precisely established by Steiner. For a further discussion see chapter end notes on pages 82–85.

18. Apparently the thought has also never crossed the mind of the subsequent more prominent scholars, as it does not seem to have been mentioned by them either. See the discussions related to Mt 2,16 and Lk 1 in the following leading works: Interp, NIB, AB, Barclay, INTPN, and Brown, *The Birth of the Messiah*, AB Ref. Lib., Doubleday, NY, 1993. None of them mention or cite Steiner anywhere in their works, though all (barely excepting Interp) post-date his remarks by at least half a century.

of one or both of the Evangelists to confirm such fact by so distinguishing their births? In reflecting upon this, it should be remembered that twentieth-century discoveries have revealed the expectation, at least among the esoteric Essenes to whom Matthew's Gospel was directed, of two messiahs, one kingly and one priestly, as elsewhere herein shown; further, Luke clearly knows of the First and Second Adam, traces his child back to Adam rather than merely to Abraham, and stresses the parental astonishment at the twelve-year-old in the temple, the only event recorded by either Gospel between Nativity and Baptism. Luke's knowledge is further clearly shown in Lk 3,23 when he says of the thirty-year-old Jesus that he was "the son (*as was supposed*) of Joseph."

In any event, when the Nathan Jesus was twelve years old, we are given the unique account of the twelve-year-old Jesus (Lk 2,41-51). The parents returned a day's journey without Jesus "supposing him to be in the company." Only "after three days" (see "Three Days") did they find him sitting in the temple confounding the savants and "amazing" all who heard him, but most especially "astonishing" his parents. No parent would be so surprised with a child they had lived with, nurtured, and presumably taught, for twelve years unless there had come over the child a dramatic change. However earthly historical the account, it is the spiritual drama of the change that causes this to be the only event given in the entire Bible of the thirty-year interval between Birth and Baptism of the person the entire Bible is focused upon. What happened to give it such significance?

Steiner goes to the "Akashic" Chronicle to give us the facts, which he says "are by no means simple." From GSL, the last part of Lect. 5:

What had happened on this occasion may also happen in a different way elsewhere in the world. At a certain stage of development some individuality may need conditions differing from those that were present at the beginning of his life. Hence it repeatedly happens that someone lives to a certain age and then suddenly falls into a state of deathlike unconsciousness. A transformation takes place: his own Ego leaves him and another Ego passes into his bodily constitution. Such a change occurs in other cases too; it is a phenomenon known to every occultist. In the case of the twelve-year-old Jesus, the following happened. The Zarathustra-Ego which had lived hitherto in the body of the [Solomon] Jesus ... in order to reach the highest level of his epoch, left that body and passed into the body of the Nathan Jesus who then appeared as one transformed. His parents did not recognize him; nor did they understand his words, for now the Zarathustra-Ego was speaking out of the Nathan Jesus. This was the time when the Nirmanakaya of Buddha united with the cast-off astral sheath and when the Zar-athustra-Ego passed into him....[19]

The transferring of the Zarathustra Ego from the Solomon child into the Nathan child is a key event. Steiner elaborates on it in JTC, Lect. 8:

When the innermost part of human nature, together with the most intensive powers of sympathy and love, had become manifest through the unsullied human substance which had been preserved until the birth of the Nathan Jesus, and when the astral body had permeated itself with the forces of Gautama Buddha, there was present in this child what we may call the most intimate inwardness of man. And then into this bodily nature there entered the individuality who above all others had seen most clearly and deeply into the spirituality of the Macrocosm. By this means the bodily instrument, the entire organism, of the Nathan Jesus was so transformed that it could be the vehicle capable of receiving into itself the Christ-extract of the Macrocosm. If this bodily nature had not been permeated by the Zarathustra-Individuality up to the thirtieth year, the eyes would not have been able to endure the substance of the Christ from the thirtieth year up to the Mystery of Golgotha; the hands would not have been capable of being permeated with the substance of the

---

19. Often it would seem that Steiner's use of the term "sheath" actually refers to one of the three bodies, i.e., physical, etheric or astral. However, here he is referring to another phenomenon in which the "sheath" is what nurtures a "body," cocoon-like, until that body is set free to become itself, so to speak. It is illustrated in GSL, Lects. 3 and 7. At the earthly birth of a child, the physical sheath, the mother's womb, is cast off and the child's physical body is set free, or born. Then at the second dentition, at about seven, the inherited etheric sheath is cast off and the etheric body set free to develop as its own being. Finally, at puberty, around fourteen (but twelve in the region of Palestine at the time), the astral sheath is discarded and the child's own astral body set free. In Lects. 3 and 4 more is said on the matter. In the normal case, the discarded etheric or astral sheath is "cast off ... [and] dissolves into the universal astral [or etheric] world ... [and] would not be suitable for incorporation in a higher Being such as Buddha in his Nirmanakaya." (Here note the application of the principle of "Spiritual Economy.") But the astral sheath of the Nathan Jesus was so special that upon being discarded it was united with the Nirmanakaya of Buddha, thus "rejuvenating the Buddhist conceptions that flowed into Christianity thereby giving them a new form" (Lect. 4).

Christ in the thirtieth year. To be able to receive the Christ, this
bodily nature had to be prepared, expanded, through the individuality of Zarathustra.[20]

To find out what happened to the Solomon Jesus child and the two
families, we continue with the last part of Lect. 5, GSL:

> Not long afterwards the mother of the Nathan Jesus died, so that
> the [Nathan] child ... was orphaned on the mother's side. As we
> shall see, the fact that the mother died and the child was left an
> orphan is especially significant. Nor could the ... Solomon child
> continue to live under ordinary conditions when the Zarathustra-
> Ego had gone out of him. [The Solomon] Joseph ... had already
> died, and the mother of the [Solomon] child, together with her chil-
> dren James, Joseph, Simon, Judas and the two daughters [Mk 6,3],
> were taken into the house of the Nathan Joseph; so that Zarathustra
> (now in the body of the Nathan Jesus-child) was again living in the
> family (with the exception of the father) in which he had incarnated.
> In this way the two families were combined into one, and the
> mother of the brothers and sisters—as we may call them, for in
> respect of the Ego they were brothers and sisters—lived in the house
> of the [Nathan] Joseph with the Jesus whose native town—in the
> bodily sense—was Nazareth.
>
> Here we see the actual fusion [see "Fusion"] of Buddhism and
> Zoroastrianism. For the body now harboring the mature Ego-soul
> of Zarathustra had been able to assimilate everything that resulted
> from the union of the Nirmanakaya of Buddha with the discarded
> astral sheath. Thus the Individuality now growing up as 'Jesus of
> Nazareth' bore within him the Ego of Zarathustra irradiated and
> pervaded by the spiritual power of the rejuvenated Nirmanakaya of
> Buddha. In this sense Buddhism and Zoroastrianism united in the
> soul of Jesus of Nazareth.
>
> When Joseph of the Nathan line also died, comparatively soon,
> the Zarathustra-child was in very fact an orphan and felt himself as
> such; he was not the being he appeared to be according to his bodily

---

20. How perfectly Steiner's words here reflect those of Paul in Heb 10,5: "... when Christ
came into the world, he said, ... a body thou has prepared for me."

descent; in respect of the spirit he was the reborn Zarathustra; in respect of bodily descent the father was Joseph of the Nathan line and the external world could have no other view. St Luke relates it and we must take his words exactly:

> Now when all the people were baptized, it came to pass that Jesus also being baptized, and praying, the heaven was opened and the Holy Ghost descended in a bodily shape like a dove upon him and a voice came from heaven which said, Thou art my beloved Son, this day have I begotten Thee. And Jesus himself, when he began to teach, was about thirty years of age....

and now it is not said simply that he was a "son" of Joseph, but: "being *as was supposed* the son of Joseph" (Luke III,21-23)—for the Ego had originally incarnated in the Solomon Jesus and was therefore not connected fundamentally with the Nathan Joseph.

"Jesus of Nazareth" was now a Being whose inmost nature comprised all the blessings of Buddhism and Zoroastrianism. A momentous destiny awaited him—a destiny altogether different from that of any others baptized by John in the Jordan. And we shall see that later on, when the Baptism took place, the Christ was received into the inmost nature of this Being. Then, too, the immortal part of the original mother of the Nathan Jesus descended from the spiritual world and transformed the mother who had been taken into the house of the Nathan Joseph, making her again virginal. Thus the soul of the mother whom the Nathan Jesus had lost was restored to him at the time of the Baptism in the Jordan. The mother who had remained to him harbored within her the soul of his original mother, called in the Bible the "Blessed Mary."

Aside from his *The Course of My Life* (CML), GSL was the first Steiner book I read. Startling as the idea of two Jesus children was, it was provisionally acceptable because it explained so many other seemingly inexplicable things in the Nativity accounts. However, the infusion of the Solomon Mary with the soul of the Nathan Mary, and then the regaining or restoration of the former's virginity, seemed extremely perplexing as I could not then make any connection. But the "Spiritual Economy" principle (which follows) relates to the matter of soul fusion, allowing the possibility for the etheric body to remold the physical. The soul passage is related in *The Fifth Gospel* (FG), Lect. 6, and the restoration of virginity is thrice related in *The Gospel of St. John and its Relation to the Other Gospels* (Jn-Rel), Lect. 10.

It may seem strange that this Nativity account has gone over into the twelve-year-old in the temple and even on briefly to the Baptism, but it seems necessary to reach ahead and show how the two Jesus children became one, and how it is that each Mary, but most especially Nathan Mary, is properly referred to as virginal.[21]

In the light of all this, we now need to look back at the significance of the numerology in the Nativity. We have already seen the significance in the 42 generations from Abraham to the Solomon Jesus of the Matthew account. In Luke, we come to the more remote ancestry of Adam and metamorphose the septenary into the zodiacal twelve, a pattern we shall see portraying the human being's reascent in the Apocalypse of John. We know that Time (evolutionary development) is expressed in terms of Seven and Timelessness[22] in terms of Twelve.[23]

---

21. Not only, from modern discoveries, can we now see that there was a pre-Christian expectation of two Messiahs, one kingly and one priestly, for Steiner has shown us that there is evidence that knowledge of the two Jesus children existed during the Christian era also. See pages 85–86 for further discussion.

22. See 12 Brit 944, "Zurvanism", showing that the concept of "limitless, eternal, uncreated time" went back to Zoroastrianism, and therein was called "Zurvan Akarana," the term from which Steiner says the word for the twelvefold zodiac derived, e.g., Z-AK.

23. Let us reflect upon certain relevant phenomena in order to appreciate the significance of both Nativity genealogies. In "Spiritual Economy," we see how Noah (Manu) brings together those who are losing their ancient clairvoyance as the most "advanced" to carry over into prehistoric Ancient India. When we come to Abraham, we are told by Steiner that this process is carried over, and that his descendants are to be those who deal with numbers (Gen 15,5 et al.), as to which see "Number-Weight-Measure." Welburn shows us in *The Book with Fourteen Seals* (BFS) that Zarathustra's eighth incarnation was as Zarathas (Nazarathos) in the sixth cent. B.C., whose obituary, according to 12 Brit 934, "Zoroaster," gave his dates as ca. 628-551 B.C. Steiner tells us that both Pythagoras and the later Jewish prophets ("Second, or Deutero-," Isaiah, Ezekiel, etc.; see Prokofieff, *The Heavenly Sophia and the Being Anthroposophia* [HSBA] placing Daniel also in this group) studied under the reincarnated Zarathustra and were influenced by his teachings during the Babylonian Captivity, 597-539 B.C. While history surrounding Pythagoras is scanty, the time frame for his life, ca. 580-500 B.C., is precisely correct for this. And we know that the Jewish prophets were present in Babylon during that time and assimilated much from that culture. That humanity's use of "number, weight and measure" can be largely traced to the ethnic descendants of Abraham is widely recognized, and that numbers, weight and measure are widely used to reflect meaning in scripture, see 4 ABD 602, "Mathematics, Algebra, and Geometry," and 4 ABD 1139, "Numbers and Counting."

At the outset of the discussion of the Solomon Jesus above, 42 generations were said to be necessary for the perfection of the three bodies of a descendent of Abraham that would be adequate to receive the Zarathustra Individuality (GSMt, Lect. 3). The requisite degree of perfection of the physical caused there to be a certain degree of perfection in the younger etheric and astral bodies, and thus could be considered the degree of perfection of the three. In Lect. 5, the matter is approached somewhat differently and refined further. To begin with, we are told, to make a long story short, that the Essenes recognized that a divine Being, the Folk-Spirit of the Hebrew people, laid into the organic constitution of Abraham the seed for the bodies that were to descend from him, and that the seed was to work through the force of the Blood, i.e., heredity. Further, the Essenes perceived a spiritual law that the influence of heredity ceases only after 42 stages: In other words, all traces of heredity have been eliminated from a human being's soul, and no influence exists, after 42 generations. This was perceived as six cycles of seven generations, with the seventh cycle of seven representing the stage of perfection. (These cycles of seven are also present in the development of individuals: every seven years a stage of development is completed.)

The hereditary aspects of the human body thus prepared for Zarathustra's return were mainly those of the physical body and the etheric body. The other two elements of the human being, the astral body and the Ego, would also have to be adequately prepared. "For an event of such stupendous importance [as the Incarnation] this could not be accomplished by *one* personality, and *two* were necessary. [This is entirely in line with the Essenic expectation of two Messiahs.] The physical body and the etheric body were prepared in the personality with whom the Gospel of St. Matthew is primarily concerned; the astral body and Ego-principle were prepared in the personality of whom the Gospel of St. Luke tells...." Here Steiner equates this division to that of the fourfold human being in a state of sleep, when the physical and etheric bodies remain in bed, while the Ego and the astral body withdraw and the astral body soars into the cosmos, the zodiacal world of the stars (hence the "astral body"; see **I-10** and also OS, Chap. 2, pp. 27-28). Unfortunately, Steiner leaves us at this seemingly mystifying point. How is it that the physical and etheric bodies are said to relate to the Matthew account and the astral body and Ego to the Luke account when we have seen that the Zarathustra Ego of the Matthew account leaves the three bodies of the Solomon Jesus to enter the three bodies of the Nathan Jesus child of the Luke account? This is an example of where one must apply what is elsewhere given in order to make sense of the statement. We have already seen (fn 17) that the Solomon child was probably at least fourteen when the Nathan child was twelve. At fourteen, the Zarathustra Ego had utilized everything it acquired by inheritance by way of the physical and etheric sheaths (fn 19), and it was ready to enter into the period of development of the astral body (see **I-26**). For that, it needed what was in the Nathan Jesus child. All development by the Zarathustra being from that point to the Baptism was in the three bodies of the Nathan Jesus.

Inasmuch as the physical and etheric bodies are related to the sevenfold Solar system and Time, the secret of 6 x 7 applies to them, while the astral body and Ego relate to timelessness and to the zodiacal forces, so that the secret of 11 x 7 applies to them. In each case, the final seven represents perfection. So in Matthew, the body prepared for the Solomon Jesus child (Zarathustra) is 6 x 7, or 42, generations, while in Luke, the body prepared for the Nathan Jesus child (the unspoiled "Second Adam") is 11 x 7, or 77 generations.[24] The fruits of the two become one after twelve years, so that by the end of that generation of thirty years, the "Son of God," the Christ, can enter at the Baptism—"You are my begotten son, today I have begotten you" (Ps 2,7; see also Mt 3,17; Mk 1,11; Lk 3,22).

Accordingly, in GSMt, Lect. 6, Steiner says that Luke's Gospel lists 77 "generations" from Adam to Jesus, pointing out the different meaning of the term "generation" as it applied to those names prior to Abraham. Before Abraham the human soul condition was different, especially the power of memory, which flowed in the "Blood" through

---

24. In the light of anthroposophical knowledge, it is hard at this point not to contemplate what went through the Christ-initiated mind of Paul as he changed the literal Hebrew "but ears hast thou *dug* for me," in Ps 40,6b, into "but a body hast thou prepared for me," in Heb 10,5c. Anthroposophy shows us that the eyes were formed by light and the ears (were "dug") by sound (compressed by the Mosaic myth into "eyes ... were opened," Gen 3,7, and "heard the sound," Gen 3,8; see also the end of **I-23**). So also does anthroposophy show us (as in this Nativity essay) how a "body" was prepared that was capable of receiving the Christ Spirit as its governing Ego when the Zarathustra Ego deferentially withdrew at the Baptism of Jesus of Nazareth. The "prepared body" that awaited the descending "dove" (Mt 3,16; Mk 1,10; Lk 3,22; Jn 1,32), the Christ Spirit, was composed of the physical, etheric and astral bodies so perfectly elaborated by the spiritual world. The "Lamb of God" that the Baptist perceived in the baptized Jesus (Jn 1,29) fulfilled what the spiritual world had foreshadowed (promised) to Abraham by the "ram, caught in a thicket by its horns" in the "land of Moriah" (Gen 22).

a series of generations, so that the individual's direct memory extended before birth and included the ancestors' experiences. Thus, a name does not refer to a single individual but to a succession of individuals connected by a common memory thread. So, in Lect. 6, he went on to say:

It will now be easier for you to realize that the 77 names enumerated in St. Luke's Gospel extend over very long periods, actually reaching back to the time when the Being we may denote as the divine-spiritual entity in man was incarnated for the first time in a human physical body. The other aspect presented in the Gospel is this.—One who in passing through the 77 stages in the Great Mysteries had succeeded in purifying his soul from everything absorbed by humanity in Earth-existence, attained the state that is possible today only when a man is free of his physical body and can live entirely in the astral body and Ego. He is able, then, to pour his being over the whole surrounding Cosmos from which the Earth itself arose. Such was the aim of the Initiation in these Mysteries. A man had then reached the level of the Divine-Spiritual Power which drew into the astral body and Ego-bearer of the Nathan Jesus.

The Nathan Jesus was to exemplify that which man receives, not from earthly but from heavenly conditions of existence. Hence the Gospel of St. Luke describes the Divine-Spiritual Power by which the astral body and Ego of the Nathan Jesus had been permeated. The Gospel of St. Matthew describes the Divine-Spiritual Power through which the inner organ for the Jahve-consciousness had been brought into existence in Abraham; and this same Power was working in the physical body and etheric body through 42 generations, constituting a line of heredity.

If Steiner ever went further to discuss the significance of the 77 names, or the Anna passage in Lk 2,36-38, I am not aware of it. However, it would seem that certain things necessarily follow from what he said above. First, note that in **I-39** Luke gives 42 + 1 generations for David through Jesus. Earlier (p. 37) we saw that (omitting David, already counted here) Luke lists 14 generations from Abraham through Jesse (as compared to 13 by Matthew). Let us now enumerate those he lists (Lk 3,23-38) from Adam (and also, for comparison, from God) through Abraham's father, Terah, and then see whether the entire Lucan list equals 77:

Terah
Nahor
Serug
Reu
Peleg
Eber
Shelah
Cainan
Arphaxad
Shem
Noah
Lamech
Methuselah
Enoch
Jared
Mahalaleel
Cainan
Enos
Seth

Adam	=	20	=			20
God	=	21	=	21	21	
1-39 (David through Jesus) =		43	=	43 or 42	or	43
Abraham through Jesse		=		<u>13</u> or <u>14</u>		<u>14</u>
Total				77	77	77

It seems certain, inasmuch as Luke understood Adam to be the "First Man," that he would have started with him and not with God. If so, it was necessary to insert one additional name, even though perhaps not historical (Arni and Admin most likely being one, as noted earlier [fn 2]), in order to get to his vital number 77. Thus, only the third total can be accepted as being in accordance with his intent, and only in this manner can it be seen that Luke was not in error in presenting what he intended to say—which was *not earthly history* but *spiritual truth.*

That such was his intent seems clearly to be confirmed by the stress upon years in the prophetess Anna passage (Lk 2,36-38). We see there that Anna had lived a total of 77 years either as a virgin or a widow (both of which have deep esoteric meaning relating to purity and devotion) and a total of 84 years ("great age," esoteric for wisdom) when she recognized the Master. According to WNWD, the name "Anna" comes from the Greek which in turn derives from the Hebrew *chana*, meaning "grace," and is expressed there in the name "Hannah" (and seems also related to the Jewish festival "Hanuka," which according to WNWD is literally *chanuka*). The number 77 thus expresses humankind's perfecting process up to the final seven years, the twelfth septenary, which comes about by virtue of "grace." Here Luke merges the concepts seven and twelve in the number 84, the product of the two.[25]

The interrelationship between the Essenic Matthew and the Buddhistic Luke, and the probability that neither was oblivious by that time of the other, seems strongly shown by another fact. We know that Paul was Luke's mentor (Col 4,14; 2 Tim 4,11; Philem 1,24). From *The Essene Odyssey* (TEO), Chaps. 12 and 14 (see also 5 ABD, "Damascus" and "Damascus Rule [CD]") we now know something of Damascus as a Nazorean (Essenite) setting and of Paul's connection with the Nazoreans after conversion. In *The Beginnings of Christianity* (BC), Chap. 11, we are told how Paul had certain relationships with Gnosticism and yet at the same time how "other scholars have urged that nearly everything in [Ephesians] can be derived from Essenism and the Dead Sea Scrolls." And not only was Paul's first Christian training in Damascus (Acts 9), but he himself tells the Galatians that he later returned to Damascus for further spiritual progress (Gal 1,17). We also have fairly clear indications that Paul followed the practices of the Nazirites (Num 6,1-21, Acts 18,18 and 21,23-26). It seems highly likely that there is a connection between the "Nazirites and Nazareth."[26] All this points toward a Paul, and thus a Luke, quite familiar with the Essenic expectation. If this be true, as it would appear, then Paul seems to be expressing the Essenic expectation in Rom 11,1-6, and if so this suggests that the "works" to

---

25. See **I-20** for the reflection of these two relationships, seven and twelve, in both macrocosm and microcosm.
26. Steiner has clearly stated (GSMt, Lect. 6, cited near the end of the "Solomon Jesus Child" discussion) that "the special concern of the pupil Netzer" was the founding of a little colony "which led a secluded existence and which then, in the Bible, received the name 'Nazareth.' There, in Nazareth—Netzereth—an Essene colony was established ... [for] those whose lives were dedicated to the ancient Nazirite order [who] lived here in fairly strict seclusion." Even if the potency of Steiner's clear statement is disregarded in this particular respect, still, we know that ancient names were given as an indication of character, and the strong tie between "Nazirite," "Netzer" and "Nazareth" is clear beyond any reasonable question. (*continued on following page*)

which he was referring were those done as a faithful descendant of Abraham during the 42 generations. That he speaks of the present status of the Covenant as applying only to "a remnant, chosen by *grace* [my emphasis]," seems powerfully connected with Luke's giving us the prophetess Anna, "Grace," to illustrate the numerological secrets of 77 and 84.

The two Jesus boys, having fused into one at "twelve" years of age, can now, as *the* Jesus of Nazareth, commence the real perfection of the human being to the stage necessary to be able to receive, at age "Thirty," the Christ Spirit at Baptism. This is expressed by Luke's saying, in Lk 2,52, that he thereafter "increased in wisdom and in stature and in favor with God and man" (**I-42** shows that this means "wisdom, beauty and strength" as metaphors for "manas, buddhi and atma," see **also I-9**).

Epilogue:

Only a few items remain to be touched upon.

First, to revisit Matthew's Solomon Jesus account, such remarkable parallels exist between it and the wanderings of the Hebrew people that it compels me to conclude that it was intentional, especially considering Matthew's "fulfillment" outlook. Steiner points to these parallels in GOSP. Abraham was chosen "to be the first human being to survey the outer physical world and to discover the unity in it." He was "the father of arithmetic, … his physical brain having at some time undergone a sort of chiselling." A nation (a "chosen people") had to be founded, based upon heredity, that was able to make the transition from ancient clairvoyance to thinking with the human brain, "to a logical grasp of the phenomena of the outer world." This was beautifully expressed in the words, "'Thy descendants shall be arranged according to the same order as the stars,' which has been carelessly translated in the Bible: 'Thy children shall be as the sand of the sea'" (cf. Gen 15,5 with Gen 22,17 and 26,4,

---

26. (*continued*) We have also the developing "Pauline" evidence. Absent anthroposophical insights, considerable confusion exists as to the source of the name "Nazareth" and its connection with "Nazarite." See 4 ABD 1049, "Nazarenes," 1050, "Nazareth," and 1051, "Nazoraeans, Gospel of the." Particularly puzzling, these indicate, is Mt 2,23 because none of the Biblical Jewish prophets refer to the Messiah being called a "Nazarene," indicating the Evangelist's knowledge of a source of prophecy other than the Biblical and clearly in accord with the Essenic expectation. Very possibly, the Evangelist was including Jeschu ben Pandira among them. Other aspects from these authorities seem to support the same connection, but these would lead us too far astray for now.

Deut 1,10, etc.).[27] To this end, reliance upon the ancient clairvoyance was ruthlessly stamped out.[28] This is vividly shown at the outset, first by the sacrifice of the Ram[29] (Isaac), a symbol of clairvoyance, and then by the expulsion from the "twelve" of Joseph, who went to (the ancient clairvoyance of) Egypt. Abraham journeyed from Chaldea to Canaan, then to Egypt because of famine (lack of clairvoyance—he went to get assistance from the outside for the lack within him) and back to Canaan. A similar journey occurred in connection with "famine" during the Joseph era. Then Moses had to attain to the gifts of ancient Egypt to provide a missing element to his people. What led Jacob to return to Egypt was Joseph's dream. What led the Bethlehem Jesus boy to Egypt was a dream of another Joseph. Matthew has the Magi also coming from Chaldea, then the dream of Joseph and the flight into Egypt, and back to Nazareth, thus retracing the pattern followed twice before; first when Abraham divided from Chaldea, then when Israel divided from Egypt, and now when the Christ stream divides from its earthly mold in the "chosen people" (see "Fission"; see also "Egypt" herein).

Second, probably no part of the Nativity accounts has so offended the modern thinking person as that of the Virgin Birth, the Immaculate Conception and the Perpetual Virginity of Mary. It is probably fair to say that it has driven humanity into at least three camps, those who reject it as preposterous, those who hold to the "literal truth" of the scripture as a matter of "faith" (implying a dichotomy between thinking and believing), and those torn by both sentiments who occupy some noncommittal middle ground. For the first time since humanity has been able to read the Bible for itself rather than relying upon the exposition of hierarchical clergy, Steiner's account of the Nativity reconciles all of these positions. Given an anthroposophical grasp of spiritual reality, it was literally a Virgin Birth and an Immaculate Conception, not because there was no physical union between the Josephs and the Marys but because of how the

---

27. That the human brain was to reflect the dome of heaven has been elsewhere herein illustrated. For instance, see **I-20** and the Appendix to "Fire" in Vol. 2.
28. Lev 19,31; Deut 18,9-22; 1 Sam 28,3,7-9; 2 K 21,6; 23,24; 2 Ch 33,6,7; Is 2,6; 8,19; 47,12-13. But a clear distinction was made between the ancient clairvoyance and these mediumistic practices, on the one hand, and "seership" or "prophecy," on the other; see Lev 19 and 1 Sam 9,9,11,18-19 as well as "Seer."
29. The ram was "caught by its horns." Moses, a clairvoyant, was depicted by Michelangelo as wearing a cap with horns, signifying his ability to use the ancient clairvoyance (see "Fading Splendor").

union came about and how the being of the primeval unspoiled soul of the Nathan Mary remained unspoiled throughout, her etheric body governing the nature of her physical body so as to either retain or restore her virginity. It was further "immaculate" in that she was not, because of her state of consciousness, subject to the same experience from union as in the case of other "fallen" human beings. The Solomon Mary is shown to have become a virgin when the Christ entered Jesus of Nazareth at the Baptism, for then the soul of the Nathan Mary indwelt that of the Solomon Mary, transforming her bodies. While Steiner apparently never said so, there is also a mysterious implication in Mt 1,25, in that Joseph "knew her not until she had borne a son." Such "knowing" bears a firm resemblance to the infection of the astral body in Gen 3,7 ("they *knew* that they were naked"; see **I-23**). In this sense, even the Solomon Mary may have remained virginal until after Jesus' birth when she conceived other children. This Mary, however, did not carry the primeval soul of the Nathan Mary at that time, so it seems possible that Matthew was telescoping into his abbreviated metaphor the result of what happened at the Baptism. In any event, anthroposophy now makes it possible to comprehend the Perpetual Virginity of Mary.

But there is another appealing possibility that would explain both the "virginity" of the Solomon Mary as well as Joseph's perplexity with her condition as Mt 1,18-25 sets them out. For this I am indebted to my friend Robert Powell's exposition on the Solomon Mary in CLC. As indicated in fn 17 (and the Nativity Appendix below), his CLC takes into account the visions of the illiterate nun Anne Catherine Emmerich. He shows their remarkable accuracy on items that are verifiable but far beyond the knowledge of all but the most scholarly students of Jewish calendrical events. At the same time he recognizes the inferiority of her visions to Steiner's Intuition (high knowledge of the spiritual world), including her failure to observe that two Jesus children were born. Because of this failure, she dismissed one of her visions indicating that "the annunciation to the Solomon Mary [took place] in the Temple, and not knowing of the *two* Marys, rejected this vision because of the annunciation to the Nathan Mary in Nazareth that took place later" (CLC, p. 131).

Emmerich's visions had included the fact that Mary had from a very young age been a "temple virgin," and still was at the time of her conception while still a "young woman" (a proper rendition of the Hebrew in Is

7,14, as RSV indicates). According to Emmerich, both the finding of a worthy prospective husband for, and then his betrothal to, this special temple virgin had been under the auspices of the temple's high priesthood. The very name "Joseph" indicates the clairvoyance of initiation, as with the patriarchal Joseph who was initiated into the Egyptian Mysteries. Here Powell infers from Emmerich's account the unique temple relationship of both Joseph and Mary, the appearance of the angel, and Joseph's later puzzlement, that in fact the betrothed couple had gone through the "temple sleep" under the guidance of its priesthood and conception had occurred during that time (see CLC, pp. 132-133; see also "Mysteries" and "Three Days' Journey" herein). There is something powerfully compelling about this in light of Mt 1,24-25, "When Joseph woke from sleep, he did as the angel of the Lord commanded him; he took his wife, but knew her not until she had borne a son." It is said that Joseph had been told by an angel in a "dream" of Jesus' divine conception (Mt 1,20), but the dream could have been a part of the initiation process. Steiner shows us that dreams in that day belonged (or could still belong) to the waking (i.e., fully conscious during "sleep") state while today they belong in the unreliable realm of sleep; see *The Teachings of Christ, The Resurrected/Reflections on the Mystery of Golgotha* (TCR), p. 3. Sensations pertaining to the body, such as are involved in the act of impregnation, would presumably not, however, intrude upon consciousness during the deathlike "temple sleep," save perhaps in terms of spiritual ecstasy, as in The Song of Solomon (Song).

Third, in concluding Lect. 6, GSMt, Steiner says:

> In the so-called "Gospel of the Egyptians" [the editor also added the 'Second Epistle of Clement'[30]] there is a passage which already in the early centuries of our era was regarded as extremely heretical, because Christian circles either did not want to hear the truth or

---

30. This "Epistle" is found in 9 Nicene-1 pp. 251-256. The passage in question is in epistle Chap. XII, p. 254, and reads, "For the Lord Himself, being asked by one when His kingdom would come, replied, 'When two shall be one, that which is without as that which is within, and the male with the female, neither male nor female.'" Here the editor's fn 5 reads, "These words are quoted (Clem. Alex., Strom., iii. 9 1.) from the Gospel according to the Egyptians, no longer extant." Here I would caution that this "well-known apocryphal Gospel of the Egyptians" is obviously not the same as the Gnostic Gospel by the same name discovered at Nag Hammadi, as to which see NHL 195.

did not want the truth to come to light.[31] Something was nevertheless preserved in an apocryphal writing where it is said in effect that salvation (the Kingdom) will come to the world when the Two become One and the Outer becomes as the Inner. This sentence exactly expresses the occult reality of which I have told you. Salvation depends upon the Two becoming One. And the Two became One in very truth when in the twelfth year of his life the Zarathustra-Individuality passed over into the Nathan Jesus and qualities that at first had been entirely inward became outward. The inwardness of soul in the Jesus of St. Luke's Gospel was profound beyond all telling. But this quality manifested outwardly too when the Zarathustra-Individuality, whose development had proceeded in the physical and etheric bodies of the Solomon Jesus, permeated that inwardness with the forces engendered by his contact with those bodies.

It cannot be too strongly emphasized that the Dead Sea Scrolls discoveries in the middle of this century, especially the document known as "The Testaments of the Twelve Patriarchs," have vindicated Steiner in the sense that they show a clear expectation on the part of the Essenes of two Messiahs. See BC, Chap. 8; *Gnosis* (GNOS), Chap. 3; and TEO, Chaps. 5 and 6.

Finally, while Steiner may not have addressed the point, it seems highly probable that 1 K 3 gives an ancient clairvoyant vision of the two Marys. There Solomon is said to have "made a marriage alliance with Pharaoh king of Egypt, [taking his] daughter" and bringing her to Jerusalem "until he had finished building his own house." Solomon next prayed for wisdom and it was given him in a "dream" vision, and immediately we are told of the account of the "two harlots." This account, in verses 16-27, seems quite accurately to portray what happened in the case of the two Jesus children. It was the Nathan Mary, the mother of the primeval "Second Adam," who died and thus turned her son over to

---

31. Illustrative of this is a passage quoted by Welburn in GNOS, Chap. 9, on "The Secret Gospel According to Mark," written by Clement in one of his "Letters" (see 3 Brit 375, "Clement, First Letter of" and 376 "Clementine Literature") which acknowledges that it is a "secret Gospel" and says, "one should not concede that the secret Gospel is by Mark, but should even deny it on oath. For 'Not all true things are to be said to all men'." We will look more fully at this in "Peter, James and John" herein.—ERS

the Solomon Mary. The Solomon Mary's son died and she thus "claimed" the son of the Nathan Mary, the son whose "three bodies" were to be inhabited at the Baptism by the Christ. These passages include the esoteric phrases "Third Day" (vs 17) and "Midnight" (vs 20). It was the very ancestor of the Solomon Jesus child to whom this dream vision was given. The fact that knowledge of it was passed on down into esoteric Essenism suggests that the reality of the two future Messiahs was made known in Israel—the apparent meaning of vs 28. The "sword" with which he was to divide the child might well be the one of which Simeon said to the Nathan Mary that "a sword will pierce through your own soul also" (Lk 2,35).

Rudolf Steiner stands at a fork in the road for humanity. Either what is made manifest by him about the Nativity and all that came therefrom is prophecy of the highest and most divine nature, or his teachings comprised some combination of abysmal ignorance and fraud. He has made it clear how necessary it now is for humanity to undertake the branch of the fork he has lighted. While many are obviously not equipped in their present incarnation to understand these things, if Steiner is right then woe[32] unto those who could but merely shrug him off out of some form of weakness, for in so doing they are also deafening their ears to the knocking of the Master. These matters are not simple, but as he often said, if there are so many complex things in the world, how can we expect the most magnificent event in the entirety of evolution to be simple.

For the first time, the Biblical Nativity accounts now constitute a magnificent, consistent whole. One who contemplates the full implications of the Nativity as here presented must see in it anew the unspeakable majesty of Jesus Christ and therein the profoundly stimulating meaning and hope which is spoken by Isaiah (Is 9,2-7):

> The people who walked in darkness have seen a great light; those who dwelt in a land of deep darkness, on them has light shined.
>
> Thou has multiplied the nation, thou hast increased its joy; they rejoice before thee as with joy at the harvest, as men rejoice when they divide the spoil.

---

32. Not in the sense used by the traditional "hell fire and damnation" preachers, but rather in the karmic consequences of failing to utilize one's Talents in a given lifetime.

For the yoke of his burden, and the staff for his shoulder, the rod of his oppressor, thou hast broken as on the day of Midian.

For every boot of the tramping warrior in battle tumult and every garment rolled in blood will be burned as fuel for the fire.

For to us a child is born, to us a son is given; and the government will be upon his shoulder, and his name will be called "Wonderful Counselor, Mighty God, Everlasting Father, Prince of Peace."

Of the increase of his government and of peace there will be no end, upon the throne of David, and over his kingdom, to establish it, and to uphold it with justice and with righteousness from this time forth and for evermore. The zeal of the Lord of hosts will do this.

APPENDIX TO "THE NATIVITY"

The genealogies in Matthew and Luke have generally been looked upon by Christian writers and theologians from the earliest days as being historically and factually inconsistent, each tendentiously putting forth its own concept of the role of Christ, that of King or Royalty in Matthew's Gospel and that of Prophet or Priest in Luke's.

"Various attempts have been made to harmonize the two genealogies," says 8 NIB 131 (Matthew), of which it gives two categories; one has Luke giving Mary's genealogy and Matthew giving Joseph's, the other applies levirate marriages and adoptions. The first is said to have been extensively refuted by John Calvin, and the second is discussed below. It must be recognized, of course, that even if the genealogies could be harmonized in one of these ways, both Gospels then purporting to describe the birth of the same child, numerous inconsistencies would remain between the other portions of the two birth accounts.

The visions of Anne Catherine Emmerich are mentioned in fn 17 as including much verity but being somewhat veiled as they applied to the two Jesus children. As Powell said of her in CHA, pp. 21-22, "She beheld with the eye of the spirit the crossing of the two lineages, the fruit of which was Jesus," but "the mystery of two children with the name Jesus—one born from the line of Solomon and the other from the line of Nathan—remained concealed from [her] spiritual gaze." In his more recent work, CLC, at pp. 56-57 he quotes Clemans Brentano's account of her actual vision as reported in *The Life of the Blessed Virgin Mary from the Visions of Anne Catherine Emmerich*, Rockford, IL, TAN Books, 1970, again recognizing its limitations in relation to Steiner's own account. Her vision falls within the first category described in the above NIB account, but it seems impressive that the spiritual world is attempting to pass this truth through to humanity, even if the pre-Steiner versions have been seen, as Paul put it, "through a mirror in a riddle" (1 Cor 13,12 [KJV-NIV—INT]).

To my knowledge, in the entire history of Christianity, only one other scenario, the second category described in the NIB account, has been postulated that could possibly reconcile the two accounts historically and factually.[33] Though that account is ancient and not widely acclaimed, it would thus be unfair to state that no such possible reconciliation, aside from Steiner's account and the Solomon-Joseph Nathan-Mary version, has ever been proposed.

The scenario is postulated in the Epistle of Julius Africanus (ca. 180-250; 1 Brit 136, "Sextus Julius Africanus") to Aristides. The text of the letter, and its editorial footnotes, as published in 6 Nicene-1 pp. 125-127 is set out below:

———————

Footnotes of the editor to the Nicene set are indicated by bold print thus, **(fn 1)**, in the text, but are copied as endnotes at the conclusion of the quoted material. The practice in the Nicene volume was to assign footnotes by the page, so that the first footnote on each page started again with 1, but I have continued the numbering sequence through the

---

33. The Anthroposophic Press, under its founding editor, Henry B. Monges, published *The Spiritual Guidance of Man* (SGM) in 1950. He added an appendix in which he makes the following statement:

> It should be realized that the early Christian theologians discussed this problem of the two different genealogies of Jesus and attempted many explanations, none of which are acceptable. Even the great St. Thomas Aquinas of the thirteenth century offered an explanation which was not tenable.

I don't know what efforts of Aquinas are referred to, nor am I acquainted with any such "early discussions" except those, perhaps, which suggested that one or the other genealogy was that of Mary instead of Joseph. Tendentious and specious, these have not been considered credible. See 6 Nicene-1 p. 139, "Elucidations," and 7 Nicene-1 p. 360, fn 8.

entirety of the epistle. While all footnotes will be indicated, only those which seem to have any meaningful relevance will be copied.

I.—THE EPISTLE TO ARISTIDES

I.

[AFRICANUS ON THE GENEALOGY IN THE HOLY GOSPELS. **(fn 1)**— Some indeed incorrectly allege that this discrepant enumeration and mixing of the names both of priestly men, as they think, and royal, was made properly, **(fn 2)** in order that Christ might be shown rightfully to be both Priest and King; as if any one disbelieved this, or had any other hope than this, that Christ is the High Priest of His Father, who presents our prayers to Him, and a supramundane King, who rules by the Spirit those whom He has delivered, a co-operator in the government of all things. And this is announced to us not by the catalogue of the tribes, nor by the mixing of the registered generations, but by the patriarchs and prophets. Let us not therefore descend to such religious trifling as to establish the kingship and priesthood of Christ by the interchanges of the names. For the priestly tribe of Levi, too, was allied with the kingly tribe of Juda, through the circumstance that Aaron married Elizabeth the sister of Naasson, **(fn 3)** and that Eleazar again married the daughter of Phatiel, **(fn 4)** and begat children. The evangelists, therefore, would thus have spoken falsely, affirming what was not truth, but a fictitious commendation. And for this reason the one traced the pedigree of Jacob the father of Joseph from David through Solomon; the other traced that of Heli also, though in a different way, the father of Joseph, from Nathan the son of David. And they ought not indeed to have been ignorant that both orders of the ancestors enumerated are the generation of David, the royal tribe of Juda. **(fn 5)** For if Nathan was a prophet, so also was Solomon, and so too the father of both of them; and there were prophets belonging to many of the tribes, but priests belonging to none of the tribes, save the Levites only. To no purpose, then, is this fabrication of theirs. Nor shall such an assertion of this kind prevail in the Church of Christ against the exact truth, so as that a lie should be contrived for the praise and glory of Christ. For who does not know that most holy word of the apostle also, who, when he was preaching and proclaiming the resurrection of our Saviour, and confidently affirming the truth, said with great fear, "If any say that Christ is not risen, and we assert and have believed this, and both hope for and preach that very thing, we are false witnesses of God, in alleging that He raised up Christ, whom He raised not up?" **(fn 6)** And if he who glorifies God the Father is thus afraid lest he should seem a false witness in narrating a marvelous fact, how should not he be justly afraid, who tries to establish the truth by a false statement, preparing an untrue opinion? For if the generations are different, and trace down no genuine seed to Joseph, and if all has been stated only with the view of establishing the position of Him who was to be born—to confirm the truth, namely, that He who was to be would be king and priest, there being at the same time no proof given, but the dignity of the words being brought down to a feeble hymn,—it is evident that no praise accrues to God from that, since it is a falsehood, but rather judgment returns on him who asserts it, because he vaunts an unreality as though it were reality. Therefore, that we may expose the ignorance also of him who speaks thus, and prevent any one from stumbling at this folly, I shall set forth the true history of these matters.]

II.

For **(fn 7)** whereas in Israel the names of their generations were enumerated either according to nature or according to law,—according to nature, indeed, by the succession of legitimate offspring, and according to law whenever another raised up children to the name of a brother dying childless; for because no clear hope of resurrection was yet given them, they had a representation of future promise in a kind of mortal resurrection, with the view of perpetuating the name of one deceased;—whereas, then, of those entered in this genealogy, some succeeded by legitimate descent as son to father, while others begotten in one family were introduced to another in name, mention is therefore made of both—of those who were progenitors in fact, and of those who were so only in name. Thus neither of the evangelists is in error, as the one reckons by nature and the other by law. For the several generations, viz., those descending from Solomon and those from Nathan, were so intermingled **(fn 8)** by the raising up of children to the childless, **(fn 9)** and by second marriages, and the raising up of seed, that the same persons are quite justly reckoned to belong at one time to the one, and at another to the other, i.e., to their reputed or to their actual fathers. And hence it is that both these accounts are true, and come down to Joseph, with considerable intricacy indeed, but yet quite accurately.

III.

But in order that what I have said may be made evident, I shall explain the interchange **(fn 10)** of the generations. If we reckon the generations from David through Solomon, Matthan is found to be the third from the end, who begat Jacob the father of Joseph. But if, with Luke, we reckon them from Nathan the son of David, in like manner the third from the end is Melchi, whose son was Heli the father of Joseph. For Joseph was the son of Heli, the son of Melchi. **(fn 11)** As Joseph, therefore, is the object proposed to us, we have to show how it is that each is represented as his father, both Jacob as descending from Solomon, and Heli as descending from Nathan: first, how these two, Jacob and Heli, were brothers; and then also how the fathers of these, Matthan and Melchi, being of different families, are shown to be the grandfathers of Joseph. Well, then, Matthan and Melchi, having taken the same woman to wife in succession, begat children who were uterine brothers, as the law did not prevent a widow, **(fn 12)** whether such by divorce or by the death of her husband, from marrying another. By Estha, then—for such is her name according to tradition—Matthan first, the descendant of Solomon, begets Jacob; and on Matthan's death, Melchi, who traces his descent back to Nathan, being of the same tribe but of another family, having married her, as has been already said, had a son Heli. Thus, then, we shall find Jacob and Heli uterine brothers, though of different families. And of these, the one Jacob having taken the wife of his brother Heli, who died childless, begat by her the third, Joseph—his son by nature and by account. **(fn 13)** Whence also it is written "And Jacob begat Joseph." But according to law he was the son of Heli, for Jacob his brother raised up seed to him. Wherefore also the genealogy deduced through him will not be made void, which the Evangelist Matthew in his enumeration gives thus: "And Jacob begat Joseph." But Luke, on the other hand, says, "Who was the son, as was supposed. **(fn 14)** (for this, too, he adds), of Joseph, the son of Heli, the son of Melchi." For it was not possible more distinctly to state the generation according to law; and thus in this mode of generation he has entirely omitted the word "begat" to the very end, carrying back the genealogy by way of conclusion to Adam and to God. **(fn 15)**

IV.

Nor indeed is this incapable of proof, neither is it a rash conjecture. For the kinsmen of the Saviour after the flesh, whether to magnify their own origin or simply to state the fact, but at all events speaking truth, have also handed down the following account: Some Idumean robbers attacking Ascalon, a city of Palestine, besides other spoils which they took from a temple of Apollo, which was built near the walls, carried off captive one Antipater, son of a certain Herod, a servant of the temple. And as the priest **(fn 16)** was not able to pay the ransom for his son, Antipater was brought up in the customs of the Idumeans, and afterwards enjoyed the friendship of Hyrcanus, the high priest of Judea. And being sent on an embassy to Pompey on behalf of Hyrcanus, and having restored to him the kingdom which was being wasted by Aristobulus his brother, he was so fortunate as to obtain the title of procurator of Palestine. **(fn 17)** And when Antipater was treacherously slain through envy of his great good fortune, his son Herod succeeded him, who was afterwards appointed king of Judea under Antony and Augustus by a decree of the senate. His sons were Herod and the other tetrarchs. These accounts are given also in the histories of the Greeks. **(fn 18)**

V.

But as up to that time the genealogies of the Hebrews had been registered in the public archives, and those, too, which were traced back to the proselytes **(fn 19)**—as, for example, to Achior the Ammanite, and Ruth the Moabitess, and those who left Egypt along with the Israelites, and intermarried with them—Herod, knowing that the lineage of the Israelites contributed nothing to him, and goaded by the consciousness of his ignoble birth, burned the registers of their families. This he did, thinking that he would appear to be of noble birth, if no one else could trace back his descent by the public register to the patriarchs or proselytes, and to that mixed race called *georae*. **(fn 20)** A few, however, of the studious, having private records of their own, either by remembering the names or by getting at them in some other way from the archives, pride themselves in preserving the memory of their noble descent; and among these happen to be those already mentioned, called *desposyni*, **(fn 21)** on account of their connection with the family of the Saviour. And these coming from Nazara and

Cochaba, Judean villages, to other parts of the country, set forth the above-named genealogy **(fn 22)** as accurately as possible from the Book of Days. **(fn 23)** Whether, then, the case stand thus or not, no one could discover a more obvious explanation, according to my own opinion and that of any sound judge. And let this suffice us for the matter, although it is not supported by testimony, because we having nothing more satisfactory or true to allege upon it. The Gospel, however, in any case states the truth.

VI.

Matthan, descended from Solomon, begat Jacob. Matthan dying, Melchi, descended from Nathan, begat Heli by the same wife. Therefore Heli and Jacob are uterine brothers. Heli dying childless, Jacob raised up seed to him and begat Joseph, his own son by nature, but the son of Heli by law. Thus Joseph was the son of both. **(fn 24)**

Notes

1. This letter, as given by Eusebius, is acephalous. A large portion of it is supplied by Cardinal Angelo Mai in the *Bibliotheca nova Patrum*, vol. iv, pp. 231 and 273. We enclose in brackets the parts wanting in Gallandi, who copied Eusebius (*Hist. Eccl.*, i, 7). On this celebrated letter of Africanus to Aristidies, consult especially Eusebius (*Hist. Eccl.*, i, 7); also Jerome, comm. on Matt. i. 16; Augustine, Retract., ii. 7; Photius, cod xxxiv, p. 22; and in addition to these, Zacharias Chrysopol. in *Bibl. P. P. Lugd.*, vol. xix, p. 751.

3. Ex. vi, 23.

4. Ex. vi, 25.

5. [Heb. vii, 14.]

6. 1 Cor xv, 12, etc.

7. Here what is given in Eusebius begins.

11. But in our text in Luke iii, 23,24, and so, too, in the Vulgate, Matthat and Levi are inserted between Heli and Melchi. It may be that these two names were not found in the copy used by Africanus.

12. Here Africanus applies the term "widow" [*kereyoysan*] to one divorced as well as to one bereaved.

14. Two things may be remarked here: first, that Africanus refers the phrase "as was supposed" not only to the words "son of Joseph," but also to those that follow, "the son of Heli;" so that Christ would be the son of Joseph by legal

adoption, just in the same way as Joseph was the son of Heli, which would
lead to the absurd and impious conclusion that Christ was the son of Mary
and a brother of Joseph married by her after the death of the latter. And second, that in the genealogy here assigned to Luke, Melchi holds the *third*
place; whence it would seem either that Africanus's memory had failed him,
or that as Bede conjectures in his copy of the Gospel Melchi stood in place
of Matthat (Migne). [A probable solution.]

18. This whole story about Antipater is fictitious. Antipater's father was not
Herod, a servant in the temple of Apollo, but Antipater an Idumean, as we
learn from Josephus (xiv, 2). This Antipater was made prefect of Idumea by
Alexander king of the Jews, and laid the foundation of the power to which
his descendants rose. He acquired great wealth, and was on terms of friendship with Ascalon, Gaza and the Arabians.

The following portions of the editorial footnotes from Eusebius' presentation of Africanus' letter, 1 Nicene-3 pp. 91-94, (i.e., see fn 1 under
Africanus above) seem pertinent also:

2. ... Of this Aristides to whom the epistle is addressed we know
nothing....

The attempt of Africanus is, so far as we know, the first critical attempt to harmonize the two genealogies of Christ. The question had
been the subject merely of guesses and suppositions until his time.
He approaches the matter in a free critical spirit (such as seems always
to have characterized him), and his investigations therefore deserve
attention. He holds that both genealogies are those of Joseph, and
this was the unanimous opinion of antiquity, though, as he says, the
discrepancies were reconciled in various ways. Africanus himself, as
will be seen, explains by the law of Levirate marriages, and his view
is advocated by Mill (*On the Mythical Interpretation of the Gospel*, p.
201 sq.); but of this interpretation Rev. John Lightfoot justly says,
"There is neither reason for it, nor, indeed, any foundation at all."

Upon the supposition that both genealogies relate to Joseph the
best explanation is that Matthew's table represents the royal line of
legal successors to the throne of David, while Luke's gives the line
of actual descent. This view is ably advocated by Hervey in Smith's
Bible Dictionary (article *Genealogy of Jesus*). Another opinion which
has prevailed widely since the Reformation is that Luke gives the

genealogy of Mary. The view is defended very ingeniously by Weiss (*Leben Jesu*, I. 205, 2d ed.). For further particulars see, besides the works already mentioned, the various commentaries upon Matthew and Luke and the various lives of Christ, especially Andrews', p. 55 sq.

3. Eusebius makes a mistake in saying that Africanus had received the explanation which follows from tradition. For Africanus himself says expressly ... that his interpretation is not supported by testimony. Eusebius' error has been repeated by most writers upon the subject but is exposed by Spitta, ibid. p. 63.

7. We know nothing more of Estha. Africanus probably refers to the tradition handed down by the relatives of Christ, who had, as he says, preserved genealogies which agreed with those of the Gospels. He distinguishes here what he gives on tradition from his own interpretation of the Gospel discrepancy upon which he is engaged.

Eusebius opens his account as follows (1 Nicene-3 p. 91):

Matthew and Luke in their gospels have given us the genealogy of Christ differently, and many suppose that they are at variance with one another. Since as a consequence every believer, in ignorance of the truth, has been zealous to invent some explanation which shall harmonize the two passages, permit us to subjoin the account of the matter which has come down to us, and which is given by Africanus ... in his epistle to Aristides, where he discusses the harmony of the gospel genealogies.

In the light of anthroposophy, one can wonder if perhaps the darkening that progressively occurred after the first century might not indicate that some of the earlier "explanations," which Eusebius alleges to have been "in ignorance of the truth," actually knew and expressed the truth which had become completely veiled by the third century. The light of Steiner's teachings might be taken as hinting strongly thus. It is notable, however, that the seeming discrepancy bothered Christians early on, as knowledge of the truth of the "Mystery" of Golgotha would take further human evolution (e.g., Jn 16,12; Hcb 5,11; 9,5) and then the revelation of truth by another prophet to appear in the early twentieth century.

Modern Christians seem inclined to ignore the genealogies as hopeless muddles. No Bible commentary has yet quoted Steiner on anything to my knowledge, presumably either out of unawareness of, or disdain for, his prophecy, more likely the former since no mention is made of him. That apparently leaves only the Africanus letter as a possible reconciliation, and no great affinity for that has developed, even where it has been noted.

Edersheim's late nineteenth century work, *The Life and Times of Jesus the Messiah*, while commencing with the Jewish world in the days of Christ, omits any reference whatsoever to the genealogies. The twentieth-century commentaries listed in the bibliography contain the following comments upon Africanus' letter as follows:

1. <u>8 Interp 81</u> (Luke)—"Early in the third century (see the letter of Julius Africanus to Aristides as quoted by Eusebius *Church History* I. 7) the theory was current that Matthew's genealogy symbolized Christ's royalty, and Luke's his priesthood."

2. <u>Barc (Luke) 41</u>—"(iii) The most ingenious explanation is as follows. In *Matthew* 1:16 Joseph's father is *Jacob*; in *Luke* 3:23 it is *Heli*. According to the Jewish law of levirate marriage (*Deut 25:5f*) if a man died childless his brother must, if free to do so, marry the widow and ensure the continuance of the line. When that happened a son of such a marriage could be called the son either of the first or of the second husband. It is suggested that Joseph's mother married twice. Joseph was in actual fact the son of Heli, the second husband, but he was in the eyes of the law the son of Jacob, the first husband who had died. It is then suggested that while Heli and Jacob had the same mother they had different fathers and that Jacob's father was descended from David through Solomon and Heli's father was descended from David through Nathan. This ingenious theory would mean that both genealogies are correct. In fact, all we can say is that we do not know."

3. <u>28 AB 497</u> (Luke)—"Even more crucial is the listing of Jesus' grandfather as Jacob in Matt 1:16 and as Heli in Luke 3:23. Various solutions have been suggested to solve this part of the problem. Julius Africanus (cited in Eusebius *Historia ecclesiastica* 1.7,2-15) explained the Lucan text by invoking levirate marriage, as in Deut 25:5-10, whereby on the death of a husband who was childless the next of kin would have intercourse with the widow to beget children in his brother's name and continue his lineage. Thus Luke 3:23 would be understood: 'Being the son, as it was supposed of Joseph, (but really) of Heli,' so that Joseph could still be the son of Jacob (according to Matthew). But the solution has many problems (on which see Brown, *The Birth*, App. I, 503-504), and in reality solves nothing."

4. <u>8 NIB 131</u> (Matthew)—"Beginning with Julius Africanus in the early third century attempts have been made to harmonize some points in the two genealogies by postulating levirite [sic] marriages or adoptions in cases where Matthew and Luke present different names (cf. Deut 25:5-10). But even if this theory (for which no evidence is offered) were to be accepted as resolving some problems, many others remain."

While not one of the listed commentaries as such, Brown, *The Birth of the Messiah*, Doubleday, NY, 1977, 1993, is a part of "The Anchor Bible Reference Library, and is that to which reference is made in #3 above. After a general discussion in which Brown points to Julius Africanus (ca. A.D. 225) as "our oldest attested witness to this [i.e., levirate] solution," he states, "Ingenious as it is, this solution faces [the following] serious difficulties:

a) Jacob and Eli would have been full or blood brothers if 'Matthan' (Matthew's name for the grandfather of Joseph and father of Jacob) and 'Matthat' (Luke's name for the same ancestor) are variants of a name borne by one man. But the father of Matthan/Matthat was *Eleazar* according to Matthew, while he was *Levi* according to Luke. Are we to assume a second levirate marriage to explain this? To avoid this difficulty, some have argued that Jacob and Eli were half brothers, with the same mother but different fathers (Matthan and Matthat respectively). Then, however, one has the dubious coincidence that their mother married two men who had almost the same names.

b) We are not certain how widely levirate marriage was practiced in Jesus' time [here his lengthy fn 2, showing gradual waning of an ancient custom, is omitted], although Mark 12:18-27 ... would suggest that it was still a known custom.

c) The whole point of the levirate marriage was that a child be born to the deceased father. Therefore, it would be very strange, if Joseph were the son of a levirate marriage, to have a genealogical list tracing his ancestry through his natural father.

d) The levirate marriage hypothesis could explain, at most, only the discrepancies at the very end of the genealogies; it offers little help with the other divergencies between the lists. If we accept the levirate hypothesis that both genealogies of Jesus are family lists traced respectively through the legal and natural fathers of Joseph, how do we explain the fact that earlier in the lists Matthew traces the descent through Zerubbabel's son Abiud, while Luke traces it through Zarubbabel's son Rhesa? Why does Matthew trace descent through David's son Solomon, while Luke traces it through David's son Nathan?

The theory of a levirate marriage solves so little and has so many difficulties that it should be abandoned as a solution in the problem of the two genealogies, and even in the more restricted problem of Jesus' overabundance of grandfathers."

Thus, we see that traditional theology has no acceptable answer and that, one exception aside, the Biblical genealogies of Jesus must remain a muddle. Rudolf Steiner's entirely plausible and coherent account offers us the only known opportunity to embrace the genealogies of the nativity accounts as powerful and accurate statements of the descent of "Jesus according to the flesh" (Rom 1,3).

CHAPTER END NOTES

17. (*continued from p. 53*) The passage quoted in the text says, "they were
about twelve." In Lect. 7 he (at least) twice refers to the Nathan Jesus, and
once to the Solomon Jesus, as having been twelve at this time, and in GSMt,
Lect. 6 he refers to the Solomon Jesus as having been twelve then. In Concerning the Nature of Christianity (CNC), he refers to the Solomon Jesus
child's death as having been "at twelve years" (Lect. 1) and "in the twelfth
year" (Lect. 4). In the GOSP lecture he says "When they were both twelve,"
with reference to the Lk 2,41-51 event. It is obvious from Luke 1 that John
the Baptist was at least six months older than the Nathan Jesus, and if either
of them (John or the Nathan Jesus) had been "in Bethlehem" or "in all that
region" (Mt 2,16), at the time Herod killed all the children under two years
of age he would have been killed, but it is unclear whether Nazareth would
have been in such region. That it was spoken of pejoratively by Nathanael in
Jn 1,46 might suggest that Herod would not have considered it possible for
the king to have come from there. Probably the "region" would have included
Jerusalem, Bethlehem, and the surroundings of both (i.e., all of Judah), but
not Nazareth. Little is known historically of this slaughter (but that does not
negate its verity, for Steiner has noted that providence caused there to be a
blackout on historical information surrounding the Christ event; e.g., most
historical figures were preserved in works of art from earlier Greek and later
Roman times, but no such contemporary item has come down as to Jesus). It
appears that the Nathan family did not long stay in either Bethlehem or Jerusalem. The circumcision (Lk 2,21) would have been on the 8th day (Lev 12,3)
and the purification and presentation (Lk 2,22) after the 40th day (Lev 12,2-
8). Presumably the Nathan family was in Bethlehem until the latter, then in
Jerusalem, after which they returned to Nazareth.

But this does not account for the safety of John! Had he been born within
two years before the approximate time of the birth of the Solomon child (Mt
2,16), he would presumably have been slaughtered in the "city of Judah"
(Lk 1,39) where he lived. In GSL, Lect. 5, Steiner says, "The births of the
two Jesus children were separated by a period of a few months. But [the
Nathan] Jesus ... and John the Baptist were both born too late to have been
victims of the so-called 'massacre of the innocents'."

Tradition for the birth of Jesus on December 25, 1 B.C. dates back to the
work of the Italian monk Dionysius Exiguus in the early sixth century.
Today scholars are generally divided between those who date it in 2 B.C.
and those who date it in or before 4 B.C., based upon certain astrological
facts relating to the death of Herod. Since only anthroposophical scholars

recognize the births of two different children, their work, which also assimilates prior knowledge, is more pertinent here. Unfortunately, the two prominent anthroposophical writers reflect a similar division. The earlier work, that of the Christian Community priest Ormand Edwards, places the birth of the Solomon Jesus child on January 6, 1 B.C., and the birth of the Nathan Jesus child on December 25, 1 B.C., (six days before the start of our current calendar on January 1, A.D. 1, there being no zero year between the two eras). The work of Robert Powell indicates high respect for Edwards and his work, but conscientiously differs based upon extensive hermetic astrological analysis (and on what is called "astrosophy," or "star wisdom"). See *Chronicle of the Living Christ* (CLC), Chaps. 1, 3 and 5. Powell dates the Solomon Jesus birth on March 5, 6 B.C., and the Nathan Jesus birth on December 6, 2 B.C.

The date of Herod's death is critical to both positions since the Solomon Jesus child's birth clearly preceded it. Secular history dates the death of Herod in 4 B.C. (see 5 Brit 879 and WNWD). Bible commentaries overwhelmingly accept the view that the Bible here refers to the wicked Herod the Great and that his reign ended in 4 B.C. Scholars searching for astronomical phenomena that could explain the Star of Bethlehem (Mt 2,2-11) have fastened upon three possible occurrences, the triple conjunction of Jupiter and Saturn in 7 B.C. first identified by Kepler, the lunar eclipse of 4 B.C., and another lunar eclipse in January, 1 B.C. (Haley's comet in 12 B.C. has also been mentioned.)

Powell's work is based upon both the insights of Rudolf Steiner and the early nineteenth-century visions of the illiterate nun Anne Catherine Emmerich as set out primarily in The Life of Jesus Christ and Biblical Revelations (LJC). (Steiner referred to her as "an extraordinarily good somnambulist," a term he used for mediumistic visions, saying that those based upon "mirror-seeing" were "undoubtedly extraordinarily correct.") Powell's work persuasively demonstrates the accuracy of many of her visions, while pointing out that Steiner's seership was higher and that some of her visions did not penetrate through to the full truth, as, for example, to the existence of two Jesus children (see *Christian Hermetic Astrology* [CHA], p. 22).

Steiner dates the Crucifixion on April 3, A.D. 33, and Emmerich's indications agree. Steiner also assures us of certain cyclical patterns, including those of one hundred years and thirds thereof (or 33 1/3 years), the life of Christ having fallen within one of these cycles, and both he and Emmerich say Jesus lived at least thirty-three years. If so, he (i.e., his "Three Bodies," being those of the Nathan Jesus child) would have been born approximately as Powell shows in December, A.D. 2, for it is less than thirty-three years from December, A. D. 1 until April, A.D. 33. Powell's dating thus seems generally acceptable for Nathan Jesus' birth.

Dating the birth of Solomon Jesus is more complicated, perplexingly so. Clearly Luke was referring to the bodily age of the Nathan Jesus child in Lk 2,42. The greatest challenge to Powell's dating on the Solomon Jesus birth comes from Steiner's many references that that child was also about twelve years old at the time of the temple incident in Jerusalem, and that the two births "were separated by a period of a few months." These statements influenced Edwards, and gave pause to Powell who was nevertheless persuaded by the cogent astrological phenomena. There is much to commend the application of the hermetic principle "As Above, So Below" to the starry phenomena in searching for the Solomon Jesus birth date. Unfortunately, the complexity of the proof makes careful investigation difficult for most. In spite of the enticing beauty and appealing logic of that pattern of phenomena, it remains difficult either to stretch the Steiner remarks implying only a few months into a period of fifty-seven months, as Powell suggests, or to ignore them altogether.

If Herod's massacre of the infants was near the end of his life, then the two births could have been separated by a period of just over two years, the Solomon birth being in 4 B.C. and the Nathan birth in late 2 B.C. This stretches Steiner's remarks, but much less than the longer period. The "Star" seen by the Magi could then have been simply the Zarathustra Individuality descending into Incarnation in Bethlehem, as the text suggests. See also GSL, Lect. 5, p. 100. This comports well with 7 Interp 257, which says (sounding almost anthroposophical), "Magi believed that a *star* could be the ... counterpart or angel ... of a great man." Many commentaries speak of stars having been associated in ancient times with the birth of significant personalities. Still, if Herod died as early as 4 B.C., even the two-plus years indicates Steiner was less than precise on the Solomon child's age and makes Powell's dating more feasible. The student who studies Powell's work must be impressed with its plausibility.

Still, another possibility exists for reconciling Steiner's statements with Powell's chronology. We know that earthly age is determined by the "Three Bodies," primarily the physical, and that the Ego itself is ageless. Only the bodies block the incarnated Ego's full consciousness within the spiritual world. We also know from both Steiner and Paul (1 Cor 13,8) that the knowledge one acquires in any given life dies with that life, and only the spiritualized elements of the three bodies is carried over and transformed into new "Talents" for a later incarnation. And while the Ego is the manager of those talents on Earth, the seat of earthly memory and knowledge is in the bodies, primarily the etheric (for memory) and astral (for conscious thinking), though the physical brain must exist to reflect that which comes into the thought process from and through one's guardian angel and the spiritual world. We reckon with the wisdom that flowed from the twelve-year-old Jesus of Nazareth after the Zarathustra Ego had entered the bodies of the Nathan Jesus child (Lk 2,46-47), but we note that it was not just his answers, but also his questions which amazed. The Zarathustra Ego would make its immense presence felt in such gifted bodies as were then available to it, because the nature of those bodies would not impede awareness in the spiritual world as normal human bodies do, and the power of that Ego to use those bodies and to recall its experiences in the spiritual world would have been unmatched among human beings. So, while the earthly "age" of the youth would be determined exclusively by the Nathan Jesus bodies, it was an "old soul" within, a soul so strong that it would develop those three bodies into a capable vehicle (Lk 2,52) and then itself step aside and let the Christ enter at the Baptism (see "Baptism-Dove").

Steiner's spiritual research may have been relatively unconcerned with the earthly age of the Solomon child, since all would be governed by the survivor's age—so important was the general concept at that time—so that he was notably imprecise with that detail in these lectures.

No position is taken here other than that the Solomon child was the older of the two and that both John and the Nathan Jesus were born after the massacre, as Steiner has stated.

21. (*continued from p. 58*) In CNC, Lect. 4, he tells us:

> You see, I have at length found, as I told you, that there are two Jesus boys. But one did not know that somewhere in history such a thing is reported, until once in North Italy we came upon a picture. There this historic fact is represented of Jesus in the temple where he taught the scribes. And there, curiously enough, is this second Jesus boy: he is departing. The one is teaching; the other who is withdrawing is not the usual Jesus boy ... whom one knows. Hence, there are two Jesus boys pictured there; so that one can say, that in certain centuries people still knew that a second Jesus boy has existed. He is departing. Since I had found it out, I could then for the first time know that these two Jesus boys are depicted there. You see, gentlemen, for centuries one had known this. But the church has never permitted such things, which thus correspond to the real truth, to get out into the open.

This lecture was not given until 1923. In Lect. 1, Steiner says that he discovered the picture in Turin *after* he had discovered the truth of the two

Jesus boys in his spiritual research, first disclosed in 1909. The painting is apparently not isolated as evidence of the existence of this former knowledge. Robert Powell, in CLC, Chap. 2, p. 64, says:

> This mysterious occurrence is depicted artistically by the Italian Renaissance painter Borgognone in his painting "The Twelve-year-old Jesus in the Temple" in the church of Saint Ambrosius, Milan. The Nathan Jesus sits in the center on a raised seat holding a discourse, surrounded by the doctors and scribes. His gaze is directed toward another child—the Solomon Jesus—on the left side of the painting. Whereas the Nathan Jesus basks in an aura of radiance arising through his inner union with the spirit of Zarathustra ("golden star"), the Solomon Jesus looks pale and weak, bereft of spirit, and appears to be making his way, in a dream-like state, away from the Nathan Jesus. A reproduction of this painting, together with many others purportedly showing the two Jesus children, is to be found in Hella Krause-Zimmer's book *Die zwei Jesusknaben in der bildenden Kunst* [The Two Jesus Children in Pictorial Art].

SPIRITUAL ECONOMY

Any SUGGESTION that Steiner's works can be segregated into those that pertain to the Bible and those that do not is unthinkable. Christ stood as the beacon light for every aspect of his life, and, when understood in the light of anthroposophy, this can be seen in all his works. One might say therefore that the Bible and Steiner both had the same lodestar—Christ. Nevertheless, it can be said that his works directed primarily to the meaning of the Bible fall most heavily within the years 1908 to 1914. While a few Bible-focused lecture cycles preceded this period, most notably *The Gospel of St. John*, clearly Steiner began to concentrate on holy scripture per se in 1908. It is also noteworthy that the last two of the five books in the Basic Anthroposophy section of Vol. 3, *Companions Along The Way*, namely, *Occult Science* (OS) and *Knowledge of the Higher Worlds and Its Attainment* (KHW), were either completed or published in 1909, and the lecture cycles *The Spiritual Hierarchies (and their reflection in the physical world)* (SH) and *Rosicrucian Esotericism* (RE) were among critically important ones completed in 1909 or shortly before. After hostilities commenced in Germany in 1914, Steiner gave few lectures of the same nature for he said that the conditions in the spiritual world did not lend themselves to the investigation of such matters at that time. After the war his lectures were directed to other pressing issues.

The above is related to properly emphasize the importance implied by the timing of the eleven lectures on spiritual economy, *The Principle of Spiritual Economy* (SE), which were given from January 21 through May 31, 1909. How the existence of this cycle and its importance escaped my attention until the research phase of this project was nearly complete, and writing begun, is simply beyond my imagination. Remembering the difficulty this deferment presented to me undoubtedly influences my introducing it early in this work.

One cannot begin to understand spiritual economy without first understanding the makeup of the human being (as described in the

"Overview" above and in **I-9**) and the course of the Ego between death and rebirth (described in **I-33** and implicit in "Karma and Reincarnation"). Recall that usually after death, first the etheric body dissolves into the etheric world (except for an extract, the fruit of the past life), then the astral body dissolves, after a period of purification, into the astral world (again, except for the extracted fruit), leaving the Ego alone to journey into the spirit world to prepare for a new life in the future.

Now, in SE, Lect. 3, Steiner tells us, "It is a principle of spiritual economy that what has once been gained cannot perish, but is preserved and transplanted on the spiritual soil of posterity."[1] Progress made in the development of any component of a human being's makeup is not lost but is preserved in other worlds. One "stores up treasures" there (Mt 6,19-20), so to speak. One way this principle applies is on an individual basis between lives, as Steiner tells us early in Lect. 1 (and also in *Reading the Pictures of the Apocalypse* (RPA), Pt. 2, Lect. 2). As the Ego descends from cosmic "Midnight" back through the astral and etheric spheres (or worlds) toward subsequent earthly incarnation, it picks up preserved extracts of the astral and etheric bodies left in these worlds from the imprint of one's prior earthly life.[2] In this manner, what has previously been perfected is not lost but carried over in transformed state.

While the individual aspect is important, SE deals primarily with the aspect of the "preservation and transplantation of spiritual treasures"

---

1. Compare this to Teilhard de Chardin's statement, in *The Phenomenon of Man* (PHEN), Book Three, Chap. 3, Sec. 1, Subsec. A (in Vol. 3), " . . . the whole history [is] there to pledge to us that a truth once seen, even by a single mind, always ends up by imposing itself on the totality of human consciousness."

2. This relates closely with the evidence presented in Powell's *Hermetic Astrology* I (HA-1). Especially pertinent are the statements by Steiner from *Life Between Death & Rebirth* (LBDR) and *The Karma of Untruthfulness*, Vol. 2 (KU-2) quoted in the early part of the writing on Powell (see Vol. 3) which Powell identifies as the "lodestar" in his research for HA1 and HA2. These significant indications by Steiner, long before computers made their demonstration practicable, are as follows:

From LBDR, Lect. 5:

> When a person passes through the gate of death he dies under a certain configuration of stars. This configuration is significant for his further life of soul because it remains there as an imprint. In his soul there remains the endeavor to enter into the same configuration at a new birth, to do justice once again to the forces received at the moment of death. It is an interesting point that if one works out the configuration at death and compares it with the configuration of the later birth, one finds that it coincides to a high degree with the configuration at the former death.

between one human or spiritual being and another human being. As Steiner said (SE, Lect. 1):

> It is, after all, clear that great differences exist when one looks at the course of human development and that the extracts or abstracts of their bodies can have different values depending on the kinds of fruit they were able to extract from life. And when we remember that there are great leaders of humanity, initiates who lead other human beings into the spiritual worlds, then we have to ask ourselves this question: What causes the accomplishments of the initiates to be preserved for the future?

So it is to the initiates who have been the great leaders of humanity that we look for the further application of the principle. Here we would do well to follow along somewhat with Steiner's presentation, starting with the old initiates—back on Atlantis. There were schools known as "oracles," where instruction was given and initiates were taught by a leader. Whether or not there were more, we know there were *seven* such oracles related to the planets (see RPA, Pt. 2, Lect. 2). The Sun Oracle, also known as the Christ Oracle, was the highest of these, and its leader was pre-eminent among all. He was known as "Manu" (see **I-59**), and we may take it that the Biblical Noah was identifiable in some manner with

---

2. (*continued*) From KU-2, Lect. 22:

> It is very significant that the dead person leaves the physical world in close connection with the constellation arising for his life from the positions of the planets.... Investigations are often made—unfortunately not always with the necessary respect and dignity, but out of egoistic reasons—into the starry constellation prevailing at birth. Much less selfish and more beautiful would be a horoscope, a planetary horoscope made for the moment of death. This is most revealing for the whole soul of the human being, for the entry into death at a particular moment is most revealing in connection with karma.

The significant difference between Powell's work and that of most Western astrologists is that the latter use the tropical zodiac, which, in contrast with ancient hermetic astrologers, has no relation to what one looks up at the starry skies and sees but relates only to the seasonal movement of the Sun.

By using the sidereal zodiac which he has defined, Powell demonstrates convincingly that persons identified by Steiner as reincarnations of particular earlier personalities are indeed that. It is a sobering demonstration, particularly to the objective, scientific mind, that the human being is, indeed, intimately related to the planetary bodies and zodiacal constellations in a unique way.

this leader. It seems pertinent to point out that the account of Noah has him taking *seven* people with him in the ark, namely, his wife, and his three sons and their wives (Gen 6,18 and 7,7). That their familial relationship is metaphorical and allegorical is virtually certain from an anthroposophical standpoint. Even Peter seems to recognize this by simply referring to the fact that he took "seven other persons" with him (2 Pet 2,5).[3]

While vast earlier migrations had taken place to lands newly arising out of the sea, "toward the end of the Atlantean era a group of advanced human beings was formed in the vicinity of what is today Ireland." Manu foresaw the impending catastrophe and set about to prepare for the preservation of the "Seed" that would go into the post-Atlantean Epoch. He "chose the best people in order to lead them into a special land. They were plain and simple people who were different from most other Atlanteans in that they had almost completely lost their clairvoyance.... The advanced people in Atlantis had begun to develop their intellect, yet they were simple people who possessed inner warmth and were deeply devoted to their leader. He took this select group east to the center of Asia, where he founded the center of the post-Atlantean culture" (SE, Lect. 1).

It is important to realize that this group was quite separate from those who had migrated earlier, before they had gathered up all that Atlantean culture was subsequently to develop. These earlier migrations to what is today the Far East were the ancestors of today's Orientals. The origin of the differences between East and West can be seen from this, and is discussed at some length in *The Evolution of the Earth and Man* (EVEM), Lect. 5. But the group Manu led to central Asia was "kept in isolation from the human beings who were unsuited to the task."

Manu accomplished the task of preserving the part of Atlantean culture that was to be carried over into the new epoch by a mysterious process of preserving the etheric bodies of the greatest leaders of the seven oracles. The process is described in the parallel accounts in SE, Lect. 1, and RPA, Lect. 2. While normally the etheric body dissipates into the

---

3. Numerous other factors support this conclusion. They include, among others: 1. the fact that Biblical personages in those ages, such as Adam, Noah, and the patriarchs, represented common memories associated with the group Ego over a period of time "as far as [a] blood relationship could be traced" (see GSJ, Lect. 4); 2. the meaning of "ark" (see "Ark"); and 3. the meaning of "animals" (see "Wild Animals").

general etheric world upon the passage of a decedent from the etheric to the astral world between lives, the law of spiritual economy provides for the preservation of the etheric (or other) body of one who has rather fully perfected it. After Manu had preserved the etheric body of the greatest initiate of each of these seven oracles, he set about to develop "the seven most outstanding people from his group" who "had the best aptitude for present-day culture" and caused the preserved etheric bodies to be brought forward into these. In Lect. 3 Steiner tells us more about the preservation and transplantation of the etheric bodies:

> While leading His small group of simple people to Asia, He carried the etheric bodies of the seven most significant initiates of Atlantis with Him. Such a thing is possible through the methods that had been developed in the mystery centers. You have to visualize this as purely a spiritual process and not in the way as if one could wrap up etheric bodies and put them into boxes for safekeeping. What is certain, however, is that etheric bodies *can* be preserved for later times....
>
> When a human being is descending to a new incarnation, he must envelop himself again with a new etheric body. Now, through the methods alluded to above, it is perfectly possible to weave into this new etheric body an old one that was preserved. And so after a diligent educational process, when the time had come, there were to emerge from the immigrants and their descendants seven individuals whose souls at their birth were sufficiently prepared to have the preserved etheric bodies of the seven greatest initiates of the Atlantean Oracles woven into their own etheric bodies....
>
> Thus we see not only that the ego but also that the second member of the supersensible constitution—the etheric body—is capable of reincarnation. The seven individuals from among the followers of the Great Initiate of the Sun Oracle were inspired human beings simply by the fact that they had received these etheric bodies containing the forces and powers of the Atlantean era. At certain times their etheric bodies were capable of letting the forces stream into themselves that unveiled the mysteries of the Sun, Mars, Saturn, and so forth. Hence they appeared to be inspired individuals, but their utterances certainly exceeded anything their astral bodies or egos were able to understand.

It was these seven who became the "seven holy rishis" of the Ancient Indian Cultural Age, and they were the seven Manu led over in the Genesis account of Noah. Manu himself was the greatest of the Sun Oracle leaders, over and above the seven. The seven were simple men, no one of whom understood the collective wisdom that came by revelation through them, but collectively they constituted what led the new Cultural Age. The one with the etheric body from the Sun Oracle leadership was always the preeminent one of the group, but none was equal to the great Manu. Even the collective seven could not grasp the exalted wisdom of the Sun Oracle as it came to him.

Some of that wisdom began to be revealed in the Ancient Persian Cultural Age (see **I-1, I-2, I-3**). As Steiner tells us in SE, Lect. 3, the founder of that culture, the great ancient Zarathustra, was "the most important disciple of the Great Initiate of the Sun Oracle" and hence able to see radiating from the Sun the "Great Aura," or "Ahura Mazdao," by which the flow of evolution was made possible. Zarathustra initiated his close disciples into the great Mysteries of the world, and two of these disciples are of special significance. To the first, Zarathustra transmitted the wisdom of "clairvoyance in the astral body, as well as the ability to perceive in one's present time frame simultaneously everything that is happening and all the mysteries spread out in both physical and spiritual space." To the second, Zarathustra transmitted "the power to read the Akashic Chronicle, and this is nothing less than the clairvoyant power of the etheric body, enabling the human being to perceive the successive phases of evolution in time." The first disciple was reincarnated as Hermes, or Hermes Trismegistos, the founder of Egyptian culture, and, through the process of spiritual economy, "the astral body of Zarathustra was transmitted to Hermes so that he could proclaim the message of higher worlds and their mysteries and incorporate them into Egyptian culture.... Hermes wore Zarathustra's astral body as if it were a garment." The other disciple was reincarnated as Moses, and he received the etheric body of Zarathustra, but a special event had to occur to make this possible.

The forces of Zarathustra's etheric body had to be awakened in this reborn disciple when he was a very small child, that is before his own individual development could come into play. For this reason, the child was placed into an ark of bulrushes that was then put into the water [Ex 2,1-10], so that he was completely cut off from the rest of the world and was unable to interact with it. That is when the forces of Zarathustra's etheric body that had been woven into him germinated and ... became illuminated.

The Ego of Zarathustra also had many reincarnations,[4] including as Zarathas (Zoroaster) in Babylon where, according to Steiner (*The Gospel of St. Matthew* [GSMt], Lect. 2), he was the teacher of Pythagoras and the "middle period prophets."[5] And we know from "The Nativity" above that all of these higher elements of Zarathustra returned again into the Solomon Jesus child of Matthew's Gospel.

So far, we have seen how the principle of spiritual economy works in the individual from one incarnation to the next, and how it works between great initiate leaders and others who come later. In Lect. 3 Steiner goes on to tell us how it also works in a third way, from higher spiritual beings into humanity. The primary example he gives is that of Noah's son Shem (Gen 6,10; see also BFS, Chap. 11). Here it might be well first to note that in **I-43** the fifth "sub-race" of the Atlantean "root race" is the original "Semites," and to be aware that Steiner tells us (e.g., *The Apocalypse of St. John* [ASJ], Lect. 8) that it was this sub-race, that of Manu (Noah), that carried (i.e., preserved the good from) the Atlantean Epoch's culture to the present Aryan (post-Atlantean) Epoch. In like manner, the sixth (Slavic) sub-race of the Aryan root race will carry Aryan culture over to the Sixth Epoch and the seventh sub-race of that Epoch will carry humanity's accomplishments over to the Seventh Epoch

---

4. Perhaps the best elaboration of these is by Welburn in *The Book with Fourteen Seals* (BFS) (see "Welburn," Vol. 3). What he calls "the book with fourteen seals" is actually the *Apocalypse of Adam* text found among the gnostic collection at Nag Hammadi (See NHL). He shows that rather than being a gnostic text, however, it was in fact an Essene writing. He plausibly identifies the various "seals" as incarnations of Zarathustra, including the one as the sixth century B.C. teacher in Babylon. One of the most intriguing aspects of this ancient document is that the first thirteen "seals" end with the statement, "And thus he came on the water," the same spiritually real expression spoken of Moses, "and she named him Moses, for she said, `Because I drew him out of the water'" (Ex 2,10).

5. As teacher of Pythagoras, see The Gospel of St. Matthew (GSMt), Lect. 2 and SE, Lect. 112; as teacher of the "middle period prophets," see GSMt, Lects. 2 and 6. Steiner says that it was three of Zarathas' students in Babylonia that reincarnated six hundred years later as the three wise men of Mt 2,1 (GSMt, Lect. 6) and that one of them was Pythagoras who also "became one of the disciples of Jesus" (SE, Lect. 11). Prokofieff, in Part 3, Chap. 2 of *The Heavenly Sophia and the Being of Anthroposophia* (HSBA) presents a plausible case that the prophet Daniel and the Persian king Cyrus were the other two.

whence, as the final fruit of the Physical Condition of Form at the last
"Trumpet," it will lead humanity toward that heavenly condition which
becomes the "Seed" for the Jupiter state after the end of Earth evolution
(see **I-1**, **I-2** and **I-3**).

This third example of spiritual economy involves the transference of
powers from an *avatar* to an otherwise exalted human being whose higher
elements are then not only *preserved* but are *preserved and multiplied* so as
to be available to subsequent humanity in manifold, if not even unlimited, quantity. What then is an "avatar?" WNWD says, "1. *Hinduism* a
god's coming down in bodily form to the earth; incarnation of a god; 2.
any incarnation or embodiment, as of a quality or concept in a person."
See also 1 Brit 734, "Avatar." Steiner says that the Christ was the greatest
of the avatars. It is interesting to see how Christianity attempts to distinguish the avatar from Christ, yet how the Oriental still sees the Christ as
an avatar.[6] This is shown in 16 Brit 284, "Christianity," in such a way
that it is easy to see that they are one and the same—when Steiner's explanation is added. In SE, Lect. 3., he identifies what an avatar is in speaking
of the role of Shem as the progenitor of the Semitic people:

> When a number of human beings are to descend from a particular
> progenitor, a special provision must be made for this in the spiritual
> world. In the case of Shem, the provision was that an etheric body was
> specially woven for him from the spiritual world, which he was to
> carry. This enabled him to bear in his own etheric body an especially
> exalted being from the spiritual world, a being who could not other-
> wise have incarnated on earth because it was incapable of descending
> into a compact physical body.... This higher being was not Shem,

---

6. Sometimes a title is an entire sermon in itself. Such is the case with the two-lecture (3-
17-07 and 5-13-08) publication *Christianity Began as a Religion But is Greater Than All
Religions* (CBRel). Religion is indeed but the chrysalis of the higher Christianity. The historical Church and what still exists today as organized Christianity is a "religion," constituting "the church" only in a lower sense, whereas in the higher sense, "the church
universal" will be attained only when, through anthroposophical insight, Christianity has
risen above the stage of being a religion (cf. Jer 31,33; Heb 10,16). Only at that stage will
it bring within its folds such as "the Oriental who still sees the Christ as an avatar," as
indeed he was. It is then that "the elect shall be gathered from the four winds" (Mt 24,31;
Mk 13,27). That this idea may not generally sit well within "ecclesiastica" today anymore
than it did in Jesus' day should not be surprising. But one should ponder how it fits with
the prophets and the Gospels. Certainly this is not to suggest that churches are not still
needful in our day. But at the same time, it suggests the philosophy toward which they
must tend if they are not to harden into a "Lot's wife" in days to come.

but it incarnated in Shem—the human being—for a special mission. Unlike ordinary human beings, this higher being did not undergo various incarnations, but descended only once into a human body. Such a being is called an avatar.... He descends but once into this world for the sole purpose of carrying out a certain mission.

The part of a human being that is indwelled by such an avatar being acquires a special character in that it is able to multiply. When a grain of seed is sown into the ground, the stalk grows from it, and the grain is multiplied into the ears of grain. In the same way, the etheric body of Shem multiplied into many copies, and these were woven into all his descendants....

But this etheric body of Shem was later used in yet another way.... In the later phase of the evolution of the Semitic people, it became necessary that a very exalted being descend to earth in order to communicate with them and provide an impetus to their culture. Such a being was the Melchizedek of Biblical history who, as it were, had to "put on" the preserved [original] etheric body of Shem—the very etheric body that was still inhabited by an avatar being.[7] Once it was woven into him, Melchizedek was able to transmit to Abraham the impulse necessary for the continued progress of Semitic culture.

In SE, Lect. 2, Steiner gives further insight into the nature of avatars:

They were beings capable of accomplishing their development in higher, more spiritual realms who did not need to descend into corporeal bodies for their further progress. However, in order to intervene in the course of human evolution, such beings can nevertheless descend vicariously into corporeal bodies such as our own....

Such a spiritual being who descends in this way into a human body in order to intervene in evolution as a human being is called

---

7. Steiner identifies Melchizedek as the reincarnated Manu (Noah) who put on the preserved etheric body of his own Atlantean son, Shem (GSMt, Lect. 4; see also Prokofieff's HSBA, Part 3, fn 9, p. 286). Moreover, Steiner says in Lect. 4 and SE, Lect. 3, that Manu also initiated Zarathustra, though he does not there explain how the founder of the first post-Atlantean Cultural Era (Ancient India) could have taught the much later founder of the second (Ancient Persia). Perhaps he spoke of the individuality (rather than the personality) in one case or the other; or maybe the different manner of counting generations prior to Abraham (see "The Nativity," in this vol. fn 3); or possibly the office rather than the person, for Steiner normally identified him only as "The Great Initiate of the Sun Oracle."

an "avatar" in the East; such a being gains nothing from this embodiment for himself and experiences nothing that is of significance for the world. This, then, is the distinction between a leading being that has emanated from human evolution and beings whom we call avatars. The latter reap no benefit for themselves from their physical embodiments, or even from one embodiment to which they subject themselves; they enter a physical body for the blessing and progress of all human beings.

All of this is just one more instance of how anthroposophy can clarify the meaning of scripture. Particularly is this true in the case of Paul's description of Melchizedek taken from Gen 14: "He is without father or mother or genealogy, and has neither beginning of days nor end of life, but resembling the Son of God he continues a priest forever" (Heb 7,3). It is the avatar character of both that enabled Paul to quote Ps 110,4 in saying of Christ, "Thou art a priest for ever, after the order of Melchizedek" (Heb 5,6).

But the Christ avatar is even further distinguished. Steiner says of it (SE, Lect. 3):

> If an avatar enters a human sheath, the essence of the host is dispersed into many replicas. In contrast to the copies of Shem's etheric body, the copies of the astral and etheric bodies of Jesus of Nazareth had another special characteristic. The copies of Shem's etheric body could be implanted only into his own descendants whereas the copies of the etheric body and the astral body of Jesus of Nazareth could be implanted into all human beings of the most diverse peoples and races. A copy of the archetypal astral and etheric bodies of Jesus of Nazareth could be implanted in anyone who through his or her personal development had become ready for this transfer, no matter what race such an individual belonged to. And we see how in this subsequent evolution of Christendom, strange developments take place behind the external historical facade, and only such developments can render the external course of events intelligible.

Steiner gives examples, summarized in **I-74**, of historical personalities who embodied copies of the etheric or astral bodies of Jesus. It was in such an etheric body that Paul perceived Christ on the Damascus road

(Acts 9,1-9; see also Gal 1,16 in KJV and in RSV footnote).[8] The concept of spiritual economy also helps us understand the depth of that scriptural passage quoted by Steiner more than any other, Paul's Gal 2,20, "Not I, but Christ in me," which tends to demonstrate the Ego and astral body, as well as the etheric body, of Jesus of Nazareth. All people who ready themselves sufficiently can "put on" one of these bodies and therefore, in spiritual reality, actually embody the Christ within. Steiner put it thus: "Yes, these imprinted copies of the Christ Jesus individuality are waiting to be taken in by human souls—they are waiting!"

---

8. While Steiner does not say explicitly that it was through an etheric body of Jesus that Paul so perceived the Christ, it seems to me implied beyond any doubt in what Steiner said in SE. This can be seen not only in the passages quoted in the text from Lect. 3, but also from the following:

> Lect. 1 (p. 5)—When the light of spiritual illumination fell on Saul-Paul near Damascus, Paul beheld the Christ that was united with the earth and knew immediately that it was He who had shed His blood at Golgotha.
>
> Lect. 2 (p. 19)—The etheric and astral bodies of Jesus of Nazareth were multiplied and the copies preserved until they could be used in the course of human evolution....When in the course of time a human being appeared who, irrespective of nationality, *was mature and suitable enough* to have his own etheric or astral body interwoven with a copy of the etheric or astral body of Jesus of Nazareth, then those bodies could be woven into that particular person's being [emphasis added].
>
> Lect. 3 (p. 51)— ... the initiate who wrote the *Heliand* ... had clairvoyant faculties, so that he was able to see Christ in a way similar to Paul's perception of Christ at Damascus. Through the event at Golgotha the Christ-Being had united Himself with the astral body of the earth, thereby infusing His power into the aura of the earth; and when Paul became clairvoyant, he could clearly perceive: The Christ *is* present! ... Only after he had seen the being that was woven into the earth with his own eyes did he change from Saul to Paul. In a similar vision, the Risen Christ ... was revealed to the writer of the *Heliand....* You may want to ask why the author of the *Heliand* was able to communicate such an image from clairvoyant perception. He was able to do this because a copy of the etheric body of Jesus of Nazareth was woven into his own etheric body.
>
> Lect. 5 (p. 65)—The Christ has liberated us from this three and a half day test.... We see the first example of this in Saul when he became Paul. What happened to him on his way to Damascus must be interpreted as something similar to an initiation. The reason that he needed only a few minutes for it was that he had attained *a certain maturity* in the preceding life [emphasis added].

[Note that Steiner here seems to have specifically included Paul within those who had reached the necessary *maturity* indicated in the passage from Lect. 2 above.]

In Lect. 8 (p. 103), Steiner indicates that it was the same spiritualized (etheric) fire that permitted Moses to see Christ in the burning bush on Sinai that also opened the eyes of Paul on the Damascus road. Later in the same lecture, after having spoken of others who have taken in the etheric or astral body of Jesus, Steiner says (p. 111): *(continued on following page)*

Does not this put special meaning in Rev 3,20, "Behold, I stand at the door and knock; if any one hears my voice and opens the door, I will come in to him and eat with him, and he with me." That this passage concludes the Seventh and last Cultural Era of the Aryan (post-Atlantean) Epoch (see **I-24** and **I-25**) is an indication of the extent to which one must progress in order to "open the door" to the Christ for full entry.[9]

If one reflects upon it, it is the joinder of Christ's earthly sacrifice, the Mystery of Golgotha, with the principle of spiritual economy that made it possible for Evangelist John to say, in Jn 3,16, "For God so loved the world that he gave his only Son, that whoever believes in him should not perish but have eternal life."

One can now begin to understand Steiner's statement in Lect. 1, "The result of this is that the whole configuration of the process of reincarnation is much more complicated than is usually supposed." And the passages of scripture that are clarified by such understanding, of which only a few have been discussed here, show that the truths of karma and reincarnation are woven deeply into the Bible when it is properly understood.

---

8. *(continued)*
   Because they bore a part of Jesus of Nazareth within themselves, they knew from a feeling of inner illumination that the Christ was alive. They knew it as well as Paul when he saw the Christ-Apparition in the blazing spiritualized fire of the heavens.
   Lect. 11 (p. 154)—Who was the first man to see Christ in the aura of the earth? It was St. Paul.... What caused Saul to become Paul? Neither the teachings nor the events that took place in Palestine, but the event at Damascus, which was of a supersensible nature.

   It seems inescapable that Paul, having become sufficiently mature, was given an etheric body of Jesus and thus was enabled to perceive him clairvoyantly. It would be hard to apply the tests laid down by Steiner in SE in describing how lesser representatives have received such an etheric body while denying it to Paul. It also seems to follow from what Steiner says in SE that those who are able to perceive Christ in the etheric in the "Second Coming" will have first received, woven into their own etheric body, a copy of the etheric body of Christ.
   Finally, the proper rendition of the Greek in Gal 1,16 has Paul recognizing that some special qualification (maturity) existed in him before he was born whereby he was "set apart" so that the Son was revealed *in* him. This clearly comports with what Steiner has said above and with the conclusion that an etheric body of Jesus was woven into his own.
9. Paul's statement in 1 Cor 15,8 that Christ's appearance to him was "as to one untimely born," takes on new meaning also in the light of this, for the etheric body of humanity was not to reach the state of such perception, absent initiation, until a much later era. In Lect. 11, Steiner refers to this passage as being "premature birth," meaning "not descending too deeply into the physical realm." But this is precisely what the reascent of humanity is to accomplish, thanks to the Mystery of Golgotha.

FORGIVEN SINS

"I HAVE BEEN SAVED AND FORGIVEN. All the burdens and consequences of my former sins are gone." So goes the substance of the claim widely professed within Christianity.

In general, this statement comports with Christian doctrine across the spectrum of Confessions. Yet, among conscientious and thinking people, Christians as well as others, a certain facet of it disquiets rather than consoles, and for the less delicate is not only a repugnance but a basis for mockery. And perhaps justifiably so, for while Christianity should represent the highest of all moralities, and forgiveness one of its noblest attributes, there is something inherently immoral about this claim, as we shall see. So subconsciously apparent to all is the ethical violation that endless qualification has been variously rationalized into it by Christian apology.

What is the immorality, and how can it be expunged? The immorality is rooted in the word "consequences." For focus consider three illustrations (there are, of course, endless more subtle shades of the problem).

First, a criminal properly convicted of murder with malice is sentenced to the maximum penalty of the law in a jurisdiction which has abolished the death sentence.[1]

Second, a person with endless personal materialistic desires and thoughtless financial profligacy runs up large debts, fully enjoying and consuming their wherewithal, then declares bankruptcy, leaving creditors totally unpaid.

Third, a highly successful professional man, married to his childhood sweetheart who gave up her own opportunity for college in order to support him through school, and father to minor children, having created an "enviable" lifestyle and saved little for family support or education, leaves his wife and family for another woman and shirks to the fullest degree possible any commitment to his former family.

---

1. The morality of the death sentence is not here in issue, but to avoid execution as a "consequence," its abolition is here postulated. The matter is complicated by the offsetting and divine "Vengeance is Mine" pronouncement, which is also avoided for now by this postulate.

In each situation, confession of sin and acceptance of Christ is made, followed by the above assertion of salvation.[2]

Typically, theology rationalizes that actions speak louder than words, thus casting doubt upon the sincerity of the confession, while at the same time acknowledging that it is possible that the latter is real and that salvation does exist, and that there is no way for humans to know the sincerity since only God knows the human heart. In this, theology has indeed patched together several spiritual and scriptural truths to rationalize its way out of what, by all appearances, is a moral atrocity. The fallback is simply to "have faith," a phrase usually mouthed along with the confession itself to establish a theologically impregnable fortress—but one that repulses humanity's more conscientious element.

The faithful shrug off this problem by saying that some things (such as knowing the mind of God on this judgment) are beyond the limits of human knowledge. On this, they collide with one of Steiner's seminal and most potent assertions, namely, that it is inappropriate to speak of any limitation on human knowledge (see *The Philosophy of Spiritual Activity* [PSA], Chap. 7). That humanity reverts to this shelter is based upon the spiritual darkness in which it still dwells. The biographical sketch of Steiner, inadequate though fair, in 11 Brit 241, hints simultaneously at Steiner's pronouncement and at the rarity of those capable of such knowledge when it characterizes anthroposophy as being "based on the notion that there is a spiritual world comprehensible to pure thought but accessible only to the highest faculties of mental knowledge." Yet it recognizes Steiner's assertion of equality in that such "ability ... [of intellect] is theoretically innate in everyone" (compare Jn 10,34, "you are gods").

The "immorality" in the above three situations is the screaming objective injustice in the "saved" person's escape from the "consequences" of the sin. This is not to deny the sincerity of the person's experience or the reality of "salvation." It is merely to recognize that from an earthly perspective, it is grossly unjust. How then can a "just God" permit it if indeed everything on Earth has its pattern and predicate in the spiritual world (see "As Above, So Below," Vol. 2, "*What Is Man?*")?

The second part (How can it be expunged?) of the initial question, can be answered only by anthroposophical insight. First, it is necessary

---

2. Presuming, in order to eliminate denominational differences, that all other doctrinal requisites such as baptism and the like are fulfilled.

to recognize that the earthly endowments of humanity have never been, are not now, and never will be, a constant, but have evolved from highly primitive to present descended state as a part of humanity's Fall, salvation and reascent (the journey of the primordial Prodigal Son of God). The corollary of this is that neither the past nor the future can be understood on the basis of the outward appearance and spiritual mentality of the present. Second, it is absolutely essential to recognize that from the time of the Fall until a distant future time of reascent (see the third through the sixth Evolutionary Epochs in **I-1** and **I-2**, the period of humanity's mineral-physical existence in its Earth Condition of Consciousness) the Individuality in each human being lives again and again on Earth.

This evolutionary change in humanity's condition is reflected in the Biblical usage of the root term "forgive." Thus, the entry "Forgiveness" in 2 ABD 831 "consists of three articles surveying the concept of forgiveness as it is presented in the Old Testament, in early Judaism, and in the New Testament, respectively."

The Old Testament usage primarily reflects the Group Ego of the people of Israel without reflecting any type of individual application; it is tied in with sacrificial offerings, priestly pronouncements, scapegoats, and the like. This was necessitated by the overall spiritual goal of preparing and purifying through the Blood of Abraham and David the receptacle for the Christ. The entirety of the thrust of forgiveness in the Old Testament was toward fulfilling the goal of the "chosen people," as the following passages illustrate.

> **Ex 32,31-33**: (31) So Moses returned to the Lord and said, "Alas, this people have sinned a great sin; they have made for themselves gods of gold. (32) But now, if thou wilt *forgive* their sin—and if not, blot me, I pray thee, out of thy book which thou has written." (33) But the Lord said to Moses, "Whoever has sinned against me, him will I blot out of my book."

The individual aspect at the end suggests that God will blot out any one individual who, by sinning, stands in the way of the mission of the chosen people; anything beyond that would seem to be an incipient reflection of the approaching time when the burning contemporary question of evolving individual responsibility in Israel was prophetically expressed in Jer 31,27-34 and Ezek 18.

1 K 8,37-40: (37) If there is famine in the land,... pestilence or [crop] blight; [enemy siege]; ... plague ... sickness .... (39) then hear thou in heaven thy dwelling place, and *forgive* ... and render to each whose heart thou knowest, according to all his ways ... ; (40) that they may fear thee all the days that they live in the land which thou gavest to our fathers. (In accord, 2 Ch 6,30.)

Again, the reference to "each heart" appears to be out of concern that the one may bring evil on the whole people.

Job: While the term "forgive" is not used in this book, the categorical assertion by Job's "friends" is that suffering is brought not only upon him but upon his entire familial domain because of some hidden sin of his.

Ps 79,9: Help us, O God of our salvation, for the glory of thy name; deliver us, and *forgive* our sins, for thy name's sake!

The community is still the obvious concern. And why is the forgiveness "for thy name's sake" rather than for the welfare of those forgiven? Surely the implication must be that the fulfillment of the covenant relationship is of benefit to God. Prophetically, the provision of the true Israel and the vehicle for the approaching Christ would appear to answer this question—the people were "a chosen race" and servants of God's purpose.

Dan 9,19: O Lord, hear; O Lord, *forgive*, ... for thy own sake, O my God, because thy city and thy people are called by thy name."

Again, the forgiveness was collective for the people "for thy own sake."

One searches the Old Testament in vain for a different thrust, one in which forgiveness is clearly either brought to, or required of, the individual unharnessed from the mission of the people. Not until the Babylonian captivity does forgiveness begin to be associated with the individual's own destiny (Jer 31 and Ezek 18) and, even then, its tone is primarily prospective.

"Forgiveness" in the New Testament comes to individual fruition and centers around one or more of the following themes:

1. The healing nature of forgiveness; e.g., Mt 9,1-8; Mk 2,1-12; Lk 5,17-26; 7,36-50; Jn 5,2-14.
2. The nature and extent of one's forgiveness is related to the manner in which one forgives others; e.g., Mt 6,12-15 and 18,21-35; Mk 11,25-26; Lk 6,37; 11,4; Eph 4,32; Col 3,13; Philem.

3. The authority of Christ (e.g., Mt 9,1-8; Mk 2,1-12; Lk 5,17-26) and his servants (e.g., Jn 20,23) on Earth to forgive sins.

4. The nature of sins that will (can) not be forgiven: Mt 12,31-32; Mk 3,28-30; Lk 12,10; Heb 6,4; 10,26; 1 Jn 5,16-17.

But given this evolutionary change, and its reflection in the Bible, we return to the initial twofold question, "What is the immorality of escaping the consequences of one's sin, and how can the immorality be expunged?"

To begin with, we need to recognize that the claim to have had the consequences of one's sin absolved requires muting the following otherwise rather loud and appealing scriptures:

Mt 5,23-26: (23) So if you are offering your gift at the altar, and there remember that your brother has something against you, (24) leave your gift there before the altar and go; first be reconciled to your brother, and then come and offer your gift. (25) Make friends quickly with your accuser, while you are going with him to court, lest your accuser hand you over to the judge, and the judge to the guard, and you be put in prison; (26) *truly, I say to you, you will never get out until you have paid the last penny.* (My emphasis)

Mt 16,27: For the Son of man is to come with his angels in the glory of his Father, and then he will repay every man for what he has done.

Gal 6,7: Do not be deceived; God is not mocked, for whatever a man sows, that he will also reap.

1 Cor 3,13-15: (13) Each man's work will become manifest; for the Day will disclose it, because it will be revealed with fire, and the fire will test what sort of work each one has done. (14) If the work which any man has built on the foundation survives, he will receive a reward. (15) If any man's work is burned up, he will suffer loss, though he himself will be saved, but only as through fire.

Few passages show more clearly the interworking of the anthroposophical principle of the preservation of an extract of the astral or etheric bodies, to the extent accomplished during a given incarnation, with the "Purifying Fire" that prepares the human Ego for entry into the spiritual world on its journey between lives (see **I-33**).

2 Cor 5,10: For we must all appear before the judgment seat of
Christ, so that each one may receive good or evil, according to what
he has done in the body.

Col 3,25: For the wrongdoer will be paid back for the wrong he has
done, and there is no partiality.

Rev 2,23b: "And all the churches shall know that I am he who
searches mind and heart, and I will give to each of you as your works
deserve."

Rev 20,12: And I saw the dead, great and small, standing before the
throne, and books were opened. Also another book was opened,
which is the book of life. And the dead were judged by what was
written in the books, by what they had done.

Rev 22,12: "Behold, I am coming soon, bringing my recompense,
to repay every one for what he has done."

Anthroposophy shows us that these scriptures must be given their full
force and effect, and that this can be done without doing violence to the
principle of salvation stated at the outset, the only modification being in
regard to the "consequences" of one's sin. And in showing how this can
be, it also "expunges" the immorality and the patent injustice of the
above creedal assertion of salvation, and gives a solid and meaningful
foundation to the claim that our God is a "just God" (Ps 145,17; Ezek,
18,25,29; Ezek 33,17-20; Jn 5,30). Nor does it do violence to the reality
that God's mercy is never ending; rather it eliminates what might be
called "cheap grace."

It is a nonsequitur to say that Christians want to escape the consequences of their acts, declining to make restitution for wrongs committed (Num 5,6-7). Restitution is a morally sound precept which Christ
did not come to repudiate. Paul requires us to "Owe no one anything,
except to love one another; for he who loves his neighbor has fulfilled
the law" (Rom 13,8). Christianity, and theologians in particular, have
long labored under the assumption, erroneous from the anthroposophical standpoint, that the "law" that Christ came to fulfill (Mt 5,17) was
the Torah. That law was merely a reflection (Heb 10,1; Heb 8,1-5; Heb
9,23-24) of the higher heavenly law, namely, the karmic law, by which
life in the physical world is regulated according to spiritual relationships.

The Sermon on the Mount, but particularly Mt 5, may be looked upon as the Magna Carta of the karmic law. In Mt 5, the fulfillment mentioned in verse 17 is followed by a series of revisions of the Torah, looked upon by practical humanity as unrealistic and infeasible, ending with the standard that one "must be perfect, as your heavenly Father is perfect." That it doesn't really mean that degree of perfection, or that such perfection is somehow accomplished for us vicariously after only one lifetime, is the necessary belief of all who reject the reality of humanity's evolution and the involvement of reincarnation and the karmic law. But the Sermon on the Mount is talking about our actions *on Earth while we dwell thereon.*

Clearly the Evangelist Matthew knew of reincarnation and its concomitant karmic law, for his entire Nativity (see "The Nativity") is predicated upon the Essenic expectation of the return of the Zarathustra Individuality. And the Evangelist could hardly have more clearly indicated that "the law" he referred to was the divine karmic law from which Moses had derived what he brought down from Mt. Sinai. How was this indicated? By having Christ declare, "Think not that I have come to abolish the law and the prophets; I have come not to abolish them but to fulfil them. For truly, I say to you, till heaven and earth pass away, not an iota, not a dot, will pass from the law until all is accomplished." Almost immediately then are given six examples where Christ not only does away with "a jot and a tittle" (KJV), but totally supplants six portions thereof by a higher spiritual law—expressive of karma, the forming of good and the healing of bad karma. It is nonsensical to say that Christ made this pronouncement (in verse 17) in bringing "the law" then to a close, for verses 18-19 are clearly prospective. And while it might be said that verse 18 is prospective only until the end of Christ's earthly mission, the same does not apply to verse 19. Nor does it do merely to say that all six of the old laws were still in effect and merely subsumed within the new, neither "relaxed" nor "broken" but strengthened. It is hard to say this with "An eye for an eye and a tooth for a tooth," but even harder to go through all the Torah and agree that every "jot" and "tittle" remained applicable after Christ began teaching. Much cerebral energy has been consumed in theological minds to reconcile the apparent inconsistencies in Mt 5, and then explain away the required "perfection" at its conclusion, but it is harmonious all the way through when seen in the light of the merciful and divine karmic law.

Let us now see how anthroposophical insight harmonizes the doctrinal claim of salvation and forgiveness of sins with God's immeasurable justice and mercy while expunging any element of immorality through the concept of unpaid debt or trespass.

To comprehend the matter more fully, one must bring in numerous other concepts, including many terms and phrases found elsewhere in this volume, such as "Karma and Reincarnation," "Lord of Karma" (i.e., Christ as), "I AM" and "Akashic." But we can get a sufficient indication for our present purpose by the following fairly simple exposition.

What is karma? It is probably fairly accurate to say that one's personal karma (as distinguished from that of humanity as a whole) is the net result of all one's prior incarnations to the extent that they have not yet resulted in the development of one's higher three states, i.e., manas, buddhi and atma, or Spirit Self, Life Spirit and Spirit Man (see **I-9**). More simply put, one is the embodiment of one's past karma and the creator of one's future karma (or such higher states). When one no longer has negative karma, one will have attained to the Buddha (cf. buddhi) state (**I-23**, **I-9**) and will not need to incarnate again (see Lk 20,34-38, esp. 36). Not only will it be shown that the immorality which is our immediate concern is expunged by anthroposophical insight, but it immediately becomes clear that the seeming inequity among human beings is an illusion, for through God's unspeakable justice, embodied in the karmic law, there is perfect equality among all human beings. One should not vainly assume that worldly good fortune is a reward, for it may well be (though not necessarily) a burden which one must overcome, as in the case of "the rich young ruler" (Lk 18,18-25), or that worldly burdens are a retribution, for they may merely be an opportunity or test given for necessary spiritual development (Job; 1 Cor 10,13).

At the very end of that period (1908-1914) of Steiner's lectures primarily directed to the Bible, in *Christ and the Human Soul* (CHS), Lect. 3 (July 15, 1914), Steiner speaks of two kinds of karma, *subjective* and *objective*. Subjective karma is personal to an individual and must be erased by some form of offsetting or retributive act in a future life. Sins that would otherwise create negative karma can be made good within the same lifetime ("Make friends quickly with your accuser, while you are going with him to court," Mt 5,25) by appropriate compensatory events (not necessarily of exactly the same character, but sufficient to erase the evil element according to the divine scales; e.g., "love covers a multitude of sins," 1 Pet

4,8). Forgiveness by Christ does not erase subjective karma, for debts incurred by an individual cannot be personally escaped "till you have paid the last penny" (Mt 5,26). On the other hand, when one accepts Christ and takes him into one's own being, then one's objective karma is taken over by Christ, who has become in our era the "Lord of Karma."

What is objective karma? When one sins, there are two kinds of consequences (though some sins, if not affecting others, may perhaps create only *objective* karma, as in the case of a lustful or covetous heart [Mt 5,29; Rom 13,9]. One is to the person who sins and to any person or creature directly affected thereby. That is *subjective* karma, which creates a debt upon the sinner that must be paid in this lifetime or another, whether or not Christ has forgiven the sins. The other type of consequence is to the world—a broader form of karma, which becomes a burden upon all humanity and creation. Every sin, however slight, actually generates evil spiritual beings (e.g., demons) or food for such evil beings, and generates a karmic burden upon humankind. It is beyond the capacity of the sinner to erase this burden, once launched, even when restitution has been made. Evil objective karma must be overcome by humanity as a whole by positive good—not restitutive action, but spontaneous, affirmative good. Thus we are told to "overcome evil with good" (Rom 12,21). Hence, once a person has sinned, overcoming the consequences to the world is beyond that person and rests upon a different agency, either humanity as a whole or Christ. These are the *objective* sins. When one's sins are "forgiven by Christ," it completely erases the objective sins. What one has loosed as evil, as bad karma upon humanity and the world, is canceled out. Those who truly take Christ into their being want to make (even have to want to make) full restitution to those harmed, in this life or another (as in the case when the harmed one has died or disappeared), but they receive the health-giving blessing of knowing in their inner ("supersensible") being that the ill of their past sins has been lifted from the shoulders of the rest of creation. This is not unrelated to Paul's statement about the "eager longing" of the rest of creation in Rom 8,19-23.

For some it will not be easy to let go of the prevailing idea that Christ immediately frees us from *all* the consequences of our sin. That he frees us from all is true, but the process is *immediate* only as it applies to objective karma, that which lies beyond the power of restitution. (It is analogous to the dropping of charges the state has against an accused in a criminal proceeding on condition that restitution be made to the injured party. Note that restitution is a matter of legal right even if the accused is convicted. The state has no power to release that civil obligation.) The prevailing idea is of long standing, though it is only doctrine formed by humanity on the basis of its darkened understanding of what is expressed in the scriptures. No scripture actually says it in explicit nullification of the many scriptural contraindications cited above. The doctrine could have arisen from any number of passages, but probably from none more powerfully than Rev 1,5b, "To him who loves us and has freed us from our sins by his blood." From the same Lazarus/John came the words, "... not that we loved God but that he loved us and sent his Son to be the expiation for our sins."(1 Jn 4,10). Yet we find he also gave us those in Rev 2,23b; 20,12 and 22,12 quoted above.

Let us recognize that this doctrine rises and falls with the belief that we each live only once. They are corollaries of each other. But we shall see in the immediately following essays how and why it was that Christ himself instructed that reincarnation was not to be taught in exoteric Christendom for two thousand years, that is until commencement of the "Second Coming" in the twentieth century, during the 2,160 year Cultural Era of the Consciousness Soul which began with the rebirth, the Renaissance, of humanity in the 15th century (see **I-19**, **I-24** and **I-25**). We have already seen how the acceptance of Christ frees us from the "objective" karma of sin. In "Lord of Karma" we shall also see how through the administration of karmic justice Christ also frees us from its "subjective" aspect. See the discussion early in that essay that starts, "How is it that Christ is Lord of Karma?"

The concept of subjective and objective sin, when fully comprehended, can be seen to fit perfectly every instance of forgiveness of sin spoken of in the Bible; to give meaning to otherwise seemingly countervailing passages such as Mt 5,23-26, Gal 6,7, and Deut 32,35; and to eliminate the immorality inherent in the concept of divine forgiveness as heretofore generally perceived. Nothing in the nature of the subjective/objective sin distinction does any violence to the concept of grace, for indeed the highest view of grace is the opportunity given to the human being under the karmic law to make good, for the sacrifice of Christ which made salvation, i.e., "perfection," ultimately possible for all of creation that wills it. Humanity can hardly come to a more effective agency for curing its evils than a full recognition of the nature and consequences of the subjective/objective sin distinction. But a fuller appreciation of such distinction must yet await an understanding of Christ as the "Lord of Karma."

KARMA AND REINCARNATION

ACCORDING TO RUDOLF STEINER (*Reincarnation and Karma* [RK], Lect. 5), a real understanding of the twin truths of Reincarnation and Karma is the one truly new element that anthroposophy presents to modern Western humanity, which before now was not ready to receive that understanding.[1] The first thing a serious student of anthroposophy (and, as we shall presently see, of the Bible also) will discover along the path is that knowledge of these two truths is essential, for everything else follows more or less as a matter of course if one is able to acquire the right insight into them.

Reincarnation and karma have gained attention in the Western world with the advent of the modern "New Age" movement, which is actually a recurring phenomenon throughout history as in fact every "Age," at its inception, is both important and "New." (None is more important or dynamically "New" than that which marked the turning point of time.) Such modern awareness is simply one of the symptoms of a deep spiritual stirring resulting from the evolutionary stage that began gradually, almost imperceptibly, to sunder old dogma in the last half of the nineteenth century.[2]

What has come forth under the name "Karma and Reincarnation," while healthy in the sense of resulting from a deep spiritual prompting, is laced, in the light of anthroposophy, with misconceptions, misapplications, misunderstandings, and half-truths and has therefore been understandably met by resistance, much of which could and should be dissolved in the light that Steiner has shed upon the matter. Other indications of these spiritual stirrings, such as unusual non-mediumistic

---

1. Actually this element was introduced by H. P. Blavatsky and the Theosophical Society in the late nineteenth century, but the Christ was left out of that presentation. Steiner was the first to show that Karma and Reincarnation were essential for an adequate understanding of the Gospels as well as the entire Biblical message.
2. See "A Time of Spiritual Awakening" in Vol. 3, *Companions Along The Way.*

visions, visitations, sightings and experiences, reassure some and disquiet others and have netted much confusion in society. Steiner predicted the coming of this circumstance later in the century if people did not become aware that the first stirrings in the evolution of a new organ for perception in the etheric world would begin to manifest in seemingly strange ways in some human beings during this time. Luciferic and Ahrimanic spirits have thus far met with considerable success in fogging the issue and generating conceptual conflict even within the Christian community.

The subject, which is far more complex than has usually been imagined, involving as it does the multifold nature (see **I-9**) of each human being, inheres in all of Steiner's twentieth-century works, but especially in the eight *Karmic Relationships* lecture cycles (KR-1 through KR-8) given during the year before his death. It is impossible to cover the scope of Steiner's teachings on reincarnation and karma in this work, but an overview of the basics is necessary before we can fully appreciate the complete Biblical confirmation of these realities.

OVERVIEW OF KARMA AND REINCARNATION

Karmic law operates upon the human being in a transforming, rhythmic ebb and flow. The fourfold Prodigal human being of today is the product of a reciprocation between time and timelessness going back at least to the dawn of the macrocosmic Saturday and running through Sunday and Monday (Old Saturn, Sun and Moon evolutions, respectively), all prior to the Earth evolution or Condition of Consciousness. Within Earth evolution, these prior three states were recapitulated in the first three Evolutionary Epochs (Polarian, Hyperborean and Lemurian; see **I-1**, **I-2** and **I-3**). The "Three Bodies" of the human being were laid down in these times, in preparation for the entry, during the Atlantean Epoch of Earth evolution, of the germinal human Ego. From the very first, rhythm was involved in all creation. By the time creation had progressed to the Lemurian Epoch, Earth evolution involved countless rhythms, from astral to solar to lunar and all the way down to the human processes of taking in and expelling the watery and gaseous elements necessary for growth and reproduction. In conjunction with the separation of the sexes which then occurred (Gen 2,18-24), the astral body became infected by the Luciferic influence resulting in the Fall (Gen 3).

Certain consequences followed. The condensing and hardening of the human form accelerated so that it became bony (thus "Adam," meaning "hard"; Gen 3,17) and could stand upright, a condition required for the formation of the human skull and body as an image of the heavenly pattern (Gen 1,26-27 and 15,5). Three divine consequences necessarily evolved for the healing, over long eons, of the fallen human condition—pain, toil and death (Gen 3,16-19). (The rhythms involved in the healing process of the respective components of the fourfold human being are given in **I-37**.)

It is the healing rhythm inherent in the "death" consequence, that between life and death, with which we are here primarily involved in the working out of human karma. Human karma itself, to the extent manifesting in reincarnation, is a phenomenon to be played out only during the portion of Earth evolution when the human being lives in mineral-physical form. Commencing in Lemurian times, it will end in the Sixth Great Evolutionary Epoch (see **I-2**).

Within this volume, it is shown that the "law" Christ came to fulfill (Mt 5,17) is not that spelled out in the "Written Word" of the Torah, but rather the higher law that exists as its pattern in the spiritual world, the "book" (see "Akashic") of which the Torah is but a "shadow" (Heb 10,1; see "As Above, So Below"). It is inherent in "the Word," Christ himself (Jn 1,1-3), emanating from the Father. The karmic law is part and parcel of that Word and/or of what it "created." Without an understanding of the law of Karma and Reincarnation, the heretofore baffling distinction between the judgment of the Father and the judgment of the Son can never be understood (see "Lord of Karma").

To introduce his vast spiritual insights to humanity, Steiner chose as his audience the one group deemed most receptive to such new insights, namely, the Theosophical Society, founded by H. P. Blavatsky. Because the Society, from which Steiner was later expelled for his emphasis upon the centrality of the Christ, had introduced Oriental concepts for the first time into the modern Western world, he retained much of the Oriental terminology, including "karma." We need first to be aware that the term "karma" is synonymous with "destiny" as Steiner assured us (see WNWD; also *Destiny* [DSTY, 1-15-15] and *The Problem of Destiny* [PRBDY, 10-24-16]). Thus, while "karma" is not itself mentioned in the Bible, "destiny" is entirely Biblical (Job 15,22, Is 65,11-12, Hos 9,13, Eph 1,5,12, 1 Th 5,9, 1 Pet 1,2,20 and 2,8; also Is 23,13 [see

"Wild Animals"]). So we must not reject the term, but rather seek to investigate more fully what it means.

Karma plays itself out in the cycle (Jas 3,6) of life and death, metaphorically akin to that of the grass which flourishes in the morning and is renewed and fades in the evening (Ps 90,5-6); it is primarily the "flesh" of the human being that fades in such manner (Is 40,6-8).

A summary of the human journey between death and rebirth is found in **I-33**. And a hint of its complexity in the formation of the human being can be found in **I-20**; there we see in the "hermetic man" the relationship of the septenary planetary system to the development of human organs, and in the "zodiacal man" the relationship between the duodecimal zodiacal regions and the parts of the human body, as well as something of the rhythmic interrelationship between these sevens and twelves. These insights have existed from more ancient times, but have eluded the grasp of modern science and intellectual thinking. Even they are but a profile of a portion of the domain in which the karmic law works.

If we are to comprehend how karma works, we must begin with an outline of what normally[3] happens in the human being's rhythmic journey between death and rebirth. Steiner presented it often and in many different modes, the most fundamental of which is probably found in *Occult Science* (OS), Chap. 3 (most of OS, including Chap. 3, is condensed in Basic Anthroposophy, Vol. 3).[4]

---

3. We can here address only the "normal" journey. There can be numerous variations, such as would occur, for instance, in the cases of highly advanced souls with special missions, on the one hand, or life destiny thwarted by particular circumstances during the preceding Earth lifetime, on the other hand.

4. Among the other better illustrations are those found in *Rosicrucian Esotericism* (RE), Lects. 4, 5, 9 and 10; *Planetary Spheres and Their Influence on Man's Life on Earth and in Spiritual Worlds* (PSI), Lect. 6; *Between Death and Rebirth* (BDR), esp. Lect. 10; *Life Between Death and Rebirth* (LBDR), All, with Lect. 7 representative; *Occult Research into Life Between Death and a New Birth* (ORL), Lect. 1; *Concerning the Technique of Karma in Life after Death and the Secret of the Human Brain* (CTK); and *The Principle of Spiritual Economy* (SE), Lect. 1). See also, *Theosophy* (THSY), Chap. 2; *Foundations of Esotericism* (FE), Lects. 16, 20 and 23; *Therapeutic Insights/Earthly and Cosmic Laws* (TIEC), Lect. 5; and *Materialism and the Task of Anthroposophy* (MTA), Lect. 13. In reality, essentially all of Steiner's works can be seen to reflect the karmic laws involved in human evolution.

In concluding his *History of the Planets* (HP), Robert Powell shows that while Christianity, in its formative first two millennia, blocked out the descending portion of the human journey into incarnation, it clearly subscribed to the ascending part. This is reflected not only in the Hierarchies explained by Paul's pupil, Dionysius the Areopagite (Acts 17,34), *Pseudo-Dionysius* (PSEUD), but also in *The Divine Comedy* of Dante (21 GB).

The soul's journey after death can be succinctly stated. Death is followed immediately by a perfect "memory tableau" in the etheric world of the entire life just ended, lasting up to about three days. The second stage, from which the Roman Catholic doctrine of Purgatory was properly, if imprecisely (see fn 11 below), taken is known in the Orient as "kamaloca," and takes place in the astral world, lasting approximately one-third of the duration of the immediate past life. Here the entire life is experienced in reverse order from death back to birth (see "Purifying Fire"). Thereafter the soul enters the spiritual world proper, which is itself divided into the lower and higher heaven (in Oriental terminology, "lower devachan" and "higher devachan"). (From the nature of his description, we may reasonably infer that the "third heaven" to which Paul was carried [2 Cor 12,2] was the higher devachan, the three being, in order, the astral world, lower devachan and higher devachan.[5]) This period customarily lasts for some centuries. Its midway and highest point is referred to as the soul's "Midnight" hour, from which it begins its descent back into incarnation as a new and unique personality.[6] In its descent, the soul traverses in reverse order the stages of its ascent, taking into the fourfold makeup of its prospective earthly personality what each realm has to offer to the soul for its own progress toward "Perfect(ion)." Now we will look at the stages in more detail.

The human Ego perceives phenomena through its astral (sense) body, but attains to earthly memory only if the astral body is able to imprint the perception upon the etheric body. Upon death, the etheric (life) body

---

5. Without anthroposophical knowledge, commentators have generally placed the first two heavens in the created world (first the atmosphere and blue dome above, and second, the starry sky), and only the "third heaven" in the spiritual. See, for instance, NICNT and 3 AB 90-94, "Heaven" and "Heaven, Ascent To."

6. While "Midnight" is a term to be separately treated later, two Gospel parables mention it in ways that seem pertinent here. Mt 25,1-13 speaks of the wise and foolish maidens who took their lamps, the foolish without oil, to meet the "Bridegroom," who is announced at "Midnight." The elements of preparedness, the light from lamps, and the number of maidens all seem significant. The number ten suggests the ten levels of "gods," the nine Hierarchies (**I-6**) plus the human being. The "Bridegroom" appears at the highest point in the soul's journey, but only to the prepared who are able to retain full consciousness. Few have attained this level as yet (cf. Rev 21,2).

Lk 11,5-8 speaks of going to a friend at "Midnight" to borrow "three loaves" for a just-arrived friend. If one reflects upon this account, it is hard not to see the arrival at "Midnight" hour of a soul who has not transformed its "Three Bodies," the "three loaves" (again, cf. Mt 13,33). Because of its importunity, "three loaves" will be "loaned" to it. In other words, at the high point of the journey between death and rebirth, arrangements are made for a new "Three Bodies" to be "loaned," that is, formed into a new personality for the soul.

separates for the first time from the physical body and is thus no longer constrained by it. The etheric body, still attached to the astral body and Ego, makes available to the Ego, through the astral body, perfect perception of the entirety of the life just ended. This perception is not subject to happiness, pain, or the like, but is entirely objective. In this tableau, nothing is lost that made an impression upon the astral body during life. As soon as the etheric body loses the form it had while connected with the physical body during life, this tableau ceases. Its duration is equal to the maximum period the person could have gone without sleep while alive (approximately one to three days). At the end of this time, the etheric body dissolves back into the general world ether, but for the soul's future incarnations an extract is preserved that contains only the "fruit" of the past life.

"There now begins for the soul an essentially different period, the period of breaking its attachment to the physical world" (RE, Lect. 4). Now the astral body and Ego alone dwell together. All the soul's sensual urges and desires are intensely present, but without the physical body's organs they cannot be satisfied. With respect to these, it is a time of unslakable "burning thirst" (Lk 16,24, Mk 9,44,48-49 and Jn 4,13-14). The soul in the astral world experiences its past life in reverse order. The soul experiences any relationship it had with another being from the viewpoint of the "other" being. Thus, in the Sermon on the Mount, we are told:

> So whatever you wish that men would do to you, do so to them; for this is the [karmic] law and the prophets. (Mt 7,12)

No soul can enter the spiritual world (lower devachan) so long as any earthly appetite, passion, desire or the like remains. This is the time of the "refiner's fire" (Mal 3,2) and, up to a point, may appropriately be considered as the fire of hell. The apocalyptic fire "prepared for the devil and his angels" (Mt 25,41,46 and Rev 20) is a far distant ultimate spiritual reality, not to be faced until long after the time for the "Grace" of reincarnation has expired (see I-2). The soul (Ego) can alleviate suffering in the astral world only to the extent that it becomes the master of the astral body's appetites, passions, desires and the like during life. Or, in one's relationship with any other (or others, including, for instance, all the suffering world, e.g., Mt 25,31-46), such alleviation will occur only to the extent the Ego acted in relation to such other(s) in accordance with the "golden rule" above (e.g., Lk 16,19-31 and 1 Jn 3,17-18). Fortunately, to the extent that the Ego governs its earthly passions, desires, and dealings with others in a

Christlike manner, the journey through the astral world can be joyful instead of painful. The period in the astral world is approximately one-third that of the past life, but more precisely equals the time spent in sleep during that life.

When the soul has worked backwards in this manner from its old age to its infancy, burning out all unworthy elements, it is now prepared to enter the spiritual world, lower devachan, the "kingdom of heaven" and "a life free from sorrow" (RE, Lect. 4). When this is understood, a higher meaning of "unless you turn and become like children, you will never enter the kingdom of heaven" (Mt 18,3), is revealed.

Contrary to a somewhat prevalent perception, the journey between death and rebirth, while in some parts a joyful, rewarding, and reassuring experience, is by no means a time of rest—unless one construes truly constructive work as rest—but is rather one of intense activity and, within limits, perception. A primary purpose of the journey is to reveal to the soul the purpose of its last life in the light of the soul's accumulated karma, the extent to which it succeeded or failed, and then, compelled by necessity, the urge to return to Earth to work in a new personality toward the overcoming of remaining karma.

While the soul works assiduously during its journey between death and rebirth, the only place where its accumulated karma can be balanced is on Earth during mineral-physical incarnation. We may aptly analogize the complete cycle by saying that the Earth is the soul's workshop, and the period between lives is spent in the planning or drawing room. Nothing worthwhile can be accomplished in the workshop without a proper plan, but no plan is worth anything unless and until it is consummated in the workshop. In order to become the "first born" or "first fruit" of humanity, humanity's pattern, so to speak, the very Son of God, the Christ Spirit, had to go into the workshop. This is the substance of such Biblical passages as Phil 2,5-7 and Heb 2 wherein Christ gave up that high spiritual state to which he was entitled, took upon himself the human form, and was sacrificially obedient to the point of the Cross itself. The Bible becomes especially radiant when read in this light, and nothing in the Bible is inconsistent with this understanding. Presumed inconsistencies arise only from placing a far too limited, parochial or temporal interpretation upon its exalted passages.

Upon death the higher human elements, the etheric and astral bodies and Ego, are liberated from the physical body. This results in an instant increase in consciousness, but as yet a consciousness that is far from complete. Immediately upon death the soul is aware of an expansion. Initially, and during the brief "memory tableau" in the etheric body, the expansion remains within close proximity of the physical world and especially in the locale of the mineral corpse. Depending upon the soul's prior advancement, this can be a difficult time of separation. While Steiner anticipated developments of the kind, we have seen in recent decades numerous instances of return from clinical death in which we are told that one floated above the body perceiving everything that was going on. This seems totally consistent with what Steiner indicated decades earlier.

After this brief tableau period in the etheric world near the Earth, the departing soul is conscious of a gradual expanding, reaching out into the Moon sphere, that spheroidal volume defined by the orbit of the Moon. This is the domain of the astral world. It is here that the untamed "Wild Animals" of the astral body fearsomely confront and torment, the "burning thirst" afflicts, and the purifying flames sear, the soul.

At the end of this astral-world period, the expansion of the soul continues into lower devachan, the lower domain of the spirit world, so that its spheroidal shape reaches out progressively from the Earth to the orbits of its nearest planetary neighbors (as though the planets and Sun orbited the Earth). Thus, the soul enters, successively, in lower devachan, the regions of Venus (esoterically called Mercury), Mercury (esoterically called Venus), the Sun, Mars, Jupiter and Saturn. The time needed for each region varies according to the needs of the soul in that region. The Mercury sphere, astronomically Venus, is where the soul's "moral qualities are expressed" (ORL, Lect. 1), qualities such as benevolence, conscientiousness and sympathy. One who lacks these in life will find loneliness here, but the moral soul will find companionship with others. The Venus sphere, astronomically Mercury, involves one's religious qualities, particularly those associated with a given religion or confession during earthly life. One given to this quality on Earth will be a social being here.

In the Sun sphere, one who was religious only in a parochial way, understanding only the perspectives of a given religion or confession, will find loneliness in this sphere, for here one is at home only from having developed on Earth "a deeper tolerance for all religious systems on earth" (ORL, Lect. 1). Indeed, Steiner tells us that "in the very essence of Christianity there lies a true tolerance for every religious system." One senses here the reality that the spiritual Sun shines on all humanity (cf. Mt 5,45; also Rom 2,14 and Acts 17,22-28). It is necessary in the Sun sphere to come to an understanding of the throne there that was emptied when the Christ descended therefrom to the Earth in the Mystery of Golgotha. Here an anthroposophical understanding becomes essential, for the emptied throne is filled by Lucifer, the "light-bearer," who himself (in contrast to his legions) was converted by the Christ when the latter's "Blood" dropped to Earth from the Cross. This is microcosmically represented in Luke's Gospel by, and is the higher meaning of, the conversion of the thief on the cross (Lk 23,39-43). (This is not to say that the thief did not convert, but rather that it was an earthly reflection of a higher spiritual development. See "As Above, So Below.") From this point forward in the journey through the outer planets (Mars, Jupiter and Saturn), the soul is led by Lucifer, but his leadership is salutary only if the soul has "the Christ impulse as a counter-balance; ... otherwise it is evil for us."

Next the soul enters the Mars sphere. The perceptive soul, so led by both Christ and Lucifer, perceives that "certain changes ... have occurred on Mars in the course of recent centuries." In short, the warlike nature of Mars has been "saved" by the Buddha, the originator on Earth of compassion, much as the Christ became the Savior of all creation. Since the beginning of the seventeenth century, "the peace substance of the Buddha flows into the Mars-sphere...." Since that time, souls that emerge rightly from the Sun sphere become permeated in the Mars sphere not with the bold "courage and energy" factor of previous times, but rather with a "Francis of Assisi ... element."[7] Aggressive courage becomes the inner strength of compassion for all beings and things.

Then one expands further into the Jupiter and Saturn spheres. But Steiner tells us that here consciousness "occurs only ... with the most advanced souls." All others go through these and later heavenly stages

> in a certain unconscious state akin to sleep. In the outer spheres, in the spheres beyond the sun, the forces are gathered which man must acquire in order to be able to work, to collaborate, in building up a new body as he approaches a new birth.

---

7. It may be recalled how this Buddha element was involved in the astral body of the Nathan Jesus child (see "The Nativity") and then how the astral body of Jesus of Nazareth later entered into the astral body of Francis of Assisi (see "Spiritual Economy," esp. where it refers to **I-74**).

The more advanced a soul becomes, that is, the more a soul has trans-formed its astral body into manas (Manna), a spiritual state, the more it can consciously collaborate with the Hierarchies in planning and fashion-ing its next incarnation during this farther journey into the spirit world.

As one expands outward through the planetary spheres, the soul is con-scious of these spheres as though they were its bodily organs during earthly life (see **I-20**, Figure 13; also the discussion of Steiner's *Occult Physiology* [OP] under "Blood" in Vol. 2, "*What Is Man?*"). Upon completion of the journey through the planetary spheres, i.e., the lower spiritual world, the soul enters higher devachan where, as before, only the most advanced soul is able consciously to participate with the Host in preparing the next earthly personality to most effectively address its remaining karma.

The "regions" of what Steiner calls "spiritland," that is, higher heaven or upper devachan, are reiterated from OS in **I-33**, and can be seen there to be a recapitulation, at a higher level, of the regions of the astral world. It is hard to escape drawing a rather precise parallel between these pro-gressions and those in virtually every water-launching in the Bible. First the voyager is on solid land, then launches upon water, next encountering a storm or danger of some sort, followed by some form of rescue, and finally perception (light). Consider, for instance, Jonah (Jon), the storm upon the Sea of Galilee (Mt 8,18,23-27, Mk 4,35-41, Lk 8,22-25) and Paul's last journey (Acts 27-28). See also "Storm/Water Launching."

After its Midnight hour, the soul is compelled to return to Earth to redress remaining karma, and the long descent to reincarnation begins; the soul journeys back through all the regions visited in its ascent, gathering in each the fruits of its sojourn there. From the highest levels to the lowest the Hierarchies work in fashioning the necessary bodies to accomplish the tasks settled upon. We have said that the fruits of the last life were pre-served in an extract of both the etheric and astral bodies. These remain at the etheric and astral levels and rejoin the descending soul upon its return, supplemented with what else may be necessary. It is sobering to reflect how the Bible hints of these extracts and their higher spiritual components (Manna and the like). We may infer such from the parables of the "Tal-ents" (Mt 25,14-30; Lk 19,12-27) as well as the Sermon on the Mount admonition to lay up "treasures in heaven, where neither moth nor rust consumes and where thieves do not break in and steal" (Mt 6,19-21).

In OS, Chap. 3, Steiner tells us of the soul's return journey to another earthly life, starting near the completion of its sojourn in higher devachan:

After death, the ego is immersed in this world, together with the harvest that it brings with it from its life in the sense world. This harvest is still united with that part of the astral body that has not been thrown off at the end of the period of purification…. The immersion of the ego in the spiritual world, together with what it has acquired in the sense world, may be compared with the insertion of a seed into the ripening earth. Just as this seed draws substances and forces from its environment in order to develop into a new plant, so, too, unfolding and growth is the very essence of the ego being embedded in the world of the spirit.—Within what an organ perceives lies hidden the force by means of which the organ itself is created.

Thus is the eye created by light, the physical body by the forces of the physical world, the ether body by those of the life world, and the astral body by those of the astral world. After death the human soul enters these regions where it perceives those forces in their own previously concealed form.

The human being is now ready to be re-created for its next incarnation. Spiritual beings of these regions work with this "Seed" so as to build it up anew as a spiritual being. "All that streams toward the ego from the spirit world now becomes not only a perfecter, but a recreator. After a certain length of time … an astral body has formed itself around the ego…. Up to the time of re-forming a new astral body, man is a witness of his own re-creation. Since the powers of the spirit land do not reveal themselves to him by means of outer organs, but from within, like his own ego in self-consciousness, he is able to perceive this revelation as long as his mind is not yet directed to an outwardly perceptible world." But the moment the astral body is formed the Ego's attention is turned outward in search of an external ether and physical body, and thereby "turns away from the revelations of the inner world. For this reason an intermediate state now begins, during which man [the Ego] sinks into unconsciousness. Consciousness can only reappear in the physical world when the necessary organs for physical perception have been formed…. Only an ego that has of itself produced life spirit and spirit man, the hidden, creative forces in the ether and physical bodies, would be able to take part consciously in the attachment of these two members." Until then, more advanced spiritual beings direct their attachment, leading the astral body to certain parents. But "before the attachment of the ether body is complete, something extraordinarily significant occurs." Those hindrances to the Ego that it experienced in reverse order after death reappear to "confront the ego anew." But instead of a past life, the Ego now sees a pre-vision tableau of its coming life showing "all the hindrances [it] must remove if [its] evolution is to make further progress. What [it] thus sees becomes the starting point of forces that [it] must carry with [it] into a new life." Thus we see the working of the law of *destiny* (i.e., *karma*).

In the discussion of the birth of the Nathan Jesus child in "The Nativity," portions of RE, Lect. 5 are quoted that show how earthly birth originates through activities in the astral world that are activated by "the being who is descending." Later in the lecture, a very beautiful reality is disclosed:

> … we must say that the reincarnating individual definitely participates in the choice of his parents…. The parents' love is therefore the answer to the child's love, it is the responsive love.

And in the next paragraph he tells us what he has said so many times, that a perfect match for the karmic needs of the reincarnating soul is not possible; the best that is attainable under earthly conditions then existing is all that can be hoped for:

> There is never a perfect correspondence between what is coming down from above to embodiment and the sheaths that this entity acquires down below. A perfect correspondence … cannot take place until man has reached the goal of his evolution,[8] when he has attained spirit man. When he has transformed the physical body into spirit man, the etheric body into life spirit, and the astral body into spirit self, man stands at the point in evolution where, with a will that is completely free, he himself chooses his final incarnation. Before this point, full accordance is not possible.

It can be seen from fn 4 that most of Steiner's works on the soul's journey between death and rebirth fell within the period that corre-

---

8. It would seem that Steiner here means the goal of earthly evolution. Anthroposophy seems to indicate that no human soul can proceed farther beyond the rest of humanity than is possible within a given planetary evolution. It is true that a soul, such as that of the Buddha, can attain a sufficiently high degree of perfection over the lower "Three Bodies" as to need no further incarnation. But it is not clear to me how one, having attained the exalted level of spirit man, is thus enabled to find a physical body through earthly hereditary forces in which reincarnation could occur if desired. Perhaps Steiner is here speaking not of a normal hereditary birth, but rather of the entry of an Ego either in substitution of, or cohabitation with, an already incarnated Ego.—ERS

sponded with his lectures specifically on the Bible, especially from 1909 to 1913. His most intense research seems to have been just before and during his 1912-1913 cycles LBDR and BDR. But in 1922 he returned for one significant reiteration in Lect. 6, the last in the cycle PSI, entitled "Christ and the Metamorphosis of Karma." It is an appropriate conclusion to our present overview, particularly in that it furnishes a rather natural bridge from Karma and Reincarnation to the next phrase, Lord of Karma. In fact, the arrangement of terms and phrases in this volume takes into account the following natural progression: Forgiven Sins; Karma and Reincarnation; Lord of Karma; and Second Coming.

In the way a human soul perceives itself, a major reversal occurs at death. During earthly life, the soul considers itself as being within the skin of its physical body. Upon death, the soul and the two higher bodies escape the physical, and perception expands in such a way that the soul sees what it had previously looked out upon as now being encompassed within its own expanse. And the heavenly bodies that it had looked out upon in their physical manifestation are now seen as merely the physical expression of spiritual beings of whom the soul now becomes conscious. During this time the soul becomes aware that the planetary beings were present inside its earthly body as its organs (**I-20**). It also becomes aware that all the elements of its earthly being are reflections of heavenly beings, not only within the planetary spheres but also within the zodiacal, and that these elements are a result of the interplay between the heavenly forces depending upon its karma.

Let us see something of the picture Steiner pours forth, in PSI, Lect. 6, of the soul in higher devachan and its return to Earth:

> ... in the sum-total of the stars which constitute the Zodiac we have a comprehensive picture of the path which Man must undergo, to build from the entire Cosmos, with the help of the Beings of the Hierarchies, the Spirit-seed of his physical body for the next incarnation.... Nothing that you can ever do on Earth can be as great and manifold as what you have to do when from the starry worlds you build this temple of the Gods, the human body.... Nor do you merely make your own body for yourself. As we shall see in a moment, you really make it so that it belongs to mankind as a whole.... Now as to how you work amid the Stars, let me describe it in more detail, only remember please what I said before. Telling

of yonder worlds sublime, I can speak only in pictures; the human concepts of our time are not so formed as to enable one to express it otherwise [cf. 2 Cor 12,1-4].

In its entirety, once more, you have to build the spiritual seed of your next physical body.[9] From the ingredients of the whole Universe you build it. When for example you are living in and with those spiritual Beings who have their physical reflection in the constellation of Aries, the Ram, you will work with the Hierarchies of Aries in forming your future head, which is indeed a Universe in itself.... And while, upon the scene of Aries, you are at work with the Hierarchy of that constellation, meanwhile the planets are shining; as they shine physically down on to the Earth, so do they shine spiritually to the other side. Say for example that you have worked your way from Aries to the next constellation—Taurus, you elaborate the region of your larynx in its connection with the lungs. Mars in the meantime, from the planetary spheres, shines up into the sphere of Taurus, and in the movements of Mars there is expressed all that you

---

9. Earlier, in the quote from ORL, it was said that in the spheres beyond the Sun consciousness "occurs only ... with the most advanced souls." Now, we are being told that here in higher devachan the soul actively engages with the Hierarchies in building up the next physical body. The more one studies Steiner, the more frequently will one come upon apparent inconsistencies. But experience with these inevitably brings the student to see that they are reconcilable, each tending to cast light upon the interpretation of the other. A bit of light seems to be shed by the following passage from LBDR, Lect. 2:

> What I have described refers to the average person. For example, in one case consciousness after death might be dimmed earlier than in another, or the condition of sleep might set in more quickly, as you will have understood from what was said previously. But a cosmic law operates so that the cosmic sleep shortens the period that we spend in the spiritual world after death. The one who enters the condition of unconsciousness earlier experiences it more rapidly. Time passes at a quicker rate for him than for one whose consciousness extends farther. Investigations of life between death and rebirth do indeed reveal that unspiritual people reincarnate relatively more quickly than others. A person who only indulges in sensual pleasures and passions, who lives strongly in what we might call his animal nature, will spend but a short time between incarnations. This is due to the fact that such a person will fall comparatively rapidly into a condition of unconsciousness, of sleep. Hence he will travel quickly between the period of death and rebirth.

Beyond this, I venture to suggest that there is a distinction between the degree of consciousness that will permit the sojourner to be dimly aware of coexistence with the Hierarchies, on the one hand, and that which ever increasingly enables the soul to take a direct part in building the next physical body, on the other hand.—ERS

did with your organs of speech, rightly or wrongly, while you were on the Earth [see Jas 3,1-12]. Every untruth which a man uttered shines at him spiritually from the planet Mars while he is working through the Taurus sphere. You may imagine therefore, what is the nature of the "memory" we there retain of our own deeds. We find it after death, written into the Universe—nay, as the very Logos, speaking from the Universe towards that other side of world-existence.

In addition to **I-20**, see also **I-56** and **I-54** in regard to the working of the Hierarchies in these regions.

> ... And so it is, to take another example, when we are going through the constellation of Leo. It is the Sun now that sheds spiritual light on all the imperfections of our heart.... So while we work and build at our future body, the language of the Planets, sounding into the cosmic spaces, utters forth the whole of our preceding life. It is so in deed and truth, strange as it may seem from an earthly standpoint. We watch the planetary movements from yonder side.... The movements form themselves into a cosmic writing, but the writing is not mute, it actually sounds into the Universe. Such is the writing of the Stars, by our own deeds inscribed into the cosmic spaces. Small wonder if on our return we prepare what will then be ... our Karma....

The longer the human being lived on Earth beyond the dim consciousness it had as a child, the longer will be the journey for it in higher devachan. In this, Steiner's remarks resemble Eccles 11,8.

> The older a man grows, the longer must he spend there. For by his longer life on Earth his higher consciousness was darkened for a longer time.... The longer this was darkened, the longer must he work to make it light again. For we must enter right fully into the light.
>
> When we are fully in the light, then comes the time between death and new birth ... described ... as the midnight hour in the spiritual life of man [see fn 6].... This is the time when our consciousness, amid the Beings of the Hierarchies in the spiritual world, is most steeped in spiritual light. Yet at this very time we also experience most deeply: Down yonder in the planetary sphere is the abiding record of all that you, man, did. You may

not abandon it, you cannot leave it thus,—so say we to ourselves—nor can you ever alter it while you are here; you can change it only by going down to Earth. And so the urge arises, to descend again to Earth.... The forces of the Moon are dawning for us once again and we resolve to follow them, so to set forth on our returning journey. If a man grew to adult life in his last incarnation, it will be centuries later.

The nearer we now come to the planetary sphere and notably to the spheres of Mercury, Venus and Moon, the more we lose the consciousness of community with the Beings of the Hierarchies.... The consciousness we enter into now contains only the *revelations* of these spiritual Beings, whereas we felt ourselves till lately living among them and within them.... Now they appear to us as if in pictures. Meanwhile the forces of the Moon arise within us.... Although not yet in a physical body, we have a premonition of living in and by ourselves, a stranger to the Cosmos....

Whilst we are going through these pictures, the spiritual seed of the physical body which we were preparing falls ever farther from us and disappears. We are obliged to witness this: ... it has gone down into a physical mother and father, entering into the forces of generation, into the stream of generation upon the physical Earth. The physical body we were preparing shrinks and contracts and falls into the streams of generation,—into a physical father and mother upon Earth,—while we ourselves as soul and spiritual being are left behind, feeling that we belong to what has fallen from us, yet cannot unite with it directly. In this condition ... we now begin to draw to ourselves the forces of the Ether that are there throughout the Cosmos; we begin to form our ether-body.... With this etheric body we then unite ourselves, when the human seed has already been for a time in the mother's womb. [Recall here what was said in "The Nativity" in regard to Lk 1,41, the babe leaping in the womb of Elizabeth.]

... What until now was but the "memory" of our own Karmic entity, we now take in as real effective forces, right into our ether-body. Therefore we afterwards appear on Earth in such a way that we of ourselves bring about the unfoldment of our destiny, our Karma. It is while passing through the Lunar forces that we conceive the longing thus to live and fulfil our Karma upon Earth.

… In present earthly time it is as I have been relating.… But we are living now in a very important period of Earth-existence, the significance of which we can understand only if we first know what has just been related.… For at this very point something of great significance is about to happen in our epoch. I will say more of it in the third part of the lecture.

In the "third part" Steiner speaks of the new age of the Archangel Michael that began in 1879 (see also **I-19**). Both this new Michaelic age and the end of the five-thousand-year Oriental dark age (Kali Yuga; see **I-46**) are discussed in A Time of Spiritual Awakening, Vol. 3. Both of these take on added significance in the light of what is said under "Lord of Karma" and "Second Coming."

Michael, we may truly say, has taken over the spiritual guidance of mankind. The fact that Michael is now entering into the soul-life and spiritual life of mankind has its visible counterpart on Earth. An ever growing number of people begin to realize that man is livingly and constantly connected, not only through his physical body with the Earth, but through his soul and spirit with the spiritual world.

Man is thus growing into conscious spiritual knowledge. This is the one aspect of the leadership of Michael, but there is also another. To be sincerely filled with spiritual knowledge also affects the human heart, the human soul. The more the light of Spiritual Science spreads, the less will it remain a mere theory; it will pour out into human feeling,—it will be present in the form of true human love, in ever widening circles.… Yet man will never understand what the leadership of Michael intends unless he goes out to meet it with his own active contribution—unless he opens out his mind to spiritual enlightenment and becomes filled with the human love which springs from such enlightenment. When he does this, then also will he realize with ever growing comprehension the significance of Michael's leadership and guidance.

The people of the Old Testament,—they too spoke of a leadership of Michael, and in so speaking they conceived Michael to be the servant of Jahve. Michael therefore, in the Old Testament times, worked with those spiritual forces which are the forces of Jahve. He was the minister of Jahve. He helped in the inexorable

fight of which I spoke before—the fight with the Ahrimanic powers. In our age on the other hand Michael is destined ever more to
become the ministering Being of the Christ. Thus when we say
that Michael's leadership now begins to regulate the historic destinies of mankind, it also signifies that the word shall presently come
true: the leadership of Christ will spread over the Earth. It is as
though Michael goes before, bearing the light of spiritual knowledge, while after Him there comes the Christ, calling man to universal, all-embracing love. Now this entails a change not only for
the Earth; it involves changes also for the life man undergoes between death and a new birth.

Since ancient times of earthly evolution it has been as I today described it. The human being prepares the spiritual seed of his own
physical body, which he takes over when he steps forth into his new
life on Earth. Now, however, since the Christ-Michael-leadership
has begun, men will be able ever increasingly to make another important decision before they come down to Earth. Today as yet
only a few will do so; a growing number will as time goes on....
Man will now learn to make a very significant decision at the moment when he has already taken on his Karma—... but is still only
setting out upon the way into the physical.... The following possibility will arise for mankind in coming time. When at the point of
descending into a new earthly life, man will be able to say to himself: "This is the body I have been preparing; yet, having sent it
down to Earth and having now received my Karma into the ether-
body which I have drawn together from the Cosmos, I see how it is
with this Karma. Through something that I did in former lives I see
that I have gravely hurt some other human being." ... And we shall
then be enabled to bring about a change in our decision,—namely
to give to the other man the body we have been preparing, while we
ourselves take on the body he prepared, whom we have injured.

Such is the mighty transition which will be taking place from
now onward in the spiritual life of men.... What we are able to
achieve on Earth will thus bring about Karmic compensation in
quite another way than heretofore.... Indeed, the Earth could
never reach her goal if this did not take place; mankind would never grow into a single whole. In preparation for future planetary
embodiments of the Earth, a time must come in earthly evolution

when it will be impossible for one individual to enjoy things on the Earth at the expense of another.... A future [must] come for the planet Earth when one human being will not want to enjoy happiness at the expense of the whole, but man will feel a member of mankind. And it will be the true spiritual counterpart of this when we shall learn to prepare the physical body even for one another.

While, as Steiner says below, these things may sound strange, they ring quite true with passages of the Bible that we have perhaps not yet come to adequately comprehend. Consider in that regard Jn 17,11,21, Eph 1,9-10 and Rom 12,5, which clearly express a "becoming one." These present a distant, rather than a present, condition; and Rom 8,18-23 projects into that far distant consciousness also envisioned by Eph 1,9-10.

> ... Moreover, as our incarnations on the Earth go on, this will lead even further. For in thus working for one another in the spirit we shall prepare for a yet later time, to tell the character of which will sound completely strange and paradoxical, yet it is true. For in that more distant future human souls even while on Earth will be able to go across into the bodies of those to whom they have done some special hurt and to receive the other soul into their own body. That will be when the Earth herself will have passed into quite new conditions. Yet it is also being prepared for by the actual and impending change of which I have been telling, and which is coming about in the spiritual world through the leadership of Michael.

SCRIPTURAL BASIS FOR KARMA AND REINCARNATION

Now we will look at some of these Biblical passages that, although Karma and Reincarnation is not directly mentioned, nevertheless convincingly (and I believe conclusively) demonstrate that the concept is scriptural in the fullest sense. (Many such concepts not directly mentioned by name in scripture have, over the centuries, been widely accepted in Christian circles and in official pronouncements, some perhaps accurately and others perhaps not. The Trinity, Immaculate Conception and other examples come readily to mind.)

1. The Composite Anthroposophical Picture of the Bible:

By far the most important evidence is not a single passage but rather the probative force and integrity of the composite picture of the full Biblical scope, from Genesis to Revelation—the Creation, Fall, Salvation and Redemption of humanity—using the term "humanity" to include all the "by-products" of humanity's creation, namely, the animal, plant and mineral kingdoms, which "groaned in travail" (Rom 8,22) awaiting redemption. See the "Overview" at the front of this volume for a concise reference to this full Biblical scope. The entirety of the vast evolutionary scheme so splendidly given by Steiner would be meaningless unless each soul was a participant essentially from the inception of humanity and had a chance to contribute to its ultimate perfection. Other pertinent terms herein include "Forgiven Sins, "Lord of Karma," "I AM" and "Akashic."

While individual passages will be discussed below, I deem this point more cogent on the Karma and Reincarnation issue than all the other Biblical references combined. For approximately the last two of the twenty-five plus years that I taught the Bible in church school, I was a convert, serious student, and advocate of Karma and Reincarnation. Having read on it extensively, I had begun a manuscript to show how Karma and Reincarnation was supported by scripture. Only in connection with that research did I come eventually upon the name of Rudolf Steiner and, in 1988, plunge into the depths of his works. So startlingly new and wonderful were the insights that I stopped the manuscript (after three hundred single-spaced typewritten pages) and eventually threw it away.

The personal library I collected during those two years included many of the prevalent and representative contemporary works on the subject.[10]

---

10. These included Cerminara, *Many Lives, Many Loves*, Marina del Rey, CA, DeVorss, 1963; Stevenson, *Twenty Cases Suggestive of Reincarnation*, Charlottesville, U. of Virginia, 1974; Head & Cranston, *Reincarnation: The Phoenix Fire Mystery*, New York, Julian Press,1977; Howe, *Reincarnation for the Christian*, Wheaton, IL, Quest, 1974; MacGregor, *Reincarnation in Christianity*, Wheaton, IL, Quest, 1978; MacGregor, *Reincarnation as a Christian Hope*, Totowa, NJ, Barnes & Noble, 1982; MacGregor, *The Christening of Karma*, Wheaton, IL, Quest, 1984; Cranston & Williams, *Reincarnation, A New Horizon in Science, Religion, and Society*, New York, Julian Press, 1984; Whitton & Fisher, *Life Between Life*, Garden City, NY, Dolphin (Doubleday), 1986; Weiss, *Many Lives, Many Masters*, New York, Simon & Schuster, 1988, all of which supported the concept of Karma and Reincarnation. Also included on the contra side was Geisler & Amano, *The Reincarnation Sensation*, Wheaton, IL, Tyndale, 1987, which took aim at such "sensation," addressing what it considered the proponents' principal arguments, especially scriptural.

With the utmost respect for the authors of those provocative works, both pro and con, I now look upon such publications much as Paul looked upon the Mosaic Law. The most notable observation about all these works is that in not one place in any of them is there any recognition of Steiner or the substance of anthroposophical insight. This fact is eerily similar to the absence of Jesus in the pages of secular history for the comparable period after Christ. "A prophet is not without honor save in his own country," Christ said, and one might add "and save in his (or her) own time."

2. Heb 9,27:

> And just as it is appointed for men to die once, and after that comes judgment,...

Most of the arguments advanced against Karma and Reincarnation are predicated upon the dogma of salvation, forgiveness, grace, resurrection, or the like. None of the scriptures cited in such arguments, however, seem to be, on their face, so literally devastating as this passage. Aside from the fact that it stands almost isolated as "authority" for the point in question, it does clearly and unequivocally say that the human being only lives "once." (We consider below the meaning of "once.") The problem, of course, is that any given sentence, standing alone, can be interpreted so as to destroy the meaning of the larger context out of which it is taken. One who goes the length hereof will find Hebrews to be a book extensively quoted in, and supportive of, this anthroposophical writing (and hardly understandable without it). The same may be said of the Pauline letters, and Paul's authorship of Hebrews will be fairly well established, over considerable scholarly reservation, in "Paul/ Hebrews." There is, of course, the clear implication of the preexistence of souls in Heb 7,3 (see fn 16 below), if we wanted to counterthrust primarily with the literal sword. The error of that course, however, is clearly recognized in scripture that not only condemns such "disputes" and "godless chatter" (Rom 14,1; 1 Tim 6,4,20; 2 Tim 2,14,16; Acts 24,12; 2 Cor 3,6) but recognizes that the written scripture will itself, in time, be displaced by a higher perception the evolving human being will gain of the spiritual world.

But having said this, let us look at the deeper meaning of Heb 9,27. It is precisely and literally correct in the anthroposophical view of Karma and Reincarnation. The "men" of whom it speaks are physical human beings, just like you and me. The "physical" body, however, though eldest and most perfected of the three bodies, comprises the least permanent aspect of a person. In anthroposophical terms, one speaks of the "personality" and also the "individuality" of a person, a distinction of immense significance for Biblical comprehension. Neither term has here our vernacular's normal connotation. The Individuality of a person is the entelechy that runs through all incarnations, the "burning bush that is not consumed," the "I Am" (Ex 3; see "I AM"). Between lives, it alone makes the full journey through the heavens and returns, shedding the three bodies on the way up and re-forming three karmically appropriate new ones on the way back toward incarnation. The "personality" is the manifestation of the "individuality" in a single incarnation only. The Individuality lives again and again; the personality lives only "once." Only those who have the developed clairvoyance to look into the soul of another person can recognize the Individuality—a task far beyond the present capacity of all but the highest Initiates of our time. So befuddling has this idea been that the Sadducees tried to trip Jesus up with the question of levirate law about the woman who had seven brothers as husbands, and neither the Sadducees nor human beings since the time of the Evangelists have understood his answer until enabled by Steiner's insights. This scripture is Point 5 below, but it illustrates the distinction.

As we saw above, the passage of the soul through the astral world (called "Purgatory"[11] by the Roman Church) is a time of judgment, for all of the personality's astralities, its passions and desires, must be burned away by the "refiner's fire" and one suffers judgment regarding every conscious earthly event, seeing one's self from the eyes the other (Mt 7,12). If one has repented and acted accordingly on Earth, then the judgment

---

11. That the astral world is what is referred to by Purgatory is clear from the fact that it is the time after death when the soul is "purged" or purified of its soiled astral nature. However, Purgatory is defined so as to make it less extensive than the anthroposophical explanation. According to 9 Brit 807, Purgatory is only for souls who have "died in a state of grace" but are not yet pure and have committed no unforgiven "mortal," as distinguished from "venial," sins. Its primary Biblical authority is 2 Macc 12,45, though New Testament implication is also seen. It was apparently a belief in the early Church but not defined "until the councils of Lyon and Florence in the Middle Ages and the Council of Trent in the Reformation." The principal difference in anthroposophy is probably that the astral world is seen as a condition that all souls pass through after death. Purgatory can therefore be anthroposophically seen as having been "carved out" of the astral world and hedged in by official definition. The two terms are thus not synonymous.

of the sin itself, when reached, is of little consequence. The karmic consequence of the forgiven sin is itself not a burden to the soul here, for the just soul desires to make restitution, and that is accomplished in future incarnations.

"Death" only occurs once for a personality, but it occurs over and over for the Individuality until the latter attains to a sufficient state of perfection of its lower bodies that it need not reincarnate again (like the Buddha). At that stage it "cannot die any more" (Lk 20,36; Rev 3,12), having thus "attain[ed]... to the resurrection" (Lk 20,35). And even here, we must differentiate between the "first death," that of the physical body, and the "second death" (Rev 20,6,14; 21,8), that of the etheric body. The "first death," in this sense, refers to the time when the physical body of human beings will be no more, and the "second death" to the far more distant time when humanity will lay aside also its "etheric body." When the etheric body is no longer needed, one who has not perfected that body will be subject to the "second death." We can see that there is much below the surface of the literal language of Heb 9,27.

3. Mt 17,1,9-13; Mk 9,2,9-13:

And after six days Jesus took with him Peter and James and John his brother, and led them up a high mountain apart.... And as they were coming down the mountain, Jesus commanded them, "Tell no one the vision, until the Son of man is raised from the dead." And the disciples asked him, "Then why do the scribes say that first Elijah must come?" He replied, "Elijah does come, and he is to restore all things; but I tell you that Elijah has already come, and they did not know him, but did to him whatever they pleased. So also the Son of man will suffer at their hands." Then the disciples understood that he was speaking to them of John the Baptist. (Mt)

On its face, this passage seems clearly to speak of the reincarnation of Elijah as John the Baptist. And as would be expected, it has been the focus of much dialectic. The Old Testament's closing prophecy was that Elijah would return "before the great and terrible day of the Lord" (Mal 4,5). Either that prophecy must be nullified, or "the great and terrible day of the Lord" had no reference (contrary to Jesus' clear implication above) to the Christ event, or Elijah was reincarnated as John the Baptist.

To get around this obvious matter, opponents of reincarnation philosophy cite two other passages. The first is the angel's message to Zechariah that Elizabeth's son "will go before [the Lord, Christ] in the spirit and power of Elijah" (Lk 1,17). The necessary inference is that, as in the case of Elisha, who sought a "double share" of Elijah's spirit and was granted that Elijah's spirit should "rest on him" (2 K 2), John the Baptist was endowed with a guiding spirit but not the "burning bush" of Elijah, his Individuality or "spirit" per se. The second is the denial by John himself that he is Elijah (Jn 1,21). From the standpoint of dialectic, both of these are most appropriately raised.

The first point pales when one notes that Luke recognized John the Baptist as the reincarnated Adam soul in telling how the babe leaped in Elizabeth's womb upon the approach of its soulmate in Mary's womb (Lk 1,44). This was Luke's way of expressing what his mentor, Paul, had expressed in the "First and Second Adam" passages. For a fuller discussion, see "The Nativity." According to Steiner, the Adam soul, as then constituted, incarnated in Israelite history as Phinehas, Elijah and John the Baptist, and still later as Raphael and Novalis (cf. Mt 17,11, "and he is to restore all things"). The most concise reference for these is Prokofieff's *Eternal Individuality* (EI). Given this recognition of reincarnation by Luke, it is doubtful he intended to weaken the thrust of the first two Gospel accounts.

The *second* point is a more impressive objection. It is addressed directly by Prokofieff in EI, which is summarized in Vol. 3. It has to do with the changing of the Individuality's guardian angel between the personalities of Elijah and John the Baptist. (The guardian angel is the immediate source of one's earthly revelation from the spiritual world.) See "Widow's Son," fn 15, herein.

Aside from this, insofar as Jesus, the Christ, asserts that John is the reincarnation of Elijah, and John denies it, whom must we credit in the final analysis? John himself gives the answer. He tells his own disciples, in almost the verbatim prophetic words of Malachi, "I am not the Christ, but I have been sent before him" (Jn 3,28), and he humbled himself at the outset, saying he was not worthy to untie the thong of the Christ's sandal (Jn 1,27).

Finally, John had Essenic connections, which we now know to have been of a highly esoteric nature, and he may well have been aware of the point Jesus made to his disciples, namely, that reincarnation was not yet to be taught in exoteric Christianity. We may infer such from Paul in Heb

9,5, and certainly the door is open to that idea in Christ's words, "I have yet many things to say to you, but you cannot bear them now" (Jn 16,12). If that is the case, then John's denial (to the priests and Levites sent by the Pharisees; Jn 1,19-25) would have been quite acceptable on the exoteric level, for there Christianity was not yet to be taught the difference between "personality" and "individuality." John the Baptist was a different personality from Elijah, even though he was the same Individuality.

Steiner developed the point that "reincarnation was not yet to be taught in exoteric Christianity" over the course of numerous lectures.[12] It is based on Jesus' statement in Jn 16,12 just cited and on the necessity to stress the critical importance of each life until humanity had matured to the Consciousness (Spiritual) Soul state (see **I-24**, **I-25** and **I-19**). The state of humanity's consciousness has never been static. What existed at the time of Abraham was far different from what existed at the time of Christ. The ancient clairvoyance had disappeared (see "Fading Splendor"). Christ made it possible for humanity to find its way back to a clairvoyant state, but this time with the mature Ego and the combined power of heart and mind, a clairvoyance developed through attaining a state of moral perfection over time (see "A Time of Spiritual Awakening" in Vol. 3).

We see the problems of early Christianity reflected also in Paul's constant struggle to wean his flock from milk onto solid food. The complexity of the ancient Melchizedek account (see "Spiritual Economy") makes it possible to comprehend the problem Paul expresses in Heb 5,11, "About this [the priestly order of Melchizedek] we have much to say which is hard to explain, since you have become dull of hearing." This "dullness" is not something for which the people of that time can be blamed—it was the Ahrimanic infection of materiality that caused the spirit world to fade away, to lose its reality, and the tangible to be perceived as ultimate reality.

All scripture has meaning on many different levels, from the most elementary or exoteric (milk) to the most esoteric (solid food). All are true according to the level of consciousness attained by the individual. It had to be thus if they were to appeal to all human beings, for the level of spiritual

---

12. Among these are *The Gospel of St. Luke* (GSL), Lect. 10; FE, Lect. 8; *The Reappearance of Christ in the Etheric* (RCE), Lect 2 and 3; *The Apocalypse of St. John* (ASJ), Lect. 7; *The Gospel of St. Mark* (GSMk), Lect. 1; *The Gospel of St. Matthew* (GSMt), Lect. 9; *The Gospel of St. John* (GSJL), (unpub. Eng. typescript); *The Bhagavad Gita and the Epistles of Paul* (BGEP), Lect. 2; and *Turning Points in Spiritual History* (TPSH), Lect. 4.

attainment varies so greatly. Christ came to save all humanity—no exceptions—so his statement in Mt 7,6 that pearls (of wisdom) should not be thrown before swine was necessarily a recognition that the highest of his teachings should be disseminated with prudence only to those able to receive it. Thus the passage in question begins (Mt 17,1 and Mk 9,2) with the statement that Jesus "led them [three unique disciples; see "Peter, James and John" herein] up a high mountain apart." To appreciate the significance of this, see "High Mountain." Clearly, this term tells us that he was giving them esoteric insight (not to mention the experiences needed to generate it).

Then in Mt 17,9 and Mk 9,9 Jesus tells the three, "Tell no one the vision, until the Son of man is raised from the dead." This is the language that has been passed down, but in *Foundations of Esotericism* (FE), Lect 8, Steiner recites it as, "Tell it to no man until I come again." The former is exoteric teaching, whereas the esoteric meaning is expressed in the latter. However, even "raised from the dead," esoterically understood, can be seen to be synonymous with "until I come again." This is so because the etheric body is the "life body," that in which humanity shall perceive Christ in his "Second Coming." The physical body is the body of "death." Only the few were able to witness the resurrection. Jesus may be considered by this command to have warranted the disclosure only in terminology carrying both an exoteric and esoteric meaning for the sake of those who could not yet bear to hear the deeper truth (Jn 16,12; Heb 5,11; 9,5; 2 Pet 3,15-16).

In the FE lecture, Steiner mentions also that the intent that Christianity not teach reincarnation for two thousand years is indicated in the miracle at the wedding at Cana, where water is turned into wine (Jn 2, discussed next). "In the old Mysteries only water was distributed, but in the Christian Mysteries wine. For in the priesthood, through the partaking of wine, knowledge of reincarnation was blotted out. Whoever partakes of wine cannot attain to any true knowledge of Manas, Buddhi and Atma, and can never directly comprehend reincarnation. By his coming again Christ means his reappearance in the sixth sub-race when he will be proclaimed by the 'Water-Man' [Aquarius]." As to the law applicable to the "old Mysteries," see Lev 10,8-11. As to the age of Aquarius, see **I-19**. See also "Second Coming."

One might well ask, why report the incident in scripture if it were not to be told until Christ comes again? And if it were reported, why only with its exoteric meaning? Both meanings are significant. It was vital that nothing be reported before the Resurrection. Christ knew that he had to drink the full cup of crucifixion that was before him, to enact upon the world stage the ancient Mystery for the eventual enlightenment and salvation of all humanity. For an exposition on this, see *Christianity as Mystical Fact* (CMF). Had this evidence of the reappearance of Elijah been proclaimed, it might have interfered with the divine plan (Lk 9,21-22). Yet, in order, after the Crucifixion and Resurrection, to convince faithful Jews that he was the Christ, it was necessary to establish the fulfillment of the Malachi prophecy of Elijah's return. Why, then, was the esoteric meaning not reported instead of the exoteric, for clearly Christ had asserted that John the Baptist *was* Elijah returned? The answer is implied by the "High Mountain" nature of what had been disclosed to them, and the fact that there were still many things the uninitiated "could not bear" (Jn 16,12). Jeremiah referred to a time when "the law" would be written on their hearts (Jer 31), and Paul (Heb 10,16-17 and 2 Cor 3) echoes the same, recognizing that the time was not yet come. The stirrings of that time are upon us with the uniquely new and authentic revelations of Rudolf Steiner, the paradigm of prophecy outlined in 1 Cor 14. Said Steiner, in *The Gospel of St. Luke* (GSL), Lect 10, "Had this teaching been proclaimed in the early centuries of Christendom in the form in which it is proclaimed today, this would have meant demanding of human evolution the equivalent of demanding a plant to produce the blossom before the green leaves."

The two thousand years that karma and reincarnation was not to be taught exoterically was not an arbitrary period. Deep spiritual reality stands behind it. It relates to the length of a "Cultural Era," the two thousand one hundred sixty (2,160) years it takes the Sun to travel through one constellation of the "Zodiac" (**I-19**). We have seen that a Cultural Era is the period required for human consciousness to evolve from one significant stage to another (**I-24**, **I-25** and **I-19**). The word "fullness" in Jn 1,16 ("And from his fullness we have all received, grace upon grace") comes from the Greek *pleroma* and means the light not just of the Eloha Yahweh but that of all seven of the Elohim (Gen 1,26; see *The Gospel of St. John* [GSJ], Lect. 4, p. 74). Each hierarchical rank must be "fully" involved for the "fullness" to be reflected in human creation and evolution. As that principle applies to a Cultural Era, it requires the full rotation through the seven archangelic regencies (Rev 2-3; see also **I-24**, **I-25** and **I-19**; cf. also **I-15**).

The first hint of human intelligence is given in Gen 3, where the serpent Lucifer, the fallen Archangel, desires to bring knowledge prematurely to the developing human being, resulting in its gaining the "tree of knowledge" but being separated from the "tree of life" (Gen 3,22-24). But without the "tree of life," that "knowledge," prematurely given, is deception, and in Rev 12,7-17 we find the Archangel Michael doing battle with that "deceiver" (vs 9). The divine intelligence, the intelligence that gives the human being true spiritual knowledge, has always been administered, within the Archangelic realm, by Michael, the Archangel of the Sun and the most exalted among the seven. The Archangels are known as "Spirits of Fire," or what Christ came to cast upon the Earth (Lk 12,49) and to baptize with (Mt 3,11; Lk 3,16; see also "Fire" in Vol. 2). The world was prepared by the Greeks for the reception and spreading of the Christian message, and this preparation came under the regency of the Archangel Michael during the era of Plato, Aristotle and Alexander (see **I-19**), ending about 200 B.C. The next Michaelic era would not begin until A.D. 1879. A whole series of events would then make it possible for the divine intelligence to enter human consciousness. The Renaissance opens the era of the Consciousness (Spiritual) Soul development, the five-thousand-year Dark Age (i.e., Kaliyuga; see **I-46** and the discussion of Deucalion in "Second Coming" below) ends in 1899, and the first Michaelic Age in the Christian era begins in 1879. These are discussed in "A Time of Spiritual Awakening" in Vol. 3 (see fn 2 above).

The significance of deferring until this first Michaelic regency in the Christian era the revelation of the divine intelligence relating to human rebirth (karma and reincarnation) is also related to the "messenger" who prepares the way for the Christ. This "messenger" (Mk 1,2; Is 40,3; Mal 3,1) is none other than the Archangel Michael. In the Christian Era, Michael acted through John the Baptist, but in the current Era he acts through Rudolf Steiner and anthroposophy, and we can hardly think otherwise than that it is this Michael whom Christ refers to as "the Spirit of truth" (Jn 16,13; 5 ABD 153, col. 2b [Betz]). We get more deeply into this in "I AM." (See there the latter part, starting in the vicinity of its fns 15 and 16 where we discuss Mk 1,2-3, especially the three bracketed paragraphs following the extract that follows these footnotes.) Steiner's works are laced with references to Michael. The anthology *The Archangel Michael* (ARCHM) can serve as a helpful introduction.

Returning to Steiner's simile, the "green leaves" were all in place when the twentieth century opened. Now, a century later, it is urgent that the blossom, the knowledge of the reality of Reincarnation and Karma, enter the minds and hearts of humanity "on earth as it is in heaven" (Mt 6,10).

4. Jn 2,1-11:

> On the third day there was a marriage at Cana in Galilee, and the mother of Jesus was there; Jesus also was invited to the marriage, with his disciples. When the wine gave out, the mother of Jesus said to him, "They have no wine." And Jesus said to her, "O woman, what have you to do with me? My hour has not yet come." His mother said to the servants, "Do whatever he tells you." Now six stone jars were standing there, for the Jewish rites of purification, each holding twenty or thirty gallons. Jesus said to them, "Fill the jars with water." And they filled them up to the brim. He said to them "Now draw some out, and take it to the steward of the feast." So they took it. When the steward of the feast tasted the water now become wine, and did not know where it came from (though the servants who had drawn the water knew), the steward of the feast called the bridegroom and said to him "Every man serves the good wine first; and when men have drunk freely, then the poor wine; but you have kept the good wine until now." This, the first of his signs, Jesus did at Cana in Galilee, and manifested his glory; and his disciples believed in him.

One can hardly come to a fuller understanding of the wedding at Cana without understanding that it signifies that Christianity was not to teach reincarnation for two thousand years. The renowned Brown, in 29 AB 101, says that of John's seven miraculous signs, "Only the Cana miracle has no parallel in the Synoptic tradition." In the light of traditional theology, where Brown is rightly preeminent, this is true. But in the light of anthroposophy, it too is connected with the above esoteric instruction given by Jesus after the Transfiguration and appearance of Elijah. And it is widely recognized that there might be a connection between the wine in this account and that in the Christian "Communion" sacrament, not otherwise mentioned in John's Gospel (for reasons more fully explained in "Peter, James and John"). Indeed, there is. Both relate to the same spiritual necessity. It is ironic that these two events, along with their related passages in regard to Noah and Melchizedek, have been relied upon in recent times to morally justify the consumption of alcoholic beverages, for when they are understood, it will be seen that the segment of humanity that would evolve toward the Second Coming must move away from the consumption of alcohol in doing so. Yet, the express sanction by Christ of the use of wine until that time was given in these two events out of spiritual necessity. And it must surely be more than coincidence that the first serious social movement directed toward prohibiting alcohol (not a correct solution to the problem in Steiner's view) arose almost simultaneously with the confluence of spiritual events discussed in this work that were centered around the beginning of the twentieth century.

Exegesis and exposition in existing commentaries on Jn 2,1-11 seem more ingenious (in the absence of deeper spiritual insight) than meaningfully inspiring. It is to the credit of much modern theology, however, that it is attempting to play down the miraculous element in such passages as this. Steiner never took the position that Christ did not in fact turn water into wine. Quite the contrary. But here as with most other seemingly miraculous incidents, he insisted upon two things. First, when one understands the true character of the Incarnation of Christ—the immense spiritual height embodied in Jesus during the "Three Years"—one can begin to see that he could control elements in ways that indeed appear miraculous to the clouded vision to which humanity had descended. Second, and more important, he lived the real events themselves as symbols. And Evangelist John was more capable than any other of setting this out in his Gospel. The symbols were "Signs," and should be seen exactly as such rather than as miracles. Most available translations properly use the term "signs" rather than "miracles" in Jn 2,11. It is a twist that the RSV is superior on this to the KJV, for the Greek term is clearly "signs." NIV speaks of "miraculous signs," to which its appended footnote says, "John always refers to Jesus' miracles as 'signs,' a word emphasizing the significance of the action rather than the marvel." Again, see CMF.

The problem has been that Christendom has not heretofore understood what the sign "signified." Hence it could only wrestle with it as one of the "miracles," and labor to gather some deeper meaning from it.

What, then, did it signify?

Prior to the point in ancient Lemuria when the Fall described in Gen 3 occurred, human beings dwelled in full communion with the gods, those described in the Bible as the Host. The infection of the astral body by Lucifer at that time (prior to the existence of the human being's Ego) precipitated a progressive and evolutionary densification of the "Three Bodies," and with it came a parallel evolutionary loss of the ancient communion, or clairvoyance. What Paul referred to as the "Fading Splendor" (2 Cor 3,13) in regard to Moses was one manifestation of this, the "end of prophecy" another (Is 29,10 and Mic 3,5-7; see also 5 ABD 489 and Jer 5,13,30-31; 14,14; 23; 29,8-9; Lam 2,9,14; Ezek 13; 22,28; Zeph 3,4). In this ancient period, one's life was not looked upon with such devotion as now for it was known that one's existence neither started at birth nor stopped at death. In short, the importance of each incarnation or life was not sufficiently valued, since one felt that failures in one life could be made up in another. But there is a progressive decline, from life to life, if one fails to use one's "Talents" fully, for circumstances on Earth change from one incarnation to another so that a lost opportunity is the same as a falling behind that compounds over time.

The Christ incarnated in Jesus of Nazareth at precisely the "Right Time," for human beings had descended so far that unless the "Seed" of salvation was then implanted by the Christ Spirit, they would be irretrievably lost.

It was vital that each human being have at least one male and one female incarnation during the time when there was no knowledge of reincarnation in order that the human being could then learn the immense significance of each incarnation. (Typically, as much as a millennium passes between incarnations, so that circumstances on Earth will have changed. Thus, in each 2,160 year Cultural Age [see **I-19**] there is time for at least one incarnation in each sexual orientation.) Hence, the exoteric teaching of only one life is seen even in the works of Paul (who knew better), as in Heb 9,27, as well as in his many references to the shortness of time.

While humanity at large was losing its clairvoyant knowledge of the spiritual world, precautions were taken by the guiding powers that there would always be on Earth some who knew the truth of these matters. This was the function of the ancient "Mysteries." Contemporaneously with Moses, the instruction was given to the Aaronic priesthood (Lev 10,8-11) as well as to the Nazarites (Num 6,1-4) that they should refrain from touching any alcohol. Alcohol prevents the eternal Ego from having control over the astral body—it causes a loss of spiritual consciousness. According to the late Werner Glas, Rudolf Steiner once said that at a certain level of spiritual development even a single glass of wine will set one back five years. Wine, even in moderation and without drunkenness, impedes the development of deeper spiritual insight (i.e., of the embryonic pineal and other glandular organs therefor). Such impediment was essential for two millennia even after the saving "Seed" was sown by Christ.

But the Mysteries had become decadent in the centuries leading up to Christ. Humanity was in a state of separation such that it began to feel the approach of "Sheol." Still, with the influence of the former prophets, there arose a stirring of expectation of deliverance. And it was indeed at the "Right Time" that Christ entered the long-prepared special "Three Bodies" of Jesus of Nazareth as the dove at his Baptism. See "Baptism-Dove."

Christ enacted "Once For All" the truths of the ancient Mysteries upon the Earth-stage (see CMF). He made it clear that there were elements of these Mysteries that the human being was not yet able to bear in that Cultural Age (see Jn 16,12, as well as Paul's Heb 9,5b). And because it was so important that all human beings thereafter have the opportunity of incarnating during a time when there was no knowledge of reincarnation, he laid it down as a matter of esoteric teaching that wine should be used in the Christian Mystery of the mass in order that there should be no knowledge among the uninitiated about reincarnation.

We are told at the outset that the wedding at Cana occurred on the "Third Day"—itself a sign of high spiritual meaning. Steiner tells us (GSJ, Lect. 10, p. 162) that the first day was the transition from the third Cultural Era (Chaldo-Egyptian) to the fourth (Greco-Roman); the second day was the transition from the fourth to the fifth (the present Germanic), and the "Third Day" will occur when humanity passes over from the fifth to the sixth (in A.D. 3574; see **I-19**), the age of Philadelphia (Rev 3,7-13). These are the three days of the human being's initiation. This is what underlies the statement in Jn 2,4, "My hour has not yet come." We are told elsewhere by Steiner, *St. John's Gospel, Notes* (GSJN) that the "Third Day" also meant "that [Evangelist] John lay three days in the sleep of Initiation, during which time the vision of the Marriage at Cana came to him; and all that follows are events seen by him in astral clairvoyance." He was, of course, speaking of the "Three Day's Journey" of Lazarus/John (Jn 11). In GSJN (p. 7) Steiner says that in the higher meaning, the sisters of Lazarus "are the conditions of consciousness in his soul," Martha being the "soul occupied with earth-life" and Mary "the divine soul." This does not for a minute suggest that they were not also the earthly sisters of Lazarus, but does more completely justify the account that Jesus "loved" them (Jn 11,5) since nowhere else in any of the Gospels is Jesus said to have "loved" anyone but Lazarus. (We elsewhere see that this term designates the relationship between teacher and pupil in the ancient Mysteries, and in the parable [Mk 10,21] of the rich "Young Man" [also ruler] it actually refers to Lazarus/John. See "Peter, James and John.") The nature of scripture is such that these need not exhaust the meaning of "Third Day" as it applies here.

Now a curious fact in John's Gospel is that two principal characters are never named (see text following reference to fn 1 in "The Nativity"). One is John (the only usage being with reference to the Baptist) and the other is Jesus' Mother. This is clearly deliberate. Its reason in the case of John will be shown in "Peter, James and John." Its reason as to his Mother is very deep. But that it is deliberate is clear from the fact that his Mother's sister is called "Mary the wife of Clopas" in Jn 19,25, and it was unusual then as now for two siblings to be given the same name. The point is that John is using the term "Mother of Jesus" in a far deeper sense than ordinary, in the sense of the Virgin Sophia, or divine Wisdom, which John was to take into himself from the Crucifixion on (Jn 19,26-27) and to express in the Gospel of John (see GSJ, Lect. 12, pp. 185-187). This is the same Mother to whom the higher meaning in Jn 2,1-11 is given. Since the time when Christ was to be fully revealed in his Second Coming was yet far in the distance, in the transition from the fifth to the sixth Cultural Age (the "Third Day"), he could say to his Mother something that he would never have said to his dear earthly Mother: "O woman, what have I to do with you?" (The common wording "what have you to do with me" is a perversion of the original meaning.) Since there were yet two millennia to run before the return of Christ to the etheric realm (Second Coming), during which time humanity was to concentrate on the importance of each life without knowledge of reincarnation, he instituted the celebration of Christian ceremonies with wine for the duration of that period and so long as he was only "remembered." But it will not be a matter of "remembrance" (1 Cor 11,24-25) to those who attain to the new vision of the Second Coming, for they will experience him directly there and know him without the necessity for such "remembrance" (see 1 Cor 11,26, "until he comes"). It will be the beginning of what Jeremiah saw (Jer 31,33-34; Heb 10,16-17).

No words are superfluous in scripture when it is taken from the "Akashic" record, which confirms the usage of "Cana *in Galilee.*" As Steiner says, (*The Gospel of St. John and its Relation to the Other Gospels*

[Jn-Rel], Lect. 9, p. 161), "Seek as you will, you can find in old Palestine within the radius then known no second Cana." It was imperative that this event be in a setting in "Galilee." Why? Because there was a mixture of "Blood" in "Galilee" and Christ was initiating the necessary spiritual change of humanity's direction away from Blood relationships toward the brotherhood of all humanity (see "All Nations" and "Races"). The earthly Mother of Jesus still represented a Blood relationship, whereas what related to Christ's "hour" was to transcend that relationship. Hence, he could say, "What have I to do with thee?"

The astral vision John gained by taking the "Mother of Jesus" into "his own home" (Jn 19,27) gave him the insights to write his Gospel. Thus, even though John's Gospel says nothing of the Transfiguration or of the "Communion" sacrament, his first "Sign" gives us the deeper elements of both. We shall see in "Peter, James and John" that he does not mention them because he was not present for either of them. (There are still other deep aspects involved in the "transubstantiation" that have become difficult for humanity to comprehend and are outside our present concern.)

Much more could be said about the Cana wedding passage (and many more terms and phrases have a bearing than those yet cited), but it will have to await development in the larger work. Those who desire to look further into what Steiner said of these matters, should see, for instance, GSJ, Lects. 4 (pp. 76-77), 5 (pp. 82-90) and 10 (p. 162); Jn-Rel, Lect. 9 (pp. 161-170); *The Gospel of St. John* (GOSPSJ, unpub. Eng. typescript), Lects. 5 (pp. 41-42) and 8 (pp. 89-92); GSJN (pp. 4-8); FE, Lects. 8 (p. 53), 23 (pp. 186-187) and 30 (pp. 246-249) and *How Can Mankind Find the Christ Again?* (HCMF), Lect. 8 (pp. 162-163).

5. Lk 20,27-38; Mt 22,23-33; Mk 12,18-27:

There came to him some Sadducees, those who say that there is no resurrection, and they asked him a question, saying, "Teacher, Moses wrote for us that if a man's brother dies, having a wife but no children, the man must take the wife and raise up children for his brother. Now there were seven brothers; the first took a wife, and died without children; and the second and the third took her, and likewise all seven left no children and died. Afterward the woman also died. In the resurrection, therefore, whose wife will the woman be? For the seven had her as wife."

And Jesus said to them, "The sons of this age marry and are given in marriage; but those who are accounted worthy to attain to that age and to the resurrection from the dead neither marry nor are given in marriage, for they cannot die any more, because they are equal to angels and are sons of God, being sons of the resurrection. But that the dead are raised, even Moses showed, in the passage about the bush, where he calls the Lord the God of Abraham and the God of Isaac and the God of Jacob. Now he is not God of the dead, but of the living; for all live to him."

For the levirate law in question, see Deut 25,5 and Gen 38,8. Luke's version above is much more explicit than the other two. Much that needs to be said about this passage is said under Point #2 above, but one critical thing needs to be added. In both the Luke and Mark passages Jesus relates his answer to Moses' "passage about the bush." He is stressing that the "bush" that burns but is not consumed is the Ego or Individuality and not the "personality." That an Individuality is not "married" is clear upon reflection. Only perishable personalities marry. We will recognize our loved ones in the spirit world, but the recognition will be of their Individuality. It is a more meaningful recognition than that of the personality only. Recognition of the Individuality implies insight into all of its former personalities, thus recognition of them in a manner of speaking. The passage also makes it clear that the "resurrection" is after one has "attain[ed] to that age," and no longer needs to reincarnate, as indicated by "for they cannot die any more." Until that "age," one is "raised" as indicated "in the passage about the bush" (see "Bush").

Anyone who doubts this latter point should search existing commentaries for an explanation of the last two sentences (vss 37-38), which are essentially identical in all three synoptic Gospels (even in Matthew as we shall see). Look there for any depth of meaning, anything that necessarily makes logical sense independent of (the tendentiousness of) established doctrine or dogma. Just how is it that these two sentences show that "the dead are raised?" For the only thing the passage about the burning bush says is that all who are descended from these three are "living," not that they have necessarily, or from that fact alone, been "raised from the dead." Now, let us look for further confirmation on this point. "Abraham, Isaac and Jacob" first collectively appeared at the conclusion of Genesis (Gen 50,24). But there it did not speak of God as specifically "the God of" these fathers. More important, with reference to the synoptic language in question, it did not speak of the "Bush." The first place in the scripture where "I am the God of your father, the God of Abraham, the God of Isaac, and the God of Jacob" is used is in Ex 3,6, the very passage about the "Bush" (and for this reason Matthew may be deemed to refer also to the "bush" passage). And the first person "I Am" was used there for the first time (see "I AM" and "Name"). Now, what is the ruler over the "Three Bodies?" It is nothing less than "the burning bush," the "I Am," the Ego, the eternal Individuality. It is the Christ-enabled and empowered "I Am" that is never consumed. It "lives" on even though it has not yet "attain[ed] to that age and to the resurrection." Clearly, it is the god of, the ruler over, "Abraham, Isaac and Jacob" who, in this instance, allegorically[13] portray the "Three Bodies." But how is it that it is "raised from the dead" in a manner distinguishable from the "resurrection" as Lk 20,34-38 clearly says? (And the Matthew and Mark passages can be no less meaningful, for they too say that the "Bush" passage shows that the dead are raised, and say nothing of "resurrection" itself.) The Ego is raised from the dead by the process of being "Born Again"[14] (Jn 3,3) on Earth as described in the first part of this essay. Doctrine and dogma to the effect that these passages refer to the resurrection, rather than to reincarnation, simply miss the deeper (esoteric) meaning that was not to come into the general comprehension of humanity until it could "bear" it (Jn 16,12) in the age of the Consciousness Soul, the age of the Second Coming and the "Lord of Karma." Christ clearly understood this, and at least Paul, Luke, and Lazarus/John (and probably others among the "Twelve" and the Evangelists) came to understand it.

---

13. This passage (Lk 20,27-38) is written by Luke, the Evangelist "beloved" (Col 4,14), initiated, by Paul. Philo (ca. 20 B.C.–A.D. 50) appears to have had an immense influence upon the New Testament writers. Particularly is this so with the two disciples initiated by Christ, Lazarus/John and Paul. His doctrine of the Logos is taken up in the Prologue of John's Gospel. And he can be seen in Paul's writings in such conceptual terms as "shadow" and "pattern." (These are illustrated in Vol. 2, in the "Conclusion" to its "Appendix to Fire" under the discussion of "The Pyramid.") Clearly Paul took up Philo's practice of seeing the underlying allegorical meaning in Mosaic writings (see Gal 4,21-31 and 1 Cor 10,1-4).
14. Obviously, then, the high, or one of the higher, meanings of being "born again" is precisely this. However, as with all scriptural passages, representing as they do the truth, they apply to various levels, so that the term can appropriately be used for certain events within a given earthly life. But even in this latter instance, the levels at which the term can be understood vary considerably, the more popular one in the modern vernacular being probably the most vulgar (however holy it in fact is).

6. <u>Jn 9,1-3</u>:

> As he passed by, he saw a man blind from his birth. And his disciples asked him, "Rabbi, who sinned, this man or his parents, that he was born blind?" Jesus answered, "*It was not that this man sinned, or his parents, but that the works of God might be made manifest in him.*" (My emphasis)

To ordinary modern thinking, four possibilities seem inherent in the birth of a blind child: *1.* Prenatal sin by the child; *2.* Prenatal sin by its ancestors; *3.* Sacrificial incarnation by the child to serve humanity through affliction, free from any personal karmic necessity (i.e., to cure the karma of humanity or to help another human being to rise); and *4.* The "luck of the draw," assuming the nullity of karma in the evolution of humanity.

Those who deny Karma and Reincarnation seem necessarily to view only 4 as being possible. Clearly they reject 1 and 3 which assume Karma and Reincarnation.[15] With all the congenital birth defects appearing today, few can doubt the causal nature of 2, but Jesus seems to have rejected this along with 1. It hardly seems appropriate to interpret his reply as simply an ignoring of the question, and the rejecters would agree with this. The rejecters thus adopt the view that it is "the luck of the draw," a view that has probably driven more conscientious people to atheism than any other. People ask if God caused some horrible event, and if not, why God allowed it to happen. Surely 4, necessarily the position of the rejecters, mauls the scriptural idea that God is just. But that is sidebar to the present Point.

To begin with, given the feebleness of the suggestion in the immediate footnote, the probability is high that the disciples assumed the reality of Karma and Reincarnation. This view is strengthened by the fact that

---

15. Geisler and Amano (note 10 above) say that "Jewish theologians of that time gave two reasons for birth defects: prenatal sin (before birth, but *not before* conception) and parental sin. They claimed that when a pregnant woman worshiped in a heathen temple, the fetus committed idolatry as well," citing Gen 25,22, and going on to say, "They also believed that the sins of the parents were visited upon the children (Ex 20,5; Ps 109,14; Is 65,6-7)." The only non-scriptural authority cited is a publication in German, inaccessible to reasonable investigation. In any event, any such sin theologically imputed to the child would be that of the parent, if any ascription of it were to be made between parent and child as the question suggests. Geisler and Amano were giving it primarily to refute the implication that the disciples accepted the reality of Karma and Reincarnation. The suggestion seems more ingenious than probable.

other scripture shows Jesus to have given his disciples esoteric training not available to the general populace—see Mt 17,1; Mk 9,2; Mt 5,1 as discussed in other Points hereunder, as well as "Mountain" and "High Mountain." In particular, see the discussion above on Point 3.

If, as thus far seems reasonable, the disciples accepted the reality of Karma and Reincarnation as indicated by their question, but Jesus denied the causality of sin by either the child or its parents (ancestors), the normal assumption by one who accepts Karma and Reincarnation would be that Point 3 applies, and by one who rejects Karma and Reincarnation that Point 4 applies. However, Steiner gives another explanation in Jn-Rel, Lect 9:

> This individuality comes over from an earlier earth life, from a previous incarnation. Hence we read, not the man's parents have sinned, nor has his own personality—the personality one ordinarily addresses as "I"; but in a previous incarnation he created the cause of his blindness in this life. He became blind because out of a former life the works of the God within him revealed themselves in his blindness. Christ Jesus here points clearly and distinctly to karma, the law of cause and effect.

The common assumption is that Karma and Reincarnation require a person in a given life to be synonymous and coextensive with his or her Ego, or "I Am." But the "I Am" is "the potential human capacity for the divine" and as such extends far beyond all that can be encompassed in any incarnated person. Many incarnations are necessary to attain to the perfection envisioned by the Biblical story. Steiner points, as merely one example, to Christ Jesus' statement, "Is it not written in your law, 'I said, you are gods'?" (Jn 10,34 referring to Ps 82,6). Steiner clearly makes here the distinction between the eternal Individuality and the one-time personality that the ordinary human being sees in another living human being. An incarnating Individuality must, along with the spiritual powers, select the parents and circumstances then available to address certain, perhaps as many as possible, defects that remain to be perfected. Seldom is it possible to accomplish more than a minute portion in any one incarnation, though remarkable progress may be made to the extent that Christ is permitted to work through one.

What then is the meaning of the words "but that the works of God might be made manifest in him"? Steiner says, "He became blind because out of a former life the works of the [g]od within him revealed themselves in his blindness." In Jn-Rel, "God" is capitalized both in the Jn 10,34 reference and in the sentence I have just quoted. But this is a matter of interpretative assumption all the way back as to the original meaning. Clearly, if we understand the scriptural impact of the "I Am" (see that phrase herein), its relationship with the deity is intimate indeed and the presence *vel non* of a capital letter inconsequential. That a karmic affliction, such as blindness, is a work of God as a matter of Grace becomes clear as we contemplate the distinction between the "judgment of the Father" and the "judgment of the Son" in "Lord of Karma."

Clearly Jn 9,1-3 is, according to the anthroposophical view, a scriptural revelation of the reality of Karma and Reincarnation.

7. Jn 3,3:

> Truly, truly, I say to you, unless one is born anew, he cannot see the kingdom of God.

At the exoteric level, this passage has the meaning given by the common understanding, that a conscious awareness of one's devotion to Christ engenders a "newness of life." Esoterically, there is the added meaning of having attained to a state of "Initiation" in accordance with the occult or esoteric path, the state attained by few by following the path called "the way" in Mt 7,13-14. The "second birth" terminology seems to have originated with that meaning in the ancient Mysteries (accord, Barclay, *The Gospel of John*, Vol. 1, p. 126), and it is likely that this meaning is the one most immediately intended by Christ for the inner circle, and most probably for Nicodemus, as indicated by the fact that he came "by night" (see "Night"). The initiates in the Mysteries had knowledge of whence they came (e.g., Know Thyself) and of Earth development, and hence knew of the cycle of rebirth, but it was a knowledge attained only by those who had followed the necessary path of preparation. Steiner's works are filled with references to the Mysteries. See CMF; also *Mystery Centers* (MC); and "Mysteries" below.

It is by virtue of Jn 3,5 that a still higher meaning is also intended by the passage. Jn 3,5 reads:

> Jesus answered, "Truly, truly, I say to you, unless one is born of water and the Spirit, he cannot enter the kingdom of God."

Steiner gives us this higher meaning in GSJ, Lect 6. During long evolutionary development the human being first came down through a gaseous state ("pneuma" originally meant air, then also spirit), then fluidic,
and finally solid. Before the human being can again attain to the state of
consciousness (but enhanced then by the "I Am") in communion with
the spirit world that it had in the beginning, ("the kingdom of God"), it
must again diffuse into and through these states, first of "water" and
then of "air or Spirit." This will involve long periods of time and many
stages of development. Reincarnation is essential to that end. Karma and
Reincarnation began with the division of the sexes in the Lemurian
Epoch. They will end together near the end of the Sixth Great Epoch of
the Mineral Physical state of Earth evolution, as portrayed in **I-2**, the
approach of the "last trumpet" (see "Trumpet[s]").

The whole context of Jn 3,1-15 is one of high elevation. First Nicodemus recognizes Jesus as having "come from God" in order to "do these
signs." Jesus then chides Nicodemus (vs 10) for being a teacher of Israel
but not understanding these Mysteries, and goes on to speak of his own
elevation into the spirit world for the sake of humanity.

Today, there is much sentiment pro and con about whether the Bible
should be taken "literally." Steiner addressed this question particularly in
his lectures on the writings of Lazarus/John. In GSJ, Lect 6, he begins his
discussion about Jn 3,5 by referring to the passage found in 2 Cor 3,6,
"The letter killeth, but the spirit giveth life," saying, "Those who quote
these words often employ them in a very peculiar manner. They find in
them a license for reading into them their own phantasy, which they call
the 'spirit of the thing,' and then they say to someone who has taken the
trouble to learn the letter before coming to the spirit: 'What have we to do
with the letter? The letter killeth, but the spirit giveth life.' One who speaks
in this manner stands on about the same level with a man who would say:
'The spirit is what truly lives, but the body is something dead. Therefore
let us destroy the body, then will the spirit become alive.' Whoever speaks
in this way does not know that the spirit is formed gradually, that the
human being must use the organs of his physical body for reception of
what he experiences in the physical world, which he then raises into spirit.
First we must know the letter, then we can kill it; likewise, when the spirit
has drawn everything it can out of the human body, the latter falls away
from the human spirit." Similarly, *The Apocalypse of St. John* (ASJ), Lect 6
and Jn-Rel, Lect 9. In *Turning Points in Spiritual History* (TPSH), Lect 4,

on Moses, while admiring the extent of the dedication and endeavors of the nineteenth century, Steiner laments the great scholarly investigation by which "the Bible was dissected and split up" into what has become the so-called "documentary hypothesis" (equally applicable to the New Testament) and the like. He looks upon it as tragic, and my personal experience is that it eventually leads one into great spiritual barrenness. It has remained for Steiner, who approximated that state of which Jeremiah prophesied (Jer 31), to bring us to a point of seeing the origin of the scriptures so that we can recognize the different literary modes of expression and see in them the "literal" truth of the message.

Steiner said often that humanity will be unable to progress much further on the upward path with Christ without coming to a knowledge and understanding of these things. The times are heavy upon us when events befalling both humanity and its environment require a higher knowledge than has heretofore been available within the ranks of Christendom (or science; as the two should become one with the increase in knowledge). When that knowledge is taken into the heart of Christendom, it will be able to show the rest of humanity the transcendency of Christianity over any religion (including Christendom as we have known it), just as Christ, who came for the salvation of all creation, stands above all humanity and the Hierarchies, the "name which is above every name" (Phil 2,9).

8. The Sermon on the Mount, Mt 5-7:

See the Commentary for detailed discussion. What is said here takes its thrust from the meaning Jesus gave to "the law" in Mt 5,17. Thus, we quote only the relevant verses:

> Think not that I have come to abolish the law and the prophets; I have come not to abolish them but to fulfill them. For truly, I say to you, till heaven and earth pass away, not an iota, not a dot, will pass from the law until all is accomplished.

To some extent I have searched in vain for an authority to cite for what I am about to propose. It may be that Steiner said it outright, though I have yet to come across such in my study. MacGregor came close to it in *The Christening of Karma*, Chap 5 (see fn 10), which he subheads with the quotation of Mt 5,17. And Steiner may as well have proclaimed it, for it would seem that one can hardly, upon serious reflection, come to any other conclusion in the light of anthroposophical insight.

What is here proposed is that the Sermon on the Mount is the *Magna Charta*, so to speak, of Christian assurance of the reality of karma and its correlative, reincarnation. It is a pyramid with all three chapters as its base, Chapter 5 as its midsection, and verse 17 thereof as its pinnacle. If one reads it with an open and unprejudiced, reverential mind, as though Karma and Reincarnation were true, it can blaze with exalted meaning never before recognized.

As a suggestion, let us start our examination with a consideration of "As Above, So Below." We will see there that "the law" of Moses is one of those lower reflections of a higher reality. "For since the law [of Moses] has but a shadow of the good things to come instead of the true form of these realities,…" (Heb 10,1), it cannot have been what Christ referred to in Mt 5,17. Too many things in the Mosaic "law" are in conflict with the supernal morality of the teachings of Christ. When one comes to realize that Israel, which in a sense commenced with Moses and the Exodus, was a nation "chosen" for the sole purpose of fashioning an earthly vehicle capable of receiving (at the Baptism) the Christ Spirit, one can see that its laws were unique to it. That they involved many advanced moralities of their day is clear, but that they jealously demanded many things designed, contrary to later Christian teachings, to keep the hereditary Blood pure and undefiled to accommodate the etheric body that came over via Noah and Melchizedek from the Shemites of Atlantis (see "Spiritual Economy") is also clear upon careful examination and reflection.

Nothing demonstrates the molting of the Israelite law better than Mt 5, "You have heard that it was said, … but I say unto you" (vss 21, 27, 31, 33, 38 and 43). And the great apostle Paul could not have stressed this critical point more than in his letters to the Romans and the Galatians.

The "Sermon" has been looked upon as "idealistic," an impractical model, precisely because it looks so far into the future and gives humanity a standard so foreign to the worldly standards by which it is wont to fashion its *modus vivendi*. Opponents of Karma and Reincarnation, particularly those who like to claim a "literal" interpretation, "de-literize" Mt 5,48, "You, therefore, must be perfect, as your heavenly Father is perfect," by bringing it into the *modus vivendi* of humanity that exists today. They say that such "perfection" is accomplished for us vicariously by simply "taking Christ into our hearts." But it is a long way from the first step of such "taking" to attaining the "perfection" that he demonstrated on behalf of the "Father." The "Sermon" begins with nine beatitudes that correspond with the ninefold human being (see **I-9**) who has attained to the ninefold "one like a son of man" (Rev 1,13-16). See "Perfect."

The principles of Karma and Reincarnation are reflected throughout the "Sermon." The "Golden Rule" (Mt 7,12) demonstrates the method by which the human being sees its errors in the astral world's "refiner's fire" (Purgatory) before it can pass on into devachan (the spirit world). Mt 7,13-14 tells of how few there are who find the difficult "way" to "life." To believe that the vast hordes who have "confessed" their sins and "professed" Christ, and have therefore begun the walk in "the newness" of life, have already attained, at death, the "perfection" required, and are thus among the "few," is a rationalization that amounts to a mockery of the "Sermon."

Nowhere does Christ more clearly demonstrate the karmic nature of the higher "law" of Mt 5,17 than by referring (in Mt 7,12) to the Golden Rule, not found in Mosaic law or the Israelite prophets, as "the law and the prophets."

This meaning is also fairly apparent in Christ's words in Lk 16,16-17:

> The [Mosaic] law and the prophets were until John; since then the good news of the kingdom of God is preached, and every one enters it violently. But it is easier for heaven and earth to pass away, than for one dot of the [higher] law to become void.

That the bracketed words correspond with Christ's intent is clear from the fact that in the Sermon he overruled the Mosaic law by higher and often inconsistent commandment. See also "Written Word." The term "violently" can be taken to refer to the conception and effort to "crash" or "force one's way" into heaven without having attained the necessary "perfection."

The law and the prophets of which Christ spoke in the "Sermon" is that higher law of which the Old Testament is merely an imperfect reflection. It is the higher karmic law written in the "Akashic" record from which indeed nothing shall pass away until he has fulfilled it. As to how that will be accomplished, see "Lord of Karma."

That this is so should be evident in Christ's statement (vs 20) that concludes the passage (Mt 5,17-20) about his coming to fulfill the law: "For I tell you, unless your righteousness exceeds that of the scribes and the Pharisees, you will never enter the kingdom of heaven." The standard of righteousness used by the scribes and Pharisees was the Mosaic law, the mere imperfect reflection (Heb 10,1). Under "Akashic" below are listed the passages that speak of the heavenly "book" where earthly deeds are recorded, and in two of those (Josh 10,13 and 2 Sam 1,17-18) the term "Book of Jashar" is used. Modern theology has yet to discover the full meaning of that term, but it has at least helped to point in the right direction. Cited there is 3 ABD 646, which states, "The term 'Jashar' is a common Hebrew word meaning 'one who [or that which] is straight, honest, just, righteous, upright.'" The first time the word "righteous" is used by Moses is in Gen 6,9, "Noah was a righteous man, blameless in his generation." The objective of Karma and Reincarnation is the attainment of the blameless, i.e., "just," state of "Perfect(ion)" (Mt 5,48). The first time the word "righteousness" is used by Moses is in Gen 15,6. In Gen 15,5 Abraham had been told that he should mold himself and his descendants after the stars, i.e., the spiritual influence of the "Twelve" features of heaven, the high pattern. Then it would be "reckoned … to him as righteousness." Only in that pattern is it to be fulfilled (Rev 21,12-14; 22,2). The second time "righteousness" is used is in Gen 18,19 where it is tied to "justice," a phrase that echoed on the lips of the prophets and must surely have been what Christ referred to in Mt 5,17. In this pattern there is no room for any misgiving about morality, for all of one's subjective debts (see "Forgiven Sins") must be paid in full (Mt 5,26). Christ is telling his close circle on the "Mountain" that the standard of "righteousness" they must follow is not that of the Mosaic law but that of the higher, Twelvefold, heavenly law of karma that requires "Perfect" justice and righteousness, as the six examples he then gives show, building up to his concluding statement that they must be "Perfect" as their "heavenly [Twelvefold Zodiacal] Father is perfect."

9. Jer 1,4-5; Gal 1,15-16; Heb 7,3; Eph 1,3-4:

Now the word of the Lord came to me saying, "Before I formed you in the womb I knew you, and before you were born I consecrated you; I appointed you a prophet to the nations." (Jer 1,4-5)

But when he who had set me apart before I was born, and had called me through his grace, was pleased to reveal his Son to [KJV says "in"] me, in order that I might preach him among the Gentiles, I did not confer with flesh and blood, nor did I go up to Jerusalem.... (Gal 1,15-16)

He [Melchizedek] is without father or mother or genealogy, and has neither beginning of days nor end of life, but resembling the Son of God he continues a priest forever. (Heb 7,3)

Blessed be the God and Father of our Lord Jesus Christ, who has blessed us in Christ with every spiritual blessing in the heavenly places, even as he chose us in him before the foundation of the world, [cf. Job 38,4,12,21] that we should be holy and blameless before him. (Eph 1,3-4)

Melchizedek[16] aside, all of these passages speak of the preexistence of a human soul or souls before their birth, and in all but one of them before they were conceived in the womb.

MacGregor, in *Reincarnation as a Christian Hope* (cited in fn 10), Chap 4, says, "Every patristic scholar knows that the doctrine of the pre-existence of the soul was openly held by some of the Alexandrian Fathers, including Clement and Origen, and that is a doctrine which, to say the least, has many affinities with a reincarnational one of the Pythagorean or Platonic type. Indeed, many centuries later, Thomas Aquinas, although he does not hold either a pre-existence or a transmigrationist theory, recognizes

---

16. See what I said about Melchizedek in "Spiritual Economy." There, particularly in fn 7 and related text, it is shown that Melchizedek was twofold in nature, so to speak. First, he was the exalted human Individuality that had led humanity into the post-Atlantean Epoch, namely, the reincarnated Manu (Noah). But in that incarnation he embodied also another critical element, for Steiner says that he "had ... 'put on' the preserved [original] etheric body of Shem—the very etheric body that was still inhabited by an avatar being." He was thus a human being in whom an avatar dwelt. I there discussed the meaning of "avatar," showing Christ, as Steiner said, to have been the highest of all avatars, uniquely so in that his "multiplied bodies" could reach to all human beings, while those of Shem could only extend to the Hebrew race.

Paul prepares us for the complexity of this situation in Heb 5,11, "About this we have much to say which is hard to explain, since you have become dull of hearing." He is talking to us, of course, for we have yet to emerge meaningfully from the darkened Intellectual Soul Condition of his own Cultural Era. I have just pointed out in the text above how the term "righteous" is used for the first time in our canon in Gen 15,6, "Noah was a righteous man, blameless in his generation." Paul thus connects Melchizedek with the Noah Individuality when he calls Melchizedek "king of righteousness" (Heb 7,2). (The Hebrew "ZDK," as in "zedek," means "righteousness," appearing frequently in the Old Testament and finding expression in the "Zadokite" priesthood, the ancient priesthood of Jerusalem, which took preeminence over the Levitical, later fictionalized as descending from Aaron; see 1 Interp 596-597; explaining why Paul subordinates Aaron in Heb 7,11.) He is called "king of Salem," normally associated with Jerusalem, but esoterically with its higher meaning (Rev 21,2; Heb 11,10; Gal 4,26; Is 52,1; 61,10). (*continued on following page*)

with his usual perspicacity, that all who have admitted the existence of the soul before birth in a body admit, at least implicitly, a reincarnationist principle [citing Aquinas, *Quaestiones disputatae, De potentia*, Qstn 3, Art. 10]. Christians in the early centuries who held such doctrines were sometimes called and may have called themselves the *pre-existiani*."

That the Individuality that incarnated as the Aquinas personality could in its later incarnation as Steiner come to a more advanced view of the matter merely reflects the evolutionary progress of humanity (see **I-24**, **I-25** and **I-19**, Aquinas preceding the early dawn of the Consciousness Soul Era, ca. A.D. 1414; also "Interlude for Steiner Individuality," Vol. 3). Aquinas does reach the same conclusion that any thinker must reach in regard to the implications of the preexistence of a soul before its incarnation, namely, that it establishes the reality of reincarnation.[17] And the scriptural passages above can then speak for themselves to the contemplative student of our time.

---

16. (*continued*) Saying "Salem" means "peace," Paul also calls Melchizedek "king of peace" (vs 2), a characterization that must surely hark back to the great Hebrew prophecy of Christ as "Prince of Peace" (Is 9,6; see also 5 ABD 905, "Salem"). These passages show why Paul characterized Jesus as being "after the order of Melchizedek (Heb 5,6,10; 6,20; 7,11,17; Ps 110,4), for the Zarathustra Ego in Jesus of Nazareth withdrew at his Baptism and the Christ, the highest of the avatars, entered as his Ego as all Gospels relate (See "Baptism/Dove"; Mt 3,16; Mk 1,10; Lk 3,22; Jn 1,33). Both Melchizedek and Jesus were therefore exalted human Individualities who had reincarnated but carried within their earthly flesh an avatar being. These beings are "without [earthly] father or mother or genealogy, and [have] neither beginning of days nor end of life." In this deeply esoteric sense, both were "of the same order" (Heb 5,10 et al.).

That Paul recognized that Jesus, like Melchizedek, had (as Steiner says above) "put on," i.e., embodied within, his earthly and human nature an avatar element is also suggested by an inspection of the original Greek in Heb 7,3. The Hebrew words there translated by RSV as "resembling" are given by KJV/NIV—INT as "but having been made like to," and KJV says "but made like unto." While semantic, these latter interpretations more clearly lend themselves to what Steiner and Paul are saying as I have outlined it above.

I have included this Melchizedek passage (Heb 7,3) as a scriptural example of the preexistence of human souls not only for the above reason, but also because theologians in general, even when denying such preexistence, have always conceded it in the case of (the avatar) Christ. However, Paul makes it clear that Melchizedek did preexist. The reader who would reject the originally Oriental avatar concept and make Melchizedek merely a human being would thus be obliged to include this as an example of the preexistence of the human soul.

17. In *The Reincarnation Sensation* (see fn 10), Geisler and Amano consider only the Jeremiah and Galatians passages, contending (questionably) that they do not establish anything more than God working on their declarant in the womb. They avoid discussing the clear implications of pre-conception existence in case they are in error.

10. Jas 3,6:

> And the tongue is a fire. The tongue is an unrighteous world among our members, staining the whole body, setting on fire the cycle of nature [fn—"Or wheel of birth"], and set on fire by hell.

Few verses (perhaps Heb 6,4, for one) have given Christian theologians greater problems. So strongly does the "wheel of birth" resemble the Oriental concept of reincarnation that the very idea that James, putatively the brother of Jesus and head of the Church in Jerusalem, might have written it is repugnant, sometimes anathema, and often (though not always) repudiated by traditional Christian thinking[18] that has not moved appreciably beyond the heritage of the Intellectual (Mind) Soul Era. Considering that each such Era spans 2,160 years, the current Consciousness (Spiritual) Soul Era having commenced with the Renaissance, ca. A.D. 1414, this lingering attitude is understandable, but even given the normal graduality of change as well as the relative newness and availability of anthroposophical insight, it must surely now become decreasingly acceptable.

See the Commentary on James for a discussion of its incredible similarity to the Sermon on the Mount. This, together with the close relationship of James[19] to the Lord, gives this language not insignificant circumstantial weight on the relationship of the Sermon on the Mount to Karma and Reincarnation. In Olivier Clement's recent, highly acclaimed work "*The Roots of Christian Mysticism*" (RCM),[20] the preface by Jean-Claude Barreau opens with the statement, "Christianity is in the first place an Oriental religion, and it is a mystical religion." Few modern theologians could seriously doubt the accuracy of that statement, it would seem.

Anthroposophy does not endorse the Oriental concept of an ever recurring cycle or "wheel of life." Rather, the wheel concept is applied in an evolutionary sense, and James' version of it, according to the

---

18. All the commentaries in my library (including Interp, AB, Barc, INTPN and NICNT) clearly recognize and variously reject what would seem to be its obvious meaning as having been intended by James.

19. Whose work, in spite of a struggle, along with the likes of Hebrews and the Apocalypse, eventually took its place in the canon by virtue of that relationship and his eminent status in the Church.

20. The biographical note on the cover reads, "Olivier Clement is one of the foremost Orthodox theologians of the day. He teaches at the Institute of St. Sergius at Paris and is a member of the Ecumenical Institute founded by *L'Institut Catholique.*"

anthroposophical view, would clearly be progressive. It is the non-progressive nature of the Oriental concept that seems most repugnant in the above cited commentaries. See Steiner's explanation, in "The Nativity" herein, of how true Buddhism (though presumably not Hinduism) was rejuvenated in this respect by the Buddha's participation in the birth of the Nathan Jesus child.

11. Gen 4,12b,15:

> (12) " … you shall be a fugitive and a wanderer on the earth.".…
> (15) Then the Lord said to him, "Not so? If any one slays Cain, vengeance shall be taken on him sevenfold." And the Lord put a mark on Cain, lest any who came upon him should kill him.

"Though brief and clear in its overall plot, the narrative of Cain and Abel bristles with problems" (1 ABD 806). If, however, one considers its place immediately after the Fall, which has afflicted all human beings, and then considers the possibility that the Cain element is present in every human being (as its allegorical interpretation suggests—compare Gal 4,21-31; see also the Appendix to "Three Bodies" discussing the "temple legend" and Gen 4-5), then the power of its message radiantly emerges when seen in the light of Karma and Reincarnation.

The divine and graceful "law" of Karma and Reincarnation is a necessity in order that the soul's "wandering" on the Earth as a consequence of the Fall (Gen 4,14) may lead to the "Perfect(ion)" required for re-entry into the paradise from which it was expelled. This requires that the Ego, while "wandering" on the Earth, take in the "I Am" of Christ (the "leaven" in Mt 13,33) to develop ("leaven") the "Three Bodies" into their higher spiritual counterparts, manas ("Manna"), buddhi and atma (**I-9**). These "bodies" are thus, so to speak, "crucified" (Mt 20,22-23 and Mk 10,38-40) into their correspondingly higher spiritual states, following, over evolutionary periods, the path that Jesus Christ, as the "First Born/ Fruits," collapsed into "Three Years."

It is well to remember that Karma and Reincarnation is the child of the division of the sexes (Gen 2,18-25) and the infection of the astral body in the Fall (Gen 3). The consequence is then spelled out further in Gen 4, after which the meaningful genealogy of Seth is spelled out in Gen 5. Even though all human beings are considered to have descended, in an earthly sense, from Adam, Cain and his descendants are notably excluded in the listing of "the generations of Adam" in Gen 5,1. Cain and his descendants disappear from the Bible after Gen 4, and are thereafter mentioned only by way of sinful example in Heb 11,4; 1 Jn 3,12 and Jude 1,11. The Cain element is surely part of the sin factor present in each human being's "members" ("Three Bodies"). See Rom 7,13-23; note especially the concept Paul brings forward in vs 21, "So I find it to be a law that when I want to do right, evil lies close at hand." Its root is Gen 4,7, "If you do well, will you not be accepted? And if you do not do well, sin is couching at the door; its desire is for you, but you must master it."

With the increase of one's anthroposophical knowledge comes first the recognition and then the inner certainty that the sine qua non to Biblical understanding appropriate for our age of the Consciousness Soul is the perception of the reality of Karma and Reincarnation. As such, it is the key to the evolutionary advancement of humanity.

The eleven scriptures above have been discussed at some length for the purpose of demonstration. But the Bible throughout will glow with richer and deeper meaning for the reader who is suffused with this new understanding. Passages will speak to the soul without the necessity for further comment. Consider, for instance:

Eccles 1,10-11:

(10) Is there a thing of which it is said, "See, this is new?" It has been already, in the ages before us. (11) There is no remembrance of former things, nor will there be any remembrance of later things yet to happen among those who come after.

Eccles 3,10-11:

(10) I have seen the business that God has given to the sons of men to be busy with. (11) He has made everything beautiful in its time; also he has put eternity into man's mind, yet so that he cannot find out what God has done from the beginning to the end.

Eccles 12,1-7:

> (1) Remember also your Creator in the days of your youth, before the evil days come, and the years draw nigh, when you will say, "I have no pleasure in them"; … (5) … because man goes to his eternal home, … (7) and the dust returns to the earth as it was, and the spirit *returns* to God who gave it. (Emphasis added)

Job 8,8-10:

> (8) "For inquire, I pray you, of bygone ages, and consider what the fathers have found; (9) for we are but of yesterday, and know nothing, for our days on earth are a shadow. (10) Will they not teach you, and tell you, and utter words out of their understanding?"

Ezek 16,59-61:

> (59) I will deal with you as you have done, who have despised the oath in breaking the covenant, (60) yet I will remember my covenant with you *in the days of your youth*, and I will establish with you an everlasting covenant. (61) Then you will *remember your ways*, and be ashamed *when I take your sisters, both your elder and your younger, and give them to you as daughters*, but not on account of the covenant with you. (Emphasis added)

We need not go on listing examples. The student will discover them in abundance as anthroposophical knowledge grows.

Further Comments on the Nature of Karma:

A high percentage of Steiner's works are laced with aspects of Karma and Reincarnation, and a significant number of lecture cycles as well as individual lectures have "karma" or "karmic" in their titles. To complement the above Overview of Karma and Reincarnation, a few salient aspects seem to merit some brief remark. Largely this is true because of the considerable extent, previously indicated, to which his insights differ from the general concept as it seems to have made its way into modern Western thinking. While other points may be equally or more qualified for inclusion under that standard, the following are given:

1. "A person is not born in a new physical body in a later millennium in order to repeat experiences already undergone, but to experience in what respects humanity has advanced in the intervening time" (GSMt, Lect 9). In accordance with this, the general scheme presented by Steiner is that an Individuality returns to earthly incarnation (as a personality) twice within each Cultural Era (2,160 years), once as a male and once as a female. He also indicated on occasion that the average is about once each 600 years,[21] but that no rule is rigidly applicable. The circumstances that may bring about variations are many. The importance of these remarks is to show that the seemingly general impression that reincarnations normally recur after short intervals is inconsistent with anthroposophy. Transmigration, as apparently envisioned in the Hindu faith is not within the anthroposophical understanding of Karma and Reincarnation.

2. Neither animals nor any of the lower kingdoms reincarnate, for the Egos of the lower kingdoms are never on the Earth (see **I-11**). Human beings reincarnate only as human beings, never as creatures of a lower kingdom. Metempsychosis or any concept involving reincarnation of a human being other than as another human being is incompatible with anthroposophy. The concept of "beasthood" in Revelation is applicable to human beings to the extent they fail during Earth evolution to take Christ into their being. The later they wait to do so, the more difficult it becomes for them to escape—hence the importance of Christianity's historical stress upon the significance of each life, and the reason it was not to teach Karma and Reincarnation for the first two millennia, until the proper state of human evolution had been reached.

3. In general, Individualities tend to reincarnate together, both individually and as groups, because of the karmic relationships between them (see Ezek 16,61).

4. All of the suffering and disease that exist on Earth are due to the karma of human beings and to the evil spiritual beings that are created or nourished thereby. Essentially, this is indicated by Gen 3, but is much more fully elaborated by Steiner. All karma has to be properly compensated for by humanity in the process of its evolution, e.g., Mt 5,18.

---

21. This period coincides closely with that in the Phoenix myth, discussed under "The Phoenix" in the Conclusion to the Appendix to "Fire," in Vol. 2 in this series.

However, see "Forgiven Sins" and "Lord of Karma" for the relationship of Christ to this compensation.

5. The principle of Karma and Reincarnation is a manifestation of the grace of God, applied over evolutionary periods of time.

6. Heredity has little to do with a personality's talents or characteristics in that the reincarnating Individuality, along with the higher powers, choose the parents for the personality. Even beyond this the effect of heredity progressively disappears during the pre-adult years so that thereafter the emerging personality is primarily a reflection of the incarnated Ego.

7. All of a person's circumstances in life are attributable to past karma, save only as one is able to modify those circumstances. The manner in which one handles those circumstances is the test for which the incarnation occurred.

8. It is detrimental to one's own future karma to take the attitude that another's circumstances are of his or her own doing and not to attempt to help alleviate the other person's difficulties to the extent it is within one's power to do so.

9. Karma can be good as well as bad.

10. Every conscious event during one's life is an opportunity either to address past karma or to create future karma, or both. A human being is the result of past incarnations, though no one incarnation can address all one's accumulated karmic debt at this stage of humanity's evolution (unless one is approaching "nirmanakaya," or buddha, status—see **I-23**).

LORD OF KARMA

As with many theological doctrines, the phrase "Lord of Karma" is not found in scripture. Steiner coined it to describe a deeply profound truth, and it provides a vital link in the unfolding account of humanity's salvation. Though he did not use Biblical language nor cite its texts, anyone familiar with scripture can recognize that his words are borne out by Holy Writ and throw radiant new light upon it, eliminating seeming conflicts. Like most such concepts, this one is interwoven with many others, for instance, "Forgiven Sins," "Karma and Reincarnation," "Second Coming," "I AM," "Bush" and "Akashic," all of which appear in this volume.

Steiner seems to have specifically referred to Christ as "Lord of Karma" only in three lectures in the fall of 1911 (*From Jesus to Christ*, [JTC], Lects. 3 and 10; *Faith, Love, Hope*, [FLH], Lect. 1). On October 7, in Karlsruhe Lect. 3, he spoke of the "Lord of Karma" for the first time:

> It is only in the twentieth century that a renewal of the Christ-Event will take place, for this is when a certain general heightening of human powers of cognition begins. It brings with it the possibility that in the course of the next 3,000 years, and without special clairvoyant preparation, more and more persons will be able to attain a direct vision of Christ Jesus.
>
> This has never happened before. Until now there have been only two... sources of knowledge concerning the Christian mysteries for persons who could not rise by training to clairvoyant observation. One source was the Gospels.... The second source of knowledge arose because there have always been clairvoyant individuals who could see into the higher worlds.... And, now from the twentieth century onwards, a third begins. It arises because for more and more people an extension, an enhancement, of their cognitional powers, not brought about through meditation, concentration and other exercises, will occur.... More and more persons will be able to renew

for themselves the experience of Paul on the road to Damascus. Hence we can say of the ensuing period that it will provide a direct means of perceiving the significance and the Being of Christ Jesus.

Now the first question that will naturally occur to you is this: What is the essential difference between the clairvoyant vision of Christ which has always been possible as a result of the esoteric development described yesterday, and the vision of Christ which will come to people, without esoteric development, in the next 3,000 years, beginning from our twentieth century?

There is certainly an important difference.... The reason is as follows.... [T]owards the end of the twentieth century, a significant event will again take place, not in the physical world, but in the world we usually call the world of the etheric. And this event will have as fundamental a significance for the evolution of humanity as the event of Palestine had at the beginning of our era.... And the occurrence of this event, an event connected with the Christ Himself, will make it possible for men to learn to see the Christ, to look upon Him.

What is this event? It consists in the fact that a certain office in the Cosmos, connected with the evolution of humanity in the twentieth century, passes over in a heightened form to the Christ. Occult clairvoyant research tells us that in our epoch Christ becomes the *Lord of Karma* for human evolution. This event marks the beginning of something that we find intimated also in the New Testament: He will come again to separate, or to bring about the crisis for, the living and the dead.[1] Only, according to occult research, this is not to be understood as though it were a single event for all time which takes place on the physical plane. It is connected with the whole future evolution of humanity. And whereas Christianity and Christian evolution were hitherto a kind of preparation, we now have the significant fact that Christ becomes the *Lord of Karma*, so that in the future it will rest with Him to decide what our karmic

---

1. An editorial footnote here reads, "Acts 10,42—To testify that He is the one ordained by God to be Judge of the living and dead. 2 Tim 4,1—Christ Jesus who is to judge the living and the dead." In *Knowledge of the Higher Worlds and Its Attainment* (KHW), Chap. 10 ("The Guardian of the Threshold"), Steiner had spoken of "the Lords of Karma" as being those who "ordain reincarnation." It was from these presumably that Christ has now recently assumed such role.—ERS

account is, how our credit and debit in life are related.... [Emphasis added]

... We know that on passing through the gate of death we separate ourselves from the physical body. The individual is at first still connected for a time with his etheric body, but afterwards he separates his astral body and also his Ego from the etheric body. We know that he takes with him an extract of his etheric body; we know also that the main part of the etheric body goes another way; generally it becomes part of the cosmic ether, either dissolving completely—this happens only under imperfect conditions—or continuing to work on as an enduring active form. When the individual has stripped off his etheric body he passes over into the Kamaloka region for the period of purification in the soul-world. Before this, however, he undergoes a quite special experience which has not previously been mentioned, because ... the time was not ripe for it. Now, however, these things will be fully accepted by all who are qualified to judge them.

Before entering Kamaloka, the individual experiences a meeting with a quite definite Being who presents him with his karmic account. And this Being, who stood there as a kind of bookkeeper for the karmic Powers, had for many men the form of Moses. Hence the medieval formula which originated in Rosicrucianism: Moses presents man in the hour of death—the phrase is not quite accurate, but that is immaterial here—Moses presents man in the hour of his death with the record of his sins, and at the same time points to the 'stern law'. Thus the man can recognize how he has departed from this stern law which he ought to have followed.

In the course of our time—and this is the significant point—this office passes over to Christ Jesus, and man will ever more and more meet Christ Jesus as his Judge, his karmic Judge. That is the supersensible event. Just as on the physical plane, at the beginning of our era, the event of Palestine took place, so in our time the office of Karmic Judge passes over to Christ Jesus in the higher world next to our own. This event works into the physical world, on the physical plane, in such a way that men will develop towards it the feeling that by all their actions they will be causing something for which they will be accountable to the judgment of Christ. This feeling, now appearing quite naturally in the course of human development, will be transformed so that it permeates the soul with a light which little by little will shine out from the individual himself, and will illuminate the form of Christ in the etheric world. And the more this feeling is developed ... the more will the etheric Form of Christ be visible in the coming centuries.

For a greater elaboration upon the appearance of Christ in the etheric world, see "Second Coming," for that is what Steiner is here referring to as a synergetic, correlated and essentially contemporaneous event. This close relationship prompted him to go to some length in the balance of Lect. 3 to stress that the appearance of Christ in the physical form was a "once for all" event, and that his return would be in the etheric world and perceivable there by those who, while still in the physical world themselves, have developed their organs of perception to that level of the new clairvoyance. The student of anthroposophy will note that most of Steiner's stress upon this particular fact was during the time when the controversy arose that eventually precipitated his separation from the Theosophical Society—its then leaders were pointing to a certain Oriental youth as the reincarnated Christ, a claim later admitted to have been spurious. Nothing more clearly marked anthroposophy as a totally Western development, differentiating it from the Oriental view. By the latter, the "cycles of life" or reincarnations are unending until one attains to Nirvana and does not have to reincarnate anymore, whereas for anthroposophy reincarnation is part of humanity's evolutionary progress to "perfection." The Oriental view is essentially a salvation for the individual, whereas the Western view recognizes the universality of Christ as the Savior of all humanity and, indeed, of all creation (Rom 8,19-23; Eph 1,9-10). This theme is taken up in Lect. 10, which again stresses the importance of humanity's taking up the insights of anthroposophy:

Just as it was necessary that the first Christ-Event should take place on the physical plane in order that the salvation of man could be accomplished, so must the preparation be made here in the physical world, the preparation to look with full understanding, with full illumination, upon the Christ-Event of the twentieth century. For a person who looks upon it unprepared, when his powers have been awakened, will not be able to understand it. The Lord of Karma will then appear to him as a fearful judgment. In order to have an illuminated understanding of this Event, the individual must be prepared. The spreading abroad of the anthroposophical world-conception has taken place in our time for this purpose, so that men can be prepared on the physical plane to perceive the Christ-Event either on the physical plane or on the higher planes. Those who are not sufficiently prepared on the physical plane, and then go unprepared through the life between death and a new birth, will have to wait until in the next incarnation, they can be further prepared through Anthroposophy for the understanding of Christ. During the next 3,000 years the opportunity will be given to men of going through this preparation, and the purpose of all anthroposophical development will be to render men more and more capable of participating in that which is to come.

Just preceding these remarks, Steiner indicated that, just as Christ had descended into hell (see "Descent Into Hell") during his entombment to lift the veil of shades ("Sheol") from "those who have fallen asleep," so also will this event in the twentieth century be perceived by those between incarnations who are prepared to do so. (On this, see 1 Pet 4,5-6 below.)

How is it that Christ is Lord of Karma? This is closely tied in with the concept of "Forgiven Sins." If one will merely think, it can become quite clear. From whence comes the power of Christ to forgive sins? The scribes and Pharisees could not understand this (see Lk 5,17-26; Mk 2,1-12; Mt 9,1-8), claiming that only God had this power. Consider, for a moment, who alone has the power to cancel a debt. No one but the creditor has the power, for only he or she provides the consideration therefor in the form of a loan or sale of goods or services on credit, or suffers the damage leading to money judgment. The "objective karma" (see "Forgiven Sins") that results from every sin is a debt to all humanity (indeed to all creation) which the sinner alone is unable to pay or erase. When Christ voluntarily descended from the heights of heaven and shed his blood on Calvary, he paid that debt once and for all (see Heb) for all who accept his offer by taking him into themselves. By virtue of this event, Christ is subrogated to the claim humanity, i.e., creation, has against the sinner. Christ is now the owner of that claim, and he alone thereby has the power to forgive it. The Father has given it into his hands because he is the only being in all of the spiritual Hierarchies above humanity that has experienced death.

In Steiner's words (CHS, Lect. 4), "Christ is the only forgiver of sins because he is the bearer of sins." This objective karma is reflected by that wonderful passage in Mt 25,40,45, "As you did it [or not] to one of the least of these my brethren, you did it to me." For there is no one else in or above all creation who can erase such objective karma save Christ by virtue of his blood and the Mystery of Golgotha.

But while Christ takes upon his own shoulders all of one's objective karma who has accepted him, it is most obvious that he has not "paid for" *all* the consequences of the same sins. Some other human being may still suffer scars received as a result of those same sins. The only one who can absolve that "subjective" debt is the human individuality who is injured. That absolution, i.e., release of debt, can be given by the injured individuality either through its personality in the present life or that incarnated in a later one. The most sublime manner of payment is for the injured individuality to forgive the sinner, as Christ commands. But if that is not done, then evil will be repaid on Earth by commensurate circumstances between the two in a later incarnation. Christ, as Lord of Karma, is the judge who presents us, when we have passed through the gate of death, with our karmic record and serves as counsellor in order for us to complete our salvation ("Perfection," Mt 5,48) by arranging the necessary karmic circumstances in future incarnations, the "wheel of birth" (Jas 3,6), to give us, as a matter of "grace," the opportunity to make restitution.

The power of objective karma is also what underlies Christ's unique power of healing. We elsewhere see that all "disposition to" illness and health is due to past karma (e.g., see *Karmic Relationships* [KR-1], Lect. 5) resulting from the sin of the Individuality or of humanity. We also know that Christ's healings were inevitably associated with a statement, expressed or implied, that one's sins (or those of one's ancestors, for instance) are forgiven. The "faith" asserted as the basis for such healing is a faith in Christ as the one who has the power to forgive sins. That this is so is shown by the fact that in each event the directive to "go and sin no more" is expressed or implied.

Upon seeing these things clearly, one can see that what Steiner found upon clairvoyant spiritual research, namely, the return of Christ as Lord of Karma, not only is vindicated by the language of scripture itself but also explains and harmonizes many aspects of it that have hitherto generated such confusion and diversity of opinion. His revelation that this is an event of the twentieth century is more fully understandable in light of what is said about timing in "Karma and Reincarnation," as well as in "Second Coming," herein.

Let us then reflect upon how scripture vindicates Steiner's revelation of Christ becoming Lord of Karma. Moreover, one can observe that the concomitant of such vindication is the illumination of passages not heretofore comprehended by (at least the exoteric) theology of all persuasions. May we also bear in mind that the hallmark of truth is that, when grasped, its light reveals meaning otherwise hidden in its locale, thus witnessing to its verity.

The key to the whereabouts of this "locale" is found in the passage quoted above, "In the course of our time... this office passes over to Christ Jesus, and man will ever more and more meet Christ Jesus as his Judge, his karmic Judge.... So in our time the office of karmic Judge passes over to Christ Jesus in the higher world next to our own." By this, Steiner identifies the "locale" as that of "judgment."

We are obliged to see from the Bible itself if Steiner is right. We will look first at current theological thinking in regard to "judging," and then discuss more widely the New Testament's usage of the concept. In order to appreciate the current state of theological understanding in regard to what the New Testament has to say about judgment, consider the following relatively recent (1992) authoritative exposition from 2 ABD 80-81 ("Day of Judgment—NT Usages"):

B. <u>NT Usages</u>

In the NT the day or time of judgment is generally associated with the future coming or Parousia of the Son of Man, the resurrection of the dead, and entrance into the kingdom of God.

1. <u>Agents of Judgment</u>. Several synoptic passages suggest that the coming Son of Man will be judge, e.g., Mark 13:26-27; Matt 25:31-46; Luke 21:36. Later NT traditions frequently name Jesus Christ as the one who will judge, e.g., Acts 10:42; 17:31; 2 Cor 5:10; 2 Tim 4:1. The coming of Jesus as judge is sometimes described as "the Day of Christ" or "the Day of the Lord," e.g., Phil 1:10; 1

Thess 5:2. See DAY OF CHRIST. Certain texts assign "the Twelve" or "the saints" (faithful Christians) a share in the task of judging "Israel" (Matt 19:28; Luke 22:30), the Church (1 Cor 5:12), the world (1 Cor 6:2), or even angels (1 Cor 6:3). Nevertheless, God himself is frequently represented as the one who will judge: Matt 18:35; John 8:50; Rom 2:2-11; 3:6; 14:10 (cf. 2 Cor 5:10); Heb 10:30-31; 1 Pet 1:17; 2:23: Rev 18:8. A few Pauline passages suggest that God and Jesus will both take part in judging: Rom 2:16; 1 Cor 4:5. In John 12:48 Jesus warns that the word he has spoken will be his hearers' judge "on the last day. "...

C. Modern Scholarly Opinion

Numerous biblical texts particularly in the NT refer to the coming day or time of judgment. Nevertheless, little scholarly attention has been devoted to this topic in contrast, for example, to closely related topics like the coming of the Son of Man and the kingdom of God. One suspects that modern scholars prefer to deal with more congenial subjects.... Scholarly squeamishness is articulated occasionally, e.g., by Dalton (1968:7): "God is primarily a God who loves, a God who saves. Hence any eschatological statement set in the context of future judgment must take into account the inadequacy of this context and must allow for this inadequacy if conclusions unworthy of God are to be avoided."

Only those willing to acknowledge as significant the eschatological orientation within apocalyptic Judaism, Jesus' teaching, and the NT churches are prepared to recognize the nature and importance of their beliefs and expectations concerning the coming time or day of judgment....

First, let us set aside the "eschatological orientation," not because it is unimportant but because my Commentary on the book of Revelation shows clearly, for the first time, what the eschatological passages in the Bible mean.

Next, observe from "C" above, eschatological views aside, that theology has generally avoided the question in its entirety— treatment symptomatic where meaning lies veiled from comprehension, as we note in many other contexts in this work.

Then we see, in both the introductory paragraph of "B" as well as in "C," that judgment is "generally associated with," or considered "closely related" to, the "coming of the Son of Man." Thus in this respect the assumption by Christ Jesus of the role of karmic judge in the twentieth century is in accord with the "general view" inasmuch as anthroposophy shows that it is also in the twentieth century when the "coming of the Son of Man" commences, namely, his reappearance in the etheric world, as to which see "Second Coming."

Our next step is to eliminate those portions of "B.1." above that are really outside the scope of our investigation, or otherwise readily explained away by it. Such portions are encompassed in the sentence about "the Twelve" or "the saints" sharing in the task of judging. Mt 19,28 and Lk 22,30 can be taken as referring to that far distant time when the twelve apostles' names will be on the twelve "foundations" (cf. "thrones") of the Holy City, representative "of the twelve tribes of the sons of Israel" (see Rev 21,12-14), a time when human evolution shall have passed from the septenary solar system of Earth evolution to the twelvefold influence of the "Zodiac" from which it came. Karma and its resulting reincarnation shall have ceased long before then (see **I-2**). The passages in 1 Cor 5 and 6 all have to do with judgment in mundane matters, as indicated not only by its context but by the circumstances Paul addressed in Corinth.

We now come to those passages where "God himself is … represented as the one who will judge." We may rightly now ask, "How do we reconcile the scriptural assertions that God is to be the judge, with those where Christ is to be the judge, particularly in view of Christ's statements that he has not come to judge, while recognizing that elsewhere he and the Epistles claim that he will judge?" Here is an illustration of that promised freedom generated by knowing the truth (Jn 8,32). For it can become readily apparent from an inspection of these passages that the judgment that comes from God is the perfect justice of the eternal law, the law of karma, whereas the justice that comes from Christ is what emanates from the taking *vel non* of Christ into one's own being whereby one's objective karma is transferred to him and only the subjective karma remains. It is with respect to that subjective karma that Christ is now becoming the administrator, replacing Moses (for much of humanity, and his counterpart for the rest), as God's agent (representing the higher karmic law—Heb 10,1).

The passages in question are considered below:

Mt 18,35:

> So also my heavenly Father will do to every one of you, if you do not
> forgive your brother from your heart.

Here one should first review the discussion of the Sermon on the
Mount (Mt 5-7) under "Karma and Reincarnation" herein. Then, in particular, consider Mt 7,1-5; 5,21-26; 6,12; Lk 6,37; Mt 18,21-22; and
Rom 14,10. The failure of one, forgiven by Christ, to forgive is a sin with
both objective and subjective karmic consequences. Again and again
Christ must be asked (e.g., Mt 6,12) to forgive us thus taking over such
objective karma. But Mt 18,35, as well as Mt 5,26 and other scriptures,
make it clear that restitution must be made in the satisfaction of our subjective karma, for here the karmic law of the "heavenly Father," as Christ
says, demands it.

Jn 8,50:

This passage is not relevant for Christ is telling the Jews that his Father
will be the one who judges whether he is telling the truth or has a demon.
However, we may reasonably infer, beyond this, that for all who reject
Christ as not telling the truth or take him for possessing a demon the full
weight of the karmic law of the Father, with all its cumulative and unforgiven sin, will indeed be the judge within the thrust of our present postulate.

Rom 2,2-11 and 3,6:

Actually, all of Rom 2 and 3 should be considered, for Paul is speaking
of the Mosaic law which he elsewhere shows (Heb 10,1 and perhaps also
Rom 2,14) is a mere reflection of the higher (karmic) law. Paul is here
saying that God (through Moses at least) will judge those who live by that
law and that such judgment is totally and perfectly "just" (as the karmic
law certainly is), and that it remains fully in effect for those who do not
take Christ into their own being (with consequent forgiveness of their
objective sins). But the burden of unforgiven objective (as distinguished
from subjective) karma is beyond normal human capacity to overcome,
hence unless and until Christ is taken into one's own being through forgiveness of objective karma, one is eventually doomed. Indeed, it would

seem that Romans can hardly be understood, in the deeper sense, unless one comes to understand the distinction Paul is making between the law applicable to objective sin and that applicable to subjective (see "Forgiven Sins"). And one must wrestle with the meaning of Rom 9 and 10, where Paul wishes he could be sacrificed for his people as a whole (not for given personalities but for the race) but then sees them as eventually coming to salvation. How frightfully cruel for those Jews who lived before that time if they are only personalities who live once and not eternal Individualities. One must surely miss Paul's meaning until the deep truth of "Karma and Reincarnation," and of the nature of "Forgiven Sins," is understood in anthroposophical light.

Rom 14,10 (cf. 2 Cor 5,10):

> Why do you pass judgment on your brother? Or you, why do you despise your brother? For we shall all stand before the judgment seat of God.

The judgment seat of God has to do with karmic justice. Therefore, just as Christ tells us in that clearly subjective-karma passage, Mt 7,1-5, "Judge not, that you be not judged," one must pay the subjective karmic debt. Paul does not excuse even himself from that judgment in this passage, "For we shall all stand before the judgment seat of God," to make just restitution for the sins we commit, even though the greater and fatal consequence of those sins has been lifted from our shoulders, for in only this manner can we attain to perfection.

2 Cor 5,10:

> For we must all appear before the judgment seat of Christ, so that each one may receive good or evil, according to what he has done in the body.

In this we see Paul's expression of Christ as the Lord of Karma. The karmic law was in effect as a part of the creative process of humanity, established by the Father (though Christ was a part of that prior to emptying himself and taking human form—Jn 1,1-3). Here Paul, as he often does, brings into his language spiritual events lying in the future, often far distant. In assigning judgment to Christ, aside from that resulting simply "from his word" (Jn 12,48 and 3,19), Paul seems to be projecting his language to the time when Christ will take over as Lord of Karma. It must be recognized that karmic debt is paid only over long periods of time so that sins committed in Paul's own day, if not previously compensated for, remain subject to the administration Christ takes over from our time on.

Heb 10,30-31:

> For we know him who said, "Vengeance is mine, I will repay." And again, "The Lord will judge his people." It is a fearful thing to fall into the hands of the living God.

Here Paul quotes Deut 32,35-36 (Moses) in one of the clearest karmic passages in all scripture, and "the living God" would seem to be the Father, as assumed by ABD above. But to whom is Paul referring as "Lord?" In the Old Testament from which he quotes, it normally means the Yahweh-eloha, but in the New it refers to Christ Jesus. Most probably he was picking up the Mosaic meaning. But what was that prophetic meaning? Let us look at Deut 32,35-36:

> (35) Vengeance is mine, and recompense, for the time when their foot shall slip; for the day of their calamity is at hand, and their doom comes swiftly. (36) For the Lord will vindicate his people and have compassion on his servants, when he sees that their power is gone, and there is none remaining bond or free.

The apparent meaning is that "vengeance" is directed toward all who sin (at this stage for both the objective and subjective karma) and "recompense" will be required, which, because they cannot remove their objective sin, assures "their doom." But the meaning of "vindicate" seems to be different, meaning to absolve and justify his people rather than to punish others. Indeed, if one observes the meaning of the term "vindicate" in a good dictionary, "justify" is what is expressed, and "punish" is designated as "obsolete" (WNWD) or very subordinate (RHCD). The Latin meaning appears to support the idea of punishment, but Latin came long after Moses' verbal pronouncement. The underlying Hebrew, though literally translated "vengeance," does not, in context, justify the idea of punishment, but rather of vindication. See TORAH, Interp and

INTPN.[2] TORAH considers it "simply a continuation of verse 34" which is a clear description of the "Akashic" record, "Is not this laid up in store with me, sealed up in my treasuries?" (Deut 32,34, RSV). And consider that the extant Hebrew manuscripts came into existence long after Moses' time and perhaps carry the meaning given in that later day (much as today we have an RSV and then a NRSV that attempt to bring current meaning in, often at the expense of original understanding). Furthermore, while it is beyond our present scope to show this, an inspection of a concordance will reveal that the primary scriptural usage of the term "vindicate" is that of "justify," not "punish." If we bear these thoughts in mind, it is quite probable that Paul is saying not only that the Father will impose the karmic judgment, but that the Christ (on the Father's behalf), as Lord of Karma, will "vindicate" or "justify" his people ("judge his people") insofar as their oppressive objective karma is concerned. And there is a basis to believe that this was precisely also Moses' prophetic pronouncement (see Jn 5,46; Lk 24,27,44; and 1 Cor 10,1-4), not understood by later Hebrew or Latin scribes or redactors.

1 Pet 1,17:

> And if you invoke as Father him who judges each one impartially according to his deeds, conduct yourselves with fear throughout the time of your exile.

This follows vss 13-16 which speak of grace and the Christ standard of conduct, namely, "holiness." Then, the juxtaposed vs 17 jumps to the Father's judgment, and we here see clearly the application of the subjective karmic law of justice "impartially according to his deeds." Peter is addressing those who have taken Christ into their beings (vss 1-2), recognizing that even they face subjective karmic judgment "according to [their] deeds." The "And *if* you invoke" does not grant an option, but recognizes that this is something they must do if they thereafter, in spite of the fact they are "sanctified … for obedience" (vs 2), fall short and sin again. Otherwise it would be pointless to present this as an option to those who, by merely invoking the ever-present forgiveness by Christ, could avoid that impartial judgment of the "Father."

---

2. At this writing, neither NIB nor AB has published its commentary volume on Deuteronomy 32.

1 Pet 2,23:

> When he was reviled, he did not revile in return; when he suffered, he did not threaten; but he trusted to him who judges justly.

Here again, as in Jn 8,50 above, it is Christ Jesus who is being judged by the Father. Immediately before, verse 22 said, "He committed no sin; no guile was found on his lips." The extent to which this is true is indicated in "The Nativity," for the etheric body of the Nathan Jesus child was not infected by original sin, and the Solomon Jesus child's Ego, even as nearly perfect as it was, dwelt in Jesus of Nazareth only until replaced by the Christ Spirit at Baptism. In any event, no Christian will debate the assertion that Christ was without sin. Therefore, he alone could submit to the full "just" judgment of the Father free of any personal karma, either objective or subjective. Given that this applies only to Christ, it does comport with, and tends to corroborate, the anthroposophical insight about the nature of karma, both subjective and objective.

Rev 18,8:

> So shall her plagues come in a single day, pestilence and mourning and famine, and she shall be burned with fire; for mighty is the Lord God who judges her.

We are approaching the end of the apocalyptic vision of Lazarus/John. Inasmuch as it is the bookend-like counterpart of the creation account in Genesis, we are probably warranted in taking "day" to be a long period of time, one ruled over by a particular spiritual Hierarchy ("god," i.e. *dei*, elsewhere herein shown to be related to *die*, or "day" in Gen 1). The point, however, is the immensity of the power of karmic judgment for those (in this case "whore Babylon" who "committed fornication" with "the kings of the earth") who have not by then taken Christ into their being so as to erase objective karma. In truth, at this point, we are far beyond the time when reincarnation occurs, and nearer that time of which Paul speaks, of salvation for the rest of creation (Rom 8,19-23; Eph 1,9-10). Those who had not previously taken in Christ are, by then, somewhat in the posture of the "rest of creation," having taken upon themselves the repugnancy of "beasthood" (e.g., Rev 13,18 and 16,2).

Our final step, then, is to examine those passages that speak of Christ Jesus as judge. It is typical of the darkness in which modern theology dwells that "B.1." above cites, for this, only "several synoptic passages," along with Acts and Pauline letters, ignoring the Gospel of John, the highest spiritual writing given to humanity according to Steiner. Only twice in its later peripheral observations does it cite John, i.e., Jn 8,50 and 12,48. We shall see that the most meaningful passages are indeed probably in John's Gospel, and we shall range even then beyond those cited in "B.1."

Let us at last observe how references to Christ Jesus as judge relate to him as Lord of Karma within the above discussion:

Jn 5,19-47:

(19) Truly, truly, I say to you, the Son can do nothing of his own accord, but only what he sees the Father doing; for whatever he does, that the Son does likewise. (20) For the Father loves[3] the Son, and shows him all that he himself is doing; and greater works than these will he show him, that you may marvel. (21) For as the Father raises the dead and gives them life, so also the Son gives life to whom he will. (22) The Father judges no one, but has given all judgment to the Son, (23) that all may honor the Son, even as they honor the Father. He who does not honor the Son does not honor the Father who sent him. (24) Truly, truly, I say to you, he who hears my word and believes him who sent me, has eternal life; he does not come into judgment, but has passed from death to life.

---

3. It is well here to bear in mind the meaning of "loves" in this context, for it means that he "shows him all that he himself is doing." Steiner has shown us that the term "loves" is used to describe what flows from teacher to student in the ancient Mysteries, and that it carried this meaning in the enactment of such Mysteries in Jn 11, which speaks of how Jesus "loved him" (Jn 11,36), and thereafter of "the disciple whom Jesus loved" (Jn 13,23; 19,26; 20,2; and 21,7,20). Aside from Mary and Martha (Jn 11,5), his sisters, Lazarus is the only one whom scriptures say, in this manner, that Jesus "loved." In so saying, I take note of Mk 10,21, the rich "Young Man," for it is my belief that this Lazarus is also the one spoken of there. Other evidence indeed exists to the effect that Lazarus was wealthy. By being so "loved," and thus the only disciple initiated by Jesus according to the ancient Mysteries (see "Three Days' Journey"), Lazarus was shown higher Mysteries by Christ than any other. It is thus that his Gospel, Epistles (for Steiner assures us they were his) and Apocalypse are preeminent as spiritual writings, it being ominously indicative of the darkness upon humanity that these works first had difficulty getting into the canon and then have been looked upon as inferior to the synoptics, or "maddening" in the case of Revelation.

(25) Truly, truly, I say to you, the hour is coming, and now is, when the dead will hear the voice of the Son of God, and those who hear will live. (26) For as the Father has life in himself, so he has granted the Son also to have life in himself, (27) and has given him authority to execute judgment, because he is the Son of man. (28) Do not marvel at this; for the hour is coming when all who are in the tombs will hear his voice (29) and come forth, those who have done good, to the resurrection of life, and those who have done evil, to the resurrection of judgment.

(30) I can do nothing on my own authority; as I hear, I judge; and my judgment is just, because I seek not my own will but the will of him who sent me. (31) If I bear witness to myself, my testimony is not true; (32) there is another who bears witness to me, and I know that the testimony which he bears to me is true. (33) You sent to John, and he has borne witness to the truth. (34) Not that the testimony which I receive is from man; but I say this that you may be saved. (35) He was a burning and shining lamp, and you were willing to rejoice for a while in his light. (36) But the testimony which I have is greater than that of John; for the works which the Father has granted me to accomplish, these very works which I am doing, bear me witness that the Father has sent me. (37) And the Father who sent me has himself borne witness to me. His voice you have never heard, his form you have never seen; (38) and you do not have his word abiding in you, for you do not believe him whom he has sent. (39) You search the scriptures, because you think that in them you have eternal life; and it is they that bear witness to me; (40) yet you refuse to come to me that you may have life. (41) I do not receive glory from men. (42) But I know that you have not the love of God within you. (43) I have come in my Father's name, and you do not receive me; if another comes in his own name, him you will receive. (44) How can you believe, who receive glory from one another and do not seek the glory that comes from the only God? (45) Do not think that I shall accuse you to the Father; it is Moses who accuses you, on whom you set your hope. (46) If you believed Moses, you would believe me, for he wrote of me. (47) But if you do not believe his writings, how will you believe my words?"

In verse 21, we are told that it is the Father who "raises the dead and gives them life," after which we are told that the Son "also... gives life to whom he will." The "raising by the Father" is by virtue of the fact of Karma and Reincarnation, where, as a matter of grace, for the purpose of restoration over time of the original pure state from which fallen, a human being lives and dies over and over again (see Lk 20,34-37). The karmic law (Mt 5,17) is established by the Father who gives life over and over that the Individuality, the "burning bush" ("Bush") may become "Perfect(ed)." This is the meaning of the mystical synoptic passage, "But that the dead are raised, even Moses showed, in the passage about the bush" (Lk 20,37; see "Karma and Reincarnation" and "Bush"). The "judgment" given by the Father to the Son (vss 22 and 27) is an administrative, saving judgment (Jn 12,47 and 3,17; see also the Jn 9,39 discussion below), as an advocate or counselor (vs 45) that Steiner calls "Lord of Karma." The "resurrection" in vs 29 should be understood in the light of Lk 20,35. The Father raises all from the dead, to give them further opportunity under the karmic law, but the Son, who "also ... gives life to whom he will," can only give it to those who accept his offer of forgiveness of their objective sins. Thus, the life given by the Father, who makes his light shine on the evil and unjust as well as the good and just (Mt 5,45), is given to all, but the life given by the Son is that of resurrection, which is available only to those who avail themselves and take him into their being and then "perfect" themselves under his guidance as Lord of Karma. The Father's life is universal to all, but carries with it the impossible burden of objective karma. The Son's life is available to those who accept his forgiveness and counsel ("whom he will," vs 21). It was the Father's love that made the Son's blood available (Jn 3,16), but the life given by the Father within the meaning of Jn 5,21 seems clearly implied to be different than that which comes through the Son.[4]

That "the Father judges no one" (vs 22) cannot be taken as contrary to the idea that one is adjudged by the law of karma established by the Father, but rather in the context that with the "purchase of salvation" by the Son, judgment is given over to the Son; thus, "but has given all judgment to the

---

4. From this extended discussion by Lazarus/John, it should now be clear beyond doubt that the distinction made in Lk 20,34-38 between the "resurrection," on the one hand, and being "raised from the dead," on the other, is a true and proper one (see "Karma and Reincarnation"; see also Heb 11,19 in the discussion under 1 Pet 4,5-6 below).

Son" (vs 22), and again, "has given him authority to execute judgment" (vs 27). That it is the Father who, in regard to karma, has theretofore been, and continues thereafter to underlie, the judge is indicated by verse 45, "Do not think that I shall accuse you to the Father; it is Moses who accuses you...." And that it is the Father's judicial authority which is exercised by Christ in regard to karma is indicated by verse 30, "I can do nothing on my own authority; as I hear, I judge; and my judgment is just, because I seek not my own will but the will of him who sent me." The judgment that is escaped by believing in Christ (vs 24) is that of the Father, not the Son (1 Cor 11,32). The two-thousand-year time lag between these statements and the movement by Christ into the post of Lord of Karma is of no consequence inasmuch as karmic law is eternal in its nature and those Individualities to whom it applies (i.e., all human beings) are of the same nature. Christ is given the post but only puts on his judicial robe, so to speak, upon his return to the etheric world—the Second Coming. That no human being would be eternally condemned prior to the age of the Consciousness Soul, nor in fact for a great time thereafter, is also in keeping with the grace involved in the long stretch of karmic justice, as clearly shown by John's Apocalypse.

Jn 3,19 and Jn 12,47-49:

> **John 3,19**: And this is the judgment, that the light has come into the world, and men loved darkness rather than light, because their deeds were evil.

> **Jn 12,47-49**: (47) If any one hears my sayings and does not keep them, I do not judge him; for I did not come to judge the world but to save the world. (48) He who rejects me and does not receive my sayings has a judge; the word that I have spoken will be his judge on the last day. (49) For I have not spoken on my own authority; the Father who sent me has himself given me commandment what to say and what to speak.

Again we see Jesus' mercy circumscribed by the karmic law of the Father, save only insofar as humanity comes to him out of "love for the light." His words of judgment are those he must speak on the authority of the Father. And his judgment is "to save" (vs 47).

Jn 8,15-16,26:

(15) You judge according to the flesh, I judge no one. (16) Yet even if I do judge, my judgment is true, for it is not I alone that judge, but I and he who sent me ... (26) I have much to say about you and much to judge, but he who sent me is true, and I declare to the world what I have heard from him.

These words, spoken in interchange with the Pharisees, seem to require no additional comment.

Jn 9,39:

Jesus said, "For judgment I came into this world, that those who do not see may see, and that those who see may become blind."

Commentaries give a rather general exoteric meaning to this passage. Our present purpose is only to consider whether it has additional, perhaps higher, meaning associated with the subject at hand. In Jn 12,47 Christ disclaims having come to judge, while here he seems to claim the contrary, so stereotypical understanding must be avoided. If, indeed, he came to save rather than to judge, then his judging must be for the purpose of saving. So here, it would seem that we may superimpose that purpose on the term so as to have, "For saving judgment I came into this world." We have already noted that the karmic law was established as a matter of "Grace." If Christ serves as Lord of Karma, thus judging humanity in administering such grace ("full of grace and truth," Jn 1,14), he does so for the purpose of saving humanity—administering the "Purifying Fire" and helping to arrange and direct the process of review and reincarnation. Those who, having just passed through the gate of death, arrive before such judge (and judgment period) will see what they did not see while on Earth, while those who are descending from the spiritual world toward reincarnation will lose the vision they had in the spiritual world as they again pass through the birth process (see **I-33**). In this sense indeed "those who do not see [will] see and ... those who see [will] become blind." It is often said, as of Homer, the "blind" poet, that one must become blind to the things of this world in order to see those in the spiritual—almost a corollary of Is 6,9-10. And in verse 41, in response to the Pharisees' inquiry if they were "also blind," Jesus answered, "If you were blind, you would have no guilt; but now that you say, 'We see,' your guilt remains." After one has entered again through birth into this world, one must, in this sense, become blind to it to see in the spiritual world (cf. Jn 3,6 et al.).

It would be wrong for me to assert that this is "the" higher meaning of the passage. But one can come, it seems, fairly to this as "a" higher understanding that accords with the concept Lord of Karma.

Jn 16,7-11:

> (7) Nevertheless I tell you the truth: it is to your advantage that I go away, for if I do not go away, the Counselor will not come to you; but if I go, I will send him to you. (8) And when he comes, he will convince [footnote of RSV says "convict," KJV says "reprove"] the world concerning sin and righteousness and judgment: (9) concerning sin, because they do not believe in me; (10) concerning righteousness, because I go to the Father, and you will see me no more; (11) concerning judgment, because the ruler of this world is judged.

Few passages offer more opportunity for shedding new light than this. We read in 29A AB 711, "Commentators have not found the detailed exposition of 8-11 easy. Augustine avoided the passage as very difficult; Thomas Aquinas cited opinions but gave none of his own; Maldonatus [?] found it among the most obscure in the Gospel." It was a deep wisdom that kept these from speaking, for humanity was indeed then not yet ready to bear it (cf. Jn 16,12). But one can look upon Steiner as the spokesman for the Spirit of Truth (Jn 16,13) now that the time is ripe (see **I-24**, **I-25** and **I-19**).

We are dealing here with the most extensive of the five Biblical uses, all Johannine, of the Greek term *Parakletos* generally given in English as "Paraclete." RSV calls it "Counselor." Others, such as KJV, traditionally have called it "Comforter." It is well to have before us the other usages (Jn 14,16,26; 15,26 and 1 Jn 2,1) which are as follows:

> (14,16-17) And I will pray the Father, and he will give you another Counselor, to be with you forever, even the Spirit of truth, whom

the world cannot receive, because it neither sees him nor knows him; you know him, for he dwells with you, and will be in you.

(14,26) But the Counselor, the Holy Spirit, whom the Father will send in my name, he will teach you all things, and bring to your remembrance all that I have said to you.

(15,26) But when the Counselor comes, whom I shall send to you from the Father, even the Spirit of truth, who proceeds from the Father, he will bear witness to me;

(1 Jn 2,1) My little children, I am writing this to you so that you may not sin; but if any one does sin, we have an *advocate* with the Father, Jesus Christ the righteous;

There is an excellent discussion of the status of scholarship on the term "Paraclete" in 5 ABD 152. Among the many possible identifications there mentioned are several that are, in a sense, compatible with the idea of Christ as the Lord of Karma. For instance, that it has to do with the "angel" Michael, or a return of Elijah, but most especially "the mediator (*melis*) in Job 33:23, translated in the Targum by the loanword *prqlyt* (Mosinckel, Johansson)" or "the fusion of two figures from the Qumran documents, Michael and 'the spirit of truth' (Betz), a fusion that, according to another scholar (Johnston), the Paraclete was designed to combat and displace, the second or successor figure in a tandem relationship: Joshua/Moses, Elisha/Elijah (Windisch), to which Bornkamm added John the Baptist/Jesus." None of these, of course, is precisely identical, but one who is familiar with the content of this work will see many esoteric connections thrusting in the direction of Steiner's Lord of Karma.

In particular, the reader is encouraged to contemplate Job 33, in which Elihu's words to Job seem to relate very closely to the function of the Lord of Karma in its relationship with the Ego or Individuality entering Kamaloca, the time of review and judgment. The Commentary herein on Job as well as the quotations above from Steiner's JTC should then be taken into account (see also Job in "Three Bodies").

It is submitted that the Lord of Karma, as described in the above-quoted passages from JTC, fills the various roles stated in all five of the Johannine passages, and in doing so reconciles and sheds a wonderful new light upon each of them.

Having now examined what Lazarus/John, "the beloved disciple," had to say about judgment, let us move on to the rest of the New Testament. (The following list includes one Old Testament passage, Is 6,11-13, but only because it is the concluding portion of Is 6,9-13, the root of important Gospel and Pauline passages in the New Testament.)

Mt 5,17-18,21-26:

(17) Think not that I have come to abolish the law and the prophets; I have come not to abolish them but to fulfil them. (18) For truly, I say to you, till heaven and earth pass away, not an iota, not a dot, will pass from the law until all is accomplished....

(21) You have heard that it was said to the men of old, "You shall not kill; and whoever kills shall be liable to judgment." (22) But I say to you that every one who is angry with his brother shall be liable to judgment; whoever insults [i.e., abuses] his brother shall be liable to the council, and whoever says, "You fool!" shall be liable to the hell of fire. (23) So if you are offering your gift at the altar, and there remember that your brother has something against you, (24) leave your gift there before the altar and go; first be reconciled to your brother, and then come and offer your gift. (25) Make friends quickly with your accuser, while you are going with him to court, lest your accuser hand you over to the judge, and the judge to the guard and you be put in prison; (26) truly, I say to you, you will never get out till you have paid the last penny.

The strong karmic character of these passages, including the meaning of "the law" in vs 17, is shown in "Karma and Reincarnation." We look at them here because they specifically relate to "judgment," as vss 21-26 demonstrate, and Steiner describes the Lord of Karma as an office relating thereto. A particularly striking corroboration of that office is that vs 18 indicates that the "fulfillment" of that higher "law," and the existence of "heaven and earth," will apparently be coterminous. If that were not so, it would seem that "till heaven and earth pass away" would be a superfluous clause. The implication is that the existence of our solar system will have served its sole purpose when all of humanity's karma has been canceled out, "accomplished," under the guidance of the Lord of Karma. That this accords with anthroposophical insight, see **I-2**, which identifies the end of the reincarnation process as the point at which the physical passes into the Astral Condition of Form and the Earth in the Mineral Physical Condition as we know it comes to an end. The Apocalypse of St. John can only be understood when one follows it in the anthroposophical light of these various succeeding conditions (see Commentary on Revelation; the chart identified herein as **I-1** was prepared by Steiner and attached at the end of the book containing his principal lecture cycle on the Apocalypse, *The Apocalypse of St. John* (ASJ).

Mt 13,37-43,47-50:

> (37) He answered, "He who sows the good seed is the Son of man; (38) the field is the world, and the good seed means the sons of the kingdom; the weeds are the sons of the evil one, (39) and the enemy who sowed them is the devil; the harvest is the close of the age, and the reapers are angels. (40) Just as the weeds are gathered and burned with fire, so will it be at the close of the age. (41) The Son of man will send his angels, and they will gather out of his kingdom all causes of sin and all evildoers, (42) and throw them into the furnace of fire; there men will weep and gnash their teeth. (43) Then the righteous will shine like the sun in the kingdom of their Father. He who has ears, let him hear. . . .
>
> (47) "Again, the kingdom of heaven is like a net which was thrown into the sea and gathered fish of every kind; (48) when it was full, men drew it ashore and sat down and sorted the good into vessels but threw away the bad. (49) So it will be at the close of the age. The angels will come out and separate the evil from the righteous, (50) and throw them into the furnace of fire; there men will weep and gnash their teeth."

Here "the close of the age" (vss 39, 40 and 49) appears to be the same as that described in Rev 20,11-15. This is at the time of the "Second Death," when not only the physical body of all human beings will have come to an end but also the etheric, again corresponding closely in point of time with the end of the reincarnation process. Jesus tells us in these passages that it will be he who will send out his angels to separate the good from the evil and throw the latter into the fire—the point at which our Earth will be extinguished by fire (2 Pet 3,10), in keeping with anthroposophical prophecy. The accounts leading up to this point in Revelation told of the angels who came as agents to carry out these end things, as in vss 41 and 49 above. The use of the metaphorical "seed" (vss 37-38) indicates the process of reincarnation (see "Seed"). That the end of our solar system is what is envisioned by all of this is certain, because Rev 21,23 and 22,5 indicate that the Sun is no longer needed, a point in keeping with the solar nature of the face of the Son of man (Rev 1,16; Mt 17,2) and the spiritual radiance from humanity's own being by then (vs 43). In all of this, the Son of man (vs 41) serves in a judicial capacity consistent with that assigned by Steiner to him as the Lord of Karma.

Mt 25,31-46; Mk 13,26-27; Lk 21,36:

Mt 25,31-46: (31) When the Son of man comes in his glory, and all the angels with him, then he will sit on his glorious throne. (32) Before him will be gathered all the nations, and he will separate them one from another as a shepherd separates the sheep from the goats, (33) and he will place the sheep at his right hand, but the goats at the left. (34) Then the King will say to those at his right hand, "Come, O blessed of my Father, inherit the kingdom prepared for you from the foundation of the world; (35) for I was hungry and you gave me food, I was thirsty and you gave me drink, I was a stranger and you welcomed me, (36) I was naked and you clothed me, I was sick and you visited me, I was in prison and you came to me." (37) Then the righteous will answer him, "Lord, when did we see thee hungry and feed thee, or thirsty and give thee drink? (38) And when did we see thee a stranger and welcome thee, or naked and clothe thee? (39) And when did we see thee sick or in prison and visit thee?" (40) And the King will answer them, "Truly, I say to you, as you did it to one of the least of these my brethren, you did it to me." (41) Then he will say to those at his left hand, "Depart from me, you cursed, into the eternal fire prepared for the devil and his angels; (42) for I was hungry and you gave me no food, I was thirsty and you gave me no drink, (43) I was a stranger and you did not welcome me, naked and you did not clothe me, sick and in prison and you did not visit me." (44) Then they also will answer, "Lord, when did we see thee hungry or thirsty or a stranger or naked or sick or in prison, and did not minister to thee?" (45) Then he will answer them, "Truly, I say to you, as you did it not to one of the least of these, you did it not to me." (46) And they will go away into eternal punishment, but the righteous into eternal life.

Mk 13,26-27: (26) And then they will see the Son of man coming in clouds with great power and glory. (27) And then he will send out the angels, and gather his elect from the four winds, from the ends of the earth to the ends of heaven.

Lk 21,36: But watch at all times, praying that you may have strength to escape all these things that will take place, and to stand before the Son of man.

The larger sections out of the three synoptic Gospels from which these passages were taken are known as the "Little Apocalypse," in which Jesus responds to a question from his disciples as to what the "signs" would be of the "close of the age" (Mt 24,3). There is a great deal in these sections, and we must defer to the Commentary a closer look at them. We bring in these passages here only because they deal with Christ Jesus in his judicial function at that end time, a function that again comports with his status as Lord of Karma. In particular we will look to see if his "signs" indicate a period corresponding with his function as Lord of Karma, beginning in the twentieth century and extending to the end of the karmic period that began with the Fall in Gen 3 and will expire at the corresponding period of the reascent. Charts **I-1** to **I-3**, which present the same scenario from three different perspectives, are helpful, probably essential, for proper focus; **I-2** in particular identifies key points.

To begin with, the statement in all three Gospel accounts that all these signs would occur before "this generation will pass away" (Mt 24,34; Mk 13,30; Lk 21,32) obviously tends to discredit the entire prophecy in the eyes of those who look to the literal meaning in our modern vernacular. We must, however, give "generation" far greater compass than the normal thirty years or so we mentally attach to it. We have seen elsewhere that prior to the time of Abraham the Biblical term "generation" did not mean the same thing that it did thereafter; and that "day" in Gen 1 did not mean twenty-four hours as we know it today. The term "generation" for present purposes must be looked at by the time period otherwise established for the "signs" themselves.

Let us take but a few examples as general indicators. What are the meanings to be ascribed to the following?

1. The separation of the sheep from the goats (Mt 25,32-33);

2. The references to wars well before the end (Mt 24,6; Mk 13,7; Lk 21,10);

3. Gathering the elect from the "four winds" (Mt 24,31; Mk 13,27);

4. The sound of a "Trumpet" (Mt 24,31);

5. The misfortune of being "with child" in those days (Mt 24,19; Mk 13,17; Lk 21,23); and

6. The Sun being darkened and the Moon not giving light and the stars falling from heaven (Mt 24,29; Mk 13,24; Lk 21,25).

The larger sections (Mt 24-25; Mk 13; Lk 21) are called the "Little Apocalypse" (2 ABD 1081) because of their apocalyptic character and obvious kinship to the longer Apocalypse of St. John. To understand these passages, we must first come to realize that they represent not information from common sources as such (as universally thought in modern theological discussion, such as the documentary hypotheses), but information from separate Mystery traditions, which necessarily bore a certain similarity to each other inasmuch as they represented true spiritual vision from different perspectives (just as there are twelve zodiacal perspectives that influence humanity). There are different levels, however, of "true spiritual vision." In scripture, we can see one such illustration by the difference between the terms "Mountain" and "High Mountain," and we recognize from of old the different levels of the nine Hierarchies. Steiner tells us that the highest spiritual vision represented in the Bible is that given to Lazarus/John, the only one initiated by Christ himself in the ancient tradition. And anthroposophical insight knows that Lazarus/John was the author of Revelation, the most complete and accurate reflection of the reascent of humanity as a counterbalance to its descent. The vision of Lazarus/John exceeded that of Moses, Ezekiel, Daniel and the three synoptic Evangelists, for we find in each of them items recognizable in Revelation but nothing approaching the complete picture given there. The creation account in the Prologue of John's Gospel goes back further in the beginning than does Genesis, and the Revelation reascent goes further and in more systematic fashion than any of the others.

The human mind does not like to be stretched any more than a human muscle likes to be tested to its aching limit. Yet if we are to think in apocalyptic terms, such stretching is mandatory. Consider Teilhard de Chardin's insistence thereon in *The Phenomenon of Man* (PHEN) from the time perspective, as well as the similar implications in *Man and Animal* (MAA), both in Cognate Writings, Vol. 3, *Companions Along The Way*. To understand the full scope, past and future, of humanity's evolution, one must contemplate charts **I-1** through **I-3**, in connection with *Occult Science* (OS), and Revelation (and to a lesser extent Genesis) in the Commentary. When this is done, one can begin to understand why prophetic revelation could be only partial up to the time of the writings of Lazarus/John. For this reason, in examining the six examples above, we shall see that they all represent events far distant from us according to our present limited vision, and further that they do not all represent the same point on the future evolutionary scale, some being telescoped into others, but that they do all fall within the time frame envisioned by humanity's emergence from the Mineral Kingdom (i.e., the Mineral Condition of Life). We shall see in the Commentary that even the Revelation takes us only up through the end of Earth evolution. The New Heaven and New Earth of Rev 21 is the Jupiter Condition of Consciousness coming into being, when the human being shall have perfected its astral body into the manas, or Spirit Self, state. Beyond that lies the development of the two higher states. While for all practical purposes Steiner's lectures on Revelation end with attainment of the Jupiter Condition, we may reasonably infer that Rev 22 is a brief vision beyond to the Jupiter Condition itself, whose purpose is the conversion of the etheric body of the human being into the buddhi, or Life Spirit, state—for Rev 22 speaks of "the river of the water of life" and of "the tree of life." Only in the Venus Condition of Consciousness will the human being work to convert the physical body (by then there is no tangible mineral-physical body, but only the non-visible "Form" or "phantom" or "pattern" to be converted) into Spirit Man, that state when humanity will have attained to the fullness of the ninefold Son of Man pictured in Rev 1,12-16 with its face "like the sun shining in full strength," according to the "I Am" pattern of the Christ.

With these understandings, let us now see how the six examples tie in with Revelation:

1. The separation of the sheep from the goats

Refer to **I-19**, **I-24** and **I-25**. See in **I-19** that Christ incarnated in the Cultural Age (Greek/Roman) of Aries (Sheep) and was thus known as the "Lamb of God" (Jn 1,29), "Agnus Dei." Note that the seventh (last) Cultural Age (American) of our present Fifth Epoch, the post-Atlantean, is that of Capricorn (Goat). Anthroposophy tells us that the sixth Cultural Age (Russian/Slavonic, or Philadelphia, Rev 3,7-13) is the one, like Noah's from Atlantis, whose representatives will carry over into the Sixth Epoch, while the seventh Cultural Age (American, or Capricorn, Rev 3,14-22) is the one that will be "spewn out" (Rev 3,16), ending with the "War of All Against All." Those who have taken Christ, the "Lamb (or Sheep) of God" into their being have written on them "the name of the city of my God, the new Jerusalem" (Rev 3,12; 21,1-2 and 22,4) and are thus "the sheep." Those who, in the Age of Capricorn, are spewn out are "the goats." There is here a form of telescoping, for "the eternal[5] fire prepared for the devil and his angels" (Mt 25,41,46) does not come until Rev 20,14-15. While those who meet the standard (Rev 3,12) in the Cultural Age of Philadelphia will have already attained preliminary assurance of salvation, there is still opportunity for others to be saved by this group between then and Rev 20,14-15, as indicated in the Revelation Commentary, though such salvation becomes progressively more difficult in view of the increasing density of the bestial nature.

2. The references to wars well before the end

We need here only point to the "War of All Against All" (**I-1** and **I-2**), the event that anthroposophy shows will be equivalent to destruction by the "fires" of Lemuria and the "floods" of Atlantis. It will result from the

---

5. While this passage clearly indicates we will suffer for our sins, many have been troubled with the idea of eternal damnation it seems to suggest. It is time to recognize that the passage should not be given that meaning.

(To prevent interrupting thought flow, the reader should consider deferring the balance of this substantively important footnote until completing the six examples in the text.) See page 207-212.

ever-increasing egoism of the human "I Am" (the Goat) that has not appropriated into itself the Christ "I Am" (Lamb, or Sheep). Those who still need further incarnation for individual perfection (cf. Rev 3,12) will be so divided that it will come down to individual against individual. As in 1, there is some telescoping since reincarnation does not end until the Sixth Epoch (see **I-2**). The resulting destruction will bring the Fifth Great Epoch, the post-Atlantean, to an end.

3. Gathering the elect from the "four winds"

In Rev 7,1 the angels standing at the "four corners" of the Earth are told to hold back the "four winds" to prevent destruction until the "hundred and forty-four thousand," a symbolic number representing 12,000 from each of the 12 tribes (all the zodiacal influences), have been "sealed."[6] This is between the sixth and seventh seals. We see from **I-25** that the seven messages (Rev 2-3) refer to the seven Cultural Ages in our present post-Atlantean Epoch, the seven seals (Rev 5-6 plus 8,1) to the seven comparable ages in the Sixth Epoch, the seven trumpets (Rev 8,2-11,15) to the seven comparable ages in the Seventh Epoch, and the seven Bowls of Wrath (Rev 16) to the seven comparable ages in the "More Perfect Astral" Condition of Form after humanity has left its Physical Condition (see **I-1**) behind. Rev 20,8 again refers to the "four corners," and so we may infer that again we are pointing to the time referred to in Mt 25,41,46 when the elect are to be gathered, between the sixth and seventh seals and the "Second Death" (Rev 20,14-15), that of humanity's etheric body (the first death having been of its physical body).

4. The sound of a trumpet

Matthew alone (Mt 24,31) here identifies the gathering of the elect to the point of time represented by one of the trumpets in Rev 8,2-11,15. We might take it to be the first, but from Paul's vision in 1 Cor 15,52 of "the last trumpet," we should probably take it as being that. Then we would probably be obliged to so identify also Paul's trumpet vision in 1 Th 4,16 and Heb 12,19. See "Trumpet(s)."

---

6. A deep meaning of "a hundred and forty-four thousand" (Rev 7,4) is shown in the Appendix to "Fire," Vol. 2.

5. The misfortune of being "with child" in those days

This has to do with the end of human reproduction as we now know it
(and with ominous indications for humanity with respect to its current
obsession with physical sexual emphasis in all walks of life, for it results
from spiritual forces inimical to those necessary to attain the evolutionary
goal of the age of Philadelphia—Rev 3,7-13). For the sake of brevity, we
refer on this point to *Eternal Individuality* (EI), Chap. 12, pp. 195-197,
where Prokofieff, with extensive footnotes (omitted in the extract below) to
Steiner's supporting works, some apparently not yet available in English,
relays that according to the Mystery of the Holy Grail as passed on by the
Rosicrucians and as given by Steiner, the true ideal of Immaculate Conception is to be attained by worthy human beings during the age of Philadelphia (the sixth Cultural Era, or Epoch as Prokofieff terms it). Prokofieff
first quotes Steiner, "The true ideal of the Holy Grail is an organ that man
will have when his reproductive power is spiritualized," then goes on:

> This new organ of reproduction ... will ... be made up of the ac-
> tivity of two transformed organs: the heart and the larynx. Rudolf
> Steiner speaks about this as follows: "There are within man organs
> of two different kinds, those which are on the way to becoming im-
> perfect and will gradually fall away and those which are still in the
> process of formation. All lower organs, the sexual organs, will fall
> away. *The heart and the larynx*, on the other hand, are organs which
> will be perfected and find their full development only in the future."
> In another lecture he speaks about this with full clarity: "Above all
> there will be a transformation *of the larynx and the heart. In future,*
> *they will be the organs of reproduction.*" The heart and the larynx are
> the new spiritual organs of reproduction whose interaction, in the
> far future, "will bring forth beings similar to man.".…
> Thus from out of the Grail Mysteries, of which the Rosicrucian
> Mysteries of modern times represent the continuation, there shines
> this sublime ideal of the distant future. This will be a time when the
> experiences of immortality and prebirth unite for man into a con-
> tinuous span of consciousness; death and birth in their present-day
> form will be finally overcome, and man himself will pass on to far
> more spiritual forms of existence. By this means, the Earth will be
> ready to unite once more with the Sun. Rudolf Steiner speaks about

this event as follows: "The Earth will then be ready to unite with the Sun…. The forces of the Moon will be overcome. At this stage man can unite with the Sun. He will live in the spiritualized Earth and at the same time be united with the power of the Sun; and he will be the conqueror of the Moon."

However … before this condition of complete spiritualization (the union with the Sun) can come about in earthly evolution, mankind will have to endure a battle and overcome the retardant Moon forces, which will enter into earthly evolution with particular power from the seventh millennium of the Christian era onwards, that is, in approximately the second half of the seventh cultural epoch, when, in accordance with what has been imparted through spiritual science, the Moon will again unite with the Earth. Rudolf Steiner speaks about this event, which will so radically change the spiritual-physical situation on the Earth, as follows: "Then a time will come in the seventh millennium…. Women will become barren; an altogether different kind and manner of earthly life will begin. It will be the time when the Moon is again approaching the Earth, when it again unites with the Earth."

As a consequence of the separation of the Moon from the Earth, there took place, at the beginning of the Lemurian epoch, the division of mankind into two sexes, and, with it, the necessity of earthly birth and death and also the final loss of the forces of immortality. By the seventh-eighth millennium, with the re-union of the Moon with the Earth, a new stage in human evolution will begin which will lead to the gradual overcoming of dual sexuality, that is, to the overcoming of birth and death in their present form, the final disappearance of which will, it is true, take place only when the Earth unites with the Sun.

In the footnotes Prokofieff refers to "the law of reflection" according to which the Sun, which separated in the "second root-race (Hyperborean)," will reunite with the Earth towards the end of the sixth root-race (the Sixth Great Epoch, the one which follows our present "post-Atlantean"). "According to [that same] law of reflection, the Moon, which left the Earth during the Lemurian epoch (the third root-race), must again unite with it by the end of our post-Atlantean period of evolution (the fifth root-race), a period which will conclude with the 'War of All Against All'."

The reader will note that on **I-2** the point at which the "Return of Moon" is indicated is ambiguous. It comes toward the end of the seventh Cultural Era of our post-Atlantean Epoch, the era called the "American," rather than at the end of the Sixth Great Epoch.[7]

While 5,000 years in the future is a long time away, it may be frightening today to consider the slowness with which humanity seems to be moving toward these goals. Much greater spiritual effort will be required in the future. There is one thing to be cognizant of here. We read in Mt 24,22 (and Mk 13,20), "And if those days had not been shortened, no human being would be saved; but for the sake of the elect those days will be shortened." In *Cosmic Memory* (CM), Chap. 13, Steiner writes, "A fact which will play a certain role in the following essays will be briefly indicated here. This concerns the speed with which the development on the different planets [here he means Conditions of Consciousness] takes place. For this is not the same on all the planets. Life proceeds with the greatest speed on [Old] Saturn, the rapidity then decreases on the [Old] Sun, becomes still less on the [Old] Moon and reaches its slowest phase on the earth. On the latter it becomes slower and slower, to the point at which self-consciousness develops. Then the speed increases again. Therefore, today man has already passed the time of the greatest slowness of his development. Life has begun to accelerate again."

So, the misfortune of "those who are with child and for those who give suck in those days" is the woe, whether male or female, of not having attained to the higher stage of reproduction through the developed heart and larynx organs. It seems apparent that those who have attained the higher level will have again become one, that is, both male and female (cf. Gen 1,27).

---

7. We note at this point that the Moon is referred to in Rev 6,12 and 8,12, evolutionary points beyond the post-Atlantean Epoch. In Rev 12,1, it is under the feet of the heavenly woman, but not in the former two references. Suffice it at this point to recognize that while some will have attained the level of reproductive conversion by the end of the age of Philadelphia and the end of their own karmic necessity to reincarnate (Rev 3,12), others will not have done so, and will need to continue battling the Moon forces. One can see this clearly in the Prokofieff passages, including Steiner quotations quoted in the text. Thus, between the time when the Moon has reunited with the Earth and that when the Sun will do so, the retardant Moon forces will still have to be overcome by a segment of humanity if it is to avoid bestiality.

6. <u>The Sun being darkened and the Moon not giving light and the stars falling from heaven</u>

We can see from the Prokofieff passage quoted under #5 that the Moon will not be giving light because it will have reunited with the Earth. The Sun will be darkened because the Earth became the spiritual Sun when Christ incarnated. From that point it will shine brighter and brighter as humanity approaches the point of reunion of Sun and Earth at the end of the Sixth Great Epoch. The "darkening" would seem to be the result of the increasing spiritual light from the Earth and the decreasing significance of the physical light from the Sun. Stars are mentioned as falling from heaven in Rev 6,13 and 8,12, near the evolutionary period when physical incarnation ceases. Quite aside from their durability as that time approaches, the human being will be expanding (cf **I-33**) out beyond the solar system, as the (or an) "Earth Star" so that other stars will not be seen as being in "heaven" by the human being who is there also. (See Prov 4,18; Is 60,19-20; Joel 2,10,31 and 3,15; Mt 13,43 and 5,14; Rev 21,23 and 22,5.)

This sampling should be sufficient to indicate clearly that the "signs" Christ gives to his disciples fit well with the period during which he is to serve as Lord of Karma.

Acts 10,42:

And he commanded us to preach to the people, and to testify that he is the one ordained by God to be judge of the living and the dead.

This passage at first blush might seem essentially neutral on the matter of Christ as Lord of Karma, compatible with the concept but not requiring it. However, ponder the significance of Christ's being called "judge of the living and the dead" in the light of what is said about that in the discussion of 1 Pet 4,5-6 below. Otherwise, it is to be noted that Luke, though "beloved" by Paul (Col 4,14), was here quoting Peter. And though Peter was one of those given the esoteric knowledge of reincarnation at the Transfiguration (see "Karma and Reincarnation"), the nature of his initiation would seem to have been lower than that of Lazarus/John and Paul (cf. 2 Pet 3,15-16); he would also have been one of those instructed not to teach reincarnation in his own time (Mt 17,9).

Acts 17,30-34:

> (30) "The times of ignorance God overlooked, but now he commands all men everywhere to repent, (31) because he has fixed a day on which he will judge the world in righteousness by a man whom he has appointed, and of this he has given assurance to all men by raising him from the dead."

> (32) Now when they heard of the resurrection of the dead, some mocked; but others said, "We will hear you again about this." (33) So Paul went out from among them. (34) But some men joined him and believed, among them Dionysius the Areopagite and a woman named Damaris and others with them.

Verses 30-31 are quoting Paul. Verse 31 in particular fits perfectly with the Lord of Karma scenario given by Steiner. One should bear in mind that Luke, Paul's understudy, then uses the same phrase in vs 32 as he used in Lk 20,35, namely, "the resurrection [of] the dead." Given the seemingly clear meaning in the Gospel passage (see its discussion in "Karma and Reincarnation") which uses like language ("for they cannot die any more") to Rev 3,12 ("never shall he go out of it"), the "fit" seems even more precise, especially considering the other Pauline passages discussed herein. The last two verses are included because of the juxtaposition of their highly significant reference to Dionysius the Areopagite, whom Steiner says established a school at Athens to teach the esoteric Christianity he learned from Paul, and whose teachings were later reduced to writing about A.D. 500 (as what is now PSEUD).

There is another reason to believe that Luke pictured Christ as the Lord of Karma in the above passage. Let us think for one moment about how Luke's parables seem to fit so well with such understanding. The Parable of the "Lost Sheep" (Lk 15,4-7) has always been popular with evangelical-minded preachers, but does it not have a deeper meaning related to karma and reincarnation? And in this instance, is not Christ the one pictured as the Shepherd who goes searching? And is not this what he does as Lord of Karma?[8] The karmic relationship is the more

---

8. The fact that this parable is also found in Mt 18,12-14 does not detract from its meaning in the Lucan context. It may even add to it by its diversity, for Mt 18,12 has the Shepherd leaving the 99 sheep "on the mountains" rather than "in the wilderness," and Mt 18,14 stresses that it is not the will of the Father that any perish, emphasizing the extent to which the love of God goes to save.

impressive in that this parable, and its parallel, the woman with the lost coins, are immediately followed by the parable of the Prodigal Son which portrays the entire elliptical scope of humanity's Fall and salvation in the light of anthroposophy. The Parable of the Widow and the Unjust Judge (Lk 18,1-8), in stressing his yielding to the importunity of the widow and then implying the greater righteousness of God, exoterically relates to the need for constant prayer, but can probably also be understood at a higher level in the light of karma and reincarnation.

Rev 6,9-11:

> (9) When he opened the fifth seal, I saw under the altar the souls of those who had been slain for the word of God and for the witness they had borne; (10) they cried out with a loud voice, "O Sovereign Lord, holy and true, how long before thou wilt judge and avenge our blood on those who dwell upon the earth?" (11) Then they were each given a white robe and told to rest a little longer, until the number of their fellow servants and their brethren should be complete, who were to be killed as they themselves had been.

Here we again have the high spiritual vision of Lazarus/John speaking. It is well to recall the various stages of human evolution represented by the four series of seven (i.e., messages, seals, trumpets and bowls of wrath) in Revelation (see the "four winds" discussion above). The seven seals refer to the Sixth Great Epoch, the one following our present post-Atlantean (**I-1**). Those here beseeching Christ about judgment are the ones who in Rev 3,12 had already come to the end of their karmically required reincarnation cycle and never have to "go out" into it again. They are the ones who have already survived the "first death," that is, they have passed beyond the point of again having physical bodies. In this sense, they have been "slain for the word of God," according to the pattern of him who was crucified as an example so that his "Name" is written on them (Rev 3,12). The very fact that they are told to "rest a little longer" is an indication that there are indeed many other Individualities who have not yet attained that point but who will before the Earth's reunion with the Sun at the end of such Epoch. These are already at the "fifth seal" and thus not far from the beginning of the "Trumpets" of the Seventh Great Epoch. The Sun becoming "black" in Rev 6,12 indicates the imminence of the reunion with the Sun, and the "full moon [becoming] like blood" indicates the end of the opportunity of humanity to overcome the Moon forces in the old reproductive organs and the end of the "Grace" of physical reincarnation opportunity.

Is 6,11-13:

(11) Then I said, "How long, O Lord?" And he said: "Until cities lie waste without inhabitant, and houses without men, and the land is utterly desolate, (12) and the Lord removes men far away, and the forsaken places are many in the midst of the land. (13) And though a tenth remain in it, it will be burned again, like a terebinth or an oak, whose stump remains standing when it is felled." The holy seed is its stump.

There is a spine-tingling time identity between the "O ... Lord ... how long" in Rev 6,10 above and Isaiah's "How long, O Lord?" in this passage. Bear in mind the words that just preceded this, Is 6,9-10, which are quoted in every Gospel, at the conclusion of Acts, and in Romans (Mt 13,14-15; Mk 4,12; Lk 8,10; Jn 12,39-41; Acts 28,26-27; Rom 11,8), and speak of those who see but do not perceive and hear but do not understand. Isaiah refers, of course, to the blindness and deafness that were entering into humanity as a result of increasing density and materiality (see "Fading Splendor"). In the above passage as well as in Rev 6,9-11, humanity is nearing that time when all physical seeing and hearing will come to an end along with the Earth's physical existence. And with this understanding, it is then easy to see that the description given to Isaiah is in keeping with the anthroposophical insight about human evolution, Karma and Reincarnation, and Lord of Karma. For it speaks of "the holy seed" (see "Seed") being "burned again" (as with the "Bush") without being destroyed. The implications of this last verse are powerful support for the idea of God's "Grace" granted through karma and reincarnation, and his unwillingness to let any pass unredeemed even though only "a tenth remain." This can have more meanings than one, of course. For one thing, the "refiner's fire" of the Kamaloca period will end with the reunion of Sun and Earth, but there will still remain the future evolutions of Jupiter and Venus when the redeemed, through their enhanced powers, will work for the redemption of the lower kingdoms, as Paul saw (Rom 8,19-23; Eph 1,9-10) and anthroposophy shows. While salvation is not assured, the length to which God goes to that end is beyond human understanding.

Mt 16,27:

> For the Son of man is to come with his angels in the glory of his Father, and then he will repay every man for what he has done.

This comports with what Steiner shows, that the coming of Christ as Lord of Karma coincides in time with the commencement of his Second Coming. And it excuses no one from being "repaid for what he has done," making no exceptions for those whose sins have been forgiven. Christ as judge, Lord of Karma, will see that subjective karma accounts are balanced.

Verse 28 which follows, "Truly, I say to you, there are some standing here who will not taste death before they see the Son of man coming in his kingdom," has been a source of puzzlement. What is it that the "some standing here" were to see? According to 8 NIB 351, four views exist in church history: the Transfiguration, Resurrection, Pentecostal experience, and Second Coming, of which the last is the more likely based upon the erroneous expectation by the Evangelist of an early "parousia." Insofar as I can determine, Steiner never seems to go along with the suggestion that the Evangelists (or Paul) were in error on this, from which one must infer instead that later Christendom has not adequately understood the Gospel message regarding the Second Coming. This is discussed near the beginning of Second Coming, which follows. The best solution is suggested near the end of that essay. The Resurrection appearances of Christ to the disciples were in the etheric body, and at the Ascension they were told that the Second Coming would be "in the same way." In a very real sense, they had already experienced his coming before they died. Verse 28 should not be permitted to cloud the relatively clear import of verse 27 as stated above.

1 Cor 4,5:

> Therefore do not pronounce judgment before the time, before the Lord comes, who will bring to light the things now hidden in

darkness and will disclose the purposes of the heart. Then every man will receive his commendation from God.

The synchronicity of Christ's "coming" and "judging" is seen again in this passage. And once more it is clear that all things hidden will be brought to light in the justice and righteousness of the Perfect (Mt 5,48) "law" (Mt 5,17) of subjective karma. It will apply to "every man" (cf. Mt 5,25-26). Judgment is to be deferred to the Lord of Karma (cf. Mt 13,24-30).

1 Cor 11,31-32:

(31) But if we judged ourselves truly, we should not be judged. (32) But when we are judged by the Lord, we are chastened so that we may not be condemned along with the world.

Need anything else be said? As Lord of Karma Christ judges so as to chasten and return one to Earth to try again to avoid condemnation, or judgment by the Father, i.e., by the karmic law. This can only refer to the subjective karma for which restitution can and must be made even by those whose objective karma has been taken over by Christ (see "Forgiven Sins").

Rom 2,16:

… on that day when, according to my gospel, God judges the secrets of men by Christ Jesus.

Romans has long been stressed by many traditional Christians in the increasingly nauseating debate of faith versus works as the worker of salvation. So long as faith is taken as something more or less synonymous and co-extensive with a public confession of belief, it has provoked the more sensitive to a feeling of something being amiss. Heretofore, the reconciliation of doctrine has tended to stress that "works," as Paul used the term, meant the "works of law" encoded in the Old Testament as propounded by the Jewish authorities, while at the same time stressing that "faith" required something more than mere intellectual assent and public confession. While these observations are not without some merit, the entire debate can be resolved in the light of anthroposophical insight.

The "law" is the higher law (Heb 10,1), the same one Jesus came to fulfill (Mt 5,17), namely, the karmic law. And its fulfillment became possible, in view of humanity's inherent sin, only because Christ, as a matter of "Grace," took away the consequence of objective karma by shouldering it himself (Rom 3,23-25) on behalf of all those who accept him (into their lives, Gal 2,20) as the one who will work their salvation. It is this acceptance that amounts to the "faith" of which Paul speaks. It in no way eliminates the karmic consequence of subjective sin, but that consequence does not stand in the way of one's salvation providing only that one make the required restitution (Mt 5,26; Lk 12,59). To the extent that one's "works" (Jam 2,18-26) not only reflect one's faith but also go about making such subjective karmic restitution, they are an essential, but they alone without such "faith" would not work salvation because the human being is unable to cure its objective karma without Christ.

Not only does this anthroposophic view accord with and help explain the "faith" salvation passages of Romans (and Galatians), as well as other Pauline passages herein, but it totally reconciles Jam 2,18-26. Consider Jam 2,24, "You see that a man is justified by works and not by faith alone." The faith element, it is true, accomplishes what the human beings cannot do for themselves, but human beings must do what they can do to take advantage of what Christ has offered. Those who would deny this will find themselves having a difficult time explaining why Paul stressed the necessity of the moral virtues so highly and lived them so fully. His commands, "If any one will not work, let him not eat" (2 Th 3,10) and "owe no one anything except to love" (Rom 13,8), can be applied at the worldly or the spiritual level.

1 Th 5,1-10:

(1) But as to the times and the seasons, brethren, you have no need to have anything written to you. (2) For you yourselves know well that the day of the Lord will come like a thief in the night. (3) When people say, "There is peace and security," then sudden destruction will come upon them as travail comes upon a woman with child, and there will be no escape. (4) But you are not in darkness, brethren, for that day to surprise you like a thief. (5) For you are all sons of light and sons of the day; we are not of the night or of darkness. (6) So then let us not sleep, as others do, but let us keep awake and be sober.

(7) For those who sleep sleep at night, and those who get drunk are drunk at night. (8) But since we belong to the day, let us be sober, and put on the breastplate of faith and love, and for a helmet the hope of salvation. (9) For God has not destined us for wrath, but to obtain salvation through our Lord Jesus Christ, (10) who died for us so that whether we wake or sleep we might live with him.

In particular, note vss 2 and 10. The unique thing about a thief is that he is Biblically pictured as coming in the night when no one is aware. (See "Thief in the Night.") Christ came that way the first time. He is coming that way the second (see "Second Coming") when he will assume the role of judge, Lord of Karma. Consider that the night is the period when one is incarnated, and the day when one is between incarnations. But those who are able to recognize him "belong to the day" (vs 8), and are with him whether in the discarnate or incarnate, i.e., waking or sleeping (vs 10), state.

2 Tim 4,1:

I charge you in the presence of God and of Christ Jesus who is to judge the living and the dead, and by his appearing and his kingdom.

Again we see Christ's "judging" and "appearing" to be contemporaneous events still then in the future, consistent with all Steiner has told us about the Second Coming and Lord of Karma. That his judgment applies to "the living and the dead" has misled many to think of an apocalyptic event wherein that judgment will be simultaneous for all souls and will be consummated from beginning to end within the scope of one brief occurrence. That interpretation is not required, for the words say that all souls will be judged but not when such judgment will occur. When one understands that the Second Coming is to occur over a broad expanse of time, then interpreting it as a single event does not fit the reality. If one is to distinguish the judgment of the Father from that of the Son, which is necessary if the matter of judgment is to make any sort of sense, then a cataclysmic, brief period of judgment does not fit the description of Christ as "counsellor," or "advocate," or the like. One cannot serve as defense counsel and judge at the same time. Beyond the long time period when Christ is to advocate and judge lies the ultimate and fearsome judgment of the Father. By directing the law of karma, in his capacity as Lord of Karma,

Christ is attempting to "save" every human being, over many incarnations, from the karmic consequence of the Father's eventual judgment (Jn 12,47). The beauty with which Lazarus/John's Apocalypse unfolds the long and evolutionary advocacy of "the Lamb" makes all this very clear.

Heb 9,27-28:

> (27) And just as it is appointed for men to die once, and after that comes judgment, (28) so Christ, having been offered once to bear the sins of many, will appear a second time, not to deal with sin but to save those who are eagerly waiting for him.

Vs 27 was discussed at some length in "Karma and Reincarnation" herein; the present remarks extend that to take into account the meaning added by vs 28. To begin with, Hebrews is probably the most extensive, certainly the most systematic, treatment of sin in the New Testament, and of how Christ, "once for all" (Heb 7,27; 9,12,28 and 10,10,12-14) paid the price for it. In vs 28, Paul again points to the "once" aspect to emphasize that Christ dealt with "sin" the first time. But in doing so, he only made the "offer" to "bear the sins." Heretofore, vs 28 has generally been skimpily dealt with on the assumption that the Second Coming is simply to confirm or claim those already saved. But the anthroposophical view accords it independent significance. For those who have "accepted his offer," and are thus "eagerly waiting for him," we are told that he came "not to deal with sin," for he had dealt with that "once for all" the first time for those who accepted his offer. Why then, if such acceptance effects salvation, was it necessary to come the second time to "save" those who have already accepted him? Surely a different verb would have been used had it simply been to "pick up" his flock. Something more is implied in the dynamic word "save," something that is in accord with Jas 2,24 ("a man is justified by works and not by faith alone"). That "something more" has to do with administering the karmic laws as to the restitution that must be made over and above the burden Christ first lifted from the sinner's shoulders—one's subjective, as distinguished from objective, sins. That function is the one he is to perform as Lord of Karma. This becomes even clearer in the passage from Heb 12 considered next.

Another important aspect of these verses is that, as part of the larger passage (vss 23-28), they give precisely the same message Steiner gave, typically in quite unbiblical language, in JTC, quoted at length near the first of this essay. The verses confirm that the Lord of Karma office passes from Moses to Christ, and that it was yet, as Paul wrote, to occur in a future time, e.g., "will appear a second time." We shall see that Christ's Second Coming and his assumption of the Lord of Karma role from Moses are both twentieth-century spiritual developments, thus fully in accord with vss 23-28.

Heb 12,22-24:

> (22) But you have come to Mount Zion and to the city of the living God, the heavenly Jerusalem, and to innumerable angels in festal gathering, (23) and to the assembly of the first-born who are enrolled in heaven, and to a judge who is God of all, and to the spirits of just men made perfect, (24) and to Jesus, the mediator of a new covenant, and to the sprinkled blood that speaks more graciously than the blood of Abel.

Hebrews is one of the books that had some problem getting into the canon, and finally did on the basis of Pauline authorship, thus being placed with Paul's other letters, albeit at the end. One of the problems was that it alone among them does not specifically identify itself as being from him. In particular, every other such letter is identified in its caption as being "of Paul," but Hebrews is not—it is simply "The Letter to the Hebrews." Scholars have raised serious objection to its Pauline authorship. It is my position that his authorship is established (see "Paul/Hebrews"). While Romans speaks most extensively about the Jews, as though to them, near consensus has it that it was addressed to Christians generally at Rome preparatory to Paul's first visit there. While Hebrews clearly applies to all humanity, it is uniquely to the Jews. That Paul wrote it out of his known anxiety for the Jews is strongly suggested not only by its title and other evidence, but by its emphasis upon Melchizedek. The esoteric nature of Melchizedek's connection with the Jews is suggested in Heb 5,11, but it is clarified by Steiner (see text and fn 7 in "Spiritual Economy"), who shows that Melchizedek took on the preserved original etheric body of Noah's son Shem, from the Atlantean evolution, in order to bring over to the Semites the necessary spiritual "impetus to their culture." An avatar still inhabited that etheric body. Melchizedek could then be given the unique descriptions of Heb 5 and 7 as being of similar character to Christ, for Christ was an avatar—by far the greatest of them all, but nevertheless of that unique spiritual character that had no earthly mother or father.

This passage commences also with a Jewish setting and continues the deeply esoteric character of the entire letter. That it is speaking of Christ as the Lord of Karma seems very clear. While Paul undoubtedly understood the mandate of Christ to Peter, James and John not to teach reincarnation exoterically until the Second Coming (Mt 17,9; see "Karma and Reincarnation"), he was here speaking, as so often elsewhere, in a manner that revealed the same esoterically. "The first-born who are enrolled in heaven" (vs 23) would seem to indicate those, such as the Buddha, possibly Enoch (Heb 11,5), and those referred to in Lk 20,35-36 and perhaps also by Augustine as having been "Christians before Christ came" (Epis. Retrac., Lib. I, xiii, 3), who, before Christ, had recognized and accepted him and had attained complete control over their astral bodies so as to be beyond the necessity of reincarnation. Then we come to "a judge who is God of all," seemingly the "Father," whose karmic law (Mt 5,17; Heb 10,1) was just, though harsh, and virtually impossible by the time of Christ to comply with by virtue of one's objective karma. Next in line are "the spirits of just men made perfect." There is a difference between being "justified" and being "just." The former term is used as a synonym for the "vindication" effected for objective karma by accepting Christ. There is a tendency in traditional Christian thinking to interpret Mt 5,48 ("You must be perfect") as impossible for the human being within one's lifetime as all still sin, but accomplished merely through accepting Christ and using one's best efforts to follow him within that lifetime. If that were true, then Paul's term "just" in vs 23 is superfluous. It seems clearly to imply not only the traditional thought of perfection through Christ, but also that one is "just" by having made restitution (e.g., Mt 5,26; Lk 12,59). The verse speaks of those who are already "just" as being then made perfect, presumably those who are "perfected" insofar as objective karma is concerned by the acceptance of Christ and who then make restitution so as to be "just." In any event, the separate status of being "just" and being "perfect" is recognized as a prelude to dwelling in the "heavenly Jerusalem" (vs 22). Finally, and most convincingly, Paul speaks of Jesus, distinguished from God the "judge," as being "the mediator of a new covenant" (vs 24). If one studies the meaning of that term, it will be obvious that a better term could not have been selected to describe the function of Lord of Karma. If acceptance of, and best effort to follow, Christ within a given life were sufficient, then no "mediator" would be required. But even under the new covenant, subjective karma must still be balanced or canceled out, which can be done only by making restitution in later lives for all the subjective karmic debt (Mt 5,26; Lk 12,59) not satisfied in prior ones.

The conclusion thus reached could hardly be more firmly nailed down than by the last verse in chapter 12, "Therefore let us be grateful for receiving a kingdom that cannot be shaken, and thus let us offer to God acceptable worship, with reverence and awe; for our God is a consuming fire." In "Purifying Fire" we see that the "consuming fire" is the "refiner's fire" which applies to every "burning bush" (i.e., Christ-enabled human Ego) in the astral world (cf. Purgatory), thereby purifying it in preparation for entry into the spiritual world where the appropriate three bodies are refashioned for another incarnation. Only when one has nothing left to purify is perfection reached.

1 Pet 4,5-6:

> (5) But they will give account to him who is ready to judge the living and the dead. (6) For this is why the gospel was preached even to the dead, that though judged in the flesh like men, they might live in the spirit like God.

This passage is one of several throughout the spectrum of New Testament authors that supported the doctrine of Christ's descent into hell. "Descended into hell" was found in the Apostles' Creed, the earliest of the three generally acknowledged Christian Creeds (Apostles', Nicene and Athanasian), but as spiritual knowledge darkened with the passage of time it was eliminated, as in the second, the Nicene (see "Apostles' Creed," and "Nicene Creed" in Brit). Even in those churches still using it today, there seems to be general discomfort with the idea, and one seldom hears elaboration upon it.

It does not meet with the common acceptance of reality that Christ could have "preached to the dead" who there in "Sheol" or "Hades" could make the necessary decision, or that their simply "hearing" it there without decision could save them, or even that they could "hear" it there. Moreover, absent karma and reincarnation, the problem of treating those who died before Christ without attaining perfection, namely, all those who experienced "Sheol," on the same basis as those who have lived since Christ, is a very insoluble one to the thinking mind, as is the idea of all the dead saints coming out of their tombs and appearing to many (Mt 27,52-53). Paul knew that such persons, as eternal Individualities, were not thus perfected, for even the Jews' most illustrious ancestors had not yet received what was promised, though they had "seen … and greeted it from afar" (Heb 11,13,39). He also knew that, prior to the "resurrection," and as a necessary means thereto, "God was able to raise men from the dead," i.e., to cause their reincarnation (Heb 11,19). But anthroposophy lets us know that those in the discarnate state were able to see much more effectively in the spiritual world what had happened at the Mystery of Golgotha and that they were thenceforth to be accorded the grace of taking in Christ in future incarnation on Earth, even though they were not on Earth when he was.

This understanding gives meaning to vs 6, for they could be "judged in the flesh like men" only when they returned to the flesh with the opportunity to accept Christ "like men" and to thereafter live on Earth reflecting that new life. The exoteric meaning, sufficient for the Church during the first two thousand years, is inadequate now that the esoteric meaning has again been revealed. For humanity has evolved beyond the Intellectual to the Spiritual (Consciousness) Soul state (**I-24, I-25** and **I-19**) and must come to the new understanding made possible thereby. And it is Christ as the Lord of Karma who thus "is ready to judge the living and the dead." That judgment occurs only upon death, but must apply to what occurs on Earth during life. Hence those to whom he preached at the time of his "descent" had to return, or be "born again." And just as his "preaching" was perceived by the dead through his "Descent Into Hell" (vs 6), so also is his Second Coming, i.e., his reappearance in the etheric world, perceivable by the dead of the twentieth century who are prepared to do so. To them, be they "living or dead" (vs 5), he can be seen. They can thus "live in the spirit like God" (vs 6), i.e., perceive there as "gods" (Jn 10,34).

Rev 2,23b and 3,2-3:

(2,23b): And all the churches shall know that I am he who searches mind and heart, and I will give to each of you as your works deserve.

(3,2-3): (2) Awake, and strengthen what remains and is on the point of death, for I have not found your works perfect in the sight of my God. (3) Remember then what you received and heard; keep that, and repent. If you will not awake, I will come like a thief, and you will not know at what hour I will come upon you.

It is important here to know, as Steiner tells us, that Rev 2,18-29 is a letter to the angel of the church in Thyatira. It is the fourth "letter" and represents the fourth Cultural Era of the post-Atlantean Epoch. It is the era in which Christ incarnated, the era in which he gave human beings his "word," which "will be [their] judge on the last day" (Jn 12,48). "All the churches ... know" this as well as the fact that he "searches mind and heart" and "will give to each ... as your works deserve." This tells what the churches "know" and what Christ "will" do in regard to karmic justice in the future. It does not purport, at that time, to execute such judgment.

Rev 3,1-6 is a letter to the angel of the church in Sardis. Being the fifth "letter," it represents the fifth Cultural Era, the present one from A.D. 1414 to 3574 (see **I-19**). Here Christ admonishes that humanity "awake," for it "is on the point of death." Steiner is the prophet who has shown us that the time for awakening is here. We are told in vs 2 that Christ's judgment has actually commenced, for he has "not found your works perfect in the sight of my God." We are reminded in Mt 5,48 that we must become "Perfect." We must here be intrigued that his "coming" is "like a thief." See "Thief in the Night." In vs 3 Christ says, "you will not know at what hour I will come upon you." In truth, he has been with us in the etheric world now for almost a century and we have not even suspected his presence, like that of a thief. It is essential that we "awake, and strengthen what remains."

Rev 22,12:

Behold, I am coming soon, bringing my recompense, to repay every one for what he has done.

When the long evolutionary periods envisioned by the Apocalypse are understood, a "coming" two millennia after the events in Palestine is a "coming soon." Illusion has existed about the meaning of the Second Coming since humanity has not understood its nature. We see here, however, in this final illustration, the recurring theme that "every one" is to be repaid "for what he has done." No exceptions are made for those who are "forgiven" (see "Forgiven Sins"). This meshes with all that has been said here. The "repayment" involves the settlement of all karmic debt, taking into account that objective karmic debt which has been paid by Christ. Fortunately, as we have seen, karma can be good as well as bad, so that "recompense" can be joyful as well. This thought is a fitting conclusion for all that has been said before in the Biblical narrative.

We have now examined those New Testament passages that speak significantly of Christ Jesus as judge. Now we can begin to see how broad and wonderful was the vision of Isaiah, who called him one upon whose shoulder the government would be, who would be called "Wonderful Counselor" (Is 9,6), upon whom the "spirit of wisdom and understanding, the spirit of counsel," etc., "shall rest," who would "not judge by what his eyes see, or decide by what his ears hear; but with righteousness" (Is 11,1-4). Here we have administration (government) that includes "counseling" and "judging." There could not be a more perfect description of the Lord of Karma who will see that "the uneven ground shall become level, and the rough places a plain" (Is 40,4) until even the extremes of the lower kingdoms are reconciled (Is 11,6-9 and 65,25; Rom 8,19-23; Eph 1,9-10).

CHAPTER END NOTE

5. (*continued from p. 188*) In spite of the fact that virtually all translations of vss 41 and 46 use either the word "eternal" or "everlasting," both appear to be incorrect. In *From Christianity to Christ* (FCC), at p. 56, Archiati, a former Roman Catholic priest, says that Mt 25,46 "should be translated in a totally different way. The *opposite* of 'everlasting' … is to be found in the Greek text: … *aionios* means 'for the period of an aeon'—this is not eternity; it refers to a time period."

The Greek word translated "eternal" in both vss 41 and 46 is *aionion* (see KJV/NIV—INT). Its noun form is *aion*. From it our "aeon," or "eon," is derived (and from *aionion* our "aeonian"). WNWD says that *aion* means "an age, lifetime, [or] eternity," but the definition it gives for our aeon speaks only of time periods and does not include the concept of eternity. MWCD and RHCD are in accord on the definition of "aeon." After studying the matter, I have come to the conclusion that the ancient Greeks seldom if ever used *aion* to mean "eternity" with the connotation we give it today. Its Greek meaning relates more to an "age" or a "lifetime" (see 1 Brit 119, "aeon"; also 17 Brit 410 "Doctrines and Dogmas, Religious; Celestial and Noncelestial Forms: Relationships of Beliefs in Angels and Demons to Views of the Cosmos," and 12 Brit 944, "Zurvanism").

William Barclay (Barc), in his 1964 *New Testament Words*, addresses the term *aionios* (same as *aionion*) at length. He says that in classical Greek its noun form, *aion*, has three meanings, namely, lifetime; age, generation or epoch; and a very long space of time. He recognizes that Plato may even have coined the word, but here Barclay seems to jump the track saying that Plato used the adjective as "the word of eternity in contrast with time." He points to Plato's *Timaeus* 37D as "the most significant of all the Platonic passages" on this term. But one who inspects that passage carefully and in context must surely come away doubting that it can have that meaning.

The passage, as translated in the GB series reads as follows:

[450] When the father and creator saw the creature which he had made moving and living, the created image of the eternal gods, he rejoiced, and in his joy determined to make the copy still more like the original; and as this was eternal, he sought to make the universe eternal, so far as might be. Now the nature of the ideal being was everlasting, but to bestow this attribute in its fullness upon a creature was impossible. Wherefore he resolved to have a moving image of eternity, and when he set in order the heaven, he made this image eternal but moving according to number, while eternity itself rests in unity; and this image we call time.

The "eternal gods" seem clearly to be subordinate to "the father and creator" and may well be taken as the equivalent of the Hierarchies (I-6). The Greek word used to describe those "gods" as "eternal" is not *aionion* but rather *aidios* (or *aidion*), which means "everlasting." The word *aionion* is used only in the later portions of the passage where it is recognized that they can be like the original only "so far as might be" but that it is impossible that any creature have the fullness of the attributes of the unchangeable creator.

The British psychologist, Maurice Nicoll, in *Living Time and the Integration of the Life*, London, Vincent Stuart Pub. Ltd., 1952, Chap. 6, writes of the "Aeon." A student of Jung, Gurdjieff and Ouspensky, his writing is reflective of their teachings, and does not seem to reflect awareness of anthroposophy. Still, what he says may help to explain Barclay's view that Plato used *aionion* as "the word of eternity in contrast with time," and to reconcile it with the conclusions herein.

What can be said in reconciliation is that in the full scope of the macrocosmic journey of the Prodigal Son there are stages that are, in a sense, unitary within themselves, and are separated from one another in quite fundamental ways. This is what was meant by the statement in the second paragraph of the General Introduction, "The origin of the human being was in the spiritual world untold expanses of time and timelessness ago." Such a period of timelessness appears to be described in Gen 2,21 by the phrase "deep sleep." In Oriental terminology it is called "pralaya." In the glossary of *Foundations of Esotericism* (FE), p. 283, pralaya is defined as "Sleep condition; Existence during a Rest-period between two Manvantaras, also called a closed orbit." In Steiner's more Western terminology, a Manvantara is a Condition of Consciousness. The entirety of Earth evolution is a single Condition of Consciousness (see **I-1**, **I-2** and **I-3)**. What separates one Condition of Consciousness from another is a condition that for lack of a more competent expression we will call a period. In the sense of spiritual evolution, it is a sort of division between manifestations, but not one that can be quantified by either time, space or existence as we know them. It is a period of total dormancy, much like that of a seed lying dormant in the soil waiting to spring back to life from its internal chaos in accordance with the akashic patterns in the spiritual world. But what existed in the earlier age (*aion*) is transformed into a progressively new and different state from what existed in the prior age (cf. 1 Cor 15,35-41). The term *aion*, in a lower sense, might then reflect a single lifetime within the larger spiritual progression or *aion*.

But just as the New Testament speaks of the "ages of the ages," so also must we recognize that the *aion* divides into smaller images of itself. The student who studies Steiner's *Occult Science* (OS) will see that the Conditions of Consciousness are fractal in nature, being themselves sevenfold and being divisible and subdivisible again and again by seven (Prov 9,1). The Revelation will give us an idea of the progression of some of these lower "ages" or *aiona*. So, when Archiati speaks of *aionios* referring to a "time period," he must be understood as speaking in a sense of what might be called "cosmic time," a measure of the progression of spiritual evolution of the Prodigal Son and the lower kingdoms.

But just as the human astral body soars into the astral world during earthly sleep between states of waking consciousness, so also may we surmise that interspersed between the larger Conditions, especially the Conditions of Consciousness (see **I-1**), the "deep sleep" of the pralaya enters into the twelvefold zodiacal realm, the image that most closely resembles what we would call eternity (Gen 15,5). Steiner tells us that the Holy City, the New Jerusalem, that St. John saw coming down out of heaven (Rev 21) is the Jupiter Condition of Consciousness. The twelvefoldedness of the zodiacal realm reveals itself as the pralaya between the Earth and Jupiter Conditions of Consciousness (ages, or aeons) approaches (Rev 21-22).

It is in *Timaeus* that Plato discusses the "Four Elements" and shows us the nature of "Fire" as the point at which the gods and the created elements meet. See **I-22**; also "Four Elements" and "Fire" in Vol. 2. Mt 25,41 uses the same *aionion* in the "eternal fire" passage. But "fire" is the lowest of the ethers, clearly a part of the creative process, and one that will be reversed over aeons, so that its meaning, as it comes from the ancient Greek, must be understood in terms of evolutionary epochs. It cannot be stretched to mean eternal or everlasting in the modern vernacular. Its meaning is that given to it in Mt 28,20, which uses the Greek *aionios*, translated "age" rather than "eternity." Obviously, that phrase could not be translated "I will be with you always, to the close of *eternity*," for in the modern vernacular eternity has no end.

That the "fire" in Mt 25,41 is temporal, i.e., of evolutionary significance, is clear from the fact that it is "prepared for the devil and his angels." That fire is more ultimate than the "refiner's [purifying] fire" of the astral world (cf. Purgatory), for it is a clear reference to the time frame foreseen in Rev 20, as recognized by the footnote in NIV. But even the fire of Rev 20 is best seen as not being eternal. For instance, though Rev 20,10 in most translations is rendered "for ever and ever," it uses the same Greek words (*aionas* and *aion-on*) that are, in KJV/NIV—INT, rendered "unto the ages of the ages." We shall see that Rev 20 is speaking of the end of Earth evolution and its "second death." But three more Conditions of Consciousness are to follow (see **I-1**). The powers of the redeemed will be unspeakably enhanced in those Conditions, and there will still be redemptions. These are well beyond our present vision. But they resonate with Paul's words in Eph 1,9-10—and Christ's in the parable of "the ninety and nine" (Mt 18,10-14; Lk 15,3-7).

It is because Christianity lost the spiritual insight of the Evangelists and had no understanding of the meaning of "ages" that it chose the modern meaning "eternal" rather than "age," unlimited rather than limited duration. Earlier in this same "Little Apocalypse" strain, Matthew speaks of the "trumpet" call (Mt 24,31). We shall see that the term "Trumpet" relates to the closing of an "age."

It is only in Matthew's Gospel that we have this passage on the judgment of the nations (Mt 25,31-46). By no means should we attribute any error to the Evangelist. One might at first think that it could be ascribed to Jerome who translated Matthew from the original Hebrew into both Greek and Latin but was not initiated to the level of being able to understand the Gospel. (This shall become quite clear in "Akashic" below. See there the *From Jesus to Christ* [JTC], Lect. 4, extract, including my footnotes.)

However, even Jerome must probably escape such criticism here (at least as to the Greek). The basic Greek term *aionion* is used dozens of times in the New Testament. Let us look at one particularly revealing instance. Luke was the only purely Greek Evangelist. In Lk 18,30, we read of those who have left much to follow Christ that they will "receive manifold more in this time, and in the *age* to come *eternal* life" (emphasis added). The noun translated as "age" is *aion*, while the adjective "eternal" is *aionion*. The adjective must be limited by the noun it is like, so it is more appropriately translated, "and in the age to come life appropriate to that age."

Obviously, since the Evangelists handed down their visionary, inspired and intuitive writings, it is enlightening to see how later translators' cosmological and epistemological views affect their translation of *aionion*. I've inspected the terms "age(s)," "eternal," "eternity," "ever," "everlasting," and "evermore" in *Nelson's Complete Concordance of the Revised Standard Version*, 2d Ed., Nashville, Thomas Nelson Publishers, 1984, and their Greek terminology reflected in KJV/NIV—INT, and compared numerous translations to see their leanings on this Greek term. Those who have no feel for the evolutionary progression of the "ages" tend to give it an eternal or everlasting meaning unless forced to do otherwise, while others tend to use the temporal concept of the passing of "ages" or "epochs," however long.

The Greek noun *aion* can mean, and its related adjective *aionion* can refer to, either an age, i.e., a period of time, however long, or an eternity, but it cannot mean or refer to both, for the two concepts are polar opposites. An age begins and ends. Eternity does neither. One word cannot describe both. These concepts are fundamental. Clearly the Greek concept of *aion* referred to measurements of cosmic time or conditions, starting with the first emanation from the father creator. (Compare Barclay's description of such emanations in the basic doctrine of Gnosticism; Barc, *The Gospel of John*, Vol. 1, p. 12.) Plato does not use *aionion* with reference to the unity of the father creator, "that which always is and has no becoming" (*Timaeus* 27D), as compared with "that which is always becoming and never is."

If ages are ever to become eternity, it must surely be when all creatures have returned to unity, a concept expressed by Paul (Rom 8,19-23 and Eph 1,9-10) that looks out even further into future evolution than is seen in the far reaches of the Revelation. For Revelation speaks of "the ages of the ages" (*aionion* repeated and often translated "for ever and ever") and makes no provision for the return of the creatures in all the lower kingdoms. If *aion* or *aionion* is ever spoken of as "eternal," surely it must be in the same non-literal sense in which we sometimes speak of it today, "a long period of time that seems endless [an *eternity* of waiting]" (WNWD, third meaning given for "eternity"), but still actually involving the element of time, cosmic or otherwise. Steiner would look at cosmic time in terms of rhythm, eliminating clocks and calendars.

The importance of this term (*aion/aionion*) is indicated by the extent to which it pervades the entirety of the New Testament. Other instances that seem particularly indicative include the following translations from the Greek in KJV/NIV—INT:

Mk 3,29: … but whoever blasphemes against the Spirit Holy, has not forgiveness unto the age [*aiona*], but is liable of an eternal [*aionion*] sin.

Mk 10,30b: … and in the age [*aioni*] coming life eternal [*aionion*].

Jn 4,14: … but whoever drinks of the water which I will give him, by no means will thirst unto the age [*aiona*], but the water which I will give him will become in him a fountain of water springing to life eternal [*aionion*].

Jn 10,28: … and I give to them life eternal [*aionion*], and by no means they perish unto the age [*aiona*], and shall not seize anyone of them out of the hand of me.

Tit 1,2-3: (2) … on(in) hope of life eternal [*aionion*], which promised the unlying God before times eternal [*aionion*] (3) but manifested times in [its] own the word of him in a proclamation …

Passages frequently translated "for ever and ever," where KJV/NIV—INT says "ages of the ages," include: Rom 16,27; Gal 1,4; Eph 3,21; Phil 4,20; 1 Tim 1,17; 2 Tim 4,18; Heb 1,8; 13,21; 1 Pet 4,11; 5,11; Jude 1,25 (before all the age [*aionios*] and now and unto all the ages [*aionias*]); Rev 1,6; 1,18; 4,9; 4,10; 5,13; 7,12; 10,6; 11,15; 14,11; 15,7; 19,3; 22,5. I find it particularly meaningful that this is almost the exclusive usage in Revelation, which addresses the succession of many ages.

Other passages using either the noun *aion* or adjective *aionion* include: Mt 12,32; 13,39; 13,40; 13,49; 18,8; 19,16; 19,29; 21,19; 24,3; Mk 10,17; Lk 1,33; 1,55; 10,25; 16,9; 18,18; 20,34; 20,35; Jn 3,15; 3,16; 3,36; 4,36; 5,24; 5,39; 6,27; 6,40; 6,47; 6,51; 6,54; 6,58; 6,68; 12,25; 12,34; 12,50; 14,16; 17,2; 17,3; Acts 13,46; 13,48; Rom 1,25; 2,7; 5,21; 6,22; 6,23; 9,5; 11,36; 16,25; 16,26; 1 Cor 1,20; 2,6; 2,7; 2,8; 3,18; 10,11; 2 Cor 4,17; 4,18; 5,1; 9,9; 11,31; Gal 1,5; 6,8; Eph 1,21; 2,7; 3,9; 3,11; Col 1,26; 2 Th 1,9; 2,16; 1 Tim 1,16; 6,12; 6,16; 2 Tim 1,9; 2,10; Tit 3,7; Philem 1,15; Heb 5,6; 5,9; 6,2; 6,5; 6,20; 7,17; 7,21; 7,24; 7,28; 9,12; 9,14; 9,15; 9,26; 13,8; 13,20 1 Pet 1,25; 5,10; 2 Pet 1,11; 3,18; 1 Jn 1,2; 2,17; 2,25, 3,15; 5,11; 5,13; 5,20; 2 Jn 1,2; Jude 1,7; 1,13; 1,21; Rev 14,6.

The weakness of the rigid "Written Word" (cf. 2 Cor 3), whose connotation changes with the passage of time, is here clearly demonstrated. And does this not also suggest that the Bible's meaning must eventually be taken from direct spiritual intuition, high prophecy such as that of Rudolf Steiner (Jer 31,33-34; Heb 10,16-17)?—ERS

SECOND COMING

IF, AS WE KNOW, along with all Christendom Paul viewed the Resurrection of Christ as central to our faith (1 Cor 15,12-19), no less so was the certainty of his return, the *parousia*, or "Second Coming" (1 Cor 16,22; 1 Th 2,19; 3,13; 4,15 and 5,23; 2 Th 2,1,8; Heb 9,28 and 10,37). But the conviction that his Resurrection was "in the body" and the expectation that his return would be likewise have, with the loss of the first century's inspired vision and the increasing focus upon the modern "scientific" mind, caused the truth to be lost by division (a "house divided," Mt 12,25-26) into opposing camps of internecine misunderstanding. On the one hand are the fundamentalists who maddeningly insist on the reconstitution, atom by atom, of the mineral-physical body not only of Christ but also of his followers "on the last day." On the other hand are the rest who, hopelessly diffused, nevertheless hold tenaciously, likewise as a matter of "faith," to some type of Resurrection and Second Coming, but cannot swallow the incredible inconsistencies assumed by the "atomic" scenario. In between, erstwhile believers slip away from firm conviction while their younger sensitive counterparts ignore Christianity as increasingly irrelevant, understandably disenchanted by both camps.

One senses that just as humanity had to sink to the "Right Time" before the Advent of Christ, Christianity had to come to this threshold of immolation before comprehension of the reconciling Truth of the Mystery of Golgotha could ripen Faith into a Faith based upon the greater certainty of Knowledge.

Anthroposophy shows us that Christ incarnated "Once for All" and that those who expect its repeat do not understand the cosmic significance of the Incarnation in the first instance. Yet, while the "atomic" scenario is indeed an Ahrimanic (delusively materialistic; see 2 Th 2,11) falsehood, it is nevertheless true that the Resurrection of Christ was in the "body," so also will be his Second Coming. Paul made a clear distinction,

of course, between "the body" and "the flesh," and it is this distinction
that is ignored by the expectation of "atomic" reconstitution. The Resurrection of Christ was of all of his three bodies, the physical, etheric and
astral, while the higher components of his Being (see **I-9**) experienced
death without themselves ever having died (Jn 11,26).

A critical distinction must here be made, however, between the Resurrection of Christ and that of humanity. The perfection of Christ was
absolute and thus during Earth evolution his Resurrection was of both
the physical and etheric bodies (ignoring as here irrelevant the less dense
astral body). The resurrection of humanity, of which Luke speaks for
instance in Lk 20,35-36, is what it will experience when the mineral-
physical body is permanently laid aside (with the end of reincarnation),
and when at the "last trumpet" (1 Cor 15; see "Trumpet[s]") the etheric
body is also laid aside, both as a result of Earth evolution leading to the
Jupiter Condition of Consciousness (see **I-1** through **I-3**), the "New
Jerusalem" of Rev 21. Earth evolution is the "Age" spoken of by Christ
(e.g., Mt 28,20; Mt 24,3; Lk 20,34). Humanity will convert its astral
body to the manas (Spirit Self) state on Jupiter, its etheric body to the
buddhi (Life Spirit) state on Venus, and its physical body to the atma
(Spirit Man) state on Vulcan. Only at the last point can the physical
body be said to be resurrected, for it only then attains the redeemed state
of its original form or pattern, what Steiner refers to as its "Phantom"
(see "Form/Phantom"). This is the state of the "one like a son of man"
portrayed in Rev 1,12-16, which during Earth evolution only the Christ
could represent. Nevertheless, his Resurrection was humanity's assurance that even that eventual state is guaranteed to those who take the
Christ "I Am" into their being. The witnesses to Christ's Resurrection
experienced both his purified, mineral-free, nonatomic, physical body
(i.e., Phantom) as well as his etheric body. They experienced this
through Christ-enabled organs of perception other than their senses as
we today know them. (Passages that seem to indicate otherwise, such as
Lk 24,43, Jn 21,13 and Jn 20,27, dealing with the eating of fish and
placing a finger in his wounds, will be seen to have a literally different
meaning than that superficially assumed. See, for instance, Point #2 in
"Peter, James and John.") In the same manner (Acts 1,11), those whose
organs are thus prepared can now experience his return, the Second
Coming, in the etheric world. Rudolf Steiner has shown us the "path"
(Mt 7,13-14) to the development of those organs of perception (e.g.,

Knowledge of the Higher Worlds and Its Attainment [KHW], as well as in numerous other works).

We need not here greatly belabor the almost universally accepted view that the early disciples expected "an imminent" return of Christ. That such did not happen is accepted. That there was an element of popular expectation at the time of Christ can hardly be denied, especially considering the eschatological and apocalyptic belief among certain segments of that society. But among the Apostolic Fathers themselves, only Judas Iscariot can be seen in the end to have gone off on this line of persuasion. During Christ's ministry, there may have been an expectation of his return among his close group, as the inquiries leading to the "Little Apocalypses" would suggest. But that they were left with this understanding after the Resurrection is not necessarily indicated, and is contrary to what we may now come to understand. What we can now see is that with the darkening of knowledge and consciousness among those Church Fathers and the larger congregation following the passage of the true apostolic group, it was seemingly taken for granted that there had been a "delay" in what had been expected (see *Christ and the Spiritual World/The Search for the Holy Grail* [CSW], Lect. 2). And the existence of such a delay, or at least of an early belief in it, has come down to us as virtually accepted doctrine to this day. But it is not justified, or at least not required, by the Biblical testimony if that is understood in the light of anthroposophical knowledge. When the Apocalypse of John is properly understood, it will be seen not only to have no necessary connection with contemporary persecution but to be inconsistent with the expectation of an early return of Christ (e.g., Rev 1,1 and Rev 22,6-7,10,12,20). So extensive was Paul's esoteric training (Gal 1,14) and spiritual insight that we also misapprehend his words to take them as indicating the imminence of an early return. His recognition of being "untimely born" (1 Cor 15,8) and his understanding, as we shall see, of deep mysteries of the faith, demand a re-evaluation of any interpretation of his sayings as betraying such an expectation on his part. His advice not to marry (1 Cor 7,9) because "the appointed time has grown very short" (1 Cor 7,29) and "the form of this world is passing away" (1 Cor 7,31) can be taken as an indication of the urgency of devoting all the time allotted to one's life in service to the Lord (cf. Heb 9,27), not to mention his recognition that sexual division would cease before the end of time. Only because we have forgotten the reality of reincarnation do we mistakenly assume that in 1 Th 4,15 ("we who are alive, who are left until the coming of the Lord, shall not precede those who have fallen asleep") Paul refers to their present incarnation. In 2 Th 2,1-12, he outlines events of the type described by Christ in the "Little Apocalypse" (Mt 25, 31-46; Mk 13, 26-27; Lk 21,36). When Paul speaks of "the last trumpet" (1 Cor 15,52; 1 Th 5,16) he demonstrates his deep esoteric knowledge of the long evolution of human consciousness. The emphasis by all the Evangelists and Paul upon the seminal pronouncement in Is 6,9-13 suggests their understanding of what can now be seen as true prophecy. It behooves me here to say only that this whole issue is quite peripheral and essentially irrelevant because the Second Coming clearly had not occurred before our time.

We will look first at what anthroposophy says about the Second Coming of Christ, and then examine how it illuminates the relevant scriptural passages. The Second Coming cannot, however, be adequately understood save in relation to other related terms herein including "Lord of Karma," "Karma and Reincarnation," "Forgiven Sins," "I AM," "Bush" and "Akashic."

Two young anthroposophic writers, Sergei O. Prokofieff and Robert Powell (in the Cognate Writings section, Vol. 3, *Companions Along The Way*), from quite different perspectives, have given us an immensely helpful exposition on the Second Coming. Both necessarily presume their readers have extensive anthroposophical background. While their contributions are of immense worth for Christian posterity, and are here highly recommended for further study, my immediate mission is to dismantle that wall heretofore separating anthroposophists and more traditional Christians. To this end, we need to look at what they say about the Second Coming.

In *The Cycle of the Year as a Path of Initiation* (CYPI), Sec. 12 ("The Modern Mysteries of the Etheric Christ") and particularly Subsec. 2 ("The New Appearance of Christ in the Etheric Realm"), Prokofieff explores Steiner's teachings. In Subsec. 2 we read:

The new appearance of Christ in the etheric realm is to be seen as the most significant event taking place in the supersensible world nearest to the Earth in the twentieth century. According to indications given by Rudolf Steiner, this event began in the year 1909 [citing *Cosmic and Human Metamorphoses* (CHM), Lect. 1], the year at the end of which the mysteries of the Fifth Gospel and—in the cycle on the Gospel of St. Luke—the mystery of the two Jesus children, were revealed for the first time.[1]

In *Hermetic Astrology, Vol. 1* (HA1), App. 2 and Chap. 3 (at pp. 76-79), as well as in HA2, Chap. 9, Powell gives extensive provocative consideration to the Second Coming as reflected in "hermetic astrology," a spiritual science for which Steiner gave the impetus so that humanity could again come to know its vital formative relationship with the "stars." In HA1 Powell writes: "Unlike the first coming of Christ, which was a physical event, i.e. incarnation by way of the baptism in the Jordan into the physical vessel provided by Jesus, the second coming is a spiritual event: the birth of Christ in the hearts and minds of human beings" (p. 76). "Jesus Christ in his second coming is now manifesting himself in the Earth's etheric aura … in a radiant light-filled etheric form" (p. 324). But human beings must prepare themselves before they will be able to behold the Second Coming: "In order for Christ to appear in the earthly realm—*the sphere of man*—human beings have first to recognize on the level of knowledge that the second coming is under way. Then, after it has become a fact of knowledge, it is a matter of *inner transformation* in order to be able to meet with Christ. This inner transformation entails a moral-spiritual development" (p. 326). Unlike Prokofieff,

---

1. Prokofieff elaborates many finer connections relating to this Second Coming, but for our purposes we note only his citations of Steiner that specifically deal with the Second Coming, namely, CHM, Lect. 1 (2-6-17); *The New Spirituality* (NSP), Lects. 6 & 7 (10-30-20 & 10-31-20); *The Search for the New Isis, the Divine Sophia* (SIS), Lect. 2 (12-24-20); *Occult Science and Occult Development* (OSOD), Lect. 2 (5-2-13); *Pre-Earthly Deeds of Christ* (PEDC) (3-7-14); *The Reappearance of Christ in the Etheric* (RCE) (13 lectures, 1 through 9 given from 1-25-10 through 10-1-11, and 10 through 14 from 10-18-17 through 11-29-17); *The Christ Impulse and the Development of Ego Consciousness* (CIDE), Lect. 5 (3-9-10); and *From Jesus to Christ* (JTC), Lect. 10 (10-14-11).

Prokofieff does not claim these as exhaustive, and the following are also additionally noted as speaking to this point: *Esoteric Christianity and the Mission of Christian Rosenkreutz* (ECMCR), Lects. 7 & 8 (11-18-11 & 11-20-11); *Faith, Love, Hope* (FLH), Lect. 1 (12-2-11); *Rosicrucian Christianity* (ROSC), Lect. 2 (9-28-11); *The Concepts of Original Sin and Grace* (OSG) (5-3-11); *The Evolution of Consciousness* (EVC), Lect. 13 (8-31-23); *Wonders of the World* (WW), Lect. 2 (8-19-11); *The Path of the Christ Through the Centuries* (PCC) (10-14-13); *Happenings at the Turn of the Millennia* (HTM) (3-7-14); *The Coming Experience of Christ* (CEC) (10-31-20); *Reading the Pictures of the Apocalypse* (RPA), Intr. & Chap 12 (5-21-09); *Earthly and Cosmic Man* (ECM), Lect. 7 (5-20-12); and *Outlooks for the Future* (OFSF) (10-31-15 through 11-7-15) (though the last three did not yet identify the event clearly to the twentieth century).

Powell places the onset of the Second Coming in 1933, based both on astronomical events and on its connection with an incarnation in this century of the future Maitreya Buddha, the current Bodhisattva of humanity (successor of the Bodhisattva who became Gautama Buddha), whose mission is to mediate the Christ Impulse issuing from the Second Coming (p. 76); see also "Robert Powell" in the Cognate Writings section, Vol. 3.

While the 1930s were indeed singled out by Steiner as highly significant to the Second Coming, the likelihood that he himself witnessed Christ in the etheric world around 1909, and was himself the Bodhisattva, seems well supported.[2] Whether it was in the etheric world, or approaching it from higher worlds, may be taken for our present purposes as too strenuous a refinement. We know from Steiner's deathbed autobiography that not long before the turn of the century, he "had stood in spirit before the Mystery of Golgotha in most inward, most earnest solemnity of knowledge," *The Course of My Life* (CML), Chap. 26. And on June 17, 1908, in a lecture at Nuremberg, *Spiritual Science, Christianity and the Future of Mankind* (SSCFM) pregnant with the approaching revelation of the Second Coming in the etheric world he had said, "And if man gives himself up to this Power [the Christ "I Am"], then he will grow again into the Spiritual World from out of which he has descended. He will rise again into that region, whereinto the Initiate can already see today."

Perhaps too much has already been said about whether it was around 1909 or 1933 that the Second Coming commenced. Sooner or later, the serious student will come upon this question, but for now, the distinction is academic, not sufficiently important to dwell further upon. That we are by now generations into that time frame is the significant point. The materialistic Ahrimanic powers have dominated the secular, and obscured the spiritual (2 Th 2,11), developments of the century, providing Christ a setting not unlike that two millennia earlier. That he has come, as yet almost universally undetected, like a "Thief in the Night" is indicated.

---

2. See Arenson, *Fruits of Earnest Study of the Lectures of Rudolf Steiner* (BQ-3). Steiner clearly said that the future Maitreya Buddha incarnated very early in the twentieth century, but he made no overt identification. Arenson's writing shows how it can refer to Steiner himself when the terminology Steiner used is properly understood. The views on the identity of the Bodhisattva have recently been given by two contrasting publications bearing the identical titles, *The Bodhisattva Question*, see BQ-1 and BQ-2. However, the beginning student should best defer the subject. We will look at it briefly under "Robert Powell" in Vol. 3.

Presently we shall look at what Steiner said about the Second Coming, then into the nature of the etheric state, and finally at the relevant scriptures. However, let us first reflect upon the possible reconciliation of some passages and concepts that tend to raise conflicting images in our minds, and see how these relate to the Second Coming. Consider, for instance, the following:

a) Ascension—e.g. Mk 16,19; Lk 24,51; Jn 20,17; Acts 1,9; 1 ABD 472.
b) "I go to prepare a place for you [in his Father's house where there are many rooms, and from whence] I will come again and will take you to myself"—Jn 14,2-3.
c) "I go away, and I will come to you ... I go to the Father"—Jn 14,28.
d) The "Counselor" and the "Holy Spirit" will be sent by the Father—Jn 14,26.
e) "I am with you always, to the close of the age"—Mt 28,20.
f) He appeared to the apostles alive "during forty days"— Acts 1,3.
g) To Paul, "I am Jesus, whom you are persecuting," appearing long after his Ascension—Acts 9,5; 1 Cor 15,8.
h) "Christ Jesus ... who is at the right hand of God"—Rom 8,34.
i) "Not I, but Christ liveth in me"—Gal 2,20.

Must we not admit that the whereabouts of the Christ after the Resurrection is problematical, and variously presented by the above passages when understood in an ordinary way? We are told that he ascended and was going to the Father, but that he would always still be here with us, and he appeared here on Earth after the Ascension, yet he is sitting at the right hand of God; and still he dwells within us, even though there is an implication that the Counselor or Holy Spirit is standing in for him during his absence. And if he is always with us, how is it that he can "come again," presumably never having left? The concept of the Holy Spirit as necessarily both distinct from and yet one with the Father and Son has, from its inception, always been called upon semantically to fill the interstices between our images.

We raise these seeming discrepancies only to point out the limitations of our level of understanding. So long as we deal, as is our custom, only with the physical and the spiritual, the harmonizing of all these concepts is indeed a challenge. They are raised here so as to get them all on the table, as being related to the "Second Coming," and so that we not be blind-sided, from a literal standpoint, by their oversight.

If we try to storm our way to comprehension, "taking it by force" (Mt 11,12), so to speak, rather than meditating upon and letting our angel help us come to an understanding in heart and mind, we shall find ourselves in the arid terrain of the Ahrimanic "Written Word" (2 Cor 3). To assist us in coming to an anthroposophic understanding of these matters, let us contemplate charts **I-9** and **I-18**. From the latter the levels of "descent" the Christ had to go through to incarnate in the flesh become apparent. Likewise, one sees that the lowest of his components before the descent was "Life Spirit," which sheds light upon his claim to be "the Life" (Jn 14,6), and that no one can get to the Father above the chart (**I-18**)without going through him, the Son, who stands at its top. If this was the Descent, then perhaps one can come to some idea of what the corresponding Ascent means. But we must recognize that the Christ, in such descent is the one and only spiritual being who has experienced all the twelve levels—the sevens have become the twelves only in him (cf. Rev). And when he took upon himself the lowliest forms, having done so free from sin and the taint of the Fall, he purified each of them (Heb 2) and, in accordance with the principle of "Spiritual Economy," left multiple copies of each so that one is abundantly available for every human soul who submits to its Christ-like nature.

When we speak, however, of "going to the Father," we must remember that the Father is present in the lowest elements of mineral-physical creation. Indeed, if one contemplates the course of the human being between death and rebirth, it can be seen that one expands into larger areas rather than leaving the former (see **I-33**) so that one has the feeling of encompassing the entirety of (i.e., being one with) what is within one's growing orbit (see *Effects of the Christ-Impulse upon the Historical Course of Human Evolution/The Occult Background of the Christmas Festival* [ECIH], *The Etheric Being in the Physical Human Being* [EBPHB], and *The Destinies of Individuals and of Nations* [DIN], Lect. 11, 4-20-15). How often we are told by Steiner that spiritual bodies interpenetrate, thus occupying the "same space" from the human perspective. At each level of Christ's descent, he is assisted, and works through and in conjunction with, the spiritual Hierarchy at that level (see **I-18**), thus having "twelve legions of angels" (Mt 26,53) at his disposal while at the lowest level. Our concept of "leaving" one sphere and "going" to another is limited to the mineral-physical where two bodies cannot occupy the same space. It is not so in the spirit world. The highest is present in all that is.

Now, if Christ, in the fourth Cultural Era, the Greco-Roman, could be comprehended by human beings only in the physical, and if the human being is evolving higher, as the Bible assures us (e.g., 2 Cor 3,18; Phil 3,21), then it is apparent that in the present Cultural Era (see **I-24** and **I-25**) he must be comprehended in the next higher state, namely, the etheric, as Steiner has said. His "First Coming" was thus in the physical, and his Second Coming will thus be in the etheric.

Let us look now at what Steiner said about the matter. While in all of the works cited above, Steiner speaks of the coming perceptions of Christ in the etheric world as the Second Coming, the most complete assembly of lectures thereon is in *The Reappearance of Christ in the Etheric* (RCE). In the first lecture he speaks of Paul's Damascus road experience as a vision (as of one "untimely born," 1 Cor 15,8) of the etheric Christ, a first fruit, in a manner of speaking, of what is now more and more to be experienced by humans who develop the necessary organ of perception. The nature of Paul's knowledge was based upon his own experience rather than what he learned from others (Gal 1,11-12). He was thus, along with others who had seen the risen Christ, an etheric "eyewitness," the only type relied upon by Luke (Lk 1,2). And just as Paul did not rely upon any written or spoken word, neither will those who now come to experience Christ in the etheric world, by raising themselves up to an etheric vision of him (Jer 31,33; 2 Cor 3; Heb 10,15-16). Souls who fail in this incarnation to prepare themselves will have to wait until they are again incarnated and will thus lose the increased consciousness during their long term in the spiritual world. The face of the Earth will have changed in the interim.

In lectures 2 through 4 Steiner speaks of spiritual science as a preparation for the new etheric vision; of the part the Maitreya Buddha will play in bringing knowledge of the Christ to humanity 5,000 years after the Buddha, Siddhartha Guatama; of why reincarnation was not to be taught in Christianity for 2,000 years; and of various mysteries of the universe, especially those dealing with cometary and lunar influences.

We have already seen in the journey of the Prodigal Son, i.e., humanity in its Fall, redemption and reascent, how stages of descent must be transformingly retraced upon reascent. Steiner opens lecture 5 by saying:

> There is a certain connection between the past and the future in the evolution of humanity.... There is a law according to which certain events are repeated in the evolution of humanity.

Steiner often mentions this. He speaks here of having done so in the last Stuttgart lectures (which do not seem to be in the Bibliography), and does so again later the same year in *Occult History* (OH), Lect. 3. More explicitly (RCE, Lect. 5, p. 79), he says,

> It is an eternal cosmic law that each individual must perform a particular deed repeatedly. He must, above all, perform the deed twice—one time as though doing the opposite of the other time. What Abraham brought down for humanity into physical consciousness he will carry up again for humanity into the spiritual world.

Immediately prior to this extract he had said,

> We stand, therefore, directly before such an evolution. We are retracing our steps, so to speak, along the path of evolution. With Abraham, consciousness of God was led into the brain; as we enter into a new age of Abraham, this consciousness of God is in turn led out of the brain and, during the next 2,500 years, we shall come gradually to know human beings who will have what the exalted secrets of initiation yield as the great spiritual teachings about the mysteries of the universe. Just as the spirit of Moses ruled in the age that has run its course up to our time, so does the spirit of Abraham now begin to reign in order that, having led humanity into a consciousness of God within the world of the senses, he may now lead humanity out again.

And immediately after the first extract he said,

> We thus see that we are living in important, essential conditions in this age, and we understand that to disseminate spiritual science today is not something one does by preference but something demanded by our times.

Notably, Abraham is the one who led humanity into the age of the intellect and vanishing clairvoyance, approximately 2,000 B.C. Now, approximately that length of time after Christ, spiritual science (founded by Steiner to publicly reveal and expand upon what had been given privately and esoterically by Christian Rosenkreutz at the threshold of the Age of the Consciousness Soul; see **I-19**, **I-24** and **I-25**) is the means of leading humanity back toward a new clairvoyance combined with intellect.[3]

In lecture 6, Steiner looks at the Sermon on the Mount, especially the beatitudes, in the light of human evolution, including the Second Coming.

Lecture 7, "The Return of Christ," notes the "signs of our times" as they relate to the Second Coming. Steiner notes that we are now the same distance into the zodiacal "sign of Pisces, the Fish" as the Advent of Christ was into the "sign of Aries, the Ram." The First Coming, in the physical world, was in Aries, hence "the Lamb of God" (Jn 1,29,36), and the Second Coming is now in the sign of the Fish, "the outer symbol for the appearance of Christ in the etheric body" (see **I-19**).

Lecture 8, "The Etheric Vision of the Future," says that just "as Christ had to have a forerunner, so spiritual science had to appear in order to prepare for this clairvoyant age."

Jumping ahead, lectures 10 through 13 deal with impediments and opposing forces. One can see in lecture 10 how etheric bodies of deceased persons have been inhabited by demonic spirits in a way that seemingly demonstrates "memories" to deceive relatives into thinking there is a communication. And one can see how the use of such bodies could explain memories certain individuals have that seem to indicate (though falsely) that they are a reincarnation of an earlier personality. (On this, consider Ian Stephenson, M.D., *Twenty Cases Suggestive of Reincarnation*, 2nd Ed., Charlottesville, Univ. of Virginia, 1974.) Ironically, but ominously similar to the position of the spiritual leaders of Jesus' day, Steiner says, "the greatest enemies to grasping the Christ impulse are the priests and clergy of the various religious faiths, no matter how strange this may sound. What keeps humanity furthest from the Christ impulse is the way

---

3. This apparent relationship between Abraham and Steiner was first mentioned in the Overview. It will be taken up in more detail in the "Interlude for Steiner Individuality," in the Cognate Writings section, Vol. 3. And we will see, in "Peter, James and John," that Christian Rosenkreutz was the reappearance of the John being, the reincarnation of the "beloved disciple" of John's Gospel.

in which the clergy and the theologians interpret this Christ impulse, because they are far from understanding what it is" (see "Shepherd[s]"). That was in 1917. I sense that there is a groping by a few clergy today for some new light—not that there is as yet much understanding, but there is perhaps a more humble openness and willingness to look at the possibilities that lie beyond, and may even conflict with, but more often elucidate, cherished tradition.

We return now to the vital ninth lecture, "The Etherization of the Blood." Ideally one should read this lecture over and over meditatively. And then having done so, to enhance understanding of its immense significance one should consider the related portions of WW, Lects. 8 and 9, and *An Occult Physiology* (OP), Lect. 4. All of these were given between March 23 and October 1, 1911, "The Etherization of the Blood" being the last, the OP lecture the first and the WW lectures intervening in late August. Something of the significance of the OP lecture can be seen in **I-86**. However, we are presently concerned primarily with that aspect of the lecture that deals with the blood, heart and pineal gland. One should not unduly fret if comprehension of these matters comes but gradually. But it is probably essential, if one is to understand how the human being can come to perceive the Christ in the etheric world, that one comprehend what Steiner is saying in these lectures. I can only feebly touch upon it in what follows. When available it will help first to contemplate the spiritual significance of blood (see "Blood" in Vol. 2, "*What Is Man?*"). In OP, Lect. 4, Steiner calls it "the noblest instrument possessed by man,… the instrument of his ego" which stands, even physically, as an intermediary between the outer world (air) and the inner (nutriment). It works through the heart organ (which was formed by primeval etheric circulation much as the etheric eye was formed by spiritual light). The etherization of the blood centers around the interplay between the organs of the heart and the pineal gland located in the vicinity of the eyes.

It will help at this point to note what are called the "lotus flowers" or "wheels" or "chakras" in the Orient. Steiner speaks of them in KHW, Chap. 6, as being "the sense-organs of the soul," just as the astral body through the nervous system is the sense organ of the physical body. A helpful discussion of the seven "lotus flowers" can be found in HA1, Chap. 5, from which **I-21** is taken. (The etheric nature of the human being's organs is also shown in **I-14**, and is further intimated in **I-76** and **I-77**. **I-86** shows the relationship of the seven traditional planets of our solar system to both the human metabolic and rhythmic systems working physically and then to the seven higher organs, glands or regions that relate to the "lotus flowers." The pituitary may be the one Powell locates at the top of the head in **I-21**, then in descending order come the pineal, larynx, heart, solar plexus, kidneys and reproductive.) The heart is seen to be the twelve-petalled lotus flower while the pineal gland is the two-petalled (*The Twelve Holy Nights and the Spiritual Hierarchies* [THNS], Sec. 2, Chap. 3). In the light of anthroposophical knowledge, we can also see that Job 40,21-22 is speaking of these: "Under the lotus plants he lies, in the covert of the reeds and in the marsh. For his shade the lotus trees cover him; the willows of the brook surround him."

In KHW, Chap. 7, Steiner says, "Only developed lotus flowers make it possible for manifestations not derived from the physical world to be imprinted [in our dream life the way sense impressions previously were]. And then the etheric body, when developed, brings full knowledge concerning these engraved impressions derived from other worlds." It is thus the etheric body that brings us true messages from the spiritual world. If we look at **I-19**, we can see that humanity has progressed from the Cultural Age of the Bull (Taurus) through that of the Lamb (Aries) to the present Fish (Pisces) and that approximately half way through the 3,000-year period of the Second Coming (as identified by Steiner), or A.D. 3574, it comes to the Waterman (Aquarius). It will be noted from **I-18** that Aquarius is associated with the etheric body. The etheric body is in a state of constant fluid motion, and its symbol is Water (cf. **I-22**, where the fourfold human being would be equated to the four elements as follows: Physical Body = Earth; Etheric Body = Water; Astral Body = Air; and Ego = Fire). Now consider Moses striking the rock and bringing forth water (Num 20,11); the Rock is identified by Paul as Christ (1 Cor 10,4) who brought forth Water and thus "showed himself holy among them" (Num 20,13; see also "Rock/Christ"). Moses was precluded from carrying the people on into their future "promised land" because his consciousness was the ancient clairvoyance (Num 20,12; see "Fading Splendor") and what is required to recognize Christ in the etheric world at the time of his Second Coming is the new clairvoyance made possible by the development of the etheric organs of perception. Of this, Paul could not yet speak in his time (Heb 9,5; also Heb 5,11 because Melchizedek had the etheric body of Shem and could thus minister to Abraham as the father of the Hebrew Folk).

Let us digress to consider this point. It is vital but generally unrecognized. We are in the age of the Consciousness Soul (A.D. 1414-3574), the parabolic mirror image, in the Prodigal Son's journey, of the age of Moses and the Sentient Soul (2907-747 B.C.); see (**I-19** and **I-24**). What was introduced during the descent of the human being in the Sentient Soul age must, since the Mystery of Golgotha, be again traversed but now so as to transform what was given earlier. The human being's "Three Bodies" must be transformed into their three spiritual counterparts, manas, buddhi and atma (**I-9**; see also Mt 13,33). This is what Paul undoubtedly refers to in the "manna, and Aaron's rod that budded, and the tables of the covenant" above which were the "cherubim of glory overshadowing the mercy seat (Heb 9,4-5). It, the age of the Intellectual Soul (**I-19** and **I-24),** was not the era for these things to be fully revealed to humanity (Paul having been "untimely born" in this respect [1 Cor 15,8]).

Thus, Paul concludes these cryptic remarks, "Of these things we cannot *now* speak in detail" (emphasis mine). I believe this statement cannot be divorced from the earlier passage (Heb 5,11) "About this we have much to say which is hard to explain since you have become dull of hearing." Heb 9,5 follows close upon the long discourse about Melchizedek (Heb 5-7), and it is in the introduction of the Melchizedek discourse that Paul says that he "has much to say which is hard to explain since you have become dull of hearing." He spoke of the "Fading Splendor" and knew that humanity was not prepared in that age (cf. Jn 16,12) to receive full understanding, save for its initiates, those with "faculties trained" (Heb 5,14; see "Mysteries"). What were these deep things about Melchizedek? Steiner has disclosed them in this Consciousness Soul age (cf. Jn 16,13). We saw something of this in "Spiritual Economy" above in the quotation from SE, Lect. 3. But in that lecture, Steiner spoke broadly only of Melchizedek as an essential teacher "for the continued progress of the Semitic culture." But this culture is broader than just its eventual Hebrew component. Abraham was blessed through Ishmael also. Still, it is through Isaac, the ancestor of the Hebrews, that the "covenant" was to be given (Gen 17,18-21; Heb 9,4). In short, it was through Isaac that the Christ was to be born who was to enable human salvation through "Perfect(ion)" of the "Three Bodies," of which Paul hinted in Heb 9,4. And Steiner, in SE, Lect. 2, identified Melchizedek, who bore the avatar-inhabited etheric body of Shem, as being sent for this mission:

In this same way, an exalted individuality had to make a strong personal effort to become one with Shem's etheric body to be able to give a definite impulse to the ancient Hebrew people. This personality was the very Melchizedek you find in Biblical history. In a way, he wore Shem's etheric body so that later he could give Abraham the impulse that you find so beautifully in the Bible. What was contained in the individuality of Shem was multiplied because an avatar being was incarnated in it, and all this became interwoven with all the other etheric bodies of the Hebrews. In addition, Shem's own etheric body was preserved in the spiritual world so that it could be borne at a later time by Melchizedek, who was to give the Hebrews an important impulse through Abraham.

It was Melchizedek who introduced into the Hebrew stream the sacrament of the bread and wine (Gen 14,18-20), the impulse which was to be perfected only by the breaking of the body of the Christ, that which was to offer redemption to all creation. Interestingly, as Noah (see "Spiritual Economy," fn 7) he was the first to plant a vineyard (Gen 9,20), and he "blessed" only his son Shem (Gen 9,26).

The book of Hebrews encountered much difficulty in entering the canon, for it alone, of Paul's extant writings, failed to identify itself as a letter to one of his churches or associates. For this and other reasons, doubt arose as to Paul's authorship. But all of such reasons disappear when it is realized that this "letter" was not to a "church" but to the Jews in dispersion to show them how Christ was the fulfillment of everything all the way back to their patriarchal ancestors and Melchizedek. Especially is this so when the depth of the mystery behind it is understood. It was a treatise no less. It also greatly aids in understanding all that was in Paul's heart as he agonized over the situation of the Jews in virtually the entire Letter to the Romans. We see the anxiety Paul felt for his own people from Rom 1,16 through Rom 11. See Rom 11,25-29:

> I want you to understand this mystery, brethren: a hardening has come upon part of Israel, until the full number of the Gentiles come in, and so all Israel will be saved;… For the gifts and the call of God are irrevocable.

Without understanding that, neither Romans nor Hebrews can be adequately comprehended, nor can any of it really be so without the understandings Steiner has brought to us. The "dullness" of Heb 5,11, the "hardening" of Rom 11,25, and the "Fading Splendor" of 2 Cor 3,13, all go to the same root which, until Steiner, has been darkened for humanity. It was the "hiding of the face of God" (see "Mysteries") of which Moses and the prophets spoke, presaged by the expulsion from the Garden (Gen 3,24) and the commitment of Cain to wandering the Earth in "Darkness" ("and from thy face I shall be hidden"; Gen 4,14).

Still the prophets spoke of the time when the new clairvoyance would return to humanity. And Jeremiah's version (Jer 31,31-34) of that new clairvoyance rang out again in Paul's treatise (Heb 10,15-16) as he fleshed out, as best he could in that darkened era, the ancient promise of which he had just spoken in Heb 9,5 and 5,11.

We can now return to the concept of moving water, which pervades the Old Testament (e.g., Gen 2,10-14; Ps 1,3), also John's Gospel. Christ tells the woman at the still well that he will give her "living water … which will become a spring in [her] welling up to eternal life" (Jn 4,10,14). Then in Jn 5,7 we see that the lame man at the pool cannot be healed until the water is made to move (how like what must happen with the "lotus flowers"). Later, Jesus appears to his disciples walking on the water (Jn 6,19, as well as all of the synoptics). And when his side was punctured, "blood and water" flowed out (Jn 19,34), both representative of the etheric body; also, the Ego first made its entrance into the human being's body through the blood. Consider as well that Moses came to Israel on the water (Ex 2,3-10), and while he was on the water the etheric body he had received from Zarathustra was illuminated (see "Spiritual Economy"). So also Zarathustra, in his many preparatory incarnations, came "on the water" (see *The Book With Fourteen Seals* [BFS]; also NHL, "The Apocalypse of Adam"). Other passages involving water come often to mind. Surely the part that water plays in bringing spiritual revelation in scripture can be seen to be full of deeper meaning considering that it is the esoteric symbol for the etheric body, which alone can begin to reveal the spiritual world to the human being. In a later volume, under "Storm/Water Launching," we will see how all the Biblical episodes of launching out upon water seem to relate directly to the stages the human soul traverses in the soul and spirit worlds between lives (see **I-33**).

In WW, Lect. 8, Steiner says, "What really do the blood circulation and the heart mean to us? They are the ether-world condensed, they are the densified forces of the etheric world!... The important and mysterious feature of Earth evolution is not only that this densification took place,... but that as regards each of our systems of organs in Earth evolution an impulse entered [i.e., via the Christ] whereby what was once etheric and had become physical, is once more dissolved, is changed back again into the ether." (Can we here but marvel that the etheric, or life, body is represented by the "Blood," which Moses also saw as being the "life" of all flesh? See Gen 9,4; Lev 17,11,14.)

Consider this passage from RCE, Lect. 9:

> When a man stands in front of us today in his waking state and we observe him with the clairvoyant eye, certain rays of light are seen streaming continually from the heart toward the head. If we wish to sketch this schematically, we must draw the region of the heart here and show the continuous streamings from there to the brain, flowing in the head around the organ known in anatomy as the pineal gland.

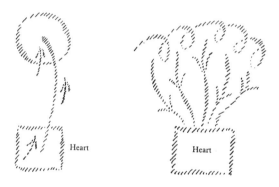

These rays of light stream from the heart to the head and flow around the pineal gland. These streamings arise because human blood, which is a physical substance, is continually dissolving itself into etheric substance. In the region of the heart there is a continual transformation of the blood into this delicate etheric substance that streams upward toward the head and flows glimmeringly around the pineal gland. This process, the etherization of the blood, can be shown in the human being throughout his waking life. It is different now, however, in the sleeping human being. When a human being sleeps, the occult observer is able to see a continual streaming from outside into the brain and also in the reverse direction, from the brain to the heart. These streams, however, which in sleeping man come from outside, from cosmic space, from the macrocosm, and flow into the inner constitution of the physical and etheric bodies … reveal something remarkable when they are investigated. These rays vary greatly in different individuals.

Moral qualities are revealed distinctly in the particular coloring of the streams that flow into human beings during sleep.... At the moment of waking or of going to sleep, a kind of struggle takes place in the region of the pineal gland between what streams down from above and what streams upward from below. When a man is awake, the intellectual element streams upward from below in the form of currents of light, and what is of moral-aesthetic nature streams downward from above. At the moment of waking or of going to sleep, these two currents meet, and in the man of low morality a violent struggle between the two streams takes place in the region of the pineal gland. In the man of high morality and an outstreaming intellectuality, a peaceful expansion of glimmering light appears in the region of the pineal gland. This gland is almost surrounded by a small sea of light in the moment between waking and sleeping. Moral nobility is revealed when a calm glow surrounds the pineal gland at these moments. In this way a man's moral character is reflected in him, and this calm glow of light often extends as far as the region of the heart. Two streams can therefore be perceived in man—one from the macrocosm, the other from the microcosm.

Before we relate this more precisely to the Blood of Christ, let us see also the parallel remarks on this process from WW, Lect. 8:

For clairvoyant sight something streams continuously out of our heart—our heart, the outcome of our blood circulation. If you see clairvoyantly the blood pulsating through the human body, then you also see how this blood becomes rarefied again in the heart, how in its finest elements—not in its coarser, but in its finer parts—it is dissolved and returns to the etheric form. Just as the blood has gradually been formed in the ether, so in the human body of the present day we have the reverse process. The blood becomes etherized, and streams of ether flow continuously from the heart towards the head, so that we see the etheric body built up in an opposite direction by way of the blood. Thus what crystallized out from the etheric during the early part of Lemuria to form the human blood circulation and the heart we now see returning to the etheric form and streaming in the human etheric body towards the brain.... [He here relates this process also to our thinking.] These etheric currents are indirectly related to a delicate and important part of the human brain called the pineal gland. They continuously lave the pineal gland, which becomes luminous and its movements as physical brain-organ respond in harmony with these etheric currents emanating from the heart.... So you see we have not only a process within the Earth which leads to solidification, but also a reverse process of rarefaction.

Continuing from RCE, Lect 9:

Just as in the region of the human heart the blood is continually being transformed into etheric substance, so a similar process takes place in the macrocosm. We understand this when we turn our eyes to the Mystery of Golgotha, to the moment when the blood flowed from the wounds of Jesus Christ. This blood must not be regarded simply as chemical substance, but by reason of all that has been described as the nature of Jesus of Nazareth, it must be recognized as something altogether unique. When it flowed from His wounds and into the earth, a substance was imparted to our earth which, in uniting with it, constituted an event of the greatest possible significance for all future ages of the earth, and it could take place only once. What happened with this blood in the ages that followed? Nothing different from what otherwise takes place in the heart of man. In the course of earthly evolution, this blood passed through a process of "etherization." Just as our blood streams upward from the heart as ether, so, since the Mystery of Golgotha, the etherized blood of Christ Jesus has lived in the ether of the earth. The etheric body of the earth is permeated by what the blood that flowed on Golgotha became. This is important. If what has thus come to pass through Christ Jesus had not taken place, man's condition on the earth could only have been as previously described. Since the Mystery of

Golgotha, however, there has existed the continuous possibility for the activity of the etheric blood of Christ to flow together with the streamings from below upward, from heart to head.

Because the etherized blood of Jesus of Nazareth is present in the etheric body of the earth, it accompanies the etherized human blood streaming upward from the heart to the brain, so that not only do these streams that I described earlier meet in man, but the human bloodstream unites with the bloodstream of Christ Jesus. A union of these two streams can come about, however, only if man is able to unfold true understanding of what is contained in the Christ impulse. Otherwise, there can be no union; the two streams then mutually repel each other, thrust each other away. In every age of earthly evolution, we must acquire understanding in the form suitable for that epoch. At the time when Christ Jesus lived on earth, preceding events could be rightly understood by those who came to His forerunner, John, and were baptized by him.... The evolution of humanity progresses, however, and in our present age it is important that man should learn to understand that the knowledge contained in spiritual science must be received and gradually be able so to fire the stream flowing from heart to brain that anthroposophy can be understood. If this comes to pass, individuals will be able to comprehend the event that has its beginning in the twentieth century: the appearance of the etheric Christ in contradistinction to the physical Christ of Palestine.

We have now reached the moment in time when the etheric Christ enters into the life of the earth and will become visible, at first to a small number of people, through a natural clairvoyance. Then in the course of the next 3,000 years, He will become visible to greater and greater numbers of people.

In the rest of the lecture, Steiner elaborates how the Maitreya Buddha will lead humanity to a fuller understanding of Christ, but the conditions will then be quite different from now. That will be in the Age of Philadelphia (Rev 3,7-13; see **I-25**, **I-24** and **I-19**). Our present Cultural Age will end about one millennium before that. The "Coming" of Christ, however, may be said to commence with the etheric and then move into even higher worlds. ECMCR, Lect. 7 (11-18-11), pp. 110-111, breaks down the progressively greater cognition of Christ as follows:

Age	World	Spiritual Cognition	Cultural Age
Intellectual	Etheric	See (Light ether)	Fifth (Present)
Feeling	Astral	Hear (Sound ether)	Sixth
Morality	Spirit	Understand (Life ether)	Seventh

Thus the three progressive levels of comprehension expressed in Is 6,9-10 will become actuality for "a number of human beings." However, while the matter is not entirely clear from what is said in ECMCR, it would appear to be proper to refer to each of these levels of perception as still involving also the etheric world, for that world is composed of all four of the different levels of ether. In *The Festivals of the Seasons* (FESTS), Lect. 14 (January 2, 1916), "Perceiving and Remembering," Steiner states, "Let us now recall that the etheric body of man naturally consists of the different kinds of ether which we have learned to distinguish. We recognize these as consisting of warmth-ether, light-ether, chemical-ether (by which the music of the spheres is communicated) and life-ether." He goes on to show how the "light body," i.e., "light-etheric body," is the one that enables our memory. It is also the "light-etheric body" that, when freed from the physical body upon death, gives the human being its brief (approximately three-day) panoramic view of the entire life just passed.

We may here recall from "The Nativity" how the Nathan Jesus child of Luke's Gospel bore the unspoiled etheric body that had been withheld from Adam as the "tree of life" (Gen 3,22-24). In *The Apocalypse of St. John* (ASJ), Lect. 9, Steiner tells us:

> And now let us consider what it is that man will contribute as the expression of his own Christ-capacity. It is the same that hovered before Paul in spirit, and that he calls "the last Adam," while he calls the first man who entered into existence in a physically visible body "the first Adam." At the end of the Lemurian epoch we already find various animals below, but man is not yet visible to external eyes; he is still etheric. He condenses, he absorbs mineral constituents and appears in his first form; the physical man gradually appears, just as water condenses into ice. Physical evolution then proceeds so far that what is earthly can dissolve and eventually disappears. Hence the man who has the etheric body appears as the "last Adam." The "first Adam" has the capacity of seeing the earth in the physical body

through the physical senses; the "last Adam," who assumes a spiritual body, is an expression of the inner Christ-capacity. Hence Christ is also called by Paul the "last Adam" [1 Cor 15,45; Rom 5, 12-14].

In the same lecture, we see that Lazarus/John, when he speaks of "heads and horns" in the Apocalypse, is using esoteric language to describe the etheric and physical bodies, respectively (Rev 13,1). We shall explore that further in the Commentary on the Apocalypse.

In *The Gospel of St. Mark* (GSMk), Lect. 9, Steiner looks at a statement of Christ found in the "Little Apocalypse" passages, "And then if any one says to you, 'Look, here is the Christ!' or 'Look, there he is!' do not believe it" (Mk 13,21; also Mt 24,23 and Lk 17,20-21). The implication is that one cannot "look" and see the Christ in the manner humanity saw him before and now "sees," but can see him upon his return only by understanding his nature at that time. Then he will descend only as low as the etheric world, where one shall "see" him only with spiritual vision—as was the case of those who witnessed his Resurrection. Steiner says much the same thing in *The Gospel of St. Matthew* (GSMt), Lect. 11, in discussing the meaning of "His body" and "His blood" at the last supper—that Christ was saying to his disciples that "they will recognize Christ more and more clearly as the Being who fills all spiritual space and was imaged in Jesus of Nazareth." Because Christ's etheric body inheres now in the entirety of our Earth, we do indeed "eat" his body and "drink" his blood when we partake of "bread and wine." In recognizing the fact of his etheric existence we help to bring him into our being.

Christ's etheric presence in all of earthly creation after his death also gives meaning to another series of his remarks as related in John's Gospel, where he says, "I go to the Father" (Jn 16,10,17,28 and 20,17). In discussing the experience of the human being in ancient days (and still faintly at the time of Christ) upon passing through the gate of physical death, Steiner says that one knew, "My etheric body is going to the Father" (*Karmic Relationships, Vol. 3* [KR-3], Lect. 5, p. 74). But we should probably not fully equate Christ's "I go to the Father" with the ancient feeling "My etheric body goes to the Father," for in the former we would seem to be dealing with the highest pinnacle of the heavenly world (especially in the case of Christ), while in the latter we are involved in the etheric world or that aspect of the Father that manifests in living Nature. We cannot here pursue in depth this distinction. It will be appropriate to do so in the Commentary and under the term "Death (Sin/Father)." That Christ remains etherically connected with the Earth while also with the highest heaven is in keeping with the fully expanded nature of the human soul at the "Midnight" hour in its journey from one incarnation to another; see **I-33** and the discussion of this journey in the overview portion of "Karma and Reincarnation" above.

The greater the scope of one's understanding of the etheric world, the more readily will one be able to comprehend how it is that the Second Coming will commence there. New insights into that world are strewn through all of Steiner's teachings.[4] In addition to what is said about the etheric body in *Theosophy* (THSY) and *Occult Science* (OS), many insights can be gained from the various Charts & Tabulations. In particular, note **I-22**, where the etheric world is seen to have a fourfold origin, namely, warmth (fire), light, chemical (or sound), and Life, in ascending order. Steiner tells us (*The Gospel of St. Luke* [GSL], Lect. 7) that the "tree of knowledge" of which the human being partook was composed of the two lower ethers (warmth and light), while the "tree of life," which was withdrawn from the human being (Gen 3,22-24), was composed of the two higher (Sound and Life). That Christ represents the "Life" suggests that through him the human being may again attain to that etheric realm (Jn 14,6).

Steiner often spoke of the Buddha, the Maitreya Buddha, and the various "ages" (e.g., 5,000-year, etc.; see **I-46**), which are generally thought of as coming to us from the Orient. We have seen the part the Buddha played in the Luke Nativity account (see "The Nativity"), and we know that the Bible's roots are out of "the East" (Gen 11,2; Mt 2,1). Somehow or other, elements within Christendom today would like to forget that, or at least to view its spiritual significance as having been erased by the New Covenant in Christ. But one fails to understand the Christ if such element is removed, for it was the soil out of which the entire Incarnation developed, and its people are among those for whom the Christ came.

---

4. Excellent references include EBPHB, *The Etheric Body as a Reflection of the Universe* (EBRU), *The Weaving and Living Activity of the Human Etheric Bodies* (WLA), *Luciferic and Ahrimanic Influences/Influences of the Dead* (LAI) and *The Driving Force of Spiritual Powers in World History* (DFSP), Lect. 6, stressing the "living" nature (the etheric body being the "life" body). One of the best single expositions on the etheric body is undoubtedly the booklet, *The Etheric Body* (EB) by Otto Wolff, M.D. SE is also a necessity for understanding how the etheric body of highly developed human beings can be used for the benefit of humanity.

What these elements of Christendom do not understand is that this ancient Oriental knowledge was not confined, even at that time, to the Orient, but was an experience of all humanity, the ancestry of the West included. Today, the myths are looked upon with folly, but in the light of anthroposophy they can be seen to reflect truths about the evolution of the human being. (See **I-58**, **I-63** and **I-85**.)

Because the Greek Prometheus myth illustrates much about the etheric body, let us look at how it reflects the same knowledge in the West (Greece) as what came down to us from the Orient. (Closely connected to this line of thinking is what has come down to us even more recently from Plato about the creation in *Timaeus* and *Critias*, as to which see Cognate Writings, Vol. 3.) The following is taken from ECM, Lect. 7:

> When the ancient Persian epoch [**I-19**, **I-24** and **I-25**] was drawing to its close and the next period was glimmering like a dawn of the future, men felt: "We shall no longer be able to experience with such intensity the Divine heritage that has come to us from the olden days of Atlantis, when with their power of inner, clairvoyant vision, men lived in communion with the worlds of Divine Spirit." ... The gaze was turned *back to the past*. What mattered most for these men were their remembrances in which living pictures arose like dreams— dreams of how the Gods had fashioned the world through the ages of Lemuria and Atlantis. They felt that these remembrances were withdrawing, were fading away from humanity and that conditions were approaching when man must work with a faculty which tells him of the outer world, clouds the bright light of the inner world of the Spirit, and compels him to look from within-outwards, if he is to master the external world. This age was drawing nearer and nearer. Those who had the deepest, clearest perception of the dawn of the new epoch were men who at that time were the knowers and sages in ancient India. They felt it in the form, as it were, of a Divine Impulse, compelling the human being to think for himself, through inner activity, about what confronts him in the physical world to which he was descending. Picturing this Impulse as a Divine Being, the successors of the first, very ancient Indian culture—those who were living now during the Second Post-Atlantean epoch—called this Being "Pramathesis." These men felt: "The God Pramathesis is drawing near, snatching human beings away from the guidance given by the

ancient Gods; God Pramathesis is causing the disappearance of all that ancient clairvoyance revealed concerning the world and is forcing man to look outwards, into the physical plane. Darkness is creeping over the world of the ancient Gods. A time is approaching when in their life of soul men will no longer be able to gaze into the world of the Gods, but when their eyes will be turned to the outer world. Kaliyuga, the 'Black Age' is approaching; the bright age of ancient Divinity is giving place to the age when the Gods of old withdraw. It is the age inaugurated by the God Pramathesis!" [**I-46**}.

Kaliyuga was said to begin at a time which lies 3,101 years before our own era—this is the time of the "Flood" according to Indian tradition. [This fits the time frame of the familiar Gilgamish epic; see "Interlude for Steiner Individuality" in Cognate Writings, Vol. 3.] For it was said that the Flood coincides with the coming of Kaliyuga, and Kaliyuga was conceived to be the offspring of the God "Pramathesis."

Kaliyuga broke in upon the world, reaching its close in our own age. Now that the ascent to the spiritual world must begin, a spiritual science has come to mankind. Kaliyuga began 3,101 years before our era, and ended in the year A.D. 1899. That is why 1899 is a year of such importance. The re-ascent to the spiritual worlds—this must be the ideal of the future.

The age preceding the onset of Kaliyuga was, however, an age characteristic of the ancient Persian epoch when the old remembrances rose up within man via the astral body. Now he was to turn to the world outside. This was a great and epoch-making transition. In the case of many human beings it came about in such a way that for a time all vision departed from them and darkness spread over their souls. This condition of darkness did not last for long periods, actually only for weeks. But men passed into this condition of sleep, and many never came out of it. Many of them perished and only relatively few were left in widely scattered regions. There is not enough time today to describe the conditions actually prevailing at that time. It can only be said briefly that owing to so large a number of human beings having succumbed, conditions were dark and sinister in the extreme and at only a few scattered places did men awaken from the great spiritual deluge that spread over their souls like a sleep. This condition of sleep was felt by most souls as a kind

of "drowning" and by only a few as a re-awakening. And then came
the "Black Age," the age devoid of the Gods.

Were these things known to other human beings on the Earth?
They were indeed. To our astonishment we find widespread evidence of knowledge among the peoples that a deluge had submerged the consciousness of men and that in the Third Post-
Atlantean epoch, through the development of the sentient soul—
in other words, outward-turned vision—an entirely new power
must have been inaugurated. The Indians divined this when they
said: Kaliyuga is the offspring of Pramathesis. And what did the
Greeks say? In Greece, "Pramathesis" becomes, "Prometheus"—
which is exactly the same. Prometheus is the brother of
Epimetheus. The latter represents one who still "looks back" into
ancient times. Epimetheus is the one whose thoughts turn backward; Prometheus sends his thoughts forward, to the world outside, to what takes place there.[5] Just as Pramathesis has his
offspring in Kaliyuga, so, too, Prometheus has his offspring. The
Greek form of "Kaliyuga" is "Kalion." And because the Greeks felt
it to be the age of Darkness, the "d" is prefixed and the word becomes "Deukalion"[6]—which is really the same word as "Kaliyuga."
This is not ingenious fancy, but an occult fact. It is clear, therefore,
that the Greeks possessed the same knowledge as the Indian sages.
This is quoted merely as an example, indicating that in their conditions of old clairvoyance, knowledge of these truths came to men
and they were able to express them in majestic pictures. The Greek
legend tells how, on the advice of his father Prometheus, Deukalion builds a wooden chest; in this he and his wife Pyrrha alone
are saved from destruction, when Zeus proposes to exterminate the
human race by a deluge. Deukalion and Pyrrha land on Parnasus,
and from them issues the new human race. Deukalion is the son of
Prometheus—and in the intervening period comes the flood, de-
noting among manifold peoples, a *condition of consciousness.*

---

5. 9 Brit 727, "Prometheus," tells us that Prometheus means "Forethinker" while
Epimetheus, his brother, means "Hindsight."—ERS
6. WNWD says, for Deucalion, that it is from the Greek word *Deukalion,* who, according
to Greek Mythology, was "a son of Prometheus and husband of Pyrrha, with whom he
survived a great flood sent by Zeus and became the ancestor of all succeeding mankind."—ERS

These wonderful pictures which have been preserved in the traditions of so many of the peoples, show us how truths concerning the evolution of humanity have survived among them.[7]

As men lived on gradually into the age of Kaliyuga, into the Third Post-Atlantean epoch, the ancient clairvoyant knowledge faded away [see "Fading Splendor"]. We who have to recapitulate the Third epoch, must bring this kind of knowledge to life once again, but in an entirely new form. The lecture given a fortnight ago (The Idea of Reincarnation and its Introduction into Western Culture) dealt with this subject. Western culture, the beginnings of which were mingled with the ancient Hebrew culture, has to concentrate primary attention on the single personality living on the physical plane between birth and death; Western culture cannot focus its main attention on the Individuality who passes through the different epochs but concentrates upon the existence of the one personality [Heb 9,27], whose life between birth and death runs its course on the physical plane, not in the higher worlds. Now that Kaliyuga has come to an end, consciousness must be imbued with the forces necessary for the further evolution of the human race; what was lost during Kaliyuga must be raised again from the depths. Our eyes must be directed more and more to the onflowing life of the Individuality. I have spoken of a series of lives in the West—Elijah, John the Baptist, Raphael, Novalis—and have shown how by the addition of knowledge derived from the spiritual worlds, we can perceive the continuous thread of the soul, the onflowing life of the one Individuality in Elijah, John the Baptist, Raphael, Novalis. [See "Novalis" in Cognate Writings, Vol. 3.]

---

7. This lecture magnificently clarifies what had seemed to be a discrepancy between the time of the Atlantean Flood (ca. 10,000 B.C.), which was the basis for the Biblical Noah account, and other traditions, such as the Babylonian Gilgamish Epic which corresponded with this Kali Yuga darkening of consciousness (3,101 B.C.) above described. To corroborate this reconciliation, see Plato's *Timaeus* in the Cognate Writings section, Vol. 3. In the opening portions of *Timaeus*, which speak of Solon's consultation with the priests of Egypt, Solon relates how, "wishing to draw them on," he told them "the most ancient things" in the Greek world, including "Phoroneus, ... 'the first man,' ... and after the Deluge, of the survival of Deucalion and Pyrrha."

To this, the priest responds, "O Solon, Solon, you Hellenes are never anything but children, and there is not an old man among you." In the following paragraph, the priest says, "those genealogies of yours ... are no better than the tales of children (for among other things) you remember a single deluge only, *but there were many previous ones.*"— ERS (Emphasis mine)

In our Movement, development of this insight must be a *conscious* aspiration, for it is a necessity in the evolution and culture of the Earth. No progress would be possible by the mere continuation of the old experiences, the old knowledge. I have emphasized often enough all that it means for the minds of men to enrich and make fruitful the heritage of ancient times by means of the new knowledge now available. It must, however, be realized that just as the transition from life inspired by the astral body to a spiritual life of soul, primarily in the sentient soul, was fraught with deep significance, so, now, we must work our way from life in the consciousness soul to life in the Spirit Self [see **I-24**, **I-25** and **I-19**]. I have intimated how this will take place by saying that during the next three thousand years, an increasing number of human beings will experience the Appearance of the Christ Impulse, will be able to experience the Christ Impulse in the spiritual worlds.

The general thrust of the above passage appeared frequently in Steiner's works. For instance, in GSL, Lect. 2, he said, "Perception of man's etheric body was quite usual in the Graeco-Latin age; numbers of people were able to see the human head surrounded by an etheric cloud that has gradually become entirely concealed within the head." But few passages elaborate it in a manner quite so appropriate for this juncture of our consideration.

We may now look at Joseph's special powers of interpretation as a holdover of this ancient clairvoyance. And we would seem to be quite justified in looking at his interpretation of Pharaoh's dream of "seven years of great plenty ... [followed by] seven years of famine [during which] all the plenty will be forgotten ... [and] unknown in the land by reason of that famine ..." (Gen 41,29-31) as a description of this loss of consciousness which led "Pharaoh [to] select a man discreet and wise, and set him over the land of Egypt" (Gen 41,33). On an even higher spiritual level the story is illustrative of the cycle of life, or wheel of birth. In advising Pharaoh to set aside grain during the good time, it is not unlike Jesus' admonition in the Sermon on the Mount (Mt 6,19-20) to "lay up for yourselves treasures in heaven."

A spine-tingling experience can reward one willing to delve into the matter of the physical body/etheric body correspondence to the tree of knowledge/tree of life (Gen 3,22-24), in recognizing that these can be seen to be demonstrated respectively by the Greek letters *Phi* and *Theta*.

Phi is the "Golden Ratio," observed by Plato, by which the pyramid, the human body, and perhaps most all of physical creation are made (*Universe, Earth and Man* [UEM], Lect. 1, pp. 14, 17 and 19; EB, p. 6). *Theta* represents the ellipse which describes the Parable of the Prodigal Son, the outgoing and return, the journey of each human soul. In support of this, see Appendix to "Fire" in Vol. 2.

Now let us look briefly at the myth of Prometheus. It has deep esoteric meaning that speaks of profound truths in the human being's evolution. Steiner often spoke of Prometheus. See *Greek and Germanic Mythology in the Light of Esotericism* (GGMLE), Lect. 1; *The Temple Legend* (TL), Lect. 4; CMF, Chap. 5; *The Influence of Spiritual Beings Upon Man* (ISBM), Lect. 1; and *Egyptian Myths & Mysteries* (EMM), Lect. 10. See also Otto Wolff's EB, pp. 9-11. The myth portrays the human being of the Fifth "Root-Race" (see **I-4**) of Earth evolution, i.e., our present post-Atlantean Epoch. Its allegorical portrayal extensively corresponds with the evolutionary facts as anthroposophy has given them. Prometheus, who steals fire (Ego) and brings it down to Earth, is chained to a rock (mineral-physical body). An eagle comes daily to gnaw at his liver, which is restored each night. Quoting Wolff, "The organ which creates life is the liver. Life—liver (*Leben—Leber* in German). The relationship of these two words is found in many languages. The liver produces life." As such it represents the life body, i.e., the etheric body. The eagle represents the astral body which, by virtue of its primeval taint (Gen 3), gnaws at the etheric body through lack of control of passions and desires, the "animals" human beings brought with them in the "Ark" from Atlantis (Gen 6,19-7,3). Each night, the etheric body is restored by sleep. Hercules, who prevails in the twelve labors of initiation, presses through to the Caucasus (the rock) in order to free Prometheus, but the centaur Chiron, man's half-animal (astral) nature (see "Wild Animals"), has to be sacrificed before Prometheus is free.

This mythical legend is but one of many from the ancient Western world that portray profound evolutionary truth.[8] Today, humanity has totally lost its comprehension of these myths. This legend shows the

---

8. It is well here to take note of what is said about "myths" in 2 Pet 1,16; 1 Tim 1,4 and 4,7; 2 Tim 4,4 and Tit 1,14. 2 Pet, in particular, is generally looked upon by scholars as having been written "in the name of" and not by "Peter," and to a considerable extent the same view is held of the so-called "pastoral" letters (i.e., Tim and Tit) in Paul's name. 2 Pet 1,16 says, "For we did not follow cleverly devised myths when we made known to you the power and coming of our Lord Jesus Christ, but we were eyewitnesses of his majesty."

necessity of the Ego (the Christ-enabled "I Am") overcoming the tainted
astral nature in order to set the human being free. When the etheric body
is thus freed, it can see the truth in the spiritual world, and that is freedom
(Jn 8,32) as Prometheus finally attained it. For our present purposes,
what the etheric body is to see in the etheric world is the Second Coming
of Christ.

When all of the above, taken in connection with the other related
terms identified early herein, is carefully considered, one can see that not
only is the etheric nature of the Second Coming compatible with the pertinent scriptural passages, but indeed its understanding clarifies what has
heretofore been mystifying about them. Such passages include at least the
following: Mt 16,28; 24-25; 26,64; Mk 13; 14,62; Lk 12,40; 17,20-21
(The "Little Apocalypse"); Jn 14,3,28; 21,22-23; Acts 1,11; 1 Cor 15,23;
16,22; 1 Th 2,19; 3,13; 4,15; 5,2,23; 2 Th 2,1-2; Heb 9,28; 10,37; Jas
5,7-8; 2 Pet 3,4,10,12; Rev 2,16,25; 3,3,11; 22,7,12,20.

At the same time that such understanding clarifies the Second Coming
passages, it also greatly clarifies Christ's appearances to the disciples after
the Resurrection itself. For among other things, Acts 1,11, "This Jesus
... will come in the same way as you saw him go into heaven," clearly tends
to equate the nature of his first appearances to that of his Second Coming.
And the accounts of his first appearances (given that passages such as Lk
24,43, Jn 21,13 and Jn 20,27 are otherwise explained herein) give clear
indication that his Resurrection, while in the "body," was in the non-min-
eral "physical body," the "phantom form," requiring a higher clairvoyance
as above indicated (see "Form/Phantom"), as well as in the etheric "body"

---

8. (*continued*) No claim is made that such "myths" are false, but merely "clever," a description that could well be explained by the darkening of consciousness which had, by
then, set in. After all, 2 Pet 3,4 speaks of "ever since the fathers fell asleep," presumably
referring to the Apostolic Fathers. And it finds it hard to understand what Paul meant in
many of his letters (2 Pet 3,15-16). While the passages in the pastoral letters refer more
disparagingly to "myths," in one case as being "godless and silly" (1 Tim 4,7), these again
can be reconciled, in their case not only by the darkening of consciousness but also by the
widening scope of Gnosticism. While there is much from Gnosticism reflected in scripture as truth, as in the Gospel of John (which doubtless influenced the lateness of its acceptance into the canon), it is also true that on a wider fringe of Gnosticism as it was
developing there were things that conflicted with the truth of the Gospel message, most
especially that the Christ had not actually incarnated in the flesh in Jesus of Nazareth. In
regard to Gnosticism, it is helpful to consider the writings of Welburn, namely, *The Beginnings of Christianity* (BC), *Gnosis* (GNOS) and BFS, as well as Robinson's NHL and
the early and popular Pagels, *The Gnostic Gospels*, Vintage, NY, 1979, 1981.

(see **I-9**). Thus, we are told of his appearances at impractically diversified spots (see SE), such as on a "mountain" (Mt 28,16; see "Mountain"); that he is "with you always, to the close of the age" (Mt 28,20); that his appearance was "in another form" (Mk 16,12); that "after he had spoken with them, [he] was taken up into heaven" (Mk 16,19; Lk 24,51); that they did not at first recognize him (Lk 24,16; Jn 20,15; Jn 20,24-28; Jn 21,4,12); that they did not recognize him until "their eyes were opened [after which] he vanished out of their sight" (Lk 24,31), to immediately appear in the presence of several, who were "startled and frightened, and supposed that they saw a spirit" (Lk 24,36-37); that he entered their presence through "shut doors" (Jn 20,19); that others than the disciples could not "see" him (Acts 9,7) and even Paul, "when his eyes were opened, ... could see nothing" (Acts 9,8); and that he appeared to Paul even after he had "ascended," many had "fallen asleep," and Paul had persecuted the Church (1 Cor 15,6-9).

The path to etheric vision is not an easy one, nor will it be walked by many as initiates (Mt 7,13-14). What is vital in our time is that correct thinking begin to mold humanity toward that day when failure to recognize the Christ in the etheric world will mean slipping toward the abyss. Regrettably, the "Faith of Our Fathers," and that "Old Time Religion," both "Epimethean" (backward looking), cannot prevent such slippage unless revitalized by these profound insights. And Heb 9,27, so relied upon to disprove karma and reincarnation, can prove to be a double-edged sword against those who so rely. For indeed, what is done in "one life" is of vital importance: the right Path must be taken during one's life on Earth if the organs of spiritual perception are to be timely developed. Conditions will not be the same in future lives, and talents not properly used will be lost (Mt 25,14-30), requiring even greater struggle ahead. Efforts properly directed will bear rich and transformed fruit, but one must not be afraid to follow Abraham's lead in this generation if one is to be fruitful, leaving the "house" that one has known, bound for "the land that I will show you" (Mt 19,29; Gen 12,1). Let us be about the task.

"I Am"

Surely no word or phrase is less understood, nor more critical to comprehension of the Bible story, than "I am." Scripturally, we first encounter it in Ex 3 where God reveals to Moses that "I Am" is his "Name" (emphasis added):

> (6) And he said, "*I am* the God of your father, the God of Abraham, the God of Isaac, and the God of Jacob." (13) Then Moses said to God, "If I come to the people of Israel and say to them, 'The God of your fathers has sent me to you,' and they ask me, 'What is his *name?*' what shall I say to them?" (14) God said to Moses, "*I AM THE*[1] *I AM.*" And he said, "Say this to the people of Israel, [the][2] '*I AM* has sent me to you.'" (15) God also said to Moses, "Say this to the people of Israel, 'The LORD, the God of your fathers, the God of Abraham, the God of Isaac, and the God of Jacob, has sent me to you': *this is my name for ever*, and thus [the] *I am* [is] to be remembered throughout all generations...."

---

1. The very diversity of interpretation on this "word" which joins the two "*I Am's*" is an indication of the darkness that has thus far precluded understanding of its meaning. Accordingly, the interpretation here used is that of Steiner, a meaning that, as we shall see, adds luster and depth to, and is thus vindicated by, every scriptural usage thereof. The "diversity" otherwise existing is reflected in the following usages (in alphabetical order, quotation marks omitted and connecting word[s] emphasized, and footnote references indicated by "Fn"):

AB (1965): I AM *WHO* I AM *and WHAT* I AM, *and* I WILL BE *WHAT* I WILL BE.

AB: (Exodus volume yet to be published).

CEV (1995): I am *the eternal God.*

  Fn—Since it ["Yahweh"] seems related to the word translated "I am," it may mean "I am *the one who is*" or "I will be what I will be" or "I am *the one who brings into being.*"

Interp (1952): (uses and compares both the KJV and RSV interpretations, see below).

KJV (1611): I AM *THAT* I AM. *(continued on following page)*

One cannot understand the Mystery of Golgotha without first coming to see that this passage discloses the Mosaic equivalent of the maxim that contemporaneously graced the portal through which every candidate for initiation into the ancient Mysteries had to pass, namely, "Know Thyself." Moses himself had been initiated into the Mysteries of Egypt (Ex 2,3-10) and of Midian (Ex 2,15-22). (See "Mysteries," as well as *Christianity as Mystical Fact* [CMF]). In this passage God has "hidden his face" (again, see "Mysteries") for some three millennia now (e.g., Deut 32,20; Ps 13,1, etc.) By understanding this, one can see a clear parallel between the plaintive cry "How long, O Lord?" in Ps 13,1 and that in Is 6,11. One can also come to understand more clearly the role that Moses played, he whose glory Paul called a "Fading Splendor."

---

1. (*continued*) <u>LB</u> (1971): (This version does not purport to be a literal translation, being guided instead by "the theological lodestar [of] a rigid evangelical position." By that standard, its preferred translation is simply, "The Sovereign God." The first clause in its footnote says, "Or, 'the Living God.'" Only the balance of its footnote purports to be a literal translation, as follows.)

Fn—Literally, "I am *what* I am," or, "I will be *what* I will be."

<u>NACB</u> (1970): I am *who* am.

Fn—apparently this utterance is the source of the word *Yahweh*, the proper personal name of the God of Israel. It is commonly explained in reference to God as the absolute and necessary Being. It may be understood of God as the Source of all created beings. Out of reverence for this name, the term *Adonai*, "my Lord," was later used as a substitute. The word LORD in the present version represents this traditional usage. The word "Jehovah" arose from a false reading of the name as it is written in the current Hebrew text.

<u>NIV</u> (1984): I AM *WHO* I AM.

Fn—Or "I *WILL BE WHAT* I *WILL BE.*

<u>NJB</u> (1985): I am *he* who *is.*

<u>NKJV</u> (1982): I AM *WHO* I AM.

<u>NRSV</u> (1990): (same as RSV, see below).

<u>RSV</u> (1952): I AM *WHO* I AM.

Fn—Or I AM *WHAT* I AM or I WILL BE *WHAT* I WILL BE.

2. This and the succeeding parenthetical additions in this and following Biblical quotes seem necessary to carry forward Steiner's meaning reflected in fn 1. Starting with the many "I am" passages in Isaiah, the reader will be left to see the meanings involved without the tiring interruptions of the text by these additions. A reader may well at first object, "Obviously God in these passages must refer to himself as 'I am' like we all do—it doesn't imply anything esoteric about it." True, but this ignores the difficulties involved in passing manuscripts and translations down through the ages when consciousness was darkening so that the original meanings are not reflected by leaving out the insertions (presumably the existence of these grammatical insertions in our language would have been merely matters of interpretation of the Hebrew). More importantly, it ignores the many powerful scriptural indications discussed herein that the "Name" of the Christ (who, as we shall see, is clearly the speaker in these passages) is the higher "I am."

This passage, "I AM *THE* I AM," can be understood only when it is seen that Moses stood at the critical point in human evolution when the Ego was making its transition from *group* or *tribal* soul to *individual* soul. Moses himself was gifted with the ancient and atavistic clairvoyance, and could not bring himself fully into the era of the developing "I Am"; hence he could not fully recognize it in the wilderness (Ex 17,6; Num 20,11-12; Deut 32; 1 Cor 10,4).

The transitional nature of the revelation is indicated by Ex 6,2-3:

> (2) And God said to Moses, "[the] *I am* [is] the LORD. (3) [It, the] *I* [Am,] appeared to Abraham, to Isaac, and to Jacob, as God Almighty [El Shaddai], but by my *name* [I Am, or] the LORD I did not make myself known to them."

While heretofore the "name" that was pronounced has been considered to be "Yahweh," it should now be realized that while it was indeed the Eloha Yahweh speaking, he here *names* himself by the "*Name*," "*I Am*." "I Am" is what Moses is instructed to call him in Ex 3,14, "Say this to the people of Israel, '[the] I Am has sent me to you'." The Elohim are the primary rulers of Earth evolution (see **I-16**). From *Occult Science* (OS) we know that the Eloha Yahweh went with the Moon when it separated from the Earth. As such he was a "moon God," and there is much documentation of this in the Hebrew tradition; but in the service of the Christ he reflected the spiritual light of Christ so that the name "I Am" was his name as a representative of the Christ (see **I-7**). We know that the Christ multifariously identified himself as the "I Am" in John's Gospel and that this *name* is identified in Revelation as that of the redeemed. We shall see that this is the *name* pointed to by Isaiah in the suffering servant passages (for Isaiah "saw his glory and spoke of him," Jn 12,41). And with this Steiner-enabled understanding of God's *name* it is also possible, as we shall see, to come to deep new insight into the meaning of Paul's "Not I but Christ *in* me" (Gal 2,20) and to see that the proper preposition in Gal 1,16 is the more literal Greek *in* and not *to*.[3]

---

3. The confusion on this little word is indicated by the following tally of its usages: "in" is used only by KJV, NIV, NJB and NKJV; "within" is used by AMPB, LB and PMEB; "to" is used by NACB, RSV and NRSV, although RSV and NRSV both show by footnote that the Greek is literally "in"; "to me and through me" is used by NEB; and "to show me his Son" is used by CEV. The Exodus volume of AB is not published.

And Paul makes it clear that the *name* referred to in Ex 6,2-3 above, which also appeared incognito to Abraham, Isaac and Jacob, was the Christ, the "I Am" (1 Cor 10,1-4).

At this point, let us pause to reflect that there is a critical dual aspect to the *name* "I Am." To correspond with the dual nature of Adam (see "First and Second Adam") there must be a higher and a lower "I Am." Inasmuch as all humanity is infected by the Fall (Gen 3), the lower "I Am" is unable by itself to raise its three bodies to a state of purity equivalent to that of their pre-Fall status. The astral body that was infected in the Garden has, over time, spread its ailment into the denser etheric body and the latter, in turn, into the physical body, so that all our "members" (Rom 7,22,23) carry within them the effects of the original sin (which occurred through the Luciferic influence before the Ego had entered into humanity). It is the task of the young Ego (Job 32,4-6) to overcome this Luciferic infection, but due to its immaturity that young Ego is not equal to the task of overcoming the deeply ingrained consequences of the infection in the older and denser bodies. From "The Nativity" we saw how the unsullied etheric body of Adam, the part held back by the heavenly powers from the densification of the first Adam, became the "provisional Ego" of the Nathan Jesus child, until at age twelve the Ego of the Solomon Jesus child (which had been that of ancient Zarathustra) entered into it, to be replaced at age "Thirty" by the descending Christ Spirit at "Baptism." Its descent had been foreseen by the ancient Zarathustra in the Great Aura ("Ahura Mazda" or "Ormuzd") of the Sun, also by the Hebrew "fathers" and by Moses and Isaiah. The Christ Spirit is the "I Am" which speaks out in John's Gospel and in the Apocalypse, and it alone is strong enough to eventually cure the "Three Bodies" ("members") of their deeply ingrained consequences of sin. In Rom 7,22, Paul says that his "inmost self" delights "in the law of God" but is unable by itself to effect the cure of his other "members." But this "inmost self," or "Ego," which he correctly identifies as his "mind" (Rom 7,23, being the same as his "I" in verse 21), has a primeval relationship to that from which it sprang, namely, the Christ. It is for this reason that Paul can speak in both Gal 1,16 and 2,20 of the Christ (i.e., the "*I Am*") *in* him. By coming to a recognition and acceptance of that Christ, the pure "I Am," the human being's own Ego joins unto itself the power of that higher primeval Ego and thereby is enabled to heal the ages of infection of its lower three bodies or "members."

Here it is well to reflect upon the significance, of old, of one's "name." To this end, see "Name," "Name Change" and "NT Names." And for further light on the nature of the "*I Am*" see the meaning of "Bush."

While "Bush" appears later herein, the other terms will not be available until later. Since they relate so closely to the "I Am," a brief discussion of them at this point seems essential. Since the Middle Ages the significance of a "Name" has undergone such a change that in our modern time we have little understanding of it. Today's human being looks out upon the world and sees in it merely a physical object in space and time. There is no tendency to think of it as existing other than in those confines, space and time. Any name given to it has no particular significance other than the fact that it is known by that name. If it is an orange, it is so only because that happens to be the name of the class of items to which it has been assigned. If it is a person, the name exists only because it was assigned at birth by the parents. The name itself has no reality apart from the person. This is so obvious that any suggestion otherwise borders on the ridiculous in the modern way of thinking.

And yet, it has not always been so. At a transitional point in human history (evolution), when this modern view began to arise, it was the center of an emotional philosophical debate known as Nominalism versus Realism. Plato and Aristotle were "realists" who saw in the name of an object something that transcended the object. For the orange, there was in the spiritual world a very real "Form" from which the tangible orange itself came into being. Moses also had this understanding. It can be found most vividly in the "after its kind" language in Gen 1,11,12,21,24,25. Throughout the time when the Bible was written this view prevailed. But this Platonic and Aristotelian conception was fading by the Middle Ages. Aquinas and other devout churchmen struggled to carry it forward, but the tendency was toward the "nominalist" idea that there was no metaphysically real existence in regard to the "Name" of an object or person. Insofar as it applied to human beings, the nominalist view seems to have been a natural development with the loss, over long periods, of the knowledge that the Ego, one's "I Am," has existed in prior lives and that its personality and its "Three Bodies" in the present life have been formed in the spiritual world as a result of these prior lives (see "Form"). The Middle Age churchmen held to the ancient understanding even though they had lost the knowledge of reincarnation. They clung to theological beliefs that had arisen earlier, without seeing the metaphysical reality behind them. See 8 Brit 753, "Nominalism," which says "In the Middle Ages ... Platonic and Aristotelian realisms were associated with orthodox religious belief."

Theologians today almost universally agree that names had greater significance in ancient than in modern times. But they have generally failed to articulate why this is so. It is all part of humanity's "Fading Splendor." When humanity comes to understand the human journey between death and rebirth, as discussed in "Karma and Reincarnation," the metaphysical reality behind the individual human being will once again be seen. The "reality" behind the sensate world, seen by ancient humanity, will again be "seen, heard and understood" (Is 6,9-10). Then, for example, will the meaning of Luke's emphasis upon the naming of the Baptist as "John" be understood (Lk 1,13,59-66).

The "Name" given to a person in the Bible is a description of the nature of the person at birth, describing the character and attributes of personality with which the person incarnated. A person who went through initiation into the Mysteries was said to have been "born again" (Jn 3,3), becoming a "New Man," whereupon a "Name Change," where appropriate, was given to indicate the person's new character and attributes. Abram became Abraham; Jacob, Israel; Simon, Peter; and Saul, Paul. We will see other examples. It is this transformation, as described in Jn 11, "the raising of Lazarus from the dead," that hides the reality of the "Name" of "the disciple whom Jesus loved" (see "Peter, James and John").

In this light, one cannot pray "in his name" who is not acting in keeping with his (Christ's) Being. The words themselves mean no more than the names given to children at their birth today. Whenever one truly prays "in his name," the prayer is always heard (Jn 14,13-14). The term "unanswered prayer" is an oxymoron if it is really "in his name." For total subservience to the Father's will is always present when one is "in his name." And it is only in this condition that one can become a "child of God" by "believing in his name" (Jn 1,12). Such belief is a matter of character, not mere verbal profession. The latter, without the former, is a fraud (1 Jn 1,6; 2,4; Mt 7,21).

Steiner called the Elohim (**I-6**), the beings called "God" in Gen 1, "Spirits of Form." They created the etheric reality behind the tangible world, and from that reality came the perishable things and creatures we perceive on Earth. Ultimately there is more reality to the "Form(s)" than to their perishable offspring. The latter has even been called "maya," illusion. The "Name" of something tangible is its higher reality in the etheric or spiritual world. With this, we can return to the "I Am."

This matter of the "name" of God is another cogent demonstration that the documentary hypotheses[4] of the Old Testament (and of the New) is the spurious offspring of the leading theology of the last two centuries. This is pointedly illustrated by the erroneous assumption that merely the awesome sounding "Yahweh" is the "name" intended by the Mosaic account rather than the mysterious phrase "I Am." Later in this essay (following the discussion on the sound "AUM"), we will return to "Yahweh" to look strictly at its meaning absent the juxtaposition of the expository "I Am" in Ex 3,14. But for now, we must preliminarily pursue a somewhat different path of analysis.

Much confusion has arisen among the scholars by the statement in Ex 6,2-3 that such "name" was not known to or used by the Hebrews before the time of Moses. Yet, clearly the term "Yahweh" appears much earlier in the book of Genesis (162 times according to 1 ZC 74). It first appears in Gen 2,4b, and in Gen 4,26 we are told, "At that time [when Adam and

---

4. According to this, the Pentateuch (or Hexateuch) is the conglomerate product of four different documents, each emanating from a different postulated historical source, generally as follows:

Document	Name	Period
J	Jahvist (or Yahwist)	9th century B.C.
E	Elohist	8th century B.C.
D	Deuteronomist	7th century B.C.
P	Priestly	6th century B.C.

The "J" source identifies the Supreme Being as "Yahweh" ("LORD" in the modern versions) and the "E" source as "Elohim" ("God" in modern versions). Thus, for instance, Gen 1 and 2,1-4a are considered to have come from the "E" document and Gen 2,4b-25 and 3 from "J." Great confusion reigns when "scholars" attempt to identify and differentiate these threads down through the respective books of "the law." Undoubtedly, to a great extent modern scholarship was driven to seek such a documentary explanation because of what, in its darkness, seemed to be parallel or duplicate accounts of the same incident. Thus, for instance, there seem to be two different creation accounts in the first three chapters of Genesis. Anthroposophy shows how this is not true, just as it shows how there is no inconsistency between the Matthew and Luke Nativity accounts. For an explanation of the documentary hypotheses, see 1 Interp 185-200 and 1 AB xx-lii. The resulting quagmire of frustration, still without meaningful light, is set out in the more recent ABRL volume *The Pentateuch*, Blenkinsopp (1992), Chap. 1, "Two Centuries of Pentateuchal Scholarship"; see also Blenkinsopp's later "Introduction to the Pentateuch," at 1 NIB 305-318. It goes without saying that Steiner is nowhere mentioned in any such scholarly work to date.

Eve were bearing their children] men began to call upon the name of the LORD."

In Barc's Exodus, App. II, we read:

> On the basis of certain phenomena in Genesis and especially on the apparently obvious interpretation of Exod. 6:1-3 . . . it has been widely held for nearly two centuries that the use of Yahweh for Israel's God began in the time of Moses, even though this theory is in contradiction to Gen 4:26 and much of the usage of Genesis. This has in turn led to a variety of theories as to the origin of the name.

More extensively, in 1 AB 37-38, we read, in regard to Gen 4,26:

> An acute problem is posed, lastly, by the laconic notice at the end of the chapter. The clause reads, "It was then that the name Yahweh began to be invoked"; not "the name *of* Yahweh," since the emphasis is precisely on the personal name and not on its eventual substitute "the Lord." But this statement is directly at variance with Exod iii 14 (E) and vi 3 (P), which indicate that the name Yahweh had not come into use until the time of Moses. Yet J employs this very name throughout Genesis; and the present passage ascribes the usage to very ancient practice.
>
> To be sure, some critics would attribute vss 25-26 to P, in view of the fact that vs 25 speaks of "Adam" (instead of "the man"), as is P's custom (see v 1ff.), aside from mentioning Elohim; cf. Noth, *Uberlieferungsgeschichte...*, p. 12, n. 26. In that case, however, the divergence from Exod vi 3 would be that much more perplexing. (There is, of course, nothing new in J's use of Elohim; cf. ix 26f.) Everywhere else, each documentary source is consistent on this point; it is only their joint testimony that gives rise to difficulties.
>
> A plausible solution may be in sight, nevertheless. Even though J traced back the name Yahweh to the dim past, while E and P attributed the usage to Moses, both views may be justified depending on the point of vantage. The worship of Yahweh was in all likelihood confined at first to a small body of searchers under the aegis of J. When Moses set out to fashion a nation out of an amorphous conglomerate of sundry ethnic and tribal elements, he had to concentrate on three major features of nationhood; a territorial base, a body

of laws, and a distinctive religion. The last was normative in more ways than one; it was necessarily the faith of the same forefathers who had already tied it to the Promised Land, with Yahweh as its fountainhead. To that extent, therefore, Yahweh revealed himself to Moses: and it is this personal revelation that both E and P celebrate. To J, however, who chronicled the progress within the inner circle of the patriarchal pioneers, the personal participation of Yahweh had been the dominant fact from the start.

Little can be said in this connection about the etymology of Yahweh. The fact that attempts to solve the problem are still being made all the time is proof that none of the preceding efforts has carried sufficient appeal. All such ventures start out with the Bible's own explication in Exod iii 14. Yet that name gloss should not be adduced as a technical etymology. It is manifestly a case of symbolism no less than the instances in Gen ii 23, iv 1, xi 9, and many other passages. On this score, at any rate, the name of Yahweh is constantly taken in vain.

Perhaps the most unequivocal indication that the intended *name* of God was "I Am" and not "Yahweh" is to be found in Revelation. Not until Steiner expounded upon that mysterious book (in *The Apocalypse of St. John* [ASJ] and *Reading the Pictures of the Apocalypse* [RPA]), in the light of his basic anthroposophic teaching, was there any treatment that carried with it significant force of reason and clarity of meaning. The chart depicted in **I-1** is taken from the ASJ lecture cycle, in which we learn for the first time (along with RPA) that the letters to the angels of the seven churches refer to the seven Cultural Eras in the present post-Atlantean Epoch (see **I-25**, **I-19** and **I-24**). (We also see that the seven seals, trumpets and bowls of wrath deal with progressively subsequent stages in humanity's evolution, reflected in **I-1**; see the Commentary.) Let us look, then, at these unequivocal passages (emphasis added):

> **Rev 2,17**: "… To him who conquers I will give some of the hidden manna, and I will give him a white stone, with a *new name* written on the stone *which no one knows except him who receives it.*"

> **Rev 3,12**: He who conquers, I will make him a pillar in the temple of my God; never shall he go out of it, and *I* will write on him the *name of my God, and the name of the city of my God, the new Jerusalem which comes down from my God out of heaven, and my own new name.*

Rev 19,12-13: (12) His eyes are like a flame of fire, and on his head are many diadems; and *he has a name inscribed which no one knows but himself.* (13) He is clad in a robe dipped in blood, and *the name by which he is called is The Word of God.*

The church in Pergamum, to whose angel Rev 2,17 is addressed, is clearly identified to Moses' Chaldo-Egyptian era. This we can see by its reference to the "hidden manna" (see "Manna"). And the "new name . . . which no one knows except him who receives it" is a clear reference to "the I Am," for as Steiner often said in reference to the above passages, the only *name* that is known to no one but the one who receives it is "I Am." There is simply no one else in all creation who could ever utter that name with reference to the one who carries it except that person alone. It is a clear reference to the Ego that the human being progressively receives during Earth evolution (see **I-72**). The "white stone" (2,17) is a contra-distinction to the original "stone tablets"—which referred not to actual rock, but to the nature of the human brain, which was developing, i.e., hardening, "rocklike," as the natural result of the process of ever-increasing densification brought about by the Fall (Gen 3) whereby humanity was given access to the "tree of knowledge" but deprived of its prior access to the "tree of life."

Only the "Second Adam" (see "First and Second Adam") could give such a "white stone," one that was unsullied, for the infection of the astral body, which occurred in the Garden of Eden (Gen 3), had the natural consequence of progressively sullying first the older etheric body and then even, in time, the still-older physical body. As the downward evolution of humanity continued, a "point of no return," was reached, the "Right Time," when it became necessary, if the abyss was to be avoided, for the highest spiritual power (the Christ) to sacrifice himself for the salvation of humanity. The Christ had to take on human form (Heb 2), so that all who called upon "his name" could be saved.

The "hidden manna" (2,17) is not physical food, nor was it in the time of Moses (again, see "Manna"), but rather "spiritual food" (1 Cor 10,3), nothing other than the first stage of enlightenment (see **I-9** and **I-35**). Only with the "new name" (Rev 2,17, Ex 3,14 and 6,2-3) revealed to humanity through Moses does such Manna become possible. It would, indeed, only become possible for humanity in the true sense when the blood of Christ (Rev 19,13) had been shed. Why this is so becomes clearer as one gains understanding of the "etherization of the blood," the continuous transformation, within all human beings, of the blood into a delicate etheric substance that streams from the heart upward into the head in the region of the pineal gland (see "Second Coming"). When one understands and takes to heart the Mystery of Golgotha, the etheric blood of Christ is incorporated into the process, and one's own spiritual organ (first the pineal gland) begins to develop, eventually reaching the point of spiritual vision ("seeing," the first stage of enlightenment or initiation). One can then "see" in the etheric world.

Rev 3,12 above has to do with the church at "Philadelphia," the sixth post-Atlantean Cultural Era, which follows our own. In that era the "manas" or Manna state will be on center stage insofar as Earth evolution is concerned (although it will not be perfected until the Jupiter Condition of Consciousness—**I-1**). To this effect, see **I-24**, supplemented by **I-25** and **I-19**. In the outgoing and return of the Prodigal Son (Lk 15,11-32), i.e., the human being in the Parable's highest application, the seven-stage process (see **I-1, I-2** and **I-3**) requires that each of the first three stages be recapitulated, in reverse order, in the last three. Thus, what was first revealed in the second Cultural Era (the Ancient Persian) must again appear in more perfect form in the sixth (the Philadelphian), and what was first revealed in the third (the Chaldo-Egyptian) must likewise reappear transformed in the fifth (our present Era). In the second, Zarathustra saw the descending Christ clearly, while in the third Moses was given the "new name" (Rev 2,17), "I Am," but in his "Fading Splendor" he did not recognize it (the life-saving "Rock") in the Wilderness. And we see in Rev 3,3, which describes our own fifth Cultural Era when the Second Coming of Christ has commenced with humanity spiritually sleeping, "If you will not awake, I will come like a thief, and you will not know at what hour I will come upon you." We fail, as did Moses, to recognize him upon his return. But in the sixth Era, Philadelphia, the clear (transformed) vision of Zarathustra returns, and we see in Rev 3,12 that the "new name," i.e., the higher "I Am," will be written on "those who conquer."

With these things in mind, it is possible to come to an understanding of the importance of the Sacrament of Communion. Typically, when the bread is offered to the communicant, the priest will refer to it as "the bread of heaven." When we begin to understand that "the I Am" is "the new name," we can begin to see the significance of a thread that runs from "the Law" through the Prophets, the Gospels and Paul to the

Revelation. We see it in the "I Am" passages. These have always commanded attention, without understanding, in John's Gospel, but they have not generally been recognized as being connected elsewhere. When we go back to Ex 3 and finally recognize that, in God's statement (3,6), "*I am* the God of your father, the God of Abraham, etc." (emphasis added) we are being introduced to the "I Am" of Christ, the "Second Adam," who, through, and only through, the understanding invitation of our own "I Am" can be conjoined to our very being in the process of perfection, then we can see that "I Am" is used with this meaning elsewhere in scripture.

When we see that the true meaning of the "I Am" was providentially cloaked in Ex 3 to "hide its face" from humanity's cognition until two millennia after the passage of the Twelve (see "Twelve"), Lazarus/John, Paul, the Mother of Jesus, Mary Magdalene, and some others (1 Cor 15,3-8), when the prophecy (1 Cor 14; cf. Ezek 33,23-33) of Steiner made it known upon the re-passage through the new age of Abraham (also discussed in "Second Coming"), then we can begin to detect its presence in other hallowed passages.

The reader must understand the extreme nature of the stricture any writing of this high level must endure. So extensive is the revelation both of scripture and of Steiner's teachings that one must enter into them long-term to gather their ever-increasing fruit. Each new insight adds gloss to every other. The character of the "I Am" or Ego pervades each such area. It is noteworthy that in the first series of Steiner's Gospel lectures, *The Gospel of St. John* (GSJ), the sixth chapter is entitled, "The 'I Am'." As magnificent and essential as it is, it can only scope a small segment of the larger picture. It opens with the passage in Jn 3,3-5, moves through the creative process of the human being's three bodies and Ego, and then expounds the meaning of the terms "son of man," "serpent," "manas" (Manna) and "buddhi." Steiner himself did not, to my knowledge, ever attempt to point out all the Biblical usages of the term "*I Am*." The range of revelation he had to pack within his one lifetime precluded total exposition in any one area or discipline; it remained to those who caught up his spirit to carry it further, and this he constantly urged as being demanded of us in our time. But he always gave the necessary tools for that task. It is with these that we look further below (but this is not to claim that he did not point, implicitly if not explicitly, on occasion, in many of these directions).

Let us look, for instance, at GSJ, Lect. 9. There Steiner tells us that just as in the case of Gal 1,16, the preposition used in Biblical translations of Jn 12,41 is in error by virtue of the failure of translators down through the ages to understand the descent of Christ and his appearance to those of old. The passage, which has reference to Is 6,10, should read as follows: "Isaiah said this because he saw his glory and spoke *with*[5] him." Clearly one must use the term "with," rather than "of" or "about," in regard to the direct conversation in Is 6,8-13. But how can it be said that it was the Christ rather than Yahweh who is referred to by Isaiah as "the Lord?" At the outset, we have only Steiner's word for it. Recall at the opening of the "Overview" how it was said that Steiner's revelations on the Bible come from his direct perception in the spiritual world, and not from the content of the Bible itself. We find him stating this in the first lecture of the first cycle (GSJ) in his Gospel series. It remains only to test out what he said and see if it proves true (cf. Deut 18,21-22).

So what about Steiner's assertion that what Isaiah saw was the Christ? When the order of the Hierarchies is recognized it becomes obvious. Paul spoke of these.[6] In Eph 1,21, after listing "all rule and authority and power and dominion" (essentially the names of the threefold second Hierarchy (see I-6), he speaks of Christ as the one "above every name that is named." Isaiah says "I saw the Lord [Christ] sitting upon a throne, high and lifted up." The Thrones are immediately above the second Hierarchy, being the third rank of the first Hierarchy. The Seraphim compose the highest rank of the first Hierarchy, and while Isaiah saw them "above" the Lord, the Lord was sitting and they "stood." But most significantly, with two of their six wings they covered their faces, and they flew calling out "Holy, holy, holy is the Lord of hosts; the whole earth is full of his glory." The Seraphim would never have been portrayed thus if it were the

---

5. Various translations use the following:

with   —   none of those cited herein
of   —   KJV, NKJV, RSV, NACB, AMPB, AB
about   —   CEV, NIV, NRSV, PMEB, NEB

Two versions get close to Steiner's meaning. NJB paraphrases, "his words referred to Jesus," and LB similarly editorializes saying, "Isaiah was referring to Jesus when he made this prediction, for he had seen a vision of the Messiah's glory." CEV adds a footnote alternative, i.e., "he saw the glory of God and spoke about Jesus."
6. Paul's Athenian convert, Dionysius the Areopagite (Acts 17,34) started a school that carried Paul's teachings of the Hierarchies down for six centuries before they were reduced to writing. See PSEUD; also I-6.

Exusiai (Elohim, or Authorities[7]) he referred to as Lord, for the Exusiai constitute the sixth rank and the Seraphim the first in the Hierarchies. Yahweh was one of the seven Elohim.

Lazarus/John and Paul were the two who were initiated directly by Christ himself. In 1 Cor 10,4 ("They drank from the supernatural Rock which followed them, and the Rock was Christ") Paul recognizes that Christ dealt directly with the people from the spiritual world before his Incarnation in the flesh. Similarly, in Jn 12,41 Lazarus/John recognized the action of Christ during Old Testament times. As we see below, Isaiah let the "I Am" passages ring out. Particularly in the suffering servant portions do we see the Christ. Consider Is 42,1, "Behold my servant, whom I uphold, my chosen, in whom my soul delights; I have put my Spirit upon him, he will bring forth justice to the nations." Could the event at the Baptism of Jesus of Nazareth, "my servant," where the dove, "my Spirit," descends upon him, be more precisely or beautifully expressed? Lazarus/John carries the "I Am" theme through his Gospel. In Jn 12,41 Lazarus/John recognized Isaiah as the one who, above all others, had seen the Christ in the spiritual world.

Steiner said "What ran through the Old Testament was like a prophecy," indicating that it was the Logos, the Christ, who gave the "name" "I

---

7. The Greek term for "authority" or "authorities" is *exusiai*. It appears profusely in the New Testament. Examples include Eph 1,21 and the other passages where Paul refers to the sixth rank of the Hierarchies, the Spirits of Form, or Elohim. These comprised, after all, the rank in charge of Earth evolution (see I-16). Christ is said to have spoken with "authority" (Mt 7,29; Mk 1,22; Lk 4,32), which is to say, with all of the controlling power of Earth evolution, or the Earth Condition of Consciousness. (Obviously, he had excess power, for this level was far below his place above all the Hierarchies, but it is really all that need be exercised during Earth evolution.) We find the Greek *exusiai* also being interpreted sometimes as "power." Most notably is this the case in Jn 1,12 ("But to all who received him, who believed in his name, he gave the power [authority, or right] to become children of God"); see 29 AB 10 and Bultmann, *The Gospel of John*, Westminster, Philadelphia, 1971, p. 57, note 5. For those, like myself, who do not read Greek, the usage asserted above can be verified by inspecting KJV/NIV—INT, and the comments made on such Greek term in 27 AB 212 (Mk 1,22) and 28 AB 544 (Lk 4,32). Steiner first alerted humanity to this understanding in *Background to the Gospel of St. Mark* (BKM), Lect. 6, pp. 96-102. There, regarding Christ's speaking with authority in the synagogue, he said "He taught in the synagogue as one of the Exousiai, as a Power and Revelation, and not as those who are here called . . . (scribes).... The people in the synagogue were very near the truth when they said: When he speaks it is as though the *Exousiai* were speaking, not merely the Archai, the Time-Spirits, or the Folk-Spirits" (i.e., the third Hierarchy). See also *Anthroposophical Studies of the New Testament* (ASNT), Chap. 3, p. 41.

Am" to Moses on Mt. Sinai (Ex 3,14). We need not here denigrate the
function of Yahweh, for the revelation of the Christ would seem to have
come through him. But the name "I Am" that Christ spoke through Yahweh was uniquely that of the Christ, the higher "I Am." The New Testament makes this abundantly clear, particularly in the Gospel and
Apocalypse of Lazarus/John. We need only look at Is 44,1-8 to gather
compelling evidence. In vs 2 we read "Thus says the Lord [Christ] who
made you, who formed you from the womb...." (see "The Nativity").
Then, compellingly, vs 6 reads "Thus says the Lord, the King of Israel and
his Redeemer, the Lord of hosts, 'I am the first and I am the last;...'" (see
also Is 41,4), and then vs 8b, "Is there a God besides me? There is no Rock;
I know not any." Clearly, "the Alpha and the Omega," the first and the
last, is Christ (Rev 1,8; 21,6; 22,13). And can there be any doubt that the
Christ is the Rock? See 1 Cor 10,4; also "Rock." Steiner has delivered us
from the effete interpretations of these passages in existing Bible commentaries. As we shall presently see, other passages in the Bible simply do not
make sense unless the name "I Am" given to Moses was that of the Christ.

There is an intriguing sentence that runs through the Old Testament
and bears a haunting similarity to the "I Am," as though to reflect an
upward looking of the lower toward the higher Ego, and an upward-lift-
ing response thereto. It is "Here am I," a mirror image of the higher counterpart, the "I Am." It was spoken of old by Abraham (Gen 22,1,11), by
Isaac (Gen 22,7), and by Jacob (Gen 31,11), all before the time of Moses.
To none of them was the higher "I Am" revealed by such name. The significance of this is pointedly reflected in Jacob's encounter with the angel
of God in Gen 32,26-29 (emphasis added):

(26) Then he said, "Let me go, for the day is breaking." But Jacob
said, "I will not let you go unless you bless me." (27) And he said to
him, "What is your name?" And he said, "Jacob." (28) Then he said,
"Your name shall no more be called Jacob, but Israel, for you have
striven with God and with men, and have prevailed." (29) Then Jacob asked him, "Tell me, I pray, your *name*." But he said, "Why is
it that you ask my *name*?" And there he blessed him.

Though it was God with whom Jacob strove, and though he saw Him
"face to face," still it was yet not time for His *name*, the "I Am," to be
revealed—and it was not. Thus Yahweh, reflecting the Christ, could say

in Ex 6,2-3 that though he had appeared to Abraham, Isaac and Jacob, by his name "I Am" he did not then make himself known. The first appearance of the patriarchal trinity Abraham, Isaac and Jacob is at the conclusion of the book of Genesis (Gen 50,24) where Joseph speaks of his own "I am" dying, but no reference to the higher "I Am" is yet given. The first identification by Christ (through Yahweh) of his *"Name"* "I Am" comes in Ex 3,6 (emphasis added):

> And he said, "[the] *I Am* [is] the God of your father, the God of Abraham, the God of Isaac, and the God of Jacob.[8]

And thereafter we find God speaking as the "I Am" throughout the Old Testament, e.g., in Ex 6,6,29 and 7,5, and again in Lev 26,44-45.

The "Here am I" passage appears again after Moses on the lips of Samuel (1 Sam 3,4-9), followed by the higher "I Am" speaking in vss 11-14. But nowhere in the Old Testament, outside of Ex 3 and 6, is the name "I Am" more clearly and profusely identified as that of the LORD than in the book of Isaiah. And no other prophet is looked to more extensively by the Evangelists than Isaiah as foreseeing and inscrutably describing the Christ. We see again the "Here am I" (Is 6,8), but this time we get an elaboration on it that, beyond all question,[9] is a foreseeing and recognition of the "I Am" as the "Name" of the LORD.

---

8. The goal of Earth evolution is to install the Christ-enabled "I Am," or Ego, as the "ruler" over the "Three Bodies." This point is first made in regard to the synoptic Gospel passages on the Levirate law—see #5 under "Karma and Reincarnation."

9. It is important to remember the relationship between the higher "I Am," the Christ, and the lower, the human Ego. The higher is the Lord of the lower, and only by putting on the higher has the human been given the "Name" of the Christ. This is the prophetic reality of the renaming of Jacob as Israel (Gen 32,24-32). The interpreters have said that "Israel" means "He who strives with God or God strives." (It can also be seen as a combination of the root [Is] of "Isis" in the Egyptian creation myth, the Egyptian Sungod "Ra," and "the common semitic [name] for the 'divinity'" [El], 4 ABD 1004.) Nevertheless (as even in the Egyptian myth) in the name Israel is implicit the fact of prevailing in the struggle. It is a prophetic indication of the taking in by the lower "I Am" of the higher, which involves the struggle of perfecting the "Three Bodies." Thus the Sun is said to rise upon him (Gen 32,31). The "servant" of whom Isaiah speaks is abundantly identified as Israel (or Jacob) but, as we have seen in Is 42,1, also describes Jesus of Nazareth upon whom the Christ Spirit, the Dove, settled. Christendom has always properly sensed that the servant passages of "second Isaiah" portrayed Jesus even while calling him "Israel." And in the end it is the "Twelve" "sons of Israel" who are the gates to the Holy City (Rev 21,12). *(continued on following page)*

The extent to which Isaiah portrays the "I Am" is reflected in the following passages therefrom (emphasis added; by now the reader should be able to see the meanings involved without the insertion of the implied parenthetical words heretofore added):

Is 6: (1) In the year that King Uzziah died I saw the Lord sitting upon a throne, high and lifted up; and his train filled the temple. (2) Above him stood the seraphim; each had six wings: with two he covered his face, and with two he covered his feet, and with two he flew. (3) And one called to another and said: "Holy, holy, holy is the Lord of hosts; the whole earth is full of his glory." (4) And the foundations of the thresholds shook at the voice of him who called, and the house was filled with smoke. (5) And I said: "Woe is me! For *I Am* lost; for *I Am* a man of unclean lips, and I dwell in the midst of a people of unclean lips; for my eyes have seen the King, the LORD of hosts!" (6) Then flew one of the seraphim to me, having in his hand a burning coal.... (7) And he touched my mouth, and said: "Behold, this has touched your lips; your guilt is taken away, and your sin forgiven." (8) And I heard the voice of the Lord saying, "Whom shall I send, and who will go for us?" Then I said, "Here *am I*! Send me." (9) And he said, "Go and say to this people: 'Hear and hear, but do not understand; see and see, but do not perceive.' (10) Make the heart of this people fat, and their ears heavy, and shut their eyes; lest they see with their eyes, and hear with their ears, and understand with their hearts, and turn and be healed." (11) Then I said, "How long, O Lord?" And he said: "Until cities lie waste without inhabitant, and houses without men, and the land is utterly desolate, (12) and the LORD removes men far away, and the forsaken places are many in the midst of the land. (13) And though a tenth

---

9. (*continued*) They have been given the name "which no one knows except him who receives it (Rev 2,17)," which is "the name . . . of the new Jerusalem" (Rev 3,12), and also of him who is clearly the Christ (Rev 19,12-13,16). See fn 13. Only the name "I Am" can meet that standard.

Elsewhere in this essay, where the Alpha and the Omega and the Rock are discussed, the Christ is clearly identified, and (in the emphasized portions of Is 41-52 below) in the references to the "name" and the giving of the name, when considered in connection with Rev 2,17; 3,12 and 19,12-13 discussed above, and in the passing through waters and flames without being overwhelmed or consumed (Is 43,2 below)—in the collective force of all of this, there seems, "beyond all question," to be the prophecy that "I Am" is the "Name" of the Lord.

remain in it, it will be burned again, like a terebinth or an oak, whose stump remains standing when it is felled." The holy seed is its stump.[10]

Deutero (and Trito) Isaiah

Is 41-52: [**41**](4) Who has performed and done this, calling the generations from the beginning? *I, the LORD*, the first, and with the last; *I am He*.... (8) But you, Israel, my servant, Jacob, whom I have chosen, the offspring of Abraham, my friend; ... (10) fear not, for *I am* with you, be not dismayed, for *I am* your God; I will strengthen you, I will help you, I will uphold you....

[**42**](1) Behold my servant, whom *I uphold*, my chosen, in whom my soul delights; *I have put my Spirit upon him*, he will bring forth justice to the nations. (5) Thus says God, the LORD, ... (6) "*I am* the LORD, I have called you in righteousness, I have taken you by the hand and kept you; I have given you as a covenant to the people, a light to the nations (7) to open the eyes that are blind, to bring out the prisoners from the dungeon, from the prison those who sit in darkness. (8) *I am the LORD, that is my name*; my glory I give to *no other*, nor my praise to graven images. (9) Behold, the former things have come to pass, and new things I now declare; before they spring forth I tell you of them." ... (16) And I will lead the blind in a way that they know not, in paths that they have not known I will guide them. I will turn the darkness before them into light, the rough places into level ground.... (18) Hear, you deaf; and look, you blind, that you may see![11] (19) Who is blind but my servant, or deaf as my

---

10. Steiner's three stages of perception, both physically and spiritually, are clearly foreshadowed here. First, Isaiah spiritually "sees" (vs 1), then "hears" (vss 3-5, "called," "voice," "said" and "lips"), then "understands" (vs 7, "touched"). Then the physical of each of these is contra-distinguished from the spiritual in vss 9-10, esp. vs 10 as follows, "eyes" vs "see," "ears" vs "hear" and "heart" vs "understand." These three stages of spiritual perception correspond with the progressive stages of initiation, namely, Imagination, Inspiration and Intuition, as anthroposophically understood. See also Is 29,9-14 reflective of the same dullness of spirit; and see "Fading Splendor."
11. Esoterically, being blind or deaf often means to be so as to the maya (illusion) of the external world while seeing or hearing in the spiritual world, e.g., Homer, the "blind poet." See also Is 43,8 below, and "Blind See."

messenger whom I send? Who is blind as my dedicated one, or blind
as the servant of the LORD? ...

[**43**](1) But now thus says the LORD, who created you, O Jacob,
he who formed you, O Israel: "Fear not, for I have redeemed you; *I
have called you by name, you are mine. (2) When you pass through the
waters I will be with you; and through the rivers, they shall not over-
whelm you; when you walk through fire you shall not be burned, and
the flame shall not consume you. For I am the LORD your God.*[12] ...

---

12. This verse is particularly indicative. The "rivers" correspond with the recurring passages
of the Ego (i.e., the "I Am") through the River Lethe, the river that causes us to lose memories of prior lives and of our intervening sojournings in the spiritual world. The root of the
word "Lethe" finds expression in so many of our words dealing, in one way or another, with
loss of consciousness. And the "fire" and "flame" relate to the burning bush which is not
consumed (Ex 3,2-3; see "Bush" and "Purifying Fire"). The "I Am" passes through all of
these. When one comes to recognize the "Name," one then sees that the "I Am," or Ego, is
not overwhelmed or consumed but passes on from life to life until perfected.

Here it seems imperative to look at Eccles 1,9-11 and 3,11b:

(**1**) (9) What has been is what will be, and what has been done is what will be done;
and there is nothing new under the sun. (10) Is there a thing of which it is said,
"See, this is new"? It has been already, in the ages before us. (11) There is no
remembrance of former things, nor will there be any remembrance of later things
yet to happen among those who come after.... (**3**)(11b) also he [God] has put eternity into man's mind, yet so that he cannot find out what God has done from the
beginning to the end.

From of old, this book was thought to be sacred, the first objection thereto having been
raised in the fifth century A.D. (2 ABD 278) when humanity's spiritual consciousness was
becoming quite dark. Obviously, by then, the book's relation to the eternal nature of the
Ego and its recurring incarnation had been lost. The name of the book itself resulted from
a struggle of translation from the Hebrew into the Greek, from which the Latin and
English versions derive (see 18 AB 193, "Ecclesiastes"). The net result, whether right or
wrong, is that there are three synonymous names, Qoheleth, Ecclesiastes, and/or
Preacher, for the one who brings us its message. Such name is used *seven* times (1,1; 1,2;
1,12; 7,27; 12,8; 12,9; 12,10). Such number can hardly be an accident (cf. Proverbs 9,1).
It is the number which stands for time, while *twelve* stands for timelessness or eternity.
From an inspection of **1-2**, in conjunction with the Commentary on Revelation, it can be
seen that the process of reincarnation comes to an end at approximately the point at
which the cycles of *seven* change into visions of *twelve*, from the septenary planetary consciousness into the twelvefold zodiacal. So long as the septenary reigns, there is repetition
and reincarnation for the purpose of perfection. The passages quoted above from Ecclesiastes could not more precisely state the nature of the human being in relation to reincarnation. Futility is expressed in the book because that is the nature of life that looks only
to what can be seen with the human being's present senses, all of which is maya, deception
or futility until it is seen in the light of what is eternal and has been forgotten (by virtue
of the River Lethe). (*continued on following page*)

(5) Fear not, for *I am* with you; I will bring your offspring from the east, and from the west I will gather you; (6) I will say to the north, Give up, and to the south, Do not withhold; bring my sons from afar and my daughters from the end of the earth, (7) *every one who is called by my name*, whom I created for my glory, whom I formed and made. (8) Bring forth the people who are blind, yet have eyes, who are deaf, yet have ears! ... (10) "You are my witnesses," says the LORD, "and my servant whom I have chosen, that you may *know and believe me and understand that I am He*.... (11) *I, I am the LORD*, and besides me there is no savior.... (13) "*I am God*, and also *henceforth I am He*.... (15) *I am the LORD*, your Holy One, the Creator of Israel, your King." ... (18) "Remember not the former things, nor consider the things of old. (19) Behold, *I am doing a new thing; now it springs forth, do you not perceive it? I will make a way in the wilderness and rivers in the desert...* (24) ... But you have burdened me with your sins, you have wearied me with your iniquities. (25) "*I, I am He* who blots out your transgressions for my own sake, and I will not remember your sins...."

[**44**] (1) "But now hear, O Jacob my servant, Israel whom I have chosen! (2) Thus says the LORD who made you, who formed you from the womb and will help you: Fear not, O Jacob my servant, Jeshurun whom I have chosen. (3) For I will pour water on the thirsty land, and streams on the dry ground; I will pour my Spirit upon your descendants, and my blessing on your offspring. (4) They shall spring up like grass amid waters, like willows by flowing streams. (5) This one will say, '*I am the LORD'S*,' another will call

---

12. (*continued*) The book is an enigma and much maligned because this fact is not recognized, having been long "forgotten." Its viewpoint is not greatly different from that of the first post-Atlantean Cultural Era, the Ancient Indian (see **I-19**, **I-24**, **I-25**, **I-1** and **I-2**), which came over "from the east" (Gen 11,2). The very placement of this book in the canon itself presents a most thrilling spectacle. Following Proverbs, it precedes the Song of Songs (or of Solomon) in which the unfulfilled longing for the Christ is expressed in terms of anticipated, albeit delayed, ecstasy. And then comes the incomparable, panoramic and prophetic vision of Isaiah, including the passage here noted. The futility expressed in Ecclesiastes is also justified, in the light of that placement, because it represents merely Wisdom, or the Eternal Feminine, which in order to bring about humanity's salvation, had to be joined to the pure Eternal Masculine represented by the Incarnation and shed Blood of the Christ, foreseen and foretold by Isaiah. Without that, the impurities from the Fall could not be cleansed (Heb 2).

himself by the *name of Jacob* and another will write on his hand, 'The LORD'S,' and *surname himself* by the *name of Israel.*" (6) Thus says the LORD, the King of Israel and his Redeemer, the LORD of hosts: "*I am* the first and *I am* the last; besides me there is no god. (7) *Who is like me?* ... (8) Fear not, nor be afraid; have I not told you from of old and declared it? And you are my witnesses! *Is there a God besides me? There is no Rock; I know not any.*"

[**45**] (1) Thus says the LORD to his anointed, to Cyrus, ... (2) "I will go before you and level the mountains, I will break in pieces the doors of bronze and cut asunder the bars of iron, (3) I will give you *treasures of darkness* and the *hoards in secret places, that you may know that it is I, the LORD, the God of Israel, who call you by your name.* (4) For the sake of my servant Jacob, and Israel my chosen, *I call you by your name, I surname you, though you do not know me.* (5) *I am the LORD, and there is no other*, besides me there is no God; I gird you, *though you do not know me*, (6) ... *I am the LORD*, and there is no other. (7) ... *I am the LORD*, who do all these things...." (18) "... *I am the LORD*, and there is no other.... (21) ... Who told this long ago? Who declared it of old? *Was it not I, the LORD?* ...."

[**46**] (3) "Hearken to me, O house of Jacob, all the remnant of the house of Israel, who have been borne by me from your birth, carried from the womb; (4) even to your old age *I am He*, and to gray hairs I will carry you. *I* have made, and *I* will bear; *I* will carry and will save.... (8) "Remember this and consider, recall it to mind, you transgressors, (9) remember the former things of old; for *I am* God, and there is no other; *I am God, and there is none like me....*"

[**47**] (10) You felt secure in your wickedness, you said, "No one sees me"; your wisdom and your knowledge led you astray, and you said in your heart, "*I am*, and there is no one besides me." (11) But evil shall come upon you, for which you cannot atone....

[**48**] (12) "Hearken to me, O Jacob, and *Israel, whom I called! I am He, I am the first, and I am the last....* " (17) Thus says the LORD, your Redeemer, the Holy One of Israel: "*I am the LORD* your God, who teaches you to profit, who leads you in the way you should go...."

[**49**] (1) ...The LORD called me from the womb, from the body of my mother *he named my name....* (5) And now the LORD says, who formed me from the womb to be his servant, to bring Jacob back to him, and that Israel might be gathered to him, for *I am* honored in the eyes of the LORD, and my God has become my strength: ... (22) Thus says the Lord God: "... (23) ... Then you will know that *I am the LORD*; those who wait for me shall not be put to shame." ... (25) Surely, thus says the LORD: "... (26) ... Then all flesh shall know that *I am the LORD* your Savior...."

[**51**] (12) "*I, I am he* that comforts you; who are you that you are afraid of man who dies, of the son of man who is made like grass, (13) and have forgotten the LORD, your Maker?... (15) For *I am the LORD* your God, who stirs up the sea so that its waves roar— the LORD of hosts is his *name.* (16) And I have put my words in your mouth, ... saying to Zion, 'You are my people.'"...

[**52**] (1) Awake, awake, ... (2) Shake yourself from the dust, arise.... (3) For thus says the LORD: "... (6) Therefore *my people shall know my name; therefore in that day they shall know that it is I who speak; here am I.*" ...

[**54**] (8) In overflowing wrath for a moment I hid my face from you, but with everlasting love I will have compassion on you, says the LORD, your Redeemer....

[**56**] (4) For thus says the LORD: "... (5) I will give in my house and within my walls a monument and *a name* better than sons and daughters; *I will give them an everlasting name which shall not be cut off....*"

[**58**] (6) "Is not this the fast that I choose? ... (7) Is it not to share your bread with the hungry, and bring the homeless poor into your house; when you see the naked, to cover him, and not to hide yourself from your own flesh? (8) Then shall your light break forth like the dawn, and your healing shall spring up speedily.... (9) Then you shall call, and the LORD will answer; you shall cry, and he will say, *Here I am....*"

[**60**] (1) Arise, shine; for your light has come, and *the glory of the LORD has risen upon you.*...(14) ... *they shall call you the City of the LORD,*[13] *the Zion of the HOLY One of Israel.*... (16) ... and you shall know that *I, the LORD, am* your Savior.... (22) ... "*I am the LORD....*"

[**62**] (2) The nations shall see your vindication, and all the kings your glory; and *you shall be called by a new name which the mouth of the LORD will give....*

[**63**] (1) ... "*It is I,* announcing vindication, mighty to save." ...

[**65**] (1) *I* was ready to be sought by those who did not ask for me; *I* was ready to be found by those who did not seek me. *I* said, "*Here am I, here am I,*" to a *nation that did not call on my name.* (2) *I* spread out my hands all the day to a rebellious people, who walk in a *way* that is not good, following their own devices; ... (5) who say, "Keep to yourself, do not come near me, for *I am* set apart from you." ...

[**66**] (18) For I know their works and their thoughts, and *I am* coming to gather all nations and tongues; and they shall come and shall see my glory.... (22) "For as the new heavens and the new earth which I will make shall remain before me, says the LORD; so shall your descendants and *your name* remain...."

It is most significant that it was Lazarus/John who both noted that Isaiah had seen and spoken *with* the Christ (Jn 12,41) and identifies him as the "I Am." And John's Gospel extensively characterizes Christ as the "I Am" (see **I-72**):

Passage	Character of the "I Am"
Jn 6,35,41,48,51	Bread of Life
Jn 8,12 and 9,5	Light of the World
Jn 10,7,9	Door

---

13. See fn 9 and the relation of the "name" ("I Am") passages in Rev 2,17; 3,12 and 19,12-13,16 to "the new Jerusalem," Rev 21,1-14.

Jn 10,11,14	Good Shepherd
Jn 11,25	Resurrection
Jn 11,25 and 14,6	Life
Jn 14,6	Way
Jn 14,6	Truth
Jn 15,1,5	Vine

Several more Johannine *"I Am"* passages deserve notation, including:

Jn 8,23 and 17,14,16	Not of this world
Jn 8,58	Before Abraham
Jn 10,36	Son of God
Jn 13,13	Teacher
Jn 13,13	Lord
Jn 13,33	With you
Jn 14,10,20	In the Father and the Father in me
Jn 18,37	A king

In each of the synoptic Gospels, the adoption of Jesus of Nazareth as "Son of God," upon exit of the Zarathustra Ego and entry of the Christ Spirit into him at Baptism,[14] is pronounced by the Father as follows (emphasis added):

Mt 3,16-17: (16) And when Jesus was baptized, he went up immediately from the water, and behold, the heavens were opened and he saw the Spirit of God descending like a dove, and alighting on him; (17) and lo, a voice from heaven, saying, "This is my beloved Son, with whom *I am* well pleased."

Mk 1,10-11: (10) And when he came up out of the water, immediately he saw the heavens opened and the Spirit descending upon him like a dove; (11) and a voice came from heaven, "Thou art my beloved Son; with thee *I am* well pleased."

---

14. Jesus is referred to as the Christ in both Nativity accounts, e.g., Mt 1,1,16-18 and 2,4; Lk 2,11,26, but if one contemplates the scope of heavenly preparation for the Incarnation of the Christ in Jesus of Nazareth (see "Nativity"), it is easy to see how the fourfold human vehicle long prepared for receiving the Christ Spirit would be thus described in anticipation of the fulfillment of its role. It is this vehicle that is the "servant" Isaiah speaks of.

Lk 3,21-22: (21) … and when Jesus also had been baptized and was praying, the heaven was opened, (22) and the Holy Spirit descended upon him in bodily form, as a dove, and a voice came from heaven, "Thou art my beloved Son; with thee *I am* well pleased."

These take on added meaning in conjunction with Ps 2,7, Is 42,1, Jn 1,12 and Rom 8,23.

The more human beings take the Christ "I Am" into their own Ego, and thereby transform the lower three bodies into the higher three states (see **I-9**), the greater the enhancement of their consciousness. When that consciousness extends beyond the gates of birth and death, then one dwells always in the Kingdom, having overcome death and the river Lethe's oblivion (Jn 1,12; Job 38,17). It is then that the three loaves (lower bodies) are fully leavened and one dwells in full consciousness in the Kingdom (Mt 13,33). The Ego, or "I Am," is after all a matter of consciousness. We see in **I-1** that there are to be a total of seven Conditions of Consciousness, of which Earth evolution is the fourth, the one in which the Ego is added to the older three bodies (members) in the human being's evolution and becomes their ruler, i.e., the God of Abraham, Isaac and Jacob (cf. Is 11,6d, "and a little child shall lead them"; also Job 32,4,6). The powerful significance of this has yet to dawn upon the bulk of humanity, from which the "Face of God," and the meaning of his "Name," thus remains "hidden."

Steiner had a great deal to say about primeval sounds, the origin of speech and the meaning of words. We cannot explore all that now, but we do note that long ago in humanity's evolution the meanings of the relatively few sounds were uniformly understood (Gen 11,1, probably mirrored in Acts 2,1-13). In one of his significant works on the subject, *Speech and Drama* (SD), a nineteen-lecture cycle, Steiner speaks in Lect. 1 of certain primeval sounds which have a haunting similarity to the sound of the "I Am." Here I refer to the Oriental meditation mantra **AUM**. Because of the relation between consciousness and the "I Am," the following extract seems pertinent:

Suppose now we want to express what is contained in **O**. In **O** we have the confluence of **A** and **U**; it is where waking up and falling asleep meet. **O** is thus the moment either of falling asleep or of awaking. When the Oriental teacher wanted his pupils to be neither asleep nor awake, but to make for that boundary between sleeping and waking where so much can be experienced, he would direct them to speak the syllable **OM**. In this way he led them to the life that is between waking and sleeping.

OM

/ \

A U M

For, anyone who keeps repeating continually the syllable **OM** will experience what it means to be between the condition of being awake and the condition of being asleep. A teaching like this comes from a time when the speech organism was still understood.

And now let us see how it was when a teacher in the Mysteries wanted to take his pupils further. He would say to himself: The **O** arises through the **U** wanting to go to the **A** and the **A** at the same time wanting to go to the **U**. So, after I have taught the pupil how to stand between sleeping and waking in the **OM**, if I want now to lead him on a step further, then instead of getting him to speak the **O** straight out, I must let the **O** arise in him through his speaking **AOUM**. Instead of **OM**, he is now to say **AOUM**. In this way the pupil *creates* the **OM**, brings it to being. He has reached a higher stage. **OM** with the **O** separated into **A** and **U** gives the required stillness to the more advanced pupil. Whereas the less advanced pupil has to be taken straight to the boundary condition between sleep and waking, the more advanced has to pass from **A** (falling asleep) to **U** (waking up), building the transition for himself. Being then between the two, he has within him the moment of experience that holds both.

It is not, perhaps, extending our contemplation too far if we suspect that in ancient times what came over "from the east" (Gen 11,2) carried with it, as the seminal "I Am," an awareness of the enhanced consciousness relating to the "**AOUM**."

We must now consider, as earlier promised, the meaning of the awe-inspiring "Yahweh" standing alone without the "I Am" appendage of Ex 3,14. Having looked at the "I Am" itself in its Biblical context, we are now in a better position to return to the meaning of this ancient sound as it emerged in humanity's consciousness out of the mists of time. All Bible scholars know that its Hebrew origin was expressed in the equivalent of the Greek Tetragrammaton, literally "four letters," YHWH, which, by extrusion through the Germanic tongue became also known as JHVH. The vowels of the Greek Adonai and the Hebrew Elohim, alternative names for God, were inserted so that we have "Yahweh," or the Germanized "Jehovah." (See WNWD.) While our New Testament came to us in Greek form, the Old Testament is available in both Hebrew (primarily the "Masoretic Text") and Greek (the "Septuagint"). Ironically, the Greek is the older of the two Old Testament texts in terms of when they were physically created, having been written down before the time of Christ, whereas the Hebrew did not come into written form until after Christ. (See WNWD and 14 Brit 780 at 786 "Biblical Literature; Old Testament Canon, Texts and Versions"). The foregoing applies to the known documents at the time our basic existing translations were made, and ignores the highly important discoveries of ancient texts in the twentieth century. The Greek word for "YHWH," or "Yahweh," is "Kyrios." These are the words that appear in our present translations as "Lord."

In a few words, what Steiner reveals to us, in an analysis similar to that of "AUM" above, is that "Yahweh" is completely synonymous with "I Am." While this obviously reconciles any element of contention as to *which* "name" was intended in Ex 3,14, and thus could clearly obviate much of the foregoing discussion, it is well that we see both angles. Steiner takes up the meaning of "Yahweh" in BKM, Lects. 4 and 11, where he focuses upon Is 40,3:

A voice cries: "In the wilderness prepare the way of the Lord, make straight in the desert a highway for our God."

Also Mk 1,3:

"the voice of one crying in the wilderness: Prepare the way of the Lord, make his paths straight—"

He stresses that in order to understand these passages one must ponder the meaning of the two words "Wilderness" and "Lord." "Wilderness" means "loneliness," or "aloneness," or "solitude," or "the desolation of the soul."[15] It is only in that condition that the "I Am" exists and can be recognized; thus those who seek the "I Am" invariably go into a "Wilderness" to do so. Steiner also points out that the term "messenger," as used in Mk 1,2 and intended by Isaiah, means a specific announcing angel[16] who was to work through John the Baptist. Let us see Steiner's own words from Lect. 11:

> Such an event in the history of humanity actually took place when the Individuality who had lived in Elijah was reborn as John the Baptist. An Angel entered into the soul of John the Baptist in that incarnation, using his bodily nature and also his soul to accomplish what no human being could have accomplished. In John the Baptist there lived an Angel whose mission was to herald in advance the Egohood that was to be present in its fullness in Jesus of Nazareth. It is of the greatest importance to realize that John the Baptist was maya and that an Angel, a Messenger, was living in him. This is indeed what the Greek says: Lo, I send my Messenger. The Messenger is an Angel. But nobody pays attention to what is actually said here. A deep mystery, enacted in the Baptist and foretold by Isaiah, is indicated. Isaiah foretold that the future John the Baptist would be maya—in reality he was to be the vehicle for the Angel, the Messenger who was

---

15. In both Is 40,3 and Mk 1,3,13, the Greek *epnuoc* is variously translated as either "wilderness" (e.g., RSV, NRSV, KJV, NKJV, LB, AMPB, PMEB, NEB and Barc) or "desert" (e.g., KJV/NIV—INT, NIV, CEV, NJB, NACB and AB). If one studies a good dictionary definition of "wilderness," it will be seen to be essentially synonymous with "desert," both indicating, along with compatible concepts, a place free from human activity. It is particularly notable in Mark's Gospel that this place, be it called "desert" or "wilderness," was full of "Wild Animals." Anthroposophy shows us that the human astral body, as it came over from Atlantis, was filled with all the animal passions. It is these which were taken into the "Ark" (the dimensions of the human physical body), no longer remaining *outside* for perception of the spiritual world. It is these which the human soul, the Ego, must confront in loneliness or desolation, separated from its prior communication with the spiritual world. The "Notes" to Mk 1,3 in 27 AB 195 say:

> There is no justification from the Hebrew text of Isa 40:3 for any punctuation of this verse which does not associate *in the desert* with *make ready.*

> *desert*: The wilderness dominates the prologue. Traditionally, the wilderness area was considered the haunt of demons, and a fitting scene for conflict between God and evil.

16. Compared, for instance, with 27 AB 195 and Barc's "Mark," 7 Interp 648 recognizes the term "angel" in this passage, e.g., "The quotation in vs 3 is from Isa. 40:3; vs 2b is from Exod. 23:20 combined with Mal. 3:1, both passages being modified ('my' *angel*, 'thy' way)." (Emphasis added)

to proclaim what man will become if he takes the Christ Impulse into himself. Angels announce in advance what man will later become. The passage in question might therefore be translated: Lo, the bestower of Egohood sends his Messenger (Angel) before you to whom Egohood is to be given.

Let us now see if we can discover the meaning of the third sentence. We must first try to picture the conditions prevailing in man's inner life when the astral body had gradually lost the power to send out its forces like feelers and to see clairvoyantly into the divine-spiritual world. Formerly, when the astral body was activated, man was able to look into that world, but this faculty was disappearing and darkness spreading within him. He had once been able to expand his astral body over all the beings of the spiritual world, but now he was inwardly desolate, inwardly isolated—the Greek word is *epnuoc.* At that time the human soul lived in isolation, in desolation. This is what the Greek text tells us: Lo, a voice seems to speak in the desolation of the soul—call it "wilderness" of the soul if you like—when the astral body can no longer expand into the divine-spiritual world. Hear the cry in the wilderness, in the desolation of the soul!

What is it that is being proclaimed in advance? First of all we must be clear about the meaning of the word *Kyrios,* when it was used in Hebrew but also still in Greek in reference to manifestations of the soul and spirit. To translate it simply as "the Lord," with the usual connotation, is sheer nonsense. In ancient times everyone using the word *Kyrios* knew perfectly well that its meaning was connected with the development of man's soul-life and its mysteries. In the astral body, as we know, are the forces of thinking, feeling and willing; the soul thinks, feels and wills. These are the three forces working in the soul but they are actually its servants. In earlier times man was under their domination and he obeyed them, but as his evolution progressed these forces were to become the servants of the Kyrios, the Ruler, the Lord—in short, of the "I." Used in relation to the soul, the word Kyrios actually meant the "I." At this stage it would no longer be true to say: "The Divine-Spiritual thinks, feels and wills in me," but rather: "I think, I feel, I will." The passage should be rendered more or less as follows.—Prepare yourselves, you human souls, to move along those paths that will awaken the Kyrios, the powerful "I" within you; listen to the cry in the solitude of the soul. Make ready the path (or way) of the "I," the Lord of the soul. Open the way for his forces so that he may no longer be the slave but the Ruler of thinking, feeling and willing. Lo, the power that is the "I" sends his Angel before you, the Angel who is to give you the possibility of understanding the cry in the solitude of the astral soul. Prepare the paths of the "I," open the way for the forces of the "I."—Such is the meaning of these significant words of the prophet Isaiah; they point to the greatest of all events in the evolution of humanity. You will now understand the sense in which he speaks about the future John the Baptist, indicating how man's soul in its solitude longs for the coming of its Lord and Ruler, the "I." Such is the real meaning of this passage and in this sense it is to be understood.

[Before returning to the text it is important to realize who the angelic "messenger" working through John the Baptist was. When Steiner said the messenger was an angel, it is as though he sensed that the revelation of angelic activity alone was a sufficient leap for his hearers at that moment. But we should not now stop there, for he elsewhere revealed that the messenger was more exalted than would be implied by the hierarchical designation "angel." We are really speaking of the angel who was to succeed the Archangel Michael, chief among the Archangels, the one related to the Sun (see **I-19**, especially its last three paragraphs), and Folk-Spirit of the Hebrew people. The student will garner more from this revelation after reading about Elijah in "Widow's Son" below, especially its fn 15 dealing with this "angel." See also *Occult Science and Occult Development*_(OSOD), Lect. 2, May 2, 1913, also found in the anthology *The Archangel Michael* (ARCHM) under the title, "Michael, The Messenger of Christ."

Aside from Gabriel, Michael is the only Archangel mentioned in the canon (Dan 10,13,21; 12 1; Jude 1,9; Rev 12,7). We see in **I-19** that there are seven archangelic regencies, each of something over three hundred years, in each Cultural Age of twenty one hundred and sixty (2,160) years (or one twelfth of a Cosmic Year, the period it takes the Sun to travel around the full Zodiac). Steiner tells us that it was not unusual in esoteric writings such as the Bible for a "day" to mean a year, and perhaps a "year," in turn, might mean a century (cf. **I-65**). It is thus curious that in speaking of Michael, Daniel refers to twenty-one days (Dan 10,13). And just after the blowing of the seventh "Trumpet" in Rev 11,15, we find the cosmic events described in Rev 12,7 where Michael appears fighting with the dragon. We will see below that each Trumpet was also associated with a 2,160-year period in a future Cultural Age. Steiner tells us that the number "one thousand two hundred and sixty days" in Rev 11,3 and 12,6 resulted from a transposition in copying whereby two thousand one hundred sixty (2,160) was incorrectly written as one thousand two hundred sixty (1,260). See Lect. 14, Sept. 18, 1924, of the cycle *The Apocalypse* (APOC-CC).

Why do I belabor the point of this two-millennia period? It is not impertinent, even though supported by the observations in "Karma and Reincarnation" above, to wonder about Steiner's assertion that karma and reincarnation were not to be taught exoterically by the Church for two thousand years; and that the "Second Coming" would start to be witnessed by some among humanity after two thousand years. The point at issue bears upon this query. The Archangel Michael is the one in charge of administering the divine intelligence, intelligence that enables direct perception of spiritual reality. The heavenly battle caused the dragon, the deceiving Luciferic and Ahrimanic forces (2 Th 2,1-11), to be thrown down to earth to do battle there against the child who was born and the rest of the woman's offspring (Rev 12,7-13). That battle would rage for the three and a half Cultural Eras left in the post-Atlantean Epoch (see **I-1**), esoterically called "a time, and times and half a time" (Rev 12,14), though this esoteric phrase may refer to the larger cycles and recurring battles between these adversaries as well. The "woman" is the heavenly Anthroposophia (**I-18**), the divine wisdom, the most holy virgin, and the child is the Christ delivered to Earth. What is important for us to realize is that the last regency of Michael before the birth of the Christ child was during the period when Greek philosophy culminated in Plato and Aristotle and then through the latter's pupil prepared the world for Paul's evangelization (**I-19**). Michael, the Sun Archangel, would not again reign until the period of three-hundred-plus years beginning in 1879. The former Folk-Spirit of the Hebrew people, the Archangel who had indwelt Elijah and then as the "messenger" (Mk 1,2; Is 40,3) speaking through

John the Baptist had prepared the way for Christ in the flesh, has become the guiding spiritual force in preparing humanity to recognize Christ in the etheric world. The former Archangel became an Archai (Time Spirit) in 1879, and was succeeded as Archangel by the former guardian angel of the Buddha (again, see fn 15 in "Widow's Son"). That combination becomes enormously powerful working together now in the first Michaelic regency since the Christian era began. This makes it possible for human intelligence to begin to rise to the level of recognizing the Christ in the etheric world, and to perceive the spiritual reality of karma and reincarnation, through the development of a new organ of spiritual perception as discussed in "Second Coming." This could not happen for two thousand years from the Incarnation, i.e., until after 1879.]

You may ask, Even if the above be true, how is it that "Yahweh" appears as "Lord" as far back in the Biblical account as Gen 2? Though it is not, indeed cannot be, seen on the basis of traditional theology as it has come down to us before (and even since) Steiner, the answer is actually quite simple in the light of anthroposophy. As we know, the entirety of the Pentateuch account is ascribed to Moses, who came into his spiritual vision as a result of his prior initiations and the revelation to him on Mt. Sinai, which included that of the "I Am." Thus, Moses, recognizing the prior existence of the "I Am," albeit unknown to human beings before Seth (Gen 4,26), and not called by such name until Moses himself (Ex 6,3), could go back and ascribe to "Yahweh," the "Lord," those prior acts performed by him. In its simplest form, this can perhaps best be seen in **I-16** where we see that the Elohim (Exusiai) are the rulers of Earth evolution. Yahweh-Eloha was the only one who descended to, and took up abode in, the Moon sphere (the other six staying in the Sun sphere); thus he was the hierarchical being charged with the entirety of Earth evolution. We see from OS, the Commentary on Genesis, and "Alpha and Omega > Creation and Apocalypse" (Vol. 2, "*What Is Man?*"), that the portion of the creation account represented by Gen 1,1-2,4a took place prior to a point in the Lemurian Evolutionary Epoch of Earth evolution (see **I-1** through **I-4**). At that point, the development of the first three Elements (Fire, Air and Water, as represented in Gen 1,2) as well as the human being's "Three Bodies" (physical, etheric and astral), had already been prepared during Earth's first three Evolutionary Epochs (Polarian, Hyperborean and Lemurian), though in far less dense condition than now, and as yet without "Form," as indicated in Gen 1,1 and 2,4b-5. Inasmuch as the Elohim (Exusiai) are the "Spirits of Form" (**I-6**), it is they who take over at the point where everything but "Form" had been accomplished, as indicated in Gen 1,1 and 2,4b-5. It is at this point that the Yahweh-Eloha comes into the picture at Gen 2,4b to stay. The reflection by the Moon of the light of the Sun is simply a manifestation on the physical level of the higher spiritual reflection by Yahweh-Eloha of the Christ who had descended by then far enough to take up abode in the Sun sphere (see "As Above, So Below). The true "I Am" was approaching, but could not enter into the human being until there was "Form" and the time was right (see "Right Time"). All of this was preparatory for the primary purpose of Earth evolution, namely, the infusion of the Ego, the "I Am," into the previously existing "bodies" as summarized in **I-14**.

The newcomer to anthroposophy will, of course, have much wrestling to do with the above until he or she is able to assimilate the basic tenets of Spiritual Science (i.e., Occult Science). Only the above brief summary can be given here. But when, with the necessary spiritual toil, that basic knowledge is taken into one's soul by one who is karmically ready (and I am certain there are vast numbers of human beings presently at that point—if they are willing to devote themselves in this incarnation to it), then all distinction between "Lord" ("Yahweh") and the higher Ego ("I Am") disappears, and Ex 3,14 (when translated "I AM *the* I AM") is seen as a perfect expression of the spiritual reality. Until Steiner, there was, to use lawyer language, "a distinction without a difference."

The recent ABD follows the commendable practice of giving the etymological meaning of the Biblical terms it expounds. Notably, by contrast, in regard to "Yahweh" it says (6 ABD 1011), "The meaning of the name is unknown." Steiner takes us back to the origins implicit in Gen 11,1 and Acts 2,8, and shows us that depth of soul-meaning (understanding) carried by the primeval sound thereof.

It is not a matter of indifference, but of salvific necessity, that a sufficient portion of humanity come to see the above-disclosed anthroposophical insight that the "I Am" is *the* "Name" of God. There is an immense tendency, anchored in the group-soul roots from which humanity has evolved, for human beings to coalesce into groupings for mutual support. And groups, to various degrees politically powerful, have a great ability to persecute those who go into the "Wilderness" of spiritual loneliness. But the prophets all went there, as did the Christ himself, and it is to those who do that the future of Christianity belongs (Mt 5,10-11), for there is where the "I Am" is found.

Steiner brings this effectively to our attention in *The EGO, The God Within and the The God of External Revelation* (EGO),[17] Lect. 1:

> It is now the task of the anthroposophical way of thinking ... that we learn to speak a language, which is really not merely understood by the human soul so long as it is in a physical body, but understood also when this soul is no longer bound to the instrument of the physical brain; for instance, either by a soul still in the body, but able to perceive spiritually, or by a soul gone through the gate of death. And that is the essential! If we bring forward those ideas which explain the world, which explain the human being, then that is a speech which cannot merely be understood here in the physical world, but also by those who are no longer incarnated in physical bodies, but live between death and a new birth. Yes, what is spoken on our anthroposophical basis is heard and understood by the so-called dead. [Cf. Gen 11,1-9 and Acts 2,1-11.] There they are fully one with us on a basis where the same speech is spoken. There we speak to all human beings. Because in a certain connection, it is chance whether a human soul is in a body of flesh, or in the condition between death and a new birth. And we learn through anthroposophy a speech comprehensible to all human beings, whether they are in the one or other condition. Thus we speak a speech within the field of anthroposophy which is spoken also for the so-called dead. We really contact the innermost kernel of man, the innermost being of man, through what we cultivate in a real sense in anthroposophical considerations, even if they appear apparently abstract. We penetrate into the soul

---

17. I am beholden to Arie Boogert, priest of the fledgling Christian Community congregation of Denver, Colorado, for bringing to my attention in early 1995 the existence of the "sometimes called 'Second Matthew Cycle of Lectures'." It consisted of twelve lectures (various cities) collected in a book in German, but apparently never so collected or designated in English. All twelve were given in 1909, thus preceding the 1910 cycle published in English as *The Gospel of St. Matthew* (GSMt). EGO consists of three lectures, at least the first two of which were among such twelve.

of man. And because we penetrate to the soul of man, we liberate man from all group-soulness, i.e., man becomes in this way more and more capable of really grasping himself in his ego, his "I." And that is the characteristic, that those who come to anthroposophy today ... appear in comparison with others who remain far from it, as if through anthroposophical thoughts, their ego would crystallize as a spiritual being, which is then carried through the gate of death. With the others, in that place where the I-being is, which remains there—which is now there in the body, and which remains after death—there is a hollow space, a nothingness. Everything else which one can take up as ideas today, will become more and more worthless for the real kernel of man's soul-being. The central point of man's being is grasped through what we take up as anthroposophical thoughts. That crystallizes a spiritual substance in man; he takes that with him after death, and with that he perceives in the spiritual world. He sees and hears with it in the spiritual world, with it he penetrates that darkness which otherwise exists for man in the spiritual world. And thereby it is brought about that when through these anthroposophical thoughts and way of thinking man develops this "I" in him today, which now stands in connection with all the world wisdom we can acquire—he develops it—he carries it over also into his next incarnation. Then he is born with this now *developed* "I," and he *remembers* himself in this developed "I" [and thus is liberated from the futile perspective set out in the Bible in Eccles 1,9-11 and 3,11]. That is the deeper task of the anthroposophical movement today, to send over to their next incarnation a number of human beings with an ego in which they remember themselves as an individual ego. They will be the human beings who form the kernel of the next period of civilization. [Here he is speaking of the Age of Philadelphia, Rev 3,7-13; see also **I-24**, **I-25** and **I-19**.] These people who have been well prepared through the anthroposophical spiritual movement, to remember their individual "I," will be spread over the whole earth [see "East, West, North & South"; also Is 43,5-7 and the gathering of the "elect" from the "four winds," Mt 24,31 and Mk 13,27.] These individual people will be scattered over the whole earth, and within the whole earth sphere will be the kernel of humanity, who will be essential for the sixth period of civilization. And so it will be the case among these people, that they will know themselves as those who in their previous incarnation strove together for the individual "I."

This is the right cultivation of that soul-faculty of which we have spoken. This soul-faculty so develops, that not only those just described will have this memory. More and more human beings will have this memory of their former incarnation—in spite of their not having developed the "I." But they will not remember an individual "I," because they have not developed it, but they will remember the group-ego, in which they have remained. Thus people will exist, who in this incarnation have cared for the development of their individual "I"—they will remember themselves as independent individualities, they will look back and say: You were this or the other. Those who have not developed the individuality will be unable to remember this individuality.

Do not think that through mere visionary clairvoyance one acquires the faculty of remembering the previous ego. Humanity was once clairvoyant. If mere clairvoyance sufficed, then all would remember, for all were clairvoyant. It is not merely a matter of being clairvoyant—humanity will already be clairvoyant in the future—it is a matter of having cultivated the ego in this incarnation, or not. If one has not cultivated it, it is not there as an inner human being; one looks back, and remembers as a group-ego, what one had in common. So that these people will say: Yes, I was there, but I have not freed myself. These people will then experience that as their FALL, as a new Fall of mankind, as a falling back into conscious connection with the group-soul. That will be something terrible for the sixth period of time; to be unable to look back to oneself as an individuality, to be hemmed in by not being able to transcend the group-soulness. If one will express it strongly, one could say: The whole earth with all it produces (this holds at least as an image) will belong to those who now cultivate their individuality[18]; those, however, who do not

---

18. Christian theologians can hardly miss the similarity between Steiner's statement here and the third beatitude, "Blessed are the meek, for they shall inherit the earth" (Mt 5,5), for few words have sent them scrambling for explanation more than the word "meek" in this context. See Barc, Vol. 1, p. 96 (Matthew). "Meek" was first used in the Bible in Num 12,3, "Now the man Moses was very meek, more than all men that were on the face of the earth," and this after he had "killed the Egyptian" and later even faced down the Pharaoh. It is then used five more times; Ps 10,17; 37,11; Is 11,4; 29,19; Mt 5,5; and "meekness" five times; 2 Cor 10,1; Eph 4,2; Col 3,12; Jas 1,21; 3,13. (*continued on following page*)

develop their individual "I," will be obliged to join on to a certain group, from which they will be directed as to how they should think, feel, will, and act. That will be felt as a fall, a falling back, in the future humanity.

So we should regard the anthroposophical movement, the spiritual life, not as mere theory, but as something which is given us in the present, because it prepares what is necessary for the future of mankind.

If we grasp ourselves aright in that point where we are now, whence we have come from out the past, and then look a little into the future, then we must say: Now the time is come where man begins to develop the human faculty of remembering backwards. It is only a question of our developing it aright, i.e., that we train in us an individual "I"; for only what we have *created* in our own soul can we remember. If we have not created it, then there only remains to us a fettering memory of a group-ego, and we feel it as a kind of falling down into a group of higher animality [the germ of eventual beasthood; see "Mark of the Beast;" something of an earlier similar memory is seemingly portrayed in Gen 6,19-7,3, as to which see also "Wild Animals"]. Even if the human group-souls are finer and higher than the animal, yet they are but group-souls. Humanity of an early age did not feel that as a fall, because they were intended to develop from group-soulness to the individual soul. If they are now

---

18. (*continued*) Steiner further elaborates on when and how this inheritance of the Earth will come about, and to whom, in *The Temple Legend* (TL), Lect. 6, near the beginning of the "Widow's Son" essay herein. That essay speaks of "passive resistance to evil," and its fn 1 cites a recent anthroposophical writing discussing Mahatma Gandhi and Martin Luther King, Jr. as modern examples of this nonviolent type that will carry humanity into its next Epoch. Steiner uses the term "fatherless" in the passage from *The Gospel of St. John and its Relation to the Other Gospels* (Jn-Rel) quoted in that essay in explaining the term "Widow's Son," and the last paragraph of the essay discusses the possibility that "fatherless," in the scriptures, can take new meaning from this understanding. At least one of the "meek" passages is used in connection with "fatherless" (see Ps 10,17-18). In the text above, Steiner identifies those who will "inherit the earth" as those who now "cultivate their individuality," and in the "Widow's Son" discussion below he identifies as one of their qualities the passive resistance to evil, a quality of a "Widow's Son," an initiate. In "Mysteries" below, under the discussion of Gen 35,4, Moses is said to have been initiated into the Mysteries of both Egypt and Midian. One can perhaps begin to understand his "meekness" (see Jas 3,13). Especially is this so when anthroposophical light begins to shine on the meaning of the various exploits of Moses in Exodus. The meaning of "Egypt" below is part of this light.

held back, they fall consciously into it, and that will be the oppressive feeling in the future of those who do not take this step aright, either now or in a later incarnation [but failure to avail of existing opportunity limits future spiritual capacity; see "Talents"]. They will experience the fall into group-soulness.

The real task of anthroposophy is to give the right impulse. We must thus grasp it within human life. If we keep in mind that the sixth period of time is that of the first complete conquest of the racial idea, then we must be clear, that it would be fantastic to think that even the sixth "race" starts from one point on the earth and develops like the earlier races. Progress is made by ever-new progressive methods of evolution appearing. By progress we do not mean that what was valid as ideas for earlier times should also hold for the future. If we do not see this, the idea of progress will not be quite clear to us. We will as it were fall again and again into the error of saying: So and so many rounds, globes, races, etc., and it all goes on revolving round again and again in the same manner [cf. Eccles 1,9-11]. One cannot see why this wheel of rounds, globes, races, etc. should always revolve again. It is a question of seeing that the word "race" is a term only having validity for a certain time. This idea no longer has any meaning for the sixth period. Races have only in themselves the elements which have remained from the Atlantean age.

In the future, that which speaks to the depths of man's soul will express itself more and more in the external nature of man; and that which man on the one side as a quite individual being has acquired, and yet, again experiences unindividually, will express itself by working out even to the human countenance; so that the individuality of man—not the group-soulness—will be inscribed for him on his countenance [see "Forehead" as well as "Mark of the Beast"]. That will constitute human manifoldness. Everything will be acquired individually, in spite of its being there through the overcoming of individuality. And we will not meet *groups* among those who are seized of the ego, but the *individual* will express itself externally. That will form the distinction between human beings. There will be such as have acquired their egoity; they will indeed be there over the whole earth with the most manifold countenances, but one will recognize through their variety how the individual ego expresses itself even into the gesture. Whereas among those who have not developed the individuality, the group-soulness will come to expression by their countenance receiving the imprint of the group-soulness, i.e., they will fall into categories similar to each other. That will be the external physiognomy of our earth: a possibility will be prepared for the individuality to carry in itself an external sign, and for the group-soulness to carry in itself its external sign.

This is the meaning of earthly evolution, that man acquires more and more the power of expressing externally his inner being. There exists an ancient script in which the greatest ideal for the evolution of the "I," the Christ Jesus, is characterized by the saying: When the two become one, when the external becomes like the inner, then man has attained the Christ nature in himself. That is the meaning of a certain passage in the so-called Egyptian Gospel.[19] One comprehends such passages out of anthroposopical wisdom.

---

19. In regard to the "Egyptian Gospel," see fn 30 (and related text) in "The Nativity." See "Akashic" below for a vivid illustration of how the darkening consciousness of the early Church Fathers caused the Bible translations now available to us, particularly Matthew's Gospel, to be so stultified as to require the prophetic insights of inspired vision like those of Steiner. We will see throughout the present work, time and again, Gen 15,5 and Ex 3,14, for example, the real meaning underlying the layered transmutations that represent our present Bible versions. It seems likely that Jerome and/or others, by misunderstanding the passage from the "Egyptian Gospel," put in one which more nearly fit their then clouded vision in Mt 18,19-20. Mt 18,19 has a literally weird and unlikely meaning. And in Mt 18,20, only *one individuality* can be referenced by "in my name," i.e., "I Am." Notably, only Matthew's Gospel contains such passages.—ERS

BUSH

THE TERM "BUSH" may be considered an appendix to the phrase "I AM," for the seminal usage of both is in Ex 3, where their meaning is clearly synonymous in the light of anthroposophical insight. To that effect, see "I AM" herein. We saw in "I AM" that the higher "I Am" is the Christ Spirit, while the lower is the human Ego.

Let us reflect for a moment upon the nature of this duality. The Parable of the Prodigal Son, in both its higher and lower applications, speaks of two sons. The larger version is that of the whole Bible story, of how the "prodigal" son (humanity) fell away and how the other Son was sacrificed in order to bring the Prodigal back into familial unity. Recall from "The Nativity" the ancient prophetic maxim that the blessing would be "when the two become one." This verity was enacted, in the sense of the process of Incarnation, as Luke tells us, in the twelve-year old scene in the temple (Lk 2,41-51). There the two Jesus children became one, Jesus of Nazareth. Lk 2,52 tells us of how this "one" "increased in wisdom and in stature, and in favor with God and man" over the period from age twelve to age "Thirty" (Lk 3,23). All four Gospels relate to us then the most divine stage of the Incarnation, when the "dove," the Christ Spirit entered into Jesus of Nazareth, and he was then more fully Jesus Christ. This is the point at which the Incarnation was essentially completed. The "two-to-become-one" vehicles were incarnated in "The Nativity," but the point at which the "Son" was adopted (or begotten) on Earth, was at the Baptism (see "Baptism-Dove"; "You are my begotten son, today I have begotten you," Ps 2,7; see also Mt 3,17; Mk 1,11; Lk 3,22, as well as Is 42,1; and cf. Jn 1,12; Rom 8,23).

The story of the outgoing and return of the Prodigal Son is one first of descent and then reascent, respectively depicted in the fullness of the Bible account under what we will see under "Fission" and "Fusion." The Old Testament is primarily a story of division or separation ("fission"), while the New Testament gives us that of reunion ("fusion"). We first

saw the spiritual principle of "the two becoming one" in "The Nativity."
See the discussion there under fn 30 and the related text from Lect. 6,
Gospel of St. Matthew (GSMt). The complex nature of this spiritual principle is shown in the passage from the Alexandrian church no later than
the fifth century A.D., in which the Lord, asked when his kingdom would
come, replies, "When two shall be one, that which is without as that
which is within, and the male with the female, neither male nor female."
See also fn 21 of "The Nativity."

This divine "oneness" is beautifully expressed in Christ's final prayer
in John's Gospel (Jn 17) in which he prays "that they may become perfectly one" (Jn 17,23) and "that they . . . may be with me where I am" (Jn
17,24). The growing union is later expressed by Lazarus/John in the magnificent evolutionary panorama of the Apocalypse. The final unity is
there expressed in terms of the New Jerusalem, the union of the bride and
bridegroom (Rev 21,2; see also "Bride/Bridegroom"), when the "Name"
of Christ was also that of the human being (Rev 2,17; 3,12; 19,12; Is
44,5; 45,3-4; 56,5; 62,2; 66,22), the higher and the lower "I Am's"
become the same "name."

Paul's entire ministry was directed toward this union of the higher and
lower "I Am's." We see it all the way from Rom 7-8 through Gal 2,20
("Not I but Christ in me") to Eph 1,9-10 when all things are united with
Christ and the Father in "oneness."

While the union of the "I Am's" is expressed at the end of the Bible, it
is equally apparent that the duality of meaning exists when the "I Am" is
first introduced in Ex 3. As we saw, it was Christ speaking to Moses. But
in truth, we had to show in "I AM" how this was so by reference to other
scriptural passages. The metaphor of the "burning bush" which "was not
consumed" appears more immediately to reflect the condition of the
human soul (Ego). In "Karma and Reincarnation" we saw how the path
of the human soul after death led first (after the brief etheric panorama)
into the astral world where the "Purifying Fire" was to burn away all
earthly desire and passion, in flames likened to "hell"—the sojourn which
found a form of expression in the Roman Catholic doctrine of Purgatory.[1]
For "the burning bush" metaphor, the salient point we saw in that journey
is how the Ego was not consumed. And it is never to be fully consumed

---

1. For the relationship of that doctrine to the astral world's "Purifying Fire," see fn 11
under "Karma and Reincarnation."

unless and until it has failed, by the time of the ultimate "Fire" (Rev 20; 2 Pet 3,7), to take into itself (i.e., become one with) the higher "I Am."

When we get to "Fire," in Vol. 2, "*What Is Man?*", we shall see more fully the meaning of Christ's statement, "I came to cast fire upon the earth" (Lk 12,49). We can then see more fully how it is that "the burning bush" on Mount Sinai was the approach of Christ, for the human being enters into oneness with the Christ through the element of "Fire," the one "element" which is still united in Earth in its duality (both etheric or spiritual, on the one hand, and mineral or earthly, on the other). The reality of this is shown by the fact that some characteristic of fire is usually present in the Bible when a human being perceives a spiritual being. It was thus in the only explicit scriptural appearance of the Seraphim, when Isaiah saw the Lord (Is 6,1-8). See also, for instance, Gen 15,17; Gen 22,1-14; Ex 3,2-3; 13,21; 1 K 18,38; 2 K 1,10-14 and 2,11 and 6,17; Is 10,17; Mt 3,11; Lk 3,16 and 12,49; Acts 2,3; 1 Cor 3,13-15; Heb 1,7; Rev 1,14 et al.; and, in addition to "Fire," see "Flaming" and "Thunder/ Lightning"; in all of which the fire element is associated with great holiness. It is the point of contact between Heaven and Earth.

Powerful confirmation that "the burning bush" refers not only to the Christ "I Am" but also to the human "I Am" is found in Jesus' response to the Sadducees' challenge to interpret the resurrection in the light of the levirate law (Lk 20,27-38). This passage is discussed under Point #5 of "Karma and Reincarnation" above, but the point here is that the lower "I Am," or human Ego, is addressed under the term "bush" in the statement (emphasis added), "But that the dead are raised, even Moses showed, *in the passage about the bush*, where he calls the Lord [i.e., the higher "I Am"] the God of Abraham and the God of Isaac and the God of Jacob. Now he is not God of the dead, but of the living; for all live to him [ie., the higher "I Am"]." Here it is the lower "I Am" which is "raised from the dead"; but the essential relationship between the higher and the lower "I Am" seems clearly implied.[2]

---

2. It is by virtue of the higher karmic "law" (Mt 5,17; see Point #8 of "Karma and Reincarnation") that the higher "I Am" came to fulfill that the lower "I Am," in order to be "perfected," is destined to pass again and again through the "refiner's fire" without being consumed. Yet, the lower "I Am," the Ego, is a higher human component than its "Three Bodies," having waited until they were duly "Formed" before descending from the spiritual world (Job 32,4) as the last which shall become first (see "Last First, First Last"). In that sense, it too is the god of the lower three, but only insofar as it becomes one with the higher "I Am."

One should not overlook the immense significance of the fact that the pronouncement, "I am the God of Abraham and the God of Isaac and the God of Jacob," first appears in Ex 3,6 in specific connection with the "Bush." Its echo reverberates throughout the Bible. It is found at least six times in the Old and five times in the New Testaments, not counting the passages "(I am the) God of your fathers," or the "God of Israel." Its meaning may also be carried over into the trio "Abraham, Isaac and Jacob" more fully explored under that phrase later, as well as in the "Three Bodies" passages below. The overriding meaning of all later usages can be taken from this passage of its origination, for it is born in connection with the "burning bush," and only later is the term "Lord" substituted for the "bush." It was previously pointed out in "Karma and Reincarnation" (Point #5) that Lk 20,37-38 had this meaning, for there all the concepts ("Bush," "God of" and the three "fathers") are linked in illustrating "that the dead are raised" (in distinction from being "resurrected" when "they cannot die any more"). Without this understanding, one misses its critical thread of meaning in Jn 8,31-59 and Rom 9,1-13. We are being told throughout the Bible that the Christ-enabled human "I Am," the (higher) Ego, is "Lord" meaning that it is "God" over the "Three Bodies." John 8,52-53 shows that the "Three Bodies" die, but the "I Am" (or "burning bush") does not. Both the Johannine and Pauline passages show that one is not a true child of Abraham who does not take in the higher "I Am" (Jn 8,39-47 and Rom 9,6-8) which is the "God" over such "fathers" or "Three Bodies."

Mark's account of the levirate law question (Mk 12,18-27) also relates Jesus' answer to "the passage about the bush." While more cryptic, its meaning is clarified by the fuller Luke version. Matthew is even more terse (Mt 22,23-32), but still compatible in meaning, though it jumps over the "bush" reference.

These represent the most pointed and clear scriptural usages of the "bush" metaphor, but from them we can garner meaning in other passages as well. If we there take "bush" to apply to the Ego, either the higher or the lower or both depending upon context, there is generally a wondrous enhancement of meaning. By the "higher Ego" is meant the Christ, the "I Am" who appeared to Moses, or the human Ego which has become fully perfected (See "Perfect") through "becoming one with" the Christ. By the "lower Ego" is meant the human Ego which is not yet so perfected—one which has not yet reached the stage of not having to reincarnate ("for they cannot die anymore ... [having become] sons of God," Lk 20,36; Jn 1,12;

Rev 3,12). Except for those exalted human beings who embody an angelic being or a perfected human soul returning in humility only to sacrificially serve others, one lives on Earth as a human being only because karmic debt remains, further perfection being required.

Gen 21,15: When the water in the skin was gone, she cast the child under one of the bushes.

This is part of the account of Hagar dispatching Ishmael into the "Wilderness," an account filled with rich symbolism. We remember from the discussion in "I AM" above that the "Wilderness" is where the "I Am" is found, and here Ishmael is placed under a "bush" in the "wilderness." For while Ishmael was not chosen to sire the line that would provide the physical body for the Incarnation of the Christ, he was blessed and did father *twelve* sons, the same number as Isaac, and both Ishmael and Isaac laid Abraham to rest (Gen 25,9). One cannot properly think of Ishmael pejoratively when the Biblical account is read in the light of anthroposophy. While it was through Isaac that Abraham's descendants were to be *named* (Gen 21,12; Rom 9,7; Heb 11,18), we can see that in the higher sense this meant that it was through him that the higher "I Am," the "*Name*" of Christ the LORD, the *Kyrios* (see "I AM"), was to come, and that the opportunity of developing the *twelvefold* zodiacal nature of the Ego promised in Gen 15,5 was not limited to Isaac's line but extended also to Ishmael. See the Commentary for the meaning of their respective "*names.*"

Deut 33,13-17: (13) And of Joseph he said, "Blessed by the LORD be his land, with the choicest gifts of heaven above,... (14) with the choicest fruits of the sun,... (15) with the finest produce of the ancient mountains, ... (16) with the best gifts of the earth and its fullness, and the favor of him that dwelt in the *bush*. Let these come upon the head of Joseph, and upon the crown of the head of him that is prince among his brothers...."

The sun wisdom, the "choicest fruits of the sun," is the natural clairvoyance that settles "upon the crown of the head" (see the discussion of the Abel and Solomon wisdom in the Appendix to "Three Bodies" below). Michelangelo depicted it in Moses by the stubs of two horns just above his hairline. We should see in this a certain significance in the "Name" Joseph. See "The Nativity." The "favor of him that dwelt in the bush" suggests that the gift is bestowed by the descending Christ for the fulfillment of his mission. The "fullness," *pleroma*, of the Elohim (Jn 1,16) is hinted.

> **Job 30,1-8**: (1) But now they make sport of me, *men who are younger than I*, whose fathers I would have disdained to set with the dogs of my flock. (2) What could I gain from the strength of their hands, men whose vigor is gone? (3) Through want and hard hunger they gnaw the dry and desolate ground; (4) they pick mallow and the *leaves of bushes*, and to warm themselves the roots of the broom. (5) They are driven out from among men.... (6) In the gullies of the torrents they must dwell, in holes of the earth and of the rocks. (7) *Among the bushes* they bray; under the nettles they huddle together. (8) A senseless, a disreputable brood, they have been whipped out of the land. (Emphasis added)

One can appreciate the great meaning of this passage, as well as that of the book of Job in its entirety (more fully shown in "Three Bodies" herein), only when one sees that it sets out the multifold nature of the human being (see **I-9**) as presented by anthroposophy.

INTPN fairly states the view the Judeo-Christian faith has developed with respect to this book in opening its Introduction thereto, "The Book of Job has to do with the most painful and unavoidable questions which can arise in human experience," stemming from the existence of arbitrary suffering and its meaning. Ask the person in the street what the book (Job) stands for. The likely response will be James' aphorism which probably expresses the extent of real knowledge modern theology has to offer on the subject (i.e., the net result of extensive treatises and the substance of the first sentence of the Introduction to Job in 15 AB xv)—"the patience of Job," Jam 5,11 (KJV), variously translated "perseverance" (NIV), "steadfastness" (RSV), "endurance" (KJV/NIV—INT) or otherwise. That knowledge, i.e., Job's "patience," is certainly valid as far as it goes, but is merely part of the problem or "Mystery," and does not alone suffice for understanding the deeper message. While I am not aware that Rudolf Steiner found the time to ever explicitly address, in any depth, the fuller meaning of this book, he does give definite pointers, such as in *From Jesus to Christ* (JTC), Lect. 5, pp. 94-97; *Supersensible Knowledge* (SKN), Lect. 3 (differently translated as the first lecture in *The Origin of Suffering/The Origin of Evil/Illness and Death* [OSOE]); *Turning Points in Spiritual History* (TPSH), Lect. 4, pp. 210-213; and *The Karma of Materialism* (KM), Lect. 3, p. 44. Other points in his works that are relevant to various portions of Job will be taken up in the Commentary or elsewhere. Notably, however, in *Manifestations of Karma* (MK), Lect. 3, p. 63, we read,

> The spiritual investigator must always in the case of illness consider, on the one hand, the share the physical body may have in this particular case, and, on the other, the share of the etheric body and the astral body; for all three principles may be involved in the disease.

I-37 is taken from MK, Lects. 3, 6 and 10, and more fully elaborates this briefly stated point. Suffice it for now to say that the human being's Fall (Gen 3) resulted in the imposition of divine remedies for each of the "Three Bodies", pain (astral body), toil (etheric body) and death (physical body), (Gen 3,16,17,19; see also #5 in "Three Bodies" below).

As one comes to a fuller understanding of anthroposophy and then investigates Job more fully, it can be seen to portray the picture of the "first Adam" (see "First and Second Adam"), before his descent into materiality, at a time when the spiritual powers exposed him to the Luciferic influence (Gen 3). The only condition was that his "life" must be "spared" (Job 2,6; cf. Cain's lament in Gen 4,13-15 immediately following the expulsion from the Garden). Reincarnation was about to begin with the Fall. Job's three friends represent, successively, his three bodies, starting from the oldest, the physical, etheric and astral (see #2 in "Three Bodies). His youngest member (Elihu), the Ego, does not make its entrance until Job 32. Immediately prior to that (Job 29-31) he yearns for the days in the Garden before he descended into materiality. What Job experiences through the body of the book is the agony of the "three bodies" and the darkening of the face of God (see "Mysteries" below). In the latter chapters of the poetic portion of the story, we see the Ego progressing toward the perfection of the "three bodies," and in the prose conclusion, Job 42,7-17, the wrath of God is directed toward the "three friends" who are obliged to offer up a "burnt offering" (i.e., themselves being purified thereby; see also "Fire" in Vol. 2). Whereupon, Job was not only restored to his former position with spiritual beings, but he was transformed by being more blessed than he was before (vs 12).

Steiner makes it clear, as does the book of Job itself, that Job suffered innocently. The human being was infected in the Garden before the Ego had descended into it, and thus was not morally responsible for what existed in its "members" (Rom 7,21-25; see *The Concepts of Original Sin and Grace* [OSG]), thus laying the just and reciprocal basis for the "Grace" that was to be later bestowed upon it freely. But the innocence of Job, as Steiner says, illustrates even more that suffering is not, in the given personality, necessarily due to the sins of that Individuality. Suffering is, in and of itself, a matter of upward transformation, spiritualization, the reascent of the human being. A soul can incarnate for the purpose of suffering to overcome the karma of humanity as a whole, or of other individuals. Job is mentioned in only three books of the Bible, Job, Ezekiel and James. Ezekiel identifies him as one of three paragons of virtue, Noah, Daniel and Job (Ezek 14,12-20; see #46 in "Three Bodies"). This would seem to justify Steiner's view, not unique to him, that Job's suffering was innocent, that is, his incarnation had a certain sacrificial character in it of "overcoming evil with good" (Rom 12,21) in curing not his own but the karma of humanity. As in Paul's case, for him to live was Christ, though, as seen in chapters 29-31, to die was gain (Phil 1,21).

When Paul said "We preach Christ crucified" (1 Cor 1,23; 2,2; see "Crucified"), he was giving Christendom a message it has yet to understand. It is implicit in his denouement where he describes Christ as the "first fruits of those who have fallen asleep" (1 Cor 15,20), for "each in his own order" (vs 23), to become kindred "fruit," must likewise suffer the crucifixion of the "three bodies" during the course of "perfection." For a normal human being this cannot be accomplished within the course of a single lifetime. We see this in the long drama of Lazarus/John's Apocalypse (Rev). See "First Born/Fruits."

In the light of anthroposophy, every single Biblical use of the term "bush(es)" (Gen 21,15; Ex 3,2-4; Deut 33,16; Job 30,4,7; Mk 12,26; Lk 6,44; 20,37; Acts 7,30,35) can be seen to involve the human Ego, the lower "I Am," either alone or in conjunction with the higher "I Am" of Christ. In the passage above, Job speaks of "men who are younger than I, whose fathers I would have disdained to set with the dogs of my flock," who "make sport of me." They only gather the "leaves of bushes," having no grasp (comprehension or vision) of the whole "bush" (Ego). Job is an old soul, such, for instance, as we have seen in Zarathustra (see "The Nativity"). These souls return to Earth sacrificially and, in humble service to humanity, suffer the barbs of others "younger," i.e., less spiritually mature, than they—in the pattern of the suffering servant, Jesus of Nazareth. We can even see in Job's reference to "the dogs of my flock" some indication of the future redemption by the Human Kingdom of the lower three Kingdoms (Rom 8,19-23; Eph 1,9-10), animals who only eat the "leaves of bushes," who, during the course of human evolution, descended prematurely into materiality and were thereby "driven out from among men" to "dwell in holes of the earth and of the rocks," merely "braying" "among the bushes" or Egos of human beings (vs 8). From another perspective, the Christ-inspired Ego is tormented by its lower "three bodies," especially by the "Wild Animals" of its astral body which "make sport" of it. It was these of which Mark spoke about Christ's temptations (Mk 1,13). But in all respects, the "bush" represents the Ego, higher, lower or both.

While the foregoing discussion essentially exhausts the scriptural usages of the term "Bush(es)," we should not stop there, for once it is seen that it is a metaphor for the Ego or "I Am," we should consider whether extending that meaning to synonyms or parallels of the literal term "bush" is warranted. For instance, "bush" and "shrub" have the same meaning, and both involve a wood element, so small trees (see "Under the Tree") also come within the scope of our search, and other passages are given enhanced meaning. (Emphasis mine)

Is 6,13: "And though a tenth remain in it, it will be *burned again*, like a *terebinth* or an oak, whose stump remains standing when it is felled." *The holy seed is its stump.*

Jer 17,5-6: (5) Thus says the LORD: "Cursed is the man who trusts in man and makes flesh his arm, whose heart turns away from the LORD. (6) He is like a *shrub* in the desert, and shall not see any good come. He shall dwell in the parched places of the wilderness, in an uninhabited salt land."

Mt 13,31-32: (31) Another parable he put before them, saying, "The kingdom of heaven is like a grain of mustard seed which a man took and sowed in his field; (32) it is the smallest of all seeds, but when it has grown it is the greatest of *shrubs* and becomes a *tree*, so that the birds of the air come and make nests in its branches."

To the same general effect are the synoptic parallels in Mk 4,30-32 and Lk 13,18-19, and the meaning may even be extended to

> **Mt 17,20**: "… For truly, I say to you, if you have faith as a grain of *mustard seed*, you will say to this mountain, 'Move from here to there,' and it will move; and nothing will be impossible to you."

Also to its parallel in Lk 17,6.

To understand the warrant for such extensions, consider the nature of a "bush," shrub, tree, or in fact of any plant. Here all that can be done is simply to point the reader in the direction for further contemplation. The Goethean conception of the "archetypal plant" furnishes an excellent starting point. In this connection, see "Johann Wolfgang von Goethe" in Cognate Writings, Vol. 3, *Companions Along The Way* as well as *Goethean Science* (GS) and *Goethe's World View* (GWV). One approaches the idea by simply asking the question, What constitutes a plant? If we look at it at any given instant in time, it will differ, just as does any other creature in the physical world to greater or lesser extent, from its state in any other instant of time. Thus, one cannot define a plant solely by describing it as a physical phenomenon analyzed at any one such instant. The plant is described more truthfully if it can be seen in its entire life cycle. But this includes the composite picture at every stage, from seed to sprout to stem to leaf to fruit and back to seed. Indeed, it is helpful to consider the immense spiritual significance of the term "Seed."[3]

The eye cannot physically "see" the "archetypal plant." To "see" it, one must use other methods of "sight." We can, of course, mentally picture each state, but what is it that we conceptualize when that has been done? We get close, in such case, to the etheric (life) body of the plant. But what we conceptualize at that point is not the etheric body, but what

---

3. The relationship of a "seed" to a "bush" is further shown in Vol. 2, *"What is Man?"* in the essay of the same title. Steiner's so-called "Astronomy Course" is condensed in that essay. In Lect. 8, the distinction between an annual and a perennial plant is shown to be analogous to the human relation to heavenly bodies. The perennial returns yearly from its root, thus having to a greater extent separated itself over time from the annual influence of the Sun as compared with the annual plant which must depend upon the Sun to germinate its "seed." The human being has, in like manner, during the course of evolution distanced itself from the direct influence of the heavenly bodies. Probably the highly intuitive Isaiah expressed this perception also in Is 6,13 when he said, "The holy seed is its "stump" (or root).

emanates from it, namely, the physical body. Yet it is not what we see with our sensate eyes as, and call in our common language, the physical body. Rather it is the spiritualized physical body discussed later under "Form/Phantom" (cf. also "Formed"). It is the unmineralized and non-densified "pattern" (see Ex 25,9,40; Num 8,4; Acts 7,44; Heb 8,5) shown us on the "Mountain" (see "Mountain," "High Mountain" and "As Above, So Below"). While the physical body is the human being's oldest "member" (see **I-14**), having represented spiritual heat on Old Saturn, its earthly manifestation to the senses is only through its densification and mineralization.

In the human, as also in the animal and plant, when the etheric (or life) body separates from the physical body, the latter reverts to its pure mineral condition (e.g., Jn 8,52-53), losing its "Form," as we see it with our sensate eyes, and disintegrating. Thus, the etheric body is what "Forms" our earthly physical bodies and causes them to retain their shape and to develop and/or heal. (Recall the application of this principle in "The Nativity," in the discussion of the virginity of the two Mary's, particularly the Solomon Mary in Matthew's Gospel.) Defective etheric bodies generally require more than one life to be healed, but defective physical conditions can be healed by a healthy etheric body. Something of the depth of this matter can be seen in **I-37**.

The "Form/Phantom" representing the spiritualized physical body is, therefore, close to what we conceptualize when we think of a plant. There is a close connection between it and the etheric body, but the latter is not a Form, for the etheric world is one of constant motion or fluidity. The fluids in our bodies are the earthly counterpart of the etheric world, but one who "sees" in the etheric world perceives motion. When our future organ of perception (associated with manas, or "Manna") is sufficiently developed, we will be able to perceive the etheric body in the plant or higher kingdoms. (Much in the Charts & Tabulations is helpful here, as, for instance, **I-9** through **I-14**.) Goethe appears to have been the harbinger of this, but his vision was limited, while that of Steiner, the prophet, went far beyond. It is only that humanity has such limited scope (see Abbott's *Flatland* [FLd]) that it has given him thus far the treatment accorded true prophets (Mt 5,12; Lk 6,23; Mt 23,37; Lk 13,34; Mt 23,34).

When one begins to see the nature of the various kingdoms in the light of anthroposophy, then even such terms as "Grass" can be seen to carry deep meaning beyond that otherwise apparent. The Bible can hardly convey its deeper meaning without these understandings. The literal language is simply part of the "hiding" process, the "occult" vehicle, inherent in its elaboration.

We teach children the ancient Greek myths, for instance, the myth of Prometheus. Why do so many in our materialistic time not accept that the Mosaic account from the same historical period, or even earlier, likewise expresses its truths in myth and allegory? When we get to spiritual adulthood, should we not "give up [these mere] childish ways" (1 Cor 13,11; see also "Milk," "Simple" and "Simple rather than Wise;" consider also Paul's instruction in Gal 4 and 1 Cor 10,1-4, and the discussion of Philo in "Egypt" below.) In the transition from the Chaldo-Egyptian Cultural Era, which our own Era mirrors (see **I-24** and **I-25**), to the critical and intervening Greco-Roman, something of the same thing was said by the Egyptian priest to Solon: "O Solon, Solon, you Hellenes are never anything but children, and there is not an old man among you.... Those genealogies of yours ... are no better than the tales of children [for among other things] you remember a single deluge only...." (*Timaeus*; see "Plato" in Cognate Writings, Vol. 3). Is it not time to come, with anthroposophical (see **I-65**) light, into an understanding of the Biblical message, given us in the form of holy myth, for spiritual adulthood in our Age?

AKASHIC

THE BRITANNICA, 1 Brit 185, has this to say:

Akashic record, in occultism, a compendium of pictorial records, or "memories," of all events, actions, thoughts, and feelings that have occurred since the beginning of time. They are said to be imprinted on Akasha, the astral light, which is described by spiritualists as a fluid ether existing beyond the range of human senses. The Akashic records are reputedly accessible to certain select individuals—e.g., a spiritualist medium who conducts a seance. Akasha allegedly transmits the waves of human willpower, thought, feeling, and imagination and is a reservoir of occult power, an ocean of unconsciousness to which all are linked, making prophecy and clairvoyance possible.

While not entirely harmonious with Steiner's comments, the above does reflect the existence of the concept, though its Oriental origin is not stated. Around the turn of this century, Steiner sensed that the Theosophical Society, as it then existed, was the most fertile field in which his spiritual insights could then be revealed. His most practical course was simply to adopt the Oriental terminology prevalent within the Society, to the extent it represented an area of spiritual insight, rather than to coin Western terms. Thus he continued to use such terminology as Karma, but with substantive revisions in meaning and application as his spiritual insight demanded. The term "Akashic record" was such an instance. He specifically did not accept that such record could be accurately read by spiritualist mediums.

Let us look first at some of the relevant things Steiner said about the "Akashic" record (generally referred to simply as "Akashic" herein), and then see what the Bible has to say about it. It is important in regard to the former to bear in mind the complex nature of the "Akashic" and that it is beyond the scope or present needs of this work to attempt a thorough treatment of it here. In her 1939 Preface to the German edition of what is now *Cosmic Memory* (CM), a group of Steiner's essays that first appeared in 1904 in the periodical *Lucifer Gnosis*, Steiner's widow, Marie, stated, "The one who wishes to obtain a clear idea of the manner in which a reading of the Akasha Chronicle becomes possible must devote himself intensively to the study of Anthroposophy." In the second essay, entitled "From the Akasha Chronicle," Steiner says, "Only a faint conception of this chronicle can be given in our language. For our language corresponds to the world of the senses." After pointing out that the script is "not ... like the dead testimony of history, but appear[s] in full *life*," he goes on,

> Those initiated into the reading of such a living script can look back into a much more remote past than is presented by external history; and—on the basis of direct spiritual perception—they can also describe much more dependably the things of which history tells. In order to avoid possible misunderstanding, it should be said that spiritual perception is not infallible. This perception also can err, can see in an inexact, oblique, wrong manner. No man is free from error in this field, no matter how high he stands. Therefore one should not object when communications emanating from such spiritual sources do not always entirely correspond. But the dependability of observation is much greater here than in the external world of the senses. What various initiates can relate about history and prehistory will be in *essential* agreement. Such a history and prehistory does in fact exist in all mystery schools. Here for millennia the agreement has been so complete that the conformity existing among external historians of even a single century cannot be compared with it. The initiates describe *essentially* the same things at all times and in all places.

From *Occult Science* (OS), Chap. IV:

> When a being reaches corporeal existence, the substance of his body disappears with his physical death. The spiritual forces that have expelled these corporeal elements from themselves do not "disappear" in the same way. They leave their impressions, their exact counterparts, behind in the spiritual foundations of the world, and he who, penetrating the visible world, is able to lift his perception into the invisible, is finally able to have before him something that

might be compared with a mighty spiritual panorama, in which all past world-processes are recorded. These imperishable impressions of all that is spiritual may be called the "Akashic Record," thus designating as the Akashic essence the spiritually permanent element in universal occurrences, in contradistinction to the transient forms of these occurrences.

Commencing in the first paragraph of the first lecture of *The Gospel of St. John* (GSJ), the first lecture-cycle in the so-called "Gospel Series,"[1] we find:

> If Spiritual Science is to fulfill its true mission in respect of the modern human spirit, then it should point out that if men will only learn to use their inner forces and capacities—their forces and capacities of spiritual perception—they will be able, by applying them, to penetrate into the mysteries of life, into what is concealed within the spiritual worlds behind the world of the senses. The fact that men can penetrate to the mysteries of life through the use of inner capacities, that they are able to reach the creative forces and beings of the universe through their own cognition must be brought more and more into the consciousness of present day humanity. Thus it becomes evident that a knowledge of the mystery of this Gospel can be gained by men, independent of every tradition, independent of every historical document.
>
> In order to make this absolutely clear, we shall have to express ourselves in quite radical terms. Let us suppose that through some circumstance all religious records had been lost, and that men possessed only those capacities which they have today; they should, nevertheless, be able to penetrate into life's mysteries, if they only retain those capacities. They should be able to reach the divine-spiritual creating forces and beings which lie concealed behind the physical world. And Spiritual Science must depend entirely upon these independent sources of knowledge, irrespective of all records. However, after having investigated the divine-spiritual mysteries of the world independently, we can then take up the actual religious documents

---

1. For the chronological list of the eleven cycles I refer to as the "Gospel Series," see the list at the end of *The Gospel of St. John and its Relation to the Other Gospels* (Jn-Rel) (p. 290). That this is not a complete list is obvious from an inspection of the Bibliography herein.

themselves. Only then can we recognize their true worth, for we are, in a certain sense, free and independent of them. What has previously been independently discovered is now recognized within the documents themselves. And you may be sure that for anyone who has pursued this path, these writings will suffer no diminution in value, no lessening of the respect and veneration due them.

In the third cycle in the Gospel series, *The Gospel of St. Luke*, (GSL), Lect. 1, we come to those three levels of spiritual perception that Isaiah (Is 6,10) calls "seeing, hearing and understanding." For parallel descriptions of these levels, see **I-31**. Steiner, as there seen, calls these, "imagination, inspiration and intuition," respectively. He says that, of the four Evangelists, only John was an Initiate in the highest sense, that of having attained to Intuition. The other three Gospel writers had attained only to the first level of spiritual perception, that of Clairvoyant Imagination (i.e., "seeing").[2] Steiner asserts that anthroposophy

---

2. Of "the other three" Steiner does say "not one of their writers expressed his message as clearly as did the writer of the Gospel of St. Luke." In regard to Luke's preface, Steiner says that "eyewitnesses" (Lk 1,2) means those who have been initiated to the first stage, that of spiritual "seeing" or clairvoyance ("Seers"). Then, however, while recognizing that "the word" has reference to the second stage, spiritual hearing or "inspiration," he points out that those with whom Luke conferred were "servants" (ministers) (see discussion at end of fn) of the word and not "possessors" of it, "people who could count less upon Inspirations than upon Imaginations in their own knowledge but for whom communications from the world of Inspiration were nevertheless available.... They could proclaim what their inspired teachers had made known to them." It seems important here to segregate out the influence upon Luke of his own teacher (Lk 4,14, "Luke the beloved ..."), Paul.

It would be wrong to say that by these words Steiner was limiting the initiation of Paul to mere clairvoyance (imagination). Rather it is better to see in "servants of the word" a reference to the fact that Luke's investigation went beyond Paul to others less inspired or intuitive who could not be elevated above "servants" (vs "possessors"). Here is not the place to be exhaustive on the subject, but there are too many indications from Steiner's work that Paul was initiated through the third stage, intuition. And there are in Luke's Gospel (and the book of Acts) too many instances of Paul's insights to believe that nothing higher than imagination and hearsay from inspiration is present.

Anthroposophists strive to penetrate words of scripture to a deeper level of meaning, a level always there according to Steiner's manifold disclosures. Paul himself said that he "was caught up to the third heaven" (2 Cor 12,2), which surely means the third level of initiation. While I have yet to find Steiner's explicit discussion on this point, it follows from his teachings. In *Saint Paul* (SP), Chap. 12, p. 238, Bock interprets (without citing any direct Steiner reference) this passage in precisely this way. It is hard to read Lect. 5 of *The Bhagavad Gita and the Epistles of Paul* (BGEP) without seeing Steiner's assertion that Paul had attained to the high level of intuition, the "third heaven." *(continued on following page)*

relies "upon no other source than that of the Initiates" (those having
attained to "Intuition," or "understanding,"—who, the Anthroposophist soon comes to realize, is essentially Steiner himself) "and that the
texts of the gospels are not the actual sources of its knowledge." And he
continues:

> The truth is that there is only one source for spiritual investigation
> when directed to the events of the past. This source does not lie in
> external records; no stones dug out of the earth, no documents pre-
> served in archives, no treatises written by historians either with or
> without insight—none of these things is the source of spiritual sci-
> ence. What we are able to read in the imperishable *Akashic Chroni-
> cle*—that is the source of spiritual science. The possibility exists of
> knowing what has happened in the past without reference to external
> records. Modern man has thus two ways of acquiring information

---

2. (*continued*) In speaking of his "First and Second Adam" revelations, Steiner says, "So
there is much in his Epistles that seems to be contradictory [cf. 2 Pet 3,15-16]. But if one
penetrates their depths one will indeed find everywhere in them the impulse coming from
the being of Christ." This "being of Christ" suggests the third level, that of "knowing,"
"touching" (Gen 32,32) or "understanding" (Is 6,10). And, while Steiner does not mention it, Luke's preface does not stop with merely "servants of the word" but goes on to say
"that you may know the truth." If, therefore, Luke had teachings from those who were
inspired, he also appears to say that he had them from those who "knew," who were intuitive. His teacher Paul was such a one. Only Paul and Lazarus/John, of the scripture
writers, were directly initiated to these levels by Christ. We are told of a third who was so
initiated, the "Young Man" of Nain, Lk 7,11-15. See "Widow's Son." The fact that Luke
is the only source of this account suggests that there was another from whom he must have
derived instruction based upon intuition. We shall see from "Peter, James and John" that
Luke also probably derived, along with the other Evangelists, testimony from Lazarus/
John upon which "knowledge" could be based.
  It is wrong to take Steiner as saying that nothing in the synoptic Gospels has its origin
in intuitive cognition, but rather that any such information is reported secondhand
whereas in John's Gospel it comes from within the soul of the Evangelist himself.
  Several modern versions have translated the Greek words *hyperetai genomenoi* "servants" rather than "ministers," and in doing so are probably closer to its literal meaning.
Those which have are NIV, NRSV, NEB and Barc. KJV/NIV—INT says "attendants becoming," and in Luke's passage in Acts 13,5 where the singular noun for *hyperetai* is
found, it is consistent, "and they also had John [as] *attendant*" (emphasis added). 28 AB
294 uses "ministers" in its text, but in its "Notes" says, "The Greek of this phrase is not
easily translated." It translates *genomenoi* as "becoming," not itself problematical, and
then says "In itself, *hyperetes* means 'a servant, helper, assistant....'" LB's loose evangelical
version says "early disciples." PMEB says "teachers"; and AMPB "ministers ...[that is of
'the doctrine concerning ...']."

about the past. He can take the documents and the historical records
when he wants to learn something about outer events, or the religious scripts when he wants to learn something about the conditions
of spiritual life. Or else he can ask: What have those men to say before whose spiritual vision lies that imperishable Chronicle known as
the "Akashic Chronicle"—that mighty tableau in which there is registered whatever has at any time come to pass in the evolution of the
world, of the earth and of humanity?

He then describes some of the difficulties involved in such an investigation, and why one who has not perceived the different elements of the
human being's nature (see **I-9**) will normally be led into error.

Again, in the first lecture of the sixth cycle, *Background to the Gospel
of St. Mark* (BKM), in the Gospel series, the same general predicate is
laid, namely, the independent search of the "Akashic" as the principal
source for knowledge of the original Gospel meaning and content. The
importance of this is illustrated in the eighth cycle, *From Jesus to Christ*
(JTC), Lect. 4:

You will understand that the anthroposophical interpretation of
the Gospels differs radically from all previous interpretations. Anyone who takes up our printed lecture-cycles on the Gospels, or re-
calls them from memory, will see that everywhere a return has been
made to true meanings, which can no longer be found simply by
reading the present-day Gospel texts. From the existing translations, in fact, we can no longer reach that which the Gospels wish
to indicate. To a certain extent, as they exist today, they are no
longer fully of use.

Later Steiner gives the following two-phased example:

When at the condemnation of Christ Jesus He was asked whether
He was a king sent from God, He replied: "Thou sayest it!"[3] Now

---

3. See Mt 27,11; Mk 15,2; Lk 23,3. Cf. Jn 18,29-19,16. Cf. also Mt 26,25 and Lk 22,70
for seemingly similar situations.—ERS

anyone who thinks straightforwardly, and does not wish to explain the Gospels according to the professorial methods of the present day, must admit that with this answer of Christ Jesus no clear sense can be connected in terms either of feeling or of reason. From the side of feeling, we must ask why Christ Jesus speaks so indefinitely that no one can recognize what He means by saying "Thou sayest it." If He means "Thou art right," there is no meaning in it, for the words of the interrogator are not a declaration but a question. How then can this be an answer full of meaning? Or, from the side of reason, how can we think that He whom we imagine to be possessed of all-comprehending wisdom should choose such a form for His answer? When, however, these words are given as they stand in the Akashic record it is not "Thou sayest it," but, "This, thou alone mayest give an answer," which means, when we understand it rightly, "To thy question I should have to give an answer that no one may ever give with reference to himself: it can be given only by someone who stands opposite him. Whether the answer is true or not true, of that I cannot speak; the acknowledgment of this truth lies not with me but with thee. Thou must say it; then and then only would it have a meaning."[4]

We can say ... that the last transcriber or translator of this passage did not understand it, because of its difficulty, and so wrote down something inaccurate. Anyone who knows how many things in the world are inexactly written down will not be surprised that here we have to do with an inaccurate version. Have we then no right, when a new epoch of humanity is beginning, to lead the Gospels back to their original form, which can be authenticated from the Akashic record? The whole thing comes out clearly—and this can be shown even from external history—if we consider in this connection the Matthew Gospel. The best that has been said about the origin of the

---

4. This point, brought powerfully home by Steiner, also bears upon the meaning of Ex 3,6, Lk 20,37, and similar passages discussed under "Bush," "I AM" and "Karma and Reincarnation." Thus Jesus is only Lord, i.e., God of Abraham, Isaac and Jacob, as well as of anyone else, to the extent that the "I Am" of that person has taken him in as such. The only one who can be "Lord," that is "the ruler," of one's "Three Bodies," i.e., of Abraham, Isaac and Jacob, is the "I Am" which is housed in those "Three Bodies." It is very similar to the question of the "Name" of the Lord, which is "I Am," since only its bearer can know it, i.e., say it. See Rev 2,17 and 19,12.—ERS

Matthew Gospel may be read in the third volume of Blavatsky's *Secret Doctrine*, a work which must be understood if we are to judge and value it correctly.[5]

There was a certain Father of the Church, Jerome, who wrote towards the end of the fourth century. From what he writes we learn something that can be fully confirmed by occult research: the Gospel of Matthew was originally written in Hebrew.[6] In the copy that Jerome had obtained, or, as we should perhaps say nowadays, in the edition he possessed, he had before him the original language of this Gospel, written in the Hebrew letters still in use, though its language was not the customary Hebrew of that time. Jerome's Bishop had given him the task of translating this version of the Matthew Gospel for his Christians. As a translator Jerome behaved in a most singular way. In the first place he thought it would be dangerous to translate this Gospel of Matthew as it was, because there were things in it which those who up to then had possessed it as their sacred writing wished to keep from the profane

---

5. It is not completely clear to me what evidence he has in mind by his reference to "external history" in the penultimate sentence. However, some external evidence related to what he then sets out does exist. For instance, we know that Jerome was the producer of the Vulgate under commission in 382 from Pope Damascus. See 12 Brit 438 "Vulgate". Furthermore, Jerome himself writes (See 3 Nicene-3, p. 362), "The Gospel also which is called the Gospel according to the Hebrews [here a footnote states that Jerome seems to regard such as "the original Hebrew Text of Matthew"], and which I have recently translated into Greek and Latin and which also Origen often makes use of...." Later (on the same p. 362) Jerome writes, "Matthew ... composed a gospel of Christ at first published in Judea in Hebrew."

Nor have I read the Blavatsky reference to see if what follows is a quote from it or Steiner's own initial assertion. In view of the fact that Steiner himself, while recognizing the truth of much that she wrote, recognizes portions of her work that were erroneous, based upon his own original spiritual research, its precise provenance does not greatly matter.—ERS

6. It seems significant that Steiner here, based upon his own "occult research," un-equivocally proclaims the origin of Matthew's Gospel to have been in Hebrew. Even our later popular commentaries equivocate on and question that, as to which see 7 Interp 240 (1951), 26 AB xliv-xlvii (1971) and Barc's Matthew, Vol 1, pp. 4-5 (1975). The later NJB (1985), at p. 1602, appears to recognize an early Gospel in "Aramaic," but by the time of its publication the twentieth-century discoveries had confirmed what Steiner said (in JTC in 1911) based upon his own occult investigation. As to these discoveries, see *The Essene Odyssey* (TEO) and Welburn's *The Beginnings of Christianity* (BC) in Cognate Writings, Vol. 3, *Companions Along The Way*. In the light of these developments, it seems strange that Professor Boring's later Introduction to Matthew, 8 NIB 124, appears to make no reference to the book's Aramaic provenance.—ERS

world.[7] He thought that this Gospel, if it were translated complete, would cause disturbance rather than edification. So he omitted the things which, according to his own and the ecclesiastical views of that period, might have a disturbing effect, and replaced them by others. But we can learn still more from his writings, and this is the most serious aspect of the whole proceeding: Jerome knew that the Gospel of Matthew could be understood only by those who were initiated into certain secrets. He knew, too, that he was not one of those. In other words, he admitted that he did not understand this Gospel! Yet he translated it. Thus the Matthew Gospel lies before us today in the dress given to it by a man who did not understand it, but who became so accustomed to this version that he afterwards condemned as heresy anything asserted about this Gospel if it was not in accord with his own rendering. These are absolute facts....

Thus we have before us the singular fact that the Gospels had to be communicated, but that Christianity could be understood only in its most imperfect form. Hence the Gospels have been subject to a method of research which can no longer determine what is historical and what is not, so that finally everything is denied. In their original form they must enter our hearts and souls.... An interpretation of the Christ-Event from the occult standpoint is thus a necessary preparation for the souls that in the near future are to experience something new, souls that are to look out on the world with new faculties. The old form of the Gospels will first receive its true value through our

---

7. That such was common in Biblical times, see Mt 7,6. See also Andrew Welburn in the Cognate Writings volume, especially the references to "The Secret Gospel According to Mark."
It appears from Welburn's discussion in GNOS, Chap. 9 that a book referred to in a letter from Clement of Alexandria to one Theodore "is actually the original text of the Gospel [of Mark] ... the esoteric Gospel of which our canonical Mark is a carefully abridged and edited version." In his letter, "Clement cites [a] passage as from the original version of the Gospel of Mark, not from an apocryphal work. Yet this version of Mark is certainly not the one we possess in the New Testament either!" In his letter to this otherwise unknown "Theodore," Clement "counsels Theodore that this is a 'secret Gospel,' and when asked about it: '... one should not concede that the secret Gospel is by Mark, but should even deny it on oath. For "Not all true things are to be said to all men".'" The text of such "secret Gospel" was discovered "in the Judean monastery of Mar Saba" by one Morton Smith in 1958, though not fully published until 1973. The "secret Gospel" appears to relate the account of the raising of Lazarus. More will be said on this in the Commentary dealing with the Gospels of Mark and John.—ERS

learning to read the Gospels with the aid of the Akashic record; through this alone will their full value be restored. In particular, the true significance of the Event of Golgotha can be fully demonstrated only by occult research. Only when the original significance of this Event is understood through occult research will the results it can have for human souls be recognized.

In the eleventh and last cycle in the Gospel series, *Christ and the Human Soul* (CHS), Lect. 3, Steiner tells us how, when one's "objective karma" (see "Forgiven Sins" and "Lord of Karma") has been taken over by Christ through the forgiveness of one's sins, then the occult researcher will not be able to find those sins in the Akashic record unless and until he or she has become permeated with Christ.

In *Life Between Death and Rebirth* (LBDR), Lect. 13, we see:

Between death and rebirth our perfections and imperfections are faithfully recorded in the Akasha Chronicle. Certain attributes are inscribed in the Moon sphere, others in the Venus sphere, others in the Mars sphere, others in the Mercury sphere, others in the Jupiter sphere, and so on. [See **I-33**; while in this passage, the "recording" is within our solar system, the Akashic seems clearly not to be limited thereto but to extend also into the zodiacal, i.e., heavenly or higher devachanic, region.] When we are returning to an incarnation in a physical body and our being is slowly contracting, we encounter everything that was inscribed on the outward journey. In this way our karma is prepared. On the path of return we can inscribe into our own being the record of an imperfection we ourselves first inscribed into the Akasha Chronicle. Then we arrive on the earth. Because there is within us everything we inscribed into our being on the return journey, and we are obliged to inscribe a great deal even if not everything, because of this our karma unfolds. Up above, however, everything still remains inscribed.

Now these inscriptions work together in a remarkable way.

Here Steiner goes into a discussion, beyond our present purposes, of how these astrological factors affect our lives in the unfolding of our karma.

Other comments upon the Akashic can be found in *At the Gates of Spiritual Science* (AGSS), Lect. 12 and its "Answers to Questions"; *Foundations of Esotericism* (FE), Lects. 10 and 21; *Genesis* (GEN), Lects. 7 and 10; and *Michaelmas and the Soul Forces of Man* (MSF), Lect 3. Countless times, of course, Steiner will simply refer to the Akashic as his source, but one must understand it to be the direct or indirect source of most of his original comments whether so stated or not. Also it should be understood that I make no claim to have addressed above substantially all, or even the major portion, of what Steiner may have said on the subject of the Akashic. The above references are, however, found in works that seem to have great relevance to our present task.

Let us now look at what the Bible has to say that appears to fit with what Steiner has expressed above about the "Akashic" and even to strongly suggest to the open mind that it is true.

First, a good many passages point generally in this direction. For instance, consider 2 Cor 3; 1 Cor 13,8c-10; 2 Cor 12,4; Heb 9,5; Jn 16,12; and Jer 31,31-34.

Even more to our point, however, is the pervasiveness with which the Biblical account speaks of a "book" in a way that virtually precludes any thought that it can be anything other than a record in the heavens. On this particular subject, I believe that Steiner is badly [8] wrong in an assertion he makes in ASJ, Lect. 4. He there sets out to "explain what a book is according to the Bible," and then says, "The word 'book' occurs in the Bible only seldom. This must not be overlooked. If you search the Old Testament, you will find the word in Genesis (V,l): This is the book of the generations of Adam.... You may then open the Bible where you will, you will only [see fn 8] find the word 'book' again in the first Gospel (Matthew I,l): This is the book of the generation of Christ Jesus.... And again the expression 'book' appears here in the Apocalypse of John. It appears where it is said that the Lamb alone is worthy to open the book

---

8. This assumes that the next quoted passage was correctly recorded and transcribed in German and then later correctly translated from the German. Perhaps it was, but the reader of any Steiner lecture series will find a preliminary editorial admonition quoting Steiner's request that copies of the lectures not be circulated beyond the immediate circle unless and until he could go back and edit them—something that the press of his mission virtually precluded. Eventually, after his death, the governing group within the Society determined that, in spite of his request, the demands for public knowledge required that they be made available in their unedited form. Thank God for that decision, for they are an unspeakable treasure rightfully belonging to all humanity!

with the seven seals. The expression 'book' has always the same significance, it is never used otherwise.... By a 'book' nothing else is ever meant
than the recording of what follows in time."

Steiner's threshold error (see fn 8) in this quotation is his assertion that
"the word 'book' occurs in the Bible only seldom" and then in the
instances he cites. If he was unaware of other occurrences, it also disqual-
ifies his statement that this is the only meaning the word has. This is not
to say he is wrong in the latter, but simply that he has not looked at all
the instances so as to be qualified to make that statement. The reader
should recall, first, that Steiner makes no claim to be a Bible student but
only to have confirmed by independent spiritual research the verity of
what he finds in the Bible and, second, that he only postulates the necessity of redeveloping the Bible account from such original spiritual source
and not that he has himself had the time to do so from beginning to end.
Fortunately, he has done enough, along with his other pronounced principles, to serve as a guide in the interpretation of passages that he has not
himself separately investigated. Both Steiner's investigative reports (and
their broader implications) and my own Bible study, are the basis of this
present undertaking.

In fact, there are numerous passages to consider (my emphasis):

Ex 32,32-33: "But now, if thou wilt forgive their sin—and if not, blot
me, I pray thee, out of thy *book* which thou has written." But the Lord
said to Moses, "Whoever has sinned against me, him will I blot out of
my *book.*"

Josh 10,13: And the sun stood still, and the moon stayed, until the
nation took vengeance on their enemies. Is this not written in the
Book of Jashar?

2 Sam 1,17-18: And David lamented with this lamentation over Saul
and Jonathan his son, and he said it should be taught to the people of
Judah; behold, it is written in the *Book of Jashar.*

Job 19,23-24: Oh that my words were written! Oh that they were
inscribed in a *book*! Oh that with an iron pen and lead they were
graven in the rock for ever!

Ps 40,7: Then I said, "Lo, I come; in the roll of the *book* it is written of me."

Ps 56,8: Thou has kept count of my tossings; put thou my tears in thy bottle! Are they not in thy *book*?

Ps 69,28: Let them be blotted out of the *book of the living;* let them not be enrolled among the righteous.

Ps 139,13-18: For thou didst form my inward parts, thou didst knit me together in my mother's womb. I praise thee, for thou art fearful and wonderful. Wonderful are thy works! Thou knowest me right well; my frame was not hidden from thee, when I was being made in secret, intricately wrought in the depths of the earth. Thy eyes beheld my unformed substance; in thy *book* were written, every one of them, the days that were formed for me, when as yet there was none of them. How precious to me are thy thoughts, O God! How vast is the sum of them! If I would count them, they are more than the sand. When I awake, I am still with thee.

Is 29,9-14,18: Stupefy yourselves and be in a stupor, blind yourselves and be blind! Be drunk, but not with wine; stagger, but not with strong drink! For the Lord has poured out upon you a spirit of deep sleep, and has closed your eyes, the prophets, and covered your heads, the seers. And the vision of all this has become to you *like the words of a book that is sealed.* When men give it to one who can read, saying, "Read this," he says, "I cannot, for it is sealed." And when they *give the book to one who cannot read*, saying, "Read this," he says, "I cannot read." And the Lord said: "Because this people draw near with their mouth and honor me with their lips, while their hearts are far from me, and their fear of me is a commandment of men learned by rote; therefore, behold, I will again do marvelous things with this people, wonderful and marvelous; and the wisdom of their wise men shall perish, and the discernment of their discerning men shall be hid."… In that day the deaf shall hear the words of a *book*, and out of their gloom and darkness the eyes of the blind shall see.

Is 30,8: And now, go, write it before them on a tablet, and inscribe it in a *book*, that it may be for the time to come as a witness for ever.

Is 34,16: Seek and read from the *book* of the Lord; Not one of these shall be missing; none shall be without her mate. For the mouth of the Lord has commanded, and his Spirit has gathered them.

Dan 7,10: A stream of fire issued and came forth from before him; a thousand thousands served him, and ten thousand times ten thousand stood before him; the court sat in judgment, and the *books* were opened.

Dan 9,2: In the first year of his reign, I, Daniel, perceived in the *books* the number of years which, according to the word of the Lord to Jeremiah [Jer 25,11-12] the prophet, must pass before the end of the desolations of Jerusalem, namely, seventy years.

Dan 10,21: But I will tell you what is inscribed in the *book of truth;* there is none who contends by my side against these except Michael, your prince.

Dan 12,1-4: "At that time shall arise Michael, the great prince who has charge of your people. And there shall be a time of trouble, such as never has been since there was a nation till that time; but at that time your people shall be delivered, every one whose name shall be found written in the *book*. And many of those who sleep in the dust of the earth shall awake, some to everlasting life, and some to shame and everlasting contempt. And those who are wise shall shine like the brightness of the firmament; and those who turn many to righteousness, like the stars for ever and ever. But you, Daniel, shut up the words, and seal the *book*, until the time of the end. Many shall run to and fro, and knowledge shall increase."

Mal 3,16: Then those who feared the Lord spoke with one another; the Lord heeded and heard them, and a *book of remembrance* was written before him of those who feared the Lord and thought on his name.

Phil 4,3: And I ask you also, true yokefellow, help these women, for they have labored side by side with me in the gospel together with Clement and the rest of my fellow workers, whose names are in the *book of life.*

Heb 10,7: cites Ps 40,7 above.

Rev 3,5: He who conquers shall be clad thus in white garments, and I will not blot his name out of the *book of life*;

Rev 13,8: And all who dwell on earth will worship it, every one whose name has not been written before the foundation of the world in the *book of life* of the Lamb that was slain.

Rev 17,8: ... and the dwellers on earth whose names have not been written in the *book of life* from the foundation of the world, will marvel to behold the beast, because it was and is not and is to come.

Rev 20,12-15: And I saw the dead, great and small, standing before the throne, and *books* were opened. Also another *book* was opened, which is the *book of life*. And the dead were judged by what was written in the *books*, by what they had done. And the sea gave up the dead in it, Death and Hades gave up the dead in them, and all were judged by what they had done. Then Death and Hades were thrown into the lake of fire. This is the second death, the lake of fire; and if any one's name was not found written in the *book of life*, he was thrown into the lake of fire.

Rev 21,27: But nothing unclean shall enter it, nor any one who practices abomination or falsehood, but only those who are written in the Lamb's *book of life*.

While Job 13,23-27 does not use the term "book," it is clearly implied by reference to an accounting ledger in which "debits" are recorded to one's account. In its discussion of Ps 40,7 (there numbered as vs 8), 16 AB 246 says that the Hebrew *alay* there used in the phrase "in the roll of the book it is written of me" is the same Hebrew word used in Job 13,26, and means "in my debit." With that in mind, one should contemplate the significance of Job 13,23-27 in the light of Karma and Reincarnation, with the effects the River Lethe has on human memory of past sin as the Prodigal Son enmeshes itself in the "Darkness" of materiality and finds the "soles of my feet" bounded by the earthly circumstantial consequences of its own past. Job 13,23-27 reads:

(23) How many are my iniquities and my sins? Make me know my transgression and my sin. (24) Why dost thou hide thy face, and count me as thy enemy? ... (26) For thou writest bitter things against

me, and makest me inherit the iniquities of my youth. (27) Thou puttest my feet in the stocks, and watchest all my paths; thou settest a bound to the soles of my feet.

On the *Book of Jashar*, mentioned in the Josh and 2 Sam citations, see 3 ABD 646. Since this ABD discussion is generally in the vein of modern Biblical criticism, it does not recognize the heavenly "Akashic" character implied by Steiner's work, but is nevertheless helpful for what it does disclose. The portion most important for our purposes is the sentence, "The term 'Jashar' is a common Hebrew word meaning 'one who [or that which] is straight, honest, just, righteous, upright.'" How could one more accurately describe the "Akashic," or heavenly "book"? Or the principle of "Karma and Reincarnation" that gives effect to the perfect justice such "book" envisions? Another point is made: "A third probable excerpt appears in 1 K 8,12-13, a couplet imbedded in Solomon's prayer at the dedication of the 'Temple,' which survives in fullest form in the LXX [Septuagint] where it appears at the end of the prayer, directing the reader to the 'Book of the Song' (Gk *biblio tes odes*)." This excerpt is recognized also in NJB in a footnote on 1 K 8,12-13. With respect to the putative title of "Book of Song," the ABD comment goes on to say, "If so [i.e., if it was called a "Book of Song"], there is some doubt whether the book ever existed in written form as such."

The Buddha, Siddhartha Gautama, is said to have come to enlightenment "under the bodhi tree," 15 Brit 265 and 28 Brit 881. This occult metaphor, though heretofore unrecognized as such, is used often in the Bible. See "Under the Tree." I have noted with considerable interest that the Song of Songs (Solomon) lists three kinds of "trees"—Apple (2,3 and 8,5), Fig (2,13), and Palm (7,7-8).[9] Inasmuch as the Song of Songs seems clearly to be an expression of the ecstatic reunion of the higher and lower "I Am" in a holy wedding like the one in Rev 21, these three "trees" could be taken as symbolizing the three stages of spiritual perception, as set out in **I-31**. Since these three are the same as Isaiah's "seeing-hearing-understanding" (Is 6,10), and since the second of these deals with "hearing" or "sound," as in the "Harmony of the Spheres," the Book of Jashar, if it is a "Book of Song," could relate to the second stage, namely, "hearing" or

---

9. See the discussion of the relationship between the palm tree and the mythical bird Phoenix in "Conclusion—The Pyramid, The Phoenix and Egypt Revisited," in Appendix to "Fire" in Vol. 2, "*What is Man?*".

"Inspiration" (as would perhaps also be true of the "Song of Songs," particularly since it is still in the longing state and not yet that of union in the holy marriage).

Finally, I propose that "Jashar" and "Akashic" are the same word from different dialects, their essential common root being "ash," upon which the emphasis in pronunciation falls. Several factors can be given in support thereof:

1. They both stand for the highest level of "righteousness." Thus, in the very section of the Sermon on the Mount in which Christ refers to this higher "law," he says (Mt 5,20), "For I tell you, unless your righteousness exceeds that of the scribes and Pharisees, you will never enter the kingdom of heaven."

2. They are both of ancient origin, probably contemporaneous.

3. The roots of the Judeo-Christian religions are "from the east" (Gen 11,2; Mt 2,1-2).

4. There is a tendency for similar sounds of a given word to carry over from one language to another.

5. As an elaboration on 2 through 4 above, we have already seen (in "Second Coming" above) how the Oriental term Kali Yuga ("dark age") was reflected in the West in the name of the god, Deucalion, the son of Prometheus, the "kali-yu" and "calio" both carrying forward the same basic sound. The Bible student should have little difficulty accepting the existence of such roots as evidence of common meaning (Gen 11,1) or accepting that the roots of the Old Testament language sprang "from the east" (Gen 11,2). In *The Genius of Language* (GL), Lect. 3, Steiner says, "All across the regions where these languages were spoken, we discover that a primeval relationship exists; we can easily imagine that at a very ancient time the primordial origins of language-forming were similar right across these territories and only later became differentiated." See also *The Realm of Language* (RL), *Changes in the Meaning of Speech* (CMS) and 22 Brit 566, "Language."

In conclusion, it is hard to imagine any serious Bible student thinking that any of the above scriptural references to "book" are speaking of a physical writing anywhere. Rather, all such references seem clearly to refer to a heavenly record of some sort, which is precisely what the "Akashic" is said to be.

"Three Days' Journey"

THE PHRASE "Three Days' Journey" appears, as we shall see, eight times in the Bible. And thus far leading commentaries, when not ignoring it, show themselves oblivious to its spiritual meaning, treating it patronizingly as either an erroneous or exaggerated expression of geographic distance or size, a "ruse for escape," or mere "dittography."[1]

We will look first at Steiner's treatment and then at the scriptural passages themselves. However, as with all Biblical language, this phrase does not exist in a vacuum and takes on added significance in relation to other terms and phrases. See especially "Mysteries" herein, as well as the various terms involving the number three ("Third Day," "Thirty," "Three Bodies," "Three Days" and "Three Years").

Fortuitously for us, William Barclay ("Barc" herein) has given us something of an entree into our subject through his original translation of 1 Cor 15,50-51 in his remarkably popular and readable *Daily Study Bible Series*:

> Brothers, I say this, that flesh and blood cannot inherit the Kingdom of God, nor can corruption inherit incorruption. Look now—
> *I tell you something which only the initiated can understand.* We shall not all die, but we shall all be changed. (My emphasis)

In his various lecture cycles on the Gospels, Steiner spoke often of what "initiation" meant within the ancient Mysteries, which themselves must be comprehended for an understanding of the very foundation of the

---

1. See 1 AB 237 (Gen 30,36), 1 NIB 715 (Ex 3,18) and 751 (Ex 8,27), 2 Interp 193 (Num 10,33), 4 AB 316 (Num 10,33), 6 Interp 888 (Jon 3,3), 7 NIB 511 (Jon 3,3) and 24B AB 230 (Jon 3,3). "Dittography," defined in none of WNWD, MWCD or RHCD, is used (in 2 Interp and in the Notes at 4 AB 316) only with respect to the second usage of "three days' journey" within Num 10,33. Presumably it means simply that the phrase used in vs 33a was unnecessarily repeated in 33b.

Gospel message (see *Christianity as Mystical Fact* [CMF]). In the first Gospel cycle, *The Gospel of St. John*, (GSJ), Lect. 4 ("The Raising of Lazarus"), he points out that the opponents of Jesus were not provoked to seek his disposal until immediately after the raising of Lazarus (see Jn 11,47-53 and 12,9-11). Let us see Steiner's language:

What is really at the bottom of it all? The raising of someone provoked the enemies of Christ Jesus to rise up against Him. Why should just the raising of Lazarus so provoke these opponents? Why does the persecution of Christ Jesus begin just at this stage? One who knows how to read this Gospel will understand that a mystery lies hidden within this chapter. The mystery concealed therein is, in truth, concerned with the actual identity of the man who says all that we find written there. In order to understand this, we must turn our attention to what in the ancient Mysteries is called "initiation." How did these initiations in the ancient Mysteries take place?

A man who was initiated could himself have experiences and personal knowledge of the spiritual worlds and thus he could bear witness of them. Those who were found sufficiently developed for initiation were led into the Mysteries. Everywhere—in Greece, among the Chaldeans, among the Egyptians and the Indians—these Mysteries existed. There the neophytes were instructed for a long time in approximately the same things which we now learn in Spiritual Science. Then when they were sufficiently instructed, they followed that part of the training which opened up to them the way to a perception of the spiritual world. However, in ancient times this could only be brought about by putting the neophyte into a very extraordinary condition in respect of his four principles—his physical, ether and astral bodies and his ego. The next thing that occurred to the neophyte was that he was put into a death-like sleep by the initiator or hierophant who understood the matter and there he remained for three and a half days. Why this occurred can be seen if we consider that in the present cycle of evolution, when the human being sleeps in the ordinary sense of the word, his physical and ether bodies lie in bed and his astral body and ego are withdrawn [see **I-9**, **I-10** and **I-33**]. In that condition he cannot observe any of the spiritual events taking place about him, because his astral body has not yet developed the spiritual sense-organs for a perception of the world in which he then finds himself. Only when his astral body and ego have slipped back into his physical and ether bodies, and he once more makes use of his eyes and ears, does he again perceive the physical world, that is, he perceives a world about him. Through what he had learned, the neophyte was capable of developing spiritual organs of perception in his astral body and when he was sufficiently evolved for the astral body to have formed these organs, then all that the astral body had received into itself had to be impressed upon the ether body just as the design on a seal is impressed upon the sealing-wax. This is the important thing. All preparations for initiation depended upon the surrender of the man himself to the inner processes which reorganized his astral body.

The human being at one time did not have eyes and ears in his physical body as he has today, but undeveloped organs instead—just as animals who have never been exposed to the light have no eyes. The light forms the eye, sound fashions the ear. What the neophyte practiced through meditation and concentration and what he experienced inwardly through them, acted like light upon the eye and sound upon the ear. In this way the astral body was transformed and organs of perception for seeing in the astral or higher world were evolved. But these organs are not yet firmly enough fixed in the ether body. They will become so when what has been formed in the astral body will have been stamped upon the ether body. However, as long as the ether body remains bound to the physical, it is not possible for all that has been accomplished by means of spiritual exercises to be really impressed upon it. Before this can happen, the ether body must be drawn out of the physical. Therefore when the ether body was drawn out of the physical body during the three and a half days death-like sleep, all that had been prepared in the astral body was stamped upon the ether body. The neophyte then experienced the spiritual world. Then when he was called back into the physical body by the Priest-Initiator, he bore witness through his own experience of what takes place in the spiritual worlds. This procedure has now become unnecessary through the appearance of Christ-Jesus. This three and a half day death-like sleep can now be replaced by the force proceeding from the Christ. For we shall soon see that in the Gospel of St. John strong forces are present which render it possible for the present astral body, even though the ether body is still within the physical, to have the power to stamp upon the etheric what had previously been prepared within it. But for this to take place, Christ-Jesus must first be present. Up to this time without the above characterized procedure, humanity was not far enough advanced for the astral body to be able to imprint upon the ether body what had been prepared within it through meditation and concentration. This was a process which often took place within the Mysteries; a neophyte was brought into a death-like sleep by the Priest-Initiator and was guided through the higher worlds. He was then again called back into his physical body by the Priest-Initiator and thus became a witness of the spiritual world through his own experience.

This took place always in the greatest secrecy and the outer world knew nothing of the occurrences within these ancient Mysteries. Through Christ-Jesus a new initiation had to arise to replace the old, an initiation produced by means of forces of which we have yet to speak. The old form of initiation must end, but a transition had to be made from the old to the new age and to make this transition, someone had once more to be initiated in the old way, but initiated into Christian Esotericism. This only Christ-Jesus Himself could perform and the neophyte was the one who is called Lazarus. "This sickness is not unto death" [Jn 11,4], means here that it is the three and a half day death-like sleep. This is clearly indicated.

You will see that the presentation is of a very veiled character, but for one who is able to decipher a presentation of this kind it represents initiation. The individuality Lazarus had to be initiated in such a way that he could be a witness of the spiritual worlds. An expression is used, a very significant expression in the language of the Mysteries, "that the Lord loved Lazarus" [Jn 11,3,36]. What does "to love" mean in the language of the Mysteries? It expresses the relationship of the pupil to the teacher. "He whom the Lord loved" is the most intimate, the most deeply initiated pupil. The Lord Himself initiated Lazarus and as an initiate Lazarus arose from the grave, which means from his place of initiation.

Soon after the GSJ cycle came that in *The Gospel of St. John and its Relation to the Other Gospels* (Jn-Rel) where in Lect. 6 we see how, over time, the mechanical method of initiation had to change due to the hardening or densification of the three human bodies:

While in Atlantean times the etheric and physical bodies were so loosely joined that the former could be withdrawn more easily than in later periods, it had now [in the Indian, Persian, Egyptian and Greek eras, progressively] become necessary in the Mysteries to place the neophyte into a deathlike sleep. While this lasted, he was either placed in a coffinlike box or bound to a sort of cross, something of that sort. The initiator, known as the hierophant, possessed the power to work upon the astral, and particularly upon the etheric body, for during this procedure, the etheric left the physical body.... Everything that had been learned through meditation and other exercises was now impressed into the etheric body while in this condition. During these three and a half days, the human being really traversed the spiritual worlds wherein the higher beings dwell. After the three and a half days had passed, the hierophant called him back, meaning that he had the power to awaken him; and the candidate brought with him a knowledge of the spiritual world. Now he could see into this spiritual world and could proclaim its truths to his fellow men who as yet did not possess the maturity to behold it themselves.

Thus, the ancient teachers of pre-Christian time had been initiated into the profound secrets of the Mysteries. There, they had been guided by the hierophant during the three-and-a-half-day period; they were living witnesses [see "Witness"] to the existence of a spiritual life and to the fact that behind the physical there is a spiritual world to which man belongs with his higher principles and into which he must find his way. But evolution proceeded. What I have just described to you as an initiation existed most intensively in the first epoch after the Atlantean catastrophe. The union of the etheric and physical bodies, however, grew ever firmer; hence, the procedure became more and more dangerous, because man's whole consciousness accustomed itself increasingly to the physical sense world. This, after all, was the purpose of human evolution: men were to become used to living in this physical world with all their inclinations and propensities.

The next significant cycle in the Gospel series was *The Gospel of St. Luke* (GSL). There, in Lect. 10, Steiner speaks of the passage in Lk 11,29-32:

The old truth was presented in comprehensible form when symbolized by the "Sign of Jonah." This symbolized the old way in which man gradually attained knowledge and penetrated into the spiritual world, or how—to use biblical terms—he became a "Prophet."

The old way of attaining Initiation was this: first the soul was brought to maturity and every necessary preparation made; then a condition lasting for three-and-a-half days was induced in the candidate, a condition in which he was completely withdrawn from the outer world and from the organs through which that world is perceived. Those who were to be led into the spiritual world were carefully prepared and their souls trained in knowledge of the spiritual life; then they were withdrawn from the world for three-and-a-half days, being taken to a place where they could perceive nothing through their external senses and where their bodies lay in a death-like condition; after three-and-a-half days their souls were summoned back again into the body and they were awakened. Such men were then able to remember their vision of the spiritual worlds and to testify of those worlds. The great secret of Initiation was that the soul, prepared by long training, was led out of the body for three-and-a-half days into an entirely different world, was shut off from the environment and penetrated into the spiritual world. Men who could bear witness to the realities of the spiritual world were always to be found among the peoples; they were men who had undergone the experience referred to in the Bible in the story of Jonah's sojourn in the whale. Such a man was made ready to undergo this experience and then, when he appeared before the people as an Initiate of the old order, he bore upon him the "sign of Jonah"—the sign of those who were able themselves to testify of the spiritual world.

This was the one form of Initiation. Christ said, in effect: "In the old sense there is no other sign save the sign of Jonah." (Luke XI, 29.) And He expressed Himself even more clearly according to the meaning of words in the Gospel of St. Matthew [see Mt 12,39-41 and 16,4]. "As a heritage from olden times there remains the possibility that without effort of his own, without Initiation, a man can develop a dim, shadowy kind of clairvoyance and through revelation from above be led into the spiritual world." The indication here is that there were also Initiates of a second kind—men who went about among their fellows and who, as a result of their particular lineage, were able to receive revelations from above in a kind of sublimated trance condition, without having undergone any special Initiation. Christ indicated that this twofold manner of being transported into the spiritual world had come down from ancient times. He bade the people to remember King Solomon—thereby pointing to an Individuality to whom, without effort on his own part, the spiritual world was revealed from above. The "Queen of Sheba" who came to King Solomon [see Lk 11,31 and Mt 12,42] was also the bearer of wisdom from above; she was the representative of those predestined to possess, by inheritance, the dim, shadowy clairvoyance with which all men were endowed in the Atlantean epoch. (See Luke XI, 31.)

Thus there were two kinds of Initiates: the one kind typified by King Solomon and the symbolic visit paid to him by the Queen of Sheba, the Queen from the South; the other kind typified by those who bore upon them the "sign of Jonah," meaning the old Initiation in which the candidate, entirely cut off from the outer world, passed through the spiritual world for a period lasting three-and-a-half days. Christ now added: "A greater than Solomon, a greater than Jonah is here"—indicating thereby that something new had come into the world. The message was not to be conveyed to the etheric bodies of men from outside, through revelations, as in the case of Solomon, nor was it to be conveyed to etheric bodies from within through revelations imparted by the duly prepared astral body to the etheric body, as in the case of those symbolized by the sign of Jonah. "Here is something which enables a man who has made himself ready for it in his Ego, to unite his being with what belongs to the kingdoms of Heaven." The forces and powers from those kingdoms unite with the virginal part in the human soul, the part that belongs to the kingdoms of Heaven and that men can destroy if they turn away from the Christ-principle, but can cultivate and nurture if they receive into themselves what streams from the Christ-principle.

... Christ wished to show that because of the new element now present in the world there can also be men who even before they die are able to behold the kingdom of Heaven. The disciples did not at first understand what this meant. Christ wanted to convey to them that *they* were to be the ones who would come to know the mysteries of the kingdoms of Heaven before natural death or the death experienced in the old form of Initiation. The wonderful passage in the Gospel of St. Luke where Christ is speaking of a higher revelation, is as follows: "But I tell you of a truth, there be some standing here, which shall not taste of death, till they see the kingdom of God" (Luke IX,27).[2]

That this happened is reflected by the fact that immediately thereafter, in all the Synoptic Gospels, comes the Transfiguration. Peter, James and John "gaze for a brief moment into the spiritual world" though "it is evident that they are still novices, for they "fall asleep immediately after being torn out of their physical and etheric bodies by the stupendous power of what was happening" (Lk 9,32; cf. Lk 22,45).

This three and a half day deathlike sleep was known as the "temple sleep." Many other Steiner passages speak of it,[3] but the above quotes suffice for our present purposes.

Now let us look at the eight Biblical passages that speak of the "three days' journey." We shall see that these eight involve only the accounts of, or surrounding, the three Biblical personages of Jacob, Moses and Jonah, who appear to have undergone this method of initiation into the Mysteries. Elsewhere we shall see that Steiner indicates that most of the Hebrew prophets did not undergo initiation into the Mysteries in their Biblical incarnations, but embodied the deep spiritual insight vested in their etheric bodies by having done so in one or more prior incarnations. (And those prophets who went to Babylon were presumably also exposed there to the teachings of Zarathas, an initiate many times over, as to which see both "middle period prophets" and "The Nativity" herein.) However, it is clear that Elijah and Elisha were initiated, and probably this is true of most of those who could be referred to as the earlier "non-writing" prophets in Israel (although Solomon and perhaps Samuel and others

---

2. This is one of sayings that, because not understood, led many erroneously to expect an early return of Jesus. Thus, see 8 Interp 172 and 7 Interp 457; but cf. 28 AB 789, 26 AB 201 and Barc's Luke 122. See generally "Second Coming" herein.
3. Included among these are *Background to the Gospel of St. Mark* (BKM), Lects. 7 (p. 118) and 8 (pp. 138-139); *Fifth Gospel* (FG), Lect. 3 (p. 51); GSJ, Lects. 8 (pp. 130-131), 10 (pp. 161-163) and 12 (pp. 175-176); *The Gospel of St. Mark* (GSMk), Lect. 7 (pp. 126-127); *The Gospel of St. Matthew* (GSMt), Lects. 2 (p. 42) and 7 (p. 130); Jn-Rel, Lects. 8 (pp. 136-137), 10 (p. 181) and 11 (pp. 211-212); *Reading the Pictures of the Apocalypse* (RPA), Lect. 2 (p.27), 4 (pp. 57-58) and 5 (p. 69); *The Principle of Spiritual Economy* (SE), Lect. 5 (pp. 64-65) and *The Karma of Materialism* (KM), Lect 5 (p. 85).

were vested with the type of atavistic clairvoyance of which Steiner speaks in the above passages). The interesting reference in Ezek 14,14,16,18,20 to "Noah, Daniel, and Job" speaks of prehistorical "prophets" or at least of those who predated the Hebrew period, stood outside of its lineage, or were merely proverbial, as Biblical commentaries generally suggest (one or more of which categories may also include Jonah).

In the order of appearance, these eight instances are as follows:

1. **Gen 30,36**: "And he [Laban] set a distance of three days' journey between himself and Jacob; and Jacob fed the rest of Laban's flock."

This occurs when the last of Jacob's twelve sons had been born and Jacob was planning his return with his family to his homeland and needed to make adequate provision therefor. An obviously spiritual journey for Jacob (Israel) is about to begin—a most appropriate time for initiation. While Laban is said to have set the "three days' journey" distance between them, it may have several "initiation" meanings: 1. Laban himself was initiated; 2. Laban caused or permitted Jacob to be initiated; or 3. Laban himself initiated Jacob so as to send him on his spiritual journey properly. The last seems the more probable since the relationship between Jacob and Laban seems similar to that between Moses and his father-in-law, Jethro, in Midian *before* the exodus.

2. **Ex 3,18**: "And they will hearken to your voice; and you and the elders of Israel shall go to the king of Egypt and say to him, 'The Lord, the God of the Hebrews, has met with us; and now, we pray you, let us go a three days' journey into the wilderness, that we may sacrifice to the Lord our God.'"

Moses, who almost certainly had already been initiated by the priests in Egypt, was further prepared by his flight into the "Wilderness" of Midian after "killing" the Egyptian. It seems equally certain that Jethro-Reuel, "the priest of Midian," was an initiate of the Midianites. This passage (Ex 3,18) is part of Moses' momentous initial (clairvoyant) trip to "the mountain of God" (Sinai-Horeb; see "Mountain" and "High Mountain"), and God himself speaks to Moses telling him what to say to Pharaoh. He was to say that the people of Israel needed to be initiated, i.e. to make a "three days' journey into the wilderness," or at least to be under the leadership of those (Moses, Aaron, etc.) who had been. The term had nothing to do with any physical distance from the scene of captivity to Sinai. Rather, it had to do with what was necessary to make them a spiritual vessel worthy of molding the earthly vehicle (Jesus) who was to receive the Christ Spirit.

3. **Ex 5,3**: "Then they said, 'The God of the Hebrews has met with us; let us go, we pray, a three days' journey into the wilderness, and sacrifice to the Lord our God, lest he fall upon us with pestilence or with the sword.'"

Here Moses and Aaron confront Pharaoh for the first time with the request imposed upon them by God in Ex 3,18.

4. **Ex 8,27**: "We must go three days' journey into the wilderness and sacrifice to the Lord our God as he will command us."

Pharaoh had proposed that Israel sacrifice to their God "within the land" (vs 25), to which Moses and Aaron speak as above, after which Pharaoh conditionally permits their request, "only you shall not go very far away...." This was "Egypt" saying to Israel that it should not progress beyond the spiritual level of "Egypt." But Israel had the divine mission of preparing the vessel to receive the Christ Spirit and much was required therefor that could not be found in that condition. The "three days' journey" passage itself is still playing out the scenario introduced in Ex 3,18. It is particularly important to remember that "Egypt" itself was strictly led by its initiated priesthood, who had made their own "three days' journey," and that the journey into the "Wilderness" was unique and characterized Israel's spiritual obligation. That archaeology has been surprisingly unable to meaningfully confirm the "Wilderness" years of Israel, or even the precise location of Sinai, is itself strong indication of the primarily spiritual nature of the "forty years" of wandering in the Wilderness.

5 and

6. **Num 10,33**: "So they set out from the mount of the Lord three days' journey; and the ark of the covenant of the Lord went before them three days' journey, to seek out a resting place for them."

Again, we are dealing with a spiritualization process of Israel, not with a geographical distance. The repetition of "three days' journey" in 33b is called "dittography," or unnecessary repetition, by 3 Interp and the Notes at 4 AB 316, though they recognize that the second usage "does not reconcile the statement with vs 21." In vs 21 the Kohathites are said to have "carried the holy things" while "the tabernacle was set up before their arrival." In vs 33b the ark is said to have gone "before them" alright, but it did so "*in* the three days' journey" (emphasis mine), thus, as seemingly recognized, keeping the second usage from being redundant. The "in," or wording of similar import, is found in most translations (e.g., KJV, NKJV, NJB, NIV, NACB, AMPB, CEV and LB), being omitted only in RSV (above), NRSV and AB. In any event, even omitting it the second time it appears in vs 33 does not lessen the term's Biblical significance.

But there is perhaps a way to view the second usage other than as superfluity while also eliminating the assumed inconsistency between verses 21 and 33b. Let us recall from the "Overview" above that the dimensions of Noah's ark (Gen 6,15) were those of the harmonious human body as it emerged from the flood of Atlantis (see also #11 in "Three Bodies" below). Steiner tells us this in the concluding Lect. 1 of *Occult Signs and Symbols* (OSS), September 13, 1907. Are we not then warranted in giving 33b the following meaning: And the I Am's physical body was put into a three and a half day deathlike sleep that the I Am might be led into its spiritual dwelling? This distinguishes the deathlike physical state from that of the other three human components that make the spiritual journey.

The Bible's use of the term "Ark" is complex and varied. See 1 ABD 386-393, "Ark of the Covenant"; which also tells us "there are two Hebrew words translated as 'ark' ... in the English: (1) *'aron.* ancient Israel's most sacred cultic object which was probably originally a box of some sort, and (2) *tebah,* the boat which Noah built. In addition to the sacred ark, *'aron* also refers to a collection box in the temple (2 Kgs 12:10,11—Eng 12:9,10; 2 Chr 24:8,10,11) and the sarcophagus of Joseph (Gen 50:26)."

TORAH is here most helpful. Under Gen 6,14 it says:

> **ark** The vessel, significantly, is called *tevah*. This key word recurs seven times here in the instructions for building the ark and seven times again in connection with the subsidence of the waters in 8:1-14 [English translations have slightly more in each instance]. Yet

tevah, in the sense of an ark, appears again in the Bible only in connection with the salvation of the baby Moses, in Exodus 2:3-5. The term suggests a boxlike craft made to float on the water but without rudder or sail or any other navigational aid. It does not use the services of a crew. The use of *tevah* is intended to emphasize that the fate of the occupants is to be determined solely by the will of God and not to be attributed to the skill of man. By contrast, the hero of the Mesopotamian stories builds a regular ship and employs boatmen to navigate it.

and under Ex 2,3 it adds:

a wicker basket The receptacle is called a *tevah*, a term that, in this sense, appears elsewhere in the Bible only as the ark in which Noah and his family were saved from the waters of the Flood. Its use here underscores both the vulnerability of its occupant and its being under divine protection. Evocation of the Flood narrative also suggests, once again, that the birth of Moses signals a new era in history.

Most translations of Ex 2,3 use the term "basket." Only KJV, NKJV and AMPB in my library use "ark" for Moses' container. In Num 10,33 we are not dealing with the Hebrew word *tebah* (or *tevah*), but the later usage of *'aron* may still reflect something of the original concept as cultic usage developed.

7. **Num 33,8**: "And they set out from before Hahiroth, and passed through the midst of the sea into the wilderness, and they went a three days' journey in the wilderness of Etham, and encamped at Marah."

This passage is a recap of the flight from Egypt through the sea, a part of the original "three days' journey" in all the Exodus passages above. The spiritual significance of this whole passage seems almost inexhaustible. In passing through the "midst of the sea", we are dealing with a "water trial." It is noteworthy that the first encampment thereafter is at "Marah," which is probably a reference to the sea (mara, meaning "sea" or water in ancient language sound), and then Elim, which seems to incorporate the word for God (El), and where the most sacred numbers appear, "twelve springs of water" and "seventy palm trees."[4] (One should bear in mind that there are three "trials" in the process of initiation, explained by Steiner in *Knowledge of the Higher Worlds and Its Attainment* (KHW), Chap. 3. They are, in order, the "fire trial," the "water trial" and the "air trial," corresponding with the first three of the four basic elements. The more advanced two also correspond with the requirements Jesus laid down in Jn 3,5 ("born of the water and the Spirit") if one is to be "born again" (Jn 3,3) and thus see the Kingdom of God. It is noteworthy also that while "Fire" is the only ether existing in physical Earth (as in our body temperature regulator) and the one where a human being meets spiritual beings (e.g., see the references in "Bush" above), the two above it are Light and Sound (or Chemical) whose respective earthly reflections are Air (Spirit) and Water. The only higher ether is Life, but to get to it one must first pass through (be "born of") the Light and Sound (Spirit and Water) ethers. This is similar imagery to what John also uses in Jn 14,6, "no one comes to the Father but by me." This can be seen graphically in the chart concluding **I-18**. The "Life" of the nation Israel thus commenced only after its "water trial," i.e., after it was "born of water."

It may also be meaningful that following their three days' journey the number of encampments until the Israelites reached Sinai was the spiritual number seven. I am not now prepared to comment on the thirty encampments listed thereafter which brought them to the plains of Moab by the Jordan, other than to note it amounts to the same sacred number three, times ten.

8. **Jon 3,3**: "Now Nineveh was an exceedingly great city, three days' journey in breadth."

It is pathetic what a literal translation of this spiritual book, so meaningful to the early Christians, and referenced by Christ in his "sign of Jonah" remarks, does to its meaning. It is so loaded with spiritual metaphors tied into the process of ancient initiation that no effort can here be made to address any significant part of them. Suffice it to say that

---

4. Again, as in fn 9 of "Akashic," see the discussion of the relationship between the palm tree and the mythical Phoenix in "Conclusion—The Pyramid, The Phoenix and Egypt Revisited," in Appendix to "Fire," Vol. 2, "*What is Man?*".

when Jonah is told to "Arise, go to Ninevah …", he was being told to make a spiritual journey amounting to initiation, to a city "three days' journey" in breadth. No city in that day could have been so wide, so to salvage the accuracy of the account it must have been a spiritual description, namely, a city one reaches only by the process of initiation. Jonah complies with this requirement, only to be commanded to go on from there, an inevitable consequence of initiation. Of course, every spiritual level lays on additional burdens. Jonah's later desire to rest in the shade reminds us of the enlightenment of arriving at the spiritual destination called "Under the Tree"—but there is no such rest, only added commitment. How unspeakably glorious is this message in such spiritual context—but it is not limited to just this, as the Commentary on this passage will show.

In summary, as mentioned above, "three days' journey" appears only in three scriptural settings, Jacob's setting out on the mission of Israel, Moses' later setting out on the Hebrew mission, and Jonah's journey to the spiritual city of Ninevah. (See "Three Bodies," #29.)

We can thus see the enormous spiritual significance of the concept of the "three days' journey." It relates to the "three days" of Jesus' entombment (although obviously it was for less than two, an otherwise tortuous anomaly to the thinking mind). And, as Steiner shows, it relates to the entombment of Lazarus, which was "a sickness not unto death" but unto the "three days' journey" of initiation by Jesus himself (although likewise obviously not for three, or three and a half, days, but four). This is not to equate the raising of Lazarus with that of Jesus, except as one spiritual level relates to a higher one—not equivalent, but of like, though embryonic, character.

Again, the "three days' journey" of ancient initiation dealt with the "temple sleep," normally three (or three and a half) days, which was part of the Mysteries of ancient times. However, it is misleading to stop there without saying that the coming of Christ brought about a different method of initiation. The "temple sleep" of ancient times would be dangerous to the human being today, for its body is more solid now. Christ's passion, death and Resurrection brought the Mysteries out into the light of day (see CMF), though this is as yet misunderstood. It was an enactment, not a repudiation, of the spiritual process of the Mysteries. The Bible speaks often of mystery (see "Mysteries"), as do the great contemporary Greek works. It is important that the human being learn the meaning of all this, for it is the essential message of the Bible—vital to the future evolutionary progress of humanity.[5]

While in "Mysteries" herein the initiation of Elijah is clearly shown, it would appear that the scriptural description of his initiation indicates that he made a "three days' journey," though such phrase itself is not used. Rather we are told (1 K 19) how in his first day he lay down "under a broom tree" (see "Under the Tree"), then in his second lodged in a "cave," and then in his third heard a "still small voice" commanding him back to the "wilderness of Damascus" (cf. Acts 9,8-19 and Gal 1,17). The word "cave" was used from ancient times to describe the initiation process. Plato used the metaphor in his celebrated "cave parable" (*The Republic*, Book VII, 7 GB 388), and the entombment process of both Lazarus and Jesus embodies the same concept. It is worthwhile to contemplate the various Biblical uses of the term "cave," shown by any good concordance. And the "still small voice" implies the spiritual "hearing" of the second aspect of initiation (see **I-31** and **I-30**, as well as the seminal passage in Is 6,9-10).

While John was "loved" and uniquely initiated by Jesus, as described in Jn 11, it seems almost certain that Paul's Damascus Road experience precipitated a similar initiation by Christ after his Resurrection.[6] This is

---

5. In this connection, the books of Daniel and Revelation are most frequently called apocalyptic and purport to speak of the future. In each a mysterious phrase is employed which has generally escaped editorial comment, namely, "a time, two times and half a time" (see Dan 7,25 and 12,7, and Rev 12,14). Obviously, this adds up to 3 1/2 "times." I have yet to find any Steiner comment on these specific passages, but it seems likely that they have some relationship to this 3 1/2 day "temple sleep" of the ancient Mysteries. They might also have reference to the larger cycles of evolution which, as clearly shown in Revelation and as explained by Steiner, occur in subdivisions of seven. Inasmuch as Christ came in the middle of the post-Atlantean Epoch of Earth Evolution and Earth Evolution is in the middle of the seven Conditions of Consciousness (see **I-1** through **I-3**) of humanity's evolution (although the present post-Atlantean Epoch is the fifth of the seven Epochs of Earth evolution), these books could be allegorizing not only the 3 1/2 day "temple sleep," but also the long evolutionary period involved before some of the things there seen are to be completed.

That the mind (or vision) of Lazarus/John contemplated the "temple sleep" seems strongly indicated in Revelation 11, which speaks of Christ's "two witnesses," whom Steiner identifies as Elijah and Moses, witnesses to the Christ at his Transfiguration. This chapter almost certainly refers to such sleep for it speaks of them lying dead in "allegorical" Sodom and Egypt for 3 1/2 days (Rev 11,9,11) after which they were raised back to life. I show herein (see "Mysteries") how the Bible indicates that Elijah had been initiated into the Mysteries, and there are strong indications that Moses had been initiated into the Egyptian Mysteries.

6. See the discussion of Paul's initiation in fn 2 of "Akashic."

indicated by the "Three Days" in Acts 9,9, as well as by comments like 2 Cor 12,2-4 (cf. SE, Lect. 5, p. 65).

The sensitive reader can come to see the urgent necessity for a revitalizing enlightenment to come upon the adumbral theology of the last two millennia, especially that of the last two centuries which sees in the "three days' journey" phrase either a description of physical dimension or a Bible pathetically in error and thus irrelevant. If the deeper truths of the Bible can be brought to the light of anthroposophical knowledge, it will take on the vital new meaning demanded by the spiritual needs of our era.

MYSTERIES

EXTENSIVE WRITING exists on the ancient "Mysteries,"[1] revealing their close relationship with Christianity while also corroborating what Steiner had to say about them, albeit without penetrating meaningfully into the reason for their origin, existence or decline. Except by Steiner (anthroposophy) only their external skeleton is perceived. One can be thoroughly exposed to the oral and written expositions of Christendom over the last two centuries without coming to any real understanding of these extensive ancient phenomena.

Someday, when anthroposophy has seeped more widely and deeply into human consciousness, there will be amazement at how extensively the ancient Mysteries and the conditions that gave rise to them and under which they functioned are stated in the Bible. That Christ incarnated for the purpose of enacting them "Once For All," not in the secret confines of the ancient practices but in the full view of all humanity, will become increasingly clear. This is the thesis Steiner developed in *Christianity as Mystical Fact* (CMF). It can now be seen that Christ disclosed it in manifold ways before his death and by his appearances to Paul and Lazarus/ John again after his Resurrection.

Humanity's loss of understanding of the Mysteries clouded its ability to comprehend what Christ was saying in these disclosures. Only a few were given the "Grace" of understanding it and seeing him at the "turning point of time." Some of these disclosures are given below (RSV; my emphasis):

> **Mt 7,13-14**: (13) "Enter by the *narrow gate*, for the gate is wide and the way is easy, that leads to destruction, and those who enter by it are many. (14) For the *gate is narrow and the way is hard*, that leads to life, and *those who find it are few*."

---

1. For instance, see 4 ABD 941, "Mystery Religions," 24 Brit 707, "Mystery Religions," and to a lesser extent 2 ABD 548, "Ephesus," and Brit Index under "Mystery" and "Mystery Religion."

Two elements are involved here in "the way" that leads to life. One is "finding" the path and the other is traversing it. Few "find" it and when they do it is "narrow and hard." This cannot refer to the masses, the "crowds" (Mt 5,1a), but describes the "way" of the initiate into the Mysteries. Christ spoke these words on the "Mountain" and only to "his disciples [who] came to him" there (Mt 5,1). First there must be a sufficient period of discipline[2] to prepare the astral body's "lotus flowers," and only then can the revelation be made within the etheric body. See the discussion of the initiation procedure in "Three Days' Journey."

> **Lk 11,29**: When the crowds were increasing, he began to say, "This generation is an evil generation; it seeks a sign, but no sign shall be given to it except the *sign of Jonah.*"

> **Mt 12,38-40**: (38) Then some of the scribes and Pharisees said to him, "Teacher, we wish to see a sign from you." (39) But he answered them, "An evil and adulterous generation seeks for a sign; but no sign shall be given to it except the *sign of the prophet Jonah.* For as Jonah was *three days and three nights* in the belly of the whale, so will the Son of man be *three days and three nights* in the heart of the earth."

See what was said about these passages in the quotation from *The Gospel of St. Luke* (GSL) in "Three Days' Journey." It would also seem that

---

2. Ponder here the similarity between "disciple" and "discipline." Both derive from the same Latin root *discipulus,* meaning "learner" or "pupil." Interestingly, in the Greek, the roots for "disciple" and "discipline" are not identical. While doubtless related in meaning, we may infer that some of those called "disciples" were not yet sufficiently "disciplined" to have fully "found" and "traversed" the "way" Jesus refers to in Mt 7,13-14. Perhaps we have been guilty of missing the deeper meaning when the Bible speaks of "discipline": Lev 26,23; Deut 4,36; 8,5; 11,2; Ps 50,17; Prov 3,11-12; 5,12,23; 6,23; 12,1; 13,24; 15,10; 19,18; 22,15; 23,13; 29,17,19; Jer 7,28; Eph 6,4; Heb 12,5-11. It is noteworthy that the term "discipline" appears more in Proverbs, which means "wisdom," than in all the other books combined. Later in this volume (see "Peter, James and John" and "Egypt") we begin to see the significance of the term "loved" as it relates to a pupil or disciple, particularly in Jn 11 and Mk 10,21 (cf. also Col 4,14). It signifies the relationship between the teacher and pupil in the Mysteries, when the former has been able to lead the latter into their deeper secrets. It was such with Lazarus/John, who, as we shall see, was also almost certainly the "Young Man" of "great possessions" in Mk 10,21-22. This relationship of being "loved" and "disciplined" are equated in Prov 3,11-12, Prov 13,24 and Heb 12,6. Paul betrays his own high enlightenment when, along with what we are given about Lazarus/John, he makes this connection in the primary New Testament passage about "discipline," Heb 12,5-11; cf. also Gal 1,14.

"generation" in vs 39 above refers not only to those then living but to the Greco-Roman Cultural Era in which humanity had sunk to the point of no longer knowing about the Mysteries or the spiritual world behind the *maya* of the mineral-physical. It would be millennia before that cognition would again arise in a later "generation," beginning with our own. Is it not remarkable that only with the beginning of the age ("generation") of the human being's Consciousness Soul (see **I-24**) was the knowledge that existed in the ancient Mysteries about the spherical shape of the Earth and its relationship to the heavenly bodies "discovered" again by Columbus and Copernicus? It was part of the renaissance, or rebirth, of human consciousness, i.e., the birth of the Consciousness Soul. Only slowly, as a newborn child, is the human being coming again into its own knowledge, lost for millennia, of what had been given to it by the spiritual world in the Mysteries. (See, for instance, the discussion of the pyramid and the phoenix in the Appendix to "Fire" in Vol. 2, *"What Is Man?"*.) And even with its rediscovery, to this very day its spiritual significance remains obscure. Powell's works on hermetic astrology (*Hermetic Astrology I* [HA1] and *Hermetic Astrology II* [HA2]) shed much light on what Steiner told us early in this century. Only slowly are we beginning to see that it was there in the Bible all along.

> **Mt 26,60-61**: (60) ... At last two came forward (61) and said, "This fellow said, 'I am able to destroy the *temple of God*, and to build it in *three days*.'"

> **Mk 15,29-30**: (29) And those who passed by derided him, wagging their heads, and saying, "Aha! You who would destroy the *temple* and build it in *three days*, (30) save yourself, and come down from the cross!"

> **Jn 2,18-19**: (18) The Jews then said to him, "What sign have you to show us for doing this?" (19) Jesus answered them, "Destroy this *temple*, and in *three days* I will raise it up."

We shall see that the higher meaning of "temple" is the "Three Bodies" which house the "I Am," and we shall come to see that all these bodies are to be purified and perfected, "transfigured," so that even the oldest and basest, the physical, is no longer mineralized in earthly existence but is resurrected in its "Form/Phantom" condition (cf. Lk 20,27-38).

"Three Days" will be seen to indicate great spiritual significance in and of itself, but as it is used here it refers to the "temple sleep" of the ancient Mysteries being carried one step further, namely, through the point of *actual* earthly death rather than mere dormancy under the watchful eye of the hierophant as in former practice. In being crucified and resurrected even through the physical body itself, the "Form/Phantom" perceived through "Grace" by some, Christ became the "First Born/Fruits" of humanity, indicating the entelechy of the Prodigal Son who takes into himself the "I Am" of the Christ. Every Prodigal Son, i.e., each of us who would be redeemed, must "drink the cup" (Mk 10,39; Mt 20,23).

On his final journey to Jerusalem, in all the synoptic accounts Jesus tells his disciples that he is to be ignominiously crucified, but that he will rise on the "Third Day" (Mt 20,17-19; Mk 10,32-34; Lk 18,31-33). In vs 34, Luke then says, "But they understood none of these things; this saying was hid from them, and they did not grasp what was said." The full "grasp" was not to come to humanity for centuries, aside from the insights ("seeing," Is 6,9-10) granted to the few who were to become "Witness" to it for posterity. Humanity was not ripe for it in that "generation" (Jn 16,12; Heb 5,11; 9,5b).

In order for Christ to give humanity a "sign" of what lay ahead for it and to become a "First Fruit," he had to "die" a real earthly death so that the final deathlike condition (Jn 11,4,11) in the "temple sleep" of the Mysteries would be carried over into the real "Death" that every human being experiences.

John's version of what the synoptics expressed (Mt 20,17-19; Mk 10,32-34; Lk 18,31-33) is given in Jn 12,32-33:

> (32) "and I, when I am *lifted up* from the earth, will draw all men to myself." (33) He said this to show by what death he was to die.

Exoterically, vs 33 meant Jesus' death on the Cross; but esoterically, as it applies to the consequential "lifting up" of each of us followers (vs 32), it means the eventual "crucifixion" of our mineral-physical body so that we do not have to "die any more" (Lk 20,36), i.e., reincarnate. The "first death" (in the context of Rev 20,6,14, i.e., the "Second Death" when the etheric body will also be permanently laid aside) will have occurred and we will be "lifted up" into the etheric existence (cf. 1 Th 5,16-17; 1 Cor 15, 51-56).

This passage carries us to the more cryptic passage where Jesus earlier expressed the knowledge of how it was necessary that he die in the manner that was to come about:

> **Jn 3,14**: "And as *Moses lifted up* the *serpent* in the *wilderness*, so must the *Son of man* be *lifted up*."

There is an analogy between the "Serpent" and the dual nature of the "Zodiac(al)" sign of the scorpion. We shall see in "Peter, James and John" that the lower "I Am," the scorpion (literally, probably Iscariot), becomes the eagle—for Lazarus/John for a time replaces Judas among the "Twelve," and his Gospel has carried the symbol of the eagle from time immemorial. And we shall see later how "Serpent" carries this double meaning. In its lower aspect it is represented by the fallen snake and the tempter, but in its higher aspect it relates to the serpent of the Oriental "kundalini fire," when the "lotus flowers" (Job 40,21-22) are so stimulated as to engender perception in the spiritual world.[3] This perception leads to the first stage of spiritual development in the human being, that called "Manna" (or manas, see **I-9**) when the Ego has gained ascendancy over the astral body. It was Moses who first brought Manna to the people (Num 11) and he who first "lifted up the serpent" in the "Wilderness" (loneliness of the soul) for their healing and life. Paul recognized this as spiritual food, 1 Cor 10,3, as did Lazarus/John, Rev 2,17. We will also see later that "Son of Man" indicates the spiritual offspring of the human Ego, i.e., "man," when it has converted its "Three Bodies" into the fullness of, and thus given birth to, the higher "I Am" of Christ (Mt 13,33).

To more fully appreciate the significance of the profuse Biblical indications about the Mysteries, we must steal a further look at the creation (evolution) of the human being. (The "Overview" gave a quite brief portrayal. An even fuller one is to be found in the first essay in Volume 2, "Alpha and Omega > Creation and Apocalypse," in its discussion of "The Creation." The fullest account must await the Commentary.)

---

3. Comprehending this, one can begin to see why Lucifer, which means "light-bearer," is also called the "serpent" in Gen 3. The profundity of this connection glows when the present role of Lucifer (as against the still unredeemed "Luciferic spirits") is observed in "Karma and Reincarnation" (where it speaks of the soul's sojourn in the Sun sphere; find it through Lk 23,39-43 in the Index).

At the point in its evolution pictured in Gen 2,15-17,

(15) The Lord God took the man and put him in the garden of Eden to till it and keep it. (16) And the Lord God commanded the man, saying, "You may freely eat of every tree of the garden; (17) but of the tree of the knowledge of good and evil you shall not eat, for in the day that you eat of it you shall die.

the human being was still in the etheric world, not yet having descended into sense-perceptible mineral (material) existence. Its being was composed of "Three Bodies," physical, etheric and astral, not yet joined by the Ego (they do not speak the name "I," Gen 3,10, until after they have eaten the forbidden fruit). Various beings of such character (i.e., also consisting of "three bodies") retarded from prior evolution, in accordance with their etheric "kind" (Gen 1,21,24,25), began to descend into materiality. These represented all the various shades of "astrality" that the human astral body encompassed (those "Wild Animals" taken into the "Ark," the post-Atlantean human physical body, in the Noah account, Gen 6,14-7,3), and as they descended into materiality the human being was able, from the "garden" to give them "Names" appropriate to their astral character. This coming into existence of the Animal Kingdom is described in Gen 2,19-20a:

(19) So out of the ground the Lord God formed every beast of the field and every bird of the air, and brought them to the man to see what he would call them; and whatever the man called every living creature, that was its name. (20) The man gave names to all cattle, and to the birds of the air, and to every beast of the field.

The human being, in its essential character, was still androgynous, a circumstance that was to change contemporaneously with the change that was to come about in its astral body. The division into sexes took place during a *pralaya*, "Deep Sleep," a "timeless" period of evolutionary transformation when there was a lull in human consciousness. This is described in Gen 2,20b-24.

Up to this point the human being dwelled in full communion with, and awareness and understanding of, the beings of the Hierarchies, angels all the way up to the Seraphim, and acted in accordance with the wishes of these higher beings. These portrayed to human consciousness the Face of God. But in this state the human being had no "knowledge" of its own, no possibility of independence. This could only be brought about by experiences, i.e., from eating the fruit of the tree of good and evil. A hierarchical being called Lucifer (meaning "light-bearer"; see fn 3) had remained behind during the Old Moon Condition of Consciousness, the stage when the human astral body was being formed (**I-14**). The account of how Lucifer, contrary to the will of the Elohim (Exusiai, or Spirits of Form), brought about the infection of the human astral body is given in Gen 3, which describes what is called the Fall.

The descent of the human being into materiality thus commenced, the closing off from it of consciousness of the spiritual world and its beings. But this loss of consciousness occurred only gradually over long eons of time during which the human Ego entered the "Three Bodies" through the "Blood," and the etheric and astral bodies slowly shrank into the developing frame of the mineral-physical body.

The separation of the sexes and descent into materiality occurred generally in the transition from Lemuria to Atlantis (see **I-2**). The Mysteries began to develop on Atlantis. Through them the guiding spiritual powers were able to communicate reality to humanity and thus to guide it in its development along proper channels. At first there was more direct involvement of spiritual beings with humans in this divine endeavor. Something of this interplay is revealed in Gen 6,1-4, "when the sons of God came in to the daughters of men." The purest and most sensitive human beings, in the sense of spiritual awareness, received revelations directly from spiritual beings and communicated these revelations to others for their direction. An instinctive recognition of this leadership existed at first. The leaders became heads of the various Mysteries and, as priests or hierophants, were able to initiate others into their secrets. All ancient peoples looked to these leaders and initiates for guidance.

But as the descent into materiality progressed, evil increased (Gen 6,5). Eventually the Atlantean Evolutionary Epoch was brought to an end, and its fruits were carried over by the highest initiate to emerge therefrom, Manu, whom we may take to be the one called Noah in the Biblical account (Gen 6-10).

Humanity continued to be guided during the prehistoric post-Atlantean Cultural Eras (Ancient Indian and Ancient Persian) by those initiated into the Mysteries. But the mineralization of the human descent was continuing. The almost perfect memory, and extensive spiritual clairvoyance, of the ancient human being gave way to an increasing intellect, and with the fading memory and clairvoyance came the need for "Writing." And as the etheric body gradually encased itself within the mineral-physical confines, especially in the head region, not only did initiation become more difficult and dangerous but the insights available even to the leadership of the Mysteries faded (see "Fading Splendor"). More and more the Mysteries became decadent. "Darkness" was settling upon humanity. Even during the period between incarnations, the human soul was shut off from experiencing the spiritual beings, the Face of God. Sheol was experienced.

The encroaching decadence of ancient Mystery centers, such as Ephesus, with its temple of Artemis, is seen in Paul's encounters (Acts 19,21-41). The greatness of the ancient Artemis is recognized, it even being said that Paul and his companions were not "blasphemers of [the] goddess" (vs 37). What is indicated is that the ancient goddess is no longer recognized because of the decadence of the temple practices.

So distant was humanity from understanding the Mysteries at the time of Christ that when he and the beings of the spiritual world enacted the substance of those Mysteries for all humanity to see upon the world stage, the event was not understood. We shall see that the New Testament fully discloses this. But what has not been seen until now (with Steiner's revelations) is that the event is still not understood by Christendom. The main channel of its doctrines, as they emerged from those with archetypal understanding, is true, but while they are piously mouthed, they remain "mysterious," and this lack of understanding will progressively enucleate the power of the Gospel message.

The pervasive Biblical references to the ancient Mysteries are not detected. Rather, they are complacently deemed to refer only to what can be garnered from a simple reading of one or more of the available modern translations. The "occult" is deemed, in many if not the full spectrum of religious persuasions, to refer only to what is sinister and evil as if a "work of the devil," only to what Steiner calls "black magic" as distinguished from "white." But the Bible shows itself, as we shall see, to be an "occult" book from beginning to end, and it also shows that those who "find" (and sufficiently pursue) its deeper meanings are initiates into the "Mystery of Golgotha," to use Steiner's phrase.

It seems especially significant that the reason the "strait (hard) and narrow way" of Mt 7,14 is trodden only by "few" is that it is not "found."

The significance of this hit me upon reading a particular translation, prompting me to investigate whether this was consistently the meaning from one translation to another. It was so in thirteen of the fourteen translations in my personal library.[4] This seems a powerful indication that part of the very difficulty of "the Way" is in "finding" it. Something is "found" only after it has been "lost" or "hidden," so it is fair to say that the "way" referred to in this passage is an "occult" ("hidden") one.

Over and over Steiner explained that it was not the intent of the higher powers that any human being should be deprived of knowledge of the Mysteries, but rather that such knowledge was beyond the reach or capabilities of those who had not yet found it. The first chapter of his vital *Occult Science* (OS), entitled "The Character of Occult Science," shows it to be open to any who is willing to meet its substantial requirements. Clearly Christ expressed the same. See Mt 7,6, especially in the light of Jn 16,12, Heb 9,5 and Is 6,9-13. While these passages show that most were not yet ready in that "generation," after Christ had dismissed the crowds he said to his disciples, "there is nothing hid, except to be made manifest; nor ... secret, except to come to light" (Mk 4,22; Lk 8,17). Immediately following both of these passages Christ stressed the importance of how his hearers "heard" (Mk 4,23; Lk 8,18), a clear recognition of Isaiah's message, Is 6,9. A typical Steiner presentation on this is from *The Occult Significance of the Bhagavad Gita* (BG), Lect. 8, as follows:

> The summits of spiritual life have at all times been concealed from the wide plain of human intelligence. So it has remained, in a certain sense, right up to our present age. It is true that one of the characteristics of our age, which is only now dawning ... will be that certain things hitherto kept secret and really known to but very few will be spread abroad into large circles. That is the reason why you are present here, because our movement is the beginning of this spreading abroad of facts that until now have remained secret from

---

4. The thirteen are RSV, KJV, NRSV, NKJV, NIV, NJB, LB, AMPB, NACB, AB, PMEB, NEB and Barc. CEV (the most recent translation) says it is not found because it is so hard to follow: "The road that leads there is so hard to follow that only a few people find it"—an indication of how subtly meaning can be changed from one translation to another. The meaning could again be reconciled if its "hidden" nature were only one of the multiple things making it hard to follow, thus removing the "Which comes first, the chicken or the egg?" test. The CEV language would seem to preclude such a multiple, but this translation seems hard to justify by the original Greek. See KJV/NIV—INT.

the masses.... The anthroposophical view ... came precisely from the feeling that certain secrets must today be poured out into all people. Until our time ... these facts remained secret not because they were deliberately kept so, but because it lay in the natural course of man's development that they had to remain secret. It is said that the secrets of the old Mysteries were protected from the profane by certain definite, strictly observed rules. Far more than by rule, these secrets were protected by a fundamental characteristic of mankind in olden times, namely, that they simply could not have understood these secrets [thus, Jn 16,12]. This fact was a much more powerful protection than any external rule could be.

Anthroposophy shows that the Christ Event was the enactment, "Once for All," of the ancient Mysteries on the stage of world history (see CMF, *The Gospel of St. Matthew* [GSMt], Lect. 9, esp. p. 151; *From Jesus to Christ* [JTC], Lects. 4, p. 73 and 6, pp. 102-105). In the GSMt lecture, Steiner said,

In the book *Christianity as Mystical Fact* I have explained the sense in which secrets of the ancient Mysteries come to light in the Gospels, and that the Gospels, fundamentally, are repetitions of the descriptions of Initiation in the Mysteries. Why, in relating events in the life of Christ, was it possible to describe the processes enacted in the Mysteries? It was possible because everything that took place in the Mysteries in the inner life of the soul, had become *historic fact*: because the Christ-Jesus-Event was a re-portrayal of symbolic rites enacted during the process of the old Initiation, but fulfilled now at the higher level of full Ego-consciousness. This fact must always be kept in mind. The similarity of episodes in Christ's life—as narrated in the Gospels—with procedures in the Mysteries will certainly be realized by those who are convinced that such procedures became historic reality through His coming, although they were enacted on an entirely different level of consciousness.

The following could also be said.—Those destined to witness the Christ Event in Palestine observed the fulfillment of the Essene prophecy and were aware of the Baptism by John, the Temptation and what followed it, the Crucifixion, and the ensuing happenings. They could say to themselves: Here is a life lived through by a sublime Being in the body of a man. What are the all-important points in this life? Certain things take place as external events and they are identical with experiences undergone in the Mysteries by candidates for Initiation. We need therefore simply turn to the canon of a Mystery-rite and there we should find the prototype of a process that may now be described as an historical fact!

Here, then, is the great secret. What had formerly been shrouded in the darkness of temple-sanctuaries, perceptible—but only in its effects—to those in the outer world possessed of spiritual vision, was now enacted as the Christ Event on the stage of world-history itself. It must of course be realized that in the days of the Evangelists, no biographies were produced of the kind familiar to us to-day. In a biography, let us say, of Goethe, of Schiller, or of Lessing, every detail of their lives is probed into and every scrap of information collected, usually resulting in a mass of unimportant data purporting to convey the essentials of a life-history. Whereas all these details hinder one from discerning the points that really matter, the Evangelists were content to describe what was of central and fundamental importance in the life of Christ Jesus, namely that in this life there was a repetition of the process of Initiation—but enacted here in the great setting of world-history.

What was taught in the Mysteries was "to a great extent … the same as what we have come to know today as anthroposophy. It differed only in that it was adapted to the customs of that time and imparted according to strict rules" (*The Gospel of St. John and its Relation to the Other Gospels* [Jn-Rel], Lect. 6, p. 102). Steiner's work contains many other descriptions of these ancient Mysteries.[5]

---

5. For further reference, see *The Gospel of St. John* (GSJ), Lect. 4; *Christ and the Human Soul* (CHS), Lect. 1, pp. 17-18; *The Fifth Gospel* (FG), Lects. 3, p. 48 and 4, p. 67; Jn-Rel, Lects. 10, pp. 188-192 and 11, pp. 209-212; *The Birth of Light* (BL), pp. 9-10; JTC, Lect. 6, pp. 102-105; *Philosophy, Cosmology & Religion* (PCR), Lect. 7, pp. 105-106; *The Principle of Spiritual Economy* (SE), Lect. 5; *The Christmas Festival in the Changing Course of Time* (CFCCT), p. 10; and *The Karma of Materialism* (KM), Lect. 3, pp. 46-47. While titles seldom are an accurate description of what is in a Steiner lecture cycle, see the Bibliography herein for those titles containing such words as "mystery," "initiation," "occult" or "esoteric." For excellent works by other anthroposophical writers, see *The Beginnings of Christianity* (BC) and *Gnosis* (GNOS), by Welburn, and *Rudolf Steiner and the Founding of the New Mysteries* (RSFNM), by Prokofieff.

Just as there were many in Jesus' day ("generation") not yet prepared to receive the deeper wisdom in the Mystery of Golgotha, while his closest disciples were urged to "enter by the narrow gate" (Mt 7,13), so also in our own time are there two paths. Most will walk the wider and easier one, and their pathway to the wisdom in the Mystery of Golgotha will be the one of evolutionary "Perfect(ion)" over many lives and eras—always exposed to the dangers of "destruction" which beset that path. Only "few" will "find" in our day the higher path. It is "narrow" and "hard." Steiner has shown us this path in his *Knowledge of the Higher Worlds and Its Attainment* (KHW).[6] In his preface to the third edition, Steiner says "It would be an error to imagine these disclosures ... to be valueless for one who lacks the inclination or the possibility[7] to pursue this path himself, ... [for it can give a basis for] confidence in the communications of the person who has done so.... [It will] help those who want their sense of truth and feeling for truth concerning the supersensible world strengthened and assured."

The study of this term "Mysteries" cannot be considered complete without considering also other closely related terms and phrases herein, such as "Three Days' Journey," "Widow's Son," and "Under the Tree," to mention only some of the more important.

Bearing in mind the evolutionary development of humanity that runs as a central theme through this entire anthroposophical work, let us now look at the extensive Biblical references to the Mysteries under the terms "mystery" (including "mysterious" and "mysteries"), "hid" (including "hidden" and "hide"), "secret," "remember" (including "remembered"; notably nothing applicable is found under "memory"), as well as some other indicative passages. One thing becomes clear as we go through them. The irony in today's religious lemming-like chant that the occult is sinister is that few themes are more pervasive in the Bible than this indicator of its occult nature.

---

6. The more recent translation is entitled *How to Know Higher Worlds.*

7. One who incarnates carrying a heavy (subjective) karmic debt may well find it practically "impossible" to reach that level during the course of the given incarnation. "Talents" or "Garments" needed may yet have to be developed. Nevertheless, recognition of the "way" must surely be helpful, as Steiner intimates, in the endeavor to attain that ultimate end.—ERS

Survey of Biblical Passages

The term "mysteries," "mysterious" or "mystery" appears in each of the passages below (RSV; emphasis mine) set out in their canonical order:[8]

Dan 2: (1) ... Nebuchadnezzar had dreams; and his spirit was troubled, and his sleep left him. (2) Then the king commanded that the magicians, the enchanters, the sorcerers, and the Chaldeans be summoned, to tell the king his dreams.... (10) The Chaldeans answered the king, "There is not a man on earth who can meet the king's demand.... (11) The thing that the king asks is difficult, and none can show it to the king except the gods, whose dwelling is not with flesh." ... (16) And Daniel went in and besought the king to appoint him a time, that he might show to the king the interpretation. (17) Then Daniel went to his house and made the matter known to Hananiah, Mishael, and Azariah, his companions, (18) and told them to seek mercy of the God of heaven concerning this *mystery*, so that Daniel and his companions might not perish with the rest of the wise men of Babylon. (19) Then the *mystery* was revealed to Daniel in a vision of the night.... (20) Daniel said: "Blessed be the name of God [see "I AM"] ... to whom belong[s] wisdom....(21) ... He gives wisdom to the wise and knowledge to those who have understanding; (22) he reveals deep and *mysterious* things...." (26) The king said to Daniel ... "Are you able to make known to me the dream that I have seen and its interpretation?" (27) Daniel answered the king, "No wise men, enchanters, magicians, or astrologers can show to the king the *mystery* which the king has asked, (28) but there is a God in heaven who reveals *mysteries*, and he has made known to King Nebuchadnezzar what will be in the latter days.... (29) To you, O king, as you lay in bed came thoughts of what would be hereafter, and he who reveals *mysteries* made known to you what is to be. (30) But as for me, not because of any wisdom that I have more than the living has this *mystery* been revealed to me, but in order that the interpretation may be made known to the king...." (47) The king said to Daniel, "Truly, your

---

8. Scriptural passages that include more than one term, such as "mystery" and/or "hidden" and/or "secret," appear only under the first term annotated.

God is God of gods and Lord of kings, and a revealer of *mysteries*, for you have been able to reveal this *mystery*."

The first thing to be noted is that the king did not ask first for an interpretation of his dream, but rather that they "tell the king his dreams." The "magicians, enchanters, sorcerers, and Chaldeans" whose services the king sought pleaded with him to tell them his dream and then they would interpret (vs 4). In the process of refusing their request and threatening them with death if they failed, the king says (vs 9; emphasis mine), "You have agreed to speak lying and corrupt words before me *till the times change.* Therefore tell me the dream, and I shall know that you can show me its interpretation." This "till the times change" seems to be a reflection of the "Fading Splendor" of prophecy.

Daniel, to show his vision was of a greater perspective than simply "the times," proceeds not only to tell the king his vision but then to interpret it (vss 31-45). It involved an "image, mighty and of exceeding brightness," of a creature whose head was of gold, its breast and arms of silver, its belly and thighs of bronze, its legs of iron, and its feet partly of iron and partly of clay. A stone from heaven, i.e., "cut out by no human hand," broke the feet bringing down the entire image in destruction, which was carried away by the wind (i.e., spirit). The stone then "became a great mountain and filled the whole earth." The term "stone" is a metaphor of much significance. While this is not the place to fully develop it, the reality of the descending Christ, seen by the initiates in the ancient Mysteries, could be described as a "stone" that became a "Mountain" (see "Rock/Christ"; cf. Acts 19,35, "the sacred stone that fell from the sky") and "filled the whole Earth." The dripping "Blood" of the crucified Christ filled the etheric substance of the Earth and is what makes the salvation of humanity possible. See "Blood" in Vol. 2, *"What Is Man?"*. Clearly Daniel's interpretation suggests that he too was an initiate who saw the descending Christ. How then does this fit with the rest of the dream?

Daniel equates the head of gold to the kingdom of Nebuchadnezzar, and then equates three successive kingdoms to the silver, bronze and iron. The last would be divided into iron and clay, the clay giving rise to the chain of destruction of all the kingdoms, whereupon the God of heaven will set up a kingdom that shall never be destroyed.

Theology, predisposed to view the prophecy through its historical lens, has generally agreed that the four kingdoms are the Babylonians,

Medes, Persians and Greeks, the last being "divided" between the Ptolemies of Egypt and the Seleucids of Antioch in Syria. See 6 Interp 387-388; 23 AB 149; and INTPN, "Daniel," pp. 35-36. All of these sources recognize that the ages of the metals derive from Ancient Indian sources, 6 Interp 385, and this is not to be taken lightly. See **I-46**. While the historical facts borrowed (seemingly retroactively) to portray the vision are perhaps those that had occurred up to the time of the writing, their use, as is so often true in scripture for disguise, is metaphorical to present a far larger perspective of truth. What had come down through these ages had to be retraced. And if the four-plus kingdoms described by reference to these ancient ages are projected out, starting with the Greco-Roman Cultural Era inaugurated by Nebuchadnezzar, we thus have

Golden Kingdom	Greco Roman Cultural Era (with its Advent)
Silver Kingdom	Germanic (Present) Cultural Era
Bronze Kingdom	Age of Philadelphia (6th) Cultural Era
Iron Kingdom	American (7th) Cultural Era

This last will be divided, bringing the War of All Against All and the end of the post-Atlantean Epoch. This interpretation would mean Daniel was foreseeing the same vision given by Lazarus/John in the last four "letters" to the angels of the churches (Rev 2,18-3,22). His later visions in Dan 7 and 12 then portray other portions of what was given to Lazarus/John more vividly in his Apocalypse.

Over and over again in the passages that follow are indications that the "mystery" involved in the Christ event is something that was foreseen in the Mysteries from of old. In that it was a "fulfillment," as Matthew's Gospel so frequently asserted, Steiner is not expressing a non-Biblical concept in saying that the Mystery of Golgotha was an enactment upon the world stage, for all to see, of the substance of the Mysteries. It seems novel only because Christendom, along with humanity in general, has lost an understanding of what was taught and accomplished in the ancient Mysteries. The extent to which Christ went to show his fulfillment of those ancient insights (prophecies) is widely recognized in his enactment of the prophecy of Zechariah (Zech 9,9; Mt 21,1-11; Mk 11,1-10; Lk 19,28-38; Jn 12,12-19).

The desire of the spiritual powers to make these things known is reflected in such passages below as Mk 4,22, discussed earlier, and the related Mt 10,26; Lk 8,17; 12,2. It is not that the effort to pierce the veil over human understanding has not occurred, but that the scales have not yet fallen from human eyes. But it will happen, and is happening, in the fullness of time. The dimming of vision took millennia. That its restoration should do the same, or that the spiritual world (as indicated by the Bible; Is 6,12-13; Jer 31,31-34; Jn 16,12; Heb 9,5 et al.) expressed this, should not be too surprising. Ominously, however, if fading insight assured the descent of humanity, failure to perceive will also impede its ascent.

> **Rom 11,25**: Lest you be wise in your own conceits, I want you to understand this *mystery*, brethren: a hardening has come upon part of Israel, until the full number of the Gentiles come in....

The "hardening" involved in this mystery is in the head region and is related to the entry of the etheric body into the physical body. This gradual development caused human memory and perception of spiritual beings to fade ("Fading Splendor") and intellect to increase. It was through Abraham and his descendants, particularly Isaac, that this hardening or progressive enhancement of intellectual thinking (like that involved in the development of arithmetic) was to occur. In the tendered sacrifice of his son Isaac, Abraham gave up the ancient clairvoyance (*Deeper Secrets of Human History in the Light of the Gospel of St. Matthew* [DSM], Lect. 2, pp. 30-36). When God gave Isaac back to him (Heb 11,19), it was to establish this line of descent (DSM, Id. and Gen 22,17). The mineralized brains (mineral = stone) of his descendants were to be the earthly instrument of the Hebrew mission as a "Chosen" race. This was foreshadowed by the "Twelve"-fold (i.e., "Zodiac[al]") dome of the skull envisioned in Gen 15,5 (see **I-20**; see also the illustrations from *Fractals* in Appendix to "Fire," Vol. 2).

If the Christ were to redeem humanity, he was destined to do so by incarnating into the race that had progressed the furthest in its "hardening" in this sense. Among them, he would make no intellectual sense whatsoever, and his "Crucifixion" would be assured—for he had to shed his "Blood" if humanity were to be redeemed. They were a stubborn, obstinate and haughty people, "stiff-necked" they are called (Ex 32,9; 33,3,5; 34,9; Jer 7,25-26; Acts 7,51), yet in spite of that God would make of them "a great nation" (Ex 32,9; 34,9) for they were to be his instrument, the channel through which the Christ, the "Dove," must enter (see "Baptism-Dove"). This was the "mystery" from of old of which Paul next speaks,

> **Rom 16,25-26**: ... according to the revelation of the *mystery* which was kept *secret* for long ages but is now disclosed and through the prophetic writings is made known to all nations....

> **1 Cor 4,1**: This is how one should regard us, as servants of Christ and stewards of the *mysteries* of God.

> **1 Cor 13,2**: And if I have prophetic powers, and understand all *mysteries* and all knowledge, ... but have not love, I am nothing.

The development of the divine love is part of the Mystery of Golgotha. Merely "understanding" it intellectually, while helpful and eventually essential, is not sufficient. The failure to also walk the "way" in this respect is ultimately fatal to the soul—it is "nothing" in the end. Its demands are upon us. Our world is crying for it—as indeed is every soul, living or "dead."

> **1 Cor 15,51**: Lo! I tell you a *mystery*. We shall not all sleep, but we shall all be changed, in a moment, in the twinkling of an eye, at the last trumpet [see "Trumpet"].[9]

> **Eph 1,9-10**: (9) For he has made known to us in all wisdom and insight the *mystery* of his will, according to his purpose which he set forth in Christ as a plan for the fullness of time, to unite all things in him, things in heaven and things on earth.

> **Eph 3,1-9**: (1) ... I, Paul, ... (2) asssum[e] that you have heard ... (3) how the *mystery* was made known to me by revelation, as I have written briefly. (4) When you read this you can perceive my insight into the *mystery* of Christ, (5) which was not made known to the sons of men in other generations as it has now been revealed to his

---

9. See the quote from Barc on this verse near the beginning of "Three Days' Journey." There Barclay substitutes for the single word "mystery" the clause "something which only the initiated can understand."

holy apostles and prophets by the Spirit.... (8) To me ... this grace was given ... (9) ... to make all men see what is the plan of the *mystery hidden* for ages in God who created all things.

Eph 6,19: ... that utterance may be given me in opening my mouth boldly to proclaim the *mystery* of the gospel....

Col 1,25-27: (25) ... I became a minister ... to make the word of God fully known, (26) the *mystery hidden* for ages and generations but now made manifest to his saints. (27) To them God chose to make known how great among the Gentiles are the riches of the glory of *this mystery, which is Christ in you.*

The passages where Paul spoke of "Christ (or God's "Son") *in* me" (Gal 1,16; 2,20) were discussed in "Spiritual Economy" and in "I AM." Paul recognized that the etheric Christ, the higher "I Am," was in him, which made it possible for him to prevail over the "Three Bodies." That is possible for everyone. Here he speaks of the "Christ *in you.*" This very reality, the etheric Christ within, as Paul says, is the "mystery." So very much is expressed in this simple statement.

Col 2,2-3: (2) ... to have the riches of assured understanding and the knowledge of God's *mystery* of Christ, (3) in whom are *hid* all the treasures of wisdom and knowledge.

Col 4,3: ... to declare the *mystery* of Christ....

1 Tim 3,16: Great indeed, we confess, is the *mystery* of our religion: He was manifested in the flesh, vindicated in the Spirit, seen by angels, preached among the nations, believed on in the world, taken up in glory.

Rev 1,20: As for the *mystery* of the seven stars....

That the ancient Mysteries were part and parcel of the fabric in which Judaism and Christianity developed is indicated, for instance, in the relationship between the Biblical account of Elijah and the ancient Mystery of Persia known as Mithraism. An account of Mithraism is given in 8 Brit 197-198 where, among other things, we are told:

1. The worship of Mithra went back far beyond the eighth century B.C., having roots even in Indian Vedic texts.

2. Initiation ceremonies took place in *caves*.

3. The initiates were organized in seven grades as follows:

(1)   Raven
(2)   Bridegroom
(3)   Soldier
(4)   Lion
(5)   Persian
(6)   Courier of (and to) the Sun
(7)   Father

4. Little is known about the initiation ceremonies, but a simulated death and resurrection was probably part of the ceremony (see "Three Days' Journey").

What is noteworthy is that, as Steiner shows (e.g., see FG, Lect. 3, p. 48;[10] Jn-Rel, Lect. 10, p. 190; and BL, p. 10), the books of Kings identify Elijah as having achieved all seven of such stages of initiation, thus:

(1) 1 K 17,4,6: He is fed by *Ravens*.

(2) 1 K 17,3-5: He goes into hiding (*Hidden One* is the second stage according to Steiner).

(3) 1 K 18,19: He confronts the prophets of Baal as a Warrior or *Soldier*.

(4) 1 K 19,9-18: Fleeing, he took refuge in a *cave*, from which he observed the wind, earthquake and fire, and then the still small voice that emboldened him, and he went out as a *Lion*.

(5), (6) and (7) 2 K 2,12: Elisha sees Elijah taken up into heaven in a

---

10. At p. 67 Steiner tells us that the Church of St. Peter in Rome stands over the site of an earlier temple of the Mithras cult.

whirlwind and cries, "My father, my father! the chariots of Israel and its horsemen!" The *Persian* is here the "true Israelite." Identification with one's folk is the point, not necessarily a Persian—reference here to Israel does that. The *Sun Hero or Sun Runner* is represented by the chariots and the horsemen. And the *Father* is the opening exclamation. (For light on the "father" principle, see *The Mystery of the Trinity/The Mission of the Spirit* [MT], Chaps. 1-4, esp. 4.)

We find Jesus himself applying this standard in his call of Nathanael in Jn 1,43-51, whom he mysteriously identifies as *"an Israelite,"* from which Nathanael immediately recognizes Christ's power as one from a higher state of initiation (for only one from a higher rank would have recognized him at the fifth or lower rank). And one might also recognize the two higher stages in the following provisions of the same passage, which suggest an even higher status for Jesus and compare to Elisha's cry to Elijah in recognition and awe. Moreover, we see that the later passage in Jn 14,8-11 is addressed to Philip who had brought Nathanael to Jesus (Jn 1, 45-46), and appears to bear upon his status as an initiate. By asking the way to the Father, Philip is inquiring about the seventh degree, and Christ, by responding that Philip has been with him a long time, suggests that Philip has by now attained the sixth degree and is indeed reaching for the seventh.

The term "the son of the widow" (see "Widow's Son") also esoterically identifies one as an initiate of the Mysteries. We find it hidden here in that same passage from 1 K 17 where the widow's son supposedly dies and is brought back by Elijah. See also 2 K 4 (Elisha).

The other closely related terms "hid," "secret" and "remember" in their various forms appear, respectively, in their canonical order in each of the passages (RSV; emphasis mine) below (the ones on "hidden" bear not only on the occult meaning, but also on the second stage of initiation above).

Under "hid":

Gen 35,4: So they gave Jacob all the foreign gods that they had …; and Jacob *hid* them under the oak which was near Shechem.

From the symbolism used here it seems highly likely that we are being told that Jacob, as the ancestral prototype for later revered Hebrews, was initiated into the Canaanite Mysteries. Later, in succession, we see Joseph being put over all the land of Egypt, suggesting his initiation (expressed through his many preparatory ordeals) into the ancient Egyptian Mysteries; Moses being initiated into the Mysteries first of Egypt and then of Midian; and Elijah (and presumably also Elisha upon whom the former's mantle fell) into the Persian Mysteries (Mithraism). "Foreign gods" implies that which came from the Mysteries of a foreign land, i.e., Canaan. "Hid" expresses the character of the ancient Mysteries. And "under the oak" is another way of expressing the phrase "Under the Tree," a spiritual term of art signifying the place within where enlightenment occurs.

> **Is 49,2**: He made my mouth like a sharp sword, in the shadow of his hand he *hid* me; he made me a polished arrow, in his quiver he *hid* me away.

If we consider only the aspect of this verse which is most pertinent here, from it the balance takes on meaning. In Is 40-48 we have the Christ speaking through Isaiah. The evidence of this is profuse. Is 41,4 and 48,12 identify the "I Am" and the "Alpha and Omega" as one and the same—clearly the Christ. See the discussion in "I AM" above. The Christ is not the servant—at least not yet as Isaiah perceived him. In Is 49, we have the servant speaking. The identity of the servant has perplexed Christendom. See 5 Interp 406-414; 20 AB xxxviii-lv; INTPN, Isaiah 40-66, pp. 126-133; and NJB 1169-1170. That the Evangelists applied the prophecy to Jesus of Nazareth is recognized; Interp Id., p. 413 and NJB 1170; but the scholars have had difficulty with the suggestion that Isaiah was in fact that prophetic, preferring instead to generalize the reference or to apply it to the nation of Israel. In that, scholarship has sold Isaiah's vision short. But it is understandable since the distinction between Jesus of Nazareth and Jesus Christ has only been made clear by the light of anthroposophy. The former did not fully become the latter until the Christ Spirit, called the "Dove," entered Jesus of Nazareth upon the withdrawal of the Zarathustra Ego at his Baptism (see "Baptism-Dove"). Lazarus/John tells us that Isaiah (he who is called "First Isaiah") spoke *with* the Christ (Jn 12,41; see the discussion in "I AM"). The descending Christ, he who was over the Hierarchies, was even then the "I Am," the "Lord," who was speaking also through the one called "Second

Isaiah" in the "servant" passages. Christ was therefore working in fashioning the vehicle (see "The Nativity") in which he was to incarnate, namely, Jesus of Nazareth. That vehicle is the "servant." The human Individuality who was to incarnate in Jesus of Nazareth, the one who had been Zarathustra of old, was a teacher of the "middle period prophets" during their Babylonian captivity. Presumably Second Isaiah was one of these. The Christ, working through that exalted teacher, inspired this worthy pupil with the vision of him who would become the servant, Jesus of Nazareth. The knowledge from this ancient source stimulated the Essenes into pregnant Messianic expectation, and led the Magi to this servant child in Matthew's Gospel.

It was the Christ who entered the servant, Jesus of Nazareth, in his thirtieth year, and "made my mouth like a sharp sword" (Is 49,2; Rev 1,16). It was the Christ who *hid* the servant in his spirit ("shadow of his hand"). The "hiding" is part of the Mystery of Golgotha. But with anthroposophical light, the identity of the servant is clear.

One needs to remember that historical facts are only tools with which a divine story is being told. And in the context of divine stories, time does not exist, hence sequence is ultimately an illusion, when sevens become "Twelves." The Genesis account is timeless in its application, as is the Bible in its entirety. The spiritual reality, the unity, in the fullness of time, is all there is. That too is the Mystery (Eph 1,9-10), and one who sees it, as Isaiah did, need not provoke himself with matters of tense. He could speak of the future servant, Jesus of Nazareth, in the present tense, but in doing so he was also speaking of the Zarathustra Individuality—a reality existing at that time.

Is 51,16: And I have put my words in your mouth, and *hid* you in the shadow of my hand....

Mk 4,22: For there is nothing *hid*, except to be made manifest; nor is anything *secret*, except to come to light.

Lk 8,17: For nothing is *hid* that shall not be made manifest, nor anything *secret* that shall not be known and come to light.

Col 2,2b-3: ... to have all the riches of assured understanding and the knowledge of God's *mystery*, of Christ, in whom are *hid* all the treasures of wisdom and knowledge.

Under "hidden":

Genesis, when understood anthroposophically, explains many otherwise "mysterious" things about human nature and evolution. The
groundwork for all the "hide" passages (including "hid" above) is laid in
Gen 3-4. At the conclusion of the Fall in Gen 3, the doorway to highest
divine knowledge is closed when the first descended human beings are
driven from the "garden" which lay to their "East" and the Cherubim and
the Seraphim's flaming sword are stationed there to "guard the way" in
order to prevent the unprepared from re-entering (Gen 3,24).

There is an interplay between Gen 3 and 4 in regard to the verb
"hide." Its first appearance is in Gen 3,8,10 where, as a consequence of
their attainment of "knowledge," Adam and Eve (i.e., the first
descended human beings) hid themselves from God and took the first
steps in separation ("Fission"). In Gen 4 the other side of that event is
reflected. In an early lecture cycle, *Temple Legend* (TL), Lects. 2 and 18,
Steiner addresses the differences between Cain and Abel. In the first
(pp. 21-22), he says,

> "Abel was a keeper of sheep." As a shepherd one accepts life as the
> Creator has presented it. One does not cultivate the herds, one tends
> them. Therefore Abel is the representative of the sex which does not
> reach spirituality through its own individual effort of understand-
> ing, but only receives it as a revelation of the Godhead and then
> merely tends it. The keeper of flocks, the guardian of that which has
> been placed on the earth, that is Abel. The one who creates things
> for himself, that is Cain.

In the second (p. 254):

> Now, there is a difference between the female priestly wisdom
> and the male aspiration. This is described to us in the legend of Cain
> and Abel. Abel was a shepherd and occupied himself with the life
> that was already there. He is the symbol of the inborn divine force
> which works in man as the wisdom which he does not acquire for
> himself, which flows into him. Cain creates something new out of
> what the world offers. He represents the passive masculine wisdom,
> which must first be fertilized from outside, which goes out into the
> world to gather wisdom and to create from what has been gathered.

Cain killed Abel; which means that male wisdom offers resistance against the female wisdom since it feels that it must subdue and re-model physical wisdom.

The descent into mineralization was underway. Since the spirit cannot dwell there (cf. Jn 3,6), it had to "hide its face." This, humanity's gradual loss of divine insight, the "Fading Splendor," had its origin from the spiritual side in the Gen 4 passage which follows. Most uses of the verb "hide" in its various forms derive from this. Cain became "a fugitive and a wanderer on the earth" (Gen 4,14). This applies to every human being. Just as their parents, they symbolize the archetypal character of each human being.[11] They and their fate are the natural offspring ("sons") of the characteristics inherent in their parents. While loss of consciousness through "death" was initiated in Gen 3,19, no human being (eternal Individuality) is given the privilege of escaping the Earth so easily, but must return to "wander" it until the condition is overcome (Gen 4,7). See the discussions elsewhere herein involving Lk 20,34-38.

Gen 4,14: Behold, thou hast driven me this day away from the ground; and from thy face I shall be *hidden*;

Josh 10,17,27: (17) And it was told Joshua, "The five kings have been found, *hidden* in the cave at Makkedah." ... (27) but at the time of the *going down of the sun*, Joshua commanded, and they took them down from the trees, and threw them into the cave where they had *hidden* themselves, and they set great stones against the mouth of the cave, which remain to this very day.

We cannot here give the above passage the full comment it deserves. It is included because it follows the notable passage about the Sun standing still (Josh 10,12-13), with the reference to its being "written in the Book of Jashar" (see "Akashic" and "Karma and Reincarnation"), and because it involves fascinating similarities to the "temple sleep" of the ancient Mysteries. It speaks in terms of "a cave" (vss 17-18,22-23,27) and of "great stones against the mouth of the cave" (vs 18; cf. the tomb of Lazarus, Jn

---

11. For a more elaborate discussion of Cain and Abel that also considers the relationship between Gen 4 and 5, see Appendix to "Three Bodies" below.

11,38-39, and that of Jesus, Mt 27,60; 28,2; Mk 15,46; 16,3-4; Lk 24,2;
Jn 20,1), and of their being brought out of the cave (vs 23), and of their
then suffering death at the hands of the multitude by being "hung upon
trees" (vss 26-27), and that they remain in the cave where they had hidden
themselves to this very day (vs 27). It also speaks of "the going down of
the sun" (vs 27) an event of significance (cf. Mk 1,32) when events are
under the auspices of the spiritual rather than the physical Sun. As with so
many parables of Christ, e.g., that of the unjust judge (Lk 18,1-8), atro-
cious stories from an earthly standpoint carry spiritual meaning of high
order. The student who studies this passage should contemplate its prophetic symbolism, for all of the elements involved in the suffering, death,
entombment, and continuing "hidden" nature of the Lazarus and
Golgotha accounts are present here. We must ask, are we not being told
that Joshua initiated these five "kings?". We must leave it there for now.

1 Sam 10,22: So they inquired again of the Lord, "Did the man
come hither?" and the Lord said, "Behold, he has *hidden* himself
among the baggage."

This refers to the time when Saul was chosen by God as the first king
of Israel. That he had "hidden" himself suggests at least an effort toward
initiation. He was then said to be "taller than any of the people from his
shoulders upward" (vs 23). If this view is correct, it illustrates that
whereas Adam and Even "hid" themselves for an ignoble reason, one can
also "hide" or be "hidden" from the world for the noble one of initiation.
Many of the passages that follow portray this feature.

The immediately succeeding passage indicates how things "hidden"
from the uninitiated (or those not blessed with ancient clairvoyance) are
known to those such as Solomon.

1 K 10,3: And Solomon answered all her questions; there was nothing *hidden* from the king which he could not explain to her. [2 Ch
9,2 is verbatim.]

Prov 2,4-5: (4) if you seek it like silver and search for it as for *hidden*
treasures; (5) then you will understand the fear of the Lord and find
the knowledge of God.[12]

---

12. Compare this with the "find" in Mt 7,14. See fn 4 above and related text.

Is 48,6b: From this time forth I make you hear new things, *hidden* things which you have not known.

Jer 33,3,5: (3) Call to me and I will answer you, and will tell you great and *hidden* things which you have not known.… (5) for I have *hidden* my face from this city because of all their wickedness.

Mt 10,26-27: (26) … for nothing is *covered* that will not be revealed, or *hidden* that will not be known. (27) What I tell you in the *dark*, utter in the light; and what you hear *whispered*, proclaim upon the housetops. [Lk 12,2-3 is almost verbatim.]

Mt 11,25: I thank thee, Father, Lord of heaven and earth, that thou hast *hidden* these things from the wise and understanding and revealed them to babes. [Lk 10,21 is verbatim. See "Simple Rather Than Wise" and "Simple."]

Mt 13,34-35: All this Jesus said to the crowds in parables; indeed he said nothing to them without a parable. This was to fulfil what was spoken by the prophet [Ps 78,2]: "I will open my mouth in parables, I will utter *what has been hidden since the foundation of the world*."

Mt 13,44: The kingdom of heaven is like a treasure *hidden* in a field, which a man found.…

Here Christ takes us all the way back to Gen 4, for it was in the "field" of human experiences (i.e., knowledge) where the "heaven" was first lost when God "hid his face" (archetypically), Gen 4,14, from the human soul.

Lk 10,22: All things have been delivered to me by my Father; and *no one knows who the Son is except the Father, or who the Father is except the Son and any one to whom the Son chooses to reveal him.* See also Mt 11,27 to the same effect.

1 Cor 2,6-7: (6) Yet among the mature we do impart wisdom, although it is not a wisdom of this age or of the rulers of this age, who are doomed to pass away. (7) But we impart a *secret and hidden wisdom of God, which God decreed before the ages for our glorification.*

1 Cor 4,5: Therefore do not pronounce judgment before the time, before the Lord comes, who will bring to light the things now *hidden in darkness and will disclose the purposes of the heart.* [Consider how completely this fits with all that was said above under "Lord of Karma" and "Second Coming."]

Rev 2,17: He who has an ear, let him hear what the Spirit says to the churches. To him who conquers I will give some of the *hidden manna*, and I will give him a white stone, with a *new name* written on the stone *which no one knows except him who receives it.*

Under "Hide":

Deut 31,17-18: (17) Then my anger will be kindled against them in that day, and I will forsake them and *hide my face* from them, and they will be devoured; and many evils and troubles will come upon them, so that they will say in that day, "Have not these evils come upon us because our God is not among us?" (18) And I will surely *hide my face* in that day on account of all the evil which they have done, because they have turned to other gods.

Several subsequent passages speak of God "hiding his face." They include Deut 32,20; Ps 10,1; 27,8-9; 30,7; 44,24; 69,17; 88,14; 102,2; Is 1,15; Mic 3,4. But the following passages also include something notable in addition:

Josh 2,16: And she [Rahab] said to them, "*Go into the hills* [see "Mountain"], lest the pursuers meet you; *and hide yourselves there three days* [See "Three Days" and "Three Days' Journey"], until the pursuers have returned; then afterward you may go your way."

2 Ch 18,24: And Micaiah said, "Behold, you shall see on that day when you go into an inner chamber to *hide* yourself [See "Three Days' Journey"]."

Ps 13,1: How long, O Lord? Wilt thou forget me for ever? How long wilt thou *hide thy face* from me?

What is especially noteworthy in this passage and the one following is the refrain from Isaiah 6,11, "How long, O Lord?"

Ps 89,46,48: (46) How long, O Lord? Wilt thou *hide thyself* for ever? How long will thy wrath burn like fire? … (48) What man can live and never see death? Who can deliver his soul from the power of Sheol?

This passage and Ps 143,7-8 below bring out the relationship between God's "hiding his face" and the encroaching shades of "Sheol." While not literally explicit, one with anthroposophical insight will see in vs 48 the suggestion that all go through repeated death, i.e., are "raised from the dead" (Lk 20,37; see "Bush").

Ps 119,18-19: (18) *Open my eyes,* that I may behold wondrous things out of thy law. (19) I am a *sojourner* on earth; *hide not thy commandments* from me!

"Open my eyes" (vs 18) and "hide not thy commandments" (vs 19) are in reality a form of typical Psalms parallelism, stating something over with the same or opposite meaning. The Psalmist wants to "see" with spiritual vision (cf. Is 6,9-10) that comes from initiation into the Mysteries. Verse 19 takes us back again to Gen 4, for a "sojourner" is a "wanderer," as Cain was when God "hid his face" (Gen 4,12,14).

Ps 143,7-8: (7) Make haste to answer me, O Lord! My spirit fails! *Hide not thy face* from me, lest I be like those who go down to the Pit. [See Ps 89 above.] (8) … Teach me *the way* [cf. Mt 7,13-14] that I should go, for to thee I lift up my soul.

Is 30,20-21: (20) And though the Lord give you the bread of adversity and the water of affliction, yet your Teacher *will not hide himself any more,* but your eyes shall see your Teacher. (21) And *your ears shall hear* a word behind you, saying, "This is *the way, walk in it*" [cf. Mt 7,13-14].

Here (vs 21) we have the "inspiration" aspect of initiation, i.e., spiritual hearing (Is 6,9-10), whereas in the Ps 119 passage above, we had the "imagination," or seeing, aspect.

Ezek 39,28-29: (28) Then they shall know that I am the Lord their God because I sent them into exile among the nations, and then gathered them into their own land. I will leave none of them remaining among the nations any more; (29) and I *will not hide my face any more from them*, when I pour out my Spirit upon the house of Israel, says the Lord God.

Mic 3,4-7: (4) Then they will cry to the Lord, but he will not answer them; he will *hide his face* from them at that time, because they have made their deeds evil. (5) Thus says the Lord concerning the prophets … (6) … it shall be night to you, without vision, and darkness to you, without divination. The sun shall go down upon the prophets, and the day shall be black over them; (7) the seers shall be disgraced, and the diviners put to shame; they shall all cover their lips, for there is no answer from God.

The "end of prophecy" is here seen, pending that distant time when vision shall again be restored, Is 6,11-12; Jer 31,31-34; Ezek 36,26-27. Those who deeply contemplate the teachings of Rudolf Steiner in connection with the scriptures can believe with the full power of their hearts and minds that he has ushered in the early budding of that time of restoration.

It should be noted that these citations under "hid," "hidden" and "hide" do not begin to exhaust all that could have been listed, such as Is 54,8, but some practical limit had to be set.

Under "secret":

Ex 7,11,22 and Ex 8,7,18 speak of the "*secret arts*" of the wise men, sorcerers and magicians of Egypt.

Deut 29,29: The *secret things* belong to the Lord our God; but the things that are revealed belong to us and to our children for ever, that we may do all the words of this law.

Mk 4,11: To you has been given the *secret* of the kingdom of God, but for those outside everything is in parables. [Mt 13,11 and Lk 8,10 are almost verbatim.]

Under "Remember":

These citations show the loss of memory of ancient traditions, akin to Plato's reference in *Timaeus* about how the Greeks have no memory (see Cognate Writings, Vol. 3, *Companions Along The Way*). The passages will be more fully appreciated if the reader will review the long quote from EGO, Lect. 1 that concludes the phrase "I AM" above, as well as fn 12 in the same discussion relating to Is 43,2 and the discussion under "Akashic," noting, for instance, that the Akashic "Book" is identified as a "*Book of Remembrance*" in Mal 3,16 (otherwise the variation "*remembrance*" is not included below). The following are illustrative (cf. Job 38,21):

Deut 32,7,18: (7) *Remember the days of old*, consider the years of many generations;[13] *ask your father, and he will show you; your elders, and they will tell you....* (18) You were unmindful of the Rock that begot you, and you forgot the God who gave you birth.

Judg 8,34: And the people of Israel did not *remember* the Lord their God, who had rescued them from the hand of all their enemies on every side.

Ps 22,27: All the ends of the earth shall *remember* and turn to the Lord.

Ps 77,4-15: (4) Thou does hold my eyelids from closing; I am so troubled that I cannot speak. (5) I consider *the days of old, I remember the years long ago*. (6) I commune [fn: Heb, my music] with my heart in the night; I meditate and search my spirit [fn: Heb, my spirit searches]: (7) "Will the Lord spurn for ever, and never again be favorable? (8) Has his steadfast love for ever ceased? Are his promises at an end for all time? (9) Has God forgotten to be gracious? Has he in anger shut up his compassion?" (10) And I say, "It is my grief that the right hand of the Most High has changed." (11) I will call to mind the deeds of the Lord; yea, *I will remember thy wonders of old*. (12) I will meditate on all thy work, and muse on thy mighty

---

13. How better than "the years of many generations" could one describe those ages before Abraham where one's "memory" included many generations—all that bore the "blood" of the eponymous ancestor? See fn 3 in "The Nativity. The passage sets the stage also for an understanding of Ps 77,5, "the days of old, I remember the years long ago."—ERS

deeds. (13) Thy way, O God, is holy. What god is great like our God? (14) Thou art the God who workest wonders, who has manifested thy might among the peoples. (15) Thou didst with thy arm redeem thy people, the sons of Jacob and Joseph.

Ps 143,1-8 (quoting only portions of vss 3,5, and 7): (3) For the enemy ... has made me sit in *darkness* like those long dead.... (5) *I remember the days of old*, I meditate on all that thou hast done.... (7) ... *Hide not thy face from me*, lest I be like those who go down to the Pit.

Eccles 5,20: For he ["every man to whom God has given wealth and possessions"] *will not much remember the days of his life* because God keeps him occupied with joy in his heart.

This passage makes more sense if the "life" is taken to be that of his Individuality rather than merely his incarnated personality.

Eccles 11,8: For if a man lives many years, let him rejoice in them all; but *let him remember that the days of darkness will be many*. All that comes is vanity.

The profound meaning of this passage is explained in "Karma and Reincarnation" herein. See the Index to locate the text where this verse is cited.

Eccles 12,1: *Remember* also your Creator *in the days of your youth, before the evil days come, and the years draw nigh, when you will say, "I have no pleasure in them."*

Is 46,9: ... *remember the former things of old*; for I am God, and there is no other.

Is 57,11: Whom did you dread and fear, so that you lied, and *did not remember me*, did not give me a thought? Have I not held my peace, even *for a long time*, and so you do not fear me?

Is 64,5: Thou meetest him that joyfully works righteousness, *those that remember thee in thy ways.*

Ezek 6,8-9: (8) Yet I will leave some of you alive. When you have among the nations some who escape the sword, and when you are scattered through the countries, (9) *then those of you who escape will remember me* among the nations where they are carried captive, when I have broken their *wanton heart which has departed from me, and blinded their eyes which turn wantonly after their idols.*

Ezek 16,59-61: (59) Yea, thus says the Lord God: I will deal with you as you have done, who have despised the oath in breaking the covenant, (60) yet I will *remember my covenant with you in the days of your youth,* and I will establish with you an everlasting covenant. (61) *Then you will remember your ways,* and *be ashamed when I take your sisters, both your elder and your younger, and give them to you as daughters,*[14] but not on account of the covenant with you.

Ezek 20,43: And there *you shall remember your ways and all the doings with which you have polluted yourselves;* and *you shall loathe yourselves for all the evils that you have committed.*

Ezek 36,31: *Then you will remember your evil ways,* and your deeds that were not good; *and you will loathe yourselves for your iniquities* and your abominable deeds.

Amos 1,9: [The people of Tyre] *did not remember the covenant of brotherhood.*[15]

Zech 10,9: Though I scattered them among the nations, yet *in far countries they shall remember me, and with their children they shall live and return.*

---

14. Does this not call to mind one of the salient aspects of "Karma and Reincarnation?" See, for instance, #3 in the "Closing Comments on the Nature of Karma."—ERS
15. Theologians seem unanimous in conceding this "covenant" to be the military-political alliance between Phoenicia (i.e., Tyre and Sidon) and Israel which was compromised (without regard to which side originated the breach) insofar as mutual relations with Assyria were concerned. Israel presumably faulted "Tyre." See 6 Interp 781; 24A AB 285-286; INTPN, Hosea-Micah, p. 89; 6 ABD 689; and NJB, p. 1525, fn n. Interp comes to this conclusion reluctantly, lacking a more convincing one. AMPB calls it a "brotherly covenant," referencing 1 K 5,1,12; 9,12,13. Less literal translations, e.g., LB and CEV, even abandon the "brotherhood" language acceding to the military-political treaty interpretation. Admittedly, from an external historical standpoint, this analysis can hardly be faulted.*(continued)*

Lk 17,26,28,30,32,37: (26) "As it was in the days of Noah, so will it be in the days of the Son of man.… (28) Likewise as it was in the days of Lot … (30) so will it be on the day when the Son of man is revealed.… (32) *Remember Lot's wife.…* (37) … Where the body is, there the eagles [fn: "Or vultures"—or possibly scorpions—see discussion of Eagle/Scorpion relationship under Jn 3,14 above] will be gathered together."

Rev 2,5: *Remember then from what you have fallen*, repent and do the works you did at first.

Rev 3,3: *Remember then what you received and heard;* keep that, and repent.

We come now to a series of passages that, while not using any of the above key words, nevertheless point to the Mysteries and those exposed to their "secrets."

---

15. (*continued*) But the anthroposophist asks if Amos didn't have a deeper spiritual concept in mind, camouflaging it in prophetic fashion in the trappings of external events. Interp, Id. says, "It is hardly possible that anyone could think of a brotherly covenant as existing between Tyre and Israel" by virtue of a mere "treaty" (1 K 5,12). What the commentaries do *not* notice is that, aside from the relationship of their respective nations, between Hiram and David *individually* a special relationship existed. It is said in 1 K 5,1, "Now Hiram king of Tyre sent his servants to Solomon, when he heard that they had anointed him king in place of his father; *for Hiram always* **loved** *David*" (RSV; emphasis mine). As we see elsewhere herein, it was typically said that the hierophant in the ancient Mysteries "loved" his most intimate pupil, the one who was able to attain to a state of initiation. Ancient kings often had this virtue. David is a worthy contemporary example.

Lest we be misled, we must take note that there were two Hirams in the Book of Kings, the king of Tyre referred to in 2 Sam 5,11 and 1 K 5 and then one in 1 K 7,13 described as "the son of a widow of the tribe of Naphtali, and his father was a man of Tyre, a worker in bronze; and he was full of wisdom, understanding, and skill, for making any work in bronze." The second of these was also known as "Hiram Abiff," legendary founder of ancient Freemasonry. See 3 ABD 203-204 for the two and the etymological roots of "Abiff," i.e., *'abi*, meaning "my master (craftsman)." Almost certainly the second of these would have been among the servants sent by the first, for 2 Sam 5,11 includes among these "carpenters and masons who built David a house." The first was probably an initiate, and the second, who was a "Widow's Son," almost certainly was. Not only so, but the second carried forward that necessary worldly wisdom characterized from Cain's archetypal son, Tubalcain, the first "forger of all instruments of bronze and iron" (Gen 4,22). Anyone who would aspire to promote "Fusion" from the historic "Fission" between this ancient Mystery (secret) wisdom and Roman Catholicism should probably begin with Steiner's lecture cycle, *The Temple Legend* (TL). "Brotherhood" is terminology most appropriate for what came forth from the ancient Mysteries that modern Freemasonry claims as its esoteric heritage. See page 364 for further discussion.

Jer 6,16-17: (16) Thus says the LORD: "Stand by the roads, and look, and ask for the *ancient paths*, where the *good way* is; and walk in it, and find rest for your souls. But they said, 'We will not walk in it.' (17) I set watchmen over you, saying, 'Give heed to the sound of the *trumpet*.' [See "Trumpet"] But they said, 'We will not give heed....'"

2 Cor 4,3: And even if our gospel is *veiled*, it is *veiled* only to those who are perishing. [Of course, the corollary is that those are perishing who do not pull back its veil, which "hides" it.]

The following three groupings should also be within this series:

1. *The Apocalypse* (ApSJn) 11 (Bock) draws a proper picture for this group as follows: "... the Old Covenant was the religion of the closed heavens.... But in the hour of Golgotha the religious principle of the veiled mystery lost its validity and power. The rending of the veil in the temple was a significant gesture of God, a telling spiritual act." Thus, see:

Ex 26,33: ... and the veil shall separate for you the holy place from the most holy.

Is 54,2: Enlarge the place of your tent, and let the curtains of your habitations be stretched out; hold not back, lengthen your cords and strengthen your stakes.

Mt 27,51: And behold, the curtain of the temple was torn in two, from top to bottom; ... [Mk 15,38 and Lk 23,45 are almost verbatim.]

Heb 6,19-20: (19) We have this as a sure and steadfast anchor of the soul, a hope that enters into the inner shrine behind the curtain, (20) where Jesus has gone as a forerunner on our behalf, having become a high priest for ever after the order of Melchizedek.

Heb 9,3,11-12,15: (3) Behind the second curtain stood a tent [fn: or tabernacle] called the Holy of Holies, ... (11) But when Christ appeared as a high priest of the good things that have come, then through the greater and more perfect tent (not made with hands, that is, not of this creation) (12) he entered once for all into the Holy Place, taking [fn: through] not the blood of goats and calves but his own blood, thus securing an eternal redemption.... (15) Therefore he is the mediator of a new covenant, so that those who are called may receive the promised eternal inheritance, since a death has occurred which redeems them from the transgressions under the first covenant.

Heb 10,19-20: (19) Therefore, brethren, since we have confidence to enter the sanctuary by the blood of Jesus, (20) by the new and living way which he opened for us *through the curtain, that is, through his flesh....*

We should remember that the highest meaning of "tent," "tabernacle" or "sanctuary," being the same as "temple" in the deeper sense, means the human bodies (see "Three Bodies"), particularly the lower bodies as changed by the Ego, through Christ, into their higher counterparts (see **I-9**). The veil or curtain is that state of spiritual unconsciousness that separates such higher counterparts from the lower.

2. The second grouping is the passages from all four Gospels, Acts and Romans that refer to the seminal remark in Is 6,9-13 about darkening the consciousness of the people so that they should not see, hear or understand for a long time. These passages are Mt 13,14-15, Mk 4,11-12, Lk 8,10, Jn 12,37-40, Acts 28,25-27 and Rom 11,7-10. See "Fading Splendor."

3. The third group are those that speak astonishingly of having seen the Lord and yet living on:

Gen 16,13: So she [Hagar] called the name of the LORD who spoke to her, "Thou art a God of seeing"; for she said, "Have I really seen God and remained alive after seeing him?"

Gen 32,30: So Jacob called the name of the place Peniel, saying, "For I have seen God face to face, and yet my life is preserved."

Ex 3,6: And Moses hid his face, for he was afraid to look at God.

Ex 33,20: "But," he said, "you cannot see my face; for man shall not see me and live."

Judg 6,22-23: (22) Then Gideon perceived that he was the angel of the Lord; and Gideon said, "Alas, O Lord God! For now I have seen the angel of the Lord face to face." (23) But the Lord said to him, "Peace be to you; do not fear, you shall not die."

Judg 13,22-24: (22) And Manoah said to his wife, "We shall surely die, for we have seen God." (23) But his wife said to him, "If the Lord had meant to kill us, he would not have accepted a burnt offering and a cereal offering at our hands, or shown us all these things, or now announced to us such things as these." (24) And the woman bore a son, and called his name Samson....

1 K 19,11-13: (11) And he said, "Go forth, and stand upon the mount before the Lord." And behold, the Lord passed by, and a great and strong wind rent the mountains, and broke in pieces the rocks before the Lord, but the Lord was not in the wind; and after the wind an earthquake, but the Lord was not in the earthquake; (12) and after the earthquake, a fire, but the Lord was not in the fire; and after the fire a still small voice. (13) And when Elijah heard it, he wrapped his face in his mantle and went out and stood at the entrance of the cave.

Is 6,5: And I said: "Woe is me! For I am lost; for I am a man of unclean lips, and I dwell in the midst of a people of unclean lips; for my eyes have seen the King, the Lord of hosts!"

More could be said here about these passages, but we will leave them with two thoughts. First, they seem to portray a simpler and more direct vision among the earlier personalities than among the later ones, reflective of the "Fading Splendor" as time went on, though a direct vision was still possible in the case of such a high visionary as Isaiah who came last among them. Second, consider the direct implications of the principle that one could not see the Lord and live. If Steiner made this observation, I'm not yet aware of it, but it would seem to follow from his teachings that in humanity's present state (including, increasingly, that during the time of the listed personalities) a human being is not able during the time of its incarnation to "see, hear and understand (i.e., know)" the spiritual beings, especially the higher ones, much less the highest. Only between lives is this increasingly possible to those sufficiently developed pursuant to the spiritual knowledge embodied in anthroposophy (including the ancient Mysteries, though consider "Sheol"). Thus, if one is to "see" the Lord it must be in the discarnate state, so that anyone who has received the grace of such sight must be "astonished" by it, as reflected in the expressions in these cases.

CHAPTER END NOTE

15. (*continued from p. 360*) In support of the more esoteric interpretation of "covenant of brotherhood," one should take note of its contextual nest of esoteric symbolism in Amos. While it can only be hinted at here, its elements include:

a) Its sevenfold series of sevens in the so-called prophecies of "doom" that are superbly discussed by Anderson and Freedman in 24A AB 199-211. The pertinent terminology is "For three transgressions ... and for four," which appears eight times, e.g., Amos 1,3 (Damascus); 1,6 (Gaza); 1,9 (Tyre); 1,11 (Edom); 1,13 (Ammon); 2,1 (Moab); 2,4 (Judah); and 2,6 (Israel). The last two should be considered as numbers 7a and 7b, representing the division that occurs at the conclusion of the seventh Cultural Era, as in Rev 3,14-22 (cf. also the division of the final kingdom in Daniel's interpretation in Dan 2 above). In this prophetic vision of Amos, Tyre represents the third Cultural Era, the Chaldo-Egyptian, which was coming to an end in the transition from Amos to Isaiah (see dates in **I-19** surrounding 747 B.C.). Thus, "three" had occurred, and four were yet to occur before the final accountability of "doom."

b) "Egypt" was a stage of evolution that lay behind (2,10).

c) "Prophets," "Young Men" and "Nazirites" are equated (2,11).

d) "Nazirites" were "made" to "drink wine," as a result of which they were unable to "prophesy" (2,12). This is particularly notable in view of what Steiner said about the loss of clairvoyance brought about by wine. The drinking of wine was something endorsed by the spiritual world, e.g., the Eucharist, until the Second Coming in order that clairvoyance would be lost for a period. It was necessary for the knowledge of "Karma and Reincarnation" to disappear until the time was ripe, until commencement of the Second Coming. We have already seen this above.

e) The blowing of a "Trumpet" is cause for spiritual alarm (see "Trumpet[s]" below) (3,6).

f) "The Lord God does nothing... without revealing his *secret* to his servants the *prophets*" (3,7; emphasis mine). Anthroposophists believe the Second Coming has been announced by Steiner as such a "prophet." That the Bible bears out what he has said can be seen to be illustrated profusely in this work.

WIDOW'S SON

THE "WIDOW'S SON," or the "Son of the (a) Widow," a phrase that usually evokes compassion, becomes instead most intriguing when its esoteric meaning is known, for its frequent presence in Holy Writ then reveals new understanding.

Rudolf Steiner deals with the esoteric meaning of the term in *The Temple Legend* (TL), Lects. 6, pp. 61, 65, 68 and 71, and 7, p. 80; *The Gospel of St. John and its Relation to the Other Gospels* (Jn-Rel), Lects. 11, pp. 211-212 and (indirectly) 2, p. 31; perhaps implicitly in regard to Jesus in *The Gospel of St. Luke* (GSL), Lect. 5, p. 108 and *The Fifth Gospel* (FG), Lects. 4, p. 72 and 6, p. 125, and probably elsewhere. TL deals intensively with Freemasonry, and is must reading for anyone who, from within or without, desires to know of its origins and deeper nature. Lecture 6, "Manicheism," as with many other references in Steiner, throws more light on the subject than has heretofore been shed within the framework of official Christendom. (See 7 Brit 775, "Mani," and 776, "Manichaeism.") (While almost homonymic and probably a namesake, the third-century A.D. "Mani" should not be confused with the prehistoric "Manu" associated with Noah as shown in "Spiritual Economy" and **I-59**, though cognate according to Lievegoed in *The Battle for the Soul* [BATSO].) In TL, Lect. 6, we find the following explanation:

> The soul was always known as the "mother" in all esoteric (mystical) teachings; the instructor was the "father." Father and mother, Osiris and Isis, those are the two forces present in the soul: the instructor, representing the divine which flows directly into man, Osiris, he that is the father; the soul itself, Isis, the one who conceives, receives the divine, the spiritual into itself, she is the mother. During the fifth Root Race [the present post-Atlantean; see **I-4** and **I-1**] the father withdraws. The soul is widowed. Humanity is thrown back onto itself. It must find the light of truth within its

own soul in order to act as its own guide. Everything of a soul nature has always been expressed in terms of the feminine. Therefore the feminine element—which exists only in a germinal state today and will later be fully developed—this self-directing feminine principle which is no longer confronted by the divine fructifier, is called by Mani the "Widow." And therefore he calls himself "Son of the Widow."

Later in the same lecture, we find the following (initially I thought Steiner's reference to the "sixth Root Race" was a misstatement, his intent being instead to the "sixth Cultural Era" of our present post-Atlantean Epoch; however, it is best to see it as a proper reference to the sixth Evolutionary Epoch of Earth evolution, particularly since the sixth Cultural Age, Philadelphia [Rev 3,7-13; see **I-1**, **I-25** and **I-24**], is the one from which the fruits of our present fifth Epoch will be carried over):

> The sixth Root Race will have the task of drawing evil back into the continuing stream of evolution through kindness. Then a spiritual current will have been born which does not oppose evil, even though it manifests in the world in its demonic form. The consciousness will have been established in the successors to the "Sons of the Widow" that evil must be included again in evolution and be overcome [see Rom 12,21], not by strife, but only through charitableness. It is the task of the Manichean spiritual stream forcefully to prepare for this. This spiritual stream will not die out, it will make its appearance in many forms. It appears in forms which many can call to mind but which need not be mentioned today. If it were to function merely in the cultivation of an inner mood of soul, this current would not achieve what it should do. It must express itself in the founding of communities which, above all, will look upon peace, love and passive resistance to evil as their standard of behavior and will seek to spread this view.[1] For they must create a receptacle,

---

1. Mahatma Gandhi and Martin Luther King, Jr. are examples of modern martyrs to this spiritual cause. See Mark E. Smith, "Anthroposophy and Nonviolence," *Journal of Anthroposophy* #60, Spring 1995, p. 5. Begging indulgence, I seize this opportunity to point out that the author of that article, though raised in a devotedly church-going family, was unable, as an adult, to accept Christ until much later he saw him in the light of anthroposophy. The author is my son.—ERS

a form, for the life which will continue to exist even without their presence.

As Steiner notes (TL, Lect. 7, entitled "The Essence and Task of Freemasonry," p. 80), "The Freemasonry Masters call themselves 'Children of the Widow'. Thus the Company of all the Masters is directly derived from the Manicheans." Steiner goes on to give the chain of development.

In Jn-Rel, Lect. 11, pp. 211-212, Steiner further explains the meaning of "Widow's Son":

> When a man was initiated in the old sense, the maternal element emerged and the paternal element remained behind; that is, the candidate killed the paternal element within himself and united with the mother in him. In other words, he killed his father within him and wedded his mother. So when the old initiate had lain three and a half days in the lethargic state, he had united with his mother and had killed the father within himself. He had become fatherless and this had to be so, for he had to renounce his individuality and dwell in a higher spiritual world. He became one with his people. But what lived in his people was precisely expressed by the maternal element. He became one with the entire organism of his people; he became exactly what Nathanael was, what was always designated by the name of the people in question—in Jewry, an "*Israelite*," among Persians a "*Persian.*"

Steiner is here speaking of Jn 1,47, discussed above in "Mysteries." Immediately preceding this statement in the same paragraph, he referred to the lifting of the etheric and astral bodies out of the physical body during the three and a half days of initiation, while the Ego was left behind. During this time, known as the "temple sleep," the physical body appeared as though dead. (See "Three Days' Journey.") It is important to note that according to Steiner, whatever the gender of one's physical body, the etheric body is the opposite. While the just-quoted passage long predated our modern commitment to non-sexist writing or speaking, in the case of one who was a man in the incarnation in question, there was a very realistic "killing" of the male, or paternal, physical element, leaving the female, or maternal, etheric element in dominance. Thus, there is high substantive spiritual essence not only to the above description, but to its reality in the highest sense. In the Bible, this is reflected by, among other things, all those passages that speak of the necessity of overcoming the "flesh" (which is distinctly different from the term "body").[2]

But we cannot stop with such relatively simplistic examination. Gen 2,18-24 tells of the time in ancient Lemuria (see **I-1**) when the division of the sexes occurred, as a part of which the Fall described in Gen 3 takes place and the "tree of life" is removed from humanity's cognition. We then enter into the Atlantean period of evolution when Cain, the male principle, kills Abel, the female principle, as described in Gen 4. The male principle applies itself to the outer world and can only receive its spiritual inspiration from without. The female principle, by contrast, remains in contact internally with the spiritual world, but as a result, in the physical world, the female element can no longer reproduce itself as it once did before the division of the sexes; it must be fertilized from without by the male element. Only gradually, in the course of evolution, has the killing of the female element been accomplished, but it was set in motion in the account in Gen 4. Still, the ancient clairvoyance remained to a great extent throughout the Atlantean period until, progressively, with Noah (Gen 6-10) we have the transition to the present post-Atlantean, or Fifth Evolutionary, Epoch (see **I-1**) with its seven Cultural Eras, of which we are in the fifth. Even in our own Epoch's earlier Eras, clairvoyance was still much more prevalent than it is in humanity's present spiritually darkened condition. But what took place had to occur, namely, the killing of the female element as humanity settled into its complete preoccupation with, and domination of, the outer, mineral-physical world. The Mystery of Golgotha had to occur at just the "Right Time" to prevent humanity's hardening beyond "the point of no return." The necessity to reestablish the female principle is absolute if humanity is to avoid beasthood (Rev 13) and the Pit. However, the return should not be to the precise condition that existed before the Fall, but rather to one that embodies the fruits of having taken dominion over the outer world and reascended therefrom. The metaphor for this is the marriage of the Bride, the renewed female element, and the Bridegroom, the Christ or eternal "I Am" (see "Bride/Bridegroom"). One does not have to

---

2. Thus, Jn 6,63; Rom 8,3-13; 1 Cor 15,50; Gal 5,13-24; 6,8-13; Eph 2,3; Phil 3,3; Col 2,23 and 1 Pet 1,24.

strain so hard to see that the female of our species has been subjugated during the post-Atlantean Epoch down to our present time. But while the germ was planted by the Christ Event and the Mystery of Golgotha, the stirrings, as though in the first pangs of labor, of a return to that female element have really only manifested themselves during the twentieth century with the end of the Kali Yuga in 1899 (see **I-46**).

To this very day, great hostility exists between the Roman Catholic Church and Freemasonry.[3] The hostility was prefigured into the spiritual transitions of our post-Atlantean Epoch, but it must come to an end with humanity's increased anthroposophical insight into its nature. The origin of the hostility is ancient, deriving from the conflict between the male Wisdom of Cain (Freemasonry) and the female Wisdom of Abel (the ancient Priesthood, now represented by the Roman Catholic Church), further represented in the division between King (male element) and Priest (female element). Solomon, the last king before the division, was nevertheless the strongest representative of the priestly Abelites. The thread of the conflict between Cain and Abel resurfaces in the Biblical account of Solomon's building of the temple, for which he sends for Hiram-Abiff. We are told in 1 K 7,13-14, "And King Solomon sent and brought Hiram from Tyre. He was the *son of a widow* of the tribe of Naphtali, and his father was a man of Tyre, *a worker in bronze*, and he was *full of wisdom, understanding, and skill, for making any work in bronze*" (my emphasis). Steiner tells us that Hiram was a descendant of Tubal-cain, the first forger of bronze and a descendant of Cain (Gen 4,22). Because of the Abel-nature of Solomon and the Cain-nature of Hiram, difficulties arose between them which involve the Queen of Sheba (hidden, it would seem, in such passages as 1 K 10,4,11, et al.). (Even the division of the kingdom that then occurred might be viewed as a sort of division between the northern male, kingly element[4] and the southern female, priestly element; see "As Above, So Below.") The basis for the above comments is to be found in Steiner's twenty-lecture cycle (May 23,1904-January 2, 1906) *The Temple Legend* (TL), subtitled "Freemasonry and Related Occult Movements." The "legend" itself,

---

3. Charles Madden, *Freemasonry—Mankind's Hidden Enemy,* TAN, Rockford, 1995.
4. While at the time I first drew this inference I was aware of Jeroboam's designation as a "Widow's Son" (1 K 11,26), the significance for this of the prophet Ahijah's action in 1 K 11,31 had not come to my attention. See the discussion of these passages in the text below.

though inherent in the cycle's entirety, is given in capsule form in Lect. 5 (pp. 50-53, incl. fn 3), and variously reiterated and elaborated in Lects. 7 (pp. 73-77), 11 (pp. 141-143), 17 (pp. 237-246) and 18 (pp. 253-263); it is also summarized in the Appendix to "Three Bodies" below.

Changing direction, let us look at two noble Individualities (i.e., entelechies, or "I Ams"). The first is that of Adam Cadmon-Phinehas-Elijah-John the Baptist-Raphael-Novalis, discussed under the heading "Novalis" in Cognate Writings, Vol. 3, *Companions Along The Way,* and expanded upon there under "Prokofieff." The incarnations of the second are set out also in Cognate Writings under the heading "Interlude for Steiner Individuality," and included Eabani-(Abraham?)-Cratylus-Aristotle-Schionatulander-Thomas Aquinas-Steiner. Particular note should be taken of the "great cosmic law," set out as a footnote in the "Interlude," "according to which each individual who accomplishes something in the service of the Guiding Powers of the world must, after a certain time, perform a similar deed in consequence of it, but in such a way now that it appears like the opposite pole of the first." The application of this cosmic law to both noble Individualities is obvious in the above references in Cognate Writings. Let us now consider how that applies in the case of the one known as Hiram-Abiff. Whether or not he was the same entelechy as Cain and/or Tubal-cain, we see from anthroposophy that his incarnations included those known as Hiram-Lazarus/John-Christian Rosenkreutz[5]-Count St. Germain;[6] and there is the distinct probability that Joshua[7] should be added to the front of this line. If Hiram, through his ancestry if not in fact his own prior incarnations, had brought the earthly craft of bronze work to humanity on its descending path, in the last three incarnations listed he clearly began to take the human being back on the ascending path of spiritual development. But it is from his enlightened status as Son of a Widow that he commenced this line of development—much as the enlightened Aristotle Individuality, the father of modern science, led humanity away from recognition of multiple Earth lives, or reincarnation, and later, as Steiner, is the one who, in the twentieth century, leads it back again to a true knowledge thereof.

---

5. For a discussion of Hiram-Lazarus/John-Christian Rosenkreutz see page 390.
6. For a discussion of Count St. Germain see page 390.
7. For a discussion of Joshua see page 391.

With the above background, let us now look, in canonical order, at instances where the Bible speaks of the Widow's Son (emphasis mine):

> **1 K 7,13-14**: (13) And King Solomon sent and brought *Hiram* from Tyre. (14) He was *the son of a widow* of the tribe of Naphtali, and his father was a man of Tyre, a worker in bronze; and he was full of wisdom, understanding, and skill, for making any work in bronze. He came to King Solomon, and did all his work.

Aside from the accomplishments of Joshua in implementing the mission of Moses in the "outer world," we see in this passage the application of wisdom to the (domination of the) "outer world" in a manner not possible for the sheer wisdom of Solomon.

> **1 K 11,26-31**: (26) Jeroboam the son of Nebat, an Ephraimite of Zeredah, a servant of Solomon, *whose mother's name was Zeruah, a widow*, also lifted up his hand against the king. (27) And this was the reason why he lifted up his hand against the king. Solomon built the Millo, and closed up the breach of the city of David his father. (28) The man Jeroboam was very able, and when Solomon saw that the young man was industrious he gave him charge over all the forced labor of the house of Joseph. (29) And at that time, when Jeroboam went out of Jerusalem, the prophet Ahijah the Shilonite found him on the road. Now Ahijah had clad himself with a new garment; and the two of them were alone in the open country. (30) Then Ahijah laid hold of the new garment that was on him, and tore it into twelve pieces. (31) And he said to Jeroboam, " *Take for yourself ten pieces; for thus says the Lord, the God of Israel, 'Behold, I am about to tear the kingdom from the hand of Solomon, and will give you ten tribes....'"*

Clearly we see the continuation, in verse 28, of the ability of Jeroboam to apply himself to the "outer world," as in the case of Hiram, and the further indication of his "wisdom" is probably suggested by the fact that the eventual opposition of Solomon forced Jereboam into "Egypt" (vs 40), an esoteric term for the ancient clairvoyance from which "Israel" had to depart, as we shall see. The emphasized conclusion of the passage relates to the division of the kingdom into kingly and priestly elements, as discussed above. The "historian(s)" who wrote the above passage left one other hidden but persuasive clue that points to the esoteric meaning of the Widow's Son. We are told in 6 AB 1084, "Zeruah," "While the identity of the king's mother is a common feature in Judean regnal formulas, it is missing from those of Israelite kings. Thus, the identification of Zeruah in 1 K 11,26 is a rare reference to an Israelite king's mother." And the significance of the break between the kingly, male, northern kingdom and the priestly, female, southern kingdom from which the Savior was to be born, is also strongly indicated by the meaning of "Zeruah." According to 6 AB 1084, "In a variant version of Jeroboam's origin," in the Septuagint's (Greek) treatment of 1 K 12,24 "Jeroboam's mother is Sarira, a 'harlot'," foreshadowing the general characterization of the northern kingdom of Israel as a "whoremonger" after other gods, namely, those of the "outer world" from the standpoint of the priestly southern kingdom of Judea. All of this plays strongly, however, into the idea of the "two becoming one" with the advent of the Christ, as more fully indicated in "The Nativity." The necessity of all the streams again converging in humanity's reascent is always emphasized in Steiner's work, and is uniquely summarized in Lievegoed's deathbed work, BATSO.

1 K 17,1-24: (1) Now Elijah the Tishbite, of Tishbe in Gilead, said to Ahab, "As the Lord the God of Israel lives, before whom I stand, there shall be neither dew nor rain these years, except by my word." (2) And the word of the Lord came to him. (3) "Depart from here and turn *eastward*, and *hide* yourself by the brook Cherith, that is *east* of the Jordan. (4) You shall drink from the brook, and I have commanded the *ravens* to feed you there." (5) So he went and did according to the word of the Lord; he went and dwelt by the brook Cherith that is *east* of the Jordan. (6) And the *ravens* brought him bread and meat in the morning, and bread and meat in the evening; and he drank from the brook. (7) And after a while the brook dried up, because there was no rain in the land. (8) Then the word of the Lord came to him. (9) "Arise, go to Zarephath, which belongs to Sidon, and dwell there. Behold, *I have commanded a widow there to feed you*." (10) So he arose and went to Zarephath; and when he came to the gate of the city, behold, *a widow* was there gathering sticks; and he called to her and said, "Bring me a little water in a vessel, that I may drink." (11) And as she was going to bring it, he called to her and said, "Bring me a morsel of bread in your hand." (12) And she said, "As the Lord your God lives, I have nothing baked, only a handful of meal in a jar, and a little oil in a cruse; and now, I am gathering a couple of sticks, that I may go in and prepare it *for myself and my son, that we may eat it, and die.*" (13) And Elijah said to her, "Fear not; go and do as you have said; but first make me a little cake of it and bring it to me, and afterward make for yourself and your son. (14) For thus says the Lord the God of Israel, 'The jar of meal shall not be spent, and the cruse of oil shall not fail, until the day that the Lord sends rain upon the earth.'" (15) And she went and did as Elijah said; and she, and he, and her household ate for many days. (16) The jar of meal was not spent, neither did the cruse of oil fail, according to the word of the Lord which he spoke by Elijah.

(17) After this the *son of the woman*, the mistress of the house, *became ill*; and his illness was so severe that there was *no breath left in him*. (18) And she said to Elijah, "What have you against me, O man of God? *You have come to me to bring my sin to remembrance,*[8] *and to cause the death of my son!*" (19) And he said to her, "Give me your son." *And he took him* from her bosom, and *carried him up into the upper chamber, where he lodged and laid him upon his own bed*. (20) And he cried to the Lord, "O Lord my God, hast thou brought calamity even upon the *widow* with whom I sojourn, by *slaying her son?*" (21) Then he stretched himself upon the child *three times*, and *cried* to the Lord, "O Lord my God, *let this child's soul come into him again*." (22) And the Lord hearkened to the voice of Elijah; *and the soul of the child came into him again, and he revived*. (23) And Elijah took the child, and *brought him down from the upper chamber* into the house, and *delivered him to his mother*, and Elijah said, "*See, your son lives*." (24) And the woman said to Elijah, "*Now I know that you are a man of God*, and that the word of the Lord in your mouth is truth."

---

8. This passage could hardly have more perfectly stated one of the aims of initiation, namely, to bring to one's "remembrance" past lives and the "sins" therein which remain as karmic debt. As of the time of Elijah, both "objective and subjective karma" remained, inasmuch as the Christ had not yet incarnated (see "Forgiven Sins"). Moreover, the son's "illness" reminds us of what afflicted Lazarus, Jn 11,2-4—ERS

While every word of this is important, the emphasized portions readily identify this passage as an initiation. What one must then come to see is that the pre-initiation personality is Naboth (1 K 21) whose Individuality is that of Elijah, Naboth's post-initiation manifestation. Before examining what Steiner said about this in more detail, it is pertinent here to note that the account in the books of Kings clearly shows Naboth/Elijah to have been initiated into the Mithraic Mysteries, as explained in "Mysteries" herein. When this is realized, it can be seen how the passage contains the critical features found in other Biblical initiations, such as that of Lazarus (Jn 11), et al.; see also "Three Days' Journey." Like other personalities who, upon receiving the insight of deep spiritual experience, have their names changed (see "Name Change"), Naboth became Elijah through the initiation by which he also became the Son of a Widow. Christ himself emphasized that the Individuality of Elijah came to one personality who was the Son of a Widow (Lk 4,26).[9]

The Elijah Individuality is so immeasurably important to the entire Bible that we must here pause to examine it more fully. For perspective, it is well to reflect upon how the Bible message revolves around the five exalted Individualities (entelechies as distinguished from personalities in a given incarnation) already identified in this work who are recapitulated in the final essay, "Pillars on the Journey," below. This Individuality is the first among those listed.

Steiner gave two excellent lectures on Naboth/Elijah. The first (December 14, 1911), "The Prophet Elijah in the light of Spiritual Science," was the fifth of six lectures published in *Turning Points in Spiritual History* (TPSH, the six being on Zarathustra, Hermes, Buddha, Moses, Elijah and Christ). The second (September 17, 1912) is Lect. 3 in *The Gospel of St. Mark* (GSMk).

Let us look at what he said in the first and longer of the two.

---

9. Literally Lk 4,26 merely says that Elijah was sent "to a woman who was a widow." Theology properly sees this as illustrative of the "prophet without honor" passage (vs 24) that precedes it. However, when the passage to which he had reference (1 K 17 and 21) is then studied it becomes obvious that, through the initiation it describes, Naboth (the personality to whom Elijah was really sent) became a Widow's Son and had his name changed, and his status as the prophet Naboth/Elijah thus took shape in a country other than Israel. In this way, the example corresponds more precisely with what Jesus had just said in vs 24.

We shall ... endeavour to portray all pertinent events first as they actually happened and later draw attention to the manner in which they are depicted in the ancient Biblical records....

We must go back in thought to those ancient Hebrew times when the brilliant epoch that marked the reign of Solomon was passed, and the kingdom of Palestine was enduring many and varied forms of privation. We must recall the troubles [with] the Philistines and other similar incidents, and transport ourselves in mind to those days when all that formerly constituted a united and centralized monarchy was already divided into the separate kingdoms of Judah and Israel, and King Ahab, who was the son of Omri, reigned in Samaria....

Between King Ahab['s father] and the King of Tyre and Sidon ... there was ... a sort of alliance [that was] further strengthened by the marriage of Ahab with Jezebel, [the latter king's daughter].... We are looking back into an age when that ancient clairvoyant gift which was in general a spiritual attribute of man in primeval times had by no means entirely disappeared among those [who] retained the fitting disposition. Now, Queen Jezebel was not only endowed with this gift, but her clairvoyant powers were of a very special order; [but these] were not always employ[ed] ... to promote that which was good and noble. While we look upon Jezebel as a kind of clairvoyant, we must regard King Ahab as a man who only under exceptional circumstances evinced a faculty [wherewith] the hidden forces of his soul could break in upon his conscious state. In olden times such manifestations were much more [widespread than today].... Ahab [sometimes] experienced visions and presentiments, but never to any marked extent, and ... only when he was confronted with some special matter connected with human destiny.

At [this] time ... a rumour had spread throughout the land that a remarkable spirit was abroad. In reality, this was ... Elijah. Few there were ... who knew precisely in what place the personality that bore this name might be found—nor did they know [how] he exerted so powerful an influence upon ... people and events.... Throughout the widest circles any reference to this mysterious being, or even the mention of his name was accompanied by a thrill of awe, and ... it was generally felt that this spirit must possess some singular and hidden attribute of greatest import [see fn 15 below]. But no man knew [how or where] it might be sought. Only certain ... initiates had true knowledge....

King Ahab was also ignorant concerning these matters, but ... experienced a peculiar feeling of apprehension, and a kind of dread overcame him whenever mention was made of [Elijah]. Ahab ... had introduced into ... Palestine a certain religious order which held to outer forms and ceremonies, ... Such information [about] Elijah as came to the followers of this pagan form of worship ... created in them a strange and peculiar feeling of fear and dismay. For [they knew of] the Jahveh-religion ... [and its] belief in One God—in One Great Spiritual Being in the cosmos, Who rules over the superperceptual realm, and Who by means of its forces makes His influence felt, and affects both the evolution and the history of mankind....

It was well known that in truth the religion of Moses contained the germ of all that one might term the Jehovah-Religion, but this fact had been grasped by the nation in a manner more or less after the fashion of a people yet in a stage of childhood or early youth. [cf. **I-65**]

The old faith ... may only be described ... as an awareness of contact with that which is invisible and superperceptual, which comes to man when he indeed apprehends and realizes his own true Ego—and it was this consciousness of the supersensible which had descended upon the people. But [it was] based upon an attempt to picture ... the workings of ... Jehovah, as conceived from their experiences of the external phenomena of life.... It was the custom to say that Jehovah acted ... in such a manner that when all nature was luxuriant and fruitful, it was a sign that He was rewarding mankind [and vice versa].

At that time about which we are speaking the nation was enduring the miseries caused by a period of dearth and starvation, and many turned aside from the God Jehovah, because they could no longer believe in His works when they saw how He treated mankind.... [To] speak of *progress* in connection with the Jahveh-conception, ... the nation must henceforth form a new Jehovah-concept embodying the old thoughts and ideas, through which must flow a fuller and a higher order of human understanding, so that all might say:—"No matter what shall take place in the outer world, ... such external events are in no way an evidence of either the wrath or the benevolence of Jehovah.... And even though we meet with the direst want and affliction, nevertheless, through those inner forces alone which dominate the soul, man shall come to the sure conviction that—HE IS."

This great revolution in religious outlook was destined to be consummated and wrought through the power of the prophet Elijah (and, as will be seen later, his spiritual force operated at times through the medium of a chosen human personality). When it is ordained that some great momentous change shall be brought about in the concepts of mankind, as was the case in Elijah's day, it is necessary ... that there be certain fitting personalities at hand in whose souls can be implanted the germ ... of those things ... ordained [to] enter into the history of mankind....

[It was] the preordained fate of the nation that the individuality known as the prophet Elijah should be the chosen one whose soul should first grasp the Jehovah-concept in the form which I have described. To this end it was essential that certain ... special forces be called up from the hidden depths of his soul—deep-seated powers as yet unknown to mankind, ... Something in the nature of a holy mystical initiation of the highest order ... must first take place in the innermost being of Elijah....

Such personalities as Elijah who are chosen [to stimulate] some momentous forward impulse stand, for the most part, isolated and alone. In olden days, however, there gathered around them certain followers, ... or Schools of the Prophets as they were called in Palestine, and which by other nations have been termed Initiation or Mystery Sanctuaries. Thus we find the prophet Elijah ... surrounded by a few earnest disciples ... [2 K 2,3,5,7,15]. [Now at that time strange events had begun to take place in the land] the people, however, had no idea where the mysterious personality might be found who had brought them about. They could only say:—"He must be here, or there,—for something unusual is happening."

Hence ... there was spread abroad ... [a] rumour ... that HE, a prophet, was actually at work, but no man knew rightly where. This uncertainty was due to the exercise of a definite and peculiar influence, which could be exerted by all such advanced spiritual beings as are found among outstanding seers....

All truly exalted spiritual personalities, such as Elijah, were endowed with this specific and highly penetrative quality which made itself felt now here, now there. [It] entered little by little into the souls of the people. It operated in such manner as to cause them to be unable to tell, at times, just where the external form of some great spiritual personality might be found. But the true followers and disciples of Elijah knew … and were … aware that his outer individuality might perchance assume a wholly unpretentious character … [in a] quite lowly station in earthly life.…

At the time [in question] the actual bearer of the spirit of Elijah was a close neighbour of Ahab's, … and [was] the possessor of a small property in his immediate vicinity; but Ahab had no suspicion that such was the case. He sought everywhere for [Elijah, but] he entirely failed … to take into consideration the simple and unassuming land-owner who lived so near him, and gave no thought as to why he should, at times, absent himself, nor where he went on these occasions. But Jezebel (being clairvoyant) had discovered that this unobtrusive personality had actually become the external physical embodiment of the spirit of Elijah, [but this] knowledge she … did not impart to Ahab [keeping] it to herself … as a secret, for reasons which will become apparent later.… In the Bible this … character … is known by the name of Naboth. We thus see that according to the investigations of Spiritual Science we must recognize in the Naboth of the Bible, the physical bearer of the spiritual individuality of Elijah.

Steiner then discusses things that take place deep within the soul of Naboth, typical of those things each Biblical prophet goes through upon receiving a call to mission, resulting in the clairvoyant development of the soul and firm resolve to "do all that in me lies." He was instructed by God to go to Ahab and say to him, "In the God Jahveh must ye have faith, until such time as He may again bring rain upon the earth" [1 K17,1; cf. Jn 4,32-34]. Naboth also knew "that henceforth he must devote himself to the further unfoldment" of the soul powers necessary for him to apprehend his full mission. "He then resolved that he would eschew no sacrifice, but [would] share in the sufferings of those who were exposed to the greatest measure of want." He gave himself "over to unceasing inner contemplation of that God who had revealed Himself to him." Confirmation came to him in the form of the following spiritual seeing and hearing:

1. He was told, "Abide in patience—endure all things—for He who feedeth mankind and thee also will of a surety provide that which thou needest; but thou must ever hold to a true faith in the soul's eternal life." At the same time

> it appeared to him ... that he was led by a hermit to the brook which is called Cherith, where he concealed himself and drank of the waters of the brook so long as any remained; and that he was nourished, so far as the conditions prevailing at the time permitted, by food which the Lord provided. It further seemed ... [that] this nutriment was brought by ravens.

2. "It was next ordained that [Naboth] should pass through a more advanced stage of development" in regard to his soul forces through "intensive contemplation" and "meditation" whereby he realized the necessity to "change utterly the nature of [his] inner being ... bring[ing] to [his] inner Ego a new life."

3. Next we read:

> Then came to [Elijah-Naboth] yet another experience which was, however, only in part a vision,[10] ... [thus] of less spiritual significance.... In the vision, it appeared to him that his God ... set him upon a journey to Zarepath [where] he met a widow who had a son and he there saw ... personified, as it were, in the fate of this widow and her son, the manner and way in which he was now to live. It seemed to his spiritual sight that their food was well-nigh spent, and even that which they had was about to be consumed, after which they would die. Then it was that he spoke to the widow as in a dream, ... using in effect those same words which, day by day, and week by week, throughout his solitary meditations, he had repeated over and over again to his own soul:— "Fear not,—from that meal which remaineth, prepare the repast which must be made ready for you and your son, and for me also. In all that may yet come to pass trust alone in that God Who doth create both joy and sorrow, and in Whom we must ever abide in faith."

_____

10. This indicates that Naboth actually went to Sidon (Phoenicia) as Jesus said (Lk 4,26).—ERS

In this dreamlike vision it was clearly impressed upon [Elijah-Naboth] that the barrel of meal would not become empty nor would the cruse of oil fail; for the oil and the meal would ever be renewed [cf. Mt 14,13-21; 15, 32-39; 16, 5-12; Mk 6, 32-44; 8,1-10, 13-21; Lk 9,10-17; Jn 6,1-14; 2 K 4,42-44; also "Feedings"]. It is worthy of note that at this point his whole soul-state ... expressed itself in the vision in such manner that it seemed to him as if his personality went to live in the upper part of the house which belonged to the widow. But in reality the inner truth was that his own soul had ... risen to a higher level.

4. And finally,

It next appeared to [Elijah-Naboth], again as in a vision, that the son of the widow lay dead. This we must regard as merely a symbolical representation of the fact that [Naboth] had overcome, and slain, as it were, the Ego which had been his up to that time.... It then happened that after the widow's son was dead, she reproached him. This signifies that his subconscious spirit reproached him, in other words, aroused in him a misgiving of his nature:—"My old Ego-consciousness has now left me—what am I to do?" In the description given of these events it is stated that he took the child unto himself and plunged unhesitatingly still further into the depths of his soul, and we are told that power was vouchsafed to him through which he brought the dead son once more to life. Then did he gain more courage to stimulate and quicken the new Ego, who was now his, by virtue of those qualities which were in the Ego that he had lost.[11]

Naboth/Elijah continued to develop the hidden soul forces. But it was now time for him "to stand before King Ahab and bring to a crisis the matter which must now be decided, namely, the victory of the new

---

11. The provisions of this paragraph can be more meaningful when one has studied the basic anthroposophic book, *Knowledge of the Higher Worlds and Its Attainment* (KHW), especially the parts dealing with the two "guardians of the threshold" (cf. Job 40-41, the Behemoth and the Leviathan).—ERS

Jehovah-concept as opposed to those beliefs that the King himself accepted" along with most of the people, "owing to the weakness of the times." We then read:

> Now, it came about, that while Ahab was making a round of his empire, anxiously observing the signs of want and distress that the personality [of Naboth-Elijah] approached him; and no man knew from whence he came.... And there was a strangeness in the manner of his speech which affected the soul of Ahab, who was not, however, aware that this man was his neighbour. More strongly than ever did the King experience that feeling of awe and dread which had always come upon him when reference was made to that great spirit known in the Bible as Elijah the prophet. Then it was that the King spoke and said:—"Art thou he that troubleth Israel" [1 K 18,17]? And Elijah-Naboth replied:—"No, not I, but thou thyself it is who bringeth misfortune and evil upon the people, and it must now be determined to which God they shall turn."
>
> So it came to pass that a great multitude of the tribe of Israel assembled upon Mount Carmel in order that final judgment should be made between the god of Ahab and the God of Elijah.[12] The decision was to be brought about by means of an external sign; but such a sign as all might plainly discern and clearly understand. To enter into details concerning these matters at the present time would, however, take us too far. It was arranged that the priests and prophets of Baal ... should be the first to offer a sacrifice. The people would then wait and see if the performance ... would lead to any communication or influence being imparted to the multitude. In other words, the people were to judge whether or not, in virtue of inherent divine powers possessed by the priests any sign was vouchsafed of the might and potency of their god.
>
> The sacrificial beast is brought to the altar.... Then Elijah-Naboth raised up his voice and said:—"This thing must now be determined—I stand alone while opposed to me are the four hundred and fifty prophets of Baal. We shall see how strong is their hold upon the people, and how great is that power which is in me."

---

12. It is notable that the word "Carmel" means "garden," "vineyard" or "orchard." 1 ABD 874.—ERS

The sacrifice is performed, and everything possible done in order to transmit to the multitude a potent influence from the priests—that all should believe in the god Baal. The ecstatic exercises are carried to such lengths that the hands and other parts of the body are cut with knives until the blood flows, so as to increase still further the awesome character of the spectacle evoked by these followers of Baal, under the frenzied stimulus of the dancing and the music. But behold! there is no sign—for Elijah-Naboth is there, and the spirit within him is at work.

In words all insufficient of expression, one might say, that while Elijah-Naboth stood thus near at hand, he caused a great spiritual power to flow forth from his being, so that he overcame and swept away all things which were opposed to him. In this case, you must not, however, imagine to yourselves the exercise of any kind of magic.

Elijah-Naboth then prepares his sacrifice [which is offered] using the full force of his soul…. The sacrifice is consummated, and achieves the fullness of its purpose, for the souls and the hearts of the people are stirred. The priests of Baal … are driven to admit defeat. *They are destroyed in their very souls by that which they had desired*, killed, as it were, by Elijah-Naboth—for Elijah-Naboth had won the day!

What follows as the natural outcome of all these events? … [Jezebel] was quite aware of the fact that the man who had done all these things was their neighbour, and that he was to be found living close at hand, that is, when he was not mysteriously absent. Now, what did Elijah-Naboth know and realize from that moment? He knew that Jezebel was powerful, and that she had discovered his secret…. He felt that henceforth his outer physical life was no longer safe. He must therefore prepare for death in the near future; for Jezebel would certainly compass his destruction.

Now, King Ahab went home, and as related in the Bible, told Jezebel about those events which had taken place upon Mount Carmel [1 K 19,1, the "sword" being the word of God, as in Mt 10,34; Lk 2,35; 1 K 3,24; Heb 4,12; Rev 1,16; et al.]; and Jezebel said:— "I will do unto Elijah that which he did unto thy four hundred and fifty prophets." Who could understand these words spoken by Jezebel [1 K 19,2] were it not for the investigations made by Spiritual Science, in whose light their meaning seems almost self-evident. [As a result of these researches it is quite clear, and this point has always been obscure, why it was that Jezebel brought about the death of Naboth, when in reality she sought to destroy Elijah. From Spiritual Science, however, we realize that she sent her threatening message to *Elijah-Naboth*, because in virtue of her clairvoyant powers, she knew full well that the physical body of Naboth was in truth the bearer of Elijah's spirit.—Ed.]

It now became necessary for Elijah to form some definite plans whereby he could avoid being immediately done to death as a result of Jezebel's revenge. He must at once arrange, that in case of this event happening, his spirit could still continue to carry on his teachings, and exert its influence upon mankind. Thus it came about when next he held commune with his soul, and while in a state of intense inner contemplation,[13] that he questioned himself thus:— "What shall I do that I may find a successor to fulfil my mission in this physical world, should my death indeed be brought about through the vengeance of Jezebel?" Then behold! a new revelation came to him, in which his inner vision was directed toward a certain quite definite personality, to whom Elijah-Naboth might pass on all that he had to bestow upon mankind—this personality was Elisha....

But soon after Elijah had chosen his successor the vengeance of Jezebel fell upon him. For Jezebel turned the thoughts of her lord toward Naboth, their neighbour, and spoke to Ahab somewhat after this fashion:—"Listen thou unto me, this neighbour is a pious man, whose mind is filled with ideas concerning Elijah. It would perhaps be well to remove him from this vicinity, for he is one of the most important of his followers, and upon him much depends."

Now the King knew nothing whatever about the secret which surrounded Naboth, but he was quite aware by this time that he was

---

13. This is portrayed in 1 K 19,4-9. We see there the "Three Days' Journey" being taken by Naboth/Elijah culminating in a "cave" experience. In the first "day's journey" he "sat down under a broom tree" (emphasis mine, see "Under the Tree"). That night he slept "under a broom tree" and "an angel touched him." Thus he entered the second day. Then he again lay down and the angel came again and touched him. Thus he entered the third day. After that he went in strength from spiritual food "to Horeb the mount of God" (see "Mountain"), where he came to a "cave, and lodged there; and behold the word of the Lord came to him."—ERS

indeed a faithful adherent of Elijah's and gave heed to his words. Jezebel next urged Ahab to try and induce Naboth to come over to his side, either by methods of persuasion or, if necessary, by exercising his power of kingly authority. She said:—"It would be a great blow to the schemes and projects of this man, Elijah, if by any means it were possible to draw him away from his intents." Jezebel knew quite well, however, that all her talk was the merest notion; what she really desired was to induce her lord to take some kind of definite and effective action. For it was not this particular move in which she was interested; her mind was bent upon a plot which was to follow: hence the advice which she tendered was of the nature of a subterfuge. After Jezebel had spoken in this manner to Ahab, the King went to Naboth and held converse with him; but behold, Naboth would not regard what he said, and replied:—"Never shall those things come to pass which thou desirest."

In the Bible the position is so represented that this neighbor of Ahab's is described as possessing a vineyard which the King coveted, and sought to acquire.[14] According to this account (1 K 21,3), Naboth said to Ahab:—"The Lord forbid it me that I should give the inheritance of my fathers unto thee." In reality, however, the actual inheritance to which reference is here made was of quite another kind to that which Naboth declined to surrender; nevertheless, Jezebel used this incident as the foundation of her revenge. She deliberately proffered false counsel, in order that the King might be discountenanced and then angered by Naboth's refusal. That such was the case becomes evident when we read that passage in the Bible (1 K 21,4), where it is written: "And Ahab came into his house heavy and displeased because of the word which Naboth the Jezreelite had spoken to him: for he had said, I will not give thee the inheritance of my fathers. And he laid him down upon his bed, and turned away his face, and would eat not bread." Think of

---

14. The depth of meaning here (1 K 21,2) seems great. Recall from fn 12 that the meaning of "Carmel" is "vineyard" or "garden," and connect this with the meaning of "Mountain." While the challenge event probably did in fact take place on Mt. Carmel, the relationship of the name and the event cannot be dismissed lightly. A "vineyard," like a "field," is a place where one works. The vineyard in which the Elijah spirit worked was the chosen Hebrew people. It was this "vineyard" that Ahab "coveted" in the deeper spiritual meaning implied by this passage.—ERS

that! Merely because the King could not obtain a certain vineyard in his neighbourhood, he refused to eat! We can only begin to understand such statements, when we are in a position to investigate the facts which underlie them.

It was at this point that Jezebel took definite steps to bring about her revenge. She started by arranging that a feast be given to which Naboth should be invited, and at which he was to be an especially honoured guest (1 K 21,12). Naboth could not refuse to be present; and at his feast it was planned that he be afforded an opportunity of expressing himself freely. Now, Jezebel was truly gifted with clairvoyant insight; with the others Naboth could easily cope, with them he could measure forces; but Jezebel had the power to bring ruin upon him. She introduced false witnesses, who declared that "Naboth did deny (blaspheme) God and the King." It was in this manner that she contrived to compass his murder; as is related in the Bible (1 K 21,13). Henceforth the outer physical personality of Elijah was dead, and no more seen upon the face of the external world.

Now, because of all that had happened the deep forces in Ahab's soul were stirred; and he was, as one might say, confronted with the grave question of his destiny, while at the same time he experienced a strange and unusual foreboding. Then Elijah, whom he had ever regarded with a feeling of awe, appeared as in a vision and revealed to him plainly how the matter stood. Here we have an actual spiritual experience, in which Ahab was accused by the spirit-form of Elijah (subsequent to his death) of having virtually himself murdered Naboth—this Naboth-Elijah. The connection with the latter personality he could but dimly realize; nevertheless, Ahab was definitely termed his murderer. In the Bible we can read the dreadful words which fell upon his soul during that awe-inspiring prophecy, when the spirit-form said:—"In the place where dogs licked the blood of Naboth shall dogs lick thy blood, even thine" (1 K 21,19); and then came yet another dire prophetic utterance:—"The dogs shall eat Jezebel by the wall of Jezreel" (1 K 21,23).

We now know that these predictions belonged to a class which finds ultimate fulfillment ... (1 K 22,35,38 [as to Ahab]; 2 K 9,30-37 [as to Jezebel]).

The lecture goes on to speak of the transference of authority over to Elisha, but that is beyond our immediate need as it regards Elijah.[15] We shall now accordingly look independently at his successor Elisha as the next Biblical example of a Widow's Son.

2 K 4,1-7: (1) Now the wife of one of the sons of the prophets cried to Elisha, "Your servant *my husband is dead*; and you know that your servant feared the Lord, but the creditor has come to take *my two children* to be his slaves." (2) And Elisha said to her, "What shall I do for you? Tell me; what have you in the house?" And she said, "Your maidservant has nothing in the house, except a jar of oil." (3) Then he said, "Go outside, borrow vessels of all your neighbors, empty vessels and not too few. (4) Then go in, and shut the door upon yourself and *your sons*, and pour into all these vessels; and when one is full, set it aside." (5) So she went from him and shut the door upon herself and *her sons*; and as she poured they brought the vessels to her. (6) When the vessels were full, she said to her son, "Bring me another vessel." And he said to her, "There is not

---

15. The later and shorter treatment of Naboth/Elijah in GSMk, Lect. 3, adds some substantive remarks of interest, especially about how the characteristics of the Elijah personality and John the Baptist manifested similarly. The spirit of Elijah was said to be a direct reflection of Yahweh (Jehovah), the Folk-Spirit of the Hebrew people, and to "have been too great to dwell altogether in the soul of his earthly form, [instead] hovering over him like a cloud; ... [going] around the whole country like an element of nature, active in rain and sunshine." Steiner suggests the mindset of Ps 104 in comprehending this spirit. Its activity after the death of Naboth is similar to its activity after the death of John the Baptist, as we see below in "Peter, James and John."

In the lengthy extract from TPSH earlier in the text, it was said it was rumored that "a remarkable spirit was abroad," and about this Steiner said, "Throughout the widest circles any reference to this mysterious being, or even the mention of his name was accompanied by a thrill of awe, and ... it was generally felt that this spirit must possess some singular and hidden attribute of greatest import." The hierarchical level from which the Folk-Spirit of a people normally comes is that of the Archangels. In the case of the Hebrews, Yahweh-Eloha "chose" them and in that sense was also their Folk-Spirit in a most exalted sense. But serving him as the normal Folk-Spirit at the Archangelic level was the Archangel Michael, and this is the great spirit that was active through Elijah. But a notable, if somewhat complex, event took place in the Elijah Individuality between its incarnation in the ninth century B.C. and then in John the Baptist. Prokofieff splendidly brings the various threads of Steiner's lectures and writings together in fn 49 to Chap. 2, *Eternal Individuality* (EI), to show why John the Baptist denied that he was Elijah (Jn 1,21). See page 391 for further discussion.

another." Then the oil stopped flowing. (7) She came and told the man of God, and he said, "Go, *sell the oil and pay your debts, and you and your sons shall live* on the rest."[16]

From 2 K 2,13 we know that the "mantle of Elijah fell on Elisha," and we can see immense similarities in the miracles they performed. We could wish that time had permitted Steiner to devote the attention to Elisha that he did to Elijah, but we know that he pointed the direction and laid the groundwork for many disciplines in which he urged his followers to carry on to new applications. In that spirit, it seems not too much to see in the above passage a Widow's Son situation for Elisha also. Obviously, the servant of the Individuality of Elisha, namely, the husband of the woman, was deceased making her a *widow*, and she was about to lose her two sons. While the "temple sleep" is not explicit here, it is perhaps implied by this telescoped version of the parallel Elijah passage and the demands of Elijah's "mantle." The balance of Chapter 4 is not quoted above but involves the raising of the son of an "old woman." It is probably not inappropriate to see in 2 K 4, especially the quoted portion above, the identification of the personality of one of the Widow's Sons with the Individuality of Elisha, just as was the case in 1 K 17 with Elijah.

> **Lk 7,11-15**: (11) Soon afterward he went to a city called Nain, and his disciples and a great crowd went with him. (12) As he drew near to the gate of the city, behold, *a man who had died was being carried out, the only son of his mother, and she was a widow*; and a large crowd from the city was with her. (13) And when the Lord saw her, he had compassion on her and said to her, "Do not weep." (14) And he came and touched the bier, and the bearers stood still. And he said *"Young man, I say to you, arise." (15) And the dead man sat up, and began to speak. And he gave him to his mother.*

The majesty of the Individuality of the "Young Man" of Nain is by no means recognizable from the exoteric reading of this passage. That this

---

16. Just as in the case of Naboth/Elijah (see fn 8), the initiation status attained by Elisha as a Widow's Son permitted the spiritual wherewithal to pay the karmic "debts" and "live." Implicit is the assumption that knowledge of those debts from past lives is now possible, in order that they may be paid. Again, the distinction between "objective" and "subjective" karma is not yet significant.

seems to have occurred early in Jesus' ministry before the authorities began to seek his life (cf. Jn 11,50 and 12,10-11) is probably Luke's way of saying this was the first initiation carried out by Jesus personally, even preceding that of Lazarus, thus indicating its immense significance.[17] This is strongly hinted by Steiner in GSL, Lect. 10, pp. 185-186, and the connection with the personality of Mani (discussed above) and the Individuality of Manu is elaborated by Lievegoed in BATSO, Chap. 6. That Individuality is there, as in TL, Lect. 6, identified as perhaps the highest "stream" in humanity's evolution. The depth of its significance is such that it is only touched upon by Luke, much as the significance of the twelve-year-old Jesus in the temple (Lk 2,41-51) pointed to a deeply veiled mystery, discussed in "The Nativity." The clear identification here in the New Testament of this youth as a Widow's Son points toward the later Mani, who identifies himself as such. What Steiner says in the two quoted passages from TL at the outset of this discussion shows the exalted status of the Individuality here involved, if it is, as indicated, that of Mani and Manu.

Before leaving the scriptural evidence, we should note the implications of the term "fatherless." The very fact of specifying this suggests that one so described (at least when identified as a male child) is a Widow's Son, else one would be identified as an "orphan." It must suffice here to point out passages that speak, always presumably with deep meaning, of the "fatherless," namely: Ex 22,24; Deut 10,18; 14,29; 16,11,14; 24,17-21; 26,12-13; 27,19; Job 5,15; 6,27; 22,9; 24,3,9; 29,12; 31,17,21; Ps 10,14,18; 68,5; 82,3; 94,6; 146,9; Prov 23,10; Is 1,17,23; 9,17; 10,2; Jer

---

17. Here it should be pointed out that there was a difference between the nature of the two initiations by Christ, those of the youth of Nain and of Lazarus. In The Gospel of St. John (GSJ), Lect. 4, Steiner shows that the thing about the Lazarus initiation that so disturbed the Jewish priests was its public character, which they considered to be a violation of the ancient Mystery traditions. Why then was no such furor stimulated by the earlier raising of this youth? In GSL, Lect. 10, Steiner states, "There are various kinds of Initiation. In one kind, immediately after the process has been completed, knowledge of the higher worlds flashes up.... In another kind ... it is only a seed that is implanted into the soul, and the individual has to wait until the next incarnation for the seed to bear fruit, only then does he become an Initiate in the real sense." He then says the youth's initiation was of the latter type, hence it would not have provided nearly the same basis for any official concern, even assuming that it came to their attention. Luke's penchant, as in Lk 2 regarding Simeon, Anna and the twelve-year-old, for pointing out things of immense esoteric spiritual significance, which would not be outwardly understood by many, surely underlaid his reporting of this incident which is also unique to his Gospel.

5,28; 7,6; 22,3; 49,11; Ezek 22,7; and Zech 7,10. We see also, in "The Nativity" that Jesus was "fatherless" long before he began his ministry, and that he committed his otherwise unattended mother to John from the Cross (Jn 19,25-27). And we are also told by Steiner that Zechariah, father of John the Baptist, a Widow's Son in the Naboth/Elijah incarnation, was slain by Herod. That these were real life situations does not detract from the probability that they reflected a deeper spiritual reality. Similarly, many spiritually exalted personalities have lost their fathers at a very early age, a curious fact which the reader may have observed.

CHAPTER END NOTES

5. One of the best accounts of Christian Rosenkreutz is in Rosicrucian Christianity (ROSC). He is referred to by Steiner again and again in numerous works, including, but not limited to, The Chymical Wedding of Christian Rosenkreutz (CWCR), Esoteric Christianity and the Mission of Christian Rosenkreutz (ECMCR), Rosicrucian Esotericism (RE) and Rosicrucian and Modern Initiation (RMI). The reasons he is not known to traditional historians, foremost among which is the requirement of serving spiritually incognito, are obvious from these accounts which, however, asseverate his earthly reality first in the thirteenth century, when he was not yet known by such name, and then again in the fourteenth. Steiner says (TL, Lect. 5, p. 50, fn 3) that the Temple Legend originated with Rosenkreutz in the fourteenth and fifteenth centuries, but insofar as the world is concerned it started with Count St. Germain and the founding of Freemasonry in the eighteenth century (accord: 10 Brit 318, "Saint-Germain, compte de").

6. Unfortunately, I do not have at my informational command all that Steiner may have said on this matter. In a letter to me dated September 4, 1995, René Querido wrote of the Hiram connection: "Rudolf Steiner gave a revised version of the Temple Legend, most probably towards the end of 1923. I have the text in a German typed copy—it has never been published, and was given to a group of friends who were preparing the Christmas Foundation meeting. At the end of the [revised version of] Temple Legend we find the following: 'Hiram Abiff was reincarnated as Lazarus and was the one who was the first to be initiated by the Christ.' I am sure that in the next few years this will be published by the Archives in Dornach, but there is no sign of it so far." That this line starting from Hiram is accepted as a verity

within anthroposophical ranks is indicated by Lievegoed in BATSO, Chap. 4, and by Rene Querido's discussion on the matter as reported in NEWS, Summer 1995, p. 26. In TL, Lect. 5 (p. 56) and ROSC (p. 12), Steiner identifies Count St. Germain as the reincarnated Christian Rosenkreutz, and his remarks in ROSC (pp. 6-8) would seem to identify the latter as the reincarnated Lazarus/John and have apparently been so taken in *Rudolf Steiner's Mission and Ita Wegman* (RSMW), Chap. 11 (p. 99). Except as above, I have been unable to resurrect the original source of my impression, from Steiner's work, that Lazarus/John was the reincarnated Hiram. That Hiram may himself have been the same Individuality as the earlier Tubal-Cain may well be suggested by the "bronze" connection when considered in the light of what Steiner had to say about the karmic significance of vocation in earlier times; see *The Karma of Vocation* (KV), Lect. 4.

7. Lievegoed, in BATSO, Chap. 4, p. 63, says, "Ehrenfried Pfeiffer has told me that Rudolf Steiner said that Joshua was an incarnation of Christian Rosenkreutz." Pfeiffer (1899-1961) as a young man worked closely with Steiner in the development of biodynamic farming. While Joshua is not clearly identified in the Bible as a Widow's Son, he is said to have been "Hoshea the son of Nun" (Num 13,8), whom "Moses called ... Joshua" (Num 13,16), both such names being variants of the name "Jesus," meaning "salvation." He is also identified (1 Ch 7,27) as the grandson of "Elishma," which probably means "El (or God) has heard" (2 AB 473) and is probably, by reason of the "ma," a feminine (i.e., maternalistic) variant of "Elisha" which means "man of God." The name "Nun" means "fish." While only a millennium of the astrological age of Pisces remained, the Cultural Age of Pisces was to start with the introduction of the spiritual teachings of Christian Rosenkreutz and the Renaissance (see **I-19**), the beginning of the 2,160 years of development of the Consciousness Soul (see **I-24**). Perhaps we have, in these names, a prophetic foreshadowing of what this Individuality was to accomplish in humanity's evolution, and thus an even more hidden indication of Joshua's being a Widow's Son.

15. (*continued from pp. 387*) According to Prokofieff, there was a "'shift' in the hierarchic Beings who inspire John which renders him incapable of recalling his previous incarnation as Elijah." We are here dealing with a changing of the guard, so to speak, brought about by an advancement procedure similar to that envisioned in **I-15**. To get to this, we must go back to the Bodhisattva who became Buddha. As a result of his last incarnation, his guardian angel was entitled to rise. Here Prokofieff quotes (see text preceding

his endnote 46) Steiner (*The Festivals and their Meaning* [FM], Lect. 5-20-13, p. 377), "When a man from being a Bodhisattva becomes a Buddha, then his Guardian Angel is, as it were, set free; it is such Angel Beings who, after the fulfillment of their mission, ascend into the realm of the Archangel Beings." Now, the Archangel who worked through Elijah was Michael, the Folk-Spirit of the Hebrew people and the "ruling Sun Archangel" (see **I-19**), thus the most advanced and chief among the Archangels. He was to advance to the rank of Archai (Time Spirit) in 1879, so that not until that time could "the place which was 'made vacant' in the Hierarchy of the Archangels as a result of Michael's ascent to the rank of Time Spirit" be filled. By virtue of his work with the Bodhisattva who became Buddha, the latter's angel became "the spiritual successor and inheritor of Michael's mission in the sphere of the Angels" (and Archangels). But "in order that he might take up his place, the Guardian Angel of the Gautama Buddha, once he had in the sixth century B.C. been freed from the task of guiding the human being that had been entrusted to him and had thereby been enabled to ascend to the rank of Archangel, had to make the sacrifice of consenting to work in the sphere of the Angels for almost a further 2,500 years, even though he was—insofar as his inner qualities were concerned—already an Archangel. It was this sacrificial deed which enabled him to participate in the manner described in the events of Palestine, though now no longer as the Guardian Angel of a Bodhisattva incarnated in a human body, but as the collaborator and guide of a Buddha working in a spirit-body. For as he continued to work in the spiritual world nearest to the Earth after the Buddha's enlightenment beneath the Bodhi tree, he was able to participate in the events of the Turning-Point of Time far more directly as an Angel than would have been possible had he been of the rank of an Archangel. Thus instead of the Archangel Michael working through Elijah, we have working through John the Baptist the particular Angelic Being who had formerly been the Guardian Angel of Gautama Buddha. However, everything has, as we have seen, now moved one Hierarchy lower."

How magnificently this observation ties in with the fact, shown by Steiner, that John the Baptist's preaching closely echoed that of the Buddha. See the portion of GSL, Lect. 6, pp. 119-120, quoted in the four paragraphs of "The Nativity" text embodying its fn 15.

TRUMPET(S)

UPON CAREFUL EXAMINATION, the "fabric" of the Bible can be seen to be "threadlike," with each term perhaps being used in various contexts, but suggesting that particular attention be given to the connotation that gives the higher meaning in each passage. This suggestion has particular force for the term "Trumpet(s)."[1] The fact that our modern Bibles use it for a variety of different Hebrew words in the Old Testament[2] does not seem to materially affect its meaning for our present purposes.

Discussing Rev 8,6, 38 AB 132 ("Revelation") makes the following observation:

> Originally the trumpet was not so much a musical instrument as an alarm. It was sounded to gather the people together, to signal, to indicate the breaking of camp, and such. Later it became a priestly instrument sounded during the liturgy.

Although I do not wholeheartedly concur with all of this observation, it may help in distinguishing various passages, but one should bear in mind

---

1. The passages in which the term "Trumpet(s)" appears (RSV) are as follows, in canonical order: Ex 19,13,16,19 and 20,18; Lev 23,24 and 25,9; Num 10,2,8-10; 29,1 and 31,6; Josh 6,4-20; Judg 3,27; 6,34 and 7,16-22; 1 Sam 13,3; 2 Sam 2, 28; 15,10; 18,16 and 20,1,22; 1 K 1,34,39,41; 2 K 9,13; 11,14 and 12,13; 1 Ch 13,8; 15,24,28 and 16,6,42; 2 Ch 5,13; 7,6; 13,12,14; 15,14; 20,28; 23,13 and 29,26-27; Ez 3,10; Neh 4,18,20 and 12,35,41; Job 39,24-25; Ps 47,5; 81,3; 98,6 and 150,3; Is 18,3; 27,13 and 58,1; Jer 4,5,19,21; 6,1,17; 42,14 and 51,27; Ezek 7,14 and 33,3-6; Hos 5,8 and 8,1; Joel 2,1,15; Amos 2,2 and 3,6; Zeph 1,16; Zech 9,14; Mt 6,2 and 24,31; 1 Cor 15,52; 1 Th 4,16; Heb 12,19; Rev 1,10; 4,1; 8,2,6-13; 9,1,13-14; and 10,7 and 11,15. In addition, "Trumpeters" appears in 2 K 11,14; 2 Ch 5,12-13; 23,13 and 29,28; and Rev 18,22.
2. An excellent discussion of this is found in 4 ABD 930 at 936-939, "Music and Musical Instruments." Four different Hebrew words, namely, *sopar, hasosera, qeren,* and *yobel,* are used in the Old Testament to express various shades of meaning for "aerophones" ("which produce sound through vibration of air in, through, or around them") in which "the lips of the player produce the vibration of air." But in the Greek Old Testament (the "Septuagint") produced several centuries B.C., the Greek word *salpinx* covers substantially all of them, so that our modern English Bibles generally use the term "trumpet" throughout.

that liturgy takes its validity by representing something more substantive and ultimate, as is suggested by such considerations as the phrase "As Above, So Below."

In any event, we should look for the highest meaning and key off that. Beyond question, the clearest exposition of this meaning is in Steiner's lecture cycle on Revelation, *The Apocalypse of St. John* (ASJ). Let us bear in mind his assertion that Lazarus/John was indeed the author of the Gospel of John, the Apocalypse of (Revelation to) St. John and the Johannine Epistles.[3] Steiner identifies John's Gospel as the most spiritually exalted writing ever given to humanity. While the citation for such assertion is presently beyond me, he clearly identifies that Gospel as the highest of the four canonical Gospels (see *The Gospel of St. John* [GSJ], Lect. 1). The reasons for Lazarus/John's high spiritual vision are given in "Three Days' Journey," where it is also noted (in the penultimate paragraph) that Paul's initiation by Christ raised his level of spiritual knowledge to a comparable plane. His rough equivalence in that respect to Lazarus/John does not necessarily raise his writings to the same height, because their missions were entirely different. Paul's high knowledge emerges in his epistles rather as "flashes" whose meanings have largely escaped humanity's knowledge prior to the revelations by Steiner, as more fully set out throughout this work. Paul's usage of Trumpet and Last Trumpet can be seen, in the light of Steiner's lectures on Revelation, to disclose a depth of spiritual knowledge far greater than could otherwise be detected from the mere literal content of his writings.

Let us then look at the meaning of this term in Revelation. There Lazarus/John gives the entire elaborate picture by which the Trumpet flashes of Paul can be comprehended. The human being, the true Prodigal Son (Lk 15,11-32), left the Father in the highest heaven, journeyed into the "far country" of its present mineral-physical condition, and, by coming to recognize the Christ event, the Incarnation and Mystery of Golgotha in the anthroposophical sense, can "come to itself" and commence its return to the Father. The descent began in, and the ascent will return to,

---

3. While 1 Jn is generally conceded to be by the same author as the Gospel, some scholars have questioned the origin of the last two epistles. However, much of the objection can be removed if it is understood, as Steiner tells us, that Lazarus/John indeed dwelt in Ephesus (and with the Mother of Jesus there during her life) until he was well past the age of one hundred. See the conclusion of "Peter, James and John" herein, under the caption "What Happened to the Two Johns?".

the twelvefold zodiacal realm or kingdom (see "Zodiac" and Twelve"), while evolution, all that is measured by time, occurs in the sevenfold solar realm. Revelation shows us the entirety of this journey; the first half, or descent, is fairly compressed in early passages, while the present and the far distant future are laid out in some detail, starting with the sevenfold solar system in which we find ourselves, then moving through four cycles of seven (letters, seals, trumpets and bowls of wrath) until the twelvefold zodiacal realm is entered with the approach to the New Jerusalem.

Steiner gives us the most helpful of all his schematics as a part of the ASJ lecture cycle. It is reproduced in **I-1** (whose introductory narrative also references **I-2**, **I-3** and **I-4**, the last containing helpful exposition relative to **I-1**). The Commentary on Revelation[4] will give a more complete picture, but the following table gives us the basis for understanding the occult meaning of Trumpet(s):

Symbol	Scripture	Chart **I-1** Description
7 Letters	Rev 2-3	7 Cultural Ages (of which the human being is in the fifth) of the Fifth Evolutionary Epoch (called post-Atlantean) of the Physical Condition of Form
7 Seals	Rev 5,1-8,1	7 Cultural Ages (or their evolutionary equivalent) of the Sixth Evolutionary Epoch of the Physical Condition of Form
7 Trumpets	Rev 8,2-11,15	7 Cultural Ages (or their evolutionary equivalent) of the Seventh Evolutionary Epoch of the Physical Condition of Form
7 Bowls	Rev 16	7 Evolutionary Epochs (or their evolutionary equivalent) of the More Perfect Astral Condition of Form of the Mineral Kingdom

4. A substantial summary of Revelation is given in "Alpha and Omega > Creation and Apocalypse," Vol. 2, *"What Is Man?"*.

In ASJ, Lect. 9 (p. 156), we are told:

... when the earth has reached its goal, when the seventh trumpet begins to sound, the following will be observed: what exists of the physical body will be dissolved like salt in warm water. Man's spirit-self [or "manas," i.e., "Manna"; see **I-9** and **I-24**] will be developed to a high degree, so that man will repeat again and again the words of Paul: Not I, but Christ in me [Gal 2,20] does everything.—Thus man will live. This will enable him to dissolve the physical nature and make the ennobled etheric into a being which can live in the astralized earth. Thus man, a new being, will live over into this spiritualized earth.

We might say that the important stage of passing over into the earth which has become spiritualized is wonderfully expressed in the Bible where it says that everything which man now accomplishes within himself in the physical body during the earth period is like a sowing whose fruit will appear when the earth has become spiritual: [here Steiner quotes 1 Cor 15,36b-40,43a,44]. Paul calls the etheric or life body, spiritual body, after the physical has dissolved and the etheric passes into the astral earth. Paul here sees beforehand the incorruptible spiritual body, as he calls it.

Most significantly, Paul refers to the *last* Trumpet (1 Cor 15,52), which has no clear meaning until one sees how it relates to the seven "trumpets" in Revelation. This also gives meaning to "meet[ing] the Lord in the air" at the "sound of the trumpet" (1 Th 4,16-17).

This thread of high meaning for Trumpet is thus woven at various spiritual levels throughout the fabric of the Bible. Particular notice is taken, however, of its use in the following passages, in canonical order rather than spiritual level (emphasis mine; bold print indicates a "term or phrase" to be covered in this work):

Ex 19,10-20: (10) And the LORD said to Moses, "Go to the people and consecrate them today and tomorrow, and let them wash their **garments**, (11) and be ready by the **third day**; for on the third day the LORD will come down upon Mount Sinai in the sight of all the people. (12) And you shall set bounds for the people round about, saying, 'Take heed that you do not go up into the **mountain** or touch the border of it; whoever touches the mountain shall be put to death [see the "third group" of scriptures concluding the discussion of "Mysteries" herein]; (13) no hand shall touch him, but he shall be stoned or shot; whether beast or man, he shall not live.' When the *trumpet* sounds a long blast, they shall come up to the mountain." (14) So Moses went down from the mountain to the people, and consecrated the people; and they washed their garments. (15) And he said to the people, "Be ready by the third day; do not go near a woman." (16) On the morning of the third day there were **thunders** and **lightnings**, and a thick **cloud** upon the mountain, and a very loud *trumpet* blast, so that all the people who were in the camp trembled. (17) Then Moses brought the people out of the camp to meet God; and they took their stand at the foot of the mountain. (18) And Mount Sinai was wrapped in smoke, because the LORD descended upon it in **fire**; and the smoke of it went up like the smoke of a kiln, and the whole mountain quaked greatly. (19) And as the sound of the *trumpet* grew louder and louder, Moses spoke, and God answered him in thunder. (20) And the LORD came down upon Mount Sinai, to the top of the mountain; and the LORD called Moses to the top of the mountain, and Moses went up.

The prophetic and evolutionary nature of this passage seems powerfully indicated by the understanding given herein to the term "trumpet," especially when the occult meaning of the words in bold print is considered. The prevalence of such words itself (enhanced by the bracketed note matter) is an indication of the purport of the passage, as is the presence of the element of fire, whose significance has been noted elsewhere herein (see "Bush"; "Fire" is one of the terms discussed in Vol. 2). Moses here telescopes many powerful New Testament themes into one brief passage. Even in the New Testament era these themes are prophetic of what will evolve over long periods of time, as can be seen from the above table illustrating the four sets of septenary symbols from Revelation. The bold words are not discussed in this volume, so it must suffice for the present merely to state succinctly their significance. As indicated in "Naked," "Garments" refers to the state attained when the lower "Three Bodies," the astral, etheric and physical, have been respectively perfected by the higher Ego into their spiritual counterparts, manas (Manna; Spirit Self), buddhi (Life Spirit) and atma (Spirit Man); see **I-9** and cf. Mt 13,33.

One cannot enter into the spiritual world without wearing these "garments" (Mt 22, 11-14). The "Third Day" is an indication of the time when a significant spiritual event is ready to happen. "Mountain" denotes the elevated human condition where spiritual perception occurs. One who has ever climbed a mountain knows that it takes persistent effort and struggle to reach its summit. "Lightning" (with which "Thunder" is always associated), "Clouds" and "Fire" are the media through which hierarchical beings, the Seraphim, Cherubim and Archai, respectively (see **I-29**), manifest in the mineral-physical world. "Fire" is also the point of contact between the mineral and spiritual conditions, the element in which the physical and etheric worlds meet. Whatever historical incidents, if any, may be indicated by, or utilized in, such account would thus be secondary and subservient to the higher spiritual message.

> **Is 18,3**: All you inhabitants of the world, you who dwell on the earth, when a signal is raised on the **mountains**, look! When a *trumpet* is blown, hear!

This passage incorporates the mandate to "look" at a signal (sign) from the "Mountains," which relates to "seeing," and to hear the "trumpet." This command to "see" and "hear" relates to the important occult message in Is 6,9-13.

> **Ezek 7,14**: They have blown the *trumpet* and made all ready; but none goes to battle, for my wrath is upon all their multitude.

> **Ezek 33,1-6**: (1) The word of the Lord came to me: (2) "Son of man, speak to your people and say to them, If I bring the sword upon a land, and the people of the land take a man from among them, and make him their watchman; (3) and if he sees the sword coming upon the land and blows the *trumpet* and warns the people; (4) then if any one who hears the sound of the *trumpet* does not take warning, and the sword comes and takes him away, his blood shall be upon his own head. (5) He heard the sound of the *trumpet*, and did not take warning; his blood shall be upon himself. But if he had taken warning, he would have saved his life. (6) But if the watchman sees the sword coming and does not blow the *trumpet*, so that the people are not warned, and the sword comes, and takes any one of

them; that man is taken away in his iniquity, but his blood I will require at the watchman's hand."

This passage is a warning both to the watchman to watch and to those who hear such warning to heed it. There is a responsibility not only for oneself, but equally so for others. The term "watch" involves "seeing," and in the prophetic sense means clairvoyant perception of what the spiritual world reveals. One who so perceives is burdened with the responsibility to make the vision and its importance known. It is well to interpret the "sword" as being the "word of God" (see the discussion of 1 K19,1 in "Widow's Son"). Given the higher meaning of "trumpet" herein, what is seen and announced by the watchman relates to the Seventh Evolutionary Epoch when humanity is nearing the end of its Physical Condition of Form (see **I-1** and **I-2**; also the passage quoted above from ASJ, Lect. 9). That alone suggests the extreme urgency and higher significance of the warning to prepare before "the sword comes and takes him away" (vs 4) from physical existence without his having put on the "garments" needed to enter the astral or spiritual condition.

> **Zeph 1,15-16**: (15) A day of wrath is that day, a day of distress and anguish, a day of ruin and devastation, a day of darkness and gloom, a day of **clouds** and thick **darkness**, (16) a day of *trumpet* blast and battle cry against the fortified cities and against the lofty battlements.

> **Zech 9,14**: Then the Lord will appear over them, and his arrow go forth like **lightning**; the Lord God will sound the *trumpet*, and march forth in the whirlwinds of the south.

> **Mt 24,31**: and he will send out his angels with a loud *trumpet* call, and they will gather his elect from the four winds, from one end of heaven to the other.

This is part of the "Little Apocalypse," discussed under Mt 25,31-46 in "Lord of Karma" herein (Point 4 addresses the trumpet call).

> **Heb 12,18-24**: (18) For you have not come to what may be touched, a blazing **fire**, and **darkness**, and gloom, and a tempest,

(19) and the sound of a *trumpet,* and a voice whose words made the hearers entreat that no further messages be spoken to them. (20) For they could not endure the order that was given, "If even a beast touches the **mountain**, it shall be stoned." (21) Indeed, so terrifying was the sight that Moses said, "I tremble with fear." (22) But you have come to Mount Zion and the city of the living God, the heavenly Jerusalem, and to innumerable angels in festal gathering [**garments?**], (23) and to the assembly of the **first-born** who are enrolled in heaven, and to a judge who is God of all, and to the spirits of just men made **perfect**, (24) and to Jesus, the mediator [see "Lord of Karma"] of a new covenant, and to the sprinkled **blood** that speaks more graciously than the blood of Abel.

Just as in 1 Cor 10,1-4 and Gal 4,22-31, Paul shows here the allegorical and prophetic nature of the Mosaic account. Again we have the "Mountain," but this time we go further to the "Perfect," which points strongly to the distant future envisioned by the "heavenly Jerusalem." And again, with the latter reference, we have Paul and John speaking of the same things. The overtones ("darkness and gloom") of the Zephaniah passage above can be seen also in this passage. Significantly, Paul says that while they have come to Jesus (who thus represents the "Perfect"), they have not yet come to the fire (i.e., the point of contact between heaven and Earth) or to the time of the Trumpet (presumably here the *last* Trumpet), or to the other indicators that the ("apocalyptic") end is near. Clearly the interpretation set out above for Ex 19,10-20 seems vindicated by this passage. Consider the relationship between Paul and Moses suggested by the concluding essay, "Pillars on the Journey."

NAKED

THE NORMAL PICTURE that springs into one's mind today when the word "Naked" is used is that of the physical human body—understandable in view of the fact that humanity's consciousness today focuses primarily, if not exclusively, upon the mineral-physical world, and what can be observed by the senses. A good dictionary gives numerous meanings, all of which are variations of "completely uncovered or exposed."

One should contemplate to what extent this term is used in the Bible (related uses such as "Nakedness" are included in the passages at the end of this discussion) with reference to the mineral-physical world observable by the senses, and to what extent it is used to describe a higher state of existence consistent with its higher message.

Since in all instances, the Bible uses the term to apply to human beings, albeit sometimes collectively in groups, it is essential to understand the composition of the human being (set out in **I-9**) in order understand how Nakedness applies to it. An understanding of the terms "I AM" and "Bush" is also a prerequisite. The Ego, or "I Am," is clothed, so to speak, in the "Three Bodies" (physical, etheric, astral). The spiritual counterpart of each body is shown opposite it in **I-9** if one connects 1 and 9 (i.e., physical body and atma, or Spirit Man), 2 and 8, etc. Then if we consider that the physical, etheric and astral bodies came into their earliest origins in the Ancient Saturn, Sun and Moon Conditions of Consciousness, or Planetary Conditions, respectively (see **I-1** and **I-4**), and that the bare germs of their spiritual counterparts were planted at the same respective stages,[1] we see that at the end of the Ancient Moon period the human being consisted only of the "Three Bodies" as well as the germs of their three spiritual counterparts.

---

1. In addition to the account in *Occult Science* (OS), this is also reflected in columns 6, 7 and 8 near the end of **I-76**.

Chart **I-14** shows that the purpose of Earth evolution, the fourth Condition of Consciousness, is the implantation and development of the human Ego, the "I Am." During the first three Evolutionary Epochs of the Mineral Physical Condition of Form of Earth Evolution (**I-1**), there is a recapitulation of the first three "Planetary" Conditions so as to re-create, in a more advanced state of existence, the "Three Bodies."[2]

Gen 1,2 describes the time in the third Evolutionary Epoch, or recapitulation ("Lemuria," see **I-1**), when the three related elements of fire, air and water exist in the etheric condition without "Form." In Gen 1,26-27, the Elohim (all seven, clearly plural as recognized in all translations), or Spirits of Form (see **I-6**), create the human being in their Image—as yet simply a "Form" without mineral substance that would be perceivable to present senses (see Gen 2,5; also "Alpha and Omega > Creation and Apocalypse," Vol. 2).

The word Naked first appears in scripture in Gen 2,25: the "man and his wife were both naked, and were not ashamed." This is immediately before the Fall in Gen 3, which caused them to become aware of their Nakedness and to be ashamed (Gen 3,7,10-11). There was no consequence to their Nakedness in Gen 2,25, but there was in Gen 3,7,10-11. What had happened in the meantime to give significance to this state?

Observe the tabulation in the last paragraph of **I-35**, which shows that during the Lemurian Epoch the Ego penetrated the astral body creating the Sentient Soul. That schematic is presented graphically by Steiner in *The Influence of Spiritual Beings Upon Man* (ISBM), Lect. 4, p. 71, as follows:

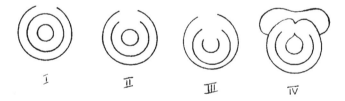

The three rings of the diagrams, from inner to outer, represent the human being's physical, etheric and astral bodies, respectively. The diagrams are identified with the following periods in the **I-35** chart:

---

2. This recap is an application of the "fractal" nature of creation, see "Fractals" in the Appendix to "Fire," Vol. 2, *"What Is Man?"*. This "fractal" nature is another manifestation of the principle "As Above, So Below."

I = Lemuria
II = First 2/3 of Atlantis
III = Last 1/3 of Atlantis
IV = Today (since Golgotha Deed)

The situation in Gen 2,25 existed at the threshold of Diagram I; in other words, before the development of the human being's soul nature (see **I-35**). The events of the Fall as described in Gen 3,1-6 then occurred. As yet, the human being had only an animal-like nature (see **I-10** and **I-11,** though its "bodies" were of a more exalted state inasmuch as they had not descended to materiality and were to become the vehicles for the human Ego), and consequently had no knowledge or consciousness of sin. Steiner elaborates this quite well in *The Concepts of Original Sin and Grace* (OSG). The human astral body was infected by "original" sin with the Fall prior to the infusion of the Ego. As the human being descended further into materiality during the Atlantean Epoch, the senses developed along with the Sentient Soul (**I-23**), and with the developing soul (i.e., Ego, or "I Am") came knowledge of Nakedness (Gen 3,7). Notably, it was not until the development of the fourth sense, that of "touch" (**I-23**), that human beings came to the knowledge in Gen 3,7, and then only after the fifth sense (hearing) in Gen 3,8 did they begin to perceive themselves, and in doing so used the first person singular pronoun, "I" (Gen 3,10-13). Three times then in Gen 3,7-11, is the term Naked used, probably signifying the progressive increase in awareness as the three embryonic stages of the human soul evolved (**I-9** and **I-35**).

We don't come to the next Biblical use of Naked until well into Exodus, at the time of the Chaldo-Egyptian Cultural Era. And here again we see the recapitulation during the post-Atlantean Epoch of the more primitive embryonic soul development during the Atlantean Epoch (see **I-24**). It is well to bear in mind the time frame of the Cultural Era in which subsequent usages of the term occur (see **I-19**) as perhaps having a significant bearing on their meaning. For instance, those that occur earlier in the Chaldo-Egyptian Era tend to emphasize the physical or sensate aspect of the term, as in Ex 28,42-43 and Lev 20,18-19, while the later usages seem to take on a progressively more exalted meaning in relation to the eternal Ego. Particularly in the Wisdom, Prophet and New Testament books is this so. But even the earlier usages can be seen to carry a higher meaning as well.

If one bears in mind that the "Three Bodies" are merely unpurified "Garments" to be shed (to the extent not purified during progressive earthly incarnations) as the Ego makes the journey between death and rebirth (see **I-33**), and that one whose "Garments" are all removed is Naked, considerable new spiritual meaning can be gathered. And in those instances where condemnation is being heaped on sinners of one variety or another who are said to have their Nakedness exposed, one can see that the converse spiritual growth can be meant, thereby giving high spiritual meaning. For instance, the failure to purify one's lower "Three Bodies" during the course of earthly incarnation means that one is not creating the type of "Garment(s)" required for spiritual advancement. Such Nakedness is most assuredly exposed during the journey between lives (**I-33**). It is then as though one were attending a wedding without the necessary "Garments" (Mt 22,11-12), not having purified any of the "bodies" in earthly lives.

Of particular interest is Gen 9,22-23. Ham, the father of Canaan, saw the Nakedness of Noah. This would seem to mean that Ham had a strong atavistic clairvoyance, enabling him to see the Individuality (Nakedness) of Noah whereas Shem and Japheth, looking to the future, covered this with their earthly "Garments" (astral and etheric bodies drawing further into the densifying physical so as to lose the ancient vision into the spiritual world). This was necessary for the post-Atlantean evolution.

Of immense importance is Mk 14,51-52, regarding the "Young Man" who fled Naked. With the intensity of a laser beam, all that is said above about the Ego seems to focus on this passage. While "Young Man" is to be the subject of a separate discussion in this work, we must touch preliminarily upon it here. Notably, the term "Young Man" is used sparingly in the Gospels, and in connection with only three incidents. The first has to do with the "rich young man" in Mt 19,16-22, the last with the youth of Nain whom Jesus initiated ("raised from the dead") in Lk 7,11-17, while this one in Mark constitutes one end of a thread whose other end shows up in the empty tomb on Easter morning (Mk 16,5). In Mk 14,51-52, the "Young Man" first wore nothing but a "linen cloth" which he yielded; in Mk 16,5 he wears a "White Robe." What a spine-tingling spectacle we are about to comprehend! The "rich young man" is Lazarus/John (see Welburn's *Gnosis* [GNOS]; also "Egypt" below, under the Philo discussion; and 4 ABD 558, "Secret Gospel of Mark"), the youth of Nain the Individuality representing the highest stream of human evolution (see *The Temple Legend* [TL], Lect. 6; *The Battle for the Soul* [BATSO]; and

"Widow's Son")—and the "Young Man" in Mark's Gospel is the Christ Spirit itself, as will be more fully discussed elsewhere (for now see *The Gospel of St. Mark* [GSMk], Lect. 9). Is it not an awesome fact that while the Gospels of Mark and Luke both relate something of the "rich young man" account (see Mk 10,17-22, but especially the "Secret Gospel of Mark" discussed in GNOS, supra; Lk 18,18-30), both of them reserve the "Young Man" terminology to demonstrate some other Individuality or Spiritual Being. Thus, we have the following:

Gospel	Young Man	Body to be Redeemed	Cultural Era
Matthew	Lazarus/John	Astral	Fourth
Luke	Youth of Nain	Etheric	Fifth-Sixth
Mark	Christ Spirit	Physical	Alpha/Omega

So in the synoptic Gospels we have the "Three Bodies" again demonstrated in connection with the high meaning of "Young Man." The Gospel of John, written by one of these "Young Men," does not employ the phrase. And only in connection with the highest of these "Young Men" is the term Naked employed, and then not for the purpose of showing that the "youth" was without the higher "Garments" but to demonstrate that he (alone) had shed, i.e., fully purified, all the lower ones, the "Three Bodies," and was worthy to wear the paragon of all "Garments," the "White Robe."

Finally, let us consider the state of Jesus at the Crucifixion. Reverent modesty has tradition covering his genitalia with a cloth (cf. Ex 28,42-43). But, as foreseen in Ps 22,18, the Gospels do not accord him that; see Mt 27,27-35; Mk 15,20-24; Lk 23,34b; Jn 19,23-24; this increased the shame (Heb 12,2) that afflicted his followers (Rom 9,33; 1 Pet 2,6; cf. Is 28,16) prior to the Resurrection. One of the most powerful preachers I've known, in one of his most powerful sermons, spoke assuredly of Christ as having been crucified completely Naked in abject worldly shame.[3]

Steiner's *Christianity as Mystical Fact* (CMF) shows that the Mystery of Golgotha was the performance of the ancient "Mysteries" in full view of

---

3. Indicative of the humiliation of the vanquished in ancient times, 2 ABD 232 at 233 ("Dress and Ornamentation") says, "The stele of Sennacherib (705-681 BCE) depicts naked male prisoners from Lachish impaled on stakes as the battle rages; after the fall of the city, naked prisoners are staked out on the ground." Cf. 2 Ch 28,15a and Is 20,4.

the world; now, however, instead of the hierophant calling the candidate for initiation back from deathlike sleep to earthly life (as in the case of Lazarus and the others—see "Widow's Son") Jesus relied upon the Father to call him back from actual earthly death to spiritual life perceivable in the etheric ("life") world by those whose vision he had prepared. One of the aspects of initiation in the Mysteries was Nakedness, at least symbolically. Steiner speaks of this in TL, Lect. 7, p. 81, to the effect that the candidate "ought to present himself in life as if he were appearing completely Naked in the eyes of his fellow men." That particular lecture had to do with Masonic rights, but in that respect they partook of the ancient Mysteries.

TEXT OF RELATED SCRIPTURES

(Emphasis mine; most emphasized words appear in "Terms & Phrases.")

Gen 2,25: And the man and his wife were both *naked* and were not ashamed.

Gen 3,7,10-11: (7) Then the eyes of both were opened, and they knew that they were *naked*; and they sewed fig leaves together and made themselves aprons.... (10) And he said, "I heard the sound of thee in the garden, and I was afraid, because I was *naked*; and I hid myself." (11) He said, "Who told you that you were *naked*? Have you eaten of the tree of which I commanded you not to eat?"

Ex 28,42-43: (42) And you shall make for them *linen* breeches to cover their *naked* flesh; from the loins to the thighs they shall reach; (43) and they shall be upon Aaron, and upon his sons, when they go into the tent of meeting, or when they come near the altar to minister in the holy place; lest they bring guilt upon themselves and die. This shall be a perpetual statute for him and for his descendants after him.

Lev 20,18-19: (18) If a man lies with a woman having her sickness, and uncovers her *nakedness*, he has made *naked* her fountain, and she has uncovered the fountain of her blood; both of them shall be cut off from among their people. (19) You shall not uncover the *nakedness* of your mother's sister or of your father's sister, for that is to make *naked* one's near kin; they shall bear their iniquity.

1 Sam 19,24: And he too stripped off his clothes, and he too prophesied before Samuel, and lay *naked* all that day and all that *night*. Hence it is said, "Is Saul also among the prophets?"

2 Sam 6,14-16: (14) And David danced **before the Lord** with all his might; and David was girded with a *linen* ephod [cf. 1 Sam 2,18]. (15) So David and all the house of Israel brought up the *ark of the Lord* with shouting, and with the *sound of the horn*. (16) As the *ark of the Lord* came into the city of David, Michal the daughter of Saul looked out of the window, and saw King David leaping and dancing **before the Lord** and she despised him in her heart.

2 Ch 28,15a: And the men who have been mentioned by name rose and took the captives, and with the spoil they clothed all that were *naked* among them;

Job 1,21a: And he said, "*Naked* I came from my mother's womb, and *naked* shall I return;

Job 22,6: For you have exacted pledges of your brothers for nothing, and stripped the *naked* of their clothing.

Job 24,7-10: (7) They lie all *night naked*, without clothing, and have no covering in the cold. (8) They are wet with the rain of the *mountains*, and cling to the *rock* for want of shelter. (9) (There are those who snatch the *fatherless* child [see "Widow's Son"] from the breast, and take in pledge the infant of the poor.) (10) They go about *naked*, without clothing; hungry, they carry the sheaves [cf. "Three Bodies"].

Job 26,6: *Sheol* is *naked* before God, and Abaddon has no covering.

Eccles 5,15: As he came from his mother's womb he shall go again, *naked* as he came, and shall take nothing for his toil, which he may carry away in his hand.

Is 20,2-4: (2) At that time the Lord had spoken by Isaiah the son of Amoz, saying, "Go, and loose the sackcloth from your loins and take off your shoes from your feet," and he had done so, walking *naked* and barefoot—(3) the Lord said, "As my servant Isaiah has walked *naked* and barefoot for *three years* as a sign and a portent against *Egypt* and Ethiopia, (4) so shall the king of Assyria lead away the Egyptians captives and the Ethiopians exiles, both the *young* and the old, *naked* and barefoot, with buttocks uncovered, to the shame of *Egypt*.

Ezek 16,7b,22,39: (7b) And you [Jerusalem] grew up and became tall and arrived at full maidenhood; your breasts were formed, and your hair had grown; yet you were *naked* and bare.... (22) And in all your abominations and your harlotries you did not *remember* the days of your *youth*, when you were *naked* and bare, weltering in your *blood*.... (39) And I will give you into the hand of your lovers, and they shall throw down your vaulted chamber and break down your lofty places; they shall strip you of your clothes and take your fair jewels, and leave you *naked* and bare.

Ezek 23,29: and they shall deal with you in hatred, and take away all the fruit of your labor, and leave you *naked* and bare, and the *nakedness* of your harlotry shall be uncovered.

Hos 2,3: lest I strip her *naked* and make her as in the day she was born, and make her like a *wilderness*, and set her like a parched land, and slay her with thirst.

Amos 2,16: " ... and he who is stout of heart among the mighty shall fall away *naked* in that day," says the Lord.

Mic 1,8: For this I will lament and wail; *I will go stripped and naked*; I will make lamentation like the jackals, and mourning like the ostriches.

Mt 25,36,38,43,44: (36) I was *naked* and you clothed me, ... (38) And when did we see thee ... *naked* and clothe thee? (43) I was ... *naked* and you did not clothe me.... (44) Then they also will answer, "Lord, when did we see thee ... *naked* ... and did not minister to thee?"

Mk 14,51-52: (51) And a *young man* followed him, with nothing but a linen cloth about his body; and they seized him, (52) but he left the linen cloth and ran away *naked*.

Acts 19,16: And the man in whom the evil spirit was leaped on them, mastered all of them, and overpowered them, so that they fled out of that house *naked* and wounded.

2 Cor 5,2-3: (2) Here indeed we groan, and long to put on our heavenly dwelling, (3) so that by putting it on we may not be found *naked*.

Rev 3,17-18: (17) For you say, I am rich, I have prospered, and I need nothing; not knowing that you are wretched, pitiable, poor, blind, and *naked*. (18) Therefore I counsel you to buy from me gold refined by fire, that you may be rich, and *white garments* [see "White Robe" and "Garments"] to clothe you and to keep the shame of your *nakedness* from being seen, and salve to anoint your eyes, that you may see.

Rev 16,15: ("Lo, I am coming like a *thief*! Blessed is he who is awake, keeping his *garments* that he may not go *naked* and be seen exposed!")

Rev 17,16: And the ten horns that you saw, they and the beast will hate the harlot; they will make her desolate and *naked*, and devour her flesh and burn her up with fire,

Gen 9,22-23: (22) And Ham, the father of Canaan, saw the *nakedness* of his father, and told his two brothers outside. (23) Then Shem and Japheth took a *garment*, laid it upon both their shoulders, and walked backward and covered the *nakedness* of their father; their faces were turned away, and they did not see their father's *nakedness*.

Ex 20,26: "... And you shall not go up by steps to my altar, that your *nakedness* be not exposed on it."

Lev 18: [Not copied herein due to its length and repetitiveness. It is forbidding the "uncovering of nakedness" of various related persons.]

Lev 20,11-21: [This is of the same tenor and seeming significance as Lev 18 above.]

Deut 28,48: therefore you shall serve your enemies whom the Lord will send against you, in hunger and thirst, in *nakedness*, and in want of all things; and he will put a yoke of iron upon your neck, until he has destroyed you.

1 Sam 20,30: Then Saul's anger was kindled against Jonathan, and he said to him, "You son of a perverse, rebellious woman, do I not know that you have chosen the son of Jesse to your own shame, and to the shame of your mother's *nakedness*? ..."

Is 47,3: Your *nakedness* shall be uncovered, and your shame shall be seen. I will take vengeance, and I will spare no man.

Is 57,8: Behind the door and the doorpost you have set up your symbol; for, deserting me, you have uncovered your bed, you have gone up to it, you have made it wide; and you have made a bargain for yourself with them, you have loved their bed, you have looked on *nakedness* [fn: "The meaning of the Hebrew is uncertain."]

Lam 1,8: Jerusalem sinned grievously, therefore she became filthy; all who honored her despise her for they have seen her *nakedness*; yea, she herself groans, and turns her face away.

Ezek 16,8,36-37: (8) When I passed by you again and looked upon you, behold, you were at the age for love; and I spread my skirt over you, and covered your *nakedness*; yea, I plighted my troth to you and entered into a covenant with you, says the Lord God, and you became mine. (36) Thus says the Lord God, Because your shame was laid bare and your *nakedness* uncovered in your harlotries with your lovers, and because of all your idols, and because of the *blood* of your children that you gave to them, (37) therefore, behold, I will gather all your lovers, with whom you took pleasure, all those you loved and those you loathed; I will gather them against you from every side, and will uncover your *nakedness* to them, that they may see all your *nakedness*.

Ezek 22,10: In you [Jerusalem] men uncover their fathers' *nakedness*; in you they humble women who are unclean in their impurity.

Ezek 23,10,18,29: (10) These uncovered her *nakedness*; they seized her sons and her daughters; and her they slew with the sword; and she became a byword among women, when judgment had been executed upon her. (18) When she carried on her harlotry so openly and flaunted her *nakedness*, I turned in disgust from her, as I had turned from her sister. (29) [See Ezek 23,29 above.]

Hos 2,9: [See Hos 2,3 above.] Therefore I will take back my grain in its time, and my wine in its season; and I will take away my wool and my flax, which were to cover her *nakedness*.

Mic 1,11: [See Mic 1,8 above.] Pass on your way, inhabitants of Shaphir, in *nakedness* and shame; the inhabitants of Zaanan do not come forth; the wailing of Bethezel shall take away from you its standing place.

Nah 3,5: Behold, I am against you, says the Lord of hosts, and will lift up your skirts over your face; and I will let nations look on your *nakedness* and kingdoms on your shame.

Rom 8,35: Who shall separate us from the love of Christ? Shall tribulation, or distress, or persecution, or famine, or *nakedness*, or peril, or sword?

THREE BODIES

W E SAW IN "MYSTERIES" how the Bible itself embodies the theme, variously expressed, that the spiritual world has "hidden its face" from humanity. Perhaps no other "term or phrase" herein exposes the reader to such sheer magnitude in Biblical usage as "threefoldedness."[1] This phenomenon must either pass one by as an unnoticed or insignificant stranger in the dark, or else whisper, speak or shout its meaning to the soul as it will. But the "Darkness" surrounding the usage can hardly be dispelled without anthroposophical light.

Not only is "three" significant standing alone, but it is a component or factor in the other holy numbers "seven" and "twelve," e.g., 4 + 3, 3 + 1 + 3, (3 x 3) + 3, 4 x 3. The significance of all of these can be seen, for instance, in **I-1**, **I-6**, **I-7**, **I-8**, **I-9**, as well as in many subsequent Charts & Tabulations.

The reader who by now has read all the foregoing portion of this volume will have come upon countless references to the "three bodies" of the human being. And by now their respective names, physical, etheric and astral, will immediately be recognized. But their immense importance to any deeper understanding of the Bible message requires that they again be portrayed at this focal point. It would be well for the reader to review the

---

1. No suggestion is here intended that other numbers appearing in scripture are not significant. Quite the contrary! In fact, the Bible surely cannot be considered to have been free from the influence that "numbers" had on the consciousness of humanity of that era. Steiner assures us that Pythagoras (ca. 580-500 B.C.) traveled to Babylon to study under Zarathas, under whom studied also Israel's "middle period prophets" (see, in Andrew Welburn, *The Book with Fourteen Seals,* the listing of the 14, esp. #viii, "Zaratas [sixth century B.C.]"). The setting of the time powerfully suggests, as do so many passages themselves, that numbers carry a hidden meaning. See also "Number-Weight-Measure." Only the lower integers "one" (presumably, since it is not collated in my concordance) and "two" are used more frequently, but by inspection would seem so often to be used less significantly. Contextually, no number seems to be more frequently emphasized than the number three in its various forms. And as can be seen, so many of its usages do not actually employ the term itself but do so by image or metaphor.

extensive descriptions in the last one-third of the General Introduction
and in the entirety, but particularly the first two-thirds, of the Overview.
The serious student will also want to read about them in *Occult Science*
(OS), Chaps. 2 and 3 and *Theosophy* (THSY), Chap. 1. One who has
assimilated all the foregoing will have the basic tools for understanding,
but in truth all of the vast reach of Steiner's revelations will continue to
add to the student's deeper discernment. Both science and religion, if they
are to meaningfully progress, must come to comprehend the momentous
reality, the pervasive reach, of the three bodies and the essential nature of
the threefold, fourfold, sevenfold and ninefold human being (as schema-
tized in **I-9**).

We are told by Moses that the Exusiai, the Elohim, whom we have
long called "God," created the heavens and the earth in six days and
rested upon the seventh (Gen 1,1-2,4a). In the first essay of Vol. 2,
"*What is Man?*", "Alpha and Omega > Creation and Apocalypse," we
look at the meaning of these "days." In Genesis, they relate to the
"earth's" creation, including all of its creatures. But at the outset, in Gen
1,2, we are told that three elements (water, air and fire) are already in
etheric existence. We have to go to the prologue of John's Gospel (Jn
1,1-3) if we are to reach further back to "the Word" that gave rise to
these three, to "all things" that were "made." So, in the larger context, in
the fractal nature of creation, there are really to be seven "days" of even
larger dimension than those described in Gen 1,1-2,4a. Abraham
brought the knowledge of this with him from Mesopotamia. See 12 Brit
555, "week." From that misty dawn of human earthly, sensate consciousness has come the names of the days of our week. The first larger
day was that of Ancient Saturn, the second Ancient Sun, and the third
Ancient Moon. And so from time immemorial has humanity called the
first three days of its seven-day week Saturday or Saturn's Day, Sunday
or Sun's Day, and Monday or Moon's Day. Before human understanding of these things faded, the other days of the week were also known to
relate to the larger "days" of creation, reflecting the fact that Earth is in
the middle, the fourth Condition of Consciousness, and that three more
will follow after the Earth ceases to exist. Tuesday (Mar's Day, or
"Mardi," as in "Mardi Gras") describes the first half of Earth evolution.
Wednesday describes the second, Mercury's (or "Woden's") Day, the
period commencing with the Incarnation of Christ, the "morning star"
(Rev 2,28) of Mercury. Thursday is Jupiter's Day, "Thor's Day," and

Friday is Venus' Day. All the seven visible planets of our Earth evolution, with its "time" measurements, are thus reflected in the days of our week. See **I-8**.

The "Seed" of the physical body was laid down during Ancient Saturn, that of the etheric body during Ancient Sun, and that of the astral body during Ancient Moon. The purpose of Earth evolution, in its entirety, as the fourth larger "day," is to implant and perfect the human Ego, the "I Am" (see "I AM"). Just as Wisdom was implanted during Ancient Moon, Love is to be implanted during the Earth Condition of Consciousness, i.e., evolution. Thus, as indicated in **I-14**, the fourfold human being relates to the four Conditions of Consciousness up through Earth evolution as follows:

Human Component	Origin
Physical body	Ancient Saturn
Etheric body	Ancient Sun
Astral body	Ancient Moon
Ego (the "I")	Earth

The coming of Christ enabled the human Ego that embraces and etherically assimilates the "Blood" of Christ to commence the "Perfection" of the three bodies, starting with the astral, then the etheric, and finally the physical. During the balance of Earth evolution, perfection will only be manifested, however, through the Consciousness Soul, the highest one-third of the human soul, or Ego (see **I-9**).[2] Manifestation of the higher three states of the sevenfold human being will occur, progressively, as follows:

---

2. What is said here refers to humanity in general. Steiner says that the initiate is one who perceives what humanity in general will come to only in the distant future. The highest initiates thus perceive far into the future. It is even possible for a soul to advance so far as to satisfy all karmic need to incarnate again. This happens when the Individuality has satisfied all karmic demands. Luke speaks of this (see Lk 20,35-36; cf. vs 37); it is also the Adam Cadmon state portrayed in **I-23**, where the astral body is completely purified. The next higher state is that of the Bodhisattva, and then of Buddhahood. The Bodhisattva returns in the personality of a servant of humanity. Many anthroposophists, including myself, feel that the Rudolf Steiner Individuality is the Bodhisattva who will become the Maitreya Buddha in the Age of Philadelphia (Rev 3,7-13; see **I-25** and **I-19**).

Future Human Component	Condition of Consciousness in Which Manifested
Manas, or Spirit Self	Jupiter
Buddhi, or Life Spirit	Venus
Atma, or Spirit Man	Vulcan (the eighth or octave, when all of creation will resonate at a higher level with the tonic in "the music of the spheres")

In the final state, that of atma, the saved of humanity will have returned to the bosom of the Father whence it first departed as the Prodigal Son, but in a condition transformed by all of its long journey into materiality. The human being will thus be ennobled as the tenth Hierarchy, just below the angels as "gods" (Jn 10,34-35; Ps 82,6), but revered by all the Heavenly Host for what it has become. This is when the "three measures of flour" will have been fully "leavened," for then the human being is back in the "kingdom of heaven" in the fullest sense (Mt 13,33).

When Christian creeds speak of "the resurrection of the body," they speak of a verity, but one that is hard for humanity to understand today. There is no resurrection of the mineral-physical body. To the extent that the three bodies become purified, their extracts are preserved and reborn as the soul reincarnates. Christ alone, as the "First Born/Fruit" of humanity, has attained to the perfection of all three bodies so that even his physical body was resurrected. But it was not his mineral-physical body![3] It was the body, i.e., the "Form/Phantom," the seed that was planted in Ancient Saturn. To "see" it, one must attain high status, or be divinely blessed, as some of his apostles were. Even to see his lower bodies requires high spiritual vision. The two who appeared in "dazzling apparel" at the tomb in Luke's Gospel were Christ's etheric and astral bodies (Lk 24,4; Jn 20,12).

---

3. Steiner speaks of what happened to the mineral-physical body of Jesus. And he asserts unequivocally that the tomb was empty. Not from any human removal was it so. He deals with this specifically in *From Jesus to Christ* (JTC), Lect. 8, and *The Fifth Gospel* (FG), Lect. 2. In a later volume, we will look at these in detail. For now, it must suffice to say that no human being witnessed the mineral-physical body of Jesus after its entombment. It did not rise, but was divinely disposed of in accordance with generally applicable laws of the physical and spiritual worlds. The physical body that was seen, the "Form/Phantom," or pattern, had no mineral content, hence could pass through closed doors (Jn 20,26) and the like.

The physical body, in its highest sense, is invisible. It is like the pattern by which the mineral-physical body is built—rather like the plans conceived by an architect. The architectural activity actually occurs in the journey between death and rebirth, based upon karmic necessity. See **I-33**. Later, the term "Form/Phantom" will be addressed. This is the pattern (cf. Heb 8,5; Col 2,17; Ex 25,40). Nothing exists within our sensate world save that it is first designed according to such a pattern in the spiritual world (Jn 1,3). The initiate, prophet or "Seer" can observe these patterns. Normal humanity, in its present state, cannot. Cf. *Flatland* (FLd).

The etheric body is also known as the life body because it is the fashioner and healer of the physical body, and when it departs from the physical body, then the laws of life cease to apply and those of the mineral world take over. The etheric body does not depart from the physical during human life. When it does depart, death immediately occurs, and the mineral-physical body commences to return to the natural mineral state.

The difference between sleep and death is the locale of the etheric body (see **I-10**). Neither the physical nor the etheric body has any perception of pain or consciousness. As a consequence, many of the most deadly illnesses do not reveal themselves by pain until well advanced and impinging upon the astral body functions. The etheric body is also the repository for the memory of events in this and former lives, which one may or may not be able to call back to consciousness. But there is no earthly consciousness in the etheric body itself. Habits and addictions created by actions of the astral body and Ego are etched into the etheric body and, in time, into the physical body. Still, the etheric body is one of (formative) forces, fluidic and always moving. To this day, science cannot explain why the human being must have sleep rather than simply rest. This necessity is symbiotic with that to reincarnate. The astral body must be restored in the "astral world" when it is outside the physical and etheric bodies during sleep. The astral body is restored by sleep, the etheric body by death. It is impossible for the human being to stay alive and conscious in the senses for more than two or three days. This is the protection divinely given to correct daily the deadly consequences of the Fall upon the three bodies, especially the astral, during one's life on Earth.

The astral body is the seat of all earthly senses, in both the human being and the animal. The nervous system is the creation and servant of the astral body. All passion and desire originate there. The astral body was infected by Luciferic influence prior to the entry of the human Ego, and it in turn infected the etheric and physical bodies, particularly as the young "I Am" succumbed to the infection's irresistible power. By the time of Christ, all human "members" (Rom 7,23) were powerless to prevail against the infection. It was too strong for the human Ego not yet strengthened by the higher "I Am" of Christ.

As we shall see below, the three bodies are addressed in the Lord's Prayer (bread/physical; debts, trespasses or guilt/etheric; temptation/astral). In *The Lord's Prayer* (LP), Steiner gives helpful descriptions, calling the physical body "a continual thoroughfare," for "in and out of it ... the substances continuously flow that are at one time of the outer world and at another time within us," and in the course of seven years are completely renewed. "The astral body ... is the vehicle of ... impulse, desire and passion, all that surges up and down in the soul as joy and sorrow, pleasure and pain. The etheric body ... is the vehicle that represents and bears within it the more lasting qualities of the soul ... [such as] temperament, character and tendencies that are persisting and continuing." He compares the etheric body to the hour hand and the astral body to the minute hand of a clock, but one can carry the simile further by equating the three bodies as

Second hand	=	astral body
Minute hand	=	etheric body
Hour hand	=	physical body

In this analogy we can begin to see how the more volatile astral body (second hand) has an impact upon the less ephemeral etheric body (minute hand), and then through it eventually even upon the dense physical body (hour hand). Normally, however, the influence of the astral upon the physical, and to a lesser extent the etheric, must carry over from one life to another. Thus consider the healing of the physical body by the etheric body as portrayed in **I-37**.

The human being who appears to our senses today is the totality of fourfold-being. It is impossible, absent all such parts, for human life to exist on Earth.[4] When the human being sleeps, the Ego and astral body

---

4. Thus, in "The Nativity" we saw that the "three bodies" of the Solomon Jesus child of Matthew's Gospel died soon after the Zarathustra Ego left it to inhabit the three bodies of the Nathan Jesus child. The scene of the twelve-year-old Jesus portraying this momentous, heaven-designed event, is thus given only in Luke's Gospel (Lk 2,41-51), as is the child's development between twelve and "Thirty" (vs 52).

withdraw from their imprisonment within the physical body, but the etheric or life body stays behind. Upon death, the etheric and astral bodies, along with the Ego, leave the physical body, but remain themselves joined together for a short time, up to about "Three Days," measured by how long the person, starting from a position of rest following sound, restorative sleep, could remain alive and conscious without returning to sleep. During this time, the joinder of the two higher "bodies" and the Ego, freed from the constraints of the physical body, makes possible a tableau of the complete life just ended, with particular reference to its destiny at birth. At the end of this period, the non-perfected portion of the etheric body falls away into the general ether of the Earth, while the perfected extract remains for the Individuality to re-enter in a future incarnation (as a "treasure laid up in heaven," so to speak, Mt 6,20).

Then the astral body and Ego enter the astral world, a sojourn that gave rise, however imperfectly, to the Roman Catholic doctrine of Purgatory. Here all of the "astralities" of the soul in the life just ended must be burned away in the "refiner's fire" (see "Purifying Fire"). Short of the ultimate fire reserved for Satan and his retinue (Rev 20,14), this can be said to be the "eternal" fires of hell (see fn 5 in "Lord of Karma"). All of one's earthly sins must here be judged by, and in the painfully purifying "Light" of, the "Lord of Karma." All of the astral body not purified on Earth must be burned, and fall away into the astral world at large. This is well portrayed in the account of "the rich man and Lazarus" (not Lazarus/John) in Luke's Gospel (Lk 16,19-31). There the consciousness of the astral body and the Ego is extreme. All the unpurified desires, addictions and shortcomings of the earthly life are felt with immeasurable urgency, but with no physical body to permit their satisfaction. Torment is severe. The "golden rule" of Mt 7,12 becomes real, for one experiences all of life's dealings from the eyes of those dealt with or affected—including those who cried for help and were denied or ignored (cf. Mt 25,31-46). What is experienced here is lived through in reverse, from the end of life back to its beginning (see "Last First, First Last"). This period lasts approximately one-third as long as the life just ended, being the amount of time spent in sleep—for during sleep the astral body was nightly shown these things. To the extent that earthly actions were in accordance with the divine, then those portions of this period in the astral world result in unspeakable joy. And just as the unpurified portion of the etheric body must fall away, so it is also with the astral body; but the perfected extract remains for future use by the soul. The individual animal, of course, has no such experience, for it has no Ego dwelling on Earth (see **I-11**).[5]

The portions of the three bodies that are purified on Earth become "Garments" that clothe the soul's "Nakedness." They are sometimes referred to as "wedding garments" (Mt 22,11-12), with special reference to that marriage of the "Bride/Bridegroom" in Rev 21,2. Ultimately then the three bodies cannot be properly thought of without their spiritual reflection on the other side of the "river"[6] of the Ego, as shown in the sevenfoldedness and ninefoldedness of the human being. Some of the passages considered below seem clearly to envision both the lower and higher aspects of the three bodies.

Before we examine the passages themselves, let us reflect upon whether there is a relationship between the three bodies and the pervasiveness of "threefoldedness" in the Bible. Taken collectively, the constancy of the recurring threefold theme can hardly fail to impress us with the seeming fact that there must be some immense spiritual significance, in our Biblical evolutionary epoch, to the number three, a significance that, though noted (see 4 ABD 1145, "Numbers and Counting"), thus far seems to have escaped detection. The number three has many obvious applications, but the mere fact that it has an application other than one directly relevant to our three bodies topic may not preclude it from also having

---

5. The animal bodies are not so refined as the human (the same is true of the even lower Plant and Mineral Kingdoms). We said earlier that the human being whose Ego departs cannot live on Earth (see fn 4), but the Animal Kingdom is different. Something of the finer development of the human body that makes it possible for the human Ego to live on Earth is discussed in "Blood," in Vol. 2.

6. See the Ego's characterization as the "river" in Ezek 47 below, the Biblical version of the ancient legend of the River Lethe which causes the human being, in crossing, to forget its past. See also Eccles 1,11; 3,11. We read, in 18 Brit 763 at 786, "European Religions, Ancient, Greek religion, Beliefs, practices, and institutions," about how the River Styx in the Elysian (Orphic) Mysteries came to be called the River Lethe:

> But the doctrines of the Orphics influenced Pindar, Empedocles, and, above all, Plato. According to the latter, the dead were judged in a meadow by Aeacus, Minos, and Rhadamanthus and were consigned either to Tartarus or to the Isles of the Blest. Long periods of purgation were required before the wicked could regain their celestial state, while some were condemned forever. The dead were permitted to choose lots for their next incarnation. Subsequently they drank from the stream of Lethe, the river of oblivion, and forgot all of their previous experiences.

We cannot help noting that the judicial panel above is threefold, and thus seems to correspond with the three bodies of the human being that must eventually be purified.

relevance thereto. If we ask how this could be so, we have but to consider the nature of creation as reflected by the discussion of "Fractals" (and its neighboring discussions) in Appendix to "Fire," Vol. 2. The fractal nature of creation is another example of the application of the spiritual principle "As Above, So Below." Inasmuch as the human being's three bodies relate back to the three Conditions of Consciousness (**I-1**) preceding Earth evolution, the magnitude of their application throughout such evolution, considering the fractal nature thereof, would seem to give a degree of relevance to Biblical passages embodying threefoldedness. Expressed another way, given the observed phenomena of the fractal nature of creation, and given that three Conditions of Consciousness preceded the one (Earth) that would create the human Ego, is it not probable that the structure into which the Ego is to enter would be threefold? And conversely, given a threefold human structure, does that not imply, under the fractal principle, a higher threefoldedness involved in its creative process? Even the development of the theological doctrine of the Trinity follows that divine pattern.

While the classification is subjective, the illustrations below are divided into the following categories:

    A. Scriptures most directly indicative of "three bodies"

    B. Scriptures readily suggestive of "three bodies"

    C. Scriptures indicative of threefoldedness

However, within each division, except for the first two examples in A, the advantages of keeping the canonical order seems to outweigh those of further classification.

One other preliminary observation seems worthwhile. The serious Bible student must admit that, absent anthroposophical understanding, numerous passages still remain mysterious. Either they have been ignored and leapt over, or given a bland and childishly trite interpretation, or they have plunged their students into the depths of erudite nonsense. They have betrayed to the minds of scholars, clergy and laymen alike no truly significant meaning. The intellectually honest must admit to wondering why they are even in scripture.

What could be more critical in this regard than a prophecy (i.e., teaching; 1 Cor 14) that brings amazing new depth of meaning to passages that have always been either obscure or simplistically understood? All possible meanings should be fairly weighed and judged. When the teachings of Steiner are fairly considered, then all the Bible passages can be seen to fit with them and with phenomena like a glove. The conscientious reader may have come to this conclusion from what has already been said herein. But the principle applies forcefully to so many of the passages we are about to examine, and how rich the meaning becomes when one does see them so revealed. And not only so, but the entire Bible message takes on an integrity of meaning so overwhelming that one comes to understand why these passages were written in this manner in the first place. It was so that, when the time was right and the Truth was finally revealed, it would fit with what had been said of old and give it richness and fullness like never before.

With that in mind, we now turn our attention to the scriptures themselves.

SCRIPTURES MOST DIRECTLY INDICATIVE OF "THREE BODIES"

Two Selected Examples:

1. **Mt 13,33**: He told them another parable. "The kingdom of heaven is like leaven which a woman took and hid in three measures of flour, till it was all leavened."

This succinct parable is a paragon of simile. How could the imagination of the three bodies, each with the germ (i.e., "leaven") of its spiritual counterpart implanted, attaining their higher states associated with the Kingdom of Heaven be more perfectly described? The reader is encouraged to investigate the commentaries on this passage. Those in the Bibliography herein, including the excellent *New Interpreter's Bible* (NIB), fall far short, by comparison with anthroposophical insight, in revealing the simple perfection of this parable's description.

Who is the "woman" who hid the leaven? Anthroposophy is her namesake. She is the holy virgin Anthropo-Sophia. See **I-18** and Prokofieff's *The Heavenly Sophia and the Being Anthroposophia* (HSBA); see also Prov 8,22-31. She is the focus of the Apocryphal Wisdom of Solomon (see 43 AB) and Wisdom of Ben Sira (see 39 AB), both found in the Catholic Bible (NJB and NACB) and some protestant versions.

The "three measures" are the "three bodies" created in the first three Conditions of Consciousness, Old Saturn, Sun and Moon. As each "body" existed in its original "Condition," it represented harmony between its inner and outer, or higher and lower, parts. Thus, on ancient Saturn, the physical body was spiritual heat that became the human phantom (see "Form/Phantom"), and at that harmonious stage comprised what is known as "atma," or Spirit Man. During the ancient Sun Condition of Consciousness, this physical body divided into its higher and lower parts. Similar processes occurred with each of the "three bodies" as Condition succeeded Condition. These ancient Conditions were recapitulated during the first Conditions of Life and Form of Earth evolution (see **I-1**). These are set out in some detail in OS and are summarized in the first essay in Vol. 2.

The "woman," Anthropo-Sophia, is a real sevenfold spiritual being who comprises the combined spiritual activity during Earth evolution of the lowest seven Hierarchies, from the Kyriotetes (Spirits of Wisdom, or Dominions; see **I-6**) down to the tenth hierarchical rank, the Human Being. The Anthroposophia is visually presented in the first two columns of the chart in **I-18**. During Earth evolution, the Anthroposophia, the combined activity of these Hierarchies, placed the "leaven," the "Seed" of the three human spiritual states, in the human being's "three bodies," the "three measures of flour." The Christ, the higher "I Am," acting through the agency of the Anthroposophia and her own agents, especially the Archangel Michael, "leavens" the three lower human "measures" into their three corresponding spiritual states. Only the first can occur as a result of Earth evolution. The purified astral body will be transformed into the bridal manas ("Manna," or Spirit Self) in the Jupiter Condition, the Holy City, the New Jerusalem (Rev 21).

The full transformation of the "three bodies" ("measures of flour") into "leavened" loaves is reflected in the sevenfold human being. It is brought about by the sevenfold nature, the "seven pillars," of the Anthroposophia. Under the "As Above, So Below" law of creation, she "has built her house, she has set up her seven pillars" (Prov 9,1). When the third "measure," the physical body, has been transformed into atma, Spirit Man, in the Venus Condition of Consciousness, then the "kingdom of heaven" will be fully present in the human being as the tenth rank in the Hierarchies (Jn 10,34; Ps 82,6).

The early Church Fathers did not dwell on this passage. Their only significant reference to it may be the brief one by Clement of Alexandria

(A.D. 153-217)[7] in *The Stromata, or Miscellaneous*, Book V, Chap. XII (2 Nicene-1 463). He opens this chapter by quoting "the truth-loving Plato," then "Orpheus, the theologian" to lay the groundwork for quoting Paul's reference to "the third heaven" (2 Cor 12,2). He then discusses Plato's *Timaeus* and comes to the "unleavened cakes" (referring to Gen 18,6) and Philo's interpretation of them.[8] Clement says that "the prophet [Moses] meant [when he ordered the cakes to be made] that the truly sacred mystic word, respecting the unbegotten and His powers, ought to be concealed." Going on he says, "And now, by the parable of the leaven, the Lord shows concealment," and he quotes Mt 13,33. What he says next is revealing (emphasis mine):

> For *the tripartite soul* is saved by obedience, through the spiritual power hidden in it by faith....

Where did this knowledge of "the tripartite soul" go between the time of Philo, Paul and Clement and the time of Steiner? The blessings of insight from the Apostolic Age faded. The teachings of Clement's student, Origen, on the pre-existence of the soul were anathematized; the darkness of the Middle Ages deepened and the Eighth Ecumenical Council in A.D. 869 declared the spirit non-existent, concluding that while the tripartite body, soul and spirit had until then been thought to compose the human being (1 Th 5,23), thereafter (in orthodoxy) only the body and soul would do so. Finally the time came when even the highest initiates on Earth had no direct spiritual vision but had to rely upon the authority of scripture, other prior writings, and the growing intellect. Such was the case in the time of the towering Aquinas. The exalted Christian Rosenkreutz (see "Pillars on the Journey") would soon thereafter incarnate,

---

7. Not the earlier first-century Clement of Rome.
8. See PHILO 101 ("The Sacrifices of Abel and Cain," para. 60). Here Philo says (my emphasis)

> Now it is very good that these three measures should, as it were, be kneaded together in the soul ... in order that so the soul ... may receive the characters of [God's] power and beneficence, and becoming initiated into the perfect mysteries, may not be too ready to divulge the divine secrets to any one, but may treasure them up in herself, and keeping a check over her speech, may conceal them in silence; for the words of the scripture are, "To make *secret* cakes;" because the sacred and mystic statements about the one uncreated Being, and about his powers, ought to be kept secret; since it does not belong to every one to keep the deposit of divine mysteries properly.

leading to the Renaissance, literally the rebirth, of humanity—the time when the Consciousness Soul (see **I-9**), the highest part of the "tripartite" soul would slowly begin to develop.

If the soul or Ego is thus threefold, surely the human being of which it is a part must be also. And if the human being and the human soul or Ego are thus threefold, does it not suggest that the body and spirit must each be threefold as well? Even the principle and processes of cell division would tell us this. It is in the fractal nature of things.

Both 8 NIB 309 and INTPN, "Matthew," p. 157 recognize the probable relationship between Christ's "three measures of flour" (Mt 13,33) and Moses' "three measures of fine meal" (Gen 18,6). Surely a marvelous depth of spiritual reality must exist in this seemingly simple, but heretofore mystifying, simile. Its most perfect application is to the three bodies of the human being.

2. **Job**: This book and its pertinence to the three bodies is too critical to be overly abbreviated. Still, the scope of the analogy is so great that only some illustrative aspects can be given.

The fractal nature of creation can be seen even in the Bible, and the book of Job is part of that vision. The out-and-back journey of the human being first from, and then to, the spiritual world can be seen in

> One verse in Mt 13,33
> One parable in Lk 15,11-32 (Prodigal Son)
> One chapter in Ezek 47 (as we will see below)
> One book in Job
> One Bible from Genesis through Revelation

If asked to epitomize the book's message, many would call to mind the hackneyed "patience of Job," Jas 5,11 (KJV; cf. RSV "steadfastness"; NIV, "Perseverance"; etc.). It addresses the question of why the seemingly righteous suffer so much, or stated differently, why there is so much inherent inequity among humanity. The answer it literally gives is, however, not really much of an answer, but is rather like the question a child would ask, Why must I do this, Mommy? and the answer, Because I said so! God is God, and that is it! But the search for the answer to Why goes on. The answer does not come from the book of Job unless one understands what it is telling us. I submit that this understanding cannot be had without the light of anthroposophical insight. Job's story is another version of the Prodigal Son parable as it applies to the evolution of the human being.

The three bodies are represented by both the three friends (Job 2,11) and the three cycles of Job's dialogue with them.

> First cycle   =   Chaps. 4 through 14
> Second cycle =   Chaps. 15 through 21
> Third cycle   =   Chaps. 22 through 27

After the three friends speak, a fourth, Elihu, enters. He "had waited to speak because they were older than he" (Job 32,4). From this it may be assumed that the other three spoke in turn from the eldest to the youngest. Thus, Eliphaz represents the physical body, Bildad the etheric body, and Zophar the astral body, while Elihu represents the Ego (the I Am), the youngest of the components of the fourfold human being. Elihu was "of the family of Ram" (Job 32,2), that is to say, of like kind with, or related to, the Lamb, the higher "I Am." (See the tabulations in **I-18** and **I-19** showing that Christ's Incarnation fell within both the Astrological and Cultural Age of Aries, the Ram or Lamb. Cf. Jn 1,29,36; Rev 5,6,12-13.) Further, Elihu, the Ego of the incarnated human being, can be seen as the alter ego of Job during the long course of the out-and-back journey during the Earth Condition of Consciousness. Elihu makes no appearance until the three friends have fully completed their threefold cycle of dialogues, and they make no further comments after Elihu. Nor does Job contend with Elihu after the latter's words (Job 32-37), but rather he then discourses only with God, to which we shall momentarily return.

Even the meanings of the "Names" of the four suggest this understanding. We find the following from ABD:

ELIPHAZ (2 ABD 471)—All the possible meanings relate to God in some manner. The more probable include "God/El is the victor," "God/El is pure/shining" and "God is fine gold." Eliphaz is identified as "the Temanite" (Job 2,11; 4,1; 15,1; 22,1; 42,7,9), Teman being known as a place of wisdom (Jer 49,7). The only one of the friends who speaks of gold is Eliphaz (Job 22,24-25), who speaks of it as "in the dust," and Job's answer refers to "the earth" as having "dust of gold" (Job 28,6). The mineral-physical body, standing alone, is indeed "dust" (Gen 3,19).

BILDAD (1 ABD 741)—The literal meaning of this name is particularly obscure. And little clarification is added by other treatises (see 15 AB 23-24 and 3 Interp 923). But if we consider that the etheric body forms or "builds" the physical, then phonetics may point us rightly. Dictionaries tell us that our word "build" comes from the Old English word *byldan*, and that Old English goes back to the middle of the fifth century A.D. And if we reflect upon the influence of the Indo-European languages even upon that, we are perhaps led back to primeval sounds relating to formative activity like that of the etheric body.

ZOPHAR (6 ABD 1167)—Though problematic, it may be related to "bird." The bird represents what frees itself from the gravity of Earth and soars into the heavens. Within the Animal and Human Kingdoms, it resembles the astral body, which takes its name from the stars it dwells among during sleep (cf. Job 33,14-18).

ELIHU (2 ABD 463)—It can be interpreted as "El/God it was indeed." Certainly this comports with Ex 3,14, "I AM the I AM," that which manifested as the burning "Bush," indicative of the Christ, as well as of the higher and lower human Egos (see "I AM).

But let us consider the construction of the dialogues with the three friends and what it implies in relation to the anthroposophical understanding of creation. We have said that the physical body is the oldest human component, going back in origin to Ancient Saturn; the etheric and astral bodies going back, respectively, to Ancient Sun and Moon. The eldest has the most to tell us. We see that in all cycles Eliphaz speaks more than the others, with Bildad speaking less, and Zophar even less. How is it, though, that Job speaks in response to each friend in every cycle (except in the third where Zophar does not speak at all)? In order to speak, Job had to be in existence during the conversation. The conversations must have occurred during Earth evolution at a time when the Ego was present within the earthly body. We have seen that the Ego progressively penetrated the three bodies during the Lemurian and Atlantean Epochs so that its presence within all three bodies, however primitively at first, effectively started with the post-Atlantean Epoch (see "Naked" and **I-35**).

We are told before any of the dialogues begin that the three friends "sat with him on the ground seven days and seven nights, and that no one spoke a word" because of his great suffering. If we go back to Gen 1,

1-2,4a, we have the seven "days" of creation up through the etheric stage of the Earth Condition of Consciousness. Nothing was yet in mineral-physical existence (Gen 2,5; see also "Alpha and Omega > Creation and Apocalypse," in Vol. 2). Truly, the three bodies have gone through these seven days and nights when no human words were spoken. We are told that these days and nights were "on the ground" (Job 2,13), but they happen after Satan has already afflicted Job (Job 2,7). We thus know that the dialogues are during the Earth Condition of Consciousness but subsequent to the Fall (Gen 3) when the astral body was infected by Lucifer, with consequent progressive infection of the older bodies, making them all subject to the hardening and descent into mineral-physical existence where pain, toil and death result (Gen 3,16-19). Though death results (Gen 3,19), the "I Am" itself does not die (Gen 4,12-15; Job 2,6). It only loses consciousness of its undying eternal nature due to its imprisonment in the mineral-physical body during incarnation.

Thus as a working hypothesis, we would seem to be warranted in ascribing the three cycles of dialogues to the first three Cultural Eras in our present (first) post-Atlantean Evolutionary Epoch.[9] We have a strong hint of this in the opening words of Job cursing the day of his birth (Job 3). He longed to go back to the spiritual world whence he had come, a theme he recapitulates in Job 29, but there it sounds more like the Prodigal Son who has "come to himself" and desires to return to his Father's fold. We have but to compare this longing in chap. 3 to that of the Ancient Indians in the first Cultural Era of our Epoch. We have said that the seven churches in Rev 2-3 represent the seven Cultural Eras. Steiner tells us that in Ancient India there was a yearning to go back, and that it was this that occasioned the complaint of the Christ against them "that you have abandoned the love you had at first" (Rev 2,4). That love was the desire to experience sensate consciousness, the desire that occasioned the Fall. Not until the second Cultural Era, that of Ancient (prehistoric) Persia did humanity, under Zarathustra's leadership, begin to apply itself meaningfully, though ploddingly, to the outer world.

The Ego in Job's account then appears in the Greco-Roman Cultural Era, that in which the Christ, the higher "I Am," walked the Earth and infused its ether with his shed "Blood." This is represented by Elihu (Job

9. We need not be concerned that I-24 assigns them slightly differently, for Job is presenting a somewhat modified profile of the same journey.

32-37), as we can see in so many ways. For instance, to the three friends he says, "It is not the old that are wise" (Job 32,9) and "My heart is like wine that has no vent; like new wineskins, it is ready to burst" (Job 32,19; Mt 9,17; Mk 2,22; Lk 5,37-38; it seems well to consider that the "old wineskins" are the "three bodies" while the "new wineskins" are the three spiritual counterparts, manas, buddhi and atma, into which the "new wine" of the higher "I Am" is to be poured for it will burst the old; however, I wonder if somewhere in the translation process the word "like" was not substituted for "needing," for in the New Testament parallels it is the inelastic old wineskin that bursts), while to Job, "The spirit of God has made me, ... I am toward God as you are" (Job 33,4-6) and "He has redeemed my soul from going down into the Pit, and my life shall see the light" (Job 33,28; Is 9,2).

In chaps. 38-39 the Lord fires ponderous questions to Job, implying his woeful inadequacy of understanding, to which Job makes no answer. One of the significant questions is, "Have the gates of death been revealed to you?" (Job 38,17). Another, after speaking of the Pleiades and Orion, "Do you know the ordinances of the heavens? Can you establish their rule on the earth?" (Job 38,33; see "Zodiac"[10]).

Job 40 and 41 cannot, it would seem, be understood without seeing in them what Steiner describes as the two Guardians of the Threshold, first the Lesser (Job 40) and then the Greater (Job 41). Steiner deals with these in *Knowledge of the Higher Worlds and its Attainment* (KHW), Chaps. 10 and 11. These "guardians" serve a role much like that of the Cherubim with the "flaming sword" of the Seraphim "at the east of the garden" (Gen 3,24). They prevent the entry of the human soul into permanent residence in the higher spiritual world until it has attained "Perfection." The Lesser Guardian is a spectral being created by the human being, normally observable only during the journey between lives. It is the composite picture of the Individuality's karmic debt. Encountering it is a terrifying experience for one not adequately prepared. Preparation involves overcoming the deficiencies of the astral body by developing the "lotus flowers."

10. Robert Powell, building upon the studies of those who first took their lead from Steiner's zodiacal indications, has powerfully demonstrated something of this "rule on the earth," while showing how the conventional practice of astrology went astray from its ancient connection with the stars and the planets. See Powell, *Hermetic Astrology I* (HA1).

The Behemoth of Job 40 is this Lesser Guardian. It is found "where all the wild beasts play" (we will see that the term "wild beasts" [see "Wild Animals"] means the unpurified animal instincts, those taken into the "Ark," the human body, in the transition from Atlantis to our present Epoch). The Lesser Guardian sends us back again and again until we have purified these. It is said that "Under the lotus plants he lies" (vs 21) and that "the lotus trees cover him" (vs 22), which is to say, one cannot pass his threshold without the development of the "lotus flowers" whereby the astral body is transformed into manas, Spirit Self, or "Manna." One who has attained this state retains full consciousness both during sleep and during the transition from earthly life at the gates of death, that is, has overcome death (cf. Job 38,17).

The Leviathan of Job 41 is the Greater Guardian. This guardian poses to the one who has fully transformed the astral body, having satisfied all personal karmic debt and overcome death, the option of enjoying what has been earned by remaining forever in the spiritual world. However, if that is opted, then the Individuality never passes by the Greater Guardian into the higher heaven. For at this point there is no interest in the individual as such, but rather in the entirety of creation. If one is to pass by the Greater Guardian, one must return to the sensible world so long as any others remain therein unredeemed. One's attained powers must be used then for others. Whether this means working from the spiritual world or returning as a lowly servant on Earth, one who is to pass the Greater Guardian must remain tied to the destiny of those still earthbound (cf. Rom 8,19-23). We see this returning illustrated by the activity of the Buddha in "The Nativity." The Greater Guardian is described as "a sublime luminous being" (KHW, Chap. 11, p. 253). Job 41 describes him in terms of light (vs 18) and says of him, "Behind him he leaves a shining wake" (vs 32) and that "He beholds everything that is high, ... king over all the sons of pride" (vs 34).

Job's final words indicate complete submission (Job 42,2-6).

We need not be troubled by the prose portions of the book, for they represent the period before the Fall and after the reascent of Job, that is to say, of the human being. As Steiner tells us, the latter state of humanity will be ennobled, transformed upward by its journey. This is clearly indicated in Job 42,7-17. It makes no difference to the account whether it was written by one or more. In its final canonized form, it tells the story of the Prodigal Son, the human being. The laborious, seemingly endless, redundant dialogues do their job in portraying what seems to us the virtually endless march of time and human evolution with its pain, suffering and death (Gen 3,16-19; 4,12-15; Job 2,6). The fact that each soul has made the long, long journey is consistent with Job 38,21 where, after reciting the very deeds of creation, God says to Job, "You know, for you were born then, and the number of your days is great!"

We have not even begun to scratch the surface of what can now be seen in Job when the light of Steiner's revelations are permitted to fall on it. Here we have only attempted to point the reader in the direction for personal study and contemplation.

Other Examples in Canonical Order:

3. **Gen 1,16**: Lights were made in the heavens, i.e., Sun, Moon and stars. We can well relate their relative influence in the following way:

Moon	Physical	Hard Shape
Sun	Etheric	Life
Stars	Astral	Feeling

4. **Gen 2,21; 15,12; 28,11,16**: Three significant "sleeps" (or "deep sleeps") occur in Genesis:

(a) The first human being (Gen 2,21) is divided into two sexes, whereby Adam, the first "hard" man (Gen 3,17), comes into existence;

(b) Abraham (Gen 15,12) is given insight into the destiny of his descendants; and

(c) Jacob (Gen 28,11,16) has his "ladder" vision.

5. **Gen 3,16,17,19**: Pain, toil and death represent, respectively, the astral, etheric and physical consequences of the Fall.

6. **Gen 6,16**: The Ark Noah was to build (whose three dimensions of 300 by 50 by 30 [vs 15] are in proportion to the physical body of the post-Atlantean human being) was to have three decks, namely, a lower, second and third.

7. **Gen 12,10-20; 20,1-18; 26,1-16**: Three times was the ruse, "She is my sister," used by Abram/Abraham and/or Isaac in dealing with the descendants of Ham's son, Egypt. The first time Abram said it to the Pharaoh in Egypt; the second Abraham said it to the Philistine king Abimelech; and the third Isaac said it to Abimelech. See the discussion on these in "Egypt." Theology has wrestled with and rationalized the immorality of this in such lustrous ancestors, but seeing it as an illustration of the development of the three bodies elevates it above immorality, vindicating the story as a wholesome verity.

8. **Gen 18,2,6**: Three "men" (i.e., angels) appeared to Abraham by the oaks of Mamre (see "Under the Tree"); and he told Sarah to take "three measures of fine meal, knead it and make cakes" (see Mt 13,33 above).

9. **Gen 40,10,18-19**: In the dreams of Joseph's fellow inmates, the butler and the baker, there were three branches that budded (cf. Heb 9,4) and began to grow grapes, and three cake baskets portending death. One can see here in the three cake baskets the three bodies that will become beastly, i.e., die, if not transformed by the Ego to become the three higher spiritual states, represented by the three budding branches. Moreover, just as is the case with Judah in Gen 38 below, Joseph here may be seen as the Ego. He came from the higher zodiacal realm of twelve, as one of Jacob's twelve sons, descended both into a pit and into "Egypt," and was later involved with two rounds of seven (good and bad years), as a result of which he was exalted more highly.

10. **Ex 21,12-14**: Moses is commanded to establish "Cities of Refuge" (see 5 ABD 657) for those who accidentally, or without willfullness, kill another, so they will be able to escape the Mosaic law of retribution. The structure of the pattern of Cities is given in those later books that show the execution of this command: Num 35,9-15; Deut 4,41 and 19,1-13; Josh 20. Three such Cities were to be established "in the land of Canaan" and three "beyond the Jordan" (Num 35,14), i.e., in the "promised land." How beautifully this very structure depicts (see "As Above, So Below") the transformation of the lower three bodies into the higher three states of the "promised land," the "Kingdom of Heaven" (cf. Mt 13,33).

11. **Josh 15,14 and Judg 1,20**: Caleb drives out the "three sons" of Anak. Anak (see 1 ABD 222) represented the daunting giants (e.g. Deut 2,10,21 and 9,2) in the Promised Land of Canaan, announced by the Hebrew spies (e.g., Deut 1,28). More pointedly, Num 13,33 identifies Anak's sons as the "Nephilim," the prehistoric Atlantean giants described in Gen 6,1-4, which accords with the evolutionary development of the human being before its three bodies had condensed and solidified to their post-Atlantean size and shape prescribed by the dimensions of the Ark (Gen 6,15) with its "three decks" (i.e., "bodies"; see Gen 6,16 above). The entire account is an earthly and metaphorical acting out of the heavenly pattern whereby the human being must "drive out" or "transform" the lower three bodies ("three sons") into the higher three spiritual states of manas-buddhi-atma (**I-9**). More immediately, however, was the necessity for Israel, in accordance with that pattern, to drive out the atavistic elements represented by the Nephilim, in order to prepare a human vehicle (Jesus of Nazareth) capable of housing the incarnating Christ (see "The Nativity").

12. **Judg 16**: Samson mocks Delilah three times (vs 15), before he gives up "all his mind" (vs 18) and loses his strength. Note that the number "seven" is used precisely three times (it appears four times but only on three occasions, in vss 7-8, 13 and 19); and also that three thousand (vs 27) looked on Samson with sport; and the dead he slew at his death were more than those whom he had slain during his life (vs 30). Moreover, it was at "Midnight" (vs 3) that "he arose and took hold of the doors of the gate of the city … and carried them to the top of the hill that is before Hebron" ("City of Four" per 3 ABD 107; i.e., enter the "I Am"). The symbolism in this chapter is incredibly descriptive of the human being's evolutionary cycle, with its three bodies, each related to a cycle of seven, and the "I Am" ("all his mind"); and the high point ("top of the hill") of each journey between lives is its "Midnight" hour (see **I-33**).

13. **Ezek 41,6; 42,3,6**: Similarly to the Ark that Noah built with three decks (see #6 above), these passages speak of "three stories" in the temple in Ezekiel's vision. Indeed, the "Temple" of the human soul (Ego, or "I Am") is composed of the threefold Body, which the Lord (the "I Am") enters and dwells within. Later herein we will see that "Temple," in the

more restrictive sense, applies only to the astral body (see #39, Rev 21,22 and 11,1-2). In that case, the lower two bodies, the physical and etheric, compose "the court outside the temple" (Rev 11,2), those parts which will not be fully "Perfected" during Earth evolution, but must await the Jupiter and Venus Conditions of Consciousness (see I-1).

14. **Ezek 47,3-6**: Ezek 47 can be seen to present the entirety of the Bible within a single chapter, from the creation to ultimate redemption. For an exposition see the Commentary. However, vss 3-6 can be seen, within that framework, to portray both the three Conditions of Consciousness (Old Saturn, Sun and Moon) prior to Earth evolution, during which the human being's three bodies had their respective origins, and the first three Evolutionary Epochs of Earth evolution (Polarian, Hyperborean, Lemurian) leading up to the time when the human being loses its atavistic clairvoyance and its "remembrance" of former things (incarnations). This is portrayed by the "eastward" (see "East") journey "through the water," which progressed in three stages, from "ankle-deep" to "knee-deep" and then "up to the loins," before becoming "a river that could not be passed through." This "river" can be seen as the legendary River Lethe that cannot be crossed by the human being's consciousness during the present Epoch. Thus, during the time of the three bodies, before the earthly development of the Ego, one could "cross" the water with consciousness, but in the fourth stage it could not be done—unless, presumably, one becomes a "Son of man," as was Ezekiel in the vision. See fn 6.

15. **Dan 3**: This seems one of the clearer visions depicting the human being's fourfoldedness. Three men, Shadrach, Meshach and Abednego, are thrown into the fiery furnace, which is so hot that it slew those who threw them into it. Yet the king then saw not three, but four, "walking in the midst of the fire, and ... not hurt." Then it says, "and the appearance of the fourth is like a son of the gods." In the period between lives, the three bodies do not survive except to the extent they have been "Perfected," (transformed). In particular, in the astral world (cf. Purgatory) the unperfected portions of the astral body are burned away in the eternal fire. But the Ego, though it suffers, is not consumed there (see "Bush"). This vision would seem to portray a perfected Ego, which means that its related bodies have also been perfected and thus are not lost but preserved. "The

appearance of the fourth" (the Ego) "like a son of the gods" bespeaks the level of spiritual development akin to that in Rev 1,12-16, which carries the "burning Bush" beyond reincarnation to the point of worthiness for the resurrection (see Lk 20,34-38).[11]

16. **Hos 1-2**: The human being's three bodies can be seen portrayed here in both their lower and higher aspects, as elements of the sevenfold human being. From that perspective, the prophetic language describes humanity's leaving the spiritual world in terms of "harlotry" simply because it was a descent or departure therefrom. There were three children of such "harlotry," identifiable to the first three Conditions of Consciousness (Old Saturn, Sun and Moon), whereby the three bodies were respectively created. The children, in order were (Hos 1):

a Son, "Jezreel," symbolizing the spiritual apostasy of Israel (vs 4);
a Daughter, "Not Pitied" (vs 6); and
a Son, "Not My People" (vs 9).

The "Names" alone portray the progressive separation of the three bodies from the spiritual realm. Then in vs 10 those to whom it is first said, "You are not my people," are assured that they are "Sons of the living God." This would seem to be the introduction of the Ego, the lower human "I Am." Next we are told in vs 11 that "one head" shall be appointed, and they will then "go up from the land." Here we can see the coming of the Christ as the higher "I Am" in the flesh. Thus ends Chapter 1. In Chapter 2 there is an immediate reversal of direction, for the second son is called "My People," and then the daughter is called "She Has Obtained Pity" (though both may be tentative, in light of vs 4, unless and until the Mother returns). But as yet, the first son is not

---

11. It is interesting that in Rev 1,12-16, the head, feet and right hand are transformed (see #32, 2 K 9,35). As Steiner has shown us, Rev 1,12-16 represents the fully perfected ninefold human being, the "Son of Man" (three threefold groupings; i.e., long robe-golden girdle-white wool, flame of fire-burnished bronze-many waters, and seven stars-two-edged sword-sun shining in full strength). Steiner also spoke of the nine beatitudes as representing the ninefold human being. We might see in them the lower "son of Man" and in Rev 1,12-16 the higher "Son of Man." Analogously, along with that higher (transformed) ninefold division of the human being, in reversed simile, are the sevenfold (or ninefold, if the hyphenated words are not combined) parts of the human mineral-physical body (i.e., breast, head-hair, eyes, feet, voice-mouth, right hand and face).

embraced. A long harangue against the Mother's harlotry follows, shading into tenderness and allurement that effectively secures her return; then in the last verse all three children are affirmed. What better interpretation of this could there be than that it is an analogy of the three bodies and the sevenfold human being?

17. **Mt 4 and Lk 4**: The synoptic Gospels unanimously say that the temptation of Jesus immediately followed the settling of the Christ Spirit, the "Dove," upon him. But that Spirit, the higher "I Am" that replaced the withdrawn Ego of Zarathustra in Jesus of Nazareth, had first to penetrate the three bodies of Jesus before he could fully carry out the Christ mission. The reader will recall that Steiner's diagram from *The Influence of Spiritual Beings upon Man* (ISBM) in "Naked" above showed how the Ego only gradually, over long eons of time, penetrated the human being's three bodies, first the astral, then the etheric and finally the physical. Since we are approaching a somewhat abstruse refinement in the relationship of the three Temptations of Jesus to the three bodies, let us first fix in our mind that the human Ego plausibly entered the youngest and rarest body (the astral) first and the oldest and densest body (the physical) last. The Christ Spirit, the highest "I Am," had also to penetrate the three bodies of Jesus in the same order. The account of this event is given in the three Temptations. However, the Ego of Christ could not have entered into full and complete possession of all three bodies unless the Ego of Zarathustra had sacrificially withdrawn. In a sense, the first entry was the substitution of Egos. We might suspect that the next entry would be in the body nearest the Ego, the astral body. And this is precisely what Steiner says in *The Gospel of St. Matthew* (GSMt), Lect. 8, p. 145. In these temptations, the respective penetrations[12] were as follows:

Astral body	=	Hunger; turning stones to bread (Mt 4,2-4)
Etheric body	=	Casting himself from the pinnacle of the temple (Mt 4,5-6)
Physical body	=	Desire to rule all the kingdoms of the world (Mt 4,7-10)

---

12. Luke's version reverses the last two temptations.

It might seem strange to us that stones and bread refer to penetration of the astral body while the desire to rule refers to penetration of the physical body. Particularly is this so when we look at the related part of **I-76** that, from a different perspective (relating to the effect of Christ's three pre-earthly deeds), reverses them to a more seemly order. Clearly, in *The Fifth Gospel* (FG), Lect. 5, pp. 92-97 and *The Four Sacrifices of Christ* (FSC) Steiner reverses the order (as in **I-76**), as does Prokofieff in *The Cycle of the Year as Path of Initiation* (CYPI), Part II, #8, pp. 63-65. It would seem that we must, however, not confuse the successive penetration by Christ of the three bodies of Jesus with the elementary nature of what comprised the Temptations. We are dealing here with two different conceptions. The first (GSMt above) speaks of the entry of the Christ Spirit into the three successive bodies of Jesus, while the others (FG, FSC and CYPI) speak of Christ's subduing those bodies. Well aware of this, in FG, p. 94, Steiner says, "The Temptation scene is, of course, included in other Gospels, but it is narrated there from different standpoints, as I have often stressed"; and at p. 97, "Remember, please, that I am relating the contents of the Fifth Gospel and there would be no point in looking for contradictory passages in the other four Gospels" (see also fn 89 to the above CYPI text). Steiner's GSMt lecture tells how it is that each penetration portrays what happens to the candidate for Initiation in regard to each of the three stages (presumably Imagination/Seeing, Inspiration/Hearing and Intuition/Understanding; cf. Is 6,9-10) and how it corresponds successively with the three Temptations of Christ as set out in Matthew's Gospel. We belabor this point only to alert the reader to what might otherwise appear as a discrepancy. The main point is to see that there is a direct relationship between the three Temptations of Christ and the human being's three bodies, and that Christ here does what is eventually required of every human being who would attain to the resurrection: he gains complete control by the Ego over the three bodies. But he had first to enter those three bodies in the same order the human being did—only Christ did it quickly. GSMt describes the entry;[13] FG, FSC and CYPI describe the subduing.

---

13. While it is not here material, Steiner elsewhere tells us that the Christ Spirit did not penetrate into the bones of Jesus until the consummation of his sacrifice.

There is even another way to view the GSMt account. Bear in mind that, in contrast to the normal human Ego, the Christ, the standard of "Perfection," had no necessity of proving itself per se. Just as the human Ego must work upon the astral body first, and physical body last, the exalted Christ had to enter the bodies prepared for fallen human beings in the same order. While stones and bread themselves relate to the physical, the astral body is the reason for the temptation to satisfy the physical body through assuagement of hunger by bread. Only in overcoming this type of temptation was the Christ able to penetrate the astral body of Jesus. It is necessary to realize that all temptations are products of the astral body. As we shall see in our study of the Lord's Prayer, the temptation passage (Mt 6,13a only, 6,13b applying to the Ego) is the one dealing with the astral body. What we must do here is look at the worldliness of the Temptations. One must eat to live. (Without the astral body's desire, the human being would starve. This temptation cannot be permanently overcome, but dwells with life itself. For this reason, Lk 4,13 indicates the tempter merely "departed from him until an opportune time.") Hence, that desire is not as removed from the spiritual world as is the maniacal desire to rule the world, the most extreme of the three.

Finally, all four Gospels say the Christ Spirit settled "on" or "upon" Jesus "like" or "as" a "Dove." So even in this tender simile, the point is brought powerfully home that the Spirit had yet to enter the body (the "three bodies"). Immediately Matthew's Gospel tells of this happening. That there are many significant facets to the Temptations is providentially indicated by the fact that they are not presented in the same way (or order) by any two Gospels, and John omits them.

18. **Mt 1,1-17**: The three cycles of fourteen generations relate to the three bodies as shown in "The Nativity."

19. **Mt 6,11-13**: Matthew here gives his version of the Lord's Prayer. It is structured to portray and lead to the "Perfection" of the sevenfold human being. In LP, Steiner says "In spiritual science [the higher principles of the human being have] always been called the higher triad, and the triangle and the square were made symbols, especially in the Pythagorean school, of the human being as he came into existence at the middle of the Lemurian epoch. The diagram [below] thus represents the constituent elements of the human being":

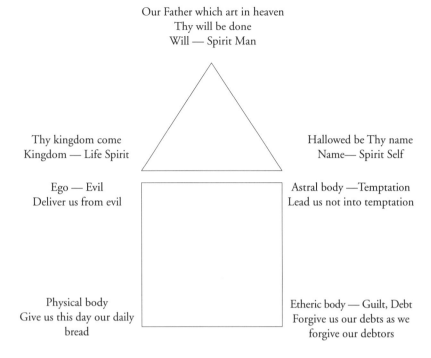

Our Father which art in heaven
Thy will be done
Will — Spirit Man

Thy kingdom come
Kingdom — Life Spirit

Hallowed be Thy name
Name— Spirit Self

Ego — Evil
Deliver us from evil

Astral body —Temptation
Lead us not into temptation

Physical body
Give us this day our daily
bread

Etheric body — Guilt, Debt
Forgive us our debts as we
forgive our debtors

He then shows how each of the seven human elements relates to the seven petitions of the Prayer. In *The Fifth Gospel* (FG), Lects. 5 and 6, he tells how the frightful ancient precursor of this Prayer was perceived in the soul of Jesus of Nazareth (Jesus before the Spirit descended upon him at his Baptism) and then how it came to expression in Jesus Christ (after the Baptism of Jesus). See also Prokofieff's *Rudolf Steiner and the Founding of the New Mysteries* (RSFNM), Chap. 3, pp. 60-70. Something of the nature of "will" and its involvement in human development is portrayed in **I-40**, and more elaborately in "Fire," Vol. 2. The Prayer will be addressed more fully in the Commentary. It must suffice for now to show its direct relationship to the three bodies, how they inhere in its petitions.

20. **Lk 2,52**: Jesus is said to have increased in wisdom, years[14] and favor. According to Steiner (see **I-42**) these reflect the development of his three bodies:

---

14. Traditionally, the Greek has been translated "stature," but more recently it has been translated more in line with what Steiner said earlier, as "age" or "years." See NRSV ("years") and KJV/NIV—INT (where the preferred Greek meaning is shown as "age").

Greek Term	Development	Body Described
Sophia	Wisdom	Astral
Helekia	Age, Status, Maturity	Etheric
Chariti	Beauty	Physical

Luke here presents the development of Jesus of Nazareth sequentially. The unspoiled etheric body of Adam (cf. Lk 3,38; 1,41; see "The Nativity") is joined, in the twelve-year-old temple scene (Lk 2,41-51), by the most advanced human Ego, that of the ancient Zarathustra. Thereby the three bodies of Jesus are, from age "Twelve" (Lk 2,42) to "Thirty" (Lk 3,23), mature enough spiritually to be able to provide a Temple, i.e., three bodies (Lk 2,52), capable of withstanding the immense ("crucifying") spiritual force of the Christ for as much as "Three Years."

21. **Lk 11,5-8**: This parable speaks of a friend coming at "Midnight" to borrow "three loaves." The significance of this passage is shown in the "Karma and Reincarnation" footnote that speaks of it. It would seem to be Luke's more elaborate expression of what is condensed into a single verse about the "three measures of flour" in Mt 13,33. Both passages envision the human being's long return journey to paradise.

22. **Jn 1,1-5**: The Christ is here described as "Life," "Word" and "Light." These express his exalted state before anything tangible to the human senses came into being, namely, the three higher ethers of life, sound (or chemical) and light. Christ himself expresses the same in Jn 14,6, "I am the Way [Light], the Truth [Word] and the Life." Later in John's Prologue (Jn 1,14) we are told that he became flesh, but more significantly it is in John's Gospel more than in any other that the significance of the higher "I Am" is expressed. If we examine **I-22** we readily see the relationship between these three higher ethers and the three lower elements, namely, earth, water and air. Thus, in Jn 1,1-5, we are being told that the three bodies are a reflection ("As Above, So Below") of his etheric being. Indeed, Jn 1,3 tells us outright that "all things were made through him, and without him was not anything made that was made." See **I-55** and **I-80**. The power of these concepts will become clearer as the contents of Volume 2, "*What is Man?*", are contemplated. It is not here suggested that Jn 1,1-5 is limited in its exaltation to the etheric world, for above

that are to be found the astral and devachanic (spiritual) worlds, and "The Word," being "with God" in the beginning, was there. We must, however, see in Jn 1,1-5 an application to the three higher etheric states that existed prior to that of "Fire," first in the descent of the human being, and then in that of the Christ. John's Prologue reflects not only the three bodies (Jn 1,1-5) but also the Ego (Jn 1,12) as shown in **I-72**:

Word (Jn 1,1)	Physical body	Old Saturn
Life (Jn 1,4a)	Etheric body	Old Sun
Light (Jn 1,4b-9)	Astral body	Old Moon
Name (Jn 1,12)	Ego ("I Am")	Earth

23. **Rev 18-20**: There are three "falls" of the evil forces representing the three bodies:

Rev 18	Babylon	Astral
Rev 19,17-21	Beast and False Prophet	Etheric
Rev 20,1-10	Satan (see "Devil/Satan")	Physical

Those Egos (human and creature souls and spirits) that have not embodied into their very being the true "I Am," the Christ Spirit, are then left to the eventual destruction of the elements by fire—Rev 20,11-15. Steiner spoke of these three falls in the last month he was able to lecture, in private talks to the priests of the Christian Community about the Apocalypse. See *The Apocalypse* (APOC-CC), Lect. 11 (September 15, 1924).

SCRIPTURES READILY SUGGESTIVE OF "THREE BODIES"

24. **Gen 1,2**: As Steiner recognized in *Genesis* (GEN), the first three elements (water, air and fire) exist in this passage in their formless etheric nature: water(s) is expressed; air is the meaning of the Greek *pneuma* or Hebrew *ruach* ("spirit" or "wind" RSV); and fire is expressed by the concept of spiritual warmth in God's "brooding" like a setting hen over the waters (1 Interp 466; Barc, Genesis, Vol. 1, p. 35; AMPB and LB). The "Spirit of God" may, in this respect, be deemed to embody the element of "Fire" which is generally present throughout scripture where a recognized spiritual being appears or is actively involved (e.g., see "Bush"). These three elements represent the recapitulation of the prior three

Conditions of Consciousness (Old Saturn, Sun and Moon) the three
bodies before they condensed further by mineralization into Earth (solids), Water and Air, respectively, to receive the human Ego during Earth
evolution. See **I-22**.

25. The Bible's recurring motif, particularly in Genesis, of precisely
three sons surely suggests the three bodies:

a)   **Gen 4**: Adam has three sons, Cain, Abel and Seth.[15] Notably,
Adam and Eve are not said to have had any female children until after
the birth of all of Cain's named descendants and Seth (Gen 5,4), so
unless Cain sired offspring from his own mother, an unlikelihood,
these archetypal scriptures suggest a meaning deeper than that associated merely with individual persons (though they may also have been
such). They can be seen to represent the three bodies as follows:

Cain is a creator of physical goods; the later Aramaic and Arabic root
    qyn means "smith" (1 ABD 806); the physical body
Abel, from the Hebrew root *hbl,* means "breath" (1 ABD 10); a less
    dense nature, hence the etheric body
Seth, the ancestor of Noah, hence of all post-Atlantean humanity,
    came last; the astral body

b)   **Gen 4,20-22**: Lamech has three sons, Jabal, Jubal and Tubal-
cain. See fn 15.

c)   **Gen 5,32; 6,10**: Noah has three sons, Shem, Ham and Japheth.
The normally assumed fact that these three are listed in the order of
their births would accord with the order of creation of the three
bodies on Old Saturn, Sun and Moon, respectively. Beyond that,
however, as in a), their "Names" also suggest that relationship:

Shem: "The Name" (5 ABD 1194), recognizing him as the epony-
    mous ancestor of all Semites; the physical body
Ham: "warm" or "hot" (3 ABD 31), suggesting the less dense etheric
    body
Japheth: from the Hebrew *yph* meaning "beautiful" (3 ABD 641),
    thus descriptive of the astral body

---

15. See the Appendix to "Three Bodies."

A somewhat different perspective is taken on these meanings from those in #20, to be compatible with the order of their ages.

d) **Gen 10**: Noah's son, Ham, had four sons, Cush, Egypt, Put and Canaan (vs 6). However Put is nowhere else mentioned in the Bible, and the other three sons are the progenitors, respectively, of the three principal Old Testament civilizations, namely, Babylon (and Assyria), Egypt (and Philistia) and Canaan (including Sodom and Gomorrah). See the discussion on these in "Egypt." Considering the early evolutionary stage Ham represented, Put could easily be seen as the incipient Ego, then too premature to yield offspring. The other three sons would then equate to the three bodies, as with so many other generations that list "three sons."

e) **Gen 11,27**: Terah has three sons, Abram, Nahor and Haran.

f) **Gen 38**: Judah has three sons, Er, Onan and Shelah, before giving birth through his deceptive daughter-in-law, Tamar, to Perez, ancestor of Jesus in Matthew's Gospel (Mt 1,3)[16]; Perez was born as a twin (Gen 38,27-30), as was Jacob.[17] The "twin" could be a reference to the zodiacal influence of Gemini (see "Zodiac"), which can be twofold in nature, i.e., two-faced. In spiritual parlance, Jacob was rather a prototype for each human being, the microcosmic reflection of the "First and Second Adam," in which the higher Ego must overcome the lower. Judah was the fourth son of Jacob (as well as being the fourth generation in Matthew's genealogy of Jesus), thus numerically fitting the image of the human Ego which comes as the human being's fourth component.

---

16. Prostitutes seem to figure mysteriously into the account of the Incarnation of Christ, his message and his most exalted followers. His ancestor Perez is conceived in this passage through an act of prostitution. The birth of the two Jesus children is foreshadowed by the account of Solomon's adjudication of the dispute between two harlots (1 K 3,16-28; see "The Nativity"). Jesus spoke with relative favor about, or with, prostitutes or women who had engaged in sexual activity of a questionable sort (Mt 21,31; Lk 7,36-50; Jn 4,7-30). Mary Magdalene, a reformed prostitute from whom seven demons had been driven by Jesus (Lk 8,2), is the one most frequently identified to have been the first witness of Christ's Resurrection. Three others who are ancestors of Jesus are Rahab (Mt 1,5; Heb 11,31; Jas 2,25; Josh 2,1), Ruth (Mt 1,5: Ruth 3) and Bathsheba (2 Sam 11-12).
17. Curiously, perhaps even significantly from our present perspective, the twin of both Jacob and Perez was associated with the color red (Gen 25,30; 38,30).

The plausibility of such purport is enhanced by three additional considerations: 1. The tribe of "Judah" is central to the Old Testament mission of creating a fitting physical body for the Christ to enter (see "The Nativity"), thus further fitting the role of the struggling human Ego. 2. Substantiation is given to this picture by the names of Judah's three sons. While ABD does not give the meaning of either "Er" or "Onan," it does for "Shelah," and meaning can to some extent be surmised for the first two. Thus, "*Er*" is presumably the primeval sound, indicating a beginning, inasmuch as its identical sound "Ur" is "a prefix meaning original, primitive" (WNWD), and identifies the geographical beginnings of the Abrahamic line (Gen 11,28-12,1), thus fitting the role of the human physical body. "*Onan*" probably takes its meaning from the same root as "onus," meaning "burden," thus signifying the karmic structure of the etheric body which reflects the "burden" of past sins, comporting with the second consequence of the Fall, "Toil" (Gen 3,16-19—pain-toil-death). Since of old the name signified one's nature (see "Name"), the event for which Onan became known (see "onanism," WNWD) is described in Gen 38,9 and clearly recognized as a "sin" (as discussed in 5 ABD 20), comporting with the idea that sin results in an "etheric" onus, as in the Fall. Additionally, the etheric body is the life, healing, and creative agent of the physical body, and this was Onan's failed mission under the levirate law (Gen 38,8; Deut 25,5-6). In 5 ABD 1191, "*Shelah*" is seen possibly to equate, etymologically, to a "weapon, a canal, or even a divine name," and the "Pool of Shelah" (Neh 3,15) is identified as the Pool of Shiloah (Is 8,6), which means "to send" as in the case of a stream of water. All of these tend to relate to the function of the astral body. 3. Finally, Perez is the son of a widow (vs 14; see "Widow's Son"), suggesting that he, like the ancestral twin Jacob, was initiated into the Mysteries, and thus a fitting ancestor for Jesus.

g) **Lev 16**: Aaron had four sons (see Lev 10,1,12) so the prevalent "three son" motif is not here used. There is nevertheless a pattern that may still bespeak the human situation reflected by that motif. Two of Aaron's sons (among his four-son, or fourfold nature) disobeyed the Lord's commands and died (Lev 10,1-2; 16,1). In the "ritual of atonement" prescribed here Aaron is to offer a "bull as a sin offering for himself" and is then to make further atonement for both himself and his house by taking two goats upon which lots shall be cast and one sacrificed; the sins of the people shall then be placed upon the head of the other, which shall be sent into the "Wilderness." The two sons who died by reason of disobedience might be taken as the human physical and etheric bodies, which are infected to death (Gen 3,19-20) by virtue of the infection of the astral body in the Fall. The bull may here be taken for the astral body, which represents the astral nature of feeling (see **I-62**). By sacrificing the bull "for himself," Aaron, now representing the astral body, is kept alive, and by the sacrifice of the one goat "for himself and for his house" and the release of the other, bearing their sins, into the "Wilderness," their atonement is accomplished. Now the goat is related to sheep (see WNWD, "goat") but in general has a more objectionable character; thus the relationship of Goat/Sheep is analogous to that of astral body/manas. The implications for the eventual "Lamb of God" thrust themselves irresistibly upon us. The goat, representing the astral nature, is two-fold, and one is sacrificed so that the other may go free into the "Wilderness." The merit of this concept is strengthened when one considers that the zodiacal realm of Capricorn (goat) equates to the astral body (see **I-18**). The only one of the three bodies over which a human being has direct control in the present Epoch is the astral body. To the extent that it is purified through the action of the "Lamb of God" it moves toward the manas state of the future Jupiter Condition of Consciousness, portrayed in Revelation as the Holy City. The Ego is thus thrust into the "Wilderness" to follow there the lead of the "Lamb of God," which takes the place of the scapegoat in bearing the sins of the human being.

h) **1 Sam 2,21**: Hannah had three sons besides Samuel.

i) **1 Sam 17,13**: The three eldest sons of Jesse, namely, Eliab, Abinadab and Shammah, i.e., the three bodies, had followed Saul into battle. Then David, the "I Am," who had prevailed over the lion and the bear (see "Wild Animals"), thereby transforming his astral body into manas (Manna), killed the giant Philistine (cf. the "sons of Anak" in #11 above) by striking him on the "Forehead" with a stone before cutting off his head.

j) **1 Sam 31,2,6**: The three sons of Saul, namely, Jonathan, Abinadab and Malchishua, were killed along with him by the Philistines, who then cut off Saul's head, i.e., his "I Am," or Ego.

26. **Gen 11-50**: There are three patriarchs, Abraham, Isaac and Jacob, representing the physical, etheric and astral natures. The original seed came from Abraham, the physical body. Isaac was offered as a sacrifice to God who gave him back to the people (Heb 11,19), thereby granting them life, the etheric body. Jacob is the very picture of the cunning astral body. In *Gospel of St. Mark* (GSMk), Lect. 6, p. 111, Steiner says, "In truth the sequence of the generations of the Old Testament peoples is analogous to the life of an individual human being." A schematic of his presentation is given in **I-68**. Steiner equates the bodily aspect of the Hebrew people to these three patriarchs and the soul to the prophets.

27. **Gen 21,25-26; 26,17-22**: Four wells (or series of wells) were the subject of controversy between Abraham and/or Isaac and the Philistines. Isaac's servants dug the last three of these, naming them, successively, as Esek ("contention"), Stinah ("enmity") and Reheboth ("broad places" or "room"). A well is a place for securing a vital for physical life and is an esoteric metaphor for what is vital for spiritual life, namely, "living water," best seen in Jn 4,1-42. The progression of wells, and the nuances of difference between their successive scenarios and names, suggests the progression from the physical body from Abraham up through the Ego in the final well dug by Isaac. The three bodies are thus inherent in the accounts.

28. **Gen 27-32**: (See Tomberg's *Anthroposophical Studies of the Old Testament* [ASOT], Chap. 4, Part 3, pp. 57-64.) In Jacob's threefold spiritual victory, he contended with:

   (a) Esau for his birthright, as father of the twelve tribes;
   (b) Laban for his wife, Rachel; and finally the
   (c) Angel at Jabbok for his "Name," Israel.

The relationship of birthright to the physical body, marriage to the Life or etheric body, and angel and "Name" to the astral body, metaphorically speaking, seems obvious. Notably, the angel never gave him its higher "Name," the "I Am."

29. Gen 30,36; Ex 3,18; 5,3; 8,27; Num 10,33; 33,8 and Jon 3,3:
Three Biblical personalities are said to have experienced a "Three Days'
Journey," namely, Jacob (Gen), Moses (Ex and Num) and Jonah (Jon),
which may thus be tabulated:

Personality	Representing	Body
Jacob	12 tribes of Israel	Physical
Moses	Hebrew People	Etheric
Jonah	Prophets	Astral

30. **Ex 1 and 2 K 17,1-6; 25,1-11:** There were three "captivities" in the
history of the Hebrew people, Egyptian (Ex 1), Assyrian (2 K 17,1-6) and
Babylonian (2 K 25,1-11). These may be taken to equate to the three
bodies progressively as follows:

Egyptian	Physical
Assyrian	Etheric
Babylonian	Astral

The Ego, the "I Am," i.e., the Christ, the true Israel, could not enter
until Israel's three bodies had first undergone these progressive stages of
development.

31. **Deut 16,16:** "Three times a year all your males shall appear before
the Lord your God at the place which he will choose; at the feast of
unleavened bread, at the feast of *weeks*, and at the feast of *booths*" (emphasis added). This passage prescribes the three appointed feasts each year, as
is also done in Lev 23. Anthroposophy permits us to see these clearly as
symbols for the human being's three bodies, as follows:

Feast	Body Symbolized
Unleavened Bread	Physical
Weeks	Etheric
Booths	Astral

"Bread" is a Biblical symbol for the physical. Jesus uses it at the last supper
to describe his physical body, and the fact that it is "unleavened" indicates

that it is the earthly and not the heavenly state to be attained when the
physical has been transformed into atma (see Mt 13,33). The Feast of
Weeks (i.e., Pentecost, or "fifty") is a period of "rest" (Lev 23,21) following
seven cycles of seven (Lev 23,15-16; Deut 16,9). The etheric nature of this
feast is shown by the "Fire" which settled upon the heads of the disciples in
Acts 2,3. "Fire" is the point of contact between the spiritual and etheric
worlds. Finally, the Feast of *Booths* elevates to the astral by the Biblical symbol of the Tabernacle ("booth" = "tabernacle"). Later, as the wanderings
ceased, the temporary, itinerant shelter of the Lord (the "I Am") came to
be called the "temple," but the meaning is here interchangeable. See "Temple." We need not otherwise here belabor that its meaning is the highest
component of the three human bodies, namely, the astral body. The Temple to be "measured" at the approach of the last "Trumpet" in Rev 11 is the
astral body, the vehicle of the "I Am," and it is the astral body that is to be
worked upon most directly by the human being during Earth evolution.
Even the etheric body will be laid aside at the time of the "Second Death,"
i.e., at the expiration of the last of the seven Conditions of Form of Earth
evolution (see **I-1**). So the Temple that must be perfected and "measured"
(Rev 11,1) is the astral body. Thus, we see that the scheme of the human
being's development, like that of the temple, is a pattern reflected on Earth
by these three Feasts (cf. Heb 8,5 and "As Above, So Below").

32. **2 K 9,35**: Regarding Jezebel we read, "But when they went to bury
her, they found no more of her than the skull and the feet and the palms
of her hands." It is submitted that these represent the following:

Skull	=	Physical body
Feet	=	Etheric body
Hands	=	Astral body

The solid bones of the head are demonstrably physical, and the skull is
the sign of the death of the physical. As to the astral, see "Washing of
Hands," which refers to *Background to the Gospel of St. Mark* (BKM),
Lect. 7, pp. 120-123, where Steiner, citing relevant scriptures, equates
this act with coming into contact with the spirit, the astral being the most
spiritual of the three bodies. Consider also Lk 24,39-40, "See my *hands*
and my *feet*, that it is *I myself*; handle me, and see; for a spirit has not *flesh
and bones* as you see that *I have*" (my emphasis). See also Jn 13,2-8, and

then especially Jn 13,9. And then, most significantly, consider Jn 20,12, commented upon by Steiner in *The Gospel of St. John* (GSJ), Lect. 12, p. 187, as follows:

> We are told that Mary Magdalene was led to the grave, that the body had disappeared and that she saw there two spiritual forms. These two spiritual forces are always to be seen when a corpse is present for a certain time after death. On the one side is to be seen the astral body, and on the other, what gradually separates from it as ether body, then passing over into the cosmic ether. Wholly apart from the physical body are two spiritual forms present which belong to the spiritual world.

> > Then the disciples went away again unto their own home. But Mary stood without at the sepulchre weeping; and as she wept she stooped down and looked into the sepulchre, and seeth two angels in white sitting....

Steiner's quote stopped in the middle of the sentence just short of what, for our purposes, is also a most significant clause, "sitting where the body of Jesus had lain, one at the head and one at the feet." In the case of Jezebel, there were no angels, just the feet and hands, the unredeemed physical symbols of the two spiritual bodies. It should be noted that Lk 24,4 also says that "two men stood by them in dazzling apparel."

33. **Mt 10,9**: In sending out the Twelve, Jesus admonished them to "take no gold, nor silver, nor copper in your belts." In BKM, Lect. 10, p. 177, Steiner explains how, in a myth sung by the European minstrels of old, these metals reflected the three bodies:

Copper	=	Physical body
Silver	=	Etheric body
Gold	=	Astral body

(Mk 6,8 and Lk 9,3 refer to them collectively only as "money.") Inasmuch as copper and tin are the components of "bronze," the following passages should be noted where Gold-Silver-Bronze are involved: Ex 25,3; 31,4 and 35,32; 2 Sam 8,10; 1 Ch 18,10 and 22,16; Dan 2,35,45; Rev 9,20.

34. Mt 17,1-8; Mk 9,2-10 and Lk 9,28-36: Jesus led Peter, James and John up a "High Mountain" where he was "transfigured" before them, and Moses and Elijah appeared. Peter suggested that they make three booths (tabernacles or temples), one each for Moses, Elijah and Jesus. A voice came from heaven, as at Jesus' Baptism, identifying him as "my Son" or "my beloved Son." Christ's "face shone like the sun" (Mt 17,2; cf. Rev 1,16) and his garments (raiment) "became white as light" (Mt 17,2), "dazzling white" (Lk 9,29). As pointed out in "Naked" above, we shall see that "Garments" refers to the three bodies. See also "White Robe," the symbol of the purified. In *The Significance of the Mass* (SMASS), Steiner tells of how the initiates in the ancient Mysteries, at the second stage of their initiation, saw the image of the human being when it was "free from desires and passions" appear with a "countenance [that] shone like the Sun; this was Osiris."

In *Foundations of Esotericism* (FE), Lect. 8, Steiner says that Peter, James and John had direct revelation at the Transfiguration of "I am the Way, the Truth and the Life." And he said, "The way = Elias, Moses = the truth, Christ = the life." Also in accord are *The Christian Mystery* (CMYST) and *The Apocalypse of St. John* (ASJ), Lect. 9, p. 161. We have already seen in #22 that this passage from Jn 14,6 describes the light, sound and life ethers, the etheric sources from which the three bodies came into materialization, as set out in **I-22**. In *The Gospel of St. Luke* (GSL), Lect. 10, pp. 186-187, Steiner indicates that the Mosaic Law could be addressed only to the astral body. Elijah, as John the Baptist, was to bring perception through momentary separation, by his immersing "Baptism," of the etheric body from the physical. But Christ, with his dazzling white "Garments," was identified as the "beloved Son," the higher "I Am," who thus had to represent the Ego. Consequently, in the three booths we do not have the physical body represented, but in its place is the Ego, so that

$$
\begin{array}{lcl}
\text{Moses} & = & \text{Astral body} \\
\text{Elijah} & = & \text{Etheric body} \\
\text{Jesus} & = & \text{Ego ("I Am")}
\end{array}
$$

35. Jn 11,1,5: The significance of the fact that Jesus is said in the Gospels to have "loved" only three persons, Lazarus and his sisters, Mary and Martha, is discussed in "Peter, James and John." Steiner indicates in *St. John's Gospel, Notes of a Lect. on* (GSJN) that Mary and Martha are the conditions of consciousness of Lazarus' soul, the divine and the earthly, respectively; and in "Egypt" below we see further that the rich youth said in Mk 10,21 to have been "loved" was one and the same as Lazarus.[18] The following relationships can then be derived:

Person	Component	Body	Soul	Spirit
Martha	Body	Physical	Sentient	Manna
Mary	Soul	Etheric	Intellectual	Buddhi
Lazarus	Spirit	Astral	Consciousness	Atma

36. **Jn 20,12 and Lk 24,4**: See the discussion in #32 above (2 K 9,35) of the "two angels in white" or "two men in dazzling apparel," as representing the etheric and astral bodies in the place where the third, the physical, had been.

37. **1 Cor 13,13**: In *Faith, Love, Hope* (FLH), pp. 11-13, Steiner shows how the three high spiritual virtues (faith-hope-love) spoken of here by Paul relate to the human being's three bodies, as follows:

Faith-Body	=	Astral body
Love-Body	=	Etheric body
Hope-Body	=	Physical body

38. **2 Cor 12,8-9**: Three times Paul besought the Lord about his "thorn in the flesh" but was told "my power is made perfect in weakness." While "flesh" might at first be deemed to represent only the physical body, it has an inherent relationship with the other two; a "thorn" would be a conscious problem only with the presence of the astral body, and many, if not most, weaknesses in the flesh have a relationship to the formative etheric body. The likelihood that the three bodies are here indicated is strengthened by the seemingly powerful and clear implications of "my

---

18. Since the discovery in 1958, and publication in 1973, of the *Secret Gospel of Mark*, discussed near the end of "Egypt," it now appears to be rather widely recognized that the original version of Mark's Gospel probably included an account of Lazarus as the rich youth in Mark 10,17-23. This is one of the many places that Steiner, in telling us the meaning of "loved" in the ancient Mysteries, strongly hinted at something not then known to Christendom (i.e., the identity of the "rich youth" in Mk 10,17-22 as Lazarus) that was established by twentieth-century discoveries made long after his death.

power is made perfect in weakness." The "weaknesses" inherent in the "three bodies" can be overcome, made "Perfect," only by the higher "I Am" of the Christ (e.g., Gal 2,20), the higher Ego that transforms the lower three bodies, the flesh, into the higher three states (**I-9**).

39. **Rev 16,19**: We are here told that "The great city was split into three parts." This is the city that falls. Earlier (vs 13) we are told of "three foul spirits" that issue from various beasts, and earlier still (vs 2) reference is made to those who bore the "Mark of the Beast," who clearly are those who have not, by that stage of evolution, completed the necessary degrees of perfection, so that their three bodies, instead of being transformed into their three spirit counterparts, are hardened into bestial characteristics. They have not put on (vs 15) the "Garments" required to avoid being exposed as "Naked."

40. **Rev 21,22; 11,1-3**: Rev 21,22 tells us that in the New Jerusalem, there will be no temple, "for its temple is the Lord God Almighty and the Lamb," the higher "I Am." And Rev 11,1-2 says (emphasis added),

> ..."Rise and *measure the temple of God*... (2) *but do not measure the court outside the temple*, leave that out, for it is given over to the nations, and they will trample over the holy city for forty-two months. (3) And I will grant my two witnesses [Moses and Elijah] power to prophesy for one thousand two hundred and sixty days,[19] clothed in sackcloth."

Jesus was mocked and condemned for saying that if the Temple were destroyed, he would raise it again in "Three Days" (Mt 26,61-68; Mk

---

19. On September 18, 1924, nine days before failing health ended his lecturing, in Lect. 14 in the cycle entitled *The Apocalypse* (APOC-CC), given exclusively to the priesthood of the Christian Community, in relation to the number 1,260 Steiner said,

> ... [This number] gave me quite a bit of trouble for awhile. For the Apocalypticer supposedly prophesies about things that will take 1,260 days. They used to speak of days when they meant years. Anyway, the Apocalypticer mentions the number 1,260. It took a lot of intensive research to discover that the 1,260 days is really a printing error, as it were, in the Apocalypse that was handed down. It should say 2,160 days. Then it agrees with what one can see today.

He is speaking in the last instance of the fact that the zodiacal year, the length of time it takes the Sun to travel completely around the Zodiac, is 25,920 years (see **I-19**), and that when divided by the "Twelve" zodiacal ages or symbols, the result is 2,160, the precise length of each Cultural Age.

15,29-32; Jn 2,19-20). John's Gospel tells us (vs 21), and Christians have come to accept without question, that he was referring to his body. Zechariah had prophesied, ... "Thus says the Lord of hosts, 'Behold, the man whose name is the Branch [Is 11,1]: for he shall grow up in his place, and he shall build the temple of the Lord'" (Zech 6,12). Notably Zechariah had been told (vs 10) to take three persons, "Heldai, Tobijah, and Jedaiah," not associated together elsewhere (e.g., 1 Ch 27,15; 9,10; 2 Ch 17,8), "from the exiles ... who have arrived from Babylonia" preparatory to his making this prophecy, as if to say that the "I Am," the "Branch," could come only if three bodies were prepared for him.

In ASJ, Lect. 9, pp. 160-161, Steiner tells us what is meant by Rev 11,1-2. The Body that immediately houses the Ego is the astral body, hence it is called "the temple of the ego within, the temple of the divinity dwelling in man, the temple of God." The goal of Earth evolution is the "Perfection" of the astral body, for work cannot be done directly on the denser etheric and physical bodies during the Earth Condition of Consciousness. Perfection of these must await the later Jupiter and Venus Conditions, respectively. The Jupiter Condition is what John saw as the "new heaven and ... new earth." During Earth evolution, "these bodies are the outer court, and must fall away, ... be thrown out. That alone that man has made does he keep. That is the temple in which are to live the new beings in the time of Jupiter existence."

The "Perfected" astral body, Manna, will be so like the "heavenly Father" that no other Temple will be required on Jupiter, where Love will be implanted in everything the way Wisdom inheres in the Earth as its heritage from Ancient Moon evolution (Mt 5,48; Rev 21,22). The "measuring rod" from Earth evolution (Rev 11,1-2) will not be necessary, but will be replaced by a rod to measure the city with its "Twelve" "gates and walls" (Rev 21,15). The physical and etheric bodies will no longer exist as they were on Earth, but will be transformed into new "spiritual bodies" (cf. 1 Cor 15,44), the "gates and walls" of the holy city, no "temple" being needed there (vs 22).

Christendom has long recognized the similarity between the fate of the nation Israel and Jesus of Nazareth (see fn 9 of "I AM" which also clearly identifies Jesus of Nazareth as the one seen by the prophet as "the suffering servant" in the so-called "second Isaiah" passages). And there is an unmistakable correspondence between the utter destruction of Judah in 587 B.C. (the third captivity; see #30 above) and what happened to the three bodies of Jesus. We can begin to see a direct correspondence between all of the examples in this essay and the three bodies of the human being during Earth evolution. Perhaps in none is the comparison more powerful than in the history of the earthly temple. There were three temples and three destructions: 1. The Solomon Temple, which underwent various changes, then destruction by the Babylonians; 2. The Temple of Zerubabbel, built by the exiles returned from Babylon, destroyed in the first century B.C. by the Romans; and 3. Herod's Temple built later in the first century B.C., destroyed by the Romans in A.D. 70 (see 6 ABD 350-369). One should not be surprised to learn that the human body has also been successively built and will be successively destroyed. We shall only learn the significance of the "Crucifixion" of Christ and his characterization as the "First Fruits" when we come to see that every human being who attains to salvation must also, in the course of time, give back each of the three bodies, must "drink the cup," so to speak (Mt 20,23; Mk 10,39).

SCRIPTURES INDICATIVE OF THREEFOLDEDNESS

41. **Gen 14,24**: Abram, immediately after his meeting with Melchizedek, says to the king of Sodom, "I will take nothing but what the *young men* have eaten, and the share of the men who went with me; let *Aner, Eshcol and Mamre* take their share" (RSV; emphasis mine). See "Young Men" and the threefold "Young Men" discussed in "Naked" (in connection with the Mk 14,51-52 passage) to which reference is also made in Mt 19,16 below, noting that such threefoldedness was prefigured in this Abram-Melchizedek passage (discussed in "Spiritual Economy").

Scholars seem to doubt the historical accuracy of this threesome as allies of Abram or that they were all included in an assumed, but lost, original writing. Each of the three is indicated to be the name of both a place and person, but with no seeming connection other than in this account. See 1 ABD 248, "Aner," 2 ABD 617, "Eshcol," and 4 ABD 492, "Mamre." They are thought to have been put together by a later writer. These circumstances are typical of those indicating that perhaps even the original writer used historical names in a non-historical way to indicate deeper spiritual truth. In the ancient Mysteries, the truth was often preserved for those qualified to receive it in ways like this. Even early Church Fathers sometimes withheld deeper insights from their flocks, and Christ not only followed this principle of the Mysteries in speaking to the crowds in parables but also admonished his disciples to exercise similar caution by not throwing "pearls before swine" (Mt 7,6; cf. Heb 9,5b and Jn 16,12).

Moreover, though not included in category #1 above, the "Names" of these three themselves, particularly in association with Abram, may well be "indicative" of the three bodies and the fourfold human being:

Name	Meaning	Human Component
Mamre	The City of Four; or the Fatted Calf (4 ABD 492)	Physical body
Eshcol	Cluster of Grapes (4 ABD 492); or Valley of Grapes (2 ABD 617)	Etheric body
Aner	Temple of the Above, or of the goddess Anat (4 ABD 492)	Astral body
Abram	Ab = From; Ram = Lamb; or A = From; Bram = Brahma	Ego ("I Am")

The "Oaks of Mamre" may signify the earthly strength of the physical body. It is the earthly foundation or house, so to speak, of the fourfold human being. And the "Fatted Calf" is indicative of what belonged to the elder son but was sacrificed by the father for the Prodigal Son, in Luke's parable (Lk 15,30, "But when this son of yours came, who has devoured your living with harlots, you killed for him the fatted calf?"). We saw in "Spiritual Economy" that Melchizedek brought the etheric body of Shem, which still embodied an avatar, over from Atlantis as the common heritage of all the Semites (Shemites). The "Wine" that Melchizedek "brought out" (Gen 14,18) rings of this etheric body not only here but throughout the Eucharist itself (see the discussion of the "etherization of the blood" in "Second Coming"). Eshcol can easily be seen to represent the etheric body in this way. Aner is related to the temple. We have just seen in #40 above that this refers, particularly in Rev 11,1-2 and 21,22, to the astral body. This leaves the first patriarch to represent, of this foursome, the highest element, the Ego.

42. **1 and 2 Sam and 1 K**: There were three kings of Israel before the division of the kingdom: Saul, David and Solomon. For a particular spiritual significance of the division of the kingdom into a male, kingly element and a female, priestly element, see "Widow's Son," fn 4 and related text through end of discussion on 1 K 11,26-31. From that we can see the necessity of the division if the nation of Israel was to fit the pattern divinely laid out for the human being itself, namely, that the "two will become one" only through the advent of the Christ, the true "I Am." We saw this in "The Nativity," where the kingly and priestly lines came together in Jesus of Nazareth. On the human level, not only must this happen through taking in the higher "I Am," but the human being long divided into two sexes must again become one through the "Perfect(ion)" the higher "I Am" makes possible.

43. **2 Sam 23,8-12**: David is said to have had "three mighty men," namely, Josheb-basshebeth, Eleazar and Shammah, and the chapter also speaks of David going into a "cave" (vs 13), a symbol of the initiation process. Then the "three mighty men broke through the camp of the Philistines, and drew water out of the well of Bethlehem which was by the gate, and took and brought it to David" (vs 16). This last sentence (vs 16) itself reveals a larger threefoldedness. The very word "philistine" means one "guided by materialism" (MWCD), indicative of the physical body. "Water" from a "well," particularly the "well of Bethlehem," symbolizes the etheric body, and the "three mighty men" phrase intimates the qualities to which the higher "I Am" leads and is consistent with the charisma that installed David as the one from whom the Messiah was to descend.

44. **Prov 30,15-31**: Four pieces of fourfold wisdom are given, each with the same introductory motif:

1. Three things are never satisfied; four never say, "Enough" (vs 15).

2. Three things are too wonderful for me; four I do not understand (vs 18).

3. Under three things the earth trembles; under four it cannot bear up (vs 21).

4. Three things are stately in their tread; four are stately in their stride (vs 29).

In each a riddle-like illustration follows. Something of this nature, a threefold item along with an independent fourth, stressed four times, is surely indicative of the human being's fourfold being (see **I-9**). Also, the fractal nature of creation is reflected. Each of the four is patterned after the sevenfold nature of each of the Conditions of Consciousness (see **I-1**). Three such Conditions preceded Earth and are thus distinct from the four which follow and about which not so much is yet understood. Consequently, deeper mystery exists about the four than the three in each case.

45. **Isaiah**: The Book of Isaiah is seen as being threefold (Is 1-39; 40-55; 56-66), having emanated from three successive authors, namely, Isaiah and two others in his spiritual wake or school (3 ABD 472-506). In a way, it is central to a larger threefoldedness in Hebrew prophecy: 1. Elijah and the other early non-writing prophets; 2. the three "major" prophets (Isaiah, Jeremiah, Ezekiel); 3. the "Twelve" "minor" prophets (Daniel through Malachi).

46. **Ezek 14,12-20**: Three times, the "three men, Noah, Daniel, and Job," are referred to; each, perhaps more than coincidentally, is involved with "three men" elsewhere herein (see #s 25c, 15 and 2). In each instance, one of three scourges is mentioned, "Wild Beasts," sword and pestilence, respectively, from which even these three men could deliver naught but themselves. Then in vs 21, a fourth scourge, famine, is added, to fulfill even more effectively judgment against sin. Yet if any survive, they are said to be vindication for all such judgment. But in what way vindicated? The traditional view seems to be that a small remnant of unrepentant sinners in Jerusalem would finally, having survived even famine, be sent into exile along with those who preceded them, and that the latter would, from the shameful character of these survivors, see that God had acted rightly in thus punishing them. Historically, the interpretation seems to fit with the facts. But if those were the historical facts, even though the prognostication came true, of what value is that as higher spiritual prophecy? Was there not also a Jeremiah, whose character was undiminished and who was not ever sent to Babylon? The famine may well represent, as perhaps in the Joseph years in "Egypt," a darkening of the spiritual world (see "Fading Splendor") during the ascendancy of the individual Ego. And those who survive without falling back into captivity

also vindicate the punishments, for those who went to Babylon had again to return to Jerusalem to work on and on toward what was "promised." Is this not how it is with the human being? An anthroposophical understanding of the heavenly law of "Karma and Reincarnation" shows us that indeed it is so.

47. **Mt 2,11**: The gifts of the magi are threefold in nature: gold, frankincense and myrrh. Steiner says that these were symbols for the riches that the pupils of Zarathustra (see "The Nativity") strove to gain in the Mysteries through the three human activities of thinking (gold), feeling (frankincense) and willing (myrrh). In **I-58** (and in *Wonders of the World* [WW], Lect. 3), the seats of these activities are seen to be the astral, etheric and physical bodies respectively.

48. **Mt 27,38; Mk 15,27; Lk 23,32-33 and Jn 19,18**: Jesus was crucified between two thieves. Thus, there were three crosses. In their deeper significance, they must surely indicate that the lower three bodies can only be transformed into the higher three states of manas, buddhi and atma by being "crucified" in their earthly, unpurified condition. Only then are the wedding "Garments" donned; only then the Bride prepared to meet the Bridegroom (Rev 21,2).

49. The following three New Testament passages or groupings are particularly indicative of the simple pervasiveness of threefoldedness, even though they might not otherwise be given much weight as individually suggesting the three bodies:

   a) **Mt 26,34,69-74; Mk 14,30,66-72 and Lk 22,34,54-62**: Peter denies Christ three times. (The single denial in Jn 18,17 need not be considered on this point, for it could even then be given a consistent meaning, i.e., "An 'I Am' I am not.") If perceived as extending to all three bodies, the denial can be taken as a total rejection.

   b) **Peter-James-John**: This triumvirate appears at the Transfiguration (Mt 17,1; Mk 9,2; Lk 9,28), in the Garden of Gethsemane (Mt 26,37; Mk 14,33), at the "raising" of Jairus' daughter (Mk 5,37; Lk 8,51), and as the audience, along with Andrew, for Jesus' "Little Apocalypse" (Mk 13,3) and the healing of Peter's mother-in-law (Mk 1,29-31).

c) **Jn 21,15-19**: Three times Jesus asks Simon if he loves him. For whatever relevance it may have on this point, one should reflect that the Greek word for "love" is different the third time from the first two, even though many if not most translations make no distinction or notation on the point. In 29A AB 1102 and KJV/NIV—INT it is given as follows:

Vs 15: agapas me ... philo se

Vs 16: agapas me ... philo se

Vs 17: phileis me ... philo se

"Agapas" (i.e., agape) is a higher, more divine form of love than is "phileis" (i.e., philo).

50. **Matthew-Mark-Luke**: The three "synoptic" Gospels can be seen as equating to the three bodies and John's Gospel to the Ego. From **I-62** in conjunction with **I-73**, the following is derived:

Gospel	Symbol	Human Component
Luke	Bull	Physical body
Mark	Lion	Etheric body
Matthew	Face of a Man	Astral body
John	Eagle	Ego

As Steiner emphasized again and again, however, one cannot assume that there is only one perspective. In *The Gospel of St. Matthew* (GSMt), Lect. 12, pp. 219-220, he explains how, in another way, each of the synoptic Evangelists attempted to reflect the spiritual activity of the particular body indicated below:

Matthew	Physical body
Mark	Etheric body
Luke	Astral body

This reversal is rather like that of the Temptations in #17.

51. **Mt 19,16-22; Mk 14,51-52 and Lk 7,11-17**: Three "Young Men" are portrayed in the four Gospel accounts, one in each citation. Their immense significance is fully shown in "Naked" above.

52. **Acts 10**: Three times Peter sees a heavenly vision of three animal kingdom groups ("animals and reptiles and birds"; cf. **I-84**), and finally the spirit told him that "three men are looking for you." It would seem that the visionary nature of this, specifically as coming from heaven or the Spirit, comports with the ninefold human being (3 X 3), the three-fold human "body," and the threefold nature of the perfected human being (manas-buddhi-atma). On the other hand, the "three men" may just reiterate the meaning of the three animal groups, for the latter suggest the three bodies:

Physical body	=	Reptiles
Etheric body	=	Animals (presumably mammals)
Astral body	=	Birds

53. **Three John Beings**: In 3 ABD 886, nine Biblical personalities are listed by the name of John, which it says "was a common Jewish name during the Hellenistic age and was especially popular among the priesthood." The first four were from the pre-Christian Maccabean era. Another is John Mark (Acts 12,12), traditionally considered to have become Evangelist Mark, who is thus known more by the latter "Name." The father of Simon Peter is called John by Evangelist John (Jn 1,42; 21,15-17), but is called Jona (e.g., Bar-Jona in Mt 16,17), or Jonah, by Matthew. Still another is the member of a high priestly family (Acts 4,6) who, in the next essay herein, is identified as one and the same person as the Evangelist John. The list of nine makes no mention of the Evangelist John, but lists John the Baptist and John the Disciple, apparently assigning the latter as the Evangelist. There are, in anthroposophical light, three major New Testament personalities who go by the name John. The amazing spiritual relationship between these three is explained in "Peter, James and John." One is sorely tempted, in the context of that relationship and the present essay, to associate them with the three bodies as follows:

John the Baptist	Etheric
John, the son of Zebedee	Physical
John, the Evangelist	Astral

54. In "Peter, James and John" below, we see that Jesus was anointed three times:

a) On his feet with ointment on Saturday before Palm Sunday by Mary Magdalene at the house of her brother Lazarus and sister Martha in Bethany (Jn 12,1-8);

b) On his head with ointment in the middle of Holy Week by a woman at the house of Simon the Leper in Bethany (Mt 26,1-13; Mk 14,1-9); and

c) On his feet by a woman with her tears at the house of a Pharisee called Simon (Lk 7,36-50). Neither the place nor the time is otherwise given. The similarity of names, i.e., Simon, suggests that it might have been at the same house in Bethany as in (b), but the time and circumstances appear different. Moreover, the identification of Simon as a leper in (b) seems clearly to distinguish him from this Pharisee, for no Pharisee would, as a leper, invite guests to his home.

APPENDIX TO "THREE BODIES"

The Bible, as we have it, seems to indicate that Adam and Eve had three sons, Cain, Abel and Seth (Gen 4,1,2,25; item #25a in "Three Bodies"; little significance is given to the fact that "other sons and daughters" were born to Adam after the birth of Seth, Gen 5,4). And so they did, but from this picture theology, without anthroposophy, again applies its formless documentary hypothesis under which the Kenan line of descent in Gen 5,12 et seq. is attributed to a different source than the Cain line in Gen 4,17-24. The anthroposophist can indeed see a difference in the two accounts, but it is a difference coming not from documents but from different stages in the descent of the human being, the Prodigal Son. Anthroposophists who read about the three sons of Adam and Eve might be troubled by the cryptic account Steiner gave in *The Temple Legend* (TL), Lects. 5 (pp. 49-59, see also Notes at 345-350), 7 (pp. 73-85), 11 (pp. 141-147), 17 (pp. 237-246) and 18 (pp. 255-263). This cycle was introduced in "Widow's Son." It will help to understand what is about to be presented if the reader will review the origin of the phrase in the passage there quoted from Lect. 6. The Cain element is that from which the passion-free direct spiritual light (the Father principle) in the soul has withdrawn (in Biblical terminology, "hidden its face," as in Mysteries). The maternal soul is thus "widowed," so that the human being in that condition is a "widow's son." While its paragons in scripture have been exalted initiates, they represent the archetypes of, and thus the term applies generally to, humanity in the fourth and fifth Cultural Eras of our post-Atlantean Epoch, the Greco-Roman (747 B.C.-A.D. 1414) and the present Germanic or European (A.D. 1414-3574); see **I-19** and **I-24**. Ours is a time of applying intellect to the outer world, an activity which is a two-edged sword. On the one hand, the Ahrimanic (Satanic, see **I-32**) temptation to materiality is overpowering. On the other, humanity must prevail over the outer world in a process of sublimation, a process which can only be accomplished through intaking the etheric "Blood" of Christ. The divine intelligence necessary for this to evolve is administered by the Archangel Michael (under his immediate predecessor who is now an Archai, a time spirit), whose regency commenced again in 1879 (see **I-19**).

The two introductory paragraphs of the passage quoted below, from TL, Lect. 5, not themselves directly a part of the legend, are included to demonstrate how a "Seed," once sown into the human soul, comes to fruition at a later time, or incarnation, as a part of the working of the wondrous "mysteries" of God (cf. Rom 11,33):

We have spoken about various legends which contain esoteric truths in the pictures which they present. These were given to man in this form at a time when he was not mature enough to receive the truths directly. These pictures took hold of man's "causal" body[20]— that part of man which bore the germ of his future Higher Manas— and thus made him ready to understand the truths directly in a future incarnation.

I would like now to show one such legend as this which dates back only a few centuries and is still extant today in many versions. It is the following. [Footnotes, though worthwhile, are omitted].

At the beginning of the fifteenth century a personality appeared in Europe who had been initiated into certain secrets in the East. This was Christian Rosenkreutz. By the time this incarnation of Christian Rosenkreutz [see "Pillars on the Journey"] had come to an end, he had initiated about ten other people into such matters as he himself

---

20. "Causal body" is defined in the glossary of Indian-Theosophical terms appended to *Foundations of Esotericism* (FE) as "the extract of the etheric and astral bodies which man bears from Earth-life to Earth-life and continually enriches."—ERS

had learned through initiation—insofar as this was possible among Europeans at that time. This small brotherhood called itself "Fraternitae Rosae Crucis," the Brotherhood of the Rose Cross. This small group of people then gave a certain legend to a larger, more exoteric fraternity, through whom it then became generally known to the world.

Christian Rosenkreutz himself had revealed certain deep secrets of the Mysteries to those people who were sufficiently prepared to receive them. But, as I said, there were not more than ten in this small circle, consisting of initiated Rosicrucians. What was taught by Christian Rosenkreutz could not be imparted to many people, but it was embodied in a kind of myth. Since it was first given out in the fifteenth century, it has often been repeated and explained in the various brotherhoods. It was told in larger brotherhoods, but was interpreted only in intimate circles.

This is the approximate content:

There was a time when one of the Elohim created a human being whom he called Eve. That Elohim united himself with Eve and she gave birth to Cain. After this, another Elohim, named Yahveh, created Adam. Adam also united himself with Eve and from this union came Abel.

Thus we see that Cain is a direct descendant of the gods, but Abel is a descendant of Adam and Eve who are human. Now the myth proceeds:

The sacrifices which Abel made to Yahveh were pleasing to him, but the sacrifices brought by Cain did not please him because the birth of Cain was not ordained by him. The result was that Cain committed fratricide. He killed Abel and for this he was excluded from communion with Yahveh. He went away into distant lands and founded his own race there.

Adam again united himself with Eve and from this union came Seth, also mentioned in the Bible, who took over the role of Abel. Thus we have two generations of mankind: the race of Cain, who was a descendant of Eve and one of the Elohim, and the other race which had human parentage and was brought into existence at the command of Yahveh.

Among the descendants of Cain are those who have been creators of art and science, as, for instance, Methuselah [Methushael, Gen

4,18], the inventor of the Tau script, and Tubal-Cain, who taught the use of working of metal ores and iron. In this line of descent, stemming from the Elohim, were all those who trained themselves in the arts and sciences.

Hiram also descended from the race of Cain, and he was the inheritor of all that had been learned by the others of his line in technology and art. He was the most significant architect we can imagine.

Out of Seth's line came Solomon, who excelled in everything which came from Yahveh. He was endowed with the wisdom of the world and all the attributes of calm, clear, objective wisdom. This wisdom can be expressed in words which go straight to the human heart and can uplift a person, but it is unable to produce anything tangible of a technical nature, in art or science. It is a wisdom which is a directly inspired gift of God and not attained from below through human passions welling up from the human will—that would be the wisdom pertaining to the sons of Cain, a legacy of the other Elohim, not Yahveh. They are the hardworking industrious ones who seek to accomplish everything through their own efforts.

The intriguing account goes on, telling of how the Queen of Sheba, who came first to and wedded Solomon, became enamored of Hiram stimulating intense jealousy between the two men, as a consequence of which Solomon conspired against Hiram. The temple was complete save for the casting of the Molten Sea for which Hiram had completed all preparations. But he had to watch three inept apprentices, angry because he had not promoted them, misdirect its casting with Solomon's complicity. As Hiram watched its disintegration in burning flames, his ancestor, Tubal-cain appeared to him saying that he should cast himself invincibly into the fire, which he did, and was thus led by Tubal-cain to Cain to be initiated into the Mystery of Fire. From Tubal-cain he received a hammer and a Golden Triangle which he was to carry round his neck. He returned and was able to complete the proper casting of the Molten Sea, whereupon the Queen of Sheba consented to become his bride. He was then attacked by the three apprentices, but before he died he managed to throw the Golden Triangle into a well. Solomon and others were worried by his disappearance. After a search he was found, and in his dying act pointed to the place where the Golden Triangle was to be found. It was brought to the Molten Sea and both were preserved together in the Holy of Holies, to be discovered there only by those who can understand the meaning of the legend of the Temple of Solomon and its Master Builder Hiram.

Before condemning the legend as contrary to the Mosaic account, several mysterious things in the Bible need be brought to mind:

First, the meaning of the tantalizing similarities between the seven generations of Cain's descendants (Gen 4) and ten of Seth (Gen 5):

Gen 4	Gen 5
1. Cain (4,1), Cf. Kenan)	1. Seth (4,25; 5,3)
2. Enoch (4,17)	2. Enosh (4,26; 5,6)
3. Irad[21] (4,18, cf. Jared)	3. Kenan (5,9; cf. Cain)
4. Mehujael (4,18)	4. Mahalalel (5,12)
	5. Jared (5,15; cf. Irad)
	6. Enoch (5,18)
5. Methushael (4,18)	7. Methuselah (5,21)
6. Lamech (4,18)	8. Lamech (5,25)
	9. Noah (5,29)
Lamech's "three sons":	
7. Jabal (4,20)	
Jubal (4,21)	
Tubal-cain (4,22)	
	Noah's "three sons" (5,32):
	10. Shem
	Ham
	Japheth

After recognizing all these similarities and the appearance of "three sons" to end both lines and their prior scholarly characterization as two different sources (J and P), the commentary at 1 NIB 380 prefers to treat them as "two separate family lines." It sees the "vengeful response of Lamech"

---

21. Curiously, one of the possible etymological meanings given in 3 ABD 448-449 is "cane huts."

to Cain's murder of Abel as indicating that Gen 5 represented a "fresh start, building upon the reference" to the origin of Yahweh worship which concludes Gen 4 (vs 26).

Second, let us consider the doctrine of the Trinity.[22] Since with it we are dealing only in terms of "doctrine," it is hard to conceive, in an earthly sense, of the Son having come forth without having a Mother as well as a Father. Nor are we without some Biblical basis for this concept, for Prov 8,22 tells us that the feminine Sophia ("wisdom") whom we may relate to the Eve concept, was the first creative act of "the Lord."[23] And if we take "Lord" here to mean the Eloha "Yahweh," then the fractal-like pattern of that creative act must derive from the highest source within the Trinity itself. The Father must have been, as modern sexist-free writing would suggest, androgynous, until divided into the fruitful male-female dualism from which the creative "Word" itself, the Christ or "Son," went out. A patriarchal society would not have found it difficult to speak, as

22. The "Trinity" is not a Bible literalism but a doctrine developed by Christianity to deal with a Mystery it could not otherwise comprehend and with certain falsities it had otherwise to encounter; see Guthrie, Jr., *Christian Doctrine*, Atlanta, John Knox, 1968, p. 89 et seq.; and to deal with paradoxes it could not otherwise handle; see MacGregor, *Philosophical Issues in Religious Thought*, Washington, D.C., University Press of America, 1979. In all of that, it is, of course, another earthly manifestation of "threefoldedness." In *The Mystery of the Trinity* (MT), Steiner explains the spiritual basis for the doctrine.
23. Under "The Birth of the Heavenly Sophia" in *The Heavenly Sophia and the Being of Anthroposophia* (HSBA), Prokofieff cogently shows from Steiner's lectures on the creation how the "heavenly Sophia" was born during the Ancient Sun Condition of Consciousness, through the sacrifice by the Kyriotetes whom Steiner calls Spirits of Wisdom (see **I-6**). During this period primal air, space and light came into being. The Archangels were "born," attained their "human status," during Sun evolution (see **I-15**), and the Archangel associated most closely with the Sun is Michael, the prince of light (see **I-19**). Yet while Prokofieff there cites the works of King Solomon as the oldest written description of the Sophia, presumably being the so-called "wisdom books" of the Bible attributed to him, he does not there relate it specifically to Prov 8,22. We might be tempted to see the name Solomon as deriving from Sun, but etymological tradition relates it (*selomoh*) instead to *salom* (or "shalom" meaning "peace") based on 1 Ch 22,9, while modern scholars relate it to *sillem* ("Make compensation") based on 2 Sam 12,14-24 (see 6 ABD 105), for our "Sol" does not derive either from Hebrew or Greek.
    Appendix 1 of HSBA is entitled "The Feminine and Masculine Principles on Earth and in the Spiritual World," which begins appropriately, "It is puzzling that earthly human beings experience the cosmic being of the Sophia as feminine." In reality, in the astral and spiritual worlds there is no such thing as a male or female being (Mt 22,30; Mk 12,25; Lk 20,35). Cf. Powell's *The Most Holy Trinosophia* (MHT). It would seem that we may speak of male and female principles, but not beings, as existing in the higher worlds. All that is said in this volume, especially relating to Prov 8,22-31, should be reconciled to this concept.

the Bible does, only of the male aspect—"sons" are everywhere, but "daughters, sisters and wives" appear only as instruments of the story.

Third, even later in the Biblical account, "when men [notice, no women] began to multiply on the face of the ground," suggesting a look back to Lemuria when mineralization, in the tenuous transition from "Fire" to air, then water, then solids, was first occurring (which led to eventual hardening, as in the meaning of "Adam"); "daughters were born to them," and "the sons of God" cohabited with them to produce off-spring of a spatially huge (giant-like or "mighty") cloud-like ("Nephilim") nature. See Gen 6,1-4. Here we have offspring produced by earthly females sired by godly or heavenly, creative male spirits. That it should have happened this way with the first earthly Eve cannot therefore be considered contrary to the Bible, unless, of course, the evolutionary nature of the human being, its descent through the higher states of existence, and eventually into the reality of reincarnation, are to be rejected—in which case theology can continue its groping in the "Darkness" for meaning to such passages as these.

Fourth, just as we wrestle with the concept of an irresistible force versus an immovable object, so might we also wrestle with the concept of a pre-creative God. How can anything be created so long as there is only a unity? For creation comes only by "Fission." Somehow the pre-creative God must have embodied within its holy being both the male and female principles, those of "Fission" and Fusion." If the divine thought of creating then somehow came into being, it would have precipitated the separation of the unity into these two principles. During the course of human descent, only the male "Fission" principle could be dominant. All growth on Earth comes from cell division, following the pattern "As Above, So Below." Eve, the female principle of oneness or unity, had to withdraw quietly into the background, and human beings of the Judeo-Christian faith, or more broadly of the monotheistic religions, came to speak only of a Father God and his Son and Spirit. But the time has begun to dawn when the female principle, Eve, Sophia, the "Mother of God" both in the beginning (Prov 8,22) and in her reflection on Earth (Lk 1,27,42-43,46), will take dominion, when the "Fusion" enabled by earthly embodiment of the Christ Spirit within the human being must bring about the reascent, transformed, to the primal heavenly union—reunion. For this Christ prayed, Jn 17,11,20-23, and on the Cross gave himself up unto the divine, death-defying Mystery of union, Eph 1,9-10.

Fifth, the female principle never thereafter departed from the Christ, the creative Word, and from the Cross he directed Lazaruz/John to take it into "his own home" (Jn 19,26-27).

Sixth, as already indicated in item #25a, Adam and Eve are not said to have had any female children, nor is even Adam said to have had any until very late (Gen 5,4), suggesting a deeper meaning to the matter of their parentage of humanity. All surviving humanity is said to have come from Seth (Gen 5 et seq.; see also Luke's genealogy [Lk 3,37-38] that jumps completely over Gen 4), even though the generations of Cain are given in Gen 4 and they are said to be the progenitors of "those who dwell in tents and have cattle" (vs 20), "those who play the lyre and pipe" (vs 21), and (implicitly) of those who forge "instruments of bronze and iron" (vs 22). Do these groups not preempt the major part of humanity, including those who are later said to have descended from Seth? Is it not significant that Philo, who so greatly influenced our New Testament writers (see "Egypt"), considered that Enoch, Methuselah and Lamech were descended from both Cain and Seth (see PHILO, pp. 132-151, at 136, "The Posterity and Exile of Cain" [40])?

We saw in "I AM" the immense theological confusion between Gen 4,26 and Ex 6,3, as to when the Eloha Yahweh was first recognized by humanity. It will be helpful to recognize that the plural Elohim did not become the primary agency of creation until after the prior three Conditions of Consciousness, Old Saturn, Sun and Moon, had passed and Earth evolution had begun (see I-16), and that the Eloha Yahweh was not separated out for recognition until the Evolutionary Epoch of Lemuria when the Moon separated from the Earth (see I-27 and OS). The Cain element down through Lamech's "three sons" appears to have been implanted (Gen 4,1-25) on the very threshold of the time when Yahweh took over from the Moon (Gen 4,26). In other words, it was a part of the sixth day of creation when the human being was first created in the etheric state and given the Cain-like "dominion" of all earthly creatures (Gen 1,26-30). That element, the Cain element, the male element was thus created by the gods and the maternal Eve before the hard "Adam" state of humanity came into being in Gen 3,17. But it was an element that would be reborn in all of humanity that came later. After the division into sexes occurred (Gen 2,18-25) and the astral body of all humanity was infected (Gen 3), Adam and Eve then had a son, Cain, who was dominated by the male influence originally born on the sixth day to Eve by the gods. Then a son, Abel was born to them embodying primarily the female principle, and in order to dominate the Earth and its creatures the male element had to subdue the female. The Individualities identified in the Cain line in Gen 4,17-24 were then born into earthly materiality as the Individualities in the Seth line in Gen 4,25-5,32.

Here we have an anthroposophical postulate that corresponds with anthroposophy's showing that there is only one creation story (Gen 1-3), only one story of Noah taking the "Wild Animals" into the "Ark" (Gen 6,19-7,3) and only one series of "sister" ruses (see item #7), each telling of the evolutionary development of the human being, a progression and not a duplication of accounts.

But let us go back and try to reconstruct what these myths (TL and Gen 4-5) are telling us.

A principle that should come easily for the Christian is that there is no spiritual growth without true sacrifice (cf. Rom 12,1; Heb, esp. 9,26). In OS, Steiner has shown us how in each stage of the development of the human being, progress could be made only by the sacrifice of the Hierarchies (**I-6**), starting with that of the Thrones on Ancient Saturn. We must start out with the assumption that all spiritual beings, in their normal state, are neither male nor female (Lk 20,34-36; Gen 1,27; 5,1-2; Mt 19,4; Mk 10,6), but androgynous, whole beings, embodying the perfect unity of both the male and female principles. What then happened to bring about a sexual human being?

While still in the etheric state, the androgynous human being of Gen 1,26-2,17, called simply "man," was brought into existence in the manner described in OS. As yet, no materialized "Blood" coursed through human veins. We are in an early race (Age) of Lemuria (**I-1**), perhaps the fourth, when Mars pulled away from the Sun complex (still containing Sun-Mars-Venus-Mercury) and passed through the Earth-Moon complex so as to leave the "Blood" component of iron in it (see the order of separation of the planets in **I-27**). That race expired in a period of rest, "pralaya," which the Bible calls a "Deep Sleep" (Gen 2,21), and the Moon separated (perhaps Lemuria's fifth race; cf. **I-27**), laying the basis for materialization. While the Eloha Yahweh is first mentioned in Gen 2,4b, "he" did not separate from the others until the Moon separated from the Earth-Moon mass, at which time "he" went from the Sun to the Moon to direct the further evolution of humanity on Earth, the other six Elohim remaining on the Sun.

We come now to what must have happened during the pralaya, the "Deep Sleep" of Gen 2,21, to bring about the sexualization of human beings. Eve was created first, that is, she was created before Adam. "Man" already existed in that etheric world, but as an androgynous being, so Eve was taken first out of that androgynous "man" (Gen 2,21-23). We are not talking about the later Eve of Gen 3. The extraction, of course, of the female element from the androgynous "man" in the etheric state would leave the male element as a separate part, so that the two would then exist separately, but at this point the action is really on Eve, the fruitful maternal element. Here, in what is buried in the Biblical account, one of the Elohim, one who was among those to remain on the Sun, had to *sacrifice* its female characteristic in order to bring about the development of a female human being in the etheric Earth. That Eloha, then being itself only of male characteristic, conjugated with Eve to produce the etheric male offspring called Cain. The being who was eventually to materialize into the hardened human being called Adam already existed in the spiritual world as the remnant of the "man" from whom Eve was created. But in order for that male element to move into the etheric Earth, it was necessary for another Eloha to sacrifice its male element, thus becoming itself predominantly female. That Eloha was Yahweh, who then went to the Moon.

But before any human being descended even into the material state that could be called hard, i.e., "Adam," those things transpired that are mentioned in "The Nativity," whereby the creative spirits withheld a portion of the unspoiled etheric bodies of both the female and the male— the etheric bodies that would, at the "Right Time," incarnate as Luke's Mary and the Nathan-Jesus child. This retention of an unsullied portion of the etheric body—the *Life* Body—is reflected in Job 2,6 where God says that Job's "life" shall be beyond Satan's (i.e., Lucifer's at this stage) power. (It is also retroactively reflected by the withdrawal of the "tree of life" in Gen 3,22-24.) Then the Fall of the human astral body occurred as described in Gen 3. Yahweh by now bore primarily a female characteristic, Moon-like. The female menstrual and human birth cycles take their characteristic from that aspect. Moreover, the characteristic and desire of Yahweh was that the human being should not descend into a hardened state, but merely touch the Earth existence to recognize its "I Am" nature. This is more fully explored under "Blood" in Vol. 2. Unity, tribe, family, were all female characteristics, as was the lunar calendar of the "chosen" Hebrew people. But Providence had it that an Archangel called Lucifer (literally "light bearer") should remain behind during the "wisdom"-developing Ancient Moon Condition of Consciousness. And this retarded spiritual being was thus more interested in bringing knowledge to the human being during the Earth Condition of Consciousness (which was to implant "love"). Lucifer thus tempted and tainted the human astral body and consequently, in turn, the etheric and physical bodies—all the "members" of the human being. As yet, no Ego had entered, so no moral guilt was implicit. In time, the counterbalancing "grace" would make the erasure of that taint possible. Thus, what came about without human moral fault would be paid for by a sacrifice without human expenditure (Heb; see *The Concept of Original Sin and Grace* [OSG]).

So Adam and Eve each became an earthly human being who could produce offspring. But already Cain was in etheric existence, just as they had earlier been. Now with the infection of the human "Bodies" consciousness began to dim (Gen 3,22-24) and human beings in time were to begin experiencing loss of consciousness through death (Gen 3,19) and implicitly through its younger sibling, sleep. But no death is said yet to have occurred when, immediately after the Garden story of Gen 3, we have Adam "knowing" Eve and producing Cain. Here we have the male etheric being of Cain brought down to Earth, not by sacrifice of an Elohim as had his parents, but rather by the earthly act of his parents. But his original etheric body was the creation of an Eloha (with Eve) other than Yahweh, that is, it was male. His earthly brother Abel, on the other hand, did not have such an etheric Body originally created by an Eloha, but being a male child bore a female etheric body (the etheric body is always of the opposite sex to the physical body in a human being). Since the female Yahweh had had nothing to do with the creation of Cain's etheric body, Cain's sacrifice was not pleasing to Yahweh.

Cain is given, literally from nowhere, a wife (Gen 4,17), which means that during that race, perhaps the sixth, probably by now that related to the Venus separation (see **I-27**), other human beings came into earthly existence, and Cain's seven generations (see above listing) came and went. Then the final Lemurian race, the seventh, perhaps related to the Mercury separation (**I-27**), brought the Lemurian Evolutionary Epoch to an end.

Those human beings prefigured into human evolution by "Name" in the sevenfold Cain genealogy of Gen 4 were then reincarnated during the Atlantean Evolutionary Epoch, each bearing the same basic character, i.e., "Name," as in the earlier stage. As we see below, one can detect the motif of seven generations, rather than ten, even in Gen 5. Several possibilities come to mind. The Enoch of Gen 4,17 becomes Enosh in Gen 5,6. The Enoch of Gen 5,18 is not a normal human being as are the others, but as the most exalted spirit from the Gen 4 Race merely enters the soul of another human being, cohabiting with the other its three bodies in an inspiring companionship (cf. the Elijah Individuality, as discussed in "Widow's Son"; and as the same Individuality did with the Twelve, especially the Beloved Disciple, after John the Baptist was beheaded [see "Peter, James and John" below). It is to be noted that Enoch's number of years is less than half that of the next shortest in Gen 5, and it has always been noted that he did not seem to die but merely "walked with God" and "was not, for God took him" (Gen 5,24). It seems plausible to consider the Enoch in Gen 5,18 to be also a reincarnation of the Enosh in Gen 5,6, but to have cohabited with Jared in view of the close relationship between Enoch and Irad in Gen 4 and Jared and Enoch in Gen 5, so that Jared gave birth to the re-ensoulment of Enoch and then in that condition sired Methuselah. Similarly, Abel might be considered as ensouled in Seth (cf. Gen 4,25), and since Cain and Abel were of the same generation, and Cain reappears as Kenan, one generation is thus eliminated in the reckoning. It seems more probable that Enosh was born to Seth in Lemuria, for it is after that birth that "men began to call upon the name of [Yahweh]" Gen 4,26, the event concluding ancient Lemuria and the Gen 4 account.

If this is true, the number of Atlantean generations then shrinks and Cain/Kenan begins that line just as he did in Gen 4. It seems powerfully significant that ages are not given in Gen 4 but are given in Gen 5, suggesting that with the Moon newly in the heavens time could be expressed in terms of years. The etheric master plan for this was laid in Gen 1,14. The Cain/Kenan line also ends with Lamech if Noah and his "three sons" are considered to be of the post-Atlantean Epoch, as suggested by the obvious seven motif, i.e., Cain is "sevenfold," Lamech in Gen 4 is "seventy-seven fold" (Gen 4,24), and in Gen 5,30 Lamech dies at "seven hundred and seventy-seven years." While born on Atlantis, we can treat Noah and his "three sons" as really post-Atlantean in character. He is said to have taken seven persons onto the "Ark" with himself (Gen 7,13; 8,18; 2 Pet 2,5), and we know that the guidance of the Ancient Indian Cultural Era, initiated by Manu (Noah), was through his "seven holy rishis."

In the Bible's numerology, Lamech's dying at the age of seven hundred seventy seven years probably suggests that his existence during Atlantis (having previously existed in the sevenfold Lemuria) had spanned the full Atlantean scope of seven races (or Cultural Eras) of seven Archangelic regencies (see **I-1**, **I-19**, and the seven angels [Archangels] of the "churches" [post-Atlantean Cultural Eras] in Rev 2-3). Lamech had a part in bringing both Lemuria and Atlantis to a close. In Gen 4,24, Lamech is associated with the number seventy-seven, while in Gen 5,31 seven hundred seventy seven; first two sevens, then three. Moreover, the number seventy-seven comprises the pregnant number "eleven" times seven (see point #2 in "Peter, James and John" for a discussion of the significance of "eleven"). The importance of the sevens for both Lamechs (Gen 4,24 and 5,31) is recognized by 4 ABD 136 which, it suggests, "makes it difficult to avoid the impression that the number is intended to convey the idea of completion." And can we not perhaps see this also in the very name Lamech which is so very like *lamedh* (or lamed), the *twelfth* letter of the Hebrew alphabet.

Another complexity, but perhaps a magnificent one, is presented if we reflect upon **I-43**. We there see that the Original Semites (whose name is generally understood to derive from Noah's son Shem) were the fifth race on Atlantis. This might suggest that Noah's "three sons" were the successive representatives of the last three races (progressively more evil) on Atlantis. There is something compelling also about the relationship between the spiritual nature of Enoch in Gen 5,22-24, as the ancestor of the Semites on Atlantis, and Melchizedek (Gen 14,18 and Heb 7,1-28) as the one who carries the etheric body of Shem over to all the Semites in the Chaldo-Egyptian Cultural Era of the post-Atlantean Epoch. Precision should not be pressed too far on these matters, but they are well to bear in mind for they open new avenues of understanding, and the Mosaic account does demand an adjustment to our modern intellectual manner of thinking.

This scenario also gives meaning to Gen 4,26b, "At that time men began to call upon the name of the Lord." This statement ends Gen 4. The Moon has separated and Yahweh has identified "herself" with it. Humanity's descent is made possible. "Blood" came into being in Gen 4 after the separation of Mars and the Moon, and thus Abel's "Blood" is the first to be spilled. The consciousness of human beings was beginning to dim, but extensive clairvoyance still existed, particularly during recurring periods of day and night, and Yahweh would have been recognized by humanity. After all, it had but shortly before dwelt with and fully known the gods. Their "face" became "hidden" only gradually. Yahweh could not have been recognized as the female goddess in direct charge of human evolution from the Moon until that point in the Lemurian Epoch when "she" had gone from the Sun to the Moon upon the latter's separation from the Earth mass.

While we, with our traditions, may squirm at calling Yahweh "she," it might be well to reflect upon what prevailed in the Cultural Era in which the Hebrew people came into being, the Chaldo-Egyptian. Moses was initiated into the Mysteries of "Egypt" which held to the male Sun god Osiris, the female Moon god Isis, and their earthly son Horus. It is especially intriguing to contemplate all the Hebrew names that seem to derive from Isis, including Isaac, Israel and Isaiah, to name but three. The lunar nature of the Hebrew people is well recognized, for Yahweh was a Moon god who reflected the light of the "fullness of the Godhead," the Elohim who dwelt, and the Christ who sojourned, in the Sun.

In closing, let us return to the legend and seek an Imagination that will reveal its meaning. It is full of the imagery of anthroposophical understanding and the Bible legend. The "temple" comprises the human being's three bodies, the "outer court" (Rev 11,2) being the physical and etheric bodies and the inner the astral body, which must be mastered by the Ego during Earth evolution so as to be transformed into Manna. These can all be seen in Paul's account, Heb 9,2-5. The Molten Sea is the fluidic etheric body within the "four corners" (Rev 7,1; 20,8; Acts 10,11; 11,5; Job 37,3; Is 11,12; Ezek 7,2) of the earthly physical body, which houses the warm human "Blood" pervaded by "Fire." The "hammer" is that used in the outer work of the physical world, not in the "temple" proper but in the quarry (1 K 6,7) and on the appointments (e.g., Ex 25,18-36; 37,7-22); see also Is 41,7; Jer 23,29; 50,23. It represents the outer world which must be both mastered and transformed by the human Ego. Ah, but the Golden Triangle, before it is tossed into the Molten Sea, represents the three bodies of the human being. Through the complicity of Lucifer and the higher spiritual world (Job 2), the casting of the Molten Sea was put in jeopardy, and it suffered the "Fire" of the astral world between lives on Earth (Lk 16,19-31), but the "Purifying Fire" was brought to proper use by the "Widow's Son" who returns enlightened to complete it "properly." When the outer body has been murdered, i.e., "crucified" (cf. Rev 10,8-11), the Golden Triangle is thrown into the repository of wisdom, the Well, and, like the Holy Grail, is found (Mt 13,44-46). It becomes truly Golden (Heb 9,4) when the three bodies have been transformed into their three higher counterparts, manas-buddhi-atma. The Kingdom of Heaven has then been attained, as summarized by Christ in Mt 13,33. Prior to that time, one returns to incarnation again and again to be able to work on the proper casting of the Molten Sea, and when that is completed there is a Wedding of the Bride and Bridegroom, i.e., the Queen of Sheba becomes one's bride (see "Bride/Bridegroom"). The legend is buried within The Lord's Prayer. The "four corners" and the Golden Triangle can be seen in its seven petitions as illustrated by the diagram in item #19 of the text.

The understanding of Gen 4-5 portrayed above must surely not be far from spiritual reality, the flowing continuity and wholeness the Bible purports to reveal from beginning to end. With it the legend of the Temple of Solomon and its Master Builder Hiram can seemingly be comprehended. Without anthroposophical light, theological understanding has yet to provide a solution to this riddle. It is a vital section of Ariadne's thread that can lead humanity to the "Fullness" of Biblical comprehension.

PETER, JAMES AND JOHN

To call "PETER, JAMES AND JOHN," a "phrase" may seem strange, as may "Abraham, Isaac and Jacob" when so treated later. But we have already seen the collective significance of the latter threesome in "Bush" above, and both groups appeared above under "Three Bodies." In a sense they are Old and New Testament counterparts, and portray the "Seed"-like "fractal"[1] nature of creation. Abraham, Isaac and Jacob became the spiritual ancestry of ancient Israel, from which sprang the specially called nation's zodiacal twelvefoldedness. Peter, James and John, representing "the Twelve," became the spiritual ancestry of the Church (i.e., Peter = Rome; James = Apostolic or Jerusalem; John = Eastern Orthodox, granting that some liberty is taken in this conditional use of the names "James and John"). From both tribes and apostles is to come the zodiacal twelvefoldedness of the Holy City (see Rev 21,12-13).

Though never in John's Gospel, Peter, James and John appear together five times in the synoptics: at the Transfiguration (Mt 17,1; Mk 9,2; Lk 9,28), in the Garden of Gethsemane (Mt 26,37; Mk 14,33), at the "raising" of Jairus' daughter (Mk 5,37; Lk 8,51), and as the audience (along with Andrew) for the healing of Peter's mother-in-law and for Jesus' "Little Apocalypse" (Mk 1,29-31 and 13,3) (thus appearing "alone" with him only "three" times).

We must pause at the outset to reflect upon why just these three—Peter, James and John—are taken by Jesus into these more intimate situations. What are we being told by this circumstance? Do these instances not relate, as indeed does the whole Bible account, to the matter of *consciousness*? How can the color red be explained to one who is blind? We have seen how the Bible is a story of the evolution of human consciousness. How do these instances reflect an intensification of that concern? They are all situations calling for new spiritual insight. And just as Jesus

---

1. See the discussion of "fractals" in the Appendix to "Fire" in Vol. 2, "What Is Man?".

recognized that not all of the masses were karmically ready to receive the message of salvation (Mt 10,11-14; Mk 6,11; Lk 9,5), nor were even many who were converted sufficiently prepared to receive the higher instruction of the "Mountain" (Mt 7,6), so also even among the "Twelve" only a smaller group could be given these most intimate teachings. Peter, James and John composed that group, though eventually only the mysterious John could be given the highest instruction. The approach to him, however, is through the three. Let us look at the three occasions in question. (We need not for now concern ourselves with those two mentioned only by Mark when Andrew was also present. Andrew was Peter's brother, and Mark was Peter's charge, thus distinguishing these instances.)

The first reported is the raising of Jairus' daughter. The account is reflected in all synoptics. Matthew alone fails to identify these three with it (Mt 9,18-26). One cannot comprehend its higher meaning without hearing what Steiner said. The following passage appears in Lect. 3 of *Building Stones for an Understanding of the Mystery of Golgotha* (BSU), pp. 57-59:

> I should like to draw your attention today to another important question. The Gospels often speak of the mysteries of the Kingdom of God or the mysteries of the Kingdom of Heaven. In what sense do they speak of mysteries? It is somewhat difficult to grasp this idea. Those who have made a careful study of the Gospels from the occult standpoint are increasingly of the opinion that every sentence in the Gospels is immutable, every detail is of the greatest moment. All criticism is reduced to silence as one penetrates ever more deeply into the Gospels from the standpoint of Spiritual Science. Now before speaking of the mystery of the Kingdom of Heaven I must draw your attention to something that is highly characteristic.
>
> In my earlier lectures on the Gospels I referred to that important passage which deals with the healing, or, one might call it, the raising of the twelve-year-old daughter of Jairus. Since we can speak openly here, I am able to refer to the deeper medical knowledge of an occult nature which is disclosed to those who study this miracle of healing from the standpoint of Spiritual Science. Christ went into the ruler's house and took Jairus' daughter who was thought to be dead by the hand in order to heal her (Matt. IX, 22-25; Mark V, 22; Luke VIII, 41). Now I must remind you that we can never arrive at

an understanding of such matters if we do not relate the passage in question to the earlier and later passages. People are only too ready to detach certain passages from their context and study them in isolation, whereas they are interdependent. You will recall that as Jesus was summoned to the daughter of Jairus, a woman who was diseased with an issue of blood for twelve years came behind Him and touched the hem of His garment and was healed. Christ felt that "virtue" had gone out of Him. He turned round and said: "Daughter, thy faith has made thee whole." We can understand these words only if we grasp in the right way the idea of faith referred to above: "Thy faith (or trust) hath made thee whole." Now this passage in the Gospels has deep implications. The woman had suffered from an issue of blood for twelve years. Jairus' daughter was twelve years old. She was sexually retarded and was unable to develop the maturity of the woman who had suffered from hemorrhage for twelve years. When Christ healed the woman He felt that "virtue" or power had issued from Him. When He entered the ruler's house He took the girl by the hand and transferred this power to her and so enabled her to reach sexual maturity. Without this power she must have wasted away. And thus she was restored to life. This shows that the real living Being of Christ was not confined to His person, but was reflected in His whole environment, that Christ was able to transfer powers from one person to another by virtue of His selfless regard for others. He was able to surrender the self in active service for others and this is reflected in the power that He felt arise in Him when the woman who had great faith touched the hem of His garment.

This mystery is related to the observation He frequently made to His disciples: "Unto you it is given to know the mystery of the Kingdom of God; but unto them that are without all these things are done in parables." (Mark IV, 11.) Let us assume that the mystery of which I have just spoken—I do not mean simply the theoretic description I have given of it, but the power that was necessary before this transference could be effected—had been imparted to the Scribes and Pharisees. What would have happened if they had been able to transfer powers from one person to another? They would not always have transferred them wisely. It is evident from the Gospels that Christ did not expect the Pharisees, still less the Sadducees, to act responsibly. When transferring this force from one person to another they would have abused it, for such was their mentality, and would have caused untold harm. This mystery therefore had to remain a secret of the Initiates.

Later in the same lecture (at pp. 66-68) he relates this human sexual development to the whole gamut of human evolution, pointing out that human beings are neither physically nor spiritually the same today as they have been in the past nor as they shall be in the future. He speaks again of the time in the latter part of our post-Atlantean Epoch (in the sixth millennium) when women "will become sterile and ... an entirely different reproductive process will exist" (cf. Lk 23,29 and Mt 24,19; Mk 13,17; Lk 21,23).

Steiner again speaks of this healing but from a slightly different perspective in *The Gospel of St. Mark* (GSMk), Lect. 3, p. 57, indicating that at this time when the Kingdom of Heaven was near "one ego must henceforth be in direct relationship with another ego."

One must also suspect that Christ perceived a karmic connection between the woman and the girl, though Steiner does not explicitly say so in these passages. In Lect. 4 of *Manifestations of Karma* (MK), he speaks of the curability and incurability of disease, saying,

> From this we see how karma works in illness and how it works to overcome illness. It will now no longer seem incomprehensible that in karma there also lies the curability or incurability of a disease. If we clearly understand that the aim—the karmic aim of illness is the progress and the improvement of man, we must presume that if a man in accordance with the wisdom which he brings with him into this existence from the kamaloca period contracts a disease, he then develops the healing forces which involve a strengthening of his inner forces and the possibility of rising higher.

Luke concludes his version of this story with Jesus charging the parents (and presumably also the disciples) "to tell no one what had happened" (Lk 8,56), a frequent admonition when something too deep for common understanding has taken place.

The next event, as reported, is the Transfiguration. We have already seen, in "Karma and Reincarnation" above, how this highly spiritual occurrence revealed the reality of karma and repeated Earth lives to Peter,

James and John, and how they were told not to say anything about this esoteric knowledge to others during that Cultural Era of the Intellectual Soul, i.e., before the "Second Coming." Clearly the Transfiguration involved a situation of enhanced consciousness on the part of the disciples. We can expect this of any experience that occurs on a "Mountain," as all the accounts report, but especially when it is said to be on a "High Mountain" as Matthew and Mark both say, Jesus having "led them up." However, later in this essay we will look at how subtly the Gospels show us the transition even then taking place in regard to the John being.

In the third and final scene, we find Peter, James and John with Jesus in Gethsemane. To appreciate this threefold sequence of events and how it reveals the demands for growing consciousness on the part of these closest disciples, we must come to a new understanding of what was taking place. Until it is seen that the "Three Years" of Christ's Incarnation in Jesus of Nazareth was an enactment upon the world arena of the stages of initiation into the ancient "Mysteries," leading humanity through their purest and profoundest depths, we will misapprehend the event. That he was to die upon the Cross was known to Jesus well before Gethsemane. Instead of the "temple sleep" of the Mysteries, the Christ must undergo actual earthly "Death," retaining full Consciousness throughout the event. He walked forthrightly into the face of his antagonists knowing this. How then can theology assume, as it has, that the "cup" that he prayed might "pass from" him was the "Crucifixion" itself (Mt 26,39; Mk 14,36; Lk 22,42)? Hear what Steiner says in GSMk, Lect. 9, pp. 168-169:

> Let us place ourselves with all humility—as we must—within the soul of Christ Jesus, who to the end tries to maintain the woven bond linking Him with the souls of the disciples. Let us place ourselves as far as we may within the soul of Christ Jesus during the events that followed. This soul might well put to itself the world-historical question, "Is it possible for me to cause the souls of at least the most select of the disciples to rise to the height of experiencing with me everything that is to happen until the Mystery of Golgotha?" The soul of Christ itself is faced with this question at the crucial moment when Peter, James and John are led out to the Mount of Olives, and Christ Jesus wants to find out from within Himself whether He will be able to keep those whom He had chosen. On the way He becomes anguished. Yes, my friends, does anyone believe, can anyone believe

that Christ became anguished in face of death, of the Mystery of Golgotha, and that He sweated blood because of the approaching event of Golgotha? Anyone who could believe that would show he had little understanding for the Mystery of Golgotha; it may be in accord with theology, but it shows no insight. Why does the Christ become distressed? He does not tremble before the cross. That goes without saying. He is distressed above all in face of this question, "Will those whom I have with me here stand the test of this moment when it will be decided whether they want to accompany me in their souls, whether they want to experience everything with me until the cross?" It had to be decided if their consciousness could remain sufficiently awake so that they could experience everything with Him until the cross. This was the "cup" that was coming near to Him. So He leaves them alone to see if they can stay "awake," that is in a state of consciousness in which they can experience with Him what He is to experience. Then He goes aside and prays, "Father, let this cup pass from me, but let it be done according to your will, not mine." In other words, "Let it not be my experience to stand quite alone as the Son of Man, but may the others be permitted to go with me."

He comes back, and they are asleep; they could not maintain their state of wakeful consciousness. Again He makes the attempt, and again they could not maintain it. So it becomes clear to Him that He is to stand alone, and that they will not participate in the path to the cross. The cup had not passed away from Him. He was destined to accomplish the deed in loneliness, a loneliness that was also of the soul. Certainly the world had the Mystery of Golgotha, but at the time it happened it had as yet no understanding of this event; and the most select and chosen disciples could not stay awake to that point.

Something of a sequel to this is given in *The Fifth Gospel* (FG), Lect. 2, where Steiner tells of how at Pentecost (Acts 2,1-12) there was a sort of awakening from the state of spiritual "Sleep" which had engulfed the disciples from the time of the Passion until then.

Let us look then at these three disciples in the light of the demand for spiritual consciousness.

At the outset it is well to remember the significance of one's "Name" and of the prevalent fact of "Name Change" in the Bible. (See "I AM," the discussion of Ex 6,2-3.) For not only in Peter's case, among these three, are we concerned here with a change of name. Of these three names, only "Peter" has no Jewish origin. In that respect, it bears some resemblance to "Paul," although that relates to the Hebrew "Saul." But both Peter and Paul are otherwise uniquely Greek words. Inasmuch as Matthew was originally written in Hebrew (as Jerome noted and Steiner insisted), it is curious that only in Matthew is Peter identified as the "rock" upon which the Church would be built (Mt 16,15-20), especially since Peter was oriented more in outlook to the Jerusalem church, at least initially (though the "Rock" was clearly a prophetic Hebrew concept; see, e.g., Gen 49,24; Num 20; Deut 32; 1 Sam 23,25,28; 2 Sam 23,3; Ps 89,26; Is 17,10 and 44,8; Hab 1,12).

The other two names are shrouded in mystery, but of the identity of Peter there is never any doubt. With James uncertainty begins to creep in, and with John it abounds. ABD (3 ABD 616) identifies at least four persons named "James," namely, the brother of Jesus and head of the Jerusalem church, the son of Zebedee, the son of Alphaeus, and the father of Judas (Lk 6,16; Acts 1,13), the first three being relatively familiar. The name derives from the Hebrew "Jacob." At least nine persons are identified as "John" in 3 ABD 886, which makes no allowance for the possibility that none of them became the revered Presbyter (Gk *presbys* = old) John in Ephesus which, as shall be shown, is the case.

In terms of spiritual "consciousness" demonstrated by these three, we see that Peter has already demonstrated a degree of this, for his "Name Change" immediately before the experience of the Transfiguration so indicates (Mt 16,13-20, esp. vs 18). Peter, taken from the Greek *Petros*, means "Rock," which as we will see in a later volume is a term for the Christ himself (1 Cor 10,4). Peter's new name characterized him as the first of the "Twelve" to recognize the Christ. When Christ says of him that "on this rock I will build my church," he is referring not to Peter as a person but to that "impulse ... in human nature" that reveals the Christ, for it is an impulse "revealed to you by the Father in Heaven, not by what you are at present as a man of flesh and blood." See *The Gospel of St. Matthew* (GSMt), Lect. 11, p. 194. While the organized church in Rome identifies itself as the representative of Peter the person, the "church universal" will come about when this spiritual impulse, the true "Rock," arises within individual human beings (cf. Jer 31,33-34 and Heb 10,16-17). Scripturally, it is within the immediate context of Peter's

"Name Change" and the Transfiguration that the sons of Zebedee begin to demonstrate their inabilities to measure up to the level of consciousness Christ had yearned to develop in them. And while Peter had recognized the Christ, he immediately thereafter showed that he was unable to comprehend the reason for the sacrifice Christ faced (Mt 16,21-23), and with James and John he too slept through the height of the Transfiguration (Lk 9,32). Light is shed on Peter's lack of comprehension by Luke 9,30-31, saying that Moses and Elijah talked with Christ "and spoke of his departure," all presumably while Peter was sleeping. The "name" James derives etymologically from Jacob, and even though that name is highly revered in Hebrew ancestry, it had no flattering meaning, and the first Jacob eventually surrendered it for the more noble one, Israel. Yet even then, it did not carry the power of recognizing the Name of Christ (see Gen 32,29, where he seeks, but is not given, the Name of his antagonist). But it is particularly the Name of "John" that we become progressively more interested in.

At first blush, it seems very odd that the sons of Zebedee were so significant in the synoptic Gospels, yet tend to pale later in relation to Peter, James the brother of Jesus, and the one to whom are ascribed the Gospel, Epistles and Apocalypse of John. For a considerable time this prompted me to postulate tentatively that the James and John who appeared along with Jesus and Peter on the three (or five) special occasions above were not the sons of Zebedee but the brother of Jesus and the author of the Johannine books. A reasonable *prima facie* case can be constructed for that scenario, though it quickly becomes vulnerable upon careful inspection. Nevertheless, the mystery surrounding these second two, most notably John, justifies our looking carefully at this threesome as a group.

Let us look briefly at James before getting to the more mysterious questions surrounding John. In large part, the relative significance of these two relates directly to the weight accorded the canonical books that bear their respective names.

For several reasons, I accept the letter of James to be the work of the brother of Jesus (Mt 13,55; Mk 6,3; Gal 1,19). It is well, however, when speaking of the "brothers" of Jesus to recognize that in the light of anthroposophy (see "The Nativity") he had no full siblings in the ordinary sense. We know that the Mother of the Nathan Jesus had no other children, and died soon after the twelve-year-old incident (Lk 2,41-51). The Father of the Solomon Jesus had already died. The Solomon Mary then joined the Nathan Joseph, and we do not know which of the four named brothers, of whom James is named first, were born of the Solomon Joseph and which of the Nathan Joseph. Assuming all were born after Jesus, then any born to the Nathan Joseph would have been relatively young during Jesus' ministry and probably not likely to have spoken out against him as indicated (Mk 3,21,31-35; Jn 7,3-9). But more significantly, from age twelve to "Thirty," Jesus of Nazareth embodied the Ego born to the Solomon parents and the "Three Bodies" born to the Nathan parents, and as such could not have had any completely full siblings. Much more significantly, however, after his Baptism when the Zarathustra Ego withdrew upon entry of the Christ Spirit, Jesus of Nazareth became Jesus Christ (see "Baptism-Dove"). Thus, in his highest component, the Ego, Jesus was then no more a brother to his "supposed" (cf. Lk 3,23) earthly siblings than He was to every other human being. How profound then becomes the question, "Who are my mother and my brothers?" (Mk 3,33; Mt 12,48).

Here is not the place to belabor all the arguments about authorship of the book of James. Two factors weigh in more heavily with me. First, James the son of Zebedee was martyred very early by Herod (Acts 12,2), probably by A.D. 44, and the other known Jameses are simply quite obscure. Second, and more important, in the light of anthroposophy I see enormous parallels between the Letter of James and the Sermon on the Mount. And while Zebedee James must surely have been among those receiving this esoteric (see "Mountain") instruction, his early death leaves the eldest "brother" of Jesus as the one most likely to have been so thoroughly indoctrinated therewith, especially in view of his primacy among those to have seen the Risen Lord (1 Cor 15,7), not to mention his natural stature within the early Church. The recently published (1995) separate AB volume on James strongly supports his authorship for other reasons also; see 37 AB 89 et seq (1995).

When we come to the Johannine authorship the plot thickens and the mystery deepens to the point of hopeless welter—up to the point where anthroposophical light begins to radiate in.

The Johannine writings, particularly the Gospel and the Apocalypse, are an ocean of spiritual perception and revelation, the Gospel being the highest yet given to humanity according to Steiner. We can here touch only upon certain relevant aspects of it, as could he, but they are enough to crack the door and emit great light.

Only gradually was Steiner able to bring out the great truths. For instance, on the deeper aspects of "Karma and Reincarnation" he had to shelve his early efforts, returning in force only in the *Karmic Relationships* (KR) series at the end of his life. One can see its early seed of his work on the Lazarus miracle in the eighth chapter of *Christianity as Mystical Fact* (CMF) in 1902, and again it is touched upon lightly in *St. John's Gospel, Notes of a Lect. on* (GSJN) (Feb 12, 1906).[2] He clearly revealed the authorship of the John Gospel in *The Gospel of St. John* (GSJ), the first of his "Gospel series,"[3] when, on May 22, 1908, he spoke on "The Raising of Lazarus." Soon thereafter, on June 17, 1908, in the introductory lecture of *The Apocalypse of St. John* (ASJ) he first clearly indicated the common authorship of the Gospel and the Apocalypse, though the seeds were also sown in CMF (Lect. 9) immediately following the discussion of Lazarus. We learn primarily from GSJ that John's Gospel is constructed with careful architectural balance so that its very middle (Chap 11) tells of the initiation of Lazarus; that, except for the prologue (Jn 1,1-18), what appears in the first half (Jn 1,19 through 10,41), though written by Lazarus/John, is the testimony of John the Baptist, whereas the balance (Jn 11-21) is the personal experience of Lazarus/John himself; that the raising of Lazarus by Jesus is a "sign" (Jn 12,18) which provoked his enemies to rise up against him (Jn 11,47-50 and 12,9-11) because he had demonstrated openly what should have remained hidden in the Mysteries;[4] that by virtue of this initiation ("Three Days' Journey"), Lazarus became a "Witness" to the high spiritual truths; that the initiation character of the event was thereafter in John's Gospel shown by the otherwise baffling but esoterically traditional terminology "the disciple whom Jesus 'loved'"; that the term

---

2. Other early lectures on John's Gospel are neither available to me nor listed in the Bibliography, but circumstances suggest that they did not go deeply yet, if at all, into this matter.

3. For the purposes of this writing, the "Gospel series" is considered to include the eleven works from 1908 to 1914 listed chronologically on p. 290 of Jn-Rel, namely, GSJ, *The Gospel of St. John and its Relation to the Other Gospels* (Jn-Rel), *The Gospel of St. Luke* (GSL), *Deeper Secrets of Human History in the Light of the Gospel of St. Matthew* (DSM), GSMt, *Background to the Gospel of St. Mark* (BKM), *The Spiritual Guidance of Man* (SGM), *From Jesus to Christ* (JTC), GSMk, FG and *Christ and the Human Soul* (CHS).

4. As Steiner said, the crime for which Socrates also was condemned to die. See 27 Brit 484 at 486, "Socrates; The accusation and its causes," which speaks of the "profanation of the mysteries."

"Wilderness" meant "solitude" or desolation of the soul; and that the true (higher) "I Am" had entered into human evolution with the coming of the Christ.

From anthroposophical understanding we learn further that from the time of the beheading of the Baptist his soul became a group-soul of the "Twelve," and that it entered particularly into Lazarus/John, for this point is made ever so poignantly in Steiner's disability-shortened "last address" (LAST) on September 27, 1924. The concluding remarks of Heidenreich's preface to LAST show more fully how this is so:

> The dramatic raising of Lazarus from the grave was an event which led to the elucidation of a different mystery. In his book *Christianity as Mystical Fact* published in 1902, Rudolf Steiner described this apparent "miracle" as an act of Initiation. In this act which represents a transitional form between the rituals of Initiation in the Mystery Temples of the ancient world and the dawning Christian era in which Initiations of this type are superseded altogether by inner development, Lazarus became Lazarus-John, "the disciple whom Jesus loved" and the author of the Fourth Gospel. Although Rudolf Steiner spoke in the years after 1902 of this event, and of the figure who passed through it, many times and from many different sides, he never referred to another incarnation of Lazarus except on an intimate occasion, the content of which became known somewhat more generally only much later, after his death. But as already stated, he never connected John the Baptist and Lazarus-John in the manner suggested in the "Last Address," and a previous incarnation of Lazarus which he indicated on the occasion mentioned above would seem to point in a different direction. Thus we are really left with a mystery.
>
> Fortunately, some light has been thrown on this through a reply which Rudolf Steiner is reported to have given to a question of Dr. Ludwig Noll, the physician who together with Dr. Ita Wegman, ... attended him during his illness. We quote the postscript printed in the most recent German edition of the "Last Address."
>
> > "According to authenticated statements, the following verbal explanation was given by Rudolf Steiner to his physician, Dr. Ludwig Noll, in connection with the 'Last Address'.

At the awakening of Lazarus, the spiritual Being, John the Baptist, who since his death had been the overshadowing Spirit of the disciples, penetrated from above into Lazarus as far as the Consciousness Soul; the Being of Lazarus himself, from below, intermingled with the spiritual Being of John the Baptist from above. After the awakening of Lazarus, this Being is Lazarus-John, the disciple whom the Lord loved."

It seems inscrutably providential that a modern discovery, that of "The Secret Gospel of Mark," has corroborated what Steiner said about the meaning of "loved" as used in John's Gospel to identify the writer of that Gospel. See the discussion of Mk 10,21 and "The Secret Gospel of Mark" later herein and near the end of "Egypt" below. In short, from that discovery the "rich young ruler" in all the synoptics (Mt 19,16-22; Mk 10,17-22; Lk 18,18-23) is now clearly to be seen as Lazarus before his initiation by Jesus.

When the above things are known, the authorship of John's Gospel becomes staggeringly clear. No person is called John in the entire Gospel except John the Baptist. In the Prologue we are told of him: "There was a man sent from God, whose name was John" (Jn 1,6). And it is immediately said, "He came for testimony, to bear witness to the light, that all might believe through him" (Jn 1,7), and that in fact he "bore witness to him" (Jn 1,15). The first statement after the Prologue then tells us, "And this is the testimony of John" (Jn 1,19a). That testimony continues uninterrupted through the entirety of the first ten chapters (Jn 1-10). What are we then told? That "everything that John said about this man was true" (Jn 10,41), and that he fulfilled the mission for which he came, "to bear witness ... that all might believe through him" (Jn 1,7), for it is said, "And many believed in him there" (Jn 10,42).Clearly we are being told that here the testimony of the Baptist, which began at Jn 1,19, ends.

Then, in the architectural middle of the Gospel, Jn 11, we are told of the initiation, the spiritual enabling, of the one who is to be the "witness" of the rest of the Gospel, Lazarus/John. After that, to the end of the Gospel we hear of the Beloved Disciple, and scholars widely agree that the one so cryptically described wrote the Gospel.

Aside from this recent discovery (see 4 ABD 558, "Mark, The Secret Gospel of"), traditional Biblical scholarship has thus far only been able to include Lazarus as one of the possibilities for authorship of John's Gospel; see 3 ABD 919, "John, The Gospel of; Date and Authorship," and 1 ABD 659, "Beloved Disciple"; Barc, The Gospel of John, p. 19; and 29 AB xcv, all of which identify Lazarus as a possibility. Others usually recognize the Gospel's purport to identify its author as the "beloved disciple" but either do not name the prospects or do not include Lazarus among them; see 8 Interp 440; 2 NICNT 290; Bultmann, *The Gospel of John*, Philadelphia, Westminster, 1971 (p. 11); and 6 Brit 587, "John, Gospel According to," and 14 Brit 854, "Biblical Literature; The Fourth Gospel: The Gospel According to John." But with the light of anthroposophical insight, all reasonable doubt is removed.

In the light of what is said above about the special relationship between the Baptist and Lazarus/John, it is remarkably notable that one recent commentary has said about the authorship of Revelation, "The candidate who seems most suitable is John the Baptist"; see 38 AB 28 (1975).

We thus take it as established beyond reasonable doubt that Lazarus, like so many other Biblical personages, underwent a "Name Change" at the time of his initiation by Jesus (Jn 11), thereby becoming "John," the author of all the Johannine corpus, including either directly or indirectly the unique last chapter (i.e., 21) of the Gospel.

It is necessary to pause here and think about the awesomeness of the assignment spiritually imposed upon the Individuality, the entelechy, behind the personalities who were "John" beings. For that we have to start with Elijah. Review again what was said about him in "Widow's Son." There we saw that the panorama of his incarnations included Adam Cadmon-Phinehas-Elijah-John the Baptist-Raphael-Novalis. In him we are thus dealing with humanity's oldest Individuality, the one Paul calls the "First Adam" (see "First and Second Adam"), whose very embryo was quickened (Lk 1,41,44) in its sixth month by the approaching embryo of its unspoiled sister soul, that of the Nathan Jesus child, whom Paul calls the "Second Adam." In "Widow's Son," we also read of the great cosmic law requiring that an Individuality who accomplished something for humanity upon its descent from the spiritual world must consequently perform a similar deed in redirecting it back to the spiritual world. Then we saw the application of that law to three distinct entities, those of John the Baptist, Lazarus/John and Rudolf Steiner. The first two figure directly into the Peter, James and John script; the third does so indirectly by being its prophetic revealer.

There is always something breathtaking about the Elijah Individuality in the Bible. Steiner tells us that he was the servant of Israel's Archangel, Michael, and became the group-soul of Israel, pervading the scene in Ahab's time as "the troubler of Israel" (1 K 18,17). He seems omnipresent. He incarnated as "Naboth" with a "vineyard," i.e., the Hebrew people; Ahab had Naboth killed so as to take control of the "vineyard" (1 K 21,1-16). But Naboth had been initiated into the Mithraic Mysteries (1 K 17; see "Widow's Son"), whereby he had a "Name Change" to "Naboth/Elijah," or simply Elijah. And even after he was dead his spirit was active and pervasive among the people until the very time that its mantle fell upon Elisha and Elijah's spirit rose to heaven in a whirlwind (1 K 21,15-2 K 2,13).

The prophet Malachi foresaw that this spirit would again become embodied, i.e., incarnated (Mal 4,5-6), in order to again carry forward the mission of Israel, and this was done as Luke's Gospel reported (Lk 1, esp. vs 17) under the mission-describing "Name" of John (Lk 1,13,59-63). And again, after he was beheaded, as he had done during Ahab's time, he entered into human activity by serving as before as a group-soul, this time of the "Twelve," but primarily and uniquely within Lazarus, who was initiated by Christ in something of the old manner to awaken in him (i.e., to subjoin his own Ego to) the Elijah spirit. So he again underwent a "Name Change" to Lazarus/John, or simply John (the Evangelist). One can see in this spiritual transaction the same thing happening with Lazarus that happened to Elisha, namely, the mantle of Elijah, the hurting and helping spirit of Adam Cadmon, fell upon him (2 K 2). Small wonder that the Gospel of John and his Apocalypse carry such an immensely deep spiritual message.

But why the name "John?" Let us defer that briefly.

We have arrived at a point beyond which credit must go largely to the late Karl Koenig, founder of the Camphill Movement (a world-wide anthroposophical initiative that addresses the needs of the trainable afflicted of all ages). I have had the privilege of inspecting a typescript English translation of a study by Koenig dated Easter, 1962. (Though apparently published in Stuttgart, Germany, in 1963, it has yet to be published in English.) It deals with the interrelationship of the three Johns, i.e., John the Baptist, John of Zebedee, and Lazarus/John, and with their respective involvement in (and with) the Gospel accounts after the death of the Baptist. Most of what follows results from the stimulating analysis he sets forth, based upon years of reflective study into, and made possible only by, the heritage of spiritual wealth left by Steiner. I am beholden also to René Querido for making me aware that any such study even existed, and to those who have custody thereof for then permitting my personal inspection.

Let us therefore construct, point by point, a skeletal framework of events that now for the first time makes an understanding of the mystery of John possible.

1. Lazarus/John is the "Beloved Disciple," and he wrote the Johannine corpus. He wrote only of his own experiences in the Gospel (the events in the first ten chapters were experienced through the Baptist who had penetrated down to his Consciousness Soul—see **I-9**). For this reason, he did not include any of the events when Peter, James and John went alone (or with Andrew) with Jesus (as listed above). Scholars have to some extent disdained John's Gospel because it said nothing about the Transfiguration, the establishment of the Eucharist or Christ's passion in the Garden. But these were omitted because Lazarus/John was not there, and moreover it was unnecessary since other Gospels addressed these from their own perspective.

2. At all times there were a zodiacal "Twelve" disciples. The variables in the list are Judas Iscariot, Lazarus/John and Matthias. The composition of the "Twelve" included one, and only one, of these three at all times, as follows:

(a) Judas Iscariot—From inception to his withdrawal at the betrayal;

(b) Lazarus/John—From the betrayal to the Ascension;

(c) Matthias—After the Ascension.

3. There were two "suppers" during Holy Week or just before, one on Saturday before Palm Sunday, as reported by John's Gospel (Jn 12,1-2), and the other on the following Wednesday, as reported by all the Gospels (Mt 26,17-21; Mk 14,12-18; Lk 22,7-16; Jn 13). The first one was in Bethany at the house of Lazarus/John, the second at the "upper room" (or cenacle/coenaculum) in Jerusalem.

4. There were two anointings of Jesus during that time period. The first was by Mary Magdalene at the first supper in Bethany, when she anointed Jesus' *feet* (Jn 12,1-8). The second was at the house of Simon the Leper in Bethany sometime after sundown of the following Tuesday, but not necessarily on Tuesday (being within "two days before the Passover"). There a woman (possibly also Mary Magdalene) anointed Jesus' *head* (Mt 26,1-13; Mk 14,1-9). (There may have been another anointing, for Lk 7,36-50 describes an anointing by a woman, but of Jesus' *feet* and with her tears rather than ointment, at a different time and under different circumstances. See "Three Bodies," #54 [c]).

5. Judas was present at both suppers as was Zebedee John, but Lazarus/ John was present only for the first supper and from the time of the foot washing at the second, but during that washing he had not yet become one of the "Twelve" and had only entered the upper room to hold the water basin for Jesus to wash the disciples' feet (including Judas'); he then remained to lie close to the Lord's bosom (Jn 13,23; 21,20).

6. Among the "Twelve," Judas, as his name "Iscariot" indicates, represented Scorpio (the scorpion, representing the "sting" of death) among the "Twelve" heavenly influences of the Zodiac. The symbol of the scorpion's higher counterpart is the "Eagle" (Rev 4,7).[5] Lazarus/John, as the "Eagle" influence, represented the one who had overcome death and thus linked his karma (destiny) to that of Judas (Scorpio = Scorpion/Eagle). Lazarus/John thus followed Judas throughout the rest of the latter's involvement in the Passion narrative, first to the house of the high priest and thence with the capturing band to the Garden (Jn 18,1-3). Lazarus/ John was thus not present with Jesus in the Garden until the time of the capture, but after that he was with Jesus all the way to the Cross, being the only one of the "Twelve" to remain with him through it all—because he alone among them, having undergone mystical death, understood all of the meaning and what Jesus had to go through. (Earlier we saw that the "cup" which Jesus sought to avoid was not death, but death without having brought any of the chosen three through the experience in a condition of being spiritually awake.)

---

5. The four Gospels have long carried with them the tradition of the four "living creatures" from the four corners of the Zodiac, i.e. John (Eagle), Luke (Bull), Mark (Lion) and Matthew (Face of a Man). See **I-62**.

We shall now look more closely at some aspects of the above, filling in the interstices where appropriate. But if one will examine the scriptures carefully it can be seen that this structure fits their deep collective wisdom more perfectly than any heretofore put forth. We have again, as in "The Nativity," an anthroposophical understanding that begins to shed an immense and brilliant light upon the Gospel accounts. As we examine the structure more fully below, one can see deep meaning coming out of passages that heretofore have been veiled in mystery—passages such as, for instance, "If it is my will that he remain until I come, what is that to you?" (Jn 21,22-23).

POINT #1:   *The Beloved Disciple as the Johannine Author*

Only a few books of the Bible have presented scholars with great challenges insofar as author identity is concerned. Some such as Job and Daniel certainly have, and in the New Testament to a certain extent Matthew and Hebrews. But none has been so enigmatic as the Gospel of John and the rest of the Johannine corpus. Only Paul contributed more volume to the New Testament canon than the heretofore mysterious "Beloved Disciple." And while Matthew, with its placement in the canon and sole claim to The Sermon on the "Mount(ain)," has historically been the most widely read Gospel, the unique spiritual quality of John's Gospel has done more to claim the hearts of humanity than any other. Surely more humans have been laid to rest with the reading of Jn 14, along with 1 Cor 15, than any other scripture. And what writer has so often been found in the testimonials of the devout as Jn 3?

It is, therefore, only understandable that so much Christian scholarship has been devoted to unveiling the identity of the mystery writer. That it has only been done, with reasonable certainty, by a modern prophet able to read the heavenly script itself when the time was right lends great credibility to Koenig's conclusion (and certainly that of others as well) that the writer intentionally placed the veil himself. That the time was right is indicated by the threefold confluence of spiritual events demonstrated by anthroposophical light: 1. the new age of Michael in 1879 (**I-19**); 2. the end of the five thousand year Kali Yuga in 1899 (see **I-46**; for the Western world's awareness of this phenomenon see the lengthy quote from *Earthly and Cosmic Man* [ECM], regarding the Prometheus myth and Deucalion, in "Second Coming"); and 3. the advent in about 1909 of the age of the Second Coming (cf. Jn 21,22-23).

There is a mysterious veiling in John's Gospel of its author's identity, which begins to appear quite deliberate. Even the circumstances of historical development after the Ascension tended to throw confusion into any effort at identification by those who came later, even immediately after the passing of "the Twelve." This was because of the nature of the "John" mission and the intertwining of the work and karma (destiny) of the three "Johns." We saw earlier in this volume how it was divinely ordained that "Karma and Reincarnation" was not to be taught in the Church for two thousand years, i.e., until the Second Coming, which dawned about 1909 but will have a long period of gradual development and recognition by humanity. There can be no question but that these things were known in the spirit world, and on Earth by at least Christ and Lazarus/John, the Beloved Disciple, and probably also by Peter and Paul based, in Peter's case, upon the instruction following the Transfiguration (Mt 17,9). Therefore Lazarus/John (directly or indirectly) could write, "If it is my will that he remain *until I come*, what is that to you?" (Jn 21,22-23). Clearly, the Beloved Disciple was to die (Jn 21,23) an earthly death before the Second Coming, so his "remaining" had to imply something other than his physical earthly existence. And that it applied to the Second Coming rather than to Christ's Resurrection is clear from the fact that all of the "Twelve" as then constituted survived until the latter, but none until the former. But lacking anthroposophical light, theology has stewed until this very day over this passage, underpinned as it has been by very literal "earthly" understandings.

The recently discovered "Secret Gospel of Mark"[6] (see Welburn, *Gnosis* [GNOS] and 4 ABD 558) shows the unique connection of Lazarus/John to all of the Gospels—and thus his importance among those who were "eyewitnesses." All four Gospels incorporate the story of this Beloved Disciple; Lazarus/John puts it in the architectural center of his Gospel, and the synoptics, as we shall soon see, place it in the chain of events that begin to show the limitations of consciousness among the three chosen disciples, especially the Zebedees. One must be struck by the

---

6. Morton Smith's scholarly *Clement of Alexandria and a Secret Gospel of Mark*, Cambridge, Harvard Univ. Press, 1973, and his popular version, *The Secret Gospel*, Clearlake, CA, Dawn Horse Press, 1982 (orig. pub. NY, Harper & Row, 1973). His later updates are "Clement of Alexandria and Secret Mark: The Score at the End of the First Decade," Cambridge, Harvard Theological Review, 1982, and "Two Ascended to Heaven—Jesus and the Author of 4Q491," in *Jesus and the Dead Sea Scrolls*, ABRL, (1992).

divine providence that hid this "Secret Gospel" for two thousand years, until the human being's Consciousness Soul was ready to mature (see **I-24**, **I-25** and **I-19**). That it came at a critical time to corroborate the teachings of the exalted but long unsung prophet Rudolf Steiner can only be a cause for deep reflection.

The very structure of John's Gospel shows its special character. First appears the clearly Platonic prologue, the lone scriptural announcement of the Logos concept, expressive of that pervasive influencer of New Testament writings, Philo of Alexandria (see "Egypt"). Then comes the testimony of the initiate of the old Mysteries, John the Baptist, vicariously entered into the Consciousness Soul of the Beloved Disciple. Then, in the very middle of the Gospel, Chapter 11 is the account of the "Three Days' Journey" of Lazarus/John. We do not hear of the Beloved Disciple before this, but from this point forward it is the pervasive theme and identification mark of the Evangelist (Jn 13,23; 19,26; 20,2; 21,7,20), veiled until the meaning of "loved" in Jn 11,3,36 and Mk 10,21 could again become known after the end of the Kali Yuga (Deucalion, or the "Dark Ages") in 1899. That John's Gospel initially ended with Chapter 20 can hardly be denied, but the nature of what is imparted in Chapter 21 is so critical for further identification and structural balance that its addition at a later point was imperative. It did not immediately lift any veil, but it left for posterity what would do so. We know, and shall see below, that Lazarus/John lived to be an extremely old man of at least one hundred years (106 according to one statement by Steiner), so he could quite well have added Chapter 21 himself later, for he himself had given us the "beloved disciple" terminology. Intervening developments could have made its necessity clear, and I lean to the view that he added it himself. But the possibility of it having been done by another under his inspiration, possibly immediately after his death (particularly in the light of Jn 21,23 and the third person style of vs 24, "his testimony"), certainly cannot be dismissed.

Let us now look at the meaning of "John" and why it was necessary that Lazarus become a "John being" upon his high initiation by Christ.

The name "John" is derived from the Hebrew *Johanan*, but by way, during the Hellenistic period, of the Greek *Ioannes*. According to 3 ABD 881, the meaning of *Johanan* was "Yahweh is or has been gracious." WNWD gives "Yahweh is gracious." Let us see how what Steiner says corresponds. In Jn-Rel, Lect. 7, p. 134, we read:

That disciple [the Beloved Disciple] does not appear in the John Gospel before the resurrection of Lazarus. Why? Because he who remained hidden behind "the disciple whom the Lord loved" was the one whom the Lord had already loved previously. He loved him so greatly because He had already recognized him—invisibly, in his soul—as the disciple who was to be awakened and carry the message of the Christ out into the world. That is why the disciple, the apostle, "whom the Lord loved" appears on the scene only beginning with the description of the resurrection of Lazarus. Only then had he become what he was thenceforth. *Now the individuality of Lazarus had been so completely transformed that it became the individuality of John in the Christian sense.* (Emphasis mine)

When Koenig asks what is meant by the emphasized words, he seems to indicate that Steiner said "John" means "the forerunner or predecessor." Perhaps Steiner said that somewhere, but if so, I don't find it in just that way, though it is indeed the net effect of what he said. The passage to which Koenig seems to me to refer is in GSJ, Lect. 4, p.74, and reads, "John the Baptist called himself—literally interpreted—the forerunner, the precursor, the one who goes before as herald of the ego. He designated himself as one who knew that this ego must become an independent entity in each individual soul, but he also had to bear witness of Him who was to come, in order that this be brought about." While Koenig's quote ends here, I find it essential to include more than this in order to reconcile the matter of "grace" indicated by the name. Steiner's actual words continue,

He said very clearly, "That which is to come is the 'I AM,' which is eternal, which can say of Itself, Before Abraham was, was the I AM." [Here it is important to remember that this passage from Jn 8,58 is in that part of the Gospel that Lazarus/John experienced vicariously through the prior experience of the Baptist who then penetrated Lazarus/John down to the Consciousness Soul.] John could say, "The I (the ego) which is spoken of here existed before me. Although I am Its forerunner, yet It is at the same time my Forerunner. I bear witness of what was previously present in every human being. After me will come One Who was before me." [Of course, here Steiner is talking about the parenthetical phrase, Jn 1,15, in the prologue.]

The significance of the change that came over Lazarus is dramatized at the transition from Jn 10 to 11. Standing alone, there is something awkward about Jn 10,41, "John did no sign, but everything that John said about this man was true." The Beloved Disciple is indeed writing the first ten chapters but through what came into his Consciousness Soul by virtue of the visitation there of the soul of the beheaded Baptist, about whom so much has already been said in this larger work. Only in this way can the significance of this sentence, which speaks of John (the Baptist) in the third person, be understood. Yet because the Beloved Disciple then knows that it is true, he can write the first ten chapters on the basis of that knowledge.

Now immediately after that, in Jn 11,1, he tells us, from that knowledge personal to himself, "Now a certain man was ill, Lazarus of Bethany." Later he has Jesus saying, "This illness is not unto death...." The illness that affected Lazarus commenced when, as the "rich young ruler" he began to see that the riches of his ancient wisdom must be sacrificed for it was a dying phenomenon. Not until this is recognized can we begin to understand the cursing of the fig tree (Mk 11,12-14,20-21 and 13,28; Mt 21,18-20 and 24,32). See "Under the Tree." The old Mysteries, i.e., the "fig tree," with their fruit, were passing away, to be replaced by the enactment on the Earth stage itself, in the full view of all humanity, of "the Mystery of Golgotha," as Steiner called it, the essence of his CMF in 1902. It was this setting, and Lazarus' former place in it, that was passing away, by reason of which "Lazarus ... was ill." He was, so to speak, the epitome of the ancient "fig tree." When he emerged, "born again" (Jn 3,3) from the old initiation into that new mystery, he was a "New Man," having seen into the fullness of the spiritual world and been brought back by Jesus the Christ, and only then could speak of himself as "the disciple whom Jesus loved."

Let us again pause in our account, this time to consider the significance of being one so "loved" by Jesus. Nowhere in all the Gospels is it said that Jesus so "loved" a person save with respect to Lazarus (and his sisters) in Jn 11 and in Mk 10,21 with respect to the man identified by Mt 19,20 as a "Young Man" and by Lk 18,18 as a "Ruler." By collapsing all synoptic versions, the person of whom Mark is speaking in 10,21 is usually called the "rich young ruler," but only in Matthew is he identified as being "young" and only in Luke as being a "ruler," while all three say in one way or another that he is "rich." Only Mk 10,21 says, as it was said of Lazarus in John's Gospel, that Jesus "loved him." The significance of this in Mark's Gospel is explained near the end of "Egypt" (find it by reference to Mk 10,21 in the Index of Scriptures Cited). From that we can see that all of the Evangelists knew of Lazarus/John and spoke of him.

In connection with the synoptic discussions about the "rich young ruler," we find what seems to have been encrypted by the Evangelists as a significant esoteric truth relating to Lazarus/John. In every one of the accounts we find what characterizes the call by Jesus of the "Twelve," namely, "come, follow me" (see Mk 10,21; Mt 19,21; Lk 18,22). The same Greek word (*akoloythei*) is used for "follow" me in all three passages. And it is used also by all three synoptics in speaking of taking up one's cross and following Jesus (Mk 8,34; Mt 10,38; Lk 9,23). But notably, it is not used in connection with the call of Peter, James and John in any of the Gospels (i.e., Mt or Mk). They each fell asleep and were not able to follow Jesus all the way to the Cross during his earthly agony—only Lazarus/John could do that, he to whom it was said, "come, follow me." The RSV uses the term "follow me" in regard to the call of Peter in Mk 1,17 and Mt 4,19, as does the KJV in Mt 4,19, but in Mk 1,17 the KJV more closely (and it would seem correctly) follows the Greek which uses entirely different words (*deyte opiso*) meaning "come after" me. Jesus does not address James and John with either of these words, but it is simply said that he "called them" (Mt 4,21; Mk 1,20), after which they "followed" him, and here the same word form is used as in the first instance above (*ekoloythesan*). In view of the subtle difference in meaning between "follow" me and "come after" me (i.e., the latter more nearly suggesting the possibility of "following" at a later time rather than immediately, with reference to understanding the full implications of the Cross), one suspects that an early copyist may have used *ekoloythesan* for James and John without appreciating the distinction between "followed" and "went after" or "responded." (Matthew, also known as Levi, is called by Jesus saying "follow me," employing the same Greek word as in Mk 10,21—see Mt 9,9; Mk 2,14; Lk 5,27). Thus we see emerging a depth to Lazarus/John that does not exist in Peter, James and John in the synoptic Gospels. Then we come to John's Gospel. There Jesus calls Philip by the same Greek word for "follow me" (Jn 1,43).[7] But most significantly, at the

---

7. See "The Gospel of Philip," discovered at Nag Hammadi, and Welburn's comments about it in GNOS.

conclusion of the John Gospel, after the threefold question to Peter, Jesus tells Peter, with the Greek word he did not use at the beginning of his ministry, "follow me" (Jn 21,19,22). And Peter, while he could not follow Jesus to the Cross, did thereafter follow him to another cross, according to tradition. Undoubtedly by the time Chapter 21 was added to John's Gospel, this historical fact was known to the aging Evangelist.

With that in mind, let us return now to look at what "John" means "in the Christian sense."

We must go to the Gospel written by Paul's "beloved" (Col 4,14) physician, Luke. There in Chapter 1, the angel tells Zechariah (vs 13), "and you shall call his name John ... (17) and he will go before him ... to make ready for the Lord a people prepared." And later in the same chapter neighbors came to see the new babe "(59) And on the eighth day they came to circumcise the child; and they [the neighbors] would have named him Zechariah after his father, (60) but his mother said, 'Not so; he shall be called John.' (61) And they said to her, 'None of your kindred is called by this name.' (62) And they made signs to his father, inquiring what he would have him called. (63) And he asked for a writing tablet, and wrote, 'His name is John.'" And then (vs 67) "Zechariah was filled with the Holy Spirit, and prophesied, saying ... (76) And you, child, will be called the prophet of the Most High; for you will go before the Lord to prepare his ways,..."

Thus, in the Christian story, the first to be named John is pointedly, and with great emphasis, so named, and the name is tied tightly to the characteristic of being an announcing messenger of the Lord.

Christ chooses one of the three John beings (his own cousin, "supposedly"), who is already so named from birth, to fill the messenger role—one who, starting with the Transfiguration, was unable to fill that role by staying spiritually awake, thus necessitating that another should be prepared to fill the role.

How does scripture tell us this? Do we simply project backwards the spiritual "Sleep" which overcame this Zebedee John (as well as Peter and James) in Gethsemane? Hardly, but we are warranted from that blatant circumstance in going back to see if what became so manifest later was more subtly expressed earlier. And in this, we are again so ably assisted by the perceptiveness of Koenig. Let us start by looking at Mark's account. Mark is the Evangelist who seems to have been closest to Peter, and thus to perhaps reflect the latter's perspective on events. Only Mark reports the presence of the threesome, Peter, James and John, in the company of Andrew, Peter's brother (Mk 1,29-31; 13,3). Undoubtedly, there was a special relationship between Peter and the Zebedee brothers, and we find these brothers appearing more frequently and with greater emphasis in Mark's Gospel than in any other. And it does seem strange, in retrospect, that any disciple who was to author so much of the Bible as the Beloved Disciple would be described in the way Zebedee John is described. Just as Andrew is normally described in all Gospels simply as "the brother of Peter," so also is Zebedee John described as "the brother of James" (but a caveat, it is the other James, Jesus' brother, so referred to in Mk 6,3). But these are the lesser circumstances. Let us look more closely at Mark's account for more telling ones.

To begin with, among Peter, James and John, it is only Peter who carries the consciousness to recognize the Christ in Jesus of Nazareth (Mk 8,27-30, more fully elaborated in Matthew's generally parallel account, Mt 16,13-20), though as noted earlier, Peter's consciousness too was limited. This event immediately precedes the Transfiguration where Jesus "led them up a high mountain" (Mk 9,2-13). Very shortly thereafter, Zebedee John says "Teacher, we saw a man casting out demons in your name, and we forbade him, because he was not following us" (Mk 9,38), and Jesus, while not reproving him, had to correct his misunderstandings and inappropriate action. The cloak of dullness which seems to be falling on Zebedee John is illustrated even more powerfully soon thereafter. In Mk 10,35-45, the Zebedee brothers come forward, having just witnessed Moses and Elijah at the right and left hand of Christ during the Transfiguration, and request that they be permitted to sit at his right and left hand in his kingdom. Christ gently but firmly shows them that they are not comprehending either the nature of that kingdom or of his mission, his "cup." (It is precisely this passage which triggered Steiner's explanation earlier herein of what the "cup" of Christ was, not that he should die, which he understood and accepted from the outset, but that he should die without having accomplished what he set out to do, without having taken any of these three with him through that event with full consciousness of its cosmic nature, reality and significance).

Note that Jesus' response to the Zebedee request is to teach all the disciples, who had become indignant toward James and John, that the greatest among them is the one who becomes the servant of all. This should be kept in mind as we look at Lazarus/John's report of the foot washing (Jn 13,1-17).

What now startles us in its clarity is that, in the light of what the "Secret Gospel of Mark" shows us, Mark's Gospel brings Lazarus/John into the picture between these last two inadequacies of Zebedee John, i.e., between the countervailing instruction about the man casting out demons in Jesus' name (Mk 9,38-40), and the request for position of privilege (Mk 10,35-45). Enter he who, from all the synoptics, is now known as the "rich young ruler," he who is clearly Lazarus/John (Mk 10,17-27). The portion of the "Secret Gospel" which tells about Lazarus is recognized as belonging between verses 34 and 35 of the canonical Mark 10. This is immediately before the Zebedee request for privilege. The general order of all these events in the Matthew account is similar to Mark's. Typically, Luke digresses therefrom, but he also includes the "rich young ruler" incident. It was something that was vital to all the Gospels, but for a reason quite different from what has been assumed by conventional theology. The synoptics too were telling of the one who was to become the Beloved Disciple, only they were hiding it because humanity was not yet ready for the fullness of that knowledge. While Steiner indicates that the Evangelists got at least the substance of their accounts clairvoyantly, none of the Gospels was written by one of the Twelve (except insofar as the Beloved Disciple served as one of them as explained below). Clearly Mark and Luke were not among the Twelve. We show herein that Zebedee John did not write John's Gospel. And even few scholars think that the apostle Matthew/Levi wrote the Gospel. Steiner has shown us that the Gospel of Matthew took its name because "everything presented in the early chapters of St. Matthew's Gospel derives from the secrets taught by Jeshua ben Pandira among the Essenes and subsequently propagated by his pupil Mathai" (see "The Nativity"; also GSMt, Lect. 6, pp. 109-111). Providence gave the Evangelists the insight to write what was appropriate for the human condition both then and as it would evolve over time. The knowledge of Lazarus/John as the Beloved Disciple was not something to be made known to all at that time. Clement of Alexandria clearly said so in his letter to Theodore, which has surfaced only in the last half of this century to reveal the "Secret Gospel's" existence. And who can quarrel with the observation that the highly initiated Lazarus/John could have made his identity more explicit had it been appropriate to do so? It was he whose Gospel gave us Christ's statement, "I have yet many things to say to you, but you cannot bear them now. When the Spirit of truth comes, he will guide you into all the truth" (Jn 16,12-13).

It is much to the credit of Koenig that, following Steiner's teachings on the meaning of "loved," he detected the subtle increase in Zebedee John's inadequacies and their relationship to the "rich young ruler" before the discovery of the "Secret Gospel" was revealed.

But long before Peter went to sleep spiritually in the Garden of Gethsemane, and immediately after Jesus said, referring to Lazarus/John, that "all things are possible with God" (Mk 10,27), we find Peter also making something of a request for recognition, "Lo, we have left everything and followed you" (Mk 10,28). Christ was beginning to perceive that even Peter, as at the Transfiguration (Lk 9,32-33), would fail to remain spiritually awake through the events of Golgotha. He began at this point to prepare Lazarus/John, and he eventually told Peter outright that he would deny him three times (Mk 14,30). Only Lazarus/John followed him spiritually awake all the way, and Jesus passed the mantle of highest spiritual insight to him from the Cross (Jn 19,25-27).

Jesus answered Peter's remark, saying that those who have left home for his sake would indeed receive their reward many times over, adding quite significantly, "But many that are first will be last, and the last first" (Mk 10,31). The first John Jesus had selected was now going to have to let another messenger, another "John," become first in service to Christ while himself becoming last. Until now, the juxtaposition of verse 31 to the manifold rewards described in vss 29-30 has seemed strange. In the light of what we can now see, as is so often true with anthroposophical insight, they tell a compelling, non-fragmented story.

So the first of the three Johns, the one Jesus chose at the outset to be the messenger, proved unable to fill that role and had to let another take it over. But with the other two Johns we have a different situation. While the Baptist was also named at birth, the Gospel places great emphasis upon the meaning of the name, given from the spiritual world, and the fact that the father's dumbness was raised only when he had followed through with the naming (Lk 1,64). And not only that, but we are told in the Gospel accounts how this one had even been the Elijah spirit of Israel. The stress upon the role, as it relates to the "Name," cannot be overemphasized. And now, with the third and last to be named "John," we have one not so named at birth, but only after his "new birth" into that role. And it begins to dawn upon us that his function has a character of being the forerunner into a far distant future, preparing the way for the Lord in the coming of the "I Am" into humanity's Consciousness Soul just as John the Baptist had entered into Lazarus/John's own being down to that level. And this is why Lazarus/John was at the foot of the Cross to take the true Mother of Jesus, the Virgin Sophia, into his very being, i.e., "his own home" (Jn 19,26-27) and was to "remain until I come" even after his own earthly death (Jn 21,22-23) by writing the Gospel of John.

In Lk 2,36-38 we are told about the prophetess Anna. In "The Nativity" we saw that the name "Anna" means "grace,"[8] which gives a majestic (though cryptic) meaning to these three verses. But this passage speaks of the birth of the Nathan Jesus child, he who carries the unspoiled etheric body of the Second Adam as a "conditional Ego" for twelve years. This is the root of what we speak of as the "Grace" of God—and here we speak of the Father God. But of the Baptist, we do not so speak. His name is "Yahweh is gracious." We know that Yahweh was the special "God" of the Hebrew people, who directed them as the Spirit of Form, one of the Elohim who took up abode on the Moon. From there he reflected the true light of the Christ, who had descended from highest heaven to the Sun—just as the Moon reflects the brighter light of the Sun in our physical world (see "As Above, So Below"). Thus, the "Grace" of God flowed through Yahweh into the birth of John the Baptist, hence his "Name," "Yahweh is gracious." The Baptist proclaimed the coming of the Christ in the flesh, the mineral-physical body of Jesus. But now, the last John, the Beloved Disciple, recognizing at the outset that Christ once came in the flesh (Jn 1,14), prepares the way for his Second Coming. That John's Gospel was to reach far into the future helps to explain its relative difficulty in getting into the canon during the "Darkness" that fell again over Christ's followers after the passage of the "Twelve." It is to "prepare the way" for the entry of the higher "I Am" as humanity matures into its Consciousness Soul.

There is probably no better place to gather an understanding of the meaning of "Grace" than in Steiner's single lecture title, *The Concepts of Original Sin and Grace* (OSG), on May 3, 1911. Steiner shows how at

---

8. Thus "John" = the Hebrew "Johanan" = Jah (or Yahweh) + Anna = Johannine = Yahweh is gracious.

the end of the first three stages of Earth evolution, in ancient Lemuria, having recapped the prior three Conditions of Consciousness, the Saturday (Saturn), Sunday (Sun) and Monday (Moon) "days" of creation, the human being consisted only of its "Three Bodies" (see **I-8** and **I-14**). It as yet had no Ego, being thus only of an animal nature (see **I-10**) and thus incapable of sin. It was at this point, just before the entry of the Ego, that the fallen Archangel Lucifer (bringer of "Light") desired, contrary to the plan of the higher spiritual world, to bring knowledge into the human being prematurely. The account of this is given in Gen 3, the infection of the astral body (the body of senses, passion and desire) and the birth of sin, along with the consequent pain, toil and death and separation from the heavenly world. The infection of the astral body then worked gradually down into the older etheric and physical bodies, so that Paul could say, in Rom 7,23, "I see in my members [his "Three Bodies"] another law at war with the law of my mind [his Ego] and making me captive to the law of sin which dwells in my members." This sin is "original sin," which infects every incarnated human being so long as it needs to incarnate (save only those who have sacrificially returned as pure unsung servants of humanity).

Inasmuch, however, as the "Three Bodies" or "members" of the human being were infected by original sin before it became a responsible being, having at that time received no Ego and being the equivalent, while as yet not having descended into mineral existence, of an animal, it cannot be blamed for the fact that its being was originally so infected. In OSG, Steiner says that in the Garden the human being could not yet act "with full moral responsibility." That it was thus infected without being morally responsible therefor is, in the perfect justice of the Father, a basis for salvation being given freely to the human being without its having earned it. This is what is called "Grace." It does not mean that the human being is saved regardless of further actions, but rather that its state of doom is lifted so that it can, in time, by taking into itself the true "I Am," the higher Ego of the Christ Being, commence to perfect its astral body into "Manna." Such is, in fact, the goal of Earth evolution. The higher states of buddhi and atma are to be the goal of the succeeding Jupiter and Venus evolutions when the mineral-physical world is no longer. But each individual is working on its etheric and physical bodies slowly and gradually by so working to "Perfect" its astral body through succeeding incarnations on Earth. One may envision the astral body as the second hand on a clock. It gradually affects the minute hand and more slowly even the hour hand. When all "Three Bodies" have been thus fully "Perfect(ed)" at the end of Venus evolution, the stage referred to by the lapidary parable of the three loaves (Mt 13,33) shall have been reached, and the ultimate "resurrection" (Lk 20,35-36) attained.

The John being who was to bring this "Grace" into the future generations was he who had previously been known as Lazarus, but no more. Truly, he could say, rightly in the third person, "Now a certain man was ill, Lazarus of Bethany" (Jn 11,1), just as Paul could say, "I know a man in Christ who fourteen years ago was caught up to the third heaven" (2 Cor 12,2), when his "Name" also was changed from Saul to Paul.

Now let us return to that place in GSJ, Lect. 4, p. 74, and take up where we left off earlier:

At this point in the Gospel [i.e., Jn 1,16] very significant words are spoken:—"For of His Fulness have we all received grace upon grace." There are men who call themselves Christians, who pass over this word, "Fulness," thinking that nothing very special is meant by it. "Pleroma" in Greek means "Fulness." We find this word also in the Gospel of St. John: "For from the Pleroma have we all received grace upon grace." I have said that if we wish really to understand this Gospel, every word must be weighed in the balance. What is then, Pleroma, Fulness? He alone can understand it who knows that in the ancient Mysteries Pleroma or Fulness was referred to as something very definite. For at that time it was already being taught that when those spiritual beings manifested themselves who during the Moon period evolved to the stage of divinity namely, the Elohim, one of them separated from the others. One remained behind upon the Moon, and thence *reflected* the power of Love until humanity was sufficiently matured to be able to receive the *direct* Light of the other six Elohim. Therefore they distinguished between Jahve, the individual God, the reflector, and the Fulness of the Godhead, "Pleroma," consisting of the other six Elohim. Since the full consciousness of the Sun Logos meant to them the Christ, they called Him the "Fulness of the Gods" when they wished to refer to Him. This profound truth was concealed in the words:—"For out of the Pleroma, we have received grace upon grace."

A lengthy paragraph follows in which Steiner speaks of the progress of the human being from the time when blood connections and the group-ego were entirely dominant, and then the stirrings toward individual freedom. He continues:

> As long as men were not yet ready to receive an independent ego, as long as they existed as members of a group, they had to be socially regulated by an outwardly revealed law. And even today men have not, in all things, risen above the group-egos. In how many things in the present are men not individual human beings, but group-beings? They are already trying to become free, but it is still only an ideal. (At a certain stage of esoteric discipleship, they are called the homeless ones.)[See "Homeless."] The man who voluntarily places himself within the cosmic activities is an individual; he is not ruled by law. In the Christ Principle lies the victory over law. "For the law was given by Moses, but Grace through Christ" [quoting Jn 1,17]. According to the Christian acceptation of the word, the soul's capacity for doing right out of the inner self was called Grace. Grace and an inner recognition of truth came into being through the Christ. You see how profoundly this thought fits into the whole of human evolution.

Thus one can see how Steiner, without ever saying that John means "Yahweh is gracious" in so many words, instead takes his hearers through an explanation that puts deep meaning upon it and shows exactly how it is so. Such "Grace" at that time in humanity's evolution demanded the service of announcing the Christ, serving as his forerunner. And from this, one also then sees how Lazarus, when he was called by Christ in the flesh into the mission of preparing the way for Christ in the etheric world (see "Second Coming"), had to be given the "Name" that went with, and described the character of, that assignment—the name "John."

Thus, of the three John beings, the Baptist prepared the way for the coming of Christ in the flesh; Zebedee John, unable to fulfill the role initially envisioned by the "Name," nevertheless served as one of the "Twelve" to the point of martyrdom; and Lazarus/John gave us the Johannine corpus which is only now to the point of becoming comprehended during the Second Coming.

POINT #2:   *The Composition of the Twelve Disciples*

At all times there were "Twelve" disciples, including successively Judas Iscariot, Lazarus/John and Matthias. Up until now it has generally been assumed, I believe, that from the time of the betrayal until the election of Matthias there were only eleven—an assumption abetted by the scriptures themselves, to wit (emphasis mine):

> **Mt 28,16**: Now the *eleven* disciples went to Galilee, to the mountain to which Jesus had directed them.

> **Mk 16,14**: Afterward he appeared to the *eleven* themselves as they sat at table;

> **Lk 24,9,33**: (9) and returning from the tomb they told all this to the *eleven* and to all the rest.... And they rose that same hour and returned to Jerusalem; and they found the *eleven* gathered together and those who were with them,

> **Acts 1,26**: And they cast lots for them, and the lot fell on Matthias; and he was enrolled with the *eleven* apostles.

Only one other time does the New Testament use the term "eleven," in Acts 2,14, "But Peter, standing with the eleven, ..." but obviously here a full complement of "Twelve" was acting.

How then can we say there were always "Twelve" acting?

Only John's Gospel gives us the answer. And only Koenig has thus far pointed it out insofar as I am aware. John shows us that Jesus appeared to the disciples three times (Jn 21,14), the first in Jn 20,19-23, the second in Jn 20,24-29 and the third in Jn 21:

> **Jn 20,19**: On the evening of that day, the first day of the week, the doors being shut where the disciples were, for fear of the Jews, Jesus came and stood among them and said to them, "Peace be with you."

> **Jn 20,26**: Eight days later, his disciples were again in the house, and Thomas was with them. The doors were shut, but Jesus came and stood among them, and said, "Peace be with you."

Jn 21,1: After this Jesus revealed himself again to the disciples by the Sea of Tiberias; and he revealed himself in this way.

The appearance cited above in Mark and Luke was in the upper room and was the first of the three. As Jn 20,24 tells us in the "doubting Thomas" passage, "Now Thomas, one of the *twelve*, called the Twin, was not with them when Jesus came" (emphasis mine). Clearly we are here being told that there were still "Twelve" disciples, although Judas has already left and Matthias has not yet been elected. The reason Mark and Luke speak of only eleven disciples is simply that Thomas was not there.

One can notice, as Koenig points out, that the appearances are described in progressively greater detail as one moves in canonical order through the four Gospels. Matthew collapses all of the appearances into a brief and general statement that "the *eleven* disciples went to Galilee, to the mountain to which Jesus had directed them." Only here do we have what, on the surface, appears to be a conflict with the statement that there were at all times "Twelve" acting. Yet upon careful consideration it is not so. First, this appearance is succinctly stated to have been upon a "Mountain." As we shall see in a later volume, that term is virtually always speaking about the spiritual, and not the physical, world. It is, so to speak, in sacred literature a term of art designating the nature of one's experience. Certainly in Matthew, perhaps more than any other, this is true. Examine the commentaries on this passage; no mountain is identified. The experiences in Galilee centered upon its "Sea," and those on a "Mountain" were of an intensely spiritual nature. Furthermore, for the disciples to have bodily gone to Galilee would have violated Christ's instructions in Acts 1,4, "And while staying with them [during the "forty days"] he charged them not to depart from Jerusalem, but to wait for the promise of the Father...."

If we so understand the "Mountain" terminology, it would seem that Mt 28,16 is speaking of the third appearance, that described in Jn 21 at the lake in Galilee. But if so, then it appears, again on the surface, that Matthew is at odds with John about the number of disciples then acting. However, if we understand Matthew in the sense that the "eleven" were to go up into the spiritual realm designated by the term "Mountain," then we can understand that Lazarus/John would not have been included, because he was already there by virtue of his status as the "beloved disciple," who alone was initiated by Christ and thereby experienced mystic death.

Again John's Gospel gives us, aided by Koenig's study, the insight to understand what has seemed mysterious. Koenig tells us that, in keeping with the other Gospels, the third appearance was just before the Ascension of Christ, which begins in Jn 21,15, "When they had finished breakfast...." This, according to Koenig, is how John describes the commencement of the Ascension scene in which Christ gives his threefold question and charge to Peter and imparts his heretofore enigmatic statement about the Beloved Disciple. This "dining" scene is a cryptic and succinct expression of the fact that the entirety of the "forty days" was a divine feeding, a spiritual communion with Christ—not unlike the divine feeding, Manna, in the "Wilderness" (1 Cor 10,3; see also "Feedings"). All the experiences in Galilee during this period were out-of-body perceptions by the disciples while they remained, as instructed, in Jerusalem, in the upper room in fact.

Perhaps Lazarus/John could see that only seven of the disciples (Jn 21,2) rose to certain spiritual heights during the third appearance, as described in Jn 21,1-14. On the other hand, one must appreciate here the relative meanings of the numbers "seven" and "Twelve." Seven is the number of creation, of time, whereas "Twelve" is the number of completion, of space. Lazarus/John brings this out in the development of the Revelation, going first through four cycles of seven before gaining the Holy City in the realm of the "Twelve." Seven applies to the physical world, twelve to the spiritual. Here he also emphasizes that there is much to be done by the "Twelve" within the sevenfold arena of the world. While the third "appearance" is symbolically brought to a close in Jn 21,14, the stress then immediately laid by the threefold charge to Peter followed by the revelation that Lazarus/John was to work on even after the death of the "Twelve" emphasizes that the spiritual world is to be attained only by the actions of his followers upon the (sevenfold) Earth.

But in spite of Jn 21,2, there were "Twelve" who witnessed the Ascension of Christ, in verse 15, when they had finished the "forty days" of spiritual communion. Clearly John is not in conflict with the synoptics by limiting the number to seven. Koenig shows this additionally by the picture Raphael painted for a tapestry intended for the Vatican which portrays the Ascension scene. Koenig's explanation will be left to a reading of his work, but here the reader is reminded that the Individuality of Raphael was the same one present in the Baptist and thus within (i.e., descended as far as) the Consciousness Soul of Lazarus/John (see "Nova-lis" and "Prokofieff" in Vol. 3, *Companions Along The Way*).

That this aspect of the Ascension has heretofore remained unapprehended undoubtedly helps to explain the paucity of theological commentary upon it, as expressed by 1 ABD 472 under the "Ascension of Christ:"

> There is "no incident in the life of Jesus at one and the same time so beset with difficulties and so essential as the Ascension." … It may well be the most neglected doctrine of the church … even though it is considered one of the most important themes in the NT, and the heavenly intercession and PAROUSIA are inexplicable apart from it … and the doctrine of God makes no sense without it.…

"Eleven"

Before bringing our reflection upon the composition of the Twelve to a close, let us look for a moment at a further significance of, and reason for, the emphasis by the synoptics, in the passages designated above, upon the number "eleven."

For this purpose, I refer to Stebbing's *The Secret of Numbers* (SN). Immediately following the title page he quotes from Steiner, without otherwise citing its source, the following:

> Those who deepen themselves in what is called in the Pythagorean sense "the study of numbers" will learn through this symbolism of numbers to understand life and the world.

Stebbing's brief discussion of the number "eleven" is as follows:

> The quality of the number Eleven is clearly seen if we place an eleven-pointed star beside a twelve-pointed star, as suggested by John W. Barton.
>
> By gazing upon the eleven-pointed star and reflecting upon it we come to feel its form as not quite satisfying. The twelve-pointed star is more harmonious.
>
> This is an indication that the eleven is not yet true perfection and does not represent the divine. On the way thereto, further hurdles have to be overcome, for perfection or completion are [sic.] not

reached easily. We can think of the several team games which demand eleven participants. They suggest imperfection with the endeavor to [r]each perfection, and this is exhibited by every team, even the best.

The number eleven is a number which in one aspect represents imperfection aiming at perfection. It can also be seen as a symbol of harmony and discord.

In this light, profound wisdom is indicated by the synoptic passages referring to the "eleven," for we know that even they were not yet "Perfect."

One who doubts the verity of this observation on the number eleven should reflect upon the meaning it gives when used in other passages of scripture. For instance, consider the following:

Gen 32,22: The same night he arose and took his two wives, his two maids, and his eleven children, and crossed the ford of the Jabbok.

Gen 37,9: Then he dreamed another dream, and told it to his brothers, and said, "Behold, I have dreamed another dream; and behold, the sun, the moon, and the eleven stars were bowing down to me."

Here Joseph represents the "Perfect(ing)" element among the sons of Jacob. Without him, they were not complete. In Gen 32,28-32, Jacob is given a new "Name" and asks the "Name" of God, but that is not given to him—the "Twelve" tribes (Jacob's "Twelve" children) were not yet to that point, but had to wait until it was first given to Moses in Ex 3. Even then, it was the mere inception of the indwelling of the individual Ego, which would not reach the realm of the twelvefold Holy City until Rev 19,12 and 21,12 (see "I AM").

Ex 26,7: You shall also make curtains of goats' hair for a tent over the tabernacle; eleven curtains shall you make.

While the tabernacle, tent and most holy place of the mercy seat, as prescribed in Ex 26 and 36, are all somewhat obscure to modern thinking, we note that in both chapters there are eleven "curtains" for the tent covering (there were ten for the tabernacle) and then a "veil" for the interior "most holy place" of the "mercy seat." A "curtain" and a "veil" both serve a similar function, that of concealing. Immediately two New Testament passages come to mind. One is Paul's reference in Heb 8,5 to Moses' account in Ex 25,40, where Paul first states that the earthly sanctuary is "a copy and shadow of the heavenly sanctuary," then goes on to quote God's instructions to Moses, "See that you make everything according to the pattern which was shown you on the mountain." The second is the Gospel account that the veil of the temple was rent as Jesus died (Mt 27,51). Why were there not a zodiacal "Twelve" curtains to begin with? Because the phrase "twelve curtains" is a spiritual oxymoron. Curtains conceal, but the "Perfect(ing)" "Twelve" reveals. Thus, the twelfth is a veil which is torn in two when the Christ by his death has revealed the heavenly pattern.

Deut 1,2: It is eleven days' journey from Horeb by the way of Mount Seir to Kadeshbarnea.

The suggestion here is that the journey to the promised land is not complete at Kadeshbarnea.

Judg 16,5: And the lords of the Philistines came to her and said to her, "Entice him, and see wherein his great strength lies, and by what means we may overpower him, that we may bind him to subdue him; and we will each give you eleven hundred pieces of silver."

Recognizing, in the light of anthroposophy, the spiritual sight ancient prophecy still held at that time, it is hard not to see a relationship between the elements of this account and those of the betrayal by Judas. (Compare the comments in "The Nativity" about the account of Solomon's great wisdom in 1 K 3,16-28.) And it was by virtue of the similar betrayal by Judas that the "Twelve" were reduced to eleven.

Mt 20,1-16: (This is the parable of the laborers in the vineyard who were hired—see vss 6 and 9—at the eleventh hour and received as much as those who had worked all day in the heat.)

In this parable, the point made by the number eleven is the imminence of the days' end, the time just before it is over. In the Commentary on

Revelation we shall see how the end is delayed until the zodiacal 144,000 have been brought in (Rev 7,4 and 14,1,3). Yet there is to be no distinction between those brought in immediately before the completion and those who came in first.

Lk 2,36-38: (This is the scene in Luke's Nativity account which tells of the prophetess Anna.)

Earlier in this essay we referred to this passage as it related to "Grace." Our point now is the emphasis Luke placed upon the distinction between the numbers "eleven" and "Twelve." This is shown in "The Nativity" in two ways. Luke's genealogy lists seventy-seven names, eleven time seven. The perfecting "Twelve" element came next with the birth of Jesus. The account of Anna has her living a zodiacal eighty-four years, "Twelve" times seven, but carving from that period seven years of marriage. The number eleven is thus implied, while she did not attain the vision of the Christ child until the zodiacal age.

The "eleven" disciples were a team seeking "Perfect(ion)" but had not yet attained it (cf. Phil 3,12-14).

The essential zodiacal character of Christ's twelvefolded institution of those who would follow him out into the world is strongly supported by John's identification of Thomas by the zodiacal identification of "the Twin" (Jn 11,16; 20,24 and 21,2). Notably, it is capitalized and used as a "Name," not necessarily indicating that he was born with a twin sibling. No other evangelist so characterized him, so we might anticipate a particularly profound meaning in this deeply spiritual Gospel, so deep that what is said here can only be the suggestion of an image.

First, "the birth of the Sun," when according to ancient Zoroastrian texts the rule of the Sun began, occurred when the Sun stood at 19 degrees Aries at the summer solstice, some time between 20,500 and 20,600 B.C., a time known also as the "exaltation of the Sun." This concept is given in somewhat greater detail in the discussion surrounding Figure 4, "The horoscope of the world," from *Hermetic Astrology I* (HA1) (under "Robert Powell" in Vol. 3). It was associated by the ancients with the nativity of the first human being. Powell plausibly suggests (p. 16) that this could mean, among other things, "the moment in history when man's consciousness awoke to the cosmic world," and in particular to the importance of the Sun for life. It most likely relates to that time in the Bible described in Gen 9,13 when the rainbow first appeared as the Sun was breaking through the primeval mists (cf. Gen 6,4, the "Nephilim"). Note from the Powell discussion that the annual "enthronement" of the Sun (summer solstice, when it is at the highest point in the sky, i.e., farthest north of the equator) has shifted since that time, due to precession, from the constellation of Aries, the "Lamb," and is today located at 5 1/2 degrees Gemini, (the "Twins"). At the time of Christ's birth it was in the sign of Cancer, the "Crab," which is also the sign of new beginnings (see **I-81**).

Second, note from **I-19** that the birth of the Christ vehicle, or "servant" (Is 42,1-4), Jesus, fell in both the "Astrological Age" and the Cultural Age of the same constellation, Aries, and that he is from ancient time called "the Lamb of God." (The Astrological Ages are determined by the zodiacal constellation the Sun is in at vernal equinox, not by its summer solstice position.)

Third, consider that inasmuch as the actual date of Christ's birth was not known to the early Church it adopted the day that from time immemorial had been referred to as the annual birth of the Sun, the date of the winter solstice. Therefore, the day for celebrating the birth of Christ is the same as that of the ancients for celebrating the annual birth of the Sun. Steiner spoke often of this. He gave many Christmas lectures, but perhaps the best source is the collection of eight Christmas lectures in *The Festivals and Their Meaning* (FM). However, this knowledge is also otherwise generally available. See 3 Brit 283, "Christmas," and 24 Brit 713, "Mystery Religions; Mystery Religions and Christianity."

If we then inspect the order of the constellations starting with Aries, Pisces, Aquarius, etc. (following the shift of the annual enthronement of the Sun since its "birth" in Aries; see HA1, p. 15), we see that the *eleventh* constellation is that of Gemini, the "Twins." In a sense, then, when one thinks of *eleven* one can think of this constellation for which Thomas seems perhaps to have been "Name(d)" (by Christ and/or Lazarus/John?).

Another way of looking at it is that Thomas was the missing number "Twelve." In that sense, he represented the doubting world. When the full complement of "Twelve" is present, then comes the understanding of the "Light," as in Isaiah's seminal "seeing, hearing and understanding" which was to be long delayed (Is 6,9-13). It is a sobering thought that, given that the enthronement of the Sun is now in Gemini, as mentioned above, humanity today could be called the "Twin", in its relationship to the heavenly bodies. We are still doubters as was Thomas, for Gemini is generally considered to represent the element of "doubt." (See, for instance, Tim Lyons, "Astrology Beyond Ego," Wheaton, Quest [The Theosophical Publishing House], 1986.) But, as seen above in "Second Coming," we have already entered the time of the reappearance of Christ in the etheric world, an event that humanity will become more aware of as the Sun's annual enthronement moves into the sign of Taurus. It will then be in the twelfth and final sign (the Age of Aquarius according to the location of the Sun at the vernal equinox), the sixth Cultural Era, that represented by the church at Philadelphia in St. John's Apocalypse (see **I-19** and **I-25**). In HA1, Chap. 3, Powell points out that according to ancient tradition the sign of Taurus relates to the human larynx (see "The zodiacal man" in **I-21**), which in turn relates to the "Word" and to the human being's future power of reproduction through the larynx.

For a list of the zodiacal signs and their traditional annual dates, as well as the fact that they became fixed long ago, see 12 Brit 926, "zodiac." See also *The Imagery of the Zodiac* (IZOD), Chap. 3.

When John has Jesus saying to Thomas, "Blessed are those who have not seen and yet believe" (Jn 20,29), does this not apply to those of us today (as "Thomases" in the sign of Gemini, the Twin) who have not yet developed our etheric bodies to the point of being able to see Christ in the etheric world during this period of the Second Coming, yet who believe that it is so—that he is there now for us, having already come again, when we are able to see him there? In the deep message of his Gospel and Apocalypse, John has remained until the Second Coming in order to reveal it to us (Jn 21,21-23).

And for those readers able to see the connection, this penultimate thought (Jn 20,29) in the Gospel's putative original conclusion closely parallels the penultimate thought in Chapter 21, Jn 21,21-23. Blessed are those who are able to "believe" that Lazarus/John who gave us the Gospel of highest spiritual insight has "remained" unidentified throughout the history of Christianity until the time of the Second Coming, and that the Individuality (Hiram Abiff) who brought the divine wisdom into earthly application in building the first temple is the same who appeared as the Beloved Disciple and then again as Christian Rosenkreutz to prepare humanity for the Age of the Consciousness Soul and the building of the higher "Temple," the purified astral body (Rev 11,1). See "Widow's Son," Appendix to "Three Bodies," and "Pillars on the Journey." The reality of this is not, after all, so far-fetched as one might tend to think.

The Second Coming is only in the etheric world. The Lazarus/John Individuality had perhaps so perfected its etheric body (as well as its astral body) that it "remained" in that world until this day of the "Second Coming" (Jn 21,22) to serve the Earth and the Christ and to be taken up again by Christian Rosenkreutz and Count St. Germain. One who reads about these latter personalities must surely suspect something akin to this. And what better than the etheric body of Lazarus/John could have made the revelations of Christian Rosenkreutz possible—those revelations that were then brought out into the open by Rudolf Steiner after the new age of the Archangel Michael had begun (in 1879) and the Kali Yuga, or five thousand year Dark Age, had ended (in 1899). It is precisely these revelations that are essential for humanity to comprehend the reappearance of Christ in the etheric world.

POINT #3:   *The Two Suppers*

There were two "suppers"[9] in Jerusalem shortly before the Passion of Christ began. One has only to read the scriptural accounts to see that this is so. John tells us clearly of two suppers; the one in Jn 12 is "six days before the Passover," while that in Jn 13 is immediately before the Passover "when Jesus knew that his hour had come to depart out of this world." This timing is borne out beyond question by the quite different events described in each passage. The first supper was in Bethany before the triumphal entry on Palm Sunday, and the second was in the upper room in Jerusalem immediately before the betrayal and Passion. The first supper is described only by John, the second by all four Gospels. Only in this way can the accounts be seen as harmonious.

POINT #4:   *The Two Anointings*

There were two anointings of Jesus during this time period. The anointing in Bethany in Jn 12 is not to be associated with the anointing at the

---

9. Koenig says there were three suppers during this period. He considers the anointing of Jesus' head at the house of Simon the Leper (Mt 26,6-13; Mk 14,3-9) to have been associated with a supper. Probably it was, but from these passages it would have to be inferred since it is not expressly stated. Luke places this, or a different, anointing at a different time and under different circumstances and specifically states that it occurred at a supper (Lk 7,36-50). But for our purposes here, the "two suppers" do not include one at the house of Simon the Leper during that period.

house of Simon the Leper, also in Bethany, reported in the synoptics. First we have the anointing by Mary Magdalene of Jesus' feet at Lazarus/John's house on Saturday (Jn 12,1-8), followed by the anointing of his head at Simon's house on Tuesday evening or Wednesday (Mt 26,1-13; Mk 14,1-9). The first is reflected in the humiliation of Jesus' washing the disciples' feet in the upper room at the last supper. As noted in fn 9, the anointing in Luke's Gospel does not appear to have occurred during this period.

POINT #5:   *Lazarus/John's Presence at the Last Supper*

As we know, the establishment of the Holy Eucharist took place at the second supper, the one in the upper room in Jerusalem. Lazarus/John was not present at that supper until he entered to carry the water basin for Christ to wash the "Twelve" disciples' feet. This accounts for the fact that John's Gospel says nothing of the initial Eucharist.

The context of this foot washing needs to be examined. There were probably at least three events during Jesus' ministry where disciples expressed a desire to seek individual preeminence among themselves. See Mt 18,1-5; Mk 9,33-37; Lk 9,46-48; Mt 20,20-28; Mk 10,35-45; Lk 22,24-27. Much confusion exists about these events, as is the case with the two suppers and the two anointings. Critical Biblical analysis over the last century and a half, in trying to reconcile seeming discrepancies between the Gospels, has tended to collapse somewhat dissimilar events which nevertheless contain common elements into a single event in order to fit them into predisposed dogma about an assumed chain of events. The practice undoubtedly sometimes produces a proper result but may well often obscure a true portrayal of developments. To some extent, the practice is the illegitimate offspring of the documentary hypothesis which also infects the modern history of Old Testament interpretation. Nowhere has the general tendency been more evident than in the effort, at least since the second century, to squeeze the perplexingly different accounts of "The Nativity" into the birth of a single child.

The self-seeking tendency among the disciples was probably a continuing problem for Jesus. From the cited passages, it appears that one occurrence took place in or around Capernaum "among the disciples" generally; another when the Zebedees asked Jesus for placement at his sides in the Kingdom (which may also have been separately advanced at a different time by their mother, "supposedly" Jesus' aunt); and still another, the one that concerns us here, during the last supper in the upper room in Jerusalem. Only Luke records this last one, but, as Koenig notes, it fits well the report, made only in John's Gospel, that Jesus then arose and proceeded to wash the feet of the "Twelve." The action is well supported by his prior statements about the desire to serve rather than to seek personal honor. Furthermore, the circumstances show that Lazarus/John indeed entered the upper room only at that time. He was not yet one of the "Twelve." He had been initiated into the higher mysteries of death, had subordinated his former great spiritual wealth in the Mysteries as well, perhaps, as worldly fortune, and already understood the spiritual imperative of being an unsung servant (which is certainly compatible with his masking of his own identity as Gospel writer so as to be understood only by the initiated), yet his Gospel gives no account of the establishment of the Eucharist which it undoubtedly would have done had he been there to take part in it. He does clearly identify (again only for the initiated) that it was he who thereafter leaned upon the bosom of the Lord.

There is immense merit in Koenig's suggestion that there had been a prearrangement between Jesus and his initiate that the latter would stand by the upper room with a water basin in order to assist Jesus with the foot washing at the proper time. Thus, as the "Twelve" were disputing about their pecking order, Jesus arose and summoned Lazarus/John (as Koenig suggests, but the communication could probably have occurred without any overt act by Jesus) to enter with the basin of water. Not only do the above Gospel accounts give the circumstances clearly supporting this scenario, but Koenig is able to go to the spiritual visions of the illiterate nun, Anne Catherine Emmerich for support (see the record of these in *The Life of Jesus Christ and Biblical Revelations* [LJC] as well as the discussion about her in the Foreword and Introduction to Powell's *Chronicle of the Living Christ* [CLC]). In fact, Koenig sees the foot washing, while addressed to all the disciples, as being especially for the benefit of Lazarus/John, who was to serve as one of the "Twelve" only for a limited time, thereafter to separate as a particular servant for the Gospel message. Koenig buttresses this suggestion by a most incisive and provocative observation, namely, that only Lazarus/John could have understood the esoteric meaning of Jn 13,18, reported only in his Gospel, citing Ps 41,9, "He who ate my bread has lifted his heel against me." We will look at that meaning in the Commentary; here I will only cite the places where Steiner gives insights into it, namely, GSJ, Lect. 7, pp. 113-115; ASJ, Lect. 6, p. 118; *Theosophy of the Rosicrucian* (TR), Lect. 14, pp. 158-159; *Reading the Pictures of the Apocalypse* (RPA), Lect. 4, pp. 60-61; GSMk, Lect. 10, p. 195. From the deep wisdom involved in this esoteric understanding has come the oft ridiculed doctrine of "transubstantiation," another of the traditions preserved by the Roman and Orthodox Catholic Churches without the source of its meaning being comprehended by many.

The posed question about who would betray the Lord has also been a point of confusion due to collapsing two different events. It has been generally heretofore assumed that the passage (Jn 13,21-26) where the Beloved Disciple asks (vs 25), "Lord who is it?" is the same event set out in the synoptics where Jesus, in response to the question of the betrayer's identity, indicates that it is one who has or is in some manner eating with him. But a careful inspection of all the passages (Mt 26,20-25; Mk 14,17-21; Lk 22,20-23; Jn 13,21-30) will indicate that the inquiry in the synoptics is during the meal, before the Eucharist (and in Luke's Gospel before the dispute), whereas in John's Gospel it appears that the meal is over, or substantially so, and one may reasonably infer that the Eucharist has previously been celebrated and that the dispute triggers the timing of the foot washing. The identification in the synoptics is not such as to demonstrate to all of the "Twelve" that it is Judas Iscariot, but merely that it is one eating with Jesus. John's Gospel does not say this, but rather that it is the one to whom Jesus "shall give this morsel when I have dipped it," thus clearly identifying Judas, and Jesus then tells him to do his deed quickly, whereupon he actually arises, completely confirming the identification. The accounts are quite different and should be understood as indicating two different events, one before the Eucharist and the foot washing and one after; Lazarus/John is present for the latter but not the former.

There is a meaningful relationship between Jn 12 and 13 in this respect, since both involve a foot washing, the first by Mary Magdalene, an anointing of the Master's feet to demonstrate his spiritual exaltation, and the second by Jesus to demonstrate the necessarily related imperative of spiritual servitude. Together they present a "now therefore" sequence, a prelude to the immensity of meaning in the Crucifixion itself.

POINT #6:   *Judas Iscariot and Lazarus/John*

What can be said about the "Name" "Iscariot"? It seems clearly to be a zodiacal identification, whatever other associations it might possibly have had. Without the benefit of anthroposophical sight, we can understand why it has not yet been recognized by traditional theology. However, in a sense it has. One Schwarz appears to have listed nine different possible interpretations, which are divided into four groups by 3 ABD 1091, "Judas Iscariot." The first group so listed is a circle known as the "Sicarii: dagger-wielding assassins." There is an obvious conceptual connection between this idea and that of the scorpion, and the essential root of both words seems both to reveal and to confirm the deeper meaning. We can see an obvious similarity between the "scar" in Iscariot and the "scor" in scorpion. And the death connection is probably carried over from ancient times in those words deriving from the Latin "caro" (flesh), such as carrion, carnage, carnal and carnivorous.

But in the spine-tingling category, we see a connection made by Paul that can give one a sense of inner certainty. In the fifteenth chapter of 1 Corinthians, so filled from start to finish with deep esoteric meaning, we find two very pertinent concepts joined in a way that brings the John beings into the picture. We have in vs 55, "O death, where is thy sting?" "Death" is represented by the First Adam (vss 21-22), the "sting" of the zodiacal Scorpion. But the zodiacal Scorpion has a higher counterpart, the zodiacal Eagle. The Christ is clearly shown in John's Gospel to be the higher "I Am." The Second Adam, as we saw in "The Nativity," incarnated as a "conditional Ego" in the "Three Bodies" of the Nathan Jesus Child, which "bodies" would eventually house, i.e., compose the Temple of, the Christ Spirit at age "Thirty." Thus, as will also be seen in "First and Second Adam," we have "death/life" as the counterpart of the zodiacal "Scorpion/Eagle." And we shall see in "Pillars on the Journey" below that "Adam, the son of God" (Lk 3,38) is the same Individuality present in John the Baptist. Thus not only is the higher "I Am" recognized by the Eagle Evangelist, Lazarus who thus had to become "John," but the lower "I Am," the "first Adam," is also represented by a "John."

Nor have we yet exhausted Paul's clues in Chapter 15, even on this narrow point. To see another, we must note the connection of the "Trumpet" (see herein) vs 52 with the passage about the "sting" and "death," and then note that in Rev 9,5,6,10 Lazarus/John says that at the sound of the fifth "Trumpet" those who do not have the appropriate seal upon their "Forehead" will suffer torture like the "sting" of a scorpion and "will seek death." See the Commentary on Revelation (condensed in

"Alpha and Omega > Creation and Apocalypse," Vol. 2) to appreciate how precisely this accords with what is said here.

As against the Scorpion (Iscariot), the character of the Eagle (Lazarus/John) is seen to represent exalting heights. Thus, in 2 Sam 1,23 (of Saul and Jonathan), "they were swifter than eagles"; Ps 103,5, "so that your youth is renewed like the eagle's"; Is 40,31, "they shall mount up with wings like eagles"; Jer 49,16, those who "nest as high as the eagles"; Prov 30,19a, "the way of an eagle in the sky, the way of a serpent on a rock" (here note, in "wisdom," the polarity of their natures); Prov 23,5, "flying like an eagle toward heaven"; Obad 1,4, "Though you soar aloft like the eagle"; Rev 8,13, "and I heard an eagle crying with a loud voice, as it flew in midheaven"; Rev 12,14, "But the woman was given the two wings of the great eagle that she might fly from the serpent" (again note the polarity of their natures). For an excellent discussion of the "living images" of the zodiacal signs of the Scorpion and the Eagle, see pp. 32 and 38 of IZOD.

What Happened to the Two Johns?

The intrigue historically surrounding the identity of the Johannine author helps to explain the trail of tradition and legend that has built up around the two John beings who survived the Baptist. And while, in light of what has been said above, we perhaps need not worry about their later destiny, some additional light may be shed and our curiosity to some extent assuaged by looking at it.

Steiner often and unequivocally tells us that Lazarus/John, the "Beloved Disciple," took the Mother of Jesus to Ephesus, where they lived until her death. Thereafter, in Ephesus the Beloved Disciple survived until well past one hundred years of age, until age 106 in fact. On the other hand, Steiner does not tell us, to my knowledge (and apparently also that of Koenig), what happened to Zebedee John.

Much has been made, one way or the other, about the implications of Mk 10,39 in this regard, namely, that both Zebedee brothers, and not just James, were martyred. There Jesus responded to the Zebedee brothers' request for special status in the Kingdom and their assertion that they were "able" to drink the "cup" by saying, "The cup that I drink you will drink; and with the baptism with which I am baptized, you will be baptized...." If it could be determined that Zebedee John was martyred, then he was probably not the John, or one of the putative two Johns, who lived in Ephesus. Such a conclusion would seem to greatly reduce the possibility that he was the Evangelist, for the tradition is very strong that the Gospel was written in Ephesus, certainly stronger than that for any other location. See 2 ABD 548-549; 8 Interp 441; 29 AB ciii; Barc (John), Vol. 1, pp. 20-23; and 9 NIB 506.

The extensive commentary on Mk 10,39, although equivocal on this point, nevertheless is fully compatible with the martyrdom of both brothers. See 7 Interp 814; 27 AB 412; NICNT (Mark), p. 381; Barc (Mark) pp. 255-256; and 8 NIB 653-654. The early martyrdom (about A.D. 44) of Zebedee James is clear from Acts 12,2. Some have considered that the failure to include in this passage the fact of his brother John's martyrdom suggests that he never died in such manner. But the earliness of Zebedee James' martyrdom and its connection with the contemporaneous arrest of Peter belies that argument. Acts also does not mention the martyrdom of countless other disciples, and especially of James the brother of Jesus, whom tradition clearly has being martyred shortly before the destruction of the temple in A.D. 70. See 3 ABD 621. The picture we see is that Zebedee John was martyred as a part of the same persecution. Clearly, such James and Zebedee John were those, along with Peter, referred to by Paul in Gal 2,9 as being at the Council of Jerusalem around A.D. 49-50, though Peter and probably Zebedee John, as we shall see, must surely thereafter have gone to Rome.

Koenig, citing a number of the early church writers, seems to establish that both Johns were banished to an island, possibly both to Patmos (a certainty for Lazarus/John), which adds to the confusion, but that the banishments were at different times. While Lazarus/John was banished under the reign of Domitian (A.D. 81-96), Zebedee John was banished under the reign of Nero (A.D. 54-68), possibly in 64. There are reports that a John apparently returned from Patmos to Jerusalem and not to Ephesus, but these probably indicate that Zebedee John returned at Nero's death to Jerusalem and there suffered martyrdom. Koenig reasonably concludes that Zebedee John went with Peter to Rome and was banished from there by Nero to Patmos, returning again to Jerusalem in A.D. 68, after which all traces are lost. But he properly remarks that the similarities in destiny are most striking, and that this fact helps to explain the confusion. It is almost as if providence assisted the "Beloved Disciple" in masking his identity for two millennia. But when one understands the significance of the "Name" John, as above set out, the similarity of destiny as well as close personal affinity is probably no mere coincidence.

Koenig's scenario seems more plausible than any other. In support of his conclusions, he refers (though usually, in the manuscript to which I am privy, without adequate citation for easy reference identification) to the following sources:

1. Eusebius' Church History;
2. Tertullian;
3. Clemens [sic.] of Alexandria;
4. Irenaeus;
5. Eusebius, in the Title of the Syrian translation and the Acts of John; and
6. Philippus Sidensis' history of the church.

Of these, I could only locate the first in my own NICENE volumes, although all the writers except the last are generally included in such sets. In addition to these six sources, Koenig quotes from Bock (surely from *Caesars and Apostles*, not yet published in English), who in turn quotes Eusebius's *Church History*, where Papias said:

At Ephesus there lived under Trajan [A.D. 98-117] a very ancient man, so old that not only his contemporaries, but also their children and grandchildren had died long ago and the great-grandchildren no longer knew who he was. They simply called him "John" or "Presbyter." They also did not know how to honor him, clothed him in precious chasubles, hung the mysterious emblem of the King and High Priest Melchizedek, a star of gold foil, the Petalon, with the unspeakable name of God on his forehead.

I do note in Eusebius' Church History, under the "Martyrdom of Symeon of Jerusalem," 1 Nicene-3, p. 163, that John, "was both a witness and a teacher, who reclined upon the bosom of the Lord, and being a priest wore the sacerdotal plate. He also sleeps at Ephesus." The "emblem" or "sacerdotal plate" almost certainly refers to that of the high priest in Ex 28,36 and 39,30, which seems to identify Lazarus/John, for he seems to have been a member of the priestly caste.[10] Aside from that plate, the passage quoted from Bock would fit well with Steiner's statement about the Evangelist's old age. But then that statement is widely corroborated by tradition anyhow, and by the very moniker "presbytr" which means "old."[11]

---

10. He was "known to the high priest" (Jn 18,15,16), and apparently for this reason was admitted to the "court of the high priest along with Jesus, while Peter stood outside at the door." And he then "went out and spoke to the maid who kept the door, and brought Peter in." The maid quizzed only Peter, but not Lazarus/John (vs 17). And we know that Luke's Gospel referred to the one Jesus was said (in Mark's Gospel) to have "loved" as being a "ruler" (Lk 18,18), implying a position of prominence consistent with that of the priests.

11. To those early church sources cited by Koenig, I would only add from the NICENE volumes:

 a. The epistle, generally recognized as spurious and from a later age, attributed to Ignatius (A.D. 30–107) to the Tarsians, Chap. 3. See 1 NICENE-1, pp. 107 & 46.

 b. The Fragments of Papias (A.D. 70-155), Chap. 1, discussed in most commentaries on this point. See 1 NICENE-1, p. 153.

 c. In the Apocrypha of the New Testament, "Acts of the Holy Apostle and Evangelist John the Theologian—About His Exile and Departure." See 8 NICENE-1, pp. 560-564.

 d. From Eusebius" Church History (same as Koenig's #1). See 1 NICENE-3:

  1. Book 3, Chap. 23, "The Apostle John and the Young Robber," p. 150.

  2. Book 3, Chap. 31, "The Death of John and Philip," pp. 162-163.

  3. Book 3, Chap. 39, "The Writings of Papias," pp. 170- 171, including editorial note 13.

EGYPT

IT IS IMPORTANT TO COME to the realization that the Old Testament, particularly Genesis, is primarily mythical and/or allegorical. The Bible is primarily and skillfully written in a literary style that portrays spiritual truth for those who have eyes to see, but in keeping with the tradition of the ancient "Mysteries," cloaks the deeper meaning from the vulgar.[1] This aspect is revealed in the Bible itself in Gal 4,24, which is speaking specifically about Genesis, and in Rev 11,8, Ezek 17,2; 20,49 and 24,3. And the pejorative references to myths in 1 Tim 1,4 and 4,7; 2 Tim 4,4; Tit 1,14 and 2 Pet 1,16 give no real basis to reject the spiritually obvious fact, because these books are seen by most as coming late, when doctrine was being formed in the face of endless speculation, and we know from Rudolf Steiner's teachings that the Christ-enabled vision of the Apostolic group (including Paul and the Evangelists) did not survive them. Nonetheless, the clearly genuine letters of Paul (e.g., Gal 4,24; 1 Cor 10,1-4) show that he understood the spiritual meaning of the Genesis and Exodus accounts.

In this regard Paul was undoubtedly well acquainted with, and perhaps strongly influenced by, Philo of Alexandria (discussed below), "the most important representative of Hellenistic Judaism" (see 9 Brit 385, "Philo, Judaeus"), whose writings, predominantly on Mosaic "Law," were primarily allegorical. In 16 Brit 258, "Christianity," we are told, "Like his elder contemporary Philo of Alexandria, also a Hellenized Jew of the dispersion, he [Paul] interpreted the Old Testament allegorically (symbolically) and affirmed the primacy of spirit over letter in a manner that was in line with Jesus' freedom with regard to the sabbath." (Cf. 2 Cor 3, also *Christianity as Mystical Fact* [CMF], Chaps. 4 and 12.)

---

1. See 4 ABD 946-965, "Myth and Mythology"; 24 Brit 710, "Myth and Mythology"; also Brit Index under the same title.

And though his writings were largely compromised, and apparently to a great extent disposed of, by later orthodoxy, there is significant evidence that Origen (ca. 185-254), "the most important theologian and biblical scholar of the early Greek church," also interpreted the Bible allegorically.[2] And even Augustine interpreted the millennium of the Apocalypse allegorically.[3]

It is submitted that the principle "Ye shall know a tree by its fruit" is applicable to the practice of Biblical interpretation, and that one should not be a slave to any particular method, but rather search for what gives the deepest corroboration of verity to the soul. The thesis of this entire work is that no exposition of the Bible story in its entirety more accords with phenomena than that given us by Steiner. And one has only to open one's eyes and heart to see that the Bible is telling us the very same thing he did, and that it is an integral whole which makes eminent sense from beginning to end—and in the process assures humanity that there is glorious purpose and hope in the entirety of all existence. In the words of St. Paul (Eph 1,9-10),

> For he has made known to us in all wisdom and insight the mystery of his will, according to his purpose which he set forth in Christ as a plan for the fullness of time, to unite all things in him, things in heaven and things on earth.

At the very time the Greeks were formulating their myths of Atlantean memories, Moses and his clan were developing their own, namely, what has come down to us in the Pentateuch and to a great extent even in the "histories," i.e., Joshua through the Chronicles. Admittedly, some "historical" facts were woven into the story, but something deeper is being told to which the facts are indentured.

Thus, just as in Gal 4 Hagar and Mount Sinai are allegorically equated as the representative of "the law" and Sarah and Christ as what superseded

---

2. 8 Brit 997, "Origen," which cites R.P.C. Hanson, Allegory and Event, 1959, as "the best study of Origen's biblical interpretation." See also Frend, The Rise of Christianity, (RoC), Chap. 11, pp. 373-377, "Origen"; 5 ABD 42 at 46, "Origen"; and 4 Nicene-1, pp. 291-292 (Origen De Principiis, Book II, Chap IX).
3. See 17 Brit 406-7, "Doctrines and Dogmas, Religious." On the varieties of Biblical interpretation, see 14 Brit 876-8, "Biblical Literature, Types of Biblical Hermeneutics." See also 11 Brit 698, "Therapeutae."

the law (i.e., the new covenant), so also must the entire Genesis account be seen as representing something far deeper and more important than a mere "historical account" (and a highly spotty and equivocal one at that, as archaeology demonstrates). It is here, in Genesis, where the tone is set and where we must take our beginnings if we are to understand the Biblical usage of certain terms. "Egypt" is one of many such terms, and the Exodus can hardly be understood if we don't thus compass ourselves aright.

First, Egypt represents the third Cultural Era in the post-Atlantean Epoch (see **I-1**, **I-24**, **I-25**, **I-85**, **I-57** and **I-58**), a time when the human being was beginning to notice the outer world more intently, but when there was still a strong atavistic inner perception of the spiritual world (compared to later Eras). Even within its own Era, Egypt seems to portray that atavistic perception vis-a-vis its Chaldean and other contemporaries. What was brought "from the East" (Gen 11,2) in the transition from the second, Ancient Persian, Cultural Era was represented in the third, Chaldo-Egyptian, Cultural Era by "Egypt," namely, an "Epimethean" backward vision as compared with the "Promethean" forward looking nature of the Chaldean patriarchs and Moses; the older Sun god and initiation rather than the younger and formative Moon (see **I-30** and **I-31**; the twelvefold zodiacal consciousness there reflected for Israel was prospective, reflecting what was to come to fruition through it).

What the human being was separating from, namely, the ancient clairvoyance, was still something needed by humanity in its evolution. One may draw a comparison with the child fed first from the breast what is vital to its growth and development, and then weaned, so that it gradually looks to harder and harder food from outer sources. The Biblical account shows a pattern of the necessity of going into Egypt for what was otherwise lacking in the background of the Jewish nation. The first such journey was that of Abraham, then Jacob and his sons, then Moses, then the flirtatious alliances of the kings, then Jeremiah (but in his case unwillingly [Jer 43,5-7]), and finally another Joseph, the father of the Solomon Jesus child, and his family. (Curiously, these comprise six journeys. The fulfilling seventh might well be the return of Christianity to its early center in Alexandria where Mark's Gospel was written and the earliest preeminent church theologians centered. The retracement and transformation of the Egyptian Cultural Era is then to occur in our own fifth Cultural Era, that of the Consciousness Soul.) Until we come to see in this panoply of "journeys" and "enslavements" the progressive account of the human being's unfolding development into the outer world (the journey of the Prodigal Son away from home), we can scarcely come to see the deeper view of the Biblical message. That it corresponds, more or less, with "historical" facts, is merely reflective of the "As Above, So Below" verity, or pattern, of creation itself.

In his excellent single lecture entitled *The Gospels* (GOSP), Steiner shows how "In Christ Jesus we really have a fusion and at the same time a rebirth of all the former spiritual streams of humanity." Recognizing many, he deals with only three, the Zarathustrian, Buddhist and Hebrew. In the part here most pertinent he deals with the Hebrew stream (the other two are visible in "The Nativity"), which was to develop logical thinking based upon observation of phenomena in the outer world. To understand this mission, and the place Egypt played in it, consider the following portions of the lecture:

> ... we must bear in mind that all clairvoyance comes about through the independent working of the etheric body, especially the etheric part of the brain. When the etheric body of the brain and the physical instrument of logical thought are strongly bound together, no clairvoyance can come about. That can only come when the etheric body keeps something back and makes it independent. When the etheric part of the brain is quite joined to the physical brain, it [the etheric body] makes use of it in the most refined way; but being thoroughly engaged in developing the physical brain it reserves nothing for the development of clairvoyance. Now it was necessary that the very quality which is connected with brain-thinking (thinking which through the brain makes logical connection between the various phenomena appearing in the world) should make its entry into humanity; for this something had to enter mankind which may be described as follows. An individual had to be selected out of mankind, in whom remained as little as possible of what was known as the old clairvoyance, but in whom, on the other hand, was developed, carved and chiselled out, to the greatest extent possible, the physical instrument of the brain. This individual was able to survey the phenomena of the outer physical world in terms of measure, number, order and harmony, and to find the unity in the external phenomena in space. Thus whereas all those who belonged to earlier civilizations gained their

knowledge of the spiritual world from within, he had to direct his gaze to the phenomena around him, to combine them in a logical way, and to weigh them. He said to himself: "The phenomena outside, when viewed as one great united picture, are seen to be parts of a great harmony." What there appears as unity, he saw as the God behind the phenomena of the physical plane. That was different from all the former conceptions of Divinity. Those who had seen God before this time, said: "Our idea of God arises within us," but this individual turned his gaze in all directions, he put the various phenomena in their right order, studied the different kingdoms of nature, and brought them into unity; in short, he was the great organizer of the world-phenomena according to number and measure, and was chosen out of all mankind for this particular work. This person who, out of all mankind, was thus selected to be the first man to survey the outer physical world and to discover the unity in it, was Abraham. Abraham or Abram was selected by the divine spiritual powers to receive this special mission of transmitting to mankind the knowledge of the forces in external phenomena connected with number and measure. He came forth from the Chaldean civilization, which had itself acquired its astrology by means of clairvoyance. Abraham, the father of arithmetic, was the first to discover this by his method of combination, through his physical brain having at some time undergone a sort of chiselling; and because of this he was entrusted with a very special mission.

Now, we must remember that this mission was not to remain with him alone, but was to become the common possession of all mankind; but as it was bound up with the physical brain, how could it belong to all? Only through physical heredity. That is to say, from Abraham had to proceed a people who were to inherit this special capacity, for as long a time as it was their mission to carry it into humanity. A nation had to be founded, not merely a civilization in which men were taught what had been clairvoyantly received. What mankind was now to receive was to be carried down through heredity to the descendants, that it might extend into all the separate parts. What was it which was thus to live on through the human organism? It was that system which was first brought to mankind by Abraham. If we look up at the stars in their order, we can by calculation ascertain their order. The thought of those who studied the Chaldean Astrology reflected the thoughts of the Gods; but now it became a question of making the transition from that to making calculations, to a logical grasp of the phenomena of the outer world. Therefore a new capacity had to be inherited by the physical human body, a capacity which could itself through the working of man's thought bring forth that which is manifested as the cosmic order. This was very beautifully expressed in the words of Him Who gave this mission to Abraham: "Thy descendants shall be arranged according to the same order as the stars,"[4] which has been carelessly translated in the Bible: "Thy children shall be as the sand of the sea."[5] It really means that the descendants of Abraham would be so organized that they would be a reflection of the stars in the heavens.

That is expressed in the twelve sons of Jacob, who are the reflection of the twelve signs of the Zodiac. Here comes the measure which is pre-figured in the heavens. In the subsequent generations this was to be the image of the numbering in the heavens. As numbers are inscribed in the heavens, so in these generations that system of numbers was to be inscribed. The deep wisdom contained in these words has been wrongly translated: Thy descendants shall be as the sand of the sea.—We can thus see the purpose of the whole mission of Abraham. In other ways also does this mission express that it is intended to be an image of the secrets of the cosmos. The first question we must put to ourselves is this:—The old dim clairvoyance was to be sacrificed at that time; that which was established in mankind from the earliest ages was to be given up. Henceforth all must come from without. In the whole of this mission the innermost feeling was that everything must now be received as a gift from without, and what was to come in as something new was to come through physical inheritance. In this way was the new mission to come to the world. Abraham himself had to receive it as a gift from God, and it came about through his first being required to sacrifice his son Isaac and then being restrained from doing so. What did he, then, actually receive from the hand of God? He received his whole mission; for if he had really sacrificed Isaac he would have sacrificed

---

4. See Gen 15,5; also "Zodiac."—ERS
5. Gen 22,17; Gen 26,4; Gen 32,12; Heb 11,12; etc.—ERS

his whole mission.[6] When Isaac was given back to him, Abraham received back his people. In Isaac he received what he himself was to
give to the world, and he received it as a gift from the divine cosmic
order [Heb 11,19]. All that followed after Abraham was therefore a
gift from God Himself. All that still remained of the gifts of clairvoyance, the last of these gifts—which was offered up willingly as a
sacrifice — is connected with the constellation of the Ram, Aries....
Thus we see the Ram at the sacrifice of Isaac [Gen 22,13]. That is a
symbolic expression for the sacrifice of the last gift of clairvoyance,
in exchange for the gift which enables man to judge the cosmic phenomena according to the laws of number and measure. [This understanding allays the moral compunction and ambivalence scholars
have long felt about the revered Father Abraham's willingness to follow the abhorrent pagan practice of infant sacrifice, let alone a loving
God's requiring it.] That is the mission of Abraham. Now, how does
this mission proceed? The last gift of clairvoyance had been offered
in sacrifice;[7] it had to be driven out of this mission, and if it still re-
appeared through inheritance, it was not tolerated, so to say, in the
direct line of succession. In Joseph we see a throw-back. He had his
dreams; he had the old gift of clairvoyance, and his brothers cast him
out. This shows how strictly the line was drawn in this whole mission. Joseph was cast out, and he wandered to Egypt in order to make
a connection with the Egyptian civilization, the other wing of our
whole cultural evolution. Joseph united in himself the general character of this mission with the remains of the old clairvoyance. In
Egypt he brought about a complete transformation by correcting the
decadent Egyptian civilization in accordance with his clairvoyant

---

6. It would seem that the inherited nature of the brain would not have been thus precluded, for Ishmael was descended from that same promise (Gen 15,5 and 21,13) and
twelvefold nature (Gen 25,12-16). But the Christ, the "I Am," the one from whom Abraham's descendants were to be "named," was to come through Isaac (Gen 21,12; Heb
11,17-19). See the discussion on this under "Bush." The "promise" would have been for
naught without this.—ERS

7. Here I must admit to a fascination with the similarity between so many Biblical names
and the Egyptian goddess "Isis," a name that seems to imply a certain connection with
clairvoyance. Prominent Biblical names include Isaac, Israel, Isaiah and Iscariot. Traditional etymology seems not to have taken any note, but then neither has traditional theology taken any note of anthroposophical insights about human evolution. Certainly, the
idea would fit Steiner's statement here, as does also his analogy of Isaac as the "etheric
body" of the developing Biblical personality (I-68).—ERS

gift. He used his gift in the service of external organization. This is what lay behind the cultural mission of Joseph to Egypt.

And now we see the playing of a curious drama. We see how those who were the missioners of the external thinking in terms of measure and numbers no longer followed the earlier path, and how through Joseph they sought the outer connection, for they sought in Egypt the reflection of what they were unable to bring forth out of themselves. They travelled thither, — and in Egypt the descendants of Abraham found what they required. There they could obtain it, and so they went there. What was necessary for the further organizing of this mission, as it could not come from within, was given from without, by means of the Egyptian Initiation.[8] Moses brought that from without and united the Egyptian culture with the particular mission of Abraham. And we see being propagated from one generation to another, a human grasp of the external world, founded on measure, number and weight. A new element had come in. This was propagated by means of blood-relationship and can only thus be propagated, for it is bound up with that which must come through inheritance.

Egypt's first appearance in the Bible (Gen 10,6) is as the name of Ham's second son. We note that Noah was the tenth generation starting with Adam (Gen 5).[9] Adam's son Abel apparently died without issue (Gen 4), and nothing further is said about Cain after Gen 4, save in Heb 11,4; 1 Jn 3,12 and Jude 1,11 (but see fn 9). Adam's only son said to have had issue was Seth (Gen 5). All three of Noah's sons, Shem, Ham and Japheth, had issue (Gen 10), but Ham is our particular concern here. Recall that Ham had seen his father's "Nakedness" (Gen 9,22; see "Naked"), thus probably indicating a predominant tendency toward atavistic clairvoyance. Ham is said to have had four sons, Cush, Egypt, Put and Canaan (Gen 10,6). Strangely, Put is mentioned nowhere else in the Bible. Ham's other three sons had issue, and it is most noteworthy that the three predominant Old Testament civilizations aside from Israel (the Shemites) come from these, namely, the Babylonians (and Assyrians)

8. Note that Joseph is said to have "put them all together in prison for three days" (Gen 42,17), an indication that they were indeed initiated into the Egyptian Mysteries. See "Three Days' Journey."—ERS
9. But see the relationship between Gen 4 and 5 in the Appendix to "Three Bodies."

from Cush, the Egyptians (and Philistines) from Egypt, and the Canaanites (including Sodom and Gomorrah) from Canaan. Also otherwise peculiar is that Noah blessed his two sons Shem and Japheth, but said nothing about Ham, instead cursing one (only) of his sons, Canaan (Gen 9,22-27). The Babylonians, the Egyptians, and the Canaanites would have had an atavistic clairvoyance, and Israel was in turn held "captive" by, and absorbed much for its growth from, the first two, but it was to take over only the land of the cursed Canaan. The rich seeds of allegorical and evolutionary truth can thus readily be seen in these unfolding lineages. See the discussion of Gen 10 in "Three Bodies" (as well as of the controversy over "wells" in #27 thereof).

It is noteworthy that Moses killed the Egyptian (Ex 2,12), and David killed the Philistine giant, Goliath (also of Egypt's lineage), by stoning him on the "Forehead" then cutting off his head (1 Sam 17,49-51). Thus each of these two outstanding leaders of Israel got his start by "killing" the Egyptian element. And in David's case, the deed is particularized right down to the "Forehead," which the stone "sank into," thus getting right to the locus of the pineal gland, the seat of both the ancient and future clairvoyant center[10]—the point of which seems to be killing the ancient to move forward to the future. And thus began the Davidic line from which the Messiah was to come.

The threefold "sister ruse" used by Abraham and Isaac (Gen 12; 20 and 26) has long troubled traditional theology. Its seeming immorality has been variously rationalized, and its redundancy has lured seekers down variant pathways of documentary hypotheses and critical analyses. But it is as Abraham said (Gen 20,12), "Besides she is indeed my sister." How could this be? The etheric body is always of the opposite sex from the physical body, and is what gives the physical body life (being also known as the "life body"). It was necessary for the etheric body to gain the benefits of the ancient spiritual insights, thus to dwell to some extent with the Egyptian (or Philistine) heritage, out of fear that otherwise it would cost the physical body its "life," i.e., its "life" mission. But in each case, after some degree of availability to the ancient influence, it was to return, and with a dramatic enhancement of benefits from the venture. In the first instance (Gen 12) the "sister" is actually taken by Pharaoh

---

10. See the discussion of "The Etherization of the Blood" and the pineal gland, midway through "Second Coming."

for his wife; in the second (Gen 20) the Philistine Abimelech was warned by God in a dream and thus did not approach her; and in the third (Gen 26) it was not even Abimelech who was attracted to her but some of his underlings whom he himself warned off after seeing Isaac fondling her. This declining involvement illustrates how the outside influence upon the "sister" etheric body is attenuated as its impact moves from working directly on the etheric body to having to work on the etheric body secondarily through the younger astral body and finally through the still younger and more remote Ego. The inherent immorality in the ruse itself is a strong hint to the alert seeker, as in Abraham's child sacrifice, that something much deeper than its surface meaning is intended. Anthroposophical insight now brings understanding not often previously to be "found."

From these beginnings, the Biblical story is replete with Egyptian involvement, and if we are to understand its significance, we must comprehend these beginnings and weave the threads of such insight into the developing picture. In doing so, we must remember the great spiritual law of reflection. Metaphorically, it can be imaged as a pathway out and back such that it must be travelled in reverse on the return journey (see **I-1** through **I-3**, and especially **I-71**). The human being, the Prodigal Son, came through Egypt in the third segment of its sevenfold journey through the first post-Atlantean Epoch. The Christ incarnated at the far point of the journey, in the fourth segment, the Greco-Roman, and we are now retracing the third in the present fifth Cultural Era. Understandably much had to be said about Egypt in the Bible, which helps to nurture us on our Way. The atavistic clairvoyance, though fading in Egypt, must be transformed through the Christ "in" us into that spiritual "seeing" toward which the redeemed must move. Our new organ of spiritual perception, when Christ-enabled, will gradually permit more and more of the redeemed to "Witness" him in his "Second Coming."

The final Biblical usage of Egypt is appropriately found in Rev 11,8, where the Temple is to be measured (Rev 11,1). It is in connection with that measurement that we are then told of the two "Witness(es)," Elijah and Moses, who make their "Three Days' Journey" (Rev 11,9), respectively, through what is "allegorically [spiritually] called Sodom and Egypt," the two main branches of Biblical involvement with the sons of Ham. The long journey through the mineral-physical world, the "flesh," is then nearing its end. Soon thereafter "the last 'Trumpet'" is to be blown. It is critical, if we are to effectively follow the Christ lead, that we come to comprehend the Way.

Steiner often spoke of the last decade of this millennium as being immensely critical from the standpoint of the spiritual evolution of humanity, from both the good and evil perspectives. From the "good," one is struck by the fact that in 1993, a meaningful seven years before the decade's expiration, an event occurred of immense significance for enhancing Biblical understanding. In that year complete and unabridged works of Philo (Philo Judeas, ca. 20 B.C. –ca. A.D. 50, "Philo of Alexandria") were, for the first time, published in English in a single, popularly priced volume (see *Philo* [PHILO] in the Bibliography). His general importance has long been recognized as a background for Christian literature, but any recognition by Biblical commentaries or critics of its full significance has escaped my attention.

We have seen above the spiritual law of "reflection" by which humanity in the present fifth Cultural Era must retrace, and transform, that which it passed through in the third (Egypt). Steiner has pointed out one of the principle negative aspects of the Egyptian Era that must now be reversed, namely, the fascination with death and the emphasis upon and preservation of the physical body. Nowhere was this more pointedly illustrated than in the process of mummification. And eerily the excavated remains of those mummies have recently fascinated vast throngs as they have been displayed with great fanfare on worldwide tour. The escalating cost of disposing of human remains is tied to our fascination with the decaying mineral body that the Ego, the burning "Bush," must necessarily abandon forever so that it can "return to dust" (Gen 2,7 and 3,19). Typically, today one tries to remember the "personality" that lived in a given incarnation, oblivious of the need to look to it only in searching for the reality of the eternal Individuality of which the former was merely a partial representation. We are still deceived by the Egyptian-like attraction to "maya," the "flesh." This is the negative we must overcome if we are to experience the overcoming of "Death" represented by the Risen Christ.

Thus, we come to Philo (of Alexandria, the leading Egyptian city founded by Aristotle's student Alexander in the Greek Era) at this critical time, for in him we see reflected the positive aspect of Egypt as it was itself evolving during the fourth Era. That positive aspect is Philo's wisdom in seeing the allegorical nature of the ancient, clairvoyantly perceived Mosaic scriptures. Once again it can be said, "Out of Egypt have I called my son" (Mt 2,15; Hos 11,1) in repetition and fulfillment of the pattern started by Abraham. How marvelous that the works of Philo have become widely available as a part of the flame of spiritual awakening fanned by Steiner.

Three writers in the Bible specifically utilize "allegories,"[11] namely, Ezekiel (Ezek 17,2; 20,49; 24,3), Paul (Gal 4,24; cf. 1 Cor 10,1-4), and Lazarus/John (Rev 11,8). The latter two can be seen to have been not only totally compatible with, but also probably strongly influenced by, Philo in this respect. Notably Ezekiel looked back upon the just ended Egyptian Era and spoke of "dry bones" (Ezek 37) in the "valley" (37,1-2) which the "spirit" (37,5-6) would one day enter, when the two kingdoms would become one (37,19; see also "The Nativity" on when the two become one), which will occur on the "Mountain(s)" (Ezek 37,22). The entirety of Chapter 37 is an allegory of great beauty in the light of Steiner's teachings. It was in the fourth Era when the Christ came, but it is in the present fifth Era when we must retrace the steps of the third on our journey back home to the spirit (i.e., Father) whence we came. To do so, we must come to see "the way." We must come to an anthroposophical understanding of the burning "Bush" to know with assurance what we are searching for, namely, to know ourselves, our entelechies or Individualities (rather than simply our one-lived earthly personalities), as "sons of God." When we come thus to know ourselves, we shall then walk as servants from life to life without death (of our consciousness) intervening—we shall have overcome death. Then only can we rejoice as sacrificial servants rather than as beings of status and privilege. Then only can we meaningfully erase the decaying, and increasingly putrefying, distinctions of sex, race and creed. Then only can Christianity rise above being simply one of the world's divisive religions and take its rightful place as the one and only path of humanity's salvation (Jn 14,6), from which the "elect" can be gathered (see "East, West, North & South").

Let us now look more closely at the evidence pointing to Philo's influence with the original Apostolic group and Evangelists and his status as a "Christian."

That Paul was thoroughly familiar with, and substantially influenced by, Philo has long been an increasing probability in my mind. It is hard to

---

11. Have we not here again a pointer at the spiritual reality of the human being's "Three Bodies?"

imagine how a hellenized Jew and Pharisee such as Saul of Tarsus had been, who "advanced in Judaism beyond many of my own age among my people, so extremely zealous was I for the traditions of my fathers" (Gal 1,14), could have been uninfluenced by so preeminent an elder in these categories as was Philo. Not only was Alexandria the largest Jewish community outside of Palestine, but Philo was himself widely known and from a wealthy family; his brother Alexander provided the gold and silver to plate the temple gates in Jerusalem and loaned money to Herod Agrippa I, father of the tetrarch Herod Agrippa II before whom Paul appeared and was found innocent (Acts 25-26). It appears (see 5 Brit 880) that save for the above loan it is unlikely that either Agrippa would have come into his official position in Judea. Furthermore, Alexander's son Marcus married the daughter (Bernice) of Herod Agrippa I, and was thus a brother-in-law of Herod Agrippa II. Bernice was with Agrippa throughout the time of his trial of Paul, for she is referred to in Acts 25,13,23 and 26,30. Paul seems to know of Agrippa's background (Acts 26,2-3) and surely must have been aware of his connections with Philo's family in Alexandria. Perhaps it even contributed to Paul's feeling of being "fortunate" to appear before him (Acts 26,2), particularly if, as here assumed, Paul was a devotee of the (primarily allegorical) teachings of Philo.

With that background we now look at Paul's terse remarks in Gal 4,21-31, identifying the Sarah/Hagar episode in Genesis as an allegory. Where might we find this more fully explained? Nowhere more than in Philo's extensive allegorical comments on Genesis. See PHILO, pp. 304-320 "On Mating with the Preliminary Studies," and "Questions and Answers on Genesis, III," pp. 848-853, paragraphs (18) through (38) dealing with Gen 16. Whatever knowledge Paul's own initiation gave him, he certainly gives his imprimatur, and would appear to acknowledge his indebtedness, to these allegorical teachings of Philo which explain in great detail what Paul says succinctly.

And when we go to Paul's identification in 1 Cor 10,1-4 of the Rock as Christ and the manna as spiritual food, we can see how these also flow from Philo's teachings. On the "Rock," see PHILO, p. 125 "That the Worse is Wont to Attack the Better" XXXI (115) and (118), and on "Manna," see p. 282 "Who is the Heir of Divine Things" VI (79).

Philo's works would indicate that virtually the entirety of the Mosaic Law has an allegorical meaning higher than its literal one, for he treats of them extensively. We shall in the course of this longer work be looking at many of these. While it has not been utilized for this term "Egypt," Philo deals with the meaning of that also and in a way quite compatible with the meanings here. But the point for now is that Paul clearly looked at the higher allegorical meanings of the Old Testament, which can inspire us to do so also.

Moreover, there is an inherent similarity in purpose between the parable (9 Brit 133) and the allegory (1 Brit 277) in that both employ fictional information to convey deeper truth. The Old Testament uses both vehicles. Most of Jesus' teachings were by parable, but some, such as that of the Prodigal Son, seem clearly more akin to allegory. That the latter has been dubbed a parable is doubtless due to the fact that its allegorical truth has generally remained hidden, absent anthroposophical light.

Among the Evangelists, we may take Luke as reflecting the thinking of Paul, and as thus being at least indirectly influenced by the hellenistic thinking of Philo, an influence readily acceptable to one already a Greek. But we will look at Peter, then to Mark and then to Lazarus/John, and in the process see the amazing conceptual links between our Gospel writers and Philo, so that virtually the entirety of the New Testament can be seen to come, in a sense, under his sway. Little wonder then that "the Christian church has been the primary preserver of the writings of Philo, who was virtually unknown in the Jewish tradition after his own time until the sixteenth century" (PHILO, Foreword, p. xiii; in accord is 5 ABD 341).

Let us embark first to Peter as the inspiration of Evangelist John Mark. Though problematic as is so often the case, the tradition is strong that Peter resided for a time in Rome and was martyred there (see 9 Brit 332, "Peter the Apostle, Saint"). Even stronger is the tradition and evidence that Mark was associated with Peter in a special way. Eusebius tells us "that Philo... became acquainted at Rome with Peter..." (Nicene-3, Vol. 1, p. 117, Chap. 17, vs 1 and editorial footnote 1). The latter footnote cites Photius as even saying "that Philo became a Christian," an assertion it says is certainly wrong. Considering that Philo died of old age during the very birthing labors of Christianity, we might perhaps say, in the sense of Augustine's recognition that there were Christians (such as Socrates and Plato) prior to the time of Christ,[12] that Philo was a Christian of such character, but we need not grovel in such semantics. Steiner says of Philo, who elaborated the doctrine of the Logos, "The platonizing Philo addresses this *logos* as Christ" (CMF, Chap. 4, p. 68;

cf. PHILO, p. 142, "The Posterity and Exile of Cain" [#101]), and he quotes a passage from Philo that speaks of "the word" as "the way to Him," "the Royal Road" (cf. Jn 14,6). In truth, Philo would himself seem to have been a part of that birthing process.

Steiner apparently makes no assertions about Peter's presence in Rome, but does confirm that Mark was his pupil and received from him the same impulse (this refers to the source of facts rather than merely to the facts themselves) of clairvoyant knowledge of the events in Jerusalem and of the Mystery of Golgotha that Peter had; thus Mark was able to generate what became his Gospel from his own authentic, clairvoyantly received spiritual knowledge (*The Gospel of St. Mark* [GSMk], Lect. 10). In the same lecture, Steiner further tells us:

> It was possible for [Mark] to be stimulated to give his description of the cosmic greatness of Christ precisely because of the place to which he had moved after he had been Peter's pupil. He moved to Alexandria in Egypt and lived there at a period when in a certain way Jewish-philosophical-theosophical learning in Alexandria had reached a certain culmination. He could take up in Alexandria what at that time were the best aspects of pagan gnosis.[13]

Certainly the spirit of Philo had to be the overriding influence in Alexandria at that time, the same spirit that had raised the concept of the Logos to the height from which Lazarus/John took it up in the Prologue of his Gospel. That Alexandria is the possible site of origin of Mark's Gospel is widely recognized (4 ABD 543). Barclay says, "Tradition has it that he went down to Egypt and founded the Church of Alexandria there" (Barc, *The Gospel of Mark*, p. 3).

It is at this point that we begin to encroach upon a most enthralling insight, revealed by the discovery during the last half century of a letter

---

12. A view previously expressed by Justin Martyr with respect to Socrates, Heraclitus and others of their kind. See 1st Apology of Justin, Chap. 46, 1 Nicene-1, p. 178; in accord, *The Four Sacrifices of Christ* (FSC), p. 12.

13. See Welburn, *The Beginnings of Christianity* (BC), Chapters 5-7, showing that Steiner spoke of the Synoptic Gospels as being representative of these existing influences:

Matthew	=	Semitic (particularly Essenic)
Mark	=	Gnostic
Luke	=	Hellenistic

from Clement of Alexandria to one Theodore in which is quoted a passage from what is now known as "The Secret Gospel According to Mark"; see 4 ABD 558, "Mark, Secret Gospel of," and fn 6 in "Peter, James and John". Welburn in the ninth and last chapter of his *Gnosos* (GNOS), shows how the passage fits precisely with Steiner's revelations to humanity early in the century. Quoted by Welburn, it reads as follows:

> They arrived at Bethany. And a certain woman, whose brother had died, was there. And coming before Jesus she prostrated herself and said to Him, "Son of David, have mercy on me."
>
> The disciples rebuked her. But Jesus was angry, and went with her into the garden, where the tomb was. And straightaway a great cry was heard from the tomb. Jesus went and rolled the stone away from the door of the tomb. And straightaway he entered, and there was the youth. He stretched forth his hand and raised him, grasping his hand. And the youth looked at him, and loved him. And he began to entreat him, that he might be with him.
>
> And going out of the tomb, they came to the house which belonged to the youth—for he was rich. And after six days, Jesus told him what to do, and in the evening the youth came to him, wearing nothing but a linen cloth. And he remained with him that night. For Jesus taught him the mystery of the Kingdom of God.
>
> And thence arising, he returned to the other side of the Jordan.

Clement of Alexandria's letter further says to Theodore that this is a "secret Gospel," and when asked about it, "one should not concede that the secret Gospel is by Mark, but should even deny it on oath. For 'Not all true things are to be said to all men'." Such attitude is typical of Clement. Clement identifies the portion quoted above as being from the original version of Mark, but it is not in the one we have. Clement himself, in the letter, states that the quoted passage fits within Mark 10 between the present vss 34 and 35 (4 ABD 558 and Welburn are both in accord).

Welburn shows that the youth was Lazarus (as many others now recognize; 4 ABD 558), and his conclusions seem to be confirmed by other observations. Note the discussion in "Three Days' Journey" of the raising of Lazarus and the meaning of the fact that Jesus is said to have "loved" him. Note then that the only other place in any of the Gospels where this statement is made with reference to Jesus' dealings with another individual (except for Lazarus' sisters, Mary and Martha, in Jn 11,5) is in Mk 10,21, where the rich "Young Man" is being told by Jesus what he lacks. Other evidence suggests that Lazarus was indeed wealthy; see Emmerich, *The Life of Jesus Christ and Biblical Revelations* (LJC), Vol. 1, p. 334. What is fascinating here is the writing by Clement of Alexandria entitled "Who is the Rich Man That Shall Be Saved?" It is quite verbose, but makes the point that one does not need to abandon all one's property so long as one abandons it as of importance within the soul, which Lazarus apparently did. There is a lengthy concluding anecdote in which the aged Evangelist John seeks to redeem a youth; one can see in it a portrayal of just such a situation as he himself, as Lazarus, must have gone through spiritually in his own youth. See 2 Nicene-1, pp. 594 and 603-4.

It is sobering to reflect that the Lazarus/John account is one of those few highly significant things reflected in all four Gospels. While neither Matthew (Mt 19,16-30) nor Luke (Lk 18,18-27) use the word "loved," they give an account of the same event. The character of the Essenes is described by Philo (see PHILO, "Every Good Man is Free," XII and XIII at pp. 689-690, and "Hypothetica," 11.1-11.18, pp. 745-746) in a manner that suggests, considering that Matthew's Gospel arose out of Essene wisdom as Steiner tells us, that Philo and Matthew were both admirers of this unique Jewish sect (see also Welburn, *The Book with Fourteen Seals* [BFS]).

It is this Lazarus/John, thus identified by Mark writing in Alexandria, who opens his own Gospel with the doctrine of the Logos (Jn 1,1,14) so preeminently expounded by Philo. For this alone the influence of Philo upon Lazarus/John is convincingly demonstrated. There is, however, a more precise esoteric bit of evidence in the latter's use of "the great city which is *allegorically* called Sodom and Egypt, where their Lord was crucified" (Rev 11,8; my emphasis). He is there speaking of the "two witnesses" (Rev 11,3), who are Moses and Elijah (Rev 11,5-6). To what does John refer but to the writings of that most renowned allegorizer of Mosaic law, Philo? For Philo specifically gives us the allegorical meanings for both Egypt (PHILO, pp. 267-8 and 847) and Sodom (pp. 226, 313 and 423), each of which relate to the outward body, senses and passions as against things of the soul.

From that we move to a topic appropriate as we near the end of the "terms and phrases" portion of this "Burning Bush" volume. What did Philo have to say about the burning "Bush?" He refers to it (PHILO,

p. 465) as "a bush or briar, a very thorny plant, and very weak and supple... entirely enveloped... by the abundant flame,... it nevertheless
remained whole without being consumed, like some impassible essence,
and not as if it were itself the natural fuel for fire, but rather as if it were
taking the fire for its own fuel." And while he at this point then says it
was a "symbol of the oppressed people, and the burning fire was a symbol of the oppressors; and the circumstance of the burning bush not
being consumed was an emblem of the fact that the people thus
oppressed would not be destroyed" by their oppressors, he elsewhere
raises the symbolism to a level applicable to the human soul or Ego.
"Moses was urged on... to investigate the causes through which the
most necessary of things in the world are brought to perfection; for seeing how many things come to an end, and are produced afresh in creation, being again destroyed, and again abiding, he marvelled, and was
amazed, and cried out, saying, 'The bush burns, and is not consumed'"
(p. 335). This rings of the same recurring nature (i.e., reincarnating) of
the process of "Perfect(ion)" of the "I Am" which is demonstrated in
the renewal of the "Grass," as in Ps 90,5-6, Is 51,12 and Mt 6,30 (with
Mt 5,48).

If we are to bring the Egyptian Philo out of the Egypt of the fourth
Cultural Era, the Greco-Roman, so that we may in our own fifth Cultural
Era retrace the emphasis of the third Cultural Era, the Egyptian, raising
ourselves above the things of the world of phenomena, "flesh," into those
of the spirit, we must see how indeed, as Philo indicated, the higher
meanings of scripture are those expressed by it allegorically. For even
Philo, recognizing this, did not have available in his Era, the spiritual
insights that dawned upon humanity when the high being who incarnated as Rudolf Steiner[14] was able to reveal the basis, which he called
"Anthroposophy," for understanding the allegorically expressed higher
meaning.

---

14. See "Pillars on the Journey."

PILLARS ON THE JOURNEY

THE OPENING CURTAIN was drawn on this volume with the startling announcement that its theme, the parable of the Prodigal Son, was the story of the macrocosmic journey of the human being. Now, at the curtain call, let us look back at those human Individualities who have emerged as Pillars on the Way; pillars, if you will, of "Fire" in the "Darkness" (Ex 13,21).

The Bible must be seen as a log of that journey (the parables in Lk 15,11-32; 11,5-8 and Mt 25,14-30 all use the "journey" metaphor in speaking of it). Rudolf Steiner has given us clear indications of certain threads of human-spiritual impulse—series of incarnations of Individualities—who have played an enormous role in the human voyage depicted in the Bible account. For those who by now have begun to sense an immense dependability in them, Steiner's revelations will not be hard to accept, and they can yield riches in the search for truth and meaning in the labyrinthine fabric of the Holy Scriptures. For others, they should be held in mind as postulates--left to ripen or not as they will during further study and contemplation.

For decades now surveys have shown the willingness on the part of a substantial percentage of professing Christians either to believe in reincarnation or to consider it with an open mind. But where have the courageous, informed voices from the pulpit been? Have these thoughtful people among the congregations not been "wander[ing] like sheep ... afflicted for want of a shepherd" (Zech 10,2; Mt 9,36; Mk 6,34)?

Between the curtains of this volume an abundance of scriptural evidence is given supporting the view that karma and reincarnation are spiritual realities. Passages have been shown to have deep meaning where before there was none. The Bible itself is seen to be an integrated account of the human journey applicable to every single individual all the way through. Many will by now have come to the realization that the Biblical vessel cannot really be embarked for the future evolutionary voyage of the human being without coming to see that karma and reincarnation have been securely loaded deep within its hold.

Steiner gave a lecture on March 6, 1910, with the title "The Reappearance of Christ in the Etheric." It is included as one of thirteen lectures now assembled under the same title (RCE). In fn 78, Chap. 4, of *Rudolf Steiner and the Founding of the New Mysteries* (RSFNM),[1] Prokofieff beautifully paraphrases a cardinal aspect of that lecture, Steiner's pronouncement of

> the great cosmic law according to which each individual who accomplishes something in the service of the Guiding Powers of the world must, after a certain time, perform a similar deed in consequence of it, but in such a way now that it appears like the opposite pole of the first.

In explaining how "Rudolf Steiner [threw] light on … the working of this great cosmic law in the mission of Abraham," Prokofieff quotes (emphasis mine; brackets are Prokofieff's):

> In the same way that in the past epoch up to our time [the second millennium after Christ] the spirit of Moses held sway, so now [the 3rd millennium after Christ] the spirit of Abraham is beginning to reign, in order that having led humanity in past times [3rd millennium BC] into a consciousness of God within the physical world, he may now lead humanity out of it again. *For it is an eternal ancient law of the cosmos that every individual who performs a particular deed must carry it out more than once: that is, at least in two periods, the second deed appearing as the opposite of the first.* What Abraham brought down to humanity, into its physical consciousness, he will carry up again into the spiritual world.

Earlier, in fn 67 of the same chapter, Prokofieff gives an excellent review of the places in Plato's works that show his teachings on reincarnation (noting that they lack, however, the clear conception of the individual "I Am"). Then Prokofieff shows how Aristotle had "a real interest in the physical world," becoming "not only the father of earthly thinking

---

1. First published (in German) by the remarkable Prokofieff when he was only twenty-seven years old.

(logic) but in a certain sense ... also the founder of the physical sciences" and in that respect "the true forerunner and herald of the coming Christianity." Steiner often pointed out that the Greeks, particularly the Plato-Aristotle-Alexander group, had prepared the way for the spread of Christianity, for it was in that world that the great apostle, Paul, was able to work, and it is in that language that our New Testament was given.

Prokofieff continues (in fn 67), "However, in order that such a relationship [the kindling by the descended Christ of the eternal, immortal "I" in every human being] with the Earth could arise, it was essential to prepare for it before the onset of the Christian era. And this was possible only through a rejection of the teaching of reincarnation in its old form with its inevitable disregard for all earthly things," and he continues this sentence by quoting from Steiner's *How Can Mankind Find the Christ Again* (HCMF), Lect. 8:

> ... [for] it is indeed the case that it was necessary for the development of humanity that for a time consciousness of repeated lives on Earth should withdraw, so that the human being could become accustomed to taking seriously and intensely just one life on Earth.

While Steiner never identified himself directly as either Abraham or Aristotle, anthroposophists clearly believe him to have been, and it would fit with this great cosmic law that he was.

It takes only a moment's reflection to realize that this "great cosmic law" has to be, for it merely states the basic law of karma. Abraham and Aristotle both lived before Christ walked the Earth. Their objective karma was inscribed in the "book" ("Akashic") before Christ came to forgive sins. Being the exalted Individualities they were, had their roles (sins or objective karma in this context) in leading humanity's descent even been forgiven by Christ in their later incarnations, still they would nobly have desired to make restitution to all humanity by correcting or transfiguring what they had first planted.

They would not have been alone in this phenomenon. Within the Bible story there are doubtless many others whom we are not yet able to identify. However, between the curtains of this book we have identified five whom we are here calling "Pillars." In regard to these five we find that: 1. a major part of the Bible story is about them; 2. a major part of the Bible was given to us directly or indirectly by them; and 3. a major part of the future of Christianity will rest upon their shoulders.[2] In these five, we are dealing only with human beings. The Christ is central. These five are merely his "servants" (cf. Is 42,1). In the listing that follows, some personalities are given in parentheses with question marks. The evidence in these instances is perhaps less complete than in the others, mainly in that we have no clear, direct statement from Steiner (insofar as I am aware) to support them. Nevertheless, they seem plausible in the light of Steiner's teachings. They are listed in chronological order based upon the initial personality given in the chain (whether in parenthesis or not).

1. Adam Cadmon
        Phinehas
            Elijah
                John the Baptist
                    Raphael
                        Novalis

2. (Cain?)
      (Tubal-cain?)
          (Joshua?)
              Hiram Abiff
                  Lazarus/John
                      Christian Rosenkreutz
                          Count St. Germain

3. Zarathustra
      Zarathas (or Zoroaster)[3]
          Jesus of Nazareth (until his Baptism by John, when this
          Individuality withdrew to permit entry of the Christ Spirit
          and thus the being we call Jesus Christ)

---

2. A good illustration of just how this may be expected is given by Prokofieff in the latter portions of *Eternal Individuality* (EI), which has to do with the first of the five listed Individualities.

3. According to Steiner, many incarnations of this Individuality occurred between the one as Zarathustra, in ancient (prehistoric) Persia, and the birth of the Solomon Jesus child. Welburn gives an excellent exploration of these in *The Book with Fourteen Seals* (BFS). We list here only the intervening incarnation of Zarathas who, according to Steiner, was a teacher of some of the "middle period prophets" in Babylonia. The name Zarathas is also variously spelled Zaratas or Zaratos, and he is often called Nazarathos.

4. Eabani[4]
   (Abraham?)
         Cratylus
            Aristotle
               Schionatulander
                  Thomas Aquinas
                     Rudolf Steiner
5. (Moses?)
      Paul[5]

---

4. The most complete account of this chain is given in *Rudolf Steiner's Mission and Ita Wegman* (RSMW), a privately printed book which, unfortunately, is presently available only to members of the Anthroposophical Society. The historic personalities known as Eabani, Cratylus and Schionatulander are less well known than the others, but at least a modicum of information is available. And in each instance it seems to fit with the evolutionary thread that manifested again in Steiner.

Eabani is another name for Enkidu in the Gilgamish epic (see 5 Brit 266). (As explained earlier in this volume, Steiner showed that the "flood" in that account had to do with a condition of the human mind and soul and was erroneously associated with the much earlier flood that finally inundated Atlantis and is described in the Biblical account of Noah.) The Gilgamish epic portrays Enkidu as a godly sort of creature, and RSMW sees in that account an indication that Enkidu was an Individuality much like the Nathan Jesus child, which did not go through the Fall. Steiner speaks at some length of Eabani (Enkidu) in *World History in the Light of Anthroposophy* (WH), Lects. 3 and 4 and *Occult History* (OH), Lect. 3. See also Sucher, *Cosmic Christianity* (COSC), Chap. 2, pp. 42-44, and cf. *The Occult Significance of the Bhagavad Gita* (BG), Lects. 6, p. 89, and 9, p. 137. It is obvious from Lect. 3 in *World History* that Eabani brought from the cosmos knowledge far exceeding that cognizable by a normal human being. The Bible student must be fascinated by the similarity between Enkidu and Engedi, an oasis and prehistoric temple site on the western side of the Dead Sea. It is mentioned some six times in the Bible: Josh 15,62; 1 Sam 23,29; 24,1; 2 Ch 20,2; Song 1,14 and Ezek 47,10.

RSMW indicates that Cratylus was an Athenian student of Heraclitus in Ephesus and was also one of Plato's teachers. If one looks at what history says about Cratylus and then at what Steiner says about the origin of language and the alphabet (see *Alphabet* [ALPH]), particularly about the significance of a "Name," one cannot help but be struck by the similarity. See Plato's *Cratylus*, 7 GB 85; 22 Brit 567, "Language"; 25 Brit 895, "Platonism" and 27 Brit 22, "Scholarship." Relevant scriptures are Gen 2,19 and 11,1-9. The significance of a "Name" surfaced in the Realism versus Nominalism philosophical schools, and the relationship of the position of Cratylus to that of Aristotle and Aquinas in support of the "realistic" nature of a "Name" is notable.

Schionatulander seems to be the most obscure of the listed personalities from a historical perspective. According to RSMW he was connected with the Grail wisdom and played a role in the Parsifal legend.

5. Steiner never to my knowledge specifically identified these two as one Individuality, but an eminent anthroposophist shared with me that he had come to such conclusion. Quite aside from an artifact he had observed (a piece of ancient, indicative statuary in southern France), one should also reflect upon the "great cosmic law," discussed earlier in this essay. In its light, Paul in his many exhortations that one is not saved by "works of law," transforms and redirects the impulse of Moses as the great law giver.

CHARTS AND TABULATIONS

PREFACE

THIS IS A "STUDY-HELPS" SECTION, intended to serve initially as a tool in the assimilation process, and thereafter as a refresher, thought-organizer, research or meditational aid. It may even help the advanced student of anthroposophy to gain some insight into the content of Rudolf Steiner's books or lecture cycles not yet studied.

It is in this latter way that I have been greatly helped by my effort to assemble this section, for I had been able to study only a fraction of Steiner's works before beginning to write this work in 1994. This is an inherent problem for anthroposophists, simply from the dimensions of Steiner's legacy. In his lectures, perhaps even more than in his writings, Steiner often dashed off graphic illustrations of what was being presented. To do any justice whatsoever to the title of this section, I deemed it necessary to go through every Steiner title in my library (then consisting of only about three hundred of the more significant titles), whether or not previously studied, merely to accumulate the large pool from which the selections herein were taken. Each illustration not previously encountered required some study of its context, so that the whole process became a primary bridge between the books previously considered and those not yet studied. In general, few of the innumerable pictorial sketches of an impressionistic sort are included. The process of selection itself required a certain editorial discipline, for every instance had purpose and meaning.

Each illustration below is identified to its source, and any related comment is only such as is necessary or appropriate to indicate a possible direction of thinking (though in some cases considerable commentary is given). The reader will always, of course, be richly rewarded in studying the original material.

I tried to put the most important charts at the first, while at the same time trying to order them in something of a logical progression. After the first several charts, it became quite difficult to adjudge relative importance; for after all, who is to determine that? And because all these matters are so inter-related, it also became more and more difficult to group them together logically. Consequently, as the sequence progresses, there may be less significance to the order.

Since this work is intended to be primarily an exploration of the Bible in the light of what is now available in English through anthroposophy, it would be a shame to foreclose full investigation by becoming bogged down too early in the game with what is indeed a complex body of knowledge. A widely loved law professor once told us students that the practice of law is a marathon—"don't burn yourselves out!" Later, as a marathoner, I learned how important it is to pace myself by my own being and capacity. While this entire work cannot begin to express all that Steiner's teachings encompassed, still this Charts and Tabulations section covers an immense amount of anthroposophy, more than can possibly be addressed in the later portions. To expect to read it through quickly and comprehendingly is to expect too much.

Source identification will be according to the abbreviations listed for all references in the "Abbreviations and Bibliography" section.

TITLES

(The prefixed "I-" is omitted from this enumeration)

1. Schematic of human being's creation, descent and reascent per ASJ
2. Schematic of human being's creation, descent and reascent per TL
3. Schematic of human being's creation, descent and reascent per FE
4. Verbal description of human being's creation, descent and reascent expanded for seven Conditions of Life
5. Geologic Time Chart
6. The nine Hierarchies
7. Interrelationships of the nine Hierarchies
8. Days of the week; their "planetary" relationships
9. The essential nature of the human being
10. The relationship of the Ego to oblivion, sleep and death; and the human being's common relationships with the lower kingdoms
11. The loci of the four components of the four kingdoms
12. The elemental beings (elemental spirits)
13. Distinctions between the mineral and physical depending on where the physical human being can be perceived
14. The four systems of the human being's physical body as expressions and descendants of Conditions of Consciousness

39. Genealogies from David to Jesus
40. The relationships between thinking, feeling and willing and birth, death and rebirth
41. Thinking, feeling and willing: the nature of their manifestation, karma and forces
42. Wisdom, Beauty and Strength—meaning
43. Atlantean and Aryan "sub-races"
44. The Conditions of Consciousness planetary evolutions
45. Christian esoteric terminology for the Conditions of Consciousness, Life and Form
46. East/West esoteric terminology for the long (e.g., 5,000 year) ages of the human being's evolution
47. The 3-fold "Logos"; The loci of consciousness of the 4 kingdoms and of elemental beings
48. Root races and their terminal causes
49. Concepts of labor in the fourth through the sixth Cultural Eras
50. Three important human stages (upright stance, speech and thought)— their nature and respective effects upon karma
51. Spiritual beings, numerous aspects of
52. The relationship of thinking, feeling and willing to various time cycles
53. Virtue development related to Conditions of Consciousness
54. Spiritual warmth/fire
55. The four temperaments and their predominant components
56. How Hierarchies work through the human being during its life on Earth and then with its Ego between lives
57. Tomberg's portrayal of Israel's three "patriarchs"
58. The human components and characteristics of four ancient myths; the elevation of human perception; the relative strength of the three human bodies and Ego
59. Ancient terminology for the 3-fold human being
60. The human being's 3-fold nature as reflected in Christianity's form
61. The human race becoming younger
62. Four kinds of pre-Christian initiates; the four Gospels and ancient symbols
63. The Cultural Eras and their prevalent myths
64. Steiner's "Turning Points" compared with Schuré's "Great Initiates"
65. Correlation of Christianity's development by century with the ages and stages of the individual human being

66. Tomberg's portrayal of the human being's encounters with the Cosmic Evil Trinity and the Cosmic Good Trinity

67. Cosmological systems relating to the different levels of consciousness (per Powell)

68. Analogy of sequential development of Old Testament peoples to the human being; the zodiacal influence reflected throughout

69. Parallel between the human being's life cycle and that of Christ's journey into and out of the mineral-physical Earth

70. Thinking-feeling-willing tabulated with other relationships

71. Portrayal of the human being's spiritual guidance during the 7 Cultural Eras

72. Reflections by the John Gospel's Prologue of the 4-fold human being and the 4 Conditions of Consciousness

73. The 4 apocalyptic animals and their most developed aspects

74. Personalities who have reflected the etheric and astral bodies of Jesus of Nazareth

75. Domains of the Hierarchies

76. The four sacrifices by Christ as reflected in the human being and the Gospels

77. The cosmic harmony reflected in the human being's 4-fold nature and in human language

78. Relationships between the human being and the plant; the different food substances and their work on the human physical body

79. Art forms and their relationships to the 7-fold human being; the human being's comprehension of musical relationships

80. The components of the human being taken into account by psychology and science, and how other components are effective agents beyond the realm of comprehension by psychology and science

81. The "Seed," the vortex, the zodiacal sign of Cancer, and the "golden mean"

82. Karmic characterizations of the human being's 4-fold being

83. Steiner, expanding on Goethe, on color

84. The 3-fold human being as related to the various types of animals

85. The nature of human perception of the Sun, and its Mysteries, in the three pre-Christian Cultural Eras

86. The reflection of the planets in the human being's physical organs

87. The "Star of David," or "Mogen (Magen) David"

88. The "Threefold Social Order"

89. The loci where the human initiate meets the Egos of the three lower kingdoms

CHARTS AND TABULATIONS

I-1 <u>Schematic of human being's creation, descent and reascent per ASJ</u>

ASJ, fold-out following terminal notes (page 228)

This chart is given primacy. Conceptualizing the creative process is probably the first, most difficult, yet most important, step in anthroposophy. It is not unlike contemplating a chart of the universe. One stretches the mind to comprehend it, yet the moment thinking is relaxed the mind reverts back toward its prior dimension. Constant stretching is required. One should not hesitate to return to this chart again and again.

Because it is so critical, different profiles of the same concept are also available in **I-2**, **I-3** and **I-4**.

The Bible, from beginning to end, is an account of the descent of the human being from the spiritual world and its return thereto, encompassing the entire evolutionary process. It assumes added resplendence when seen in the light of anthroposophy. And humanity itself is then seen as the paradigm of the Prodigal Son. Anthroposophy is nothing but that "knowledge of truth" (Jn 8,32) which is vital if the human being is to "come to himself" (Lk 15,17). These three charts portray that same path, which Rudolf Steiner has lighted for the first time since the age of the human being's intellectual maturity.

(While more fully treated later, it may be helpful here to refer to the "twenty-four elders" frequently mentioned in Revelation [e.g., Rev 4,4,10, Rev 5,8, Rev 11,16, Rev 19,4 et al.]. These are identified by Steiner [ASJ Lect. 5] as twenty-four members of the spiritual Hierarchies who attained their respective "human" [i.e., consciousness] states in the twenty-four successive Conditions of Life that have preceded our present one, i.e., seven each on Old Saturn, Old Sun and Old Moon plus the first three Elementary Kingdoms of the Earth Condition of Consciousness. All these elders come from the Hierarchies [see **I-6**], but in considering this, one must realize that there are seven levels within each rank of each Hierarchy, thus seven "elders" would come from a single rank in the list of nine Hierarchies. More is said about the "twenty-four elders" in **I-12** and **I-15**.)

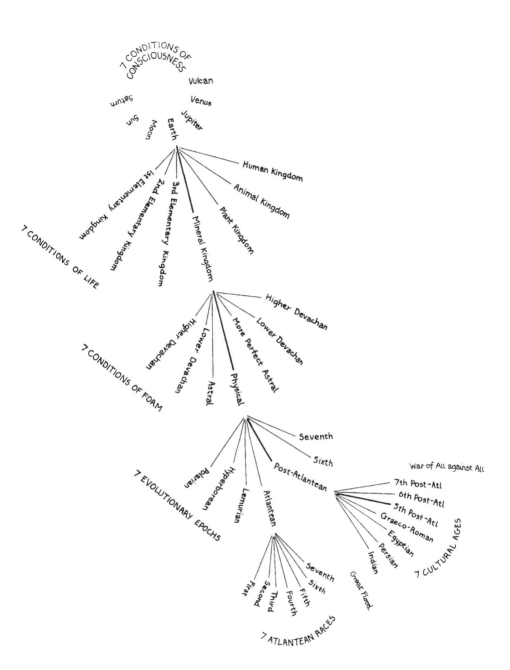

I-2 <u>Schematic of human being's creation, descent and reascent per TL</u>

TL, between Notes 3 and 4 of Lecture 11 (page 385)

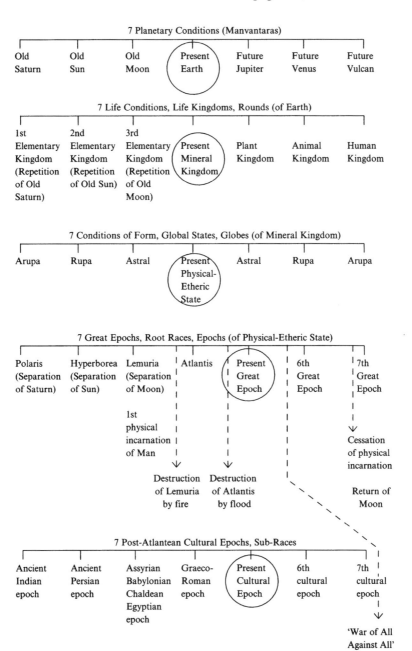

I-3 Schematic of human being's creation, descent and reascent per FE

FE, concluding the "Schematic Survey of the Stages of World-Evolution" found after Lect. 31 (pp. 270-271, but all of the Survey is helpful)

FURTHER DIAGRAM OF EVOLUTION

Planetary Evolutions

| Old Saturn | Old Sun | Old Moon | Earth | Future Jupiter | Future Venus | Vulcan |

Example of: 1 Round of 7 Globes
(or Conditions of Form)
The Descent to Physical Manifestation

Anthroposophical Terms

Arupa Plane	Archetypal	Upper Devachan	Higher Spiritual World
Rupa Plane	Intellectual	Lower Devachan	Lower Spiritual World
Astral Plane	Plastic Astral		Astral World
Physical Plane			Physical World

Old Saturn 7 Rounds of 7 Globes		Old Sun	Old Moon
	Arupa \ Devechan	7 Rounds of 7 Globes	7 Rounds of 7 Globes
	Rupa /		
	Astral		
	Physical		
	Plastic Astral \	As Under Old Saturn	As under Old Saturn
	Intellectual Devechan		
	Archetypal /		

EARTH (FOURTH PLANETARY EVOLUTION)

Short Pralaya	Short Pralaya	Short Pralaya		Short Pralaya		Short Pralaya	Short Pralaya
Recapitulation of old Saturn	Recapitulation of Old Sun	Recapitulation of Old Moon	Fourth Round			Fifth Round	Sixth Round	Seventh Round

Polarian
Hyperborean
The Present
Lemurian
Atlantean (7 Sub-Races
1st Post Atlantean (7 Cultural Epochs)
2nd Post Atlantean
3rd Post Atlantean

| Pralaya | FUTURE JUPITER | Pralaya | FUTURE VENUS | Pralaya | VULCAN | Long Pralaya |

| Fifth Planetary Evolution | Sixth Planetary Evolution | Seventh Planetary Evolution |

The Final 666 occurs in the Sixth Globe of the Sixth Round

I-4 <u>Verbal description of human being's creation, descent and reascent</u> <u>expanded for seven Conditions of Life</u>

Derived from foregoing three items

<u>7 (Planetary) Conditions of Consciousness (Manvantaras)</u>
(Old) Saturn, Sun, Moon, (Present) Earth, (Future) Jupiter, Venus, Vulcan
<u>7 Conditions of Life (Kingdoms or Rounds)</u>
(Old) 1st Elementary Kingdom, 2nd Elementary Kingdom, 3rd Elementary Kingdom, (Present) Mineral Kingdom, (Future) Plant Kingdom, Animal Kingdom, Human Kingdom
<u>7 Conditions of Form (Globes)</u>
(Old) Arupa, Rupa, Astral, (Present) Physical-Etheric, (Future) Astral, Rupa, Arupa
(*Arupa = Higher Devachan; Rupa = Devachan.*
Deva means spirit; Devachan = Spiritland.)
<u>7 Great Epochs (Root Races)</u>
(Old) Polaris, Hyperborea, Lemuria, Atlantis, (Present) 5th Great Epoch, (Future) 6th Great Epoch, 7th Great Epoch
<u>7 Cultural Ages (Eras or Sub-Races)</u>
(Ancient) Indian, Persian, Egyptian, Graeco-Roman, (Present) 5th Cultural Era a/k/a Germanic, (Future) 6th Cultural Era a/k/a Slavic, 7th Cultural Era a/k/a American

Charts **I-1**, **I-2** and **I-4**, in describing Conditions of Life (Kingdoms or Rounds), use the term "Elementary Kingdom." In THSY Chap. 5, Steiner gives the following explanation of humanity's 7 Life Conditions:

(1) Archetypal formless beings—*1st elementary kingdom*;
(2) Shape-creating beings—*2nd elementary kingdom*;
(3) Soul beings—*3rd elementary kingdom*;
(4) Created shapes (crystal forms)—*mineral kingdom*;
(5) Forms sensibly perceptible in which shape-creating beings are active—*plant kingdom*;
(6) Forms sensibly perceptible in which shape-creating and soul beings are active—*animal kingdom*;
(7) Forms sensibly perceptible in which shape-creating and soul beings are active, and in which spirit fashions itself in form of thought within the sense world—*human kingdom*.

I-5 Geologic time chart   WNWD 585

MAIN DIVISIONS OF GEOLOGIC TIME			PRINCIPAL PHYSICAL AND BIOLOGICAL FEATURES
ERAS	**PERIODS or SYSTEMS**	**Epochs or Series**	
CENOZOIC	Quarternary	Recent 12,000*	Glaciers restricted to Antarctica and Greenland; extinction of giant mammals; development and spread of modern human culture.
CENOZOIC	Quarternary	Pleistocene 600,000	Great glaciers covered much of N America & NW Europe; volcanoes along W coast of U.S.; many giant mammals; appearance of modern humans late in Pleistocene.
CENOZOIC	Tertiary	Pliocene 10,000,000	W North America uplifted; much modernization of mammals; first possible apelike humans appeared in Africa.
CENOZOIC	Tertiary	Miocene 25,000,000	Renewed uplift of Rockies & other mountains;** great lava flows in W U.S.; mammals began to acquire modern characters; dogs, modern type horses, manlike apes appeared.
CENOZOIC	Tertiary	Oligocene 35,000,000	Many older types of mammals became extinct; mastodons, first monkeys, and apes appeared.
CENOZOIC	Tertiary	Eocene 55,000,000	Mountains raised in Rockies, Andes, Alps, & Himalayas; continued expansion of early mammals; primitive horses appeared.
CENOZOIC	Tertiary	Paleocene 65,000,000	Great development of primitive mammals.
MESOZOIC	Cretaceous 135,000,000		Rocky Mountains began to rise; most plants, invertebrate animals, fishes, and birds of modern types; dinosaurs reached maximum development & then became extinct; mammals small & very primitive.
MESOZOIC	Jurassic 180,000,000		Sierra Nevada Mountains uplifted; conifers & cycads dominant among plants; primitive birds appeared.
MESOZOIC	Triassic 230,000,000		Lava flows in E North America; ferns & cycads dominant among plants; modern corals appeared & some insects of modern types; great expansion of reptiles including earliest dinosaurs.
PALEOZOIC	Permian 280,000,000		Final folding of Appalachians & central European ranges; great glaciers in S Hemisphere & reefs in warm northern seas; trees of coal forests declined; ferns abundant; conifers present; first cycads & ammonites appeared; trilobites became extinct; reptiles surpassed amphibians.
PALEOZOIC	CARBONIFEROUS	Pennsylvanian 310,000,000	Mountains grew along E Coast of North America & in central Europe; great coal swamp forests flourished in N Hemisphere; seed-bearing ferns abundant; cockroaches & first reptiles appeared.
PALEOZOIC	CARBONIFEROUS	Mississippian 345,000,000	Land plants became diversified, including many ancient kinds of trees; crinoids achieved greatest development; sharks of relatively modern types appeared; land animals little known.
PALEOZOIC	Devonian 405,000,000		Mountains raised in New England; land plants evolved rapidly; large trees appeared; brachiopods reached maximum development; many kinds of primitive fishes; first sharks, insects, & amphibians appeared.
PALEOZOIC	Silurian 425,000,000		Great mountains formed in NW Europe; first small land plants appeared; corals built reefs in far northern seas; shelled cephalopods abundant; trilobites began decline; first jawed fish appeared.
PALEOZOIC	Ordovician 500,000,000		Mountains elevated in New England; volcanoes along Atlantic Coast; much limestone deposited in shallow seas; great expansion among marine invertebrate animals; all major groups present; first primitive jawless fish appeared.
PALEOZOIC	Cambrian 6000,000,000		Shallow seas covered parts of continents; first abundant record of marine life, esp. trilobites & brachiopods; other fossils rare.
PRE-CAMBRIAN	Late Precambrian (Algonkian)*** 2,000,000,000		Metamorphosed sedimentary rocks, lava flows, granite; history complex & obscure; first evidence of life; calcareous algae & invertebrates.
PRE-CAMBRIAN	Early Precambrian (Archean)*** 4,500,000,000		Crust formed on molten earth; crystalline rocks much disturbed; history unknown.

* Figures indicate approx. number of years since beginning of each division. ** Mountain uplifts generally began near the end of a division. *** Regarded as separate eras.

I-6 The nine Hierarchies

OS, Chap. 4 (pp. 122-128); CM, Essay xiv, "The Life of Saturn"; SH, Lect. 5; SB, Intro. by Querido (p. 17); UEM, Lect. Aug 7, 1908 (p. 63)

The spiritual Hierarchies, of which there are nine between the Trinity (Father-Son-Holy Spirit) and the human being, are as follows:

Name Given by Steiner	Christian Esotericism	Biblical Greek (Heb)
1. Spirits of Love	Seraphim	Seraphime
2. Spirits of Harmony	Cherubim	Cherubime
3. Spirits of Will	Thrones	Thronos
4. Spirits of Wisdom	Dominions	Kyriotetes
5. Spirits of Motion	Mights	Dynamis
6. Spirits of Form	Powers (Authorities)	Exusiai (Elohim)
7. Spirits of Personality	Principalities (Primal Beginnings)	Archai
8. Spirits of Fire (Folk)	Archangels	Archangeloi
9. Sons of Life (or of Twilight)	Angels (Messengers)	Angeloi

It is noted that in the most basic work, OS, Steiner identifies his Spirits of Motion to the Christian esoteric term "Powers," and equates his Spirits of Form to "Authorities." However, in all the other works of his identified above, he conforms to the above listing in this regard.

An excellent article by Jennifer Mellett, entitled "The Spiritual Hierarchies as Depicted in the Florence Baptistry Dome and by Dante," appeared in the informal publication entitled "Anthroposophy in Texas" in recent years, though I do not have the date of the issue. It has a most helpful tabulation entitled, "Different Systems of Ordering the Angelic Hierarchies," which shows the terms used by Dionysius the Areopagite, Dante in *Paradiso* and in *Il Convivio*, Steiner, Brunetto Latini (Dante's teacher) and Gregory the Great in *Moralia* and in *Homilies*. The terminology is generally in line with that above, though with some variations. Others who wrote on these Hierarchies, according to Querido's Introduction to SB, include John of Salisbury, Bishop of Chartres, Thomas

Aquinas, and Albertus Magnus. As Querido points out, by the sixteenth century, humanity (i.e., materialistic Christianity) had lost this spiritual view of the universe.

I-7 <u>Interrelationships of the nine Hierarchies</u>

ASOT, Chap. 2 (pp. 16-17; it would have been helpful had the controversial Tomberg identified Steiner sources for these)

Each of the Primal Beings (Father, Son and Holy Spirit) is active in each of the three Hierarchies, but one Hierarchy is its chief domain, and one rank in each Hierarchy is its chief agency therein, as follows:

	<u>Father</u>	<u>Son</u>	<u>Spirit</u>
<u>1st Hierarchy</u>	**X**		
Seraphim		x	
Cherubim			x
Thrones	x		
<u>2d Hierarchy</u>		**X**	
Dominions	x		
Dynamis			x
Exusiai		x	
<u>3d Hierarchy</u>			**X**
Archai	x		
Archangels		x	
Angels			x

This chart helps to clarify the lines of spiritual agency that run through the Hierarchies down to humanity. For example, the Exusiai belong to the Christ (Son) Hierarchy and are moreover the agency of Christ therein. When Christ is said to speak with "authority" (Mt 7,29; Mk 1,22; Lk 4,32), the Greek term used is *Exusiai*, and this rank is also known as "Authorities." We know, furthermore, from Table **I-6**, that the Hebrew term for a member of this rank is "Elohim." These are the Spirits of Form, of whom Yahweh is one, who are spoken of (in the plural) in the creative (i.e., "formative") work in Genesis (as in Gen 1,1).

I-8 Days of the week; their "planetary" relationships

CD, Enclosure with 41; AGSS, Lect. 9 (p. 86); HI-2, Lect. 8; 12 Brit 555, "week"

The whole progress of the human being's evolution through the seven Conditions of Consciousness was laid down by the ancient initiates in the names of the days of the week, as follows:

Old Saturn	Saturn's Day	Saturday
Old Sun	Sun's Day	Sunday
Old Moon	Moon's Day	Monday
Earth:		
Mars	Mar's Day	Tuesday
Mercury	Mercury's Day	Wednesday
Jupiter	Jupiter's Day	Thursday
Venus	Venus' Day	Friday

Vulcan (not formed because it is a repeat, as the octave is the repeat of the tonic)

The above-cited references explain with consistency the transition to our Anglo-Saxon words for these evolutionary periods and their namesake gods. Mars represents the first half of Earth evolution, up until the time of Christ, and Mercury the last half. Mercury is, as shall be seen, the "morning star" referred to in Rev 2,28, representing the last half of Earth evolution which commenced with the incarnation of Christ.

I-9 The essential nature of the human being

OS, Chap. 2 (The Essential Nature of the Human Being)

The human being may be described as being composed of 3, 4, 7 or 9 divisions, as follows:

3-Fold	4-Fold	7-Fold	9-Fold
	Physical	Physical	Physical
Body	Etheric	Etheric	Etheric
	Astral	Astral	Astral

3-Fold	4-Fold	7-Fold	9-Fold
			Sentient Soul
			Intellectual Soul
Soul		Ego	Consciousness
			(Spiritual Soul)
	Ego		
		Spirit Self	Spirit Self
		(Manas)	(Manas)
Spirit		Life Spirit	Life Spirit
		(Buddhi)	(Buddhi)
		Spirit Man	Spirit Man
		(Atma)	(Atma)

The essential nature of the body and soul components is as follows:

Component of Human Being	Essential Nature of Component
Ego	Lasting or eternal individuality
Astral body	Seat of consciousness, passions & desires
Etheric (Life) body	Seat of life
Physical body	Seat of, or pattern for, mineral accumulation

I-10 <u>The relationship of the Ego to oblivion, sleep and death; and the human being's common relationships with the lower kingdoms</u>

OS, Chap. 2 (p. 30-35); THSY, Chap. 1

Human Being absent Ego	=	Oblivion
Human Being absent Ego and astral body	=	Sleep
Human Being absent Ego, astral & etheric bodies	=	Death

Or

Ether body	=	Life
Astral body	=	Consciousness
Ego	=	Memory*

Thus

The human being has a(n)	In Common With the
Physical body	Mineral
Etheric body	Plant
Astral body	Animal
Ego	—

* What would seem to be memory in an animal is not memory in the sense that the human being has a memory, but is based upon a function of the astral body. The cause for what appears to be memory in an animal always comes from a presently existing circumstance giving rise to need based upon experience. Absent such a circumstance (such as its master's presence, hunger, etc.), the animal cannot call up from within the same conscious feeling as can a human being.

I-11 The loci of the four components of the four kingdoms

SB, Lect. 8 (p. 153); AGSS, Lect. 5 (p. 46)

Each of the four "kingdoms" observable by the human being's physical senses is itself a fourfold being, the difference between them being the locus of their respective "bodies":

	Human being	Animal	Plant	Mineral
Upper Devachan	—	—	—	Ego
Lower Devachan	—	—	Ego	Astral
Astral Plane	—	Ego	Astral	Etheric
Physical Plane	Ego	Astral	Etheric	Physical
	Astral body	Etheric	Physical	
	Etheric body	Physical		
	Physical body			

The same is expressed another way in UEM, Lect. 3, (Aug 6, 1908, pp. 37-43):

	EGO	ASTRAL	ETHERIC	PHYSICAL
Mineral	Where all astral rays unite in highest devachan	Ray-like forms into infinity of cosmos	Surrounds physical	Enclosed
Plant	Group Ego in center Earth— lowest devachan	Surrounds	Enclosed	Enclosed
Animal	Group Ego is in astral world surrounding	Enclosed	Enclosed	Enclosed
Human being	Enclosed	Enclosed	Enclosed	Enclosed

According to Steiner, "For human existence to become possible it was necessary for the Earth, in its mineral nature, to suffer infinite pain—for infinite pain was bound up with this solidification of the Earth's substance. This is why Paul says [Rom 8,22], '... the whole creation groaneth and travaileth in pain ... awaiting the adoption ....'"

I-12 The elemental beings (elemental spirits)

ISBM, Lect. 8; MWS, Lect. 5; MSCW, Lect. 9; NATS; WEEB

One of the more difficult concepts to comprehend is the distinction between Mineral Kingdom (i.e., Condition of Life) and Physical Condition of Form—see **I-1**, **I-2** and **I-3**, the "Basic Charts" above. This will appear more extensively later, but the distinction is inherent in this chart, which will require more than normal discussion at this point. It has to do with what are known as "Elemental Spirits (Beings)," a subject touched upon, otherwise mysteriously, by Paul (Gal 4,3,9 and Col 2,8,20). As is evident from the Basic Charts, the "Physical" Condition of Form appears in every Condition of Life within every Condition of Consciousness. It has thus, prior to the present Condition of Form, appeared 24 times (e.g., as in "24 elders"). We are in the 25th such appearance, and there will be another 24 hereafter before the end of the 7 Conditions of Consciousness. Out of these 49 appearances, only 7 will have occurred in the combined Mineral Physical Conditions, but only once, namely in the Earth Condition of Consciousness, will this occurrence have been such that it could be perceived by any of the senses of the human being as presently constituted. Just as there are spiritual beings (e.g., **I-6**) above the human being that are not visible to the human being's present senses, so are there beings below it that are not visible. The critical point is that "the material form of beings through which no Ego glows cannot be visible in our evolutionary phase" (ISBM, Lect. 8, p. 130). Each of the 4 "kingdoms" presently visible to the human being is endowed with an Ego, as indicated in **I-11**. Just as we cannot, except as it comes to expression in the mineral-physical, see the etheric or astral body or Ego (or even the physical body in its archetypical form, absent the mineral condition), so also we cannot today see those beings that are below these 4 "kingdoms," but they exist just as do those that are above. They are also known as "nature spirits."

"What we call Elemental Beings lack Ego, but they have developed a principle below the physical body. We can say, therefore, that the principles 3, 2, 1 and minus 1 are developed in them. But there are not only beings which begin at the third principle. We have also those which begin at 2 and then have minus 1 and minus 2. And then we have still others whose highest principle is the same as the human being's lowest [the physical]" (ISBM, Lect. 8, p. 131). The following table (ISBM, p. 138) shows all the forms of nature spirits:

	Phys body & above	Below
Gnomes	1	3
Undines	2	2
Sylphs	3	1
Salamanders	4	0

It is fair to ask why salamanders are not visible since they have something in the nature of an Ego (though none of such principles is enclosed within, in the sense described in **I-11**). It is discussed in the cited sources, but is too complex for summary here.

(Grieg's "Peer Gynt Suite" is a portrayal of the trolls in the mines. WNWD shows the word "troll" to be from Middle High German, then later from Norwegian, and to mean [Scand. Folklore] any of a race of supernatural beings, variously conceived of as giants or dwarfs, living underground or in caves; obviously, these are the same as the "gnomes" of which Steiner speaks.)

As we shall see, three domains (thinking, feeling and willing) compose all human activity on Earth. In MWS, Lect. 5 (same as Lect. 7 in NATS), Steiner shows how all these domains are made possible by "elemental spirits," as follows:

Action	Result	Ascending	Descending	Locus
Thinking	Truth	Spirit-fools	Gnomes	Earth
Feeling	Beauty	Ugly-beings	Sylphs & Undines	Water & Air
Willing	Good	Bashful beings	Salamanders	Warmth

Small wonder Paul did not long dwell on "elemental spirits" for the very perceiving of the concept of them demands a grappling in the half-light. But of their existence Paul clearly indicated and Steiner insists. There is a subtle hint in Samson's riddle, about the honey from the lion's carcass (Judg 14,5-18), of the polarities that exist in the above table. For in the table, thinking (the ability to hold thoughts in mind) relies upon spirit-fools, appreciation for beauty upon ugly-beings, and stimulation by good and moral thoughts upon those most highly disdained, the bashful beings. The descending elemental spirits disdain the ascending, increasingly as one moves from the top down in the table. There is apparently an ahrimanic and luciferic nature in both the ascending and descending elemental spirits. The ascending elemental spirits were "perceptible as a real animal world" during the Ancient Moon Condition of Consciousness, "visible to the senses" in a manner of speaking, but are moving in the opposite direction, into the spiritual realm, ascending, though "admittedly through their Luciferic and Ahrimanic natures." The descending elemental spirits, on the other hand, "will one day become visible to the senses."

But this table gives only one of many arenas in the mineral-physical world affected by the activities of the elemental spirits, as the works cited at the first of this chart show.

In MSCW, Lect. 9 (p. 142), Steiner indicates that, "When man is going through his development in the life between death and a new birth," the message (as part of the Creative Word) received by man from these respective beings is as follows:

Chorus of	Their Activity	That Seeks in Human Being a
Gnomes	Strive to awaken	System of movement
Undines	Think in the spirit	Metabolic organization
Sylphs	Live and create breathing existence	Rhythmical system
Salamanders (Fire spirits)	Receive in love the will-power of the gods	System of Nerves and Senses

I-13 Distinctions between the mineral and physical depending on where the physical human being can be perceived

CL, Lect. 7 (p. 97)

Another way of relating the distinction between the mineral and physical states is as follows:

Higher spirit world, higher Devachan plane	World of perception of physical human nature on Saturn
Spirit world, Devachan plane	World of perception of physical human nature on Sun
Soul world, astral plane	World of perception of physical human nature on Moon
Physical plane	World of perception of physical human nature on Earth

I-14 The four systems of the human being's physical body as expressions and descendants of Conditions of Consciousness

ISBM, Lect. 8 (pp. 128-129) and Lect. 10 (pp. 163-165); UEM, Lect. 10, Aug 14, 1908 (p. 151); Jn-Rel, Lect. 3 (p. 41)

Body System (i.e., Instrument)	"Body"	Origin
Physical body and organs working purely mechanically	Physical	Saturn
Gland Organs	Etheric	Sun
Nerve Organs	Astral	Moon
Blood (Circulatory) System	Ego	Earth

I-15 Hierarchical attainment of "human" status on the three former Conditions of Consciousness

OS, Chap. 4 (pp. 125-129)

Note again the discussion in **I-1** of the "24 elders." Recall that we are now in the 25th Condition of Life. The human being first attained "human" status (acquired an Ego, consciousness of self, the "I Am" [Ex 3,14]) about midway through the 25th, but all spiritual beings in the 9 Hierarchies above the human being also went through the equivalent of a "human" state during a particular Condition of Life, and thus bear the human within themselves. So there are 24 "elders" who passed this way before the human being.

However, one must conclude that there are 7 levels of "elders" within each hierarchical level. Each hierarchical being is, like the human being, a 7-fold being that moves one step higher with each Condition of Life, and thus, like the human being, attains to its self-awareness (human) level in its own 4th evolutionary Condition of Life within its own evolutionary Condition of Consciousness, which does not coincide with the human being's except once every 7 levels, each group of which is then characterized here as a hierarchical level. Thus, there are in Steiner's description of the hierarchical levels active on *Saturn* several that have as their lowest member the astral body at various descending stages of development. So, just as the human being receives its Ego in its 4th Condition of Consciousness (*Earth*), but more specifically in its 4th Condition of Life (Mineral Kingdom) thereof, so also during any one of the human being's Conditions of Consciousness there would be 7 elders generally classified during that time as receiving their "human" or "Ego" or "self-awareness" state during that 7-stage Condition. All 7 of these elders would be referred to as a single hierarchical level, but at 7 different stages of development (and each stage, as in the case of the human being itself, would encompass innumerable such spiritual beings within it). Within this framework then, it can be said (see for instance, page 125 where Steiner mentions that the Spirits of Personality reach "human" status on *Saturn*) that one hierarchical level reaches human status during each Condition of Consciousness and specifically as follows:

Spiritual Being	Attains Human Status On
Principalities (Spirits of Personality)	Saturn
Archangels (Spirits of Fire)	Sun
Angels (Sons of Life, Sons of Twilight)	Moon
Human Being	Earth

Those hierarchical beings higher than Principalities thus attained human status prior to *Saturn*. While they continue to advance, such levels are beyond those we need here discuss.

I-16 <u>The ruling Hierarchies on Earth and its three former Conditions of Consciousness, respectively</u>

UEM, Lect. 4 (pp. 52-53)

In the same way that Elohim (Gen 1,1), or Exusiai, ruled the Earth evolution, so also did higher Hierarchies rule prior incarnations of the Earth.

<u>Ruling Hierarchical Level</u>	<u>Condition of Consciousness</u>
Exusiai (Elohim), Authorities	Earth
Dynamis, Powers or Mights	Moon
Kyriotetes, Dominions	Sun
Thronos, Thrones	Saturn

It was the sacrifice by the ruling Hierarchy during each such period that made the development of the human being possible during that period, i.e., physical (Saturn), etheric (Sun), astral (Moon) and Ego (Earth), respectively.

I-17 <u>Relationship of human evolution to the various planetary orbits</u>

SH, Lect. 5 (p. 63); HA2, Chap. 8 (pp. 294-5)

The entire descent of the human being from the spiritual world represents, in a manner of speaking, a condensation to ever denser states of existence, and the reascent will involve the volatilization to ever rarer states. Our solar system reflects this entire process. Leaving aside, for now, the more recently discovered planets of Pluto, Neptune and Uranus, none of which is visible to the naked eye, the structure of our solar system itself illustrates the progression of human evolution. The orbits of the planets represent the dimensions of the successive Conditions of Consciousness. Those from the periphery in toward Earth preceded the Incarnation of Christ, hence represented processes of densification. The Incarnation of Christ made it possible for humanity (to the extent it takes Christ into itself) to begin the reverse process. The ultimate objective, to the extent it lays within the 7 Conditions of Consciousness, is reunion with the Sun, which is itself a body of (rarified) spiritual beings.

The anthroposophist Robert Powell portrays the following scenario in HA2:

The manvantaras [periods of manifestation as opposed to pralayas, periods of rest] of Orphic cosmology and the stages of human evolution

Orbit of	Orbit of (Condition of Consciousness)
1. Pluto (Phanes)	
2. Neptune (Night)	
3. Uranus (Ouranos)	
4. Saturn (Kronos)	Saturn (*Saturn*)
5. Jupiter (Zeus)	Jupiter (*Sun*)
6. Mars (Dionysos)	Mars (*Moon*)
7. Earth	Earth (*Earth*)
8. Venus	Venus (*Jupiter*)
9. Mercury	Mercury (*Venus*)
10. Sun	Sun (*Vulcan*)

Thus, according to Steiner's cosmology, the 7 stages of evolution relating to the development of the human being are:

Saturn (which took place within the orbit of planet Saturn)
Sun (which took place within the orbit of planet Jupiter)
Moon (which took place within the orbit of planet Mars)
Earth (which is taking place within the orbit of Earth)
Jupiter (which will take place within the orbit of planet Venus)
Venus (which will take place within the orbit of planet Mercury)
Vulcan (which will take place in the sphere of the Sun)

According to Steiner, in ancient times, due to a particular change in the perspective from which the order of the interior planets is observed (i.e., from Earth or from Sun), as Powell says, "the names of Venus and Mercury became interchanged, so that esoterically considered the orbit of the Earth lies between that of Mars and Mercury. In the light of this consideration the validity of the designation of the two halves of Earth evolution as 'Mars' and 'Mercury' can be seen." (See **I-8**.)

I-18 Human and other hierarchical and Trinitarian relationships to the zodiac

Steiner spoke often about the "Zodiac," about how consciousness of its influence had gradually been lost as the human being descended from spiritual consciousness into materialistic consciousness, about how modern astrology was merely dilettantism, and about how the former consciousness would one day again be regained as knowledge. And he left many guideposts in that direction, so that now, after many decades of dedicated research by his disciples, we have the recent, amazing works of Robert Powell on "hermetic astrology." The substance of these will be touched upon later. The foregoing is mentioned here only to awaken the reader to the fact of the influence of the Zodiac (the "fixed stars" beyond our Solar System) upon the human being. The truth of this is strewn through the Bible when the meaning of its passages is understood. We get an inkling of it when Yahweh tells Abram, in Gen 15,5 (according to a modern translation), "'Look toward heaven, and number the stars, if you are able to number them.' Then he said to him, 'So shall your descendants be.'"

From what follows, one can see that Christ, the "Mystical Lamb," represents the highest of the twelve "animals" of the Zodiac, and as such is also called, "the Son." Above him is the Father, so that the macrocosmic Word behind the Zodiac had 12 sons, and thus microcosmically Jacob had 12 sons, as did Ishmael, and Christ had 12 disciples. None of these are mere coincidence, but represent truth inscribed into all that we call "creation."

"In the same way that Christ has *the Constellation of the Ram* as the source of His spiritual emanations in our cosmos [citing ISBM, Lect. 2] ... so does the Sophia have *the Constellation of the Virgin* as the source of her spiritual emanations in the macrocosm ..." (Prokofieff, THNS, Sec. 2, Chap. 1, p. 86). In the ancient Mysteries, known to the Magi, "there was a prophetic indication of the event that would take place when the sun stood at midnight between December 24 and 25 in the *sign of the Virgin* ..." (EIE). Inasmuch as all spiritual beings are 7-fold (ISBM, Lect. 2 and Prov 9,1), Christ could only become an incarnated human being (i.e., descend to the physical state) by entering therein *through the Constellation of the Virgin.*

For now, it must suffice merely to set out certain tabulations from ISBM, Lect. 2 (esp. p. 32); SIS, Lect. 2; EIE; THNS, Sec. 1, Chaps. 1 and 2, Sec. 2., Chap. 1 (esp. p. 86).

7-Fold Human Being	Hierarchy	Zodiacal Symbol Animal *(Latin)*	Animal *(English)*	7-fold "Mystical Lamb"
	Son/Christ	Aries	Ram (Lamb)	12th member
	Holy Spirit	Taurus	Bull	11th member
	Seraphim	Gemini	Twins	10th member
	Cherubim	Cancer	Crab	9th member
	Thrones	Leo	Lion	8th member
7th Spirit Man	Kyriotetes	Virgo	Virgin	7th member
6th Life Spirit	Dynamis	Libra	Scales	6th member
5th Spirit Self	Exusiai	Scorpio	Scorpion	
4th Ego	Archai	Sagittarius	Archer	
3rd Astral Body	Archangels	Capricorn	Goat	
2nd Etheric Body	Angels	Aquarius	Waterman	
1st Physical Body	Human Being	Pisces	Fishes	

The human being's highest "fold" is represented by the cosmic sign of the Virgin, to be attained at the conclusion of the Venus Condition of Consciousness. The human being will then have attained to the state of the Cosmic Virgin "Sophia"—thus, "Anthropo-Sophia," the Holy Virgin who gave birth to the Christ in the physical state.

I-19   Powell's hermetic astrological charts and tabulations

HA1, Chap. 3

The length of time required for the Sun to travel its complete cycle through the 12 constellations of the Zodiac is 25,920 years (an astronomical fact). The average length of time allocable to each constellation is thus 25,920/12, or 2160 years.

In *Sidereal Zodiac* (SZ), Robert Powell updates "the original definition of the zodiac by Babylonian astronomers" to our own time by formally defining it "for the epoch 1950.0, in line with conventional astronomical practice" (p. 12). That practice, however, appears to involve some other changes from Babylonian practice, changes made by the Greek Hipparchus by the second century B.C. One of these is the use of the "ecliptic" rather than the "zodiacal belt" as a frame of reference. In SZ, p. 1, Powell states:

In modern astronomy the zodiacal belt is defined in relation to the path of the Sun through the fixed stars, which path is taken as the middle of the belt, so that the zodiacal belt, usually taken to be 16 degrees wide, by this definition extends 8 degrees north and 8 degrees south of the path of the Sun. The zodiacal belt is thus a belt of fixed stars along the middle of which runs the path of the Sun and contains also the paths of the Moon and the five planets known to the ancients through naked eye observation—Mercury, Venus, Mars, Jupiter, and Saturn.

Another is given by Powell as follows (SZ, pp. 9-10):

> The vernal point, i.e., the location of the Sun in the ecliptic at the time of vernal equinox, was adopted in Greek astronomy as the beginning of the ecliptic, apparently because the vernal equinox was considered by Greek astronomers as the start of the year. This represents another point of difference between Greek and Babylonian astronomy. Since the Babylonian year consisted of twelve or thirteen lunar months, the start of the year was related to a lunar phenomenon, namely the appearance of the first new Moon of the year, which was, generally speaking (at least in later Babylonian times), the new Moon falling nearest to the vernal equinox. However, as early as the fifth century B.C., the Greek astronomer Euctemon defined a seasonal calendar, consisting of twelve (approximately) equal solar months, related to the solar phenomena of equinoxes and solstices. The months in Euctemon's calendar have the same names—the equivalent Greek names—as the signs of the zodiac in Babylonian astronomy. Thus the solar month commencing on the day of the vernal equinox was called by Euctemon the month of Aries. Similarly, the solar month commencing on the day of the summer solstice was called the month of Cancer.... This calendrical system is still in vogue today in astrology.

Christians will readily recognize the lunar nature of the Yahweh faith, since the Passover, and the Christian Easter celebration, are both related to the vernal equinox in terms of its proximity to the new Moon. At the time these systems were established, it was Aries that was arising at sunrise on the eastern horizon at the vernal equinox, but today this is no longer true due to the precession of the equinoxes (an astronomical fact that conventional astrology ignores). See 4 Brit 534, "equinox" and "equinoxes, precession of the," and 1 Brit 551, "Aries."

Because humanity must come to recognize the "ages" preordained by its relationship to the heavenly bodies (as the outward manifestation of spiritual beings and their forces), it is important to understand that it is the "vernal point" that determines the dates of the "ages." It is based upon the zodiacal sign rising in the eastern sky at sunrise at the vernal (spring) equinox. Due to the "precession of the equinoxes," this point retrogresses one degree each 72 years so that an "age" consists of 2,160 years and a "zodiacal year" of twelve ages consists of 25,920 years.

In order to relate to the reality of the changing relationship of the heavenly bodies to the Earth by taking the precession of the equinoxes into account, Powell defines the "sidereal zodiac" by fixing it in relation to the brightest star in the zodiacal belt, Aldebaran, located approximately in the middle of the constellation Taurus (as the eye of the bull), placing the zero point exactly 45 degrees west of Aldebaran on that date, i.e., 1950 (pp. 27 and 32). His portrayal of the sidereal zodiac, so defined, is shown below:

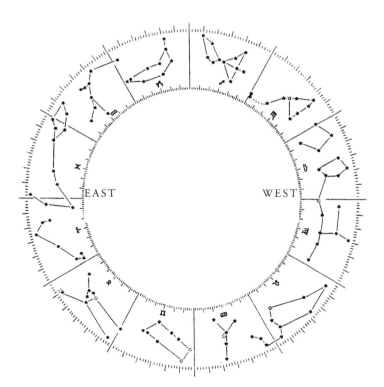

Based upon such chart, the dates of the "Astrological Ages" are thus as follows:

Aquarius		23,546-21,386 B.C.
Capricorn		21,386-19,226
Sagittarius		19,226-17,066
Scorpio		17,066-14,906
Libra		14,906-12,746
Virgo		12,746-10,586
Leo		10,586- 8,426
Cancer		8,426- 6,266
Gemini		6,266- 4,106
Taurus		4,106- 1,946 B.C.
Aries	B.C.	1,946- 215 A.D.
Pisces	A.D.	215- 2,375
Aquarius		2,375- 4,535

However, there is a time lag of approximately 1,200 years (1,199 to be exact) between each "Astrological Age" in the heavens and its respective Cultural Age on Earth, so that the seven respective Cultural Ages of the post-Atlantean Epoch are as follows:

Cultural Age	Dates	Civilization
Cancer	7227-5067	Indian
Gemini	5067-2907	Persian
Taurus	2907- 747 B.C.	Chaldo-Egyptian
Aries	747-1414 A.D.	Greco-Roman
Pisces	1414-3574	European
Aquarius	3574-5734	Russian-Slavonic
Capricorn	5734-7894	American

This time lag is explained by the fact that transformation to a new state of consciousness is not effected instantaneously. Rather, it proceeds initially in subconscious strata as a cultural impulse which manifests in a new Cultural Age only when it has reached a certain level. The time lag is an expression of the time taken for the transformation of consciousness to take effect.

This time lag is determined by a remarkable phenomenon in the heavens that Powell identifies as "the Venus Pentagram," which makes a complete rotation of the sidereal zodiac in 1,199 years. It is explained in HA1, pp. 58-63 and pictured below:

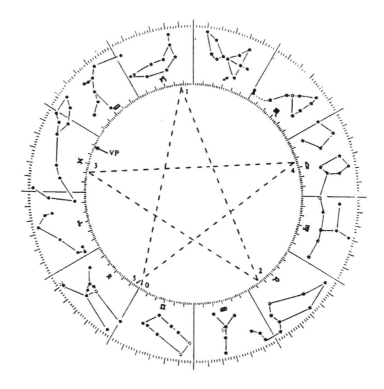

During each Cultural Age (2,160 years), there is a rotation of leadership among the Archangels in the following order, using their Christian names: Oriphiel, Aneal, Zachariel, Raphael, Samael, Gabriel, Michael. While each Cultural Age is ruled over by a Time Spirit (Archai), the Archangels, as Folk-Spirits, have predominance according to such lesser cycles therein. It is not yet completely clear to me just how these lesser cycles fit within the larger 2,160 year cycle. The clearest indication of timing is that the current cycle is that of Michael which began in 1879. If we divide 2,160 by seven, we get 308.57 years. Yet on one occasion (notebook entry dated Aug. 18, 1924, editorially footnoted in TFP, Lect. 7), Steiner gave a different breakdown. The two tabulations are compared below:

	TFP, Lect. 7	308.57 year
Gabriel	1879-1510	1879-1570
Samael	1510-1190	1570-1262
Raphael	1190- 850	1262- 953
Zachariel	850- 500	953- 645
Anael	500- 150	645- 336
Oriphiel	A.D. 150- 200 B.C.	336- 28
Michael	200-	A.D. 28- 281 B.C.

Support for both of these approaches would seem to exist in KR-6, Lect. 8 (July 19, 1924). In this lecture, Steiner clearly indicated, however, that Michael was in rulership at the time Alexander the Great (356-323 B.C.) founded Alexandria (cf. KR-8, Lect. 6). I have opted to set out the general indications about archangelic rulership, in spite of being unable presently to give fuller explanation of this apparent discrepancy.

Tradition also assigns (see KR-3, Lect. 11; RSMW, Chap. 11, p. 96; MOT, Letter 13, p. 367) to each Archangel a special relationship to one of the chief planets, so that the order of the Archangels is also the order of the days of the week (see **I-8**):

Oriphiel	Saturn	Saturday
Anael	Venus	Friday
Zachariel	Jupiter	Thursday
Raphael	Mercury	Wednesday
Samael	Mars	Tuesday
Gabriel	Moon	Monday
Michael	Sun	Sunday

I-20 The microcosmic reflections of the zodiacal and planetary natures in the human being (and in the apostolic groupings)

RH, Lect. 13 (pp. 178-179) and Lect. 7; SSFS, Lect. 3; SM, Lect. 8; MBSP; MLO, Lects. 5 and 6; HA1, Figs. 13 and 23, Tab. 16; MSZ; TI, Lects. 3 and 7; OH, Lect. 5

The zodiacal nature is microcosmically reflected (e.g., Gen 15,5; Ezek 1,22) in the human being in multifarious ways. The 12 constellations seen under the dome of the firmament are reflected under the dome of the human being's skull. As Steiner has said (e.g., RH, Lect. 13, pp. 178-179) there are 12 principal nerves that originate in the head. This is true, but only as part of the picture. One can confirm (e.g., 24 Brit 811-821, "Nerves and Nervous Systems") that the peripheral nervous system is made up of 3 parts, namely, the cranial nerves, the spinal nerves and that part of the autonomic (involuntary) nervous system that is outside the brain and spinal cord. These three are the "Trinity" above the zodiac. The highest of these three are the cranial nerves, of which there are indeed 12 pairs as follows:

1. Olfactory
2. Optic
3. Oculomotor
4. Trochlear
5. Trigeminal
6. Abducens
7. Facial
8. Vestibulocochlear
9. Glossopharyngeal
10. Vagus
11. Accessory
12. Hypoglossal

Next are the 31 pairs of the spinal nerves (cf. **I-86** re vertebrae), roughly reflective of the division of each of the 12 constellations into degrees, or months into days. The greater consciousness (in an earthly sense) is located in the cranial nerves, the middle consciousness in the spinal nerves, and the unconscious (involuntary) in the autonomic nerves.

In quite another way the 12-fold zodiacal nature is reflected in the number of senses in the human being. Typically thought to be five in number (sight, hearing, smell, taste and touch), in reality there are 12 senses (the order, for now, listed in RH, Lect. 7):

1. Touch
2. Life
3. Movement
4. Balance
5. Smell
6. Taste

7. Sight
8. Warmth
9. Hearing
10. Word (Speech)
11. Thought
12. Ego

That there are 12 is a microcosmic reflection of the 12 macrocosmic (zodiacal) forces. One may get the idea there is a correspondence between a particular zodiacal constellation and a particular human sense. Initially this idea could come from the fact that on occasion Steiner himself makes such an identification for a particular purpose (e.g., see MLO and MBSP). One could be thrown into quite a state of confusion by Steiner's apparent inconsistency from one lecture series to another. Davidson adverts to this potential conflict in MSZ, and seems to explain it by suggesting that one must seek the macrocosmic-microcosmic connection on an individualized basis. It would seem, however, that Steiner, himself, has given us a more precise explanation, or at least a complementary one, in RH, Lect. 7. There he first draws a circle on which he lists, in the above order the 12 senses around the periphery, as follows:

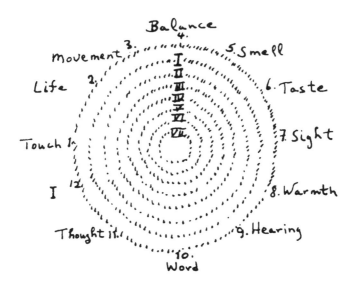

He then asserts that there are 7, and only 7, life processes:

1.   Breathing
2.   Warming
3.   Nourishing
4.   Secreting
5.   Maintaining
6.   Growing
7.   Reproducing

which he portrays by 7 successively interior, concentric circular paths within the initial (zodiacal) circle, as follows:

Prior to drawing either diagram, Steiner had pointed out that each of the 12 senses flows through each of the life processes, and that no one such sense could manifest in an organ (such as the ear) without the presence of all of these forces. Thus, we see that not only are our 12 senses a reflection of the 12 zodiacal constellations, but also of the 7 planetary forces, and that all of these interact in a manner reflective of the way the bodies of our solar system travel through the forces of the constellations.

That the rhythm of the zodiac is reflected in the human being is indicated by the following (see MK, Lect 2, p. 36 et al.; HI, Lect. 7; PM, Lect. 10; TIEC, Lects. 1 and 4; EVC, Lects. 11 and 12; EVEM, Lects. 10 and 14); CHM, Lect. 2; MSCW, Lect. 10; CHM, Lect. 2): A solar year, time required for Sun to travel its complete cycle through the 12 constellations of the zodiac is *25,920 years* (see **I-19**); the length of human life at approximately age 70 (Ps 90,10) is *25,920 days*; and the average number of times a human breathes in a day is *25,920 breaths*.

Nor does the microcosmic reflection even stop there, for in MLO, Lect. 6, Steiner shows how the human being's 3 systems—thinking, feeling and willing—are a trinity reflective of the 12 zodiacal forces, as follows:

UPPER MAN

1	Upright Position	♈
2	Direction forwards	♉
3	Symmetry	♊
4	Upper Arm	♐
5	Elbow	♑
6	Lower Arm	♒
7	Hands	♓

MIDDLE MAN

1	Head and Feet, Twins	♊
2	Breast enclosure	♋
3	Interior, Heart	♌
4	The second Interior part of man	♍
5	Balance	♎
6	Organs of Reproduction	♏
7	Thigh	♐

LOWER MAN

7	Feet	♓
6	Leg	♒
5	Knee	♑
4	Thigh	♐
3	Organs of Reproduction	♏
2	Balance	♎
1	Kidneys, Solar Plexus	♍

And in SM, Lect. 8, he illustrates how each of the human being's senses, though active in all 3 soul forces (thinking, feeling and willing), is predominantly related to one of them, as follows:

<u>Thinking</u>	<u>Feeling</u>	<u>Willing</u>
Ego	Warmth	Balance
Thought	Sight	Movement
Speech	Taste	Life
Hearing	Smell	Touch

   Not only is this 12-fold, 7-fold and 3-fold macrocosmic nature reflected in the microcosm of the human being's physical makeup, but Steiner tells us (HCT, Lect. 3) that it is also reflected in humanity's thinking through 12 World Outlook Shades (Zodiac), 7 World Outlook Moods (Planets) and 3 World Outlook Tones. (He adds that one additional Tone, namely, "Anthropomorphism," is in reality a harmony of these 3, as they are reflected within the human being itself.) The Tones are reflective as follows:

Sun	Theism
Moon	Intuitionism
Earth	Naturalism

The Shades and Moods are portrayed in the following diagram:

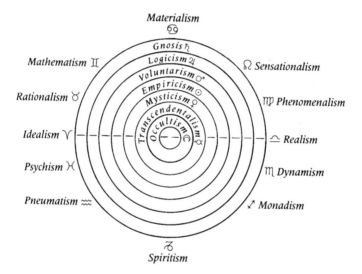

   We can then see the same 12-fold, 7-fold, 3-fold and even 1-fold nature reflected in the 12 apostles, as follows:

12-fold	Matthew, Mark and Luke Gospels
7-fold	John 21,2
3-fold	Peter, James and John (at Transfiguration, Gethsemane, etc.)
1-fold	Evangelist John (identified elsewhere herein)

I-21 Powell's charts and graphs showing "the hermetic man" (planetary relationships of the human being's organs) and "the zodiacal man" (zodiacal relationships of the human being's physical body)

HA1, Figs. 13 and 23 and Tab. 16

In his HA1, Robert Powell shows how ancient tradition has associated the human being's soul organs ("lotus flowers," "chakras" or "wheels") with the planets and its physical body with the Zodiac, in what are referred to as "the hermetic man" and "the zodiacal man." The former is portrayed in his Figure 13 and the latter in Table 16 and Figure 23.

Table 16
The zodiacal melothesia

Early in the hermetical-astrological tradition the twelve signs of the zodiac were placed in correspondence with various parts of the human body, as indicated in the following tabulation:

ZODIACAL SIGN	PART OF THE BODY
Aries	head
Taurus	larynx region
Gemini	shoulders and arms
Cancer	breast region
Leo	heart and back
Virgo	Solar plexus and stomach region
Libra	hips and pelvic region
Scorpio	region of reproductive organs
Sagittarius	thighs
Capricorn	knees
Aquarius	calves and ankles
Pisces	feet

Figure 13
The hermetic man

The hermetic man—the planetary archetype of the human being—
shows the correspondance between the planets and the lotus flowers.

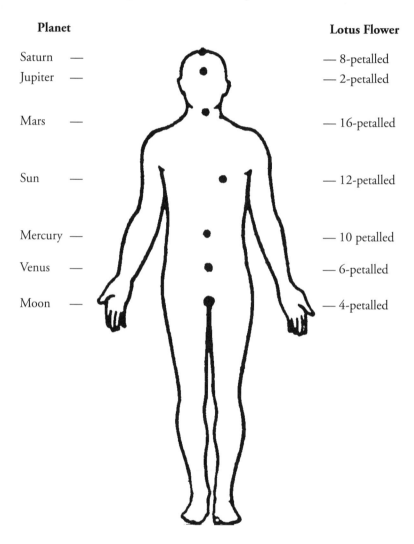

Planet		Lotus Flower
Saturn —		— 8-petalled
Jupiter —		— 2-petalled
Mars —		— 16-petalled
Sun —		— 12-petalled
Mercury —		— 10 petalled
Venus —		— 6-petalled
Moon —		— 4-petalled

Figure 23
The zodiacal man

The zodiacal man, from a fifteenth century Shepherd's Calendar, showing the correspondence between the twelve signs of the zodiac and parts of the body—see Table 16 for a tabulation of this correspondence.

(Reproduced from Fred Gettings, *The Hidden Art*, London, 1912, p. 24.)

I-22 The elementary states, the ethers and elements

GEN, Lects. 2, 4 and 7; FE, Lects. 5, 6, 9 and 28; EoB; NEOA

The elementary states within our Earth existence (i.e., Earth Consciousness-Mineral Kingdom-Physical Form, as per **I-1**) are as follows:

Solid (Earth)

Watery

Gaseous

Warmth

Light (ether)

Chemical or Sound (ether)

Life (ether)

Steiner indicates that it is in the Earth that we have to look mainly for solid, fluid and gas, that warmth is shared by Earth and Sun, and that the three ethers are of Sun nature (GEN, Lect. 7). Lect. 4 ends with the following tabulation:

Saturn	Sun	Moon	Earth
Warmth or Fire	Light	Sound	Life
	Warmth	Light	Sound
	Air	Warmth	Light
		Air	Warmth
		Water	Air
			Water
			Earth

The form of the chart seems difficult to fathom. In Lect. 2, Steiner, speaking of the human being's descent from the spiritual to the material world in a process of densification, points out that whenever there is a descent there is a corresponding ascent. "Thus, when we descend from warmth into the denser, we come to the gaseous condition; if we ascend, we come to light. Ascending still further, beyond the light we come to a yet finer etheric condition, … something which is not really recognizable in the ordinary sense-world. We get only a kind of external reflection of it." He then discusses how the chemical/sound ether manifests in the "Chladni" sound-figure experiment when fine powder is placed on a metal plate and the bow of a violin is then drawn across the plate.

This process of descent and offsetting ascent would seem to illustrate the principle of "Fission," which is so amply demonstrated in scripture. I have constructed the following chart in an effort to more clearly illustrate the process:

```
Saturn              Sun            Moon            Earth

                                                   Life
                                                    /
                                   Sound
                                     /          \
                     Light                          Light
                       /             \          /
Warmth (Fire)                      Warmth
                       \             /          \
                     Air                            Air
                                     \          /
                                   Water
                                                    \
                                                   Earth
```

As can be seen, the process from Saturn to Earth is one of descent from a state of warmth, which has required "Fission." It would seem that the reascent of the human being will require "Fusion," a principle also demonstrated in scripture.

But just as there are (invisible) elemental spirits below, as well as spiritual Hierarchies above, the human being, so also there are (invisible) conditions of matter below, as well as above, those we call gas, fluid and solid. Steiner refers to them (in EoB) as constituting the "sub-physical" world, which he sets out as follows:

Astral World . . . . the province of Lucifer

Lower Devachan . . . . the province of Ahriman

Higher Devachan . . . . the province of Asuras

Life Ether

Chemical Ether

Light Ether

sub-physical Astral World
               electricity

sub-physical Lower Devachan
                    magnetism

sub-physical Higher Devachan
               terrible forces of destruction

In the lecture he had pointed out that, just as a human being is in a state of growth until the 35th year and thereafter is in a state of decay, so also is matter in the same pattern. Up until the Atlantean Epoch, matter was in a progressive process, but decay has set in with the post-Atlantean Epoch. "Light is being destroyed in this post-Atlantean age of the Earth's existence, which until the time of Atlantis was a progressive process. Since then it has been a process of decay. What is light? Light decays and the decaying light is *electricity*. What we know as electricity is light that is being destroyed in matter. And the chemical force that undergoes a transformation in the process of Earth evolution is *magnetism*. Yet a third force will become active and if electricity seems to work wonders today, this third force will affect civilization in a still more miraculous way. The more of this force we employ, the faster will the Earth tend to become a corpse and its spiritual part prepare for the Jupiter embodiment.... [I]t is necessary for the Earth to be destroyed, for otherwise the spiritual could not become free."

In NEOA, Lect. 1, Unger, keying off Steiner's EoB lecture, gives the following schematic of how the subsensible world is constituted:

                                              Life Ether

                         Chemical Ether

            Light Ether

Warmth   Gaseous   Fluid
Ether   Condition   Condition   Solid Condition

              Electricity
              (Lucifer)

                               Magnetism
                               (Ahriman)

                                                Third Force
                                                (Asuras)

Steiner's EoB lecture was in 1911. Unger's were between 1968 and 1978. In his Lect. 2, Unger expresses the view that nuclear energy, of itself, is not yet the "Third Force." Rather, "there is embodied [in it], somewhat prematurely, some small part of the future forces which have been spoken of … the 'tip of the iceberg.'"

I-23 Glossary of theosophical/anthroposophical terminology and charts & tabulations of the various relationships described; also the scriptural sequence of development of the human being's "five" senses

FE, Lects. 5, 6, 9, 28 and Glossary of Indian-Theosophical Terms

FE is a series of 31 lectures by Steiner in the fall of 1905. No stenographer was present, so FE is based upon notes taken by those in attendance. The earliness of these lectures accounts for the presence of much Eastern terminology, though Steiner had already begun to substitute anthroposophical terminology in his THSY (1904). Because the "ethers" in **I-22** are not well understood in the scientific community or by modern humanity, it is deemed worthwhile to explore them further here. To that end, the following comparative terminology is taken from the Glossary:

Theosophical Literature	Anthroposophical Literature
1. Physical Plane	The same, also: physical world, world of understanding
2. Astral Plane	The same, also: Soul World or Land, Imaginative World, Elementary World
3. Devachan or Mental	The same, also: Spirit Land, Plane Spiritual World, World of the Harmony of the Spheres, World of Inspiration
Rupa-Devachan	Lower Devachan, Lower Spiritual World, also Heavenly World
Arupa-Devachan	Higher Devachan, Higher Spiritual World, World of true Intuition
4. Shushupti or Buddhi Plane	Buddhi Plane, also World of Foreseeing
5. Nirvana Plane \	
6. Para-nirvana Plane — Nirvana Plane	
7. Maha-para-nirvana Plane /	

"This world above the World of Foreseeing is of such a nature 'that in accordance with truth and uprightness its name may not be given in European languages, for it would not do to choose just any name for what in Oriental languages is called Nirvana and which is higher than the World of Foreseeing'" (CIDE, Lect. 1).

In FE, Lect. 5, Steiner says, "In ordinary life we differentiate three bodily conditions [solid, fluid and gas]. Theosophical writings add to these four other finer conditions of matter. The first element which is finer than air is the one which causes it to expand, which always increases its spatial content. What expands the air in this way is warmth; it is really a fine etheric substance, the first grade of ether, the Warmth Ether. Now follows the second kind of ether, the Light Ether. Bodies which shine send out a form of matter which is described in Theosophy as Light Ether. The third kind of ether is the bearer of everything which gives form to the finest matter, the formative ether, which is also called the

Chemical Ether. It is this ether that brings about the union of oxygen and hydrogen. And the finest of all the ethers is what constitutes life: Prana, or Life Ether."

The 7 conditions of matter and the correlative planes upon which their "life" can be perceived are as follows:

Condition of Matter	Plane upon which Perceived
Life Ether	Physical Plane
Chemical Ether	Astral Plane
Light Ether	Mental (Devachan) Plane
Warmth Ether	Buddhi Plane
Air (Gas)	Nirvana Plane
Water (Fluid)	Paranirvana Plane
Earth (Solid)	Mahaparanirvana Plane

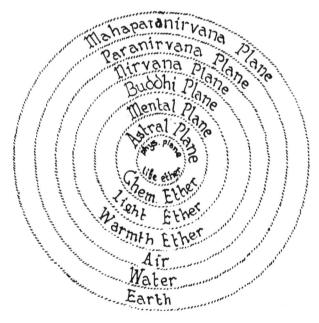

"Just as the child today has the old human being beside man who is at another stage," so there are 7 different ascending ranks of beings to which the human being belongs, as follows:

1. Elemental Beings
2. Adam (human beings)
3. Adam Cadmon (human beings with purified astral bodies)
4. Bodhisattvas
5. Nirmanakayas
6. Pitris
7. Gods

There are 12 senses of which 5 are already physical and 2 others will become so during further Earth evolution. The 2 that will become so are located in the pituitary gland and the pineal gland. The human being's higher principles, atma-buddhi-manas, developed on Saturn-Sun-Moon, respectively. The human being has now descended to the 4th stage, Kama-manas, or Intellectual Soul. On Saturn, only one "sense" was present, smell. The 7 Conditions of matter and the correlative planes upon which their "lives" can be perceived have been indicated above. To these are added the correlative 7 senses:

Planes of Perception	Conds. of Matter	Senses
1. Physical Plane	Life ether	Smell
2. Astral Plane	Chemical ether	Taste
3. Mental Plane	Light ether	Sight
4. Buddhi Plane	Warmth ether	Touch
5. Nirvana Plana	Air (Gas)	Hearing
6. Paranirvana Plane	Water (Fluid)	Pituitary Gland
7. Mahaparanirvana Plane	Earth (Solid)	Pineal Gland

It is worth noting that the sequence of the first 5 senses above is identifiable in Gen. 2 and 3 as follows:

Smell	Gen 2,7	Relates to "breathing"
Taste	Gen 3,6	"Ate" the fruit
Sight	Gen 3,7	"Eyes ... were opened"
Touch	Gen 3,7	"Knew" their nakedness
Hearing	Gen 3,8	"Heard the sound ... of God walking"

I-24 Progressive development of the human being's 9-fold nature charted through the present post-Atlantean Epoch

OH, Lect. 3; GSMk, Lect. 4; MTA, Lect. 11

As to the Mineral Physical Conditions of Earth evolution, we are now in the 5th "Evolutionary Epoch," namely, the post-Atlantean (see **I-1**), which is in turn divided into 7 Cultural Eras, of which we are also in the 5th, the one following the Greco-Roman (see **I-19**). Each aspect ("fold") of the 9-fold nature of the human being is the primary target for humanity's development through the post-Atlantean Epoch, as follows:

Atlantis	=	Physical body
Post-Atlantean:		
Indian	=	Etheric body
Persian	=	Sentient or Astral body
Chaldo-Egyptian	=	Sentient Soul
Greco-Roman	=	Intellectual or Mind Soul
Present	=	Spiritual or Consciousness Soul
6th Cultural Era	=	Manas or Spirit Self
7th Cultural Era	=	Buddhi or Life Spirit
After Catastrophe	=	Atma or Spirit Man

This is not to say that the development is completed during the indicated Cultural Era, for the human being will not attain to the state of manas or Spirit Self, proper, prior to the Jupiter Condition of Consciousness (see **I-1**), which is far in the future. Prior to the commencement of the Ego (soul) state in the Chaldo-Egyptian period, higher spiritual beings, in the state of atma (during the Indian Era) worked on the Etheric Body, and in the state of buddhi (during the Persian Era) worked on the astral body, and in the state of manas or "Manna" (during the Chaldo-Egyptian era, e.g., Ex 16,31; Num 11,7; Jn 6,31; 1 Cor 10,3; cf. Rev 2,17) worked on the Sentient Soul, for the Ego was not yet then strong enough to make itself felt independently, which became possible only during the Greco-Roman Era (the Christ era).

I-25 Relationship of the 7 "churches" of the Apocalypse to the 7 Cultural Eras of the post-Atlantean Epoch

ASJ, Lect. 3

The 7 "churches" of the Apocalypse are identified with the 7 Cultural Eras of the post-Atlantean Evolutionary Epoch (see **I-1** and **I-19**) as follows:

	"Church"	Cultural Era	Rev Ref.
1.	Ephesus	Indian	2,1-7
2.	Smyrna	Persian	2,8-11
3.	Pergamum	Chaldo-Egyptian	2,12-17
4.	Thyatira	Greco-Roman	2,18-29
5.	Sardis	Present (European)	3,1-6
6.	Philadelphia	6th (Slavic-Russian)	3,7-13
7.	Laodicea	7th (American)	3,14-22

I-26 The human being's 9-fold nature as related to its 9 septenaries (7-year periods) and their planetary correspondences

HA2, Chap. 7, esp. Fig. 16; KR-5, Chaps. 5, 6 and 7; BKM, Lect. 3

The nine 7-year periods ("Septenaries") of the human being's life, their relationship to the human being's 9-fold being, and their planetary correspondences are as follows:

Ages	9-Fold Being	Planet	Characteristic	Outer Manifes-tation
0- 7	Physical body	Moon	Will	Change of Teeth
7-14	Etheric body	Mercury	Intelligence	Puberty
14-21	Astral body	Venus	Love	Adulthood
21-28	Sentient Soul \			
28-35	Intelligence Soul -	Sun	Selfhood	
35-42	Consciousness / Soul		(Ego)	
42-49	Spirit Self	Mars	Speech	
49-56	Life Spirit	Jupiter	Thought	
56-63	Spirit Man	Saturn	Memory	

I-27 <u>Steiner's exposition on the organic order and character of the traditional planets; Powell's on the outer three planets</u>

HA2, Chap. 8; ISBM, Lect. 3

Modern minds will require us to treat of the outer planets, Uranus, Neptune and Pluto, which were not a part of the ancient cosmology in the same way as those within the orbit of Saturn. Steiner (ISBM, Lect. 3) said,

> In the numerous popular accounts of the origin of our planetary system one is first led back to a kind of original mist, to a vast fog-like structure, a nebula, out of which our sun and its planets have somehow agglomerated, although for the driving force in this process only physical forces, as a rule, are taken into account. This is called the "Kant-Laplace theory," though it is somewhat modified today.... The modified Kant-Laplace theory may definitely hold good as an external event, but within the whole forming of globes, within this whole crystallizing of the separate cosmic globes, spiritual forces and spiritual beings were at work....
>
> When our Earth came forth from the purely spiritual devachanic state and received for the first time a kind of externally perceptible existence, it was not like it is today. In fact, seen externally, it could really be pictured as a kind of great primordial nebula, as our physical science describes. Only we must think of this primordial mist as immense, far greater than the present earth, extending far beyond the outermost planets now belonging to our solar system—far beyond Uranus. To spiritual science what is seen coming forth from a spiritual condition is not merely a kind of physical mist. To describe it as a kind of mist and nothing more is about as sensible as if a man who has seen another should reply to a question as to what he saw: I saw muscles which are attached to bones and blood—simply describing the physical aspect. For in the primordial mist there were a multitude of spiritual forces and spiritual beings....
>
> When you add the fact that not only these various beings were united with the original nebula, but a whole series more, standing at very varied stages of evolution, then you will understand that not only these cosmic bodies, earth, sun, moon, separated from the nebula, but

other cosmic bodies too. Indeed they all agglomerated as separate globes because scenes of action had to be found for the varying stages of evolution of the different beings.

Thus there were beings at the very beginning of our Earth who were scarcely fitted to take part in further development, who were still so young in their whole evolution that any further step would have destroyed them. They had to receive a sphere of action, so to speak on which they could preserve their complete youthfulness. All other fields of action existed to give dwelling-places to those who were already more advanced. For the beings who arose last of all during the Moon existence, and who therefore had stayed behind at a very early evolutionary stage, a field of action had to be separated out. This scene of action was the cosmic body which we call "Uranus," and which therefore has but slight connection with our earthly existence. Uranus has become the theater for beings which had to remain at a very backward stage.

Then evolution proceeded. Apart from Uranus, all that forms our universe [*Ed.*, solar system] was contained in an original pap-like mass. Greek mythology calls this condition "Chaos." Then Uranus separated out, the rest remaining still in the Chaos.

The Kant-LaPlace theory still has considerable "scientific" validity. See 10 Brit 941, "solar nebula." Steiner does not mention Pluto, which was "scientifically" discovered in 1930. His above remarks leave room for it to have been in a pre-evolutionary mass in similar manner to Uranus (see AM, Lect. 1) and Neptune, a matter to which we shall return momentarily.

Steiner then says that the other "planets" separated out in the following order and character:

1. Saturn, for those beings who stood in their development at the stage we human beings stood at during Old Saturn (our present Saturn thus being the only planet to have any nominal connection with an earlier Condition of Consciousness);

2. Jupiter, for beings of "a certain stage of development";

3. Sun, for the most advanced beings, taking with it all but Earth and Moon (which remained together);

4. Mars, whose spiritual beings pulled away from the Sun and, in the process of reaching its outer orbit, passed through the (still joined) Earth and Moon, leaving behind what later developed into iron (a necessary component of human blood, which then came into existence, the fluid sap of living beings having theretofore been chlorophyll which contains no iron);

5. Moon, separating from Earth to remove retarded beings and permit the evolution of those beings (human) who remained, leaving Earth alone as it now is;

6. Venus and Mercury, for those Fire-Spirits (Archangels) who, though far above human beings, had not advanced far enough to endure the Sun existence, Mercury in the neighborhood of the Sun being the more advanced of the two and Venus between Mercury and Earth.

For the sake of visual clarification, Figure 20 from HA2 presents the heliocentric (Sun-centered) view of our solar system:

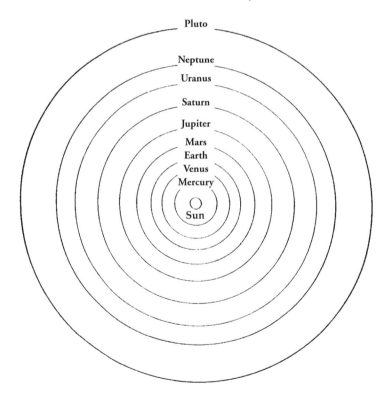

Returning to the 3 outer planets, Steiner clearly indicates that Uranus separated and that, as of that point, "all that forms our [solar system] was contained in an original pap-like mass." Assuming that Neptune had previously separated, it need not have been mentioned for the purposes of the human being's evolution through the 7 classical planetary states. As of the time he spoke (1908), Pluto had not been "scientifically" discovered, and the state of his teachings was still too preliminary to go into the detail of any outer planets. For this, however, we are beholden to his disciples whose teachings have, to a considerable extent, culminated in the works of Robert Powell.

Powell tells us, "According to Orphic cosmogony, a divine dynasty of six generations [of gods] are said to have held in turn the rule of the universe. These six are: Phanes, Night, Ouranos, Kronos, Zeus and Dionysos.... A series of *manvantaras*, or planetary periods [occurred], each drawing successively closer towards the Sun. The first ..., Phanes, took place within the orbit of Pluto ... the second ..., Night, ... within the orbit of Neptune," the third within the orbit of Uranus. In between each such manvantara, a period of cosmic rest (*pralaya*) occurred. During these 3 early manvantaras there were laid down the following respective elements:

Pluto	Life	(Primal love/will)
Neptune	Sound	(cosmic harmony)
Uranus	Light	(cosmic intelligence)

During these three manvantaras, however, the human being did not exist, not even in a rudimentary form. For this reason, [these] planets ... represent qualities that are superhuman ..., but which nevertheless pervade the cosmic existence in which the human being is embedded.

Powell described these 3 higher stages of consciousness in HA1, Chap. 4:

Lunar consciousness	Illumination
Solar consciousness	Inspiration
Zodiacal consciousness	Union (Intuition)

The fact that these states of consciousness are beyond the human being's present evolution is reflected in the physical sphere by the fact that these 3 planets are not visible to the naked eye, as are all the others.

In his Table 19 (see **I-17**), Powell gives the manvantaras of Orphic cosmology and the stages of human evolution:

Orbit of	Condition of Consciousness
1. Pluto (Phanes)	
2. Neptune (Night)	
3. Uranus (Ouranos)	
4. Saturn (Kronos)	Old Saturn
5. Jupiter (Zeus)	Old Sun
6. Mars (Dionysos)	Old Moon
7. Earth	Earth
8. Venus	(Future) Jupiter
9. Mercury	(Future) Venus
10. Sun	(Future) Vulcan

What, then, if anything, do Uranus, Neptune and Pluto have to do with the human being?

Whereas the Sun, Moon and 5 planets are incorporated into the human being's astral and etheric bodies via the lotus flowers and organs, respectively, Uranus, Neptune and Pluto work from beyond, at a level transcending normal human behavior. Just as there is an inherent polarity in all creation, so do these outer forces call the human being's higher self as follows:

Uranus	cosmic intelligence
Neptune	cosmic harmony
Pluto	cosmic life

But at the same time these represent forces of hindrance, for they have become *trapped* as negative forces within the interior of the Earth, and are now being released through technology for technological progress, posing grave dangers to the future of humanity and planet Earth through their release. The discoveries of these 3 planets are linked in a remarkable way with the discoveries of forces (see **I-22**) connected with them:

Uranus discovered in 1781—Galvani in 1780 began experiments leading to discovery of *electricity*, which is essentially *trapped light*;

Neptune discovered in 1846—Faraday in 1845 concluded that all matter must contain *magnetism*, which is essentially *trapped sound*;

Pluto discovered in 1930—in 1932 came artificial splitting of the lithium nucleus by neutron bombardment, leading to discovery of *atomic power*, which is essentially *trapped life*.

The classical planets are connected with cosmic forces that have densified in the Earth to become the following metals (see also HI, Lect. 9, OP, Lect. 8 and AOMR, p. 30):

Saturn	Lead
Jupiter	Tin
Mars	Iron
Venus	Copper
Mercury	Quicksilver (Mercury)
Sun	Gold
Moon	Silver

In the same way, the transcendental planets that have densified have become trapped within the interior of the Earth as follows:

Uranus	Electricity
Neptune	Magnetism
Pluto	Atomic Power

The polarities involved, depending upon the human being's moral development, or lack thereof, are:

Trapped Light	(Electricity)	Illumination
Trapped Sound	(Magnetism)	Inspiration
Trapped Life	(Atomic Power?)	Intuition (Union)

I-28 The interior of the Earth

EC, Lect. 16; AGSS, Lect. 14; DCOM; ASOT, Chap. 7, Sec. 1

Just as the human being is 9-fold (**I-9**), so also is the Earth. While modern Christianity plays down the early church concept of Christ's descent to the underworld (see 2 ABD 156), we will consider its significance herein. Steiner concludes EC, Lect. 16 with the following diagram:

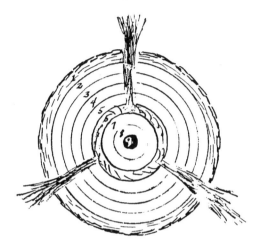

THE INTERIOR OF THE EARTH

1. Mineral crust
2. Negative life
3. Inverted consciousness
4. Circle of forms
5. Circle of growth
6. Circle of fire
7. Circle of decomposition
8. Circle of fragmentation
9. Ego-centric-egoism

I-29 Elements or events in which the Hierarchies manifest during Earth evolution

GEN, Lects. 6 and 8; UEM, Lect. 4; MFS, Lect. 5; see also **I-22**:

This chart attempts to identify the elements or events in which the 9 Hierarchies respectively manifest during Earth evolution. The identifications clearly indicated by Steiner's lectures are set out in bold print, while those based upon inference are in normal print. Inference is used for the Dynamis and Kyriotetes, and to some extent also for the Thrones, although in the case of the latter, Steiner clearly says that during Earth evolution they manifest in the element of solids. Because of the implications of **I-22**, I have also inferred that in relation to the Seraphim and Cherubim, the Thrones may represent the polarity of the terrible forces of destruction. With such admonition, this inference seems justified to complete the picture. Accordingly:

Spiritual Being	Manifestation	Supporting Reference
Seraphim	**Lightning**	GEN, Lects. 6 & 8
	Fire	MFS, Lect. 5
Cherubim	**Clouds**	GEN, Lects. 6 & 8
	Air (Wind)	MFS, Lect. 5
Thrones	**Solid matter/**	GEN, Lects. 6 & 8;
Thrones	Fission-Fusion	**I-22**
Kyriotetes	Life (Ether)	**I-22**
Dynamis	Chemical/Sound	
	(Ether)	**I-22**
Exusiai	**Light** (Ether)	UEM, Lect. 4
Archai	**Fire**	UEM, Lect. 4
Archangels	**Air (Wind)**	UEM, Lect. 4
Angels	**Water**	UEM, Lect. 4

An example of how one might think Steiner sometimes contradicts himself can be seen in BL where (p. 11) he says, "in reality the Spirits of Wisdom [Kyriotetes, above, or Dominions] manifest themselves through the light, which the ancient religion considered to be the garment of wisdom." However, in UEM, Lect. 4, we are told that the Spirits of Wisdom were in command during Old Sun evolution just as the Exusiai are in command of Earth evolution (see **I-16**). This gives them a connection with light, which in a sense is supernal or ancestral to the light manifested during Earth evolution, and is compatible with their earthly manifestation in the Life Ether (as above) since even our scientists tell us that all life on Earth must come from the Sun.

I-30 Levels of consciousness during Chaldo-Egyptian Cultural Era

HA1, Chap. 4

Three levels of consciousness were reflected among the peoples of the Chaldo-Egyptian Cultural Era:

Babylonian	Lunar Consciousness
Egyptian	Solar Consciousness
Israelite	Zodiacal Consciousness

The Babylonian calendar was lunar, its days starting at sunset. The Egyptian calendar was solar, its days starting at sunrise. Israel brought in the "sacrifice of the Ram" (Gen 22,13) and the 12 tribes, both reflecting the zodiacal.

I-31 Stages of consciousness

HA1, Chap. 5; HA2, Chap. 8

The stages of spiritual consciousness may be described as follows:

Type	Perception	Per Plato	Per Steiner
Terrestrial	No Perception	—	—
Lunar	Seeing	Doxa	Imagination
Solar	Hearing	Dianoia	Inspiration
Zodiacal	Touching (Understanding/ Certainty)	Episteme	Intuition

"Doxa" is hypothetical knowledge; "Dianoia" is a greater degree of knowing supported by logical arguments and supporting facts; "Episteme" is 100% certainty which cannot exist short of zodiacal consciousness.

A human being's incarnation process is a kind of recap of the stages of evolution:

Period	Recapped in	Develops
Saturn	Zodiac	Archetype of Phys. Body; Image (zodiacal man)
Sun	Planetary	Astral body; Likeness (hermetic man)
Moon	Conception/ Birth	Etheric body; per 10 lunar orbits of sidereal zodiac (**I-86**)
Earth	Birth/Death	Physical body

I-32 Lucifer and Ahriman

LA; Jn-Rel, Lect. 5; AD; BWM; DCOSP

Two Biblical terms, "Devil" (diablos) and "Satan" (satan), are generally considered virtually interchangeable, and not without some superficial justification in scripture itself, but in esotericism they have quite different meanings, which are polar opposites but which work together for an evil result so that in the popular mind (as well, perhaps, as in that of the scribes preceding even our earliest extant manuscripts) they are indistinguishable. Ahriman was first recognized by Zarathustra (1 Brit 168, "Ahriman"). In Goethe's *Faust* he is known as "Mephistopheles." Steiner says this is a term derived from two Hebrew words, "Mephiz" (Corrupter) and "Topel" (Liar). Anthroposophy makes a clear distinction: "Devil" equals "Lucifer" and "Satan" equals "Ahriman." Hardly any anthroposophical work can be found that has no reference to a "Luciferic" or an "Ahrimanic" influence. Consequently, neither the references cited above nor the illustrative characteristics listed below can be considered all-inclusive. They are given only as a bare indication of the influence or reflection of each:

Lucifer	Ahriman	Ref.
Tendency to spiritualize	Tendency to materialize	
Force	Matter	KM
Fallen Archangels	Fallen Archai	See Below
Electricity, or fallen light ether	Magnetism, or fallen chemical ether	**I-22**
False motive	Belief in chance	MK
Serpent	Beast	Gen,Rev
False spiritualization	Reliance upon physical world	
Inner conceit	Illusions about external world	MK
Circulatory System	Nervous System	BWM

It has been deceptively difficult to characterize these beings as to the Hierarchy from which each "fell." It seems clear that Lucifer fell during Ancient Moon and Ahriman during Ancient Sun, but their actual rank, the Condition of Consciousness during which they had attained the "human" stage (see **I-15**), is deemed to be the preceding Condition in each case. Thus, Ahriman is from the rank of the Archai (see *The Apocalypse* [APOC-CC], Lects. 11 and 18), which attained this status on Ancient Saturn though he appears to have fallen during Ancient Sun (*Manifestations of Karma* [MK], Lect. 7, pp. 166-167). Since Lucifer appears (MK) to have fallen during Ancient Moon, it would seem that he belongs to the rank of Archangels, which attained "human" status during Ancient Sun (**I-15**). This would accord with his desire to implant "Light," for the controlling Hierarchy of the Sun Condition was the Spirits of Wisdom (**I-16**), and he was able to fight on somewhat the same plateau as the Archangel Michael.

I-33 Course of the Ego between death and rebirth; Regions of soul and spirit worlds

OS; THSY; LBDR; RE, Lects 4 and 5; TIEC, Lect. 5; MTA, Lect. 13; MM, Lect. Two; DCOM; HoP, Sec. 5; BDR, Lect. Ten; PSI, Lect. 6; EVC, Lect. 10; HSBA, App. 5; CTK; ORL, Lect. 1

To understand the hidden reflection (as we shall see elsewhere herein) in numerous Biblical passages of the course taken by a human being between death and rebirth, a tabulation is given here of the progressive stages of that journey. First a brief recap of fundamentals is set out.

Component of Human Being	Essential Nature of Component
Ego	Lasting or eternal Individuality
Astral body	Seat of consciousness, passions and desires
Etheric (Life) Body	Seat of life
Physical Body	Seat of, or pattern for, mineral accumulation

State of Consciousness	Components joined
Waking	Ego and all 3 bodies, i.e., astral, etheric (life) & physical
Sleeping	Etheric (life) and physical (the astral & Ego separating therefrom)
Death	Physical, the minerals of which, absent life body, proceed to disintegrate (the Ego and astral & etheric bodies having separated)

Course of the Ego between Death and Rebirth

1. Etheric world, for approximately 3 days, during which the etheric body remains attached with the astral body and Ego permitting a panaramic review, in reverse, of the life just past.

2. Astral world, for approximately 1/3 the length of the person's life (equal to the time spent sleeping), during which the Ego remains attached with the astral body. This is the period of purification, or burning fire, known in the Roman Church as Purgatory, also sometimes in anthroposophy as "the soul world," and in Eastern religions as "kamaloca." The attachment of the Ego and astral body permits a review, also in reverse, of the life just past, actually of what is experienced during sleeping periods (nightly reviews beyond waking consciousness) by the Ego and astral bodies during that life; characteristic of this review is placement in the position of those with whom one dealt, in the sense of Mt 7,12 (the Golden Rule).

3. Spiritland, or "Devachan" as it is known in Eastern terminology, which can be entered only after all desires and passions have been eliminated in the astral world. The only component that can enter here is the Ego itself, along with the part of its 3 "bodies" (astral, etheric and physical) that the Ego has been able to convert to the respective higher 3 spiritual components of the future, i.e., manas (Spirit Self), buddhi (Life Spirit) and atma (Spirit Man). The Ego's consciousness during its sojourn in Spiritland is dependent upon the extent to which it has perfected its "Three Bodies," but only manas (the purified astral body) can meaningfully be developed during Earth evolution; consider here the parable in Mt 13,33, "The kingdom of heaven (is) like leaven which a woman hid in three measures of flour, till it was all leavened."

4. "Cosmic midnight" when the Ego has ended its spiritual ascent and begins its descent to another incarnation for the purpose of, and resolved toward, further perfection (Mt 5,48).

5. The Descent, which retraces the stages of the ascent, during which the elements of one's "Three Bodies" are formed, including finally the choice of time, place and parentage, from what is then available on Earth.

Pathway of the Ego's Course Through the Heavens

	Stage of Ego's Journey	Space Into which Ego Expands
1.	Etheric World	Proximity of Earth and Physical Body
2.	Astral World	Orbit of Moon (though both Mercury and Venus orbits have both astral and spiritual character)
3.	Lower Devachan	Successive spheres reaching out to the "planets" in the order of their distance from the Earth (remembering that in times past occultism reversed the order of Venus and Mercury), thus, the Mercury sphere, Venus sphere, Sun sphere, Mars sphere, Jupiter sphere and Saturn sphere
4.	Higher Devachan	Zodiacal sphere, among the stars of the 12 formative constellations.

Nature of the 7 Regions of the Astral (Soul) World

	Soul World Region	Earthly Counterpart
1.	Burning Desire	Solid physical bodies
2.	Mobile Sensitivity	Liquids
3.	Wishes	Gases
4.	Liking and Disliking	Warmth
5.	Soul Light	Light (Ether)
6.	Active Soul Force	Sound (or Chemical, Ether)
7.	Soul Life	Life (Ether)

Nature of the 7 Regions of Devachan (Spiritland)

	Spiritland Region	Form it Assumes on Earth
1.	"Solid Land"	Physical
2.	"Oceans & Rivers & Blood Circulation"	Life
3.	"Atmosphere"	Sensation—Raging Tempest/ Battlefield
4.	"Warmth"	Thought
5.	"Light"	Wisdom

6. & 7. See Note immediately below

Note—In OS, Chap. 3, where the above is related, Steiner says of Regions 6 and 7, "descriptions will be found in a later part of this work." It is not totally clear to what he was referring, but presumably it was to what is implied in Chap. 6 dealing with the future Jupiter and Venus Conditions of Consciousness. Inasmuch as they will not mature during Earth evolution, it would have been inappropriate for him to designate a form for their earthly manifestation. Inasmuch, however, as Region 5 ("Light") dealt with the first ether, it would seem that Regions 6 and 7 would deal with Sound and Life Ether, respectively. We shall see, indeed, that the Biblical passages first referred to appear only to go through these first 5 stages applicable to Earth evolution.

I-34 The stages of universal evolution

ISBM, Lect. 2

Everything in the universe is connected. The stages of universal evolution from bottom to top are:

1. Planetary
2. Fixed Star (Solar)
3. Zodiacal
4. Sacrifice (to give birth to Planetary, as in Old Saturn)

Macrocosmically, the "heavenly ladder" of Gen 28,12 speaks of the fact that zodiacal forces "rain" down continuously into planetary existence, first descending, then ascending. When a planetary existence starts, there are no ascending zodiacal forces but all descend. At midpoint they are in balance (Libra = scales, the midpoint in Earth's Planetary existence—see **I-18**). Since the middle of the Atlantean Age (**I-1**), or the middle of Earth evolution, there are now 7 ascending forces (constellations) and 5 descending, as follows:

Ascending	Descending
Aries	Scorpio
Taurus	Sagittarius
Gemini	Capricorn
Cancer	Aquarius
Leo	Pisces
Virgo	
Libra	

When, at the end of the Venus evolution (in the Vulcan Condition), the Earth itself will have become a Sun (Fixed Star), there will no longer be any descending forces; all will be ascending.

Our "Zodiac," and indeed the universe of heavenly bodies as they exist today, came into being as a part of this evolutionary procedure. What today permeates all beings as warmth is known in occultism as "fire." An "ocean of flame" had arisen through the Sacrificial stage of the prior planetary existence, and from this ocean arose the constellations of our "Zodiac" as they are today—but they were not the same during the Saturn existence. Everything that is contained in the zodiacal stage is under the sign of "duration," whereas all comprised within planetary existence is under the sign of "time." Not even the farthest reaches of the mind can conceive of changes having taken place in the Zodiac, because they are not measured in terms of "time." Forces working in the Zodiac remain, relatively speaking, fixed and permanent, but these concepts are only relative. Planetary existence belongs to the sphere of the finite, zodiacal to that of infinitude—relatively speaking, but for our purposes sufficiently accurate.

A being who has just passed the midpoint of equilibrium in the receiving of zodiacal forces, where the ascending is just beginning to preponderate, is said to have an Ego. It is this condition that permits something to begin working from within, so that a receiving creature begins to radiate life into the universe. This is reflected in the Biblical account from beginning to end. But it is apparent that even in the middle of the Atlantean evolution the stage had just begun where the Ego could start to emerge in rudimentary form from its prior group nature. It is not possible to understand the force of Ego development without knowing its relationship to the forces of the Zodiac and the Christ force, the Sacrificial Lamb, which stands above them (see **I-18**).

I-35 The hierarchical sacrifices and the approach and entry of the human being's Ego

ISBM, Lects. 3 and 4

We have already seen, in **I-27**, the order in which the "planets" of our solar system separated from the original "pap-like mass." When the Sun separated (along with what later became Mars, Venus and Mercury) from the Earth-Moon mass, the exalted spiritual beings who led the Sun (Sun-beings) were the Exusiai (Gk) or Elohim (Heb) or Spirits of Form (Steiner). They were 7 in number (or groups), of whom Yahweh was the most exalted. When needed by humanity later, spiritual forces caused the Moon to separate from the Earth, at which time Yahweh left the domain of the Sun and took abode on the Moon. The Moon-forces, under Yahweh's leadership, as a Spirit of Form, give the human being form; forces that give form proceed from the Moon, while those that continually alter the form proceed from the Sun; thus, the development of the Ego-human being had to proceed from the Moon (Yahweh) because it involves consciousness of self which can only come from separation, which in turn can only come from the development of form. Hence, one begins to come to an understanding of how compelling is the interpretation and meaning of Ex 3,14, "I AM the I AM."

These Spirits of Form (Exusiai or Elohim) have played an important part from the beginning of the human being's evolution. They stand 4 levels above the human being in the Hierarchies. This means that during Earth evolution the lowest element of their 7-fold being would be Spirit Self in the human being, the stage just higher than the Ego. We saw, in **I-15** the evolutionary stage at which the 3 intervening Hierarchies (Angels, Archangels and Archai) attained their "human" or Ego status. Consistent with this pattern, we can thus see from an inspection of the **I-18** chart that on Old Saturn the Spirits of Form (Elohim) had no physical body, their lowest being the etheric. On Saturn, they "rayed in fructifying life-saps" and the warmth substance rayed these back again, giving "mirror-pictures," thus even then giving the human being a "likeness" (Gen 1,26) of its Godhead.

On Old Sun the Elohim no longer need the etheric body, which they relinquish to the human being, endowing its physical body with an etheric body, a portion of that given up by the Elohim. This advance from Saturn to Sun is portrayed by the ancient Greek myth of Gaea (Saturn) and atmosphere Chronos. The lowest member of the Elohim on Old Sun is now the astral body, which manifests through the raying of instincts, desires and passions (of a higher nature). The myth of the Titans relates to this astral event.

On Old Moon, the Elohim lay aside their astral body, relinquishing it to the human being, so that their Ego is their lowest member. On Old Moon these Elohim have only pure Egos. On Old Moon, all that we call "human being" has gradually flowed down out of its environment, from the outside, not from within it.

In Earth evolution, the Elohim sacrifice the lowest body they had on Old Moon, their Ego, to the human being, and thus the human being is able for the first time to take within itself something for further development, its own Ego. The lowest member the Elohim, namely Yahweh at this point, have is Spirit Self, or manas (which in the Bible is called Manna). From this we see the significance not only of the bringing and giving of "the I Am" in Ex 3,14, but also of the coming of the scriptural Manna (Ex 16, Num 11, et al.) and of the statement by Christ that the kingdom is now to be found "within" the human being (Lk 17,21).

The approach and entry of this Ego into the human being during Earth evolution is shown in the following table (see diagram in "Naked"):

Period	Ego penetrates	Creating
Lemuria	Astral body	Sentient Soul
1st 2/3 Atlantis	Etheric body	Intellectual Soul
Last 1/3 Atlantis	Physical body	Consciousness Soul
Golgotha Deed	Works on Astral	Manas
Golgotha Deed	Works on Etheric	Buddhi

While Christ's Deed on Golgotha made it possible for the human being to develop both its manas and buddhi, the wisdom that is all around us, e.g., in a piece of the thigh bone, manifests the manasic nature of the lowest member of the Yahweh being.

I-36 Powell's "birth chart"

HA1, Table 10, p. 184

In this remarkable work and its sequel, HA2, Robert Powell demonstrates by verifiable examples the influence of the heavenly bodies in the area of reincarnation. He gives three levels of what he calls "the birth chart," as follows:

Level	Astrological Designation	Corresponding to	Centered in
house system	wheel of life	etheric body	Earth (life body)
geocentric chart (Earth centered)	map of the soul	astral body (vehicle of soul)	Moon
hermetic chart (heliocentric)	map of the the spirit	spirit-Individuality (vehicle of spirit)	Sun

It is helpful to consider that the "geocentric" chart is a lunar, or "Moon's eye," view, while the "hermetic" chart is a solar, or "Sun's eye," view but with the Earth as the Sun since the time of Christ's (earthly) Incarnation.

I-37 Relationship of "healing" to the different "bodies" and "kingdoms"

MK, Lects 3, 6 and 10

As implied by its very name, "Anthroposophy" or "Anthropo-Sophia," i.e., "human being-wisdom," no aspect of humanity's being or existence is beyond the reach of anthroposophy, including medicine and the healing arts. Steiner often lectured just to medical personnel, as he did freely with all disciplines afforded by time and interest. Pertinences are littered throughout his lectures and writings. One cannot have failed to observe them in passing through this Charts & Tabulations section, as, for instance, in **I-14** and **I-20**. Some works by other anthroposophical writers in the Bibliography are also illustrative, e.g., AAM, Vols 1-3, AAC, AOMR, CMHm, EB; and the latest complete catalogue from the Anthroposophic Press will always list numerous others.

A purely physical body, e.g., a stone or a corpse, is unable to heal itself or to repair an injury, hence we cannot even speak in this case of disease and healing. Above that level, however, we generally have to look for the principle of inner healing power in the etheric body. The following chart illustrates the period necessary for the etheric body to heal the physical when, for instance, it is externally mutilated:

Bodies	Kingdom	Period Necessary for Etheric to Heal Physical
Physical	Mineral	None—no healing occurs
Phys + Etheric	Plant	Quickly, depending upon nature of plant, i.e., perennial, tree, etc.
Phys + Etheric + Astral	Animal / \	Triton—little pain, prompt replacement Crab—next casting off of shell Mammal—Pain, but healing is in offspring
Phys + Eth + Ast + Ego	Human	Pain, but healing is in next life

One obvious question immediately arises. Why is healing in the offspring of a mammal and in the next life of the human? Short of referring to the Basic Anthroposophy books, the answer lies in the locus of the Ego (see **I-11**). Animals do not reincarnate, for the locus of their Ego "is not in this world."

Another question (which incidentally seems to have obvious implications for the "scientific" practice of experimentally testing drugs for human application by first applying them to animals) is, How is it that as we rise higher in the animal and human kingdoms, we find that the healing forces of the etheric body have to make greater efforts to manifest themselves? This depends upon the fact that the etheric body is bound to the physical body in very different ways as we progress up the ladder. The lower we go (including the plant kingdom), the looser is the connection between physical and etheric. At the lower level, the union is such that the physical body is unable to react upon the etheric body, and the latter remains untouched. The nature of the etheric body is that of activity, generation and growth. The more intimate the union between physical and etheric, as we progress up the ladder, the more the forces of the physical react upon the etheric body. An injury to the physical body is thus simultaneously an injury to the etheric body. But the higher we go, the more do we also have to bring into consideration, not only the activity of the etheric and physical bodies, but also that of the astral body (the seat of pain, passion, etc.). Where an astral body is active, external impressions are reflected into the inner experiences. The more active the astral body is, the more a being opens itself to the external world, and the increasing activity of this body causes the etheric body to have to use much stronger forces to make injuries good. If we then pass from animals to the human being, we bring in the matter of the incarnated Ego and the ability to distinguish good from evil. Through purely individual motives the Ego comes into touch with the world in various ways, making various impressions upon the astral body, which in turn acts upon the etheric body. Both now suffer these reactions. In the journey of a human being between death and rebirth (see **I-33**), an extract of the etheric body is left over on the ascent and picked up again on the descent, so that in the new existence the results of the prior experience is present in the etheric body, which imprints it upon the physical body also. The same extract principle applies also to the astral body, but we are so built that while emotions and attitudes may relate to prior lives, normal consciousness does not extend from one life to another (Eccles 1,11 and 3,11).

In the case of the human being, matters of healing become extremely complex, for they relate, in the case of general health and disease, and even in case of external accident, to prior lives, and we begin to see how some things can be healed in this life and some cannot but must have their consequence in another. Anthroposophy goes into great detail on these, but we cannot go into it here.

The ability of the human Ego to work upon, "heal," the lower bodies in one lifetime is progressively less as one descends from astral to etheric to physical, somewhat like the way the hands of a clock affect each other. This brings us to the relationship of pain to serious illness in regard to the astral and etheric bodies. We may state it thus:

Health   =   Sleeping of astral (pain-free) and etheric bodies (as well as physical, which always sleeps)

Illness   =   Awakening of astral body (pain)

Serious
Illness   =   Awakening of etheric body (pain-free);

Death   =   Awakening of physical body, i.e., the phantom, form, or resurrection body, absent its mineral accumulation (remembering that a distinction must be made between the physical and mineral bodies—see **I-1**, Condition of Life versus Condition of Form)

Thus our most deadly illnesses, such as malignancy and heart disease, do not identify their onset with pain, and are more difficult to cure in one lifetime.

While it can only be hinted at here, there is a relationship between the locus of the illness and where the cure is to be sought, as follows:

Illness	Cure
Astral body	Animal kingdom
Etheric body	Plant kingdom
Physical body	Mineral kingdom

I-38 Significant characteristics, powers and perceptions of the magi, shepherds and prophets relating to the Nativity

SIS, Lect 3; Mt 2,1-12; Lk 2,8-20; Isaiah through Malachi

In the Nativity accounts, we have three groups of persons who displayed unusual powers of perception, the magi, the shepherds and the prophets. The following table sets out some of their significant characteristics, powers and perceptions:

<u>Magi</u>	<u>Shepherds</u>
Starry heavens	Earth's depths
Mineral world	Human soul
Plant world	Animal life
Prenatal faculties	After-death faculties
Intellect	Will
\	/

Prophets

I-39 <u>Genealogies from David to Jesus</u>

Mt 1,6-17; Lk 3,23-31

According to these Gospel accounts, the lines of descent from David to Jesus, with points of departure at the level of David's son, were as follows:

<u>Gospel of Matthew</u>	<u>Gospel of Luke</u>
David	David
Solomon	**Nathan**
Rehoboam	Mattatha
Abijah	Menna
Asa	Melea
Jehoshaphat	Eliakim
Joram	Jonam
Uzziah	Joseph
Jotham	Judah
Ahaz	Simeon
Hezekiah	Levi
Manasseh	Matthat
Amos	Jorim
Josiah	Eliezer
	Joshua
Jechoniah	Er
Shealtiel	Elmadam
Zerubbabel	Cosam

Abiud	Addi
Eliakim	Melchi
Azor	Neri
Zadok	Shealtiel
Achim	Zerubabbel
Eliud	Rhesa
Eleazar	Joanan
Matthan	Joda
Jacob	Josech
Joseph	Semein
Jesus	Mattathias
	Maath
	Naggai
	Esli
	Nahum
	Amos
	Mattathias
	Joseph
	Jannai
	Melchi
	Levi
	Matthat
	Heli
	Joseph
	Jesus

Total $2 \times 14 = 28$ $42 + 1 = 43$

Knowledge of the significance of the distinction between these 2 totally different genealogies was lost to Christianity early in the post-Christian era, to be regained only through the insights of Rudolf Steiner and anthroposophy. Consequently the genealogies are ignored by today's theology as inconsequential mumblings, but today's theology does not understand the nature of the incarnation of Christ. It is critical that this be remedied, and that the insights of anthroposophy gain a hold within humanity if its salvation is to be accomplished.

I-40 <u>The relationships between thinking, feeling and willing and birth,</u>
<u>death and rebirth</u>

SM, Lects. 2, 4 and 5

This chart can barely hint at all that underlies it in the lectures. I debated including it, yielding only to the feeling that it betrays a pearl of great value. Its scope includes the befuddling subject of psychology, upon which the insights of anthroposophy are badly needed (as with most other disciplines).

Steiner says the famous "I think therefore I am" is one of the greatest errors of (then) recent philosophy, for thinking is not the "sum" but the "non-sum" of the "I Am." Certainly this accords with Paul (1 Cor 13,8-9). Steiner has so thoroughly elsewhere shown that thinking is circumstantial evidence of the existence of the "I Am," that his statement could not be pejorative.

Already it has been said that the 3 areas of human activity are thinking, feeling and willing. Steiner here reasonably identifies thinking, or mental picturing, as an image activity. The Eloha (i.e., Spirit of Form, Exusiai) Yahweh identifies itself, of course, to Moses as "the I AM" (Ex 3,14), and in Gen 1,26 the Elohim purport to make the human being in their "image." We thus have a scriptural basis for seeing in the human being's thinking something that is brought into its existence from the prenatal aspect. Mental picturing is an image of all the experiences gone through before one's birth, and the process cannot be understood unless one is clear on this. And just as mirror images (1 Cor 13,12) are spatial, so one's life between death and rebirth is reflected in time between birth and death, as Steiner's drawing (the first of three) depicts:

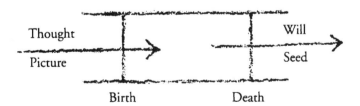

The wise sage (Eccles 3,11) depicted this so well: "He has put eternity into the human being's mind, yet so that he cannot find out what God has done from the beginning to the end." This becomes quite clear when one realizes that the "He" of whom the sage speaks is Yahweh who identified himself as the "I Am." Thus, the "I Am" has put into our minds what they give us. Human beings today subconsciously fear to face this truth because they conceive of the "I Am" as a monstrous egoism, but they have not recognized its significance, nor will they until the perfection (Mt 5,48) of the great "I Am" in Christ is accepted as their standard. It is this human beings shy away from, while still purporting to proclaim him (Mt 7,21). Not until humanity comes to recognize its own individual and collective responsibility (Mt 5,25-26) imposed by "the law" (Mt 5,17) of karma can it find its way toward what is its ultimate destiny if its salvation is to be attained.

Steiner next investigates the activity of the human being's will in the same way. Psychologists, he says, always find the content of will as coming from mental picturing, conscious or subconscious. But Steiner says that will has no real content of its own, for it is nothing else but the "Seed" in us of what after death will be reality of spirit and soul (see above diagram). Thus, while mental picturing is an image from prenatal life, will is the "Seed" of something that appears later. A "Seed" is something more than real, and an image is something less than real; a "Seed" does not become real until later, though it carries within it the germ of what will appear later as reality, so that the will is indeed of a very spiritual nature. (One should bear in mind that Steiner elsewhere says that most of the normal person's will actions are not subject to one's consciousness, though they are nevertheless one's own actions.) Thus far, we have divided the human being's soul life into thinking (mental picturing) and willing, which is in the nature of a "Seed." Between these lies a boundary, which is the whole life of the physical human being (see above diagram) who reflects back the prenatal as mental pictures, and who does not allow the will to fulfill itself, thereby keeping it continuously as nothing more than "Seed."

Now we come to feeling, the third area of human activity, and this Steiner divides into antipathy and sympathy (with indifference lying in between as the absence of feeling). If we encounter some person, philosophy, or what not, for the first time, we may respond in one of three ways, namely, with sympathy, antipathy or indifference. Indifference

suggests no prenatal connection (though it may entail future consequence). We must be clear that certain forces in the human being reflect
back the prenatal reality and hold the after-death reality in "Seed,"
namely, antipathy and sympathy. When we incarnate, by entering the
physical world we cannot remain in the spiritual world. In being brought
down into the physical world we develop an antipathy for everything
spiritual so that we radiate back the spiritual, prenatal reality in an antipathy of which we are unconscious. Thereby we transform the prenatal element into a mere mental picture or image (thought). On the contrary, we
unite ourselves in sympathy with what radiates out toward our later existence as the reality of will after death. We create the "Seed" of soul life as
a rhythm of sympathy and antipathy.

The first diagram can now be brought forward as follows:

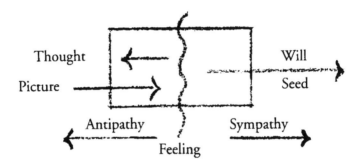

What is rayed back in antipathy is the whole of the prenatal experiences, which has the character of cognition. In coming up against antipathy, cognition is thereby reduced to mental picturing. Our mental
picture must, in a measure, correspond to the force that has remained in
us from the prenatal experience. If that prenatal experience, and consequent antipathy, is sufficiently strong, a memory image arises. Memory
is only heightened antipathy. When, along with memory, the image element is held fast, the concept arises, thus completing the side of the soul's
activity connected with prenatal life.

Now we go over to the Willing/"Seed" side, taking up first the feeling
of sympathy. Just as our thinking depends upon antipathy, so our willing
depends on sympathy. If sympathy is sufficiently strong, as with the
antipathy that becomes not only mental picture but also memory, then

out of sympathy arises imagination (a form of picturing). And if imagination is sufficiently strong (which is only unconscious in ordinary life), to permeate the being right down into the senses, then one gets the ordinary picture forms through which mental pictures of outer things arise (such as the whiteness of chalk). All of this starts in the will.

The being of the human being cannot be comprehended unless one understands the difference between sympathy and antipathy in the human being. Everything pertaining to the soul is expressed and revealed in the body, where its antipathy/thinking element is bound up with the nervous system. Antipathy, memory and concept from pre-natal life form the nervous system in this life. Thus, all talk of classifying nerves as sensory and motor is meaningless, which Steiner has also expressed in other contexts. Similarly, the activities of willing, sympathy, imagination and outer picture-forming are all bound to the "Seed" condition, which can never come to completion but must perish at the moment it arises, for it has to remain a "Seed," losing itself in its bodily nature in the form of "Blood." "Blood" is a "very special fluid," which would whirl away as spirit if we were able to remove it from the human body so that it still remained "Blood" and was not destroyed by other physical agencies—an impossibility while bound to earthly conditions. Because of this, "Blood" has to be destroyed to keep it from whirling away as spirit. For this reason we have perpetually within us both formation and destruction of "Blood" through in-breathing and out-breathing. "Blood" wants to become ever more spiritual, nerve ever more material.

Steiner tabulates both sides of these soul and bodily processes as follows:

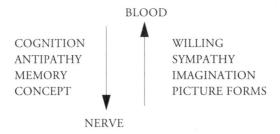

He goes on in this Lect. 2 to explain how the processes of antipathy and sympathy find expression in the body, as a reflection of the cosmos, but we will not presently venture further into that.

In Lect. 4, we are told how the will works in the three bodily principles, as follows:

Body	How Will Works
Physical	Instinct
Etheric	Impulse
Astral	Desire

Having now shown the nature of the three soul activities, thinking,
feeling and willing, we are told, in Lect. 4, and readily recognize, that
they flow into each other, merge and interpenetrate. Between thinking
on the one hand and willing on the other, we find the activity of feeling.
We can say that from a certain central boundary all that is sympathy/will-
ing and all that is antipathy/thinking stream forth. But then we see that
sympathy/willing works back into thinking, and antipathy/thinking
works over into willing. The human being is thus a unity because these
principles play over into each other, and between them lies feeling, which
is related to both. In soul life, one cannot keep thinking and willing
strictly apart, and even less can each be separated from feeling. We come
then to the third and last diagram:

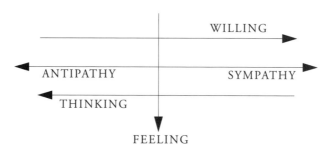

I-41 Thinking, feeling and willing: the nature of their manifestation,
karma and forces

FE, Lect. 21

Manifestation	Event	Karma	Forces (see **I-4**)
Physical Plane	Deeds	Form	Arupa Plane
Astral Plane	Feelings	Opportunities	Rupa Plane
Devachan Plane	Thoughts	Character	Astral Plane

I-42 <u>Wisdom, Beauty and Strength—meaning</u>

FE, Lect. 22; Jn-Rel, Lect. 2; JTC, Lect. 8

Human life is a continuous process of being enveloped in what surrounds us: Involution—Evolution. The part of us that we gain for ourselves from the outside world is immortal. We have come into being through the world and are beginning to build up in ourselves the mirror of a new world. The highest degree of perfection that we have put out from ourselves, that we have established around us, this we shall take with us. Therefore the Rosicrucians said: "Form the world in such a way that it contains within itself Wisdom, Beauty and Strength; then Wisdom, Beauty and Strength will be reflected into us." Thus,

Wisdom	into	Manas
Beauty (including Piety & Goodness)	into	Buddhi
Strength	into	Atma

Such is the assertion of Lk 2,52, "And Jesus increased in wisdom and in stature, and in favor with God and man" (RSV).

I-43 <u>Atlantean and Aryan "sub-races"</u>

FE, Lect. 24 and Glossary

In Eastern occultism, the 7 main epochs of the Condition of Form in Earth evolution were (see **I-1** through **I-3**): 1. Polarian, 2. Hyperborean, 3. Lemurian, 4. Atlantean, 5. Aryan (post-Atlantean; i.e., "of Aries," see **I-18**), and the following two are always called the 6th and 7th Root Races. The "sub-races" within the Atlantean and Aryan epochs are as follows:

	<u>Atlantean</u>	<u>Aryan</u>
1.	Rmoahals	(Old) Indian
2.	Tlavtlis	(Old) Persian
3.	Toltecs	Chaldo-Egyptian
4.	Turanians (Original)	Greco-Roman
5.	Semites (Original)	Germanic
6.	Akkadians	Slavic
7.	Mongols	Anglo-American

I-44 The Conditions of Consciousness planetary evolutions

FE, Lect. 24

The purpose of the various single planetary evolutions is to develop successive Conditions of Consciousness (**I-1** through **I-3**) as follows:

Planetary Evolution	Condition of Consciousness	Demonstrated Today By Consciousness of
Old Saturn	Deep Trance	Minerals
Old Sun	Dreamless Sleep	Plants
Old Moon	Dream-filled Sleep	Animals
Earth	Waking/Object	Human being
Jupiter	Imagination (Psychic or conscious picture consciousness [astral])	Earth + Moon
Venus	Inspiration (super-psychic or conscious life-consciousness [etheric])	Sound/Music of the Spheres
Vulcan	Intuition (Spiritual or self-conscious universal consciousness)	Identification of Self with Spiritual Beings

I-45 Christian esoteric terminology for the Conditions of Consciousness, Life and Form

FE, Lect. 25

In Christian esotericism, the following names are given:

A Planetary Condition (Condition of Consciousness) = *Power*
A Condition of Life (Round) = *Kingdom*, Wisdom
A Condition of Form (Globe) = *Glory*, Splendor

These terms, not present in the scriptural Lord's Prayer (see Mt 6,9-13; Lk 11,2-4) or in Roman Catholic liturgy, were added in most Protestant churches (see 7 Brit 478, "Lord's Prayer").

I-46 East/West esoteric terminology for the long (e.g., 5,000 year) ages of the human being's evolution

FE, Glossary and Lect. 26; RCE, Lect. 2

In esotericism, the ages (of diminishing length; cf. Mt 24,22; Mk13,20) of the human being's evolution (from a certain early point) are as follows:

Western Term	Oriental Term	Period (Approx.)
Golden Age	Krita Yuga	Atlantis
Silver Age	Treta Yuga	Atlantis/Indian/Persian
Bronze Age	Dvapara Yuga	Persian/Chaldo-Egyptian
Dark Age	Kali Yuga	3,101 B.C. to A.D. 1899
Our Age-future		1899 A.D. to ca. A.D. 4,399*

*(or A.D. 4,399 till the end of our present post-Atlantean Epoch)

These are not recognized in Brit., which deals only with their historical or literary meaning, but they are recognized in RHCD (in Classical Mythology), as follows:

Golden Age   the 1st and best of the 4 Ages of the human being; an era of peace and innocence

Silver Age   the 2nd of the 4 Ages of the human being: characterized by an increase of impiety and of human weakness

Bronze Age   the 3rd of the 4 Ages of the human being, marked by war and violence

Iron Age   the last and worst of the 4 Ages of the human being, characterized by danger, corruption, and toil

(MWCD also recognizes all four "ages," but more mundanely.)
And WNWD also recognizes the first two, as follows:

Golden Age   an imaginary early age in which humanity was ideally happy, prosperous, and innocent

Silver Age   the second age of the world, inferior to the earlier Golden Age

I-47 The 3-fold "Logos"; the loci of consciousness of the 4 kingdoms and of elemental beings

FE, Lect. 27

Three "Logos" underlie a planetary chain as follows:

3rd Logos produces forms by means of combining
2nd Logos gives life to forms
1st Logos produces consciousness "out of nothing" but experiences
          from prior planetary chain

and may thus be further tabulated as follows:

3rd Logos	Form	Saturn
2nd Logos	Life	Sun
1st Logos	Consciousness	Earth

All four kingdoms (human being through mineral) have their life on the physical plane but their consciousness at different levels (**I-11**), as follows:

Human being's consciousness	Physical
Animal consciousness	Astral
Plant consciousness	Lower Devachan
Mineral consciousness	Higher Devachan

The human being's consciousness is enclosed within the head in frontal brain; the focal point of the animal's consciousness lies in front of the head in the astral; plant consciousness is at the center of the Earth (thus its "head," or root, goes down, **I-78**); and mineral consciousness is in Higher Devachan.

Elemental Beings (**I-12**) have their consciousness in all four forms of the physical plane and their body in the astral world. What the natural scientist today calls laws of nature are the "thoughts" of beings who "think" on the physical plane but have their bodies on the astral plane. The forces of nature are creative beings and natural laws are their "thoughts."

I-48 Root races and their terminal causes

FE, Lect. 28

Root Races and their causes of destruction (generated by evil):

Lemurian	Fire
Atlantean	Water
Aryan	Air (turbulence)

I-49 Concepts of labor in the fourth through the sixth Cultural Eras

FE, Lect. 28

The concept of labor as it has been, is, and will be, in the fourth through the sixth Cultural Eras of the post-Atlantean epoch are as follows:

Cultural Era (Sub-Race)	Concept of Labor
Greco-Roman work	Slave
Germanic (present)	Commodity (**I-88**)
Slavonic	Free offering

I-50 Three important human stages (upright stance, speech and thought)—their nature and respective effects upon karma

FE, Lect. 16

Very important stages for the human being, their nature as reflected today, and their respective effects upon karma, are as follows:

Stage of Development	Nature	Effect on Karma of
Standing upright	Deeds	Individual
Speech	Words	Nation or Tribe
Thinking	Thoughts	Humanity (Planet)

I-51 Spiritual beings, numerous aspects of

SB, Lects. 1-5

When one, with strength of soul, is able to penetrate (i.e., to lift the veil of) the perceptions of the sense world, then the elements of the sense world spring to life as moral perceptions. Something deeper than the vision of the eyes, the hearing of the ears, or the intellectual power of brain-thinking then works within one—a deeper "seeing, hearing and understanding" akin to what is spoken of in Is 6,9-10, the tentacles of which reach throughout the Bible. Such a one comes into a region in which, gradually, one begins to perceive manifold beings that live and work behind the mineral kingdom. The etheric world gradually appears, differentiated in its details. The etheric world of physical nature differs from that of a human being, the latter being a unity and the former a plurality. The beings one meets there in this etheric world are the "elemental spirits" already mentioned, for instance, in **I-12**.

There are four classes of elemental spirits:

1. Those who appear to such "sight" to have a form, and who are the nature spirits of solid substance, earth.

2. Those whose form is mobile or constantly changing, who are associated with motion or metamorphosis, as in the case of cloud formation, rain falling, mist rising, water tossing in a waterfall and giving out spray, plants coming forth in spring, the power of growth, and the like; these are the nature spirits of fluid substance, water.

3. Those who have no form but appear flashing up like lightning or meteors, now seen, now gone, and who are involved in the gradual fading or dying of the plant world; these are the nature spirits of gaseous substance, air.

4. Those, also without form, best portrayed by the nature of a "Seed," for these are the protectors of the germs of all the kingdoms of nature, who make it possible that the same beings continually reappear on our Earth, and that they are brought into contact with the warmth of our planet; these are the nature spirits of warmth, fire.

Collectively, the nature spirits may be said to govern the nature forces.

Thus, while the etheric body of the human being is a unity, that of the Earth is a 4-fold plurality, with each fold a multiplicity.

When one is then able to draw aside the veil of the etheric body of the Earth, one comes again to moral impressions and, penetrating further, to a perception of a new order of spiritual beings. These have command over the nature spirits, having the task of directing the appropriate nature spirits to their activities at the right time. These spiritual beings are the astral body of the Earth. They govern all the periods or cycles of time, those of day and night, seasons of the year, the forces rotating the Earth on its axis, and everything connected with rhythmic return. They are called Spirits of the Cycles of Time. Just as Nature Spirits represent the Earth's etheric body and govern Nature Forces, so these Spirits of the Cycles of Time (also a multiplicity) represent the Earth's astral body and govern the Laws of Nature.

To be able to navigate to the still higher region of the Earth that corresponds to the human Ego, one must pass through the shoals of multiplicity to what is again an undivided spirit, the Planetary Spirit. And just as it is undivided, so must one, to perceive it, feel oneself united with the whole of the planet rather than with any particular territory or the like. The task of the Planetary Spirit is to bring the Earth into mutual relation with the other heavenly bodies—into a right relationship with the cosmos.

All of the foregoing may be roughly portrayed in summary by the following chart:

Name of Spirit Manifestation	Realm it Governs	Nature of Body or Division it Represents
Planetary Spirit	Meaning of Nature	"I" or Ego
Spirits of the Cycles of Time	Laws of Nature	Astral body
Nature Spirits	Nature Forces	Etheric body
Sense World	Perceptions	Physical body

We must now consider how the spirit manifestations set out in this chart relate to the Hierarchies (see **I-6** and **I-7**). In descending order, the Hierarchies are First Hierarchy (Seraphim, Cherubim, Thrones), Second Hierarchy (Dominions or Kyriotetes, Dynamis, Exusiai) and Third Hierarchy (Archai, Archangels, Angels).

This relationship is summarized in the following chart:

Hierarchy	Outer Life	Inner Life	Offspring
First	World-creation	Creation of Beings	Spirits of the Cycles of Time
Second	Self-creation	Stimulation of Life	Group-Souls of Plants/Animals
Third	Manifestation	Being filled with Spirit	Nature Spirits
Humanity	Sense Perception	Inner Life	Children

As human beings we have the possibility of leading inner lives quite independent of our outer lives. When we lose ourselves in the external world, we have perceptions, and when we withdraw from the external world we have independent inner lives. Beings of the third Hierarchy have manifestation instead of perception, and in this manifestation or revelation they experience themselves. Instead of an inner life, they experience higher spiritual worlds, i.e., they are filled with the spirit. Thus, in the chart, what is sense perception to a human being is manifestation or revelation to beings of the third Hierarchy. When a person has inner experiences that do not coincide with external perceptions, the result is a lie. But the possibility of untruth does not exist in the third Hierarchy as long as its members retain their nature. (Lucifer did not so retain his nature, hence untruth became a possibility for him.) To experience themselves, they must manifest. Angels manifest in guiding individual human beings, Archangels by directing the vision of groups of human beings, and Archai by giving leadership to humanity in successive epochs.

Beings of the third Hierarchy continually bring forth offspring that are of a lower order because they have other tasks to accomplish that require a lower order. The respective natures of the Nature Spirits produced by this Hierarchy are as follows:

Spirit-Being	Domain of Offspring
Archai	Earth/solids
Archangels	Water
Angels	Air

Beings of the second Hierarchy not only manifest their own being, but this manifestation remains as something independent that separates from these beings themselves. As the inner beings of the third Hierarchy change, so also their external manifestations change. But it is different with the second Hierarchy. What they experience is detached from them and acquires independent existence. They create, as it were, an impression of themselves, making themselves objective, in a sort of image, and in this, life is stimulated. The stimulation of life is always the result of such a self-creation. The nature of activity of each level with the second Hierarchy is as follows:

Spirit-Being	Nature of Activity
Exusiai (Elohim) Spirits of Form	Form of living creatures, Plants/Animals/Human being
Dynamis (Mights) Spirits of Motion	Changing form of living creatures
Kyriotetes (Dominions) Spirits of Wisdom	Meaning of outward appearance (of form and movement) of living creatures

The offspring of the second Hierarchy, detached but living beings of a lower order sent down into the kingdoms of nature, are the group-souls of the individual plant and animal species.

While beings of the third Hierarchy are perceived by one's astral body as a vision or imagination in spiritual light (spiritual "seeing"), beings of the second Hierarchy are perceived by one's etheric body in something like tone, "music of the spheres" (spiritual hearing). Beings of the first Hierarchy are perceived with even greater difficulty. To perceive beings of the first Hierarchy, one must plunge down into the being of other creatures in a form of "knowing or understanding" (comparable to the "seeing" or "hearing" of the lower two Hierarchies). "Knowledge" of the three levels of the first Hierarchy is thus gained as follows:

Knowledge of	Gained by Plunging Down Into
Thrones/Spirits of Wisdom	Human Beings or Higher Animals
Cherubim/Spirits of Harmony	Lower Animals or Plants
Seraphim/Spirits of Love	Lifeless Creatures (e.g., stones)

Beings of the second Hierarchy can create something like an image of themselves, a living creature, but it remains a living image only so long as it remains connected to them, otherwise falling into decay. By contrast, beings of the first Hierarchy can also objectify themselves by image, but when this is detached it continues to exist in the world though they sever themselves from it. Thus, a higher degree of objectivity is attained by them than by the second Hierarchy.

The inner being of this first Hierarchy is in the action of creation, in forming independent beings. Creation of worlds is their outer life; creation of beings is their inner life.

They, too, create offspring of a lower nature which are sent down into the kingdoms of nature in the form of the Spirits of the Cycles of Time.

Thus have we touched upon all the components of the first two charts. However, Lect. 5 concludes with a helpful explanation of the relationship of the hierarchical world with our cosmos. If we take as the lowest principle of a 9-fold being which has the Holy Trinity as its highest 3-fold component, we start at the level of the Exusiai (Elohim)/Spirits of Form. The form of our Earth is their creation. The following chart expresses these relationships:

Hierarchical Strata	Cosmic Function	Human Equiv.
Exusiai (Spirits of Form)	Formation of Earth/Planets	Physical body
Dynamis (Spirits of Motion)	Changing form (livingness) of Earth/Planets	Etheric body
Kyriotetes (Spirits of Wisdom)	Consciousness of Earth/Planets	Astral body
Thrones (Spirits of Will)	Impulse driving Earth/Planets through space	Sentient soul

Cherubim (Spirits of Harmony)	Harmony of movement between one planet and another	Intellectual soul
Seraphim (Spirits of Love)	Harmony between fixed stars in the cosmos	Consciousness soul
Holy Spirit \ /	Creates for itself sheaths	Manas
Son Spirit	in the different planetary	Buddhi
Father Spirit / \	systems for the bodies of divine beings	Atma

I-52 <u>The relationship of thinking, feeling and willing to various time cycles</u>

MWS, Lect. 2; SCM, Lect. 2

The relationship of the human being to the cosmos is further involved in how the threefoldedness of the human being's activities, thinking, feeling and willing, is related to the daily, yearly and lifetime cycles. Our thoughts, whether we are foolish or clever, are the small change carried out daily, but only to the regions closest to the Earth. Our feelings, i.e., our heart-nature, is carried out yearly farther into the cosmos, at Christmas, which is reflected by the tendency at this midwinter time to look at the year and resolve what the next year shall be like. Both of these are strictly regulated in time. But our will, which is left in the hands of humanity itself, must be borne out into the cosmos by the human being itself, which is done when it passes through the gate of death. Thus, the relationship of these three to the time periods when they are carried out into the cosmos (cycles), and the manner in which they are then carried out, may be tabulated as follows:

Activity	Cycle	Manner by which Carried Out
Thoughts	Daily	Sleep
Feelings	Yearly	Christmas
Willing	Lifetime	Death

The parts of the cyclical year disclosed to the ancient human being the nature of the human being, as follows:

Spring	=	Physical body
Summer	=	Etheric body
Autumn	=	Astral body
Winter	=	Ego

I-53 Virtue development related to Conditions of Consciousness

RH, Lect. 5

When the human being's evolution has progressed through the seven Conditions of Consciousness (see **I-1** through **I-3**), it will have completed the consummate development of the realms of justice, truth/wisdom, beauty and morality. The development of each such realm is initiated in a particular Condition of Consciousness and completed in the third one thereafter (spanning four Conditions). They may thus be seen as follows:

Saturn	Justice			
Sun	Truth/Wisdom	Justice		
Moon	Beauty	Truth/Wisdom	Justice	
Earth	Morality	Beauty	Truth/Wisdom	Justice
Jupiter		Morality	Beauty	Truth/ Wisdom
Venus			Morality	Beauty
Vulcan				Morality

I-54 Spiritual warmth/fire

WH, Lect. 8

Steiner tells of how, in the waning days of the Greco-Roman epoch (the time that gave us the likes of Dante and Aquinas, who last spoke of the spiritual Hierarchies—see **I-6**), the Rosicrucian master, when sought out by students, might give them an understanding of themselves, from a particular perspective. "Behold the stones!" he would say (Shades of Christ! Cf. Lk 19,40). They can exist on Earth by themselves by virtue of Earth forces—but none of the human being's bodies can do so—only the mineral kingdom. If the human being's soul leaves, then all of its "bodies," physical, etheric and astral, are destroyed, driven back to their home, and what is left dissolves to mineral "dust" (Gen 3,19). Our "Three Bodies," physical, etheric and astral, "are not of this world" (Jn 8,23 and 18,36). The master brought this home to the student in what distills to the following chart:

Originating Hierarchy	Body of Man	Incremental Element Utilized by This Body on Earth
1st Hierarchy	Physical	earth/solid/mineral
2nd Hierarchy	Etheric	water/fluid
3rd Hierarchy	Astral	air/gaseous

And then the students could see that they were inhabitants of the Earth purely and solely because of the element of warmth/fire that they bear within. Into none of the baser elements (earth, water or air) could the soul nature be brought, but only into the element of warmth. Our English translations have lost the meaning of Gen 1,2 in this respect, for it says, literally (see 1 Interp 466), that the Spirit was "brooding upon" the face of the waters, a term that paints a picture of providing warmth, as it was also in "fire" that Moses saw the "I Am" in the burning bush (Ex 3,14) and it was with "fire" that the disciples were inflamed by the Holy Spirit (Acts 2,2-3). We are here, of course, speaking of an element rarer than that of the heat of molecular action—the element that regulates the human being's body temperature, for instance, regardless of its environmental temperature (see 2 Brit 317, "body heat").

A moment's reflection will show how the order of the human being's creation from these four elements can still be seen in regard to the maintenance of its life. The element of warmth dwells constantly in it, and leaves at the instant of death. The other three elements must be constantly taken in and then expelled if one is to stay alive. Life exists many days without solid intake, a much shorter time without fluid intake, but only a matter of a few minutes without gas (oxygen) intake. Similarly, the period of time involved in processing these essential elements (in and out) through the body varies in direct proportion to the length of time life can exist without them.

I-55 The four temperaments and their predominant components

RMC, Chap. 16

Steiner spoke of the four temperaments, so helpfully expounded upon by Harwood, which derive from the fact that one of the human being's 4-fold components (physical, etheric or astral body, or Ego) will predominate over the others. Whichever predominates in a person characterizes the person as that temperament type, as summarized in the following chart:

Temperament	Predominant Component
Choleric	Ego
Sanguine	Astral
Melancholic	Etheric
Phlegmatic	Physical

I-56 How Hierarchies work through the human being during its life on Earth and then with its Ego between lives

KR-1, Lect. 6; KR-5, Lect 7

The following chart (from KR-1) portrays how the Hierarchies work through the human being during its life on Earth:

Hierarchy	Organization	Activity	Consciousness	Karma
Third	Head	Thinking	Waking	
Second	Rhythmic	Feeling	Dreaming	Inner
First	Motor	Willing	Sleeping	Outer (Destiny)

The following chart (from KR-5) portrays, how the Hierarchies work with the human being's Ego in the astral and lower devachan regions of its journey through the heavens between death and rebirth (see **I-33**):

Hierarchy	Organization	Planetary "Sphere(s)"
Third	Motor	Moon/Mercury/Venus
Second	Rhythmic	Sun
First	Head	Mars/Jupiter/Saturn

I-57　Tomberg's portrayal of Israel's three "patriarchs"

ASOT, Chap. 3, Sec. 2

The following chart portrays, according to Tomberg, why one patriarch would not suffice to supply the primary impulse for the history of Israel, and thus why the Bible speaks of "the God of Abraham, of Isaac and of Jacob," as well as how the threefold stream of inheritance through the generations of Israel began.

Father	Astral	Abraham Impulse	Thought
Son	Etheric	Isaac Impulse	Life (Feeling)
Holy Spirit	Physical	Jacob Impulse	Will

Thus the thought of the Father, the Sacrifice of the Son, and the Victory of the Spirit are mirrored in history and the Bible, for the Old Testament is primarily of Abraham's thought, the New Testament of Isaac's sacrifice, and the Apocalypse of the future victory of the Spirit.

I-58　The human components and characteristics of four ancient myths; the elevation of human perception; the relative strength of the three human bodies and Ego

WW, Lect. 3

The anthroposophist sees deep meaning in the ancient myths, sees that the ancients understood more than humanity today of its own origin and descent from the spiritual world. The following chart reflects something of that ancient understanding:

Ancient God	Human Component	Character
Persephone	Ego	"The cycle of the grain, pictured in the myth of Persephone, was thought to be parallel to the cycle of man." 24 Brit 707, "Mystery Religions, … Eleusinian." She was carried off by Pluto (Hades, or Sheol) into the depths of the Earth, ate a pomegranate seed, a symbol of death and birth, and thus could not be released, thereafter spending 1/3 of the year with Pluto and the rest with her heavenly mother, Demeter.
Zeus	Astral body	Rainbow, clouds, thunder, lightning and other meteorological phenomena.
Poseidon	Etheric body	Oceans, storms and hurricanes, more closely bound up with Earth than Zeus in widths of space.
Pluto (Hades, Heb. Sheol)	Physical Body	Solid matter, associated with death.

It will be seen, from their respective characteristics, that the "astral/etheric/physical bodies" are the seats of the Ego's *thinking/feeling/willing*.

We have seen (**I-20**) how all of the human being's 12 senses microcosmically reflect the spiritual world. Steiner elsewhere (e.g., KHW) shows how one may develop one's soul to a point where each sense is elevated so that, for instance,

> Sight becomes clairvoyance
> Hearing becomes clairaudience
> Tasting becomes clairsipience, etc.

He describes how such a clairsipient experiences his or her own 3-fold being, as follows:

Physical	=	Bitter
Etheric	=	Delicate, sweet, pleasant
Astral	=	Tasteless—rather the experience is one of breathlessness, fear or dread.

While Steiner does not here make any such identification, one can see that this understanding will be enlightening when we come to the Apocalypse of John, where we are told (Rev 10,9-10) that the scroll, when eaten, "will be bitter to your stomach, but sweet as honey in your mouth" (see ASJ, Lect. 8, p. 147; OSC, p. 5; and Bock's Aps Jn, p. 85).

We have already seen (**I-19**) one way that the pentagram (5-pointed star) is significant in astrological understanding, and we shall see many Biblical uses. Steiner uses that understanding to close this lecture. He draws the following diagram,

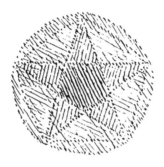

which he uses to express the relative strength of the forces of the human being's "Three Bodies," by showing that such forces are represented by the areas within their respective geometrical figures, as follows:

Physical	=	small pentagon (dark center);
Etheric	=	5 triangles with bases on the sides of the small pentagon;
Astral	=	large pentagon
Ego	=	circle around outer points of triangles.

I-59 Ancient terminology for the 3-fold human being

BSU, Lect. 7

The 3-fold nature of the human being can be expressed by the following three words, all of which mean "human being," but carried much different meanings for those who initiated the terms:

Manushya (Sanscrit) = The human being as spirit

Anthropo (Greek)   = The human being as soul (psychic)

Homo (Greek)   = The human being as physical (procreated)

("Manushya" obviously comes from "Manu," who, according to the mythology of India was "the first man and author of an important Sanscrit code of law." If one examines the myth, it would seem likely that he is one and the same as the Biblical Noah, a point to which credence is given by 7 Brit 798, "Manu," from which the last quote is taken.) Considering that words originally had meaning according to their sounds (e.g., Gen 11,1), the vestiges of many of which can still be traced through Indo-European and other languages, it would seem significant that the sound and meaning of "manu" seems to have found its way into the Oriental "manas" and its Biblical equivalent, Manna; into the name of the 3rd-century Persian, Mani (Manes, or Manichaeus) (about whom Steiner says in this lecture of April 19, 1917, "unfortunately it is not yet permissible today to unveil the ultimate secrets of this doctrine, even in our present circle"); and, according to WNWD, into the native Polynesian term, "mana," meaning "the impersonal supernatural force to which certain primitive peoples attribute good fortune, magical powers, etc."

I-60 The human being's 3-fold nature as reflected in Christianity's form

HCMF, Lect. 2

Christianity itself, in order to address itself to the 3-fold nature of the human being, was poured into

The Body	of	Romanism
The Soul	of	Judaism
The Spirit	of	Hellenism

but there is something shadowlike about all of these, something Luciferic and Ahrimanic, which must be distinguished from true Christianity itself. These shadows today are reflected in the following tabulation:

Part	Mold	Institution	Shadow
Body	Romanism	Church (Roman or other)	Antiquated Ecclesiasticism
Soul	Judaism	Freemasonry	Antiquated Symbolism
Spirit	Hellenism	Aristotelian Materialism	Antiquated Materialistic Science

I-61 The human race becoming younger

HCMF, Lect. 3; AM, Lect. 5; AHE, Lect. 1

As yet another way in which the human being has changed with the passage of time, Steiner here tells us that the human race is gradually becoming younger. He is not talking about the demographics of the average age of then living persons. Rather he is referring to a phenomenon that may have escaped our attention, namely, the capacity of a human being, simply by being born, to develop wisdom through its physical body up to a certain age. This fact is totally obvious in the early years of life, but continues long beyond what we might otherwise think. However, it is in this respect that we are getting younger. In other words, the age at which we cease to gain wisdom from our physical bodies is much younger now than in earlier post-Atlantean times. Steiner gives the following ages:

Cultural Era	Wisdom Acquired Until Age
Old Indian	56
Old Persian	49
Chaldo-Egyptian	42
Greco-Roman	35
Germanic	28

Then he points out the wonderful fact that the age of Christ Jesus when he passed through death on Golgotha coincides with the age to which humanity had fallen back at that time; and that the particular age at which humanity now stands (at the time of the lecture in 1918) is 27 years. (Each Cultural Age lasts approximately 2,160 years, so that the

length of time to which a one-year decline is attributable is 308.57
years—the length of each archangelic period as per **I-19**.)

I-62 Four kinds of pre-Christian initiates; the four Gospels and ancient
    symbols

GMCP; GOSP; Jn-Rel, Lect. 3; EI, Chap. 9, p. 127, fn 353

There were four kinds of Pre-Christian initiates, as follows:

Activity	Service	Gospel that Represents	Ancient Symbol
Thinking	Sage	John	Eagle (Scorpion)
Feeling	Healer	Luke	Bull
Willing	Magi	Mark	Lion
Harmony	Leader	Matthew	Face of Man

Today, because their meaning has been largely lost to humanity's consciousness, the four ancient symbols above are generally either ignored or
treated as insignificant in Gospel commentary. Their vestigial authenticity
is widely acknowledged, but as something traditional whose meaning has
become clouded. See 14 Brit 818, "Biblical Literature,… Ezekiel," and
26 Brit 69, "Prehistoric Peoples and Cultures, Evolutionary Development." It was a thrill to me to discover, after first studying this matter, this
symbolism on a statuary feature of the four Gospels in our local cemetery.
    Each of these symbols represents a stage of the human being's prehis-
toric Atlantean evolution, and the respective dispositions of mind that
descended therefrom. The earliness of this stage is reflected in the vision
of Ezekiel (Ezek 1,10) and even more clearly in that of John (Rev 4,7),
which immediately follows the original crystallization of minerals from
the sea (Rev 4,6). That these four Gospels are merely representative of an
even larger division of humanity which is to be harmonized by the Christ
is clearly indicated by an inspection of these symbols and their places in
the Zodiac. If one reflects upon the ordering of the constellations in the
sky, it will be seen that these four are equally spaced among the twelve so
as to represent, in effect, the "four corners" of the entire group (see **I-18**
and **I-19**). Each is a river (of several confluent streams) so that the New

Testament begins with "four rivers" as does the Old (Gen 2,10). The apparent inconsistencies between the Gospels begins to disappear when one understands these things.

I-63 The Cultural Eras and their prevalent myths

JTCL

The terminology for the clairvoyance of old was as follows:

Cultural Era		Prevalent Myth
Persia	=	Mithra
Egypt	=	Isis & Osiris
Greece	=	Dionysus

I-64 Steiner's "Turning Points" compared with Schure's "Great Initiates"

TPSH; GI

It is helpful to see, in tabular and chronological order, a listing of great spiritual leaders of post-Atlantean times. For this, the two above-cited books are most helpful, from which the following lists are taken (their common personalities in bold):

STEINER'S "TURNING POINTS"	SCHURÉ'S "GREAT INITIATES"
Zarathustra	Rama
Hermes	Krishna
Buddha	**Hermes**
Moses	**Moses**
Elijah	Orpheus
Christ	Pythagoras
	Plato
	Jesus (Christ)

Neither is, nor purports to be, all-inclusive. It should be noted that there is a difference of approach. One is, indeed, "turning points," and the other primarily gives the leading initiate of a particular Mystery School, e.g., Brahman (Krishna), Egyptian (Hermes), Dionysus (Orpheus), Delphi (Pythagoras), Eleusis (Plato).

I-65 Correlation of Christianity's development by century with the ages and stages of the individual human being

HA1, App. II

Robert Powell has clarified something implicit in Steiner's message, namely, that there is a correspondence between a year in the life of an individual and a century in the life of Christianity. We have already seen **(I-19)** how the Venus Pentagram makes a complete rotation of the 12 signs of the sidereal zodiac in 1199 yrs, which essentially equals a 100-year rhythm multiple cosmically. He combines this with the life of Christ at 33 1/3 yrs (see also INE, Lect. 3), which established a new rhythm such that it is an integer of the rhythm of 100. He identifies Father Pietro Archiati (see NEWS, Winter 94-95, p. 12 for biographical sketch) as the first, insofar as he knows, to have pointed out such correspondence. Inasmuch as the most important rhythm in human biography is the 7-yr rhythm, he applies it to develop such correspondence into the following pattern:

Period of A.D. Era	Stage of Christianity's Development
0/33 to 700/733:	*infancy* of Church (guided by Church Fathers)
700/733 to 1400/1433:	*childhood* of Church (emergence of the Holy Roman Empire)
1400/1433 to 2100/2133:	*youth* of Church (rebellion and conflict)
2100/2133 onwards:	*adulthood* (flourishing of true Christianity)

He applies this correspondence to further developments in Church history as they relate to the rhythms (time required to orbit the sidereal zodiac) of the respective planets, but this would overly extend the present chart.

I-66 <u>Tomberg's portrayal of the human being's encounters with the Cosmic Evil Trinity and the Cosmic Good Trinity</u>

ASOT, Chap. 5, Sec. 2

We have already encountered expressions of the domain of evil in charts **I-22**, **I-27**, **I-28** and **I-32**. In this one, Tomberg speaks of "The Trinity of Cosmic Evil," composed of Lucifer, Ahriman and the Azura (or Asura or Adzura), in the following descending order:

Evil Spirit	Brings Ego Out of	Into
Lucifer	Waking	Dreaming
Ahriman	Dreaming	Sleeping
Azura	Sleeping	Death

The time of the human being's encounter with Azura is still in the distant future. We shall see a Biblical reflection of this in Daniel and Revelation. At present, the conflict between Good and Evil has not yet descended into the human being's physical body, though it is mirrored there by what takes place in the higher members. If, for instance, as a result of this conflict the gall-bladder or liver becomes ill, the cause is not to be sought in the physical body, but in the astral-etheric region. At present, the human being's three encounters with the cosmic good do not reach down to the physical body, but are reflected in the following tabulation:

When	Trinity	Through its Spiritual Agency	The human being's Being
Daily at Night	Holy Spirit	Angel	Ego
Annually at Christmas	Son	Archangel	Astral body
Lifetime at Death	Father	Archai	Etheric body

But the scenes of conflict between the Holy Trinity and the Trinity of Evil are as follows:

The human being's Being	Holy Trinity	Evil Trinity	Through its Spiritual Agency
Astral body	Holy Spirit	Lucifer	Fallen Archangel
Etheric body	Son	Ahriman	Fallen Archai
Physical body	Father	Azura	Fallen Exusiai

As to the "Spiritual Agency" in both these tabulations, see **I-7**.

I-67 <u>Cosmological systems relating to the different levels of consciousness (per Powell)</u>

HA2, Chap. 4 Table 5

Cosmological systems relating to different levels of consciousness are as follows:

Level of Consciousness	Cosmological System	Applying to (Dimension)
Terrestrial	Heliocentric (Copernican)	Spatial (Physical)
Lunar	Babylonian (Ptolemaic)	Temporal
Solar	Egyptian (Tychonic)	Causal (correspondence between macrocosm & microcosm)
Zodiacal	(None named)	Being

I-68 <u>Analogy of sequential development of Old Testament peoples to the human being; the zodiacal influence reflected throughout</u>

GSMk, Lect. 6

Steiner points out how the sequence of the development of the Old Testament peoples is analogous to the life of an individual human being in so many ways. We may tabulate it somewhat as follows:

Human Component	Biblical Personality
Physical body	Abraham
Etheric body	Isaac
Astral body	Jacob
Sentient Soul \	
Intellectual Soul	Elijah/Sons of Maccabees/John the Baptist
Consciousness Soul /	
Manas/Buddhi/Atma	Christian Era

In this pattern, the 12-fold zodiacal influence runs as a thread through body, soul and spirit, as follows:

Body	=	Twelve sons of Jacob
Soul	=	Twelve sons of Maccabees
		([1 Macc 2,2 = 5] + [2 Macc 7,1 = 7] = 12)
Spirit	=	Twelve apostles

That the clairvoyance of the spiritual state comes upon the twelve apostles is clearly indicated in Mark's Gospel (as in Mt and Lk) when the feedings follow immediately upon announcement of the beheading of John the Baptist, showing that the soul of John the Baptist became thereafter the group-soul of the Twelve (and we shall see later the connection of "the Twelve" with the Twelve Sons of the Maccabees). The Elijah connection is made clear by the fact that immediately after the beheading Christ feeds the 5,000, then the 4,000, asking the apostles if it is now clear what has happened (Mk 8,21). What has happened in this context is the bestowal of the soul of Elijah upon the Twelve. The "feedings" are used to illustrate this because they pick up the thread of the "increase in bread" which is found first with Elijah (1 K 17,8-16) and then again with Elisha (2 K 4,1-7) after he had received the spirit of Elijah (2 K 2,9-15). Then follows the clairvoyance of Peter's confession of the Christ (Mk 8,27-30), the Transfiguration appearance of Moses, Elijah and Christ (Mk 9,2-13), and later the appearance of the resurrected Christ (Mk 16).

These might be taken as the manas-buddhi-atma states, respectively, inasmuch as the feedings relate to the Manna experience (Ex 16, Num 11), the designation of Peter as "the Rock" to the experience of the water from the rock (the Christ) in the "Wilderness" (Num 20,11, 1 Cor 10,4), and the Resurrection as the attainment of the full 9-fold status of the Son of Man (Rev 1,12-16).

I-69 <u>Parallel between the human being's life cycle and that of Christ's journey into and out of the mineral-physical Earth</u>

FG, Lect. 3

The 7-stage process of the human being's cycle from conception to upper devachan (for the upper four levels, see **I-33**) is paralleled by Christ's entry into the Earth as the Spirit of the Earth and the taking of his body back into the spirit world. That his Baptism was his "Conception" in this process, see Lk 3,22 (fn in RSV), as well as Ps 2,7. The process can then be tabulated as follows:

Baptism	=	Conception
3 years	=	Gestation (embryo)
Mystery of Golgotha	=	Birth
40 days	=	Etheric panorama (Etheric World)
Ascension	=	Kamaloca (Astral World)
Pentecost	=	Devachan (Lower Spiritland)
End of Age	=	Devachan (Higher Spiritland)

I-70 <u>Thinking-feeling-willing tabulated with other relationships</u>

CHS, Lect. 1

The three human activities (forces) can be further tabulated as follows:

Activity	Spirits of	1 Cor 13	Given By
Will	Will (Thrones)	Faith	Law
Thinking	Wisdom (Kyriotetes)	Hope	Mysteries
Feeling	Love/Harmony (Seraphim & Cherubim)	Love	Christ

I-71 <u>Portrayal of the human being's spiritual guidance during the 7 Cultural Eras</u>

SGM, Lect. 3

In the evolution of the human being, it was necessary that the Hierarchies withdraw more and more from direct guidance up through the period in which Christ incarnated. Thereafter, in accordance with the pattern of evolution, the subsequent periods have and will reflect the former periods as the human being (the Prodigal Son) returns to the spiritual fold of the Father. The post-Atlantean spiritual guidance of the human being may thus be portrayed as follows:

Indian	=	Archai
Persian	=	Archangels
Egyptian	=	Angels
Greco-Roman	=	None
5th post-Atlantean	=	Angels
6th post-Atlantean	=	Archangels
7th post-Atlantean	=	Archai

I-72 <u>Reflections by the John Gospel's Prologue of the 4-fold human being and the 4 Conditions of Consciousness</u>

GSJ, Lect. 2; Jn-Rel, Lect. 3

The 4-fold human being (see **I-9**) and the four Conditions of Consciousness (**I-1** through **I-3**) up through Earth evolution are reflected in the Prologue (verses 1-18) of the Gospel of John, as shown in the following tabulation:

Word (Jn 1,1)	Physical body	Old Saturn
Life (Jn 1,4a)	Etheric body	Old Sun
Light (Jn 1,4b-9)	Astral body	Old Moon
Name (Jn 1,12)	Ego ("I Am")	Earth

John's Gospel, of course, emphasizes Jesus as "the I Am," but John's Apocalypse (written, by the same author known as "John") makes it clear that the "Name" of Jesus is "the I Am," for it is the only "Name" that is known, and can be spoken, only by the one who bears it (see Rev 2,17; 3,12; 19,12).

I-73 The 4 apocalyptic animals and their most developed aspects

RPA, Lect. 3

Reflecting further on the four animal symbols of Rev 4,7 (see **I-62**), Steiner's remarks can be tabulated as follows:

People	Most Developed Aspect
Bull	Physical body, i.e., digestive (metabolic) system
Lion	Etheric body, i.e., circulatory system
Man Face	Astral body, i.e., brain and nervous system
Eagle	Ego

I-74 Personalities who have reflected the etheric and astral bodies of Jesus of Nazareth

SE, Lect. 2 and 3

During the course of this work we will see the application of the important principle of "Spiritual Economy," the subject of the cited lecture series. This principle provides for the preservation and multiplication of an extract of one or several members (such as, particularly, the etheric or astral bodies) of an avatar or of other eminent initiates who have attained to a high level of perfection. We shall see the application of this principle in the case of Shem and in connection with the Biblical Nativity accounts, among others. The working of this principle in the preservation and multiplication of the etheric and astral bodies of Jesus of Nazareth has enabled Christianity to progress through periods much like those of the development of an individual human being. The intimate history of Christian development is connected with this fact, as tabulated below:

Period (A.D.)	Developmental Plane	Representative Personalities
Golgotha to 400	Physical	Irenaeus, Papias, Augustine
500 to 1,100	Etheric	Author of the Heliand [see 5 Brit 811, "Heliand" & 14 Brit 793, "Biblical Literature, ... Later and modern versions: continental, German," and John Scotus Erigena
1,100 to 1,500	Astral	Francis of Assisi, Elizabeth of Thuringen, the Scholastics, Meister Eckhart, Johannes Tauler
1,600 to present and beyond	Ego	None mentioned by Steiner

I-75 Domains of the Hierarchies

BKM, Lect. 6

Domains (areas of work) of the Hierarchies are as follows:

Hierarchical Rank	Domain
Angels	Individuals
Archangels	Folk
Archai	Time Periods
Exusiai and above	Forces and Kingdoms of Nature

I-76 The four sacrifices by Christ as reflected in the human being and the Gospels

FSC; PEDC; FSCace; CYPI, Chap. 2

This chart is deeply esoteric. Those with considerable prior anthroposophical understanding will readily fathom most of it, but others, even those with extensive familiarity with scripture, can scarcely be expected to do so merely from the chart itself. Nevertheless, to those who are prepared and ready, it may well begin to flicker light, which in time could grow into understanding. Indeed, many significant scriptural passages, such, for instance, as the babe leaping in Elizabeth's womb (Lk 1,44), the "first and second Adam" (Rom 5,12-14; 1 Cor 15,21-22,45,47-49) and the dragon/ Michael conflict (Rev 12), can hardly be understood without these insights.

Steiner tells us that there have been four sacrifices by Christ. The first occurred in Lemuria, the next two in Atlantis, and the fourth (Golgotha) in post-Atlantean times; only the fourth was in the physical realm, the prior ones having been "the three supersensible deeds of Christ." With the insight of these four sacrifices, we can now extend the tabulation in **I-20**, as follows:

Sacrifice by Christ	What was Preserved	Reflected in Gospels By
First	12 Senses of Physical body	12 disciples (Mt/Mk/Lk)
Second	7 Organs of Etheric body	7 disciples (Jn 21,2)
Third	3 Activities of Astral body	3 disciples—Transfiguration, Gethsemane
Fourth	Oneness of Ego	1 disciple—Evangelist John (elsewhere identified)

The following 8-column tabulation is an optional consideration being derived, to a considerable extent, from Tomberg's FSCace, with the background provided by Steiner especially in FSC and PEDC, and made somewhat more comprehendible by Prokofieff's CYPI, Chap. 2. Though highly controversial, and perhaps not always reliable, Tomberg's writings can challenge deep contemplation. The beginning student is justified in jumping over these eight columns, for they may give pause even to the most experienced anthroposophist. And even for that one, it would be helpful to read all of the cited works, for space does not permit adequate elaboration. Among other things it would be well to bear in mind the fractal nature of creation, the concept of the Logos and the Prologue of John's Gospel, and maybe even thrust back to the misty thought presented halfway through the Appendix to "Three Bodies" below: The Father must have been, as modern sexist-free writing would suggest, androgynous, until divided into the fruitful male-female dualism from which the creative "Word" itself, the Christ or "Son," went out. (The male "Son," as well as the female Virgin Sophia, Wisdom [Prov 8,22], were previously "with God" [Jn 1,1-2], indeed, were comprised in God.) I make no claim to inerrancy in this tabulation, but offer it as an attempted crystallization of the several profound works above. I suggest the reader inspect both rank and file, row and column, no title or heading being adequate for any. In doing so, a pattern may seem to take shape in each direction. The four sacrifices of Christ can be seen as reflected therein.

1	2	3	4
Saturn	Sun	Moon	Earth
Father	Son	Holy Spirit	Jesus Christ
Trinity	Logos	Redeemer	Jesus Christ
Warmth	Air	Water	Earth

5	6	7	8
Cold	Will "My God" (Mt 27,46)	Feeling Gethsemane (Mt 26,36-46)	Thinking "Do this in" (Lk 22,19)
Lonely	Thrones	Archangelic Jesus (Jesus-Being)	Archangelic Jesus (Jesus Being)
Memory	Physical	Etheric	Astral
Repeat	Atma seed	Buddhi seed	Manas seed

But with or without contemplating the 8 columns, the Earth evolution deeds of Christ can be charted as follows:

CB = Christ Being (Son)
JB = Jesus Being (archangelic)
JC = Jesus Christ (earthly)]:

(a)	(b)	(c)	(d)
Lemuria	Early Atlantis	Late Atlantis	Earth
JB	JB	JB	JC
Upright	Speech	Consonantal Speech	Death
Will	Feeling	Thinking	

While CB (the Christ Being/Son) is not directly reflected in such tabulation, note (from **I-7**) that the archangelic rank is the chief agency of the Son's Hierarchy (the 2nd Hierarchy) in Earth evolution.

We then see that immediately after the Christ Spirit enters into Jesus of Nazareth so that he becomes Jesus Christ (JC), he is driven by the evil forces into loneliness (the "Wilderness"), where he is confronted by all the temptations that humanity faces; he overcomes them, thereby harmonizing in the human being all its previous gifts, as follows:

Deeds Harmonized	Temptation	Threatened By	Prevail By
Physical—Lemuria	3rd	Ahriman (stones)	Intuition
Etheric—Early Atlantis	2nd	Lucifer & Ahriman (pinnacle)	Inspiration
Astral—Late Atlantis	1st	Lucifer (kingdoms)	Imagination
Ego—Mystery of Golgotha\(Eternal Individuality)	4th	Antichrist (Evil Personality)	All 3 together

Thus, as is so often true, Steiner's various descriptions of Christ, which might at first seem contradictory, are resolved as follows:

Description	Being Involved
The Fullness of the Elohim	(JC) Jesus Christ
A Being, active on Old Sun as leader of Archangels	(JB) Jesus Being
The Logos	(CB) Christ Being

In comparing this chart with **I-35**, one notes that as the Ego was penetrating the astral body during Lemuria, the physical body senses were being harmonized by the first supersensible deed of Christ. During early Atlantis, the Ego was penetrating the etheric body as its organs were being harmonized by the second deed. In late Atlantis, the Ego was penetrating the physical body as the astral body's three forces were being harmonized by the third deed.

I-77 <u>The cosmic harmony reflected in the human being's 4-fold nature and in human language</u>

ALPH; OROH, Lect. 2; SD, Lect. 1

In Is 6,9-13, it is obvious that Isaiah is speaking of a threefold perceptivity (seeing/hearing/understanding) that was being (and was all but) lost and that would someday be regained, a fact explicitly recognized in all four Gospels, the conclusion of Acts, Romans and Jeremiah, and implicitly in countless other ways in the Bible. The lost "hearing" aspect was the atavistic clairaudience of old, which would someday again be regained as a possession of the Christ-Inspired Ego ("I Am"). Then the cosmic connections will be "heard" as the "music of the spheres," and the universal language lost in Babel (Gen 11,1-9) will again be understood (Acts 2,8). We will see how our consonants derive from the "Zodiac," our vowels from the planets, and our "h" and "w" from experiencing planetary revolution, and how the cosmic harmony is actually found in our 4-fold being as follows:

In Our	As The
Physical body	Echo of the "Zodiac"
Etheric body	Echo of the Planetary Movements
Astral body	Experience of the Planetary Movements
Ego	Perception of the Echo of the "Zodiac"

I-78 <u>Relationships between the human being and the plant; the different food substances and their work on the human physical body</u>

NH, Lect. 1; EVEM, Lect. 6; NS, Part II, Sec. 24

As with every domain of existence, anthroposophy sheds great light upon the matters of nutrition and healing (as already indicated in **I-37**). While it is clearly beyond the scope of this work to dwell on this extensively, certain important relationships are reflected in Steiner's following drawing (see also **I-47**):

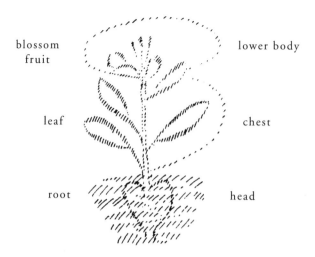

blossom   lower body
fruit

leaf   chest

root   head

Generally speaking, for nutrition and healing the pertinent part of a plant is that which corresponds with the part of the human body in the above drawing. The human head in particular needs minerals, and these are basically provided by the part of the plant that corresponds to the human head, namely, the root, which is in the Earth, the locus of minerals. In like manner, fruits from the top of the plant are good for the intestines, corresponding with the lower body of the human. The following chart indicates how the different types of food substances work on the body:

Food Substance	Works On
Protein	Abdominal Organs
Fats	Heart and Blood Vessels
Carbohydrates	Lungs, Throat, Palate
Minerals	Head

I-79 Art forms and their relationships to the 7-fold human being; the human being's comprehension of musical relationships

ALMW, Lect. 2; INMET, Lect. 5; NOA

Steiner shows how the different art forms, and the impulses behind them, are related to the 7-fold structure of the human being, as follows:

Art Form	Human Component	Character
Architecture	Physical body	Space body; serves external impulses
Sculpture	Etheric body	Harmonious; closely involved with external structure, but rhythmic & involving forces of fluidity
Painting	Astral body	Sensual expression; more fluid, while yet giving expression to space
Music	Ego	Expressive of ourselves when pressed down into the astral body, but as if in the subconscious there, not yet encompassing the higher inner members in conscious expression; moves from space to time
Poetry	Spirit Self	Higher expression of Ego, involving some fidelity to time, but not so much as in music
Eurythmy	Life Spirit	Still higher expression of Ego, but both more fluid and spatial than poetry

Steiner did not go on with a seventh, perhaps implying that the eurythmy he had initiated was itself the latest such expression. (If I correctly understood him, Sergei O. Prokofieff suggested in a recent lecture that the "Social Art" would be the seventh, while anthroposophy itself would be the octave expressive of the entire range of the arts.) It is probably not wise to anchor to any one such scheme. Steiner himself, in the allegorical lecture NOA, gave the following septenary sequence: Dancing, Acting, Sculpture, Architecture, Painting, Music, Poetry.

To show the complexity of each "body," he then says it is as if each component, such as the astral body, were itself 7-fold such that one fold related to each of the seven components themselves in a system of laws for each such relationship. Musically expressed, it would be as though the astral body were the tonic in its scale relationship with the musical intervals of the second, third, fourth, etc. Thus, the interval of the third would be experienced in the part of the astral body which corresponds with the astral body itself. Bearing in mind that the 9-fold human being is reduced to the 7-fold by combining components 3-4 and 6-7, the simile is thus expressed in the following tabulation:

-				
-				
-				
Fifth	-	Consciousness Soul		
Fourth	-	Intellectual Soul		
			/	Sentient Soul
Third	-	Astral body		
			\	Astral body
Second	-	Etheric body		
Tonic	-	Physical body		

The modification from 9-fold to 7-fold thus introduces the division between the major and minor scales, so that, for instance, the third in the left hand column represents the major third and that in the (implied) right hand column the minor third.

To experience a musical work depends upon the inner musical activity of the astral body, but while we listen to the music with our Ego we sink the experience into our astral body, i.e., into the subconscious. Steiner carries us further by supposing that we do not need to hear the physical sound of tones, but are able to listen to the creative activity of the cosmos—the universal music, or the "music of the spheres." We have developed the spiritual strength of our astral body so that it is playing our own being. This thought was alive in human beings of ancient times, and in pointing this out one is also pointing to how materialistic we have become. Humanity is no longer aware that the astral body is a musical instrument. "There was a time when men said, 'A man once lived who was called John,' and this John was able to transport himself into a state of spiritual consciousness in which he could hear the music of the heavenly Jerusalem. They said, 'All earthly music can only be a copy of the heavenly music which began with the creation of mankind.'" But some saw that humanity had absorbed impulses that had darkened the celestial music. This insight into the relationship between external, materialistic music and its heavenly prototype was still beautifully expressed in the 10th and 11th centuries when the following words were written:

> Ut queant laxis
> resonare fibris
> mira gestorum
> famuli tuorum
> solve polluti
> labii reatum,
> S. J. (Sancte Johanne)

which translates, "So that thy servants may sing with liberated vocal cords the wonders of thy works, pardon the sins of the lips which have become earthly [or, "which have become capable of speech"]—O Saint John." And from this has been extracted what we today sing in the scale as "ut(do)-re-mi-fa-sol-la-si(ti)."

While the above comes from ALMW, in INMET Steiner goes on to show how the human being's ability to experience the various intervals has developed, and is developing, only as its evolution proceeds through the ages. Prior to the Atlantean Epoch, the human being could not experience any interval of less than nine (beyond the octave), and the human being has still not come to the point of being able to experience the octave. Gradually, the human being's ability to experience the intervals has progressed downward according to the following tabulation:

Age	Smallest Interval Experienced
Atlantis	7th
1st through 3rd post-Atlantean (Old Indian through Chaldo-Egyptian)	5th
4th & 5th post-Atlantean Greco-Roman & Present Ages)	3rd (Maj/min)

The ability to express major and minor moods in music thus began only in the fourth Age when the ability to experience the third was reached. Only in the future will the human being be able to experience the interval of the second (which may explain the general inability to appreciate the "discord" introduced by "modern classical" music, such as that of Sergei S. Prokofieff [grandfather of anthroposophist Sergei O. Prokofieff] and others); and even more distant is the time when the human being will experience the fullness of the tonic and the octave.

Steiner gives numerous other intriguing relationships of music to the reality of the human being's evolution, but the above must suffice for this present work.

I-80 <u>The components of the human being taken into account by psychology and science, and how other components are effective agents beyond the realm of comprehension by psychology and science</u>

BBUS; PM

Modern psychology (and science) considers only one part of the human being's body (the solid) and one part of its soul (the Ego), and thus cannot come to an understanding of how they work upon each other. The divisions of body (left side below) and soul (right side below) are reflected in the following chart:

warmth body	ego soul realm
air body	dream consciousness
fluid body	sleep consciousness
solid body	

The deeper, and effective, relationships of the upper three components of the body are reflected in the following:

4-fold Component	Activity	Body Component	Spiritual Component
Ego	Will	Warmth-Organism	Warmth Ether
Astral body	Feeling	Air-Organism	Light Ether
Etheric body	Thinking	Fluid-Organism	Chemical (Tone or Sound) Ether

While much in the above charts is beyond our scope, the bridge between universal spirituality and the human being's physical being starts with the top line of the last chart, and the Warmth-Organism. The bridge is then built by moral ideas and destroyed by theoretical thoughts, as reflected by the following analyses:

Moral
Ideas   Stimulate the Warmth-Organism
           Producing in the Air-Organism—sources of *Light*
           Producing in the Fluid-Organism—sources of *Tone*
           Producing in the Solid-Organism—"Seed(s)" of (etheric) *Life*.

Theoretical
Thoughts   "Cool down" the Warmth-Organism
           "Paralyze" the sources of Light
           "Deaden" the sources of Tone
           "Extinguish" (etheric) Life.

Realizing that thinking lies in the nerve sense, feeling in the rhythmic, and willing in the metabolic, an important aspect of the relationship between these areas and our prior lives is reflected in the following Steiner drawing:

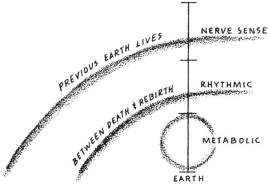

In order to connect the cycle, we must realize that by the phrase "previous Earth lives," Steiner is speaking of what is carried over from them, primarily what came from the willing (metabolic) element (which, in the first tabulation of this chart, relates to the "Ego—Will—Warmth-Organism—Warmth Ether" category). Our thoughts and our knowledge, to the extent they do not play down into the will element (the "deed" element) do not become the "Seed" of our future spiritual (or worldly existence). As Paul said in 1 Cor 13,8, our "knowledge" does indeed pass away, and this happens with our death in this life; only our will, or deed, element (the true reflector of "love"), the "eternal seed," passes over. One must, of course, and will immediately see that our moral thoughts and our feelings are activators of our will (deed) element. But thoughts and feelings that we do not carry forth into the outer world in the form of deeds do not carry forward in any positive sense.

Steiner carries this forward, saying that there is no eternal conservation of matter or energy, for matter is transformed into semblance and semblance is raised to reality by will—all by the human being who stands as the supreme achievement of the cosmos. It is only because of unwillingness to consider things summarized in this chart that ideas of the imperishability of matter and energy were invented. If they were imperishable, there would be no moral world order. As always, this chart is but a hint, a pointer, and it would be unwise to overlook the fact that a more thorough explanation is available in the lecture texts.

I-81 The "Seed," the vortex, the zodiacal sign of Cancer, and the "golden mean"

SKN, Lect. 11; ONMI, Lect. 3; EC, Lect. 11; GSMt, Lect. 11

In so many contexts of anthroposophy (e.g., **I-80**), as in the Bible, the concept of the "Seed," or that which dies and then is reborn completely new, is to be found. It is a deeply occult and spiritual concept, foreign to the guidelines of the laboratory—"of a different world." It relates quite closely to that third step of the Rosicrucian path known as knowledge of "the occult script," widely represented by the sign of the "*vortex.*" This can be thought of as two intertwined figure 6's," of which Steiner says (in SKN, Lect. 11):

This sign is used for indicating and also characterizing a certain type of event that can occur both physically and spiritually. For example, a developing plant will finally produce seeds from which new plants similar to the old one can develop. To think that anything material passes from the old plant to the new is materialistic prejudice without foundation and will eventually be refuted. What passes over to the new plant is formative forces. As far as matter is concerned, the old plant dies completely; materially its offspring is a completely new creation. This dying and new coming-into-being of the plant is indicated by ... a vortex, (drawn) so that the two spirals do not touch.

Many events ... correspond to such a vortex. For example, ... the transition from the ancient Atlantean culture to the first post-Atlantean culture was such a vortex. Natural science only knows the most elementary aspects of this event. Spiritual science tells us that the space between Europe and America, which is now the Atlantic Ocean, was filled with a continent on which an ancient civilization developed, a continent that was submerged by the Flood. This proves that what Plato referred to as the disappearance of the Island of Poseidon is based on facts; the island was part of the ancient Atlantean continent. The spiritual aspect of that ancient culture vanished, and a new culture arose. The vortex is a sign for this event; the inward-turning spiral signifies the old civilization and the outward-turning the new.

As the transition took place from the old culture to the new, the sun rose in the spring in the constellation of Cancer [see **I-19**]—later ... in Gemini ... then in ... Taurus and later still in ... Aries. But the transition from Atlantis to post-Atlantis took place under the constellation of Cancer, whose sign is the intertwining spirals—a sign you find depicted in calendars.

Elsewhere (ONMI, Lect. 3), he refers to the vortex as "the symbol of the spiralling movement of humanity's impulses throughout the ages," drawing it as follows:

In the thirteenth century, one Leonard Pisano, a/k/a Fibonacci, discovered a number sequence that today is widely referred to in the scientific and investment worlds, and in other disciplines, as "the Fibonacci ratio." The extent of its applicability in phenomena of widely varying type is amazing. See 7 Brit 279, "Leonardi, Piero," and 25 Brit 5-6, "Number Games," and Appendix to "Fire," Vol. 2., "*What Is Man?*". When the ratio is graphed, it portrays precisely one of the spirals of the vortex. We find this spiral not only in the action of the markets and of social tastes, but in such phenomena of nature as the spiraling vortices of heavenly bodies and galaxies, the structure of the sea shell, the human ear, the pyramids, the human body and endless other examples. It is, indeed, referred to as "the golden section" or "the golden mean" and seems to be inherent in the created world and in the creating process. It is an expression of the principle of the "seed," of "reincarnation," so aptly put by Paul in 1 Cor 15,36-37. That humanity has thus far managed to avoid applying it to Biblical understanding is simply a manifestation of the "seeing and hearing without seeing, hearing or understanding," as Isaiah saw it from the Seraphim so long ago.

I-82 <u>Karmic characterizations of the human being's 4-fold being</u>

    KV, Lect. 5

    The following characterizations, were given by Steiner in a lecture on karma:

Physical body:	Creative of the life situation
Etheric body:	Formative
Astral body:	Transformative
Ego	Transformative of the life situation

I-83 <u>Steiner, expanding on Goethe, on color</u>

C, Lects. 1 and 2; ARTM, Lects. 7 and 8

In the realm of color, we again find Steiner and the "scientific" view to be at odds as to its nature or objectivity. The Newtonian approach to color is based on the spectrum and the measurement of wave lengths. Steiner basically adopted and carried further Goethe's approach to color. There are two types of colors, "image" and "lustre," exemplified by the following:

<u>Image Colors</u>	<u>Lustre Colors</u>
Green	Yellow
Peach-blossom	Blue
White	Red
Black	

Image colors, as their name implies, are an image of something, namely, Green—plant; Peach-blossom—human soul; White—light and Black—lifeless. These are derived as follows:

<u>Green</u>—comes from the plant, which owes its existence to the fact that it has, in addition to its physical body, an etheric (life) body. The etheric body is not green; the green is to be found in its physical body. Although green belongs to the plant in a most intimate way, it is not the essential nature of the plant, for that lies in the etheric body. It is the mineral nature that appears as green. Therefore, *green represents the lifeless image of the living*.

<u>Peach-blossom</u>—one's human nature is revealed by the way the soul flows into one's physical form in the color of one's skin. Thus, *peach-blossom represents the living image of the soul*.

<u>White</u>—inasmuch as light gives us something of our own spirit, our "I Am," we can say that *white or light represents the soul's image of the spirit*.

Black—carbon represents black (though it also represents a diamond under certain circumstances). A carbonized plant is dead. Black shows itself alien to life. The soul deserts us when blackness is within us, the spirit can flourish. It can penetrate the blackness and assert itself within it. However spirit is the only thing that can be brought into it. Thus, *black represents the spiritual image of the lifeless.*

Steiner gives us the following drawing, in which the outer circle represents the "Illuminant," the middle circle the "Shadow-thrower," and the inner circle the "Image:"

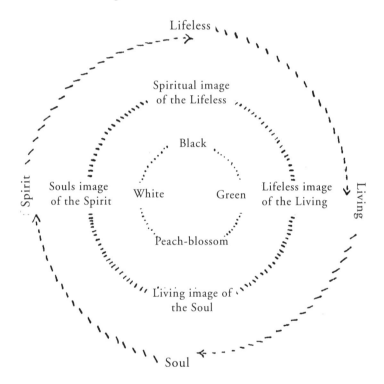

The outer circle thus moves clockwise from twelve o'clock through the cycle of nature from the lifeless to the living, to the ensouled beings, and finally to beings of spirit.

He then depicts the lustre colors by the following characteristics:

Yellow must shine outward;
Blue shines inward;
Red is uniform throughout in its stillness.

These lustre colors are illustrated by the following:

While black, white, green and peach-blossom are images or pictures of something, yellow, blue and red are lustrous, something shines from them, as follows:

Yellow is the lustre of the *spirit*;
Blue is the lustre of the *soul*;
Red is the lustre of the *living*.

I-84 The 3-fold human being as related to the various types of animals

SEWE, Lect. 10; MAE, Lect. 8

In the last few years of his life, Steiner began to show humanity how to make practical application of anthroposophy in the various walks and disciplines of life. Among those was the field of education, where he founded what today is widely recognized as the Waldorf School system. It takes into account the true developmental progress of a child and what is appropriate at each age and stage. He stressed, in the teaching process, "how necessary it is to develop living ideas—ideas that are drawn from actual reality and not from something that has no existence in itself." He stressed the pictorial character of teaching in the earlier years—pictures tied to reality. It is particularly fascinating to see how, using this method, one could realistically explain not only the mineral and the plant, but also the animal and the human being to a child so that a true picture of the evolution of each comes naturally into the young mind.

Steiner drew the following illustration of the 3-fold being of the human being to explain the origin of the human being in relation to the various types of animals of which the human being was the synthesis:

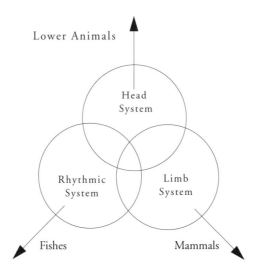

Lower Animals

Head
System

Rhythmic
System

Limb
System

Fishes   Mammals

He then says that by an unprejudiced view of the crustaceans (e.g., shellfish, oysters, etc.—"invertebrates"), the lower animals represent the principle of the human head in its most primitive form, as they are all head principle. Then he moves to those with a spine (e.g., fish, the "vertebrates"), the middle class of animals, which he says are entirely spine creatures; we might compare these to the human lymph organization—the human being's middle (circulatory, or fluid) system. Finally, we come to the higher animals, the mammals, whose entire being is dominated by the specially developed organization of the limbs and metabolism, some (such as cows) being a digestive system and others (such as lions or camels) a limb system, both of the same nature as the human being's lower system, the metabolic-limb system.

This also gives a real insight into the evolution of the human being and animal.

> Human development began with something which finally emerged as the head, but this happened during very ancient times when outer conditions of the earth were entirely different from what they are today. There was as yet plenty of time … for these early stages … to develop into what has become the present head. One can follow this development if one looks at human embryology which shows that, with regard to its head organization, the human being has undergone a long evolution. The head organization began at a time which is still represented by today's mollusks. Today's mollusks, however,

are late arrivals in evolution. As they now have to develop under less favorable outer conditions, they cannot achieve the density of the human head, but have to remain at the stage of a soft-bodied animal surrounded by a hard shell. In today's completely different external conditions they still represent early stages of the human being's head organization.

He then goes on similarly through the middle and higher classes of animals, then adds, "This point of view will enable you to understand that the current theory of the human being's descent is correct, but only with regard to the head. For the head does stem from forebears who had a remote resemblance to the lowest animals of today. And yet, these forebears were again quite different from our present day crustaceans because these latter creatures have to exist under such different external conditions."

It is then not difficult to see how both Bible and science can be brought together, for the human being has taken into its "Ark" all of the animal kingdom (Gen 6,19-7,3), and the order of development of the human being and animals accords with that recognized today by geology. (See **I-5**; the invertebrates appeared two billion years ago, then the first primitive fish 500 million years ago, then the first small and primitive mammals 135 million years ago. We shall see that the order of appearance corresponds to the systems of the human being's physical being and of its embryological development, but as we shall also see, Steiner does not appear to accept the time frames involved in present geological science.)

I-85 The nature of human perception of the Sun, and its Mysteries in the three pre-Christian Cultural Eras

PSI, Lect. 1

For all of the darkening that existed in the age of St. Augustine, and to which he himself was largely subject, he nevertheless retained certain insights from old that have been largely lost in Christendom today. Among them was the knowledge that the Christ Spirit had descended from the highest heavens toward its day of incarnation, staying for a significant part of this journey in the Sun sphere. It was from this that Sun worship properly originated, based upon the sure knowledge of the ancient initiates that the Christ Spirit dwelt in the Sun at that time. On this, Augustine said (CMF, Lect. 13), "What is now called the Christian religion already existed among the ancients and was not lacking at the very beginnings of the human race. When Christ appeared in the flesh, the true religion already in existence received the name of Christian" (Epis. Retrac., Lib. I, xiii, 3).

According to Steiner, the following three pre-Christian periods recognized, to a diminishing extent, this Sun nature:

Cultural Era	Nature of Perception
Ancient Persian	Originally by Zarathustra, not the Zarathustra of whom history tells, but much more ancient. The one of history is the last of a succession of Zarathustra's pupils. The original Zarathustra, was, in relation to all initiates that came after him, more lofty and more sublime. He was also called "Zoroaster," literally "the Radiant Star," for he looked upon the spiritual cosmic Sun, seeing therein the source of all the forces that make the Earth and its inhabitants. He had knowledge of everything that took place on the Earth because he was able to experience the *Spiritual Being* of the Sun, i.e., the One later called the Christ. It was this "Radiant Star" (the Zarathustra spiritual Individuality) whom the Magi were able to see in the Matthew nativity account (Mt 2,2).
Chaldo-Egyptian	The human being still looked up to the Sun, seeing it no longer as *radiant*, but rather only as *shining*, illuminating the Earth with its light. The human being spoke in those times of *Ra*, whose representative on Earth was *Osiris*. Elsewhere we shall again look at *Ra* in connection with the name "Israel" (Is—Isis, widow of Osiris; ra—Ra; El—Canaanite god, e.g., a 3-fold god) along with "Ishmael" (same as Is and El, plus ma-Maat, daughter of Ra).

Greco-Roman   The human being had lost all power of looking
                   into the Mysteries of the Sun and could see only
                   the effect of the Sun's influence in the Earth's
                   environment—the ether surrounding it—and
                   this they (i.e., their initiates) called *Zeus*.

Steiner characterizes these collectively as "the threefold sun," representing
the three stages in the cultural evolution of humanity when something of
the Christ Spirit was recognized in regard to the Sun.

I-86 The reflection of the planets in the human being's physical organs

    OP, Lects. 4 and 8

One significant way the human being reflects its planetary system
within his body is shown by the following Steiner sketches:

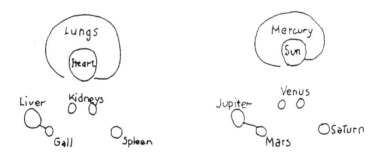

The related lecture text explains the correlation. The noblest instrument
possessed by the human being is said to be its "Blood," which is the
instrument of its Ego. Before any sort of nutrient can be taken in from
the plant or animal kingdoms, which have their own rhythms, its rhythm
must be modified to correspond with the human rhythm. The digestive
organs involved in this process are the spleen, gall bladder and liver,
whose main collective function is to repel what constitutes the particular
inner nature of this food. These organs thus adapt the laws of the outside
world, from which we take our food, to the inner organization or rhythm
of the human being. There must, however, be a continual living reciprocal activity of the human being with the outside world, though these
three organs are placed in opposition to it. What is thus fed into the

"Blood" (Ego) system must be balanced by what represents the outside world. This is accomplished by the lung system through which oxygen enters the "Blood" directly from the outer world, assisted by the kidney system. Thus, we have the spleen-liver-gallbladder (inner) system balanced by the lung-kidney (outer) system. The blood system (Ego) with the heart as its central point is placed in the middle where these two opposing systems are brought into balance for the sustenance of the human being.

It can be seen that the outer planets are associated with what comes from food and the inner two planets with what comes from air and "Blood" purification. Just as the Ego, in its spiritual connection, presupposes the physical, etheric and astral bodies, so also the physical blood-system (Ego), in its physical side, presupposes these two counterbalancing systems, portrayed as follows:

Spiritual	Physical
Physical	Blood-heart
Etheric	Spleen-liver-gallbladder system
Astral	Lung-kidney system

There is a further powerful indication of these relationships. In **I-27** we saw the relationships of the various metals to the planet from which they originated. We now see that where one of the above organisms manifests too strong an inner vitality, it must be counterbalanced, which can be brought about by a proper application of these metals (which is beyond our present scope). We thus see the outer cosmic system duplicated in our inner cosmic system.

This is not the only manifestation of the planetary system in our earthly being. Another one, for instance, is that set out in **I-21** where the planets are shown to have a relationship to the seven "lotus flowers" (Pituitary, Pineal, Larynx, Heart, Solar Plexus, Kidney, Reproductive). Another is the relationship between the number of spinal vertebrae and days in the monthly cycle of the Moon. In RMI, Lect. 5, Steiner numbers the vertebrae at 28 to 30. While trying to get a better fix on the number, it is also fascinating to distinguish (see 24 Brit 810, "The Spinal Cord," and 815, "Spinal Nerves," "Nerves and Nervous Systems") between vertebrae and spinal nerves (see **I-20**), as follows:

Type	Number Vertebrae	Nerves
Cervical	7	8
Thoracic	12	12
Lumbar	5	5
Sacral	5	5
Coccygeal	3	1
Total	32	31

However, the Coccygeal vertebrae are described as "vestigial" and as "rudimentary and occasionally absent," so they would not seem to be of significance in this count. If they are eliminated, the total vertebrae count is 29, which corresponds approximately to the 27 1/2 days in the lunar month, the median (between 29 and 27 1/2) being close to 28, a number divisible by the planetary seven. Thus our bony skeleton relates primarily to the Moon forces, while the higher nervous system relates more closely to the 30+ days derived by dividing the year by the zodiacal Twelve. Steiner sketched (RMI, Lect. 5) the following illustration of how the ancient initiates saw in the formation of the human spine a copy of the monthly movement of the Moon, "of the streams that the Moon sends down continually upon the Earth":

The editor/translator of RMI notes that in German the same word is used for "rotations" and "vertebrae," and even our English word is taken from the Latin *vertere* (to turn). The relationship of the lunar month to human embryology is amazing. Only a hint of it is given in the fact that the human gestation period of approximately 275 days comprises ten lunar months (**I-20**).

I-87 The "Star of David," or "Mogen (Magen) David"

RMI, Lect. 5

As shown in "Three Bodies," the Bible extensively and pervasively demonstrates the 3-fold body, revealed for our time by Rudolf Steiner. A small portion of that evidence is given in the patriarchal and monarchic accounts of Genesis and Kings. When the Jews referred to their blood-line, it was always to their fathers, "Abraham, Isaac and Jacob" (Ex 3,6, et al.). It is noteworthy that the first identifying expression of this three-some was immediately before the declaration by their God, "I AM the I AM" (Ex 3,14). The Book of Kings tells us that there were three, and only three, kings of the undivided Israel, namely, Saul, David and Solomon. In these we see a line of progressively greater spiritual (one might even say occult) insight, or "wisdom."

Our purpose in this chart is to look at the symbol known as the (six-pointed) "Star of David," or "Mogen (Magen) David," meaning "Shield of David." We are told, 3 Brit 911, "David, Star of":

> The symbol—which historically was not limited to use by Jews—originated in antiquity, when, side by side with the five-pointed star, it served as a magical sign.... In the Middle Ages [it] appeared with greater frequency among Jews but did not assume any special religious significance.... The term *Magen David* ... gained currency among medieval Jewish mystics, who attached magical powers to King David's shield just as earlier (non-Jewish) magical traditions had referred to the five-pointed star as the "seal of Solomon." Kabbalists popularized [its use] against evil spirits... from the 17th century on [it] became ... a general sign of Judaism, though it has no biblical or Talmudic authority.

In the Commentary we will look at the "Key of David" (Rev 3,7), but here we note that Steiner refers to this symbol as "Solomon's Key," and to explain it he sketches the following portrayal:

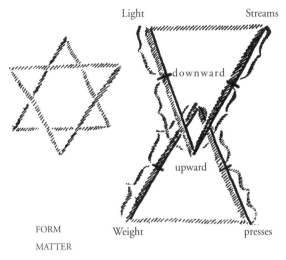

Light   Streams

downward

upward

FORM   Weight   presses

MATTER

He tells us that there was a small and lonely school somewhere in Central Europe, apparently "in the early decades of the nineteenth century," led by a "Master." What this Master taught was acknowledged by Steiner to have included matters later "disclosed" to him through spiritual science (anthroposophy). In his teaching, the Master used the above symbols, which came to him from ancient times, with the words (at the points of the triangles) in Hebrew. As a mode of meditative training, he would

get the pupils to assume a certain attitude with their physical bodies. The body itself had to "draw" this symbol. He made them stand with their feet far apart, and their arms stretched out above. Then, by lengthening the lines of the arms downwards and the lines of the legs upwards, these four lines (darker in the diagram) came to view in the human organism itself. A line was then drawn to unite the feet, and another to unite the hands above; and these two joining lines had to be felt as lines of force. The pupil became conscious that they do really exist; it became clear to him that currents pass, not unlike electro-magnetic currents, from the left finger-tips to the right finger-tips, and again from the left foot to the right. So that in actual fact the human organism itself writes into space these two intersecting triangles.

The pupil had then to learn to feel what lies in the words: "Light streams upwards, Weight bears downwards."

According to Steiner, the pupil was gradually thus brought to experience something "practiced over and over again in the ancient Mysteries, … namely, that he could feel the very marrow within the bones of his limbs (see dark lines in diagram)." And then, we are told, the teacher put into the following words what the pupils were experiencing:

> Behold the man of bone,
> And thou beholdest Death.
> Look within the bones,
> And thou beholdest the Awakener—

Compare Heb 4,12 which speaks of the "word of God … piercing to the division of soul and spirit, of joints and marrow.…"

If one considers the above symbol in the light of these remarks, it is quite apparent that it portrays the Fall, salvation, and ascension of the human being, which is the theme of the Bible from Gen 1 to Rev 22, the ultimate application of the Parable of the Prodigal Son, the story of two sons, the "prodigal" first Adam, who fell, and the second Adam, his sister soul, who, by serving the Christ, brought him to his senses and made his return possible. The first Adam was "the son of God" (Lk 3,38) and the second was "the Son of God." The reality of the Fall, redemption and eventual ascension is central to the teaching of anthroposophy.

I-88　The "Threefold Social Order"

TSO; ESP, Lect. 3; WE

At the request of various prominent Europeans at the end of World War I, Steiner lent his energies to developing and propounding a system of social renewal for the devastated continent. His radical ideas turned out to be premature and were rejected, as he may well have expected, though typically he poured his heart and soul into the effort to bring them to pass.

It is this author's conviction that the human being has arrived at a spiritual crossroads at which a growing comprehension of anthroposophical truth is essential if progress is to be made on the upward path to salvation, rather than continuing on the downward path to perdition and the abyss represented by the materialism of our age—a materialism that frightfully often afflicts most grievously those among our religious who least expect it and are most certain of their own personal salvation, as was true in Biblical times.

A corollary of the materialistic outlook of our times is the political reality that Steiner's social proposals stand no chance of being adopted so long as his underlying insights into the nature of the human being and the Christ are not understood. It is also my judgment that the conflicts so obvious in the world will never be overcome until that day when this true nature is recognized and put into effect in the social system. These conflicts exist from the individual all the way up to the international level. The only eventual hope for attaining the spiritual age to come is the implementation of Steiner's "threefold social order."

The threefold fundamental problems in society's structure are:

1. Spiritual life is felt as an ideology;
2. Labor is treated as a commodity;
3. Economic conditions govern human labor.

It is noted that both Capitalists, on the one hand, and Communists, Socialists, and the Labor Movement, on the other, are equally guilty of regarding labor as a commodity. Neither approach is a part of the proposed new order.

The "social question" divides itself into three distinct parts:

1. A healthy form of spiritual life;
2. Right way to incorporate labor into community;
3. Proper place and function of economic life.

Essential comparisons are set out below:

Social Life	3-Fold Being	The 3 Human Organisms
Economic system	Body	Metabolic/Limb
Public rights	Soul	Rhythmic
Individuality	Spirit	Head/Nervous

No good can be done in the social movement unless we are willing to give reality its due. It is essential that the human being's activities within the body social must be in line with the conditions of its organic life. Steiner did not attempt to get into the minute details of implementation, saying that these would have to be worked out within the various units involved. Still, the principles and guidelines are sufficiently definite to point the way for humanity when it is sufficiently prepared spiritually to take this step.

The separate spheres of political, economic and spiritual life as they exist today must be brought together, for, as Bock (ApSJn, Chap.10) points out, they will each, standing alone, fall with Babylon (Rev 18) as follows:

Kings (Rev 18,9)	=	Political
Merchants(Rev 18,11)	=	Economic
Sailors (Rev 18,17b)	=	Spiritual

The heavenly city foreseen by the prophet (Is 11,1-9 and 66,17-25) cannot coexist with them.

The post-Atlantean Cultural Age of Philadelphia (Rev 3,7-13) can hardly be attained by humanity until the conflicts inherent in any lesser system are overcome. See **I-49**.

I-89 The loci where the human initiate meets the Egos of the three lower kingdoms

GOSPSJ, Lect. 5

The following is a complement to, and paraphrase of, **I-ll**, but with emphasis upon the human being's components and consciousness:

Human Ego of the	World	Human Consciousness of the Egos of the
Physical body	Higher	Spiritual Minerals
Etheric body	Lower	Spiritual Plants
Astral body	Astral	Animals (also angels)
Individual body	Physical	Day Consciousness

The human being who is initiated into the higher worlds is conscious of the Egos that dwell in those worlds. In this lecture Steiner speaks of there being an Ego of each of the human bodies. To activate it, the individual Ego must permeate the body in question, and in doing so becomes conscious in that body's world. He concludes the lecture with a 3-fold simile, which may be charted as follows:

The Ego of the	That Dwells In the Following World	May be Compared to a Car's
Etheric body	Lower Devachan	Engineer
Astral body	Astral	Driver
Individual body	Physical	Owner

ABBREVIATIONS AND BIBLIOGRAPHY

Cross-Reference Table

(from abbreviations to chronological bibliography)

Abbrev-iation	Earliest Date	Abbrev-iation	Earliest Date	Abbrev-iation	Earliest Date
AA	01-11-16	AQL	01-19-07	BMFE	11-02-08
AAF	1910	ARCHM	Anthol.	BMRSH	07-17-21
AART	08-23-21	AREF	11-25-86	BNS	09-27-20
ABMI	11-27-13	ARNS	01-01-21	BPS	09-23-23
ABTCC	02-18-13	ARTM	05-27-23	BSE	11-23-05
AC	07-13-14	AS	03-16-21	BSEH	11-06-17
ACCOE	09-28-19	ASJ	06-15-08	BSU	03-27-17
ACDB	01-19-14	ASLF	02-16-13	BT	09-15-20
ACG	06-29-21	ASP	03-07-07	BUDC	05-31-09
ACHC	02-23-18	ASQ	1905	BWIS	12-05-08
ACOM	01-23-23	ASSMT	04-11-21	BWM	11-20-14
AD	10-27-19	ASSW	1898	BWMAG	11-10-06
AE	10-17-20	ATM	05-27-23	C	07-26-14
AEAKC	05-20-24	ATMD	01-06-23	CA	02-03-12
AEC	05-01-09	AUTOB	09-09-07	CAHE	11-05-22
AEL	Anthol.	AVA	04-09-22	CASE	1917
AET	06-22-22	AWASJ	10-10-04	CATO	11-06-08
AF	09-20-16	AWD	10-19-08	CBRel	03-17-07
AFT	08-24-23	AWHC	05-08-12	CCC	04-15-23
AGRIC	06-07-24	BANDC	08-13-14	CCMS	01-02-24
AGSS	08-22-06	BaW	12-05-08	CConf	12-24-23
AHE	05-29-17	BBB	01-12-23	CCWL	12-13-07
AIL	01-19-24	BBIR	09-06-18	CD	Anthol.
ALECT	10-11-21	BBUS	12-17-20	CEC	10-31-20
ALFS	09-19-14	BCCMA	03-05-24	CED	06-25-24
ALG	03-30-18	BCHS	12-22-18	CEHE	01-09-12
ALMW	12-28-14	BD	10-25-14	CEU	04-12-21
ALPH	12-18-21	BD-2	01-23-20	CEVC	08-05-22
ALT	02-17-24	BDR	11-05-12	CFCCT	12-22-10
AM	01-04-18	BECD	11-23-15	CFE	02-09-24
ANIMS	03-16-07	BEEK	02-03-23	CFFAK	07-16-21
ANMO	06-10-23	BG	05-28-13	CFM	11-24-21
AOT	03-28-21	BGEP	12-28-12	CGS	1899
AP	11-05-17	BKM	10-17-10	CHE	02-15-09
APOC	01-16-05	BL	12-19-04	CHLS	03-10-08
APOC-CC	09-05-24	BLAT	01-30-15	CHM	02-06-17

CHS	07-12-14	CTME	12-19-15	ECON	01-08-22
CHWC	03-25-22	CURR	09-06-19	ECSCD	02-22-16
CIBU	02-13-15	CWCR	1917	EDCH	1907
CIDE	10-25-09	CWEM	02-09-23	EDCL	01-22-18
CINIT	07-11-06	CWIM	05-02-23	EE	04-08-24
CIU	ca. 1890	CWN	01-26-19	EEC	04-02-22
CL	09-10-15	CWORD	11-16-07	EFA	06-21-22
CLD	11-09-16	CY	03-31-23	EFEM	04-19-24
CLPAM	07-22-22	DAQA	04-10-21	EGO	12-04-09
CM	1904	DAA	06-02-14	EGOEXC	08-12-21
CMF	1902	DAG	06-15-09	EIE	12-23-17
CML	12-08-23	DBS	10-15-11	EK	12-11-10
CMMSES	11-12-21	DCFGLE	10-23-21	EKHW	02-02-23
CMNS	12-22-08	DCOSP	01-01-09	EKING	12-04-07
CMOD	05-29-15	DDC	02-11-06	ELEC	01-28-23
CMPCE	02-10-23	DE	10-26-18	ELW	Sep 1922
CMRP	05-17-23	DEST	1919	EMD	05-03-24
CMS	09-11-20	DFC	08-05-21	EML	04-26-18
CMSW	11-06-16	DFSP	03-11-23	EMM	09-02-08
CMYST	02-09-06	DIE	10-15-23	EMSS	01-09-15
CNC	04-21-23	DIN	09-01-14	EMTI	05-06-09
CNY	12-21-19	DMAP	02-29-12	ENH	10-20-23
COHLBD	12-16-08	DOS	06-24-22	ENHS	03-13-13
CONFN	11-09-14	DPHL	09-14-18	EoB	10-01-11
CoS	1912	DSGRD	08-30-22	EOONY	12-31-18
COSMC	11-24-15	DSM	11-01-09	ERIN	04-28-10
COST	10-08-06	DSTY	01-15-15	ESD	03-20-13
CPAM	09-20-18	DT	08-21-19	ESI	11-27-12
CPGJ	12-27-15	DTFFN	05-15-21	ESOTD	12-07-05
CPN	08-23-15	DTSLT	01-09-21	ESP	08-09-19
CPSK	05-27-22	DWTN	10-11-19	ESR	03-06-13
CRA	Anthol.	DWU	02-10-18	ESSB	10-09-22
CRLA	05-18-15	EA	02-03-13	ESSS	Anthol.
CRSP	Anthol.	EACT	04-12-07	EVC	08-19-23
CSEE	03-13-10	EAML	03-25-23	EVEM	06-30-24
CSF	02-29-08	EAR	10-23-11	EVIL	01-15-14
CSMG	06-14-06	EASTER	04-12-06	EVS	06-24-24
CSMY-1	09-23-21	EBPHB	04-20-15	EVSG	02-19-24
CSPT	06-10-17	EBRU	06-13-15	EW	Apr 1922
CSSS	1924	EC	05-25-06	EWLCI	12-24-21
CSSZ	05-17-24	ECE	09-20-22	EWM	09-03-20
CSW	12-28-13	ECIH	05-07-15	EWRC	02-05-21
CT	11-29-18	ECM	03-19-12	FA	08-29-21
CTC	05-06-12	ECMCR	09-17-11	FAM	10-26-22
CTK	12-15-12	ECMS	04-21-24	FAS	12-25-23

FAT	08-22-24	GFRS	12-07-11	HI-1	10-19-22
FBAF	07-09-22	GGMLE	10-07-04	HI-2	12-30-22
FBFN	07-14-22	GIMT	01-03-19	HMAUT	10-18-04
FCRE	01-15-16	GL	12-26-19	HMLA	03-12-20
FDE	11-22-19	GMA	01-02-15	HMT	10-17-18
FDEP	07-24-21	GMCP	11-19-09	HNFW	12-22-17
FDLD	11-16-15	GMGS	06-27-21	HPP	10-23-08
FDSW	04-06-23	GMSD	11-15-17	HPR	06-14-18
FE	09-26-05	GOSP	11-14-09	HQCA	06-25-22
FESTS	03-19-07	GOSPSJ	11-16-07	HSAS	11-10-10
FG	10-01-13	GPT	08-28-21	HSBRSU	03-15-17
FIRE	01-01-23	GS	1883	HSDTB	05-08-14
FJAIB	01-03-15	GSAPM	02-02-08	HSF	08-20-16
FKDLD	06-01-24	GSJ	05-18-08	HSHS	05-30-04
FLFN	03-20-09	GSJL	06-26-05	HSIB	01-08-11
FLH	12-02-11	GSJN	02-12-06	HSKSW	06-28-23
FM	12-14-05	GSL	09-15-09	HSLD	11-26-14
FMCI	10-28-21	GSLL	04-23-14	HSRWE	04-29-22
FMD	08-10-10	GSMk	09-15-12	HSU	02-20-17
FN	1895	GSMt	09-01-10	HTM	03-07-14
FOA	11-28-21	GSR	10-22-08	HUHT	05-26-22
FOT	1925	GSS	03-01-24	HVE	07-17-24
FOTF	11-25-23	GWV	1897	IaM	04-29-09
FPG	11-16-11	HAECK	10-05-05	IASQ	02-04-19
FPOA	Nov 1921	HART	10-08-16	ICIC	12-23-21
FQ	10-22-06	HATR	09-13-18	ICWH	03-20-13
FQ-2	05-27-24	HAUSW	04-18-14	IDM	12-15-04
FSA	10-05-23	HBBSS	08-02-22	IEPM	08-25-12
FSC	06-01-14	HBLA	11-29-21	IEVE	04-16-06
FSD	09-29-17	HBRB	12-12-14	IFM	01-21-23
FSDT	12-13-18	HBRPL	07-01-22	IGP	11-29-17
FSI	10-17-19	HBSNS	01-14-16	IH	03-03-10
FSLS	06-10-13	HCFI	06-16-21	IIFPH	12-03-07
FSR	10-18-18	HCMF	12-22-18	IIWEM	09-18-16
FSSP	11-17-22	HCPE	02-01-20	IK	01-26-09
FTEMP	03-04-09	HCSI	04-07-20	ILA	11-14-19
FV	01-31-15	HCT	01-20-14	ILE	05-30-15
FVE	Oct 1923	HDIFC	10-16-18	IMP	02-20-20
FWPR	02-03-16	HDSL	11-23-11	IMW	02-11-23
GAM	10-21-16	HEA	02-02-24	INDP	1899
GBG	01-26-11	HEAA	07-21-23	INE	12-12-19
GCNC	10-02-16	HEPA	06-03-15	INH	07-01-21
GEM	02-08-20	HGK	03-09-13	INM	04-06-14
GEN	08-17-10	HHEBR	09-05-15	INMET	12-03-06
GET	1903	HHF	02-13-20	INTE	04-05-19

IPCP	01-07-17	LBTR	12-02-08	MGRSM	03-24-22
IPPG	10-31-23	LBYD	12-15-12	MH	05-06-23
ISBM	01-06-08	LC	12-23-19	MHB	10-09-16
ITTO	05-31-19	LCEGA	05-30-23	MHPOK	06-25-24
JAC	11-15-13	LCFR	Jun 1903	MHU	04-09-20
JB	01-09-13	LCOS	09-11-15	MI	12-06-19
JBP	11-04-11	LD	10-27-10	MIANG	01-08-14
JCPET	12-28-15	LDV	02-13-13	MICHM	08-17-24
Jn-Rel	06-24-09	LECPAR	05-05-13	MICK	03-14-15
JOC	11-29-21	LECT	05-16-12	MIGR	1904
JSQ	11-09-18	LEUR	08-26-23	MK	05-16-10
JTC	10-05-11	LEWC	10-05-19	ML	12-04-22
JTCL	10-04-11	LHE	05-19-17	MLEG	03-02-13
KC	08-12-24	LMS	12-03-22	MLO	06-02-12
KCC	01-25-24	LMW	12-17-12	MLSE	12-12-19
KHW	1904	LNCA	01-13-24	MM	03-21-10
KI	04-14-22	LP	01-28-07	MMHM	05-03-18
KM	07-31-17	LPROB	11-26-10	MMS	06-22-19
KMSB	10-31-22	LRM	06-05-13	MNNFC	01-05-23
KMSBT	07-22-19	LS	Oct 1923	MNS	01-20-23
KMSR	02-06-20	LSEII	04-15-23	MOHEB	03-03-11
KOB	06-20-24	LSIS	06-28-23	MOWS	05-05-21
KR-1	02-16-24	MAE	08-05-23	MP	07-15-23
KR-2	04-06-24	MAK	11-12-10	MPCW	01-28-17
KR-3	07-01-24	MAMT	12-25-17	MPL	08-15-21
KR-4	09-05-24	MANAT	07-18-20	MPLS	09-02-23
KR-5	03-29-24	MATD	03-12-10	MPPF	09-14-23
KR-6	01-25-24	MATHO	06-21-04	MPPP	01-26-19
KR-7	06-07-24	MBD	05-16-23	MPU	09-17-22
KR-8	08-12-24	MBRE	02-14-18	MR	01-30-13
KSBU	11-03-22	MBSP	07-22-21	MRWSW	12-01-07
KSH	03-20-20	MBSS	02-25-18	MS-1	10-14-09
KU-1	01-04-16	MC	11-23-23	MS-2	10-14-09
KU-2	01-01-17	MCBTW	07-08-21	MSCW	10-19-23
KV	11-04-16	MCR	11-18-11	MSF	09-27-23
LA	04-01-19	MCTKC	03-27-15	MSLSWD	03-21-22
LAD	01-26-13	MDMA	1901	MST	02-24-18
LAD-2	06-21-23	MDRAM	01-01-10	MSTM	08-24-18
LAI	12-03-16	MEC	02-03-13	MSYMB	10-07-07
LAIHE	11-28-20	MEEC	12-07-22	MT	07-23-22
LAST	09-27-24	MENSR	10-13-23	MTA	04-02-21
LBBD	02-02-15	MEW	12-07-19	MTAT	05-25-05
LBDNB	02-18-16	MFR	01-26-23	MU	03-21-18
LBDR	10-26-12	MFS	06-07-10	MULS	02-12-18
LBLD	10-10-13	MG	12-17-13	MWLSS	03-18-08

MWS	11-26-22	OPSYCH	08-17-18	PF-11	01-18-19
MYST	12-25-07	ORD	04-23-13	PF-12	01-19-19
MYSTD	11-22-15	ORIGE	02-20-08	PHE	10-17-04
MYSTG	12-02-06	ORL	02-17-13	PHIT	08-28-23
NASQ	09-15-19	OROH	10-13-14	PIFAH	09-17-10
NATS	05-16-08	OS	Dec 1909	PIPT	01-06-21
NB	10-08-23	OSAGG	03-22-05	PKC	05-27-14
NC	02-21-23	OSC	05-18-07	PKHW	11-26-21
NCOM	10-24-23	OSG	05-03-11	PL	12-03-05
NE	03-21-12	OSOD	05-01-13	PLK	11-21-09
NEK	04-09-12	OSOE	11-08-06	PLSS	02-07-20
NETFA	02-27-21	OSPF-1	09-04-16	PM	09-08-24
NF	01-25-16	OSPF-2	09-09-16	PMC	02-02-15
NH	07-31-24	OSPF-3	09-10-16	PMFT	12-26-08
NMSE	12-23-13	OSPF-4	09-11-16	PNEUM	04-01-22
NOA	10-28-09	OSPWC	07-02-20	PNM	11-09-11
NOI	1880	OSS	09-13-07	PNT	01-10-15
NS	Anthol.	OVN	01-11-12	PNUT	12-17-08
NSD	09-08-19	PA	08-17-08	PoN	01-08-09
NSHDH	05-21-21	PACM	12-24-17	POPOCC	06-28-06
NSLS	06-08-13	PARA	04-26-06	POT	09-12-19
NSP	10-17-20	PARIS	05-25-24	PP	12-31-23
NUMG	10-21-13	PARS	07-29-06	PPMC	01-04-15
NY	03-23-19	PARTS	09-29-20	PRBD	02-05-15
OAB	01-07-13	PAS	04-08-22	PRBDY	10-24-16
OAMR	08-28-24	PAT	08-21-19	PSA	1894
OAWLS	01-18-12	PBA	07-08-20	PSE	01-15-15
OCC	10-19-07	PCC	10-14-13	PSI	04-24-22
OEVIL	01-18-07	PCR	09-06-22	PSJB	10-27-08
OFG	10-21-13	PD	04-17-14	PSM	10-13-06
OFGH	11-16-13	PE	12-12-20	PSP	02-25-12
OFSF	10-31-15	PEDC	03-07-14	PSRTA	02-15-18
OGSJ	06-26-05	PELA	03-10-20	PSYC	09-13-15
OH	12-27-10	PEM	03-05-20	PT	10-07-20
OI	04-12-12	PET	11-19-22	PTT	01-18-09
OIL	10-21-21	PF-1	09-30-16	PWDLC	02-22-11
OMC	09-10-23	PF-2	12-10-16	PYR	02-17-10
OMCHD	05-19-07	PF-3	01-27-17	QH	01-14-09
OML	05-23-12	PF-4	11-02-17	QW	01-21-22
OMN	10-10-15	PF-5	11-03-17	RABG	01-23-23
ONL	01-23-10	PF-6	11-04-17	RBCEPC	06-30-22
ONMI	01-01-22	PF-7	09-27-18	RBCT	01-16-16
ONS	12-24-22	PF-8	09-28-18	RBLD	02-16-16
OP	03-20-11	PF-9	09-29-18	RC	07-06-23
OPSS	10-26-16	PF-10	01-17-19	RCATH	05-30-20

RCE	01-25-10	SBMEM	07-11-19	SLP	02-04-07
RCHB	07-20-23	SBPD	05-14-08	SLSR	02-04-16
RCI	08-31-18	SBPSE	05-11-19	SLWA	ca. 1920
RCULT	12-02-21	SC	01-15-12	SM	08-21-19
RD	11-29-15	SCDI	12-19-07	SMASS	03-17-05
RDC	08-06-21	SCE	03-15-24	SMCHH	11-06-21
RE	06-03-09	SCON	11-24-21	SMRC	02-20-10
RED	04-13-24	SCT	06-12-19	SMS	03-26-08
RETSS	04-20-20	SCUSC	01-18-20	SMW	12-19-04
RH	07-29-16	SD	09-05-24	SOA	09-12-20
RHW	11-25-21	SDM	04-20-23	SOFT	06-25-18
RI	01-12-16	SE	01-21-09	SPLS	11-27-14
RK	01-23-12	SED	04-04-13	SPQ	04-21-19
RL	07-17-15	SELFT	12-07-05	SPTREL	12-14-20
RLSS	04-13-23	SEM	03-14-12	SPTWSB	10-22-21
RM	1916	SESL	04-13-19	SPV	09-12-15
RM-2	06-28-21	SEWE	12-23-21	SQ	03-30-19
RMFS	03-16-15	SF	10-24-19	SQPSL	03-28-19
RMI	01-04-24	SFM	05-28-12	SQQC	03-16-19
RMLSS	05-19-13	SFPM	12-16-15	SRHO	10-20-22
RMOTH	08-16-15	SGE	08-16-22	SRIF	05-05-18
RMWE	01-29-21	SGM	06-06-11	SRMR	Anthol.
RN	01-27-23	SGSM	02-11-11	SRP	12-08-10
ROC	04-28-23	SH	04-12-09	SS	04-08-11
ROSC	09-27-11	SHBAE	02-06-24	SSAE	11-27-19
RP	1914	SHBU	11-01-22	SSBGW	07-10-05
RPA	04-22-07	SHCMH	05-14-24	SSBR	1914
	05-09-09	SHF	11-26-20	SSCFM	06-17-08
RS	09-10-17	SHK	1905	SSFS	08-06-20
RSI	12-01-13	SI	01-05-20	SSKSU	10-23-19
RSK	1912	SIDP	09-10-23	SSLA	01-23-21
RSO	1919	SIHM	09-22-22	SSM	03-21-20
RSRNM	12-31-21	SIHMC	10-12-19	SSMAN	11-12-23
RSVL	Anthol.	SIP	07-27-23	SSMB	10-14-22
RSWS	Anthol.	SIS	12-23-20	SSNPT	03-13-15
RT	05-22-20	SITW	10-12-05	SSNS	03-01-13
RTGE	04-30-18	SJT	06-24-23	SSRM	03-06-11
RWB	04-29-08	SK	1886	SSSPT	01-30-17
RWLA	03-28-05	SKADA	09-27-23	ST	08-24-13
RWM	12-02-07	SKCE	02-02-23	STUTT	06-09-20
RYA	12-12-21	SKN	10-11-06	SUBCF	05-09-15
SAF	12-12-18	SKSPPT	1918	SUMC	01-09-16
SAI	05-06-18	SKWL	11-16-23	SUPP	06-12-21
SALTMS	01-13-23	SLCR	Jul 1921	SUSS	10-04-19
SB	04-03-12	SLL	12-21-19	SWECC	07-16-22

SWM	01-14-23	TWW	Anthol.	WSIHE	06-06-16
SWMR	03-13-24	TYP	07-20-24	WSIM	02-26-16
SWS	08-24-19	UEM	08-04-08	WSO	09-07-19
TASS	11-13-09	UH	12-04-09	WSOC	11-17-06
TAT	11-03-04	UNEM	10-09-21	WSWS	12-27-11
TAY	01-06-23	VIEN	06-18-22	WTL	03-04-11
TBG	01-19-23	VLS	02-26-14	WW	08-18-11
TCAT	11-13-08	VM	Anthol.	WWHE	12-25-21
TCR	04-13-22	VT	05-16-16	YAL	06-09-24
TCSM	11-16-08	VTK	09-17-15	YCF	12-27-10
TEW	06-01-22	WAAE	06-30-23	YG	10-03-22
TFP	08-11-24	WAMAB	10-09-18	YP	07-20-24
TFWRS	04-14-23	WARK	Anthol.	YSN	01-17-24
TGG	01-21-24	WBG	08-19-16	ZS	12-30-17
THEOSC	10-01-06	WC	03-01-20		
THSY	1904	WCAD	11-13-10		
TI	06-06-16	WCAH	07-17-24		
TIEC	06-24-21	WCR	11-16-05		
TIG	01-19-05	WCY	05-23-15		
TK	1892	WDB	09-22-23		
TL	05-23-04	WDIOA	11-10-06		
TLTK	07-24-15	WDLA	12-01-21		
TM	08-29-15	WE	07-24-22		
TMMM	09-02-23	WEA	Anthol.		
TNM	02-01-21	WEAN	02-23-21		
TOR	1903	WEC	02-25-11		
TPA	07-20-23	WEDA	Anthol.		
TPBR	05-05-09	WEEB	Anthol.		
TPHO	11-27-20	WESVS	12-21-13		
TPI	11-30-06	WFRSL	01-31-19		
TPMH	01-24-19	WH	12-24-23		
TPSC	04-16-12	WHA	03-16-11		
TPSH	01-19-11	WHG	02-09-11		
TPWD	02-02-19	WHIT	06-09-08		
TR	05-22-07	WHSFD	04-28-23		
TSA	08-28-22	WLA	03-20-16		
TSESE	03-05-14	WMCWB	10-21-07		
TSHE	10-04-18	WNSA	06-07-14		
TSO	Apr 1919	WMSIN	09-06-20		
TSOL	02-15-21	WMSS	10-23-09		
TSR	1919	WNSA	06-07-14		
TSS	Apr 1921	WNY	12-31-14		
TTIM	12-12-11	WPG	04-09-23		
TTLB	04-03-05	WRU	11-18-17		
TWTP	07-15-21	WSA	07-24-20		

Abbreviations used for Anthroposophical publishers are as follows:

AM	Anthroposophical Movement Weekly News
AMLY	Anthroposophic Monthly
ANS	Anthroposophic News Sheet, Dornach, Switzerland
AP	Anthroposophic Press, Hudson, NY
APC	Anthroposophic Publishing Co., London
AQ	Anthroposophic Quarterly
AR	Anthroposophic Review
FB	Floris Books, Edinburgh, Scotland
GB	Golden Blade (An anthroposophic periodical published by FB)
GBR	Garber Communications, Blauvelt, NY
JA	The Journal of Anthroposophy, Dripping Springs, TX
KBDF	Bio-Dynamic Farming & Gardening Ass'n, Kimberton, PA
MP	Mercury Press, Chestnut Ridge, NY
NEWS	Newsletter, Anthroposophical Society in America
RSP	Rudolf Steiner Press, London
RSPB	Rudolf Steiner Publications, Blauvelt, NY
RSPC	Rudolf Steiner Publishing Co., London
SBC	Steiner Book Centre, North Vancouver, Canada
TC	Threefold Commonwealth, London
TLP	Temple Lodge Press, London
U.E.T.	See next paragraph

Publication dates are for English editions only. A majority of the Steiner titles below were not in print during my own library accumulation. On these, loan copies were provided by the Rudolf Steiner Library. In many instances these copies contained on their face no data on publication, nor was it available on the Library's catalogue listings. In these instances, if the document was in typescript form I usually assumed it was unpublished. In the most common of these situations, the publication data is given as "unpublished English typescript" and abbreviated "U.E.T." Where publication data uses one of the publishing company abbreviations above or is otherwise shown in the normal format (i.e., city, publisher name, year), it is believed to be reliable. In all other cases, the data is simply the best practically available to me in compiling this list and cannot, as such, be deemed fully reliable.

The reader should bear in mind that this Bibliography is part of the initial volume of a series to be published. The bibliographical section in later volumes will include only supplements to the original list and references cited in the volume itself.

Abbreviations are used only where the full title has been used previously in the same essay. Space considerations preclude the use of both an alphabetical and chronological arrangement on Steiner's works. The chronological is deemed more useful. Consequently, the date of the earliest lecture (or publication if originally a writing) is given immediately following each Steiner abbreviation in the Cross-Reference Table. From that, the title, publishing information and location can be readily found in the Bibliography data. Works other than Steiner's and Steiner Biographies are arranged alphabetically.

Steiner Writings and Lectures:

Earliest Date	# & Location of Lectures	Title & Abbreviation
1880	Letter/bklet	*Nature and Our Ideals*, MP, 1983 (NOI)
1883	Book	*Goethean Science*, MP, 1988 (GS)
1886	Book	*The Science of Knowing*, MP, 1988 (SK)
11-25-86	Essay	*Atomism and its Refutation*, no pub. data given (AREF)
ca. 1890	Article	*Credo—The Individual and the Universe*, Proteus Quarterly (Post 1948) (CIU)
1892	Book	*Truth and Knowledge*, 2d Ed., RSPB, 1981 (TK)
1894	Book	*The Philosophy of Spiritual Activity*, AP, 1986 (PSA)
1895	Book	*Friedrich Nietzsche, Fighter for Freedom*, 2d Rev. Ed., RSPB, 1985 (FN)
1897	Book	*Goethe's World View*, MP, 1985 (GWV)
1898	Article	*Another Secret of Shakespeare's Works*, MP, 1985 (ASSW)
1899	Essay	*The Character of Goethe's Spirit as shown in the Fairy Story*, GBR, 1991 (at the end of FTSL below) (CGS)
1899	Essay	*Individualism in Philosophy*, MP, 1989 (INDP)
1901	Book	*Mysticism at the Dawn of the Modern Age*, 2d Ed., RSPB, 1980 (MDMA)
1902	Book	*Christianity as Mystical Fact*, 2d Ed., AP, 1972 (CMF)
1903	Extracts	*Guidance in Esoteric Training*, 3rd Ed., RSP and AP, 1994 (GET)
1903	Articles (3)	*Theosophy and German Culture / Occult Investigation of History Reincarnation and Senility*, (Eng. typescript from journal *Luzifer*, 1903) (LCFR)
June 1903	Essay	*Lucifer*, (Eng. typescript from journal *Luzifer*, 1903) (LCFR)
1904	Book	*Cosmic Memory*, RSPB, 1959 (CM)
1904	Book	*Knowledge of Higher Worlds and its Attainment*, 3rd Ed., AP, 1947 (KHW)
1904	Book	*Theosophy*, AP, 1971 (THSY)
1904	1-Berlin	*On the Migrations of the Races*, (Eng. typescript from German Gaa-Sophia: Volkerkunde, 1904) (MIGR)
05-23-04	20-Berlin	*The Temple Legend/Freemasonry & Related Occult Movements*, RSP, 1985 (TL)

05-30-04	1-Berlin	*The History of Spiritism, Hypnotism* and *Somnambulism,* AP & RSP, 1943 (HSHS)
06-21-04	1-Amsterdam	*Mathematics ad Occultism,* (weekly news sheet "Anthroposophical Movement," 7-8-28) (MATHO)
10-07-04	4-Berlin	*Greek and Germanic Mythology in the Light of Esotericism,* U.E.T. (GGMLE)
10-10-04	3-Berlin	*On Apocalyptic Writings, with special reference to the Apocalypse of St. John,* U.E.T. (AWASJ)
10-17-04	13-Berlin	*Planetary and Human Evolution,* (U.E.T. of unpub. German notes) (PHE)
10-18-04	8-Berlin	*History of the Middle Ages Until the Time of the Great Inventions and Discoveries,* U.E.T. (HMAUT)
11-03-04	1-Berlin	*Theosophy and Tolstoi,* (U.E.T. from German text in Nachrichtenblatt, 1946) (TAT)
12-15-04	1-Berlin	*The Inner Development of Man,* AP, 1970 (IDM)
12-19-04	1-Berlin	*The Birth of the Light,* MP, 1984 (BL)
12-19-04	4-Berlin	*Supersensible in Man and World* (Lect. 4 is same as BL but diff. trans.), RSPB, 1964 (SMW)
1905	Essays	*Anthroposophy and the Social Question* (see also MHB), MP, 1982 (ASQ)
1905	Book	*The Stages of Higher Knowledge,* AP, 1967 (SHK)
01-16-05	2-Cologne	*The Apocalypse,* U.E.T. (APOC)
01-19-05	1-Dusseldorf	*The Idea of God* (Extracts), U.E.T. (TIG)
03-17-05	1-Cologne	*The Significance of the Mass,* U.E.T. (SMASS)
03-22-05	1-Dusseldorf	*The Old Sagas of the Gods,* U.E.T. (OSAGG)
03-28-05	2-Berlin	*Richard Wagner in the Light of Anthroposophy,* ANS, 1-10-37 (RWLA)
04-03-05	1-Berlin	*The Ten Leafed Book,* U.E.T. (TTLB)
05-25-05	1-Berlin	*Medical Training and Anthroposophy,* West Nyack, NY, Free Deeds, Sept. 1962 (MTAT)
06-26-05	1-Berlin	*On the Gospel of St. John,* (U.E.T. from unpub. German notes) (OGSJ)
07-10-05	1-London	*The Spiritual-Scientific Basis of Goethe's Work,* Spring Valley, NY, St. George Pub., 1982 (SSBGW)
09-26-05	31-Berlin	*Foundations of Esotericism,* RSP, 1983 (FE)
10-05-05	1-Berlin	*Two Essays on Haeckel,* AP & Rudolf Steiner Pub. Co., Eng., (no pub. date given) (HAECK)
10-12-05	1-Berlin	*The Situation of the World,* ANS, 9-9-45 (SITW)
11-16-05	1-Berlin	*The Wisdom Contained in Religions,* U.E.T. (WCR)
11-23-05	1-Berlin	*Brotherhood and the Struggle for Existence,* 2d Ed., MP, 1980 (BSE)

12-07-05	5-Berlin	*Esoteric Development*, AP, 1982 (ESOTD)
12-07-05	12-Various	*Self-Transformation*, RSP, 1995 (SELFT)
12-08-05	1-Cologne	*Parsifal and Lohengrin*, (Notes) U.E.T. (PL)
12-14-05	29-Various	*The Festivals and their Meaning*, RSP, 1992 (FM)
02-09-06	1-Dusseldorf	*The Christian Mystery*, U.E.T. from Das Christliche Mysterium (no pub. data) (CMYST)
02-11-06	1-Dusseldorf	*Dante's Divine Comedy*, ANS, 5-10-36 (DDC)
02-12-06	1-Cologne	*St. John's Gospel, Notes of a Lect. on*, U.E.T. (GSJN)
04-12-06	1-Berlin	*Easter*, U.E.T. (EASTER)
04-16-06	1-Berlin	*The Interior of the Earth and Volcanic Eruptions*, U.E.T. (IEVE)
04-26-06	1-Berlin	*Paracelsus* ANS, 9-21-41 (PARA)
05-25-06	18-Paris	*An Esoteric Cosmology*, GBR, 1987 (EC)
06-14-06	1-Paris	*Cosmogony* (found at back of RPA), AP, 1991 (CSMG)
06-28-06	11-Leipziz	*Popular Occultism*, U.E.T. (POPOCC)
07-11-06	1-Leipzig	*Christian Initiation*, U.E.T. from Nachrichtenblatter, Nov. 1946 (CINIT)
07-29-06	1-Landin	*Parsifal*, U.E.T. (PARS)
08-22-06	14-Stuttgart	*At the Gates of Spiritual Science*, 2d Ed., RSP and AP, 1986 (AGSS)
10-01-06	1-Berlin	*Theosophy and Science*, U.E.T. (THEOSC)
10-08-06	1-Berlin	*Concerning the Objections of Science to Theosophy*, U.E.T. (COST)
10-11-06	13-Berlin	*Supersensible Knowledge*, MP, 1988 (SKN)
10-13-06	1-Leipzig	*Precious Stones and Metals: Their Connection with the Evolution of the Earth and of Humanity*, U.E.T. from *Das Christliche Mysterium* (no pub. date given) (PSM)
10-22-06	1-Berlin	*The Food Question*, U.E.T. from unpub. French notes (FQ)
11-08-06	3-Berlin	*The Origin of Suffering / The Origin of Evil, Illness and Death*, SBC, 1980 (OSOE)
11-10-06	1-Leipzig	*Wagner's Development of the Ideas on Art and Schopenhauer on Music*, U.E.T. (WDIOA)
11-10-06	1-Leipzig(?)	*Black and White Magic* (Answer to a Question), U.E.T. (BWMAG)
11-17-06	1-Hamburg	*Woman and Society*, RSP, 1985 (WSOC)
11-30-06	1-Cologne	*The Three Paths of Initiation*, U.E.T. (TPI)
12-02-06	1-Cologne	*The Mystery of Golgotha*, U.E.T. (MYSTG)
12-03-06 to 03-16-23	7-various	*The Inner Nature of Music and the Experience of Tone*, AP, 1983 (INMET)

1907	Essay	*The Education of the Child,* RSP & AP, 1965 (EDCH)
01-18-07	1-Stuttgart	*The Origin of Evil,* ANS, 6-24-45 (OEVIL)
01-19-07	1-Stuttgart	*Answers to Questions after Lecture,* U.E.T. (AQL)
01-28-07	1-Berlin	*The Lord's Prayer,* AP, 1970 (LP)
02-04-07	1-Karlsruhe	*The Structure of the Lord's Prayer,* RSP, 1971 (SLP)
03-07-07	1-Dusseldorf	*The Adept-School of the Past,* ANS, 8-0-41 (ASP)
03-16-07	2-Leipzig	*The Animal Soul/The Four Human Group Souls,* U.E.T. (ANIMS)
03-17-07	2-Munich	*Christianity Began as a Religion but is Greater than all Religions,* APC, 1959 (CBRel)
03-19-07	19-Various	*The Festivals of the Seasons,* APC, 1928 (FESTS)
04-12-07	1-Berlin	*Easter and the Awakening to Cosmic Thought,* AQ, no pub. date given (EACT)
04-22-07	4-Munich	*Reading the Pictures of the Apocalypse—Part l,* AP, 1991 (RPA)
05-18-07	1-Munich	*Occult Seals and Columns,* U.E.T. (OSC)
05-19-07	1-Munich	*The Oneness of Man and Cosmos; Human Development and Its Relations with the Cosmic-Planetary Development,* ANS, 4-18-48 (OMCHD)
05-22-07	14-Munich	*Theosophy of the Rosicrucian,* 2d Ed., RSP, 1966 (TR)
09-09-07	1-Barr/Alsace	*Autobiographical Sketch* (for Schure), NEWS Spring 1975 (AUTOB)
09-13-07	4-Stuttgart	*Occult Signs and Symbols,* AP & RSP, 1972 (OSS)
10-07-07	4-Berlin	*Myths and Symbols: The World Ash: Yggdrasil/The Mongolian Legend/The Hermaphrodite/Man's Victory Over the Physiognomy of Death: The Skeleton/The Flight of Birds/Et al.,* GB, 1957 (MSYMB)
10-19-07	1-Berlin	*On Chaos and Cosmos,* U.E.T. (OCC)
10-21-07	1-Berlin	*White Magic Contrasted With Black,* U.E.T. (WMCWB)
11-16-07	?-Basel	*The Creative Word* (Private Notes taken during cycle GOSPSJ), U.E.T. (CWORD)
11-16-07	8-Basel	*The Gospel of St. John,* U.E.T. (GOSPSJ)
12-01-07	1-Nuremburg	*Man's Relationship With the Surrounding World/ Physical and Moral Laws,* ANS, #9 (MRWSW)
12-02-07	1-Berlin	*Richard Wagner and Mysticism,* AQ #5, per R. S. Library (RWM)
12-03-07	2-Munich	*Illusory Illness and the Feverish Pursuit of Health,* AP, 1969 (IIFPH)
12-04-07	1-Berlin	*The Elementary Kingdoms. The Nature of the Elementary Beings, Their Activities and Influence,* ANS, 3-29-36 (EKING)

12-13-07	1-Berlin	*Christmas/A Contemplation out of the Wisdom of Life/Vitaesophia*, MP, 1982 (CCWL)
12-19-07	1-Cologne	*The So-Called Dangers of Initiation*, ANS, 5-4-41 (SCDI)
12-25-07	1-Cologne	*The Mysteries, a poem by Goethe*, MP, 1987 (MYST)
01-06-08	11-Berlin	*The Influence of Spiritual Beings Upon Man*, AP, 1961 (ISBM)
02-02-08	1-Frankfurt	*The Group Souls of Animals, Plants and Minerals*, U.E.T. (GSAPM)
02-20-08	1-Cassel	*The Origin of Evil*, U.E.T. (ORIGE)
02-29-08	1-Berlin	*Concerning the Spirits of Form*, ANS, 9-20-36 (CSF)
03-10-08	1-Arnheim	*The Course of Human Life Seen in the Light of Spiritual Science*, ANS, 4-27-47 (CHLS)
03-18-08	1-Munich	*Man and Woman in the Light of Spiritual Science*, AR, #2 (MWLSS)
03-26-08	1-Berlin	*Sun, Moon and Stars*, ANS, 3-29-36 (SMS)
04-29-08	1-Munich	*The Relationship between Worlds and Beings/The Perception of Higher Beings*, ANS, 5-24-36 (RWB)
05-14-08	1-Munich	*Shadow Beings, Phantoms and Demons Created by Man Himself*, ANS, 8-30-36 (SBPD)
05-16-08	12-Various	*Nature Spirits*, RSP, 1995 (NATS)
05-18-08	12-Hamburg	*The Gospel of St. John*, Rev. Ed., AP, 1962 (GSJ)
06-09-08	1-Cologne	*Whitsuntide*, U.E.T. (WHIT)
06-15-08	13-Nuremberg	*The Apocalypse of St. John*, 4th Ed., RSP & AP, 1977 (ASJ)
06-17-08	1-Nuremburg	*Spiritual Science, Christianity and the Future of Mankind*, London, TC, 1921 (SSCFM)
08-04-08	11-Stuttgart	*Universe, Earth and Man*, RSP, 1987 (UEM)
08-17-08	1-Stuttgart	*Philosophy and Anthroposophy*, MP, 1988 (PA)
09-02-08	12-Leipzig	*Egyptian Myths and Mysteries*, AP, 1971 (EMM)
10-19-08	1-Berlin	*The Astral World and Devachan*, U.E.T. (AWD)
10-22-08	4-Berlin	*Goethe's Secret Revelation and the Riddle of Faust*, RSPC, 1932 (GSR)
10-23-08	1-Berlin	*History of the Physical Plane and Occult History*, pub. data unclear, typescript form (HPP)
10-27-08	1-Berlin	*Concerning the Nature of Pain, Suffering, Joy and Bliss*, AN, 9-22-46 (PSJB)
11-02-08	9-Berlin	*The Being of Man and His Future Evolution*, RSP, 1981 (BMFE)
11-06-08	1-Munich	*Carnegie and Tolstoi*, pub. data missing from R. S. Library copy (CATO)
11-16-08	2-Various	*The Ten Commandments/The Sermon on the Mount*, AP, 1978 (TCSM)

12-02-08	1-Breslau	*Life Between Two Reincarnations*, ANS, 6-5-38 (LBTR)
12-05-08	1-Hamburg	*The Bible and Wisdom*, SBC, 1941 (BWIS)
12-16-08	1-Nuremberg	*A Chapter of Occult History: With Special Reference to the Life Between Death and Rebirth*, AQ, 1969 (COHLBD)
12-17-08	1-Berlin	*Problems of Nutrition*, U.E.T. (PNUT)
12-22-08	1-Berlin	*The Christmas Mystery: Novalis, The Seer*, MP, 1985 (CMNS)
12-26-08	2-Berlin	*The Poetry and Meaning of Fairy Tales*, MP, 1989 (PMFT)
01-01-09	2-Berlin	*The Deed of Christ and the Opposing Spiritual Powers/Mephistopheles and Earthquakes*, SBC, 1954 (DCOSP)
01-08-09	1-Munich	*Problems of Nutrition*, AP, 1969 (PoN)
01-14-09	1-Berlin	*Questions of Health*, U.E.T. (QH)
01-18-09	1-Karlsruhe	*Practical Training in Thought*, 2d Ed. AP, 1966 (PTT)
01-21-09	11-Various	*The Principle of Spiritual Economy*, AP & RSP, 1986 (SE)
01-26-09	1-Berlin	*Illness and Karma*, U.E.T. (IK)
02-15-09	1-Berlin	*Christianity in Human Evolution*, AP, 1944 (CHE)
03-04-09	1-Berlin	*The Four Temperaments*, AP & RSP, 1987 (FTEMP)
03-20-09	1-Berlin	*Friedrich Nietzsche* (Extract), U.E.T. (FLFN)
04-12-09	10-Dusseldorf	*The Spiritual Hierarchies and Their Reflection in the Physical World*, AP, 1970 (SH)
04-29-09	1-Berlin	*Isis and Madonna*, MP, 1987 (IaM)
05-01-09	1-Berlin	*Ancient European Clairvoyance*, GB, no pub. date given (AEC)
05-05-09	1-Berlin	*Two Pictures by Raphael*, U.E.T. (TPBR)
05-06-09	1-Berlin	*The European Mysteries and The Initiates*, AQ, Spring, 1964 (EMTI)
05-09-09	12-Kristiania	*Reading the Pictures of the Apocalypse—Part 2*, AP, 1991 (RPA)
05-31-09	5-Various	*From Buddha to Christ*, AP & RSP, 1978 (BUDC)
06-03-09	10-Budapest	*Rosicrucian Esotericism*, AP, 1978 (RE)
06-15-09	1-Breslau	*The Dedication of an Anthroposophical Group*, ANS, 5-22-38 (DAG)
06-24-09	14-Kassel	*The Gospel of St. John and Its Relations to the Other Gospels*, 2d Ed., AP, 1982 (Jn-Rel)
09-15-09	10-Basle	*The Gospel of St. Luke*, Rev. Ed., AP, 1962 (GSL)
10-14-09	18-Berlin	*Metamorphoses of the Soul/Paths of Experience*—Vols. 1 & 2, 2d Ed., RSP, 1983 (MS-1 & MS-2)

10-23-09	12-Berlin	*The Wisdom of Man, of the Soul, and of the Spirit/ Anthroposophy, Pyschosophy, Pneumatosophy,* AP, 1971 (WMSS)
10-25-09	7-Berlin	*The Christ Impulse and the Development of Ego Consciousness,* AP, 1976 (CIDE)
10-28-09	1-Berlin	*The Nature and Origin of the Arts,* MP, 1992 (NOA)
11-01-09	3-Berlin	*Deeper Secrets of Human History in the light of the Gospel of St. Matthew,* Rev. Ed., RSP & AP, 1957 (DSM)
11-13-09	1-Stuttgart	*The Tasks and Aims of Spiritual Science,* APC, 1960 (TASS)
11-14-09	1-Stuttgart	*The Gospels,* Eng. typescript; unclear if otherwise published (GOSP)
11-19-09	1-Zurich	*The Gospel of St. Matthew and the Christ-Problem,* ANS, 6-22-47 (GMCP)
11-21-09	1-St. Gallen	*Problems of the Law of Karma,* ANS, 6-25-42 (PLK)
Dec 1909	Book	*Occult Science—an Outline,* 3rd Ed., AP, 1972 (OS)
12-04-09	4-Various	*The Universal Human,* AP, 1990 (UH)
12-04-09	3-Munich	*The EGO, The God Within and The God of External Revelation,* RSPC & AP, no pub. date given (EGO)
1910	Book	*Anthroposophy (A Fragment),* AP, 1996 (AAF)
01-23-10	1-Strassburg	*Extract From Lecture at the Opening of the "Novalis" Lodge,* U.E.T. (ONL)
01-25-10	13-Various	*The Reappearance of Christ in the Etheric,* AP, 1983 (RCE)
02-17-10	1-Berlin	*Prayer,* 3rd Ed., AP, 1977 (PYR)
02-20-10	1-Dusseldorf	*The Sermon on the Mount and the Return of Christ,* U.E.T. (SMRC)
03-03-10	1-Berlin	*Illness and Healing,* U.E.T. (IH)
03-12-10	1-Munich	*The Mission of Anger, Truth and Devotion,* ANS, 7-4-54 (MATD)
03-13-10	1-Munich	*Comets and their Significance for Earthly Existence,* ANS, #9 (CSEE)
03-21-10	11-Vienna	*Macrocosm and Microcosm,* Rev. Ed., RSP & AP, 1985 (MM)
04-28-10	1-Berlin	*Error and Insanity,* U.E.T. (ERIN)
05-16-10	11-Hamburg	*The Manifestations of Karma,* 3rd Ed., RSP, 1984 (MK)
06-07-10	11-Christiana	*The Mission of Folk-Souls,* GBR, 1989 (MFS)
08-10-10	4 Plays	*Four Mystery Dramas,* SBC, 1973 (FMD)
08-17-10	10-Munich	*Genesis,* RSP, 1982 (GEN)

09-01-10	12-Berne	*The Gospel of St. Matthew*, 4th Ed., RSP & AP, 1965 (GSMt)
09-17-10	3-Various	*Three Lectures on the Mystery Dramas*, AP, 1983 (MDRAM)
09-17-10	4-Various	*Self-Knowledge re "The Portal of Initiation"/ Faust's Ascension into Heaven, etc.*, U.E.T. (PIFAH)
10-17-10	13-Various	*Background to the Gospel of St. Mark*, 3rd Ed., RSP & AP, 1968 (BKM)
10-27-10	1-Berlin	*Life and Death*, U.E.T. (LD)
11-10-10	2-Berlin	*The Human Soul and the Animal Soul/The Human Spirit and the Animal Spirit*, pub. data unclear (HSAS)
11-12-10	1-Numerberg	*Morality and Karma*, ANS, 10-15-44 (MAK)
11-13-10	1-Nuremberg	*The Wisdom Contained in Ancient Documents and in the Gospels/The Event of the Christ*, ANS, 6-27-37 (WCAD)
11-26-10	1-Bremen	*Life Problems*, ANS, 6-4-41 (LPROB)
12-08-10	1-Berlin	*The Spirit in the Realm of Plants*, MP, 1984 (SRP)
12-11-10	1-Munich	*Effects of Karma*, ANS, 6-30-35 (EK)
12-22-10	1-Berlin	*The Christmas Festival in the Changing Course of Time*, AP, 1988 (CFCCT)
12-27-10	6-Stuttgart	*Occult History*, RSP, 1982 (OH)
12-27-10	1-Stuttgart	*Yuletide and the Christmas Festival*, AQ, Winter 1974 (YCF)
01-08-11	1-Frankfurt	*The Human Soul's Innermost Being and its Relationship with the Spiritual World*, ANS, 9-3-44 (HSIB)
01-19-11	6-Berlin	*Turning Points in Spiritual History*, RSPB, 1934 (TPSH)
01-26-11	1-Berlin	*Galilei, Giordano Bruno and Goethe*, ANS 2-22-42 (GBG)
02-09-11	2-Berlin	*What Has Geology to Say About the Origin of the World?/The Face of the Earth*, U.E.T. (WHG)
02-11-11	1-Munich	*The "Son of God" and the "Son of Man,"* U.E.T. (SGSM)
02-22-11	1-Basle	*Patience, Wisdom, Devoutness and Life-Confidence*, ANS, 7-20-47 (PWDLC)
02-25-11	1-Zurich	*The Work of the Ego in Childhood/A Contribution Towards an Understanding of Christ*, AQ, Winter, 1976 (WEC)
03-03-11	1-Berlin	*Mendelssohn's "Overture of the Hebrides?,"* ANS, #6 (MOHEB)
03-04-11	1-Hanover	*"I Am the Way, the Truth and the Life,"* U.E.T. (WTL)

03-06-11	1-Bielefeld	*The Significance of Spiritual Research for Moral Action*, AP, 1981 (SSRM)
03-16-11	1-Berlin	*What Has Astronomy to Say about the Origin of the World?*, U.E.T. (WHA)
03-20-11	8-The Prague	*An Occult Physiology*, 3rd Ed., RSP, 1983 (OP)
04-08-11	1 Bologna	*Seeing with the Soul*, MP, 1996 (SS)
05-03-11	1-Munich	*The Concepts of Original Sin and Grace*, RSP, 1973 (OSG)
06-06-11	3-Copenhagen	*The Spiritual Guidance of Man*, AP, 1950 (SGM)
08-18-11	10-Munich	*Wonders of the World, Ordeals of the Soul, Revelations of the Spirit*, RSP, 1963 (WW)
09-17-11	13-Various	*Esoteric Christianity and the Mission of Christian Rosenkreutz*, 2d Ed., RSP, 1984 (ECMCR)
09-27-11	2-Neuchatel	*Rosicrucian Christianity*, MP, 1989 (ROSC)
10-01-11	1-Basle	*The Etherization of the Blood*, 4th Ed., RSP, 1971 (EoB)
10-04-11	1-Carlsruhe	*From Jesus to Christ*, RSPC, no pub. date given (JTCL)
10-05-11	10-Karlsruhe	*From Jesus to Christ*, RSP, 1973 (JTC)
10-15-11	1-Stuttgart	*Dedication of the Building at Stuttgart*, U.E.T. (DBS)
10-23-11	6-Berlin	*Evolution in the Aspect of Realities*, GBR, 1989 (EAR)
11-04-11	2-Leipzig	*Jeshu Ben Pandira*, AP & RSP, 1942 (JBP)
11-09-11	1-Berlin	*Prophecy, Its Nature and Meaning*, APC, 1950 (PNM)
11-16-11	1-Berlin	*From Paracelsus to Goethe*, U.E.T. (FPG)
11-18-11	8-Various	*The Mission of Christian Rosenkreutz*, RSPC, 1950 (MCR)
11-23-11	1-Berlin	*The Hidden Depths of Soul Life*, U.E.T. (HDSL)
12-02-11	2-Nuremberg	*Faith, Love, Hope*, SBC, no pub. date given (FLH)
12-07-11	1-Berlin	*Good Fortune, Its Reality and its Semblance*, APC, 1956 (GFRS)
12-12-11	1-Berlin	*The Temple is—Man!*, APC, 1951 (TTIM)
12-27-11	6-Hanover	*The World of the Senses and the World of the Spirit*, SBC, 1979 (WSWS)
1912	Book	*The Calendar of the Soul*, 2d Ed., AP, 1988 (CoS)
1912	Book	*A Road to Self Knowledge/(1913) The Threshold of the Spiritual World*, 3rd Ed., RSP, 1975 (RSK)
01-09-12	1-Munich	*Cosmic Ego and Human Ego*, AP & RSP, 1941 (CEHE)
01-11-12	1-Munich	*Overcoming Nervousness*, AP, 1969 (OVN)
01-18-12	1-Berlin	*The Origin of the Animal World in the Light of Spiritual Science*, U.E.T. (OAWLS)

01-23-12	5-Various	*Reincarnation and Karma/Their Significance in Modern Culture*, SBC, 1985 (RK)
02-03-12	1-Breslau	*Conscience and Astonishment*, ANS, #6 (CA)
02-25-12	5-Various	*Psychoanalysis and Spiritual Psychology*, AP, 1990 (PSP)
02-29-12	1-Berlin	*Death in Man, Animal and Plant*, U.E.T. (DMAP)
03-14-12	1-Berlin	*The Self-Education of Man in the Light of Anthroposophy*, U.E.T. (SEM)
03-19-12	8-Berlin	*Earthly and Cosmic Man*, GBR, 1986 (ECM)
03-21-12	1-Berlin	*The Nature of Eternity*, AQ, Summer, 1972 (NE)
04-03-12	14-Helsinki	*Spiritual Beings in the Heavenly Bodies & in the Kingdoms of Nature*, AP, 1992 (SB)
04-09-12	1-Helsingfors	*The National Epics with especial attention to the Kalevala*, U.E.T. (NEK)
04-12-12	1-Helsingfors	*Occultism and Initiation*, ANS, 5-9-43 (OI)
04-16-12	2-Stockholm	*The Three Paths of the Soul to Christ*, AP & RSP, 1942 (TPSC)
05-06-12	1-Cologne	*Christ in the Twentieth Century*, AP, 1971 (CTC)
05-08-12	1-Cologne	*Ancient Wisdom and the Heralding of the Christ Impulse*, AQ format (AWHC)
05-16-12	1-Munich	*Lecture* (untitled; but involves Buddha, Christ, Death, and the Nature of the Second Coming), ANS, 1937 (LECT)
05-23-12	2-Copenhagen	*On the Meaning of Life*, AP (NY & London), 1928) (OML)
05-28-12	3-Norrkoping	*The Spiritual Foundation of Morality*, AP, 1995 (SFM)
06-02-12	10-Oslo	*Man in the Light of Occultism, Theosophy and Philosophy*, GBR, 1989 (MLO)
08-25-12	7-Munich	*Initiation, Eternity and the Passing Moment*, AP, 1980 (IEPM)
09-15-12	10-Basel	*The Gospel of St. Mark*, AP & RSP, 1986 (GSMk)
10-26-12	16-Various	*Life Between Death & Rebirth*, AP, 1968 (LBDR)
11-05-12	10-Berlin	*Between Death and Rebirth*, 2d Ed., RSP, 1975 (BDR)
11-27-12	1-Munich	*The Errors of Spiritual Investigation*, U.E.T. (ESI)
12-15-12	1-Bern	*Concerning the Technique of Karma in Life after Death and the Secret of the Human Brain*, no pub. data given (CTK)
12-15-12	13-Various	*Life Beyond Death*,RSP, 1995 (LBYD)
12-17-12	1-Zurich	*Love and its Meaning in the World*, APC, 1960 (LMW)

12-28-12	5-Cologne	*The Bhagavad Gita and the Epistles of Paul*, AP, 1971 (BGEP)
01-07-13	1-Berlin	*Olaf Aesteson, The Awakening of the Earth-Spirit*, U.E.T. (OAB)
01-09-13	1-Berlin	*Jacob Boehme*, AP & RSP, 1942 (JB)
01-15-12	1-Zurich	*Sleep and Clairvoyance*, ANS, 4-11-54 (SC)
01-26-13	1-Linz	*Life After Death/Necessity for Realizing the Spiritual in Life/Spiritual Language/Heredity*, U.E.T. (LAD)
01-30-13	1-Berlin	*The Mission of Raphael*, U.E.T. (MR)
02-03-13	4-Berlin	*The Mysteries of the East and of Christianity*, GBR, 1989 (MEC)
02-03-13	1-Berlin	*The Essence of Anthroposophy*, U.E.T. (EA)
02-13-13	1-Berlin	*Leonardo DeVinci*, U.E.T. (LDV)
02-16-13	1-Tuebingen	*Anthroposophy as a Substance of Life and Feeling*, ANS, Easter, 1937 (ASLF)
02-17-13	2-Stuttgart	*Occult Research into Life Between Death and a New Birth*, AP, 1949 (ORL)
02-18-13	1-Stuttgart	*About Horses That Can Count and Calculate*, ANS, 7-26-36 (ABTCC)
03-01-13	2-Frankfurt	*Spiritual Science and Natural Science in their Relation to Life's Mysteries*, U.E.T. (SSNS)
03-02-13	1-Frankfurt	*The Mission of Life on Earth as a Gateway to the World Beyond*, ANS, 1938 (MLEG)
03-06-13	1-Berlin	*Errors in Spiritual Investigation*, U.E.T. (ESI)
03-09-13	1-Munich	*How can we Gain Knowledge of the Supersensible Worlds?*, ANS, #2 (HGK)
03-13-13	1-Augsburg	*The Essence and Nature of the Human Soul and the Riddle of Death*, ANS, 9-29-35 (ENHS)
03-20-13	2-Hague	*Introductory and Concluding Word to Lectures in the Hague*, U.E.T. (ICWH)
03-20-13	10-Hague	*The Effects of Spiritual Development*, RSP, 1978 (ESD)
04-04-13	1-Berlin	*Self-Education: Autobiographical Reflections 1861-1893*, MP, 1985 (SED)
04-23-13	1-Essen	*On the Relationship with the Dead*, Dornach, Goetheanum News, Mar/Apr 1971 (ORD)
05-01-13	2-London	*Occult Science and Occult Development/Christ at the Time of the Mystery of Golgotha & Christ in the Twentieth Century*, 4th Ed., RSP, 1983 (OSOD)
05-05-13	1-Paris	*Lecture Given in Paris*, U.E.T. (LECPAR)
05-19-13	1-Stuttgart	*Raphael's Mission in the Light of the Science of the Spirit*, ANS, 7-21-35 (RMLSS)

05-28-13	9-Helsingfors	*The Occult Significance of the Bhagavad Gita*, AP, 1968 (BG)
06-05-13	1-Helsingfors	*Lecture to Russian Members*, ANS, 1-4-41 (LRM)
06-08-13	1-Stockholm	*Nature and Spirit in the Light of Spiritual-Scientific Knowledge*, ANS, 10-27-35 (NSLS)
06-10-13	1-Stockholm	*The Freedom of the Soul in the Light of Spiritual Scientific Knowledge*, ANS, 11-10-35 (FSLS)
08-24-13	8-Munich	*Secrets of the Threshold*, AP & RSP, 1987 (ST)
10-01-13	7-Various	*The Fifth Gospel*, 2d Ed., RSP, 1968 (FG)
10-10-13	2-Bergen	*Links Between the Living and the Dead/ Transformation of Earthly Forces into Clairvoyance*, RSP, 1973 (LBLD)
10-14-13	1-Copenhagen	*The Path of the Christ through the Centuries*, AQ, Summer, 1975 (PCC)
10-21-13	1-Berlin	*The Necessity of Understanding the Mystery of Golgotha Anew*, ANS, 1949 (NUMG)
10-21-13	7-Berlin	*On the "Fifth Gospel"*, ANS, #17 (OFG)
11-15-13	1-Hamburg	*Jesus and Christ*, AP, 1976 (JAC)
11-16-13	1-Hamburg	*On the Fifth Gospel* (Hamburg), U.E.T. (OFGH)
11-27-13	2-Berlin	*About Death/The Meaning of the Immortality of the Human Soul*, U.E.T. (ABMI)
12-01-13	1-Basle	*Results of Spiritual Investigation*, RSPB, 1971 (RSI)
12-17-13	2-Cologne	*The Mystery of Golgotha*, U.E.T. (MG)
12-21-13	1-Bochum	*The Winter of the Earth and Spiritual Victory of the Sun*, ANS, 12-20-36 (WESVS)
12-23-13	1-Berlin	*Newborn Might and Strength Everlasting*, AP, 1977 (NMSE)
12-28-13	6-Leipzig	*Christ and the Spiritual World/ The Search for the Holy Grail*, RSP, 1963 (CSW)
1914	Book	*Riddles of Philosophy*, AP, 1973 (RP)
1914	Essay	*Spiritual Science: A Brief Review of its Aims and of the Attacks of its Opponents*, London, John M. Watkins, 1914 (SSBR)
01-08-14	1-Berlin	*Michangelo*, U.E.T. (MIANG)
01-15-14	1-Berlin	*On Evil*, R. S. Library Newsletter, Vol. IV #3/4, Issue 15/16, 1996 (EVIL)
01-19-14	1-Berlin	*On the Anthroposophists' Colony in Dornach* (Berlin), U.E.T. (ACDB)
01-20-14	4-Berlin	*Human and Cosmic Thought*, RSP, 1961 (HCT)
02-26-14	1-Berlin	*Voltaire in the Light of Spiritual Science*, U.E.T. (VLS)
03-05-14	1-Stuttgart	*The Three Super-Earthly Spiritual Events Preceding the Mystery of Golgotha / "The Effects of the Christ Impulse in the Development of Humanity"*, U.E.T. (TSESE)

03-07-14	1-Pforzheim	*Happenings at the Turn of the Millennia* (Extract), U.E.T. (HTM)
03-07-14	1-Pforzheim	*Pre-Earthly Deeds of Christ*, SBC, 1947 (PEDC)
04-06-14	8-Vienna	*The Inner Nature of Man*, RSP, 1994 (INM)
04-17-14	7-Various	*The Presence of the Dead on the Spiritual Path*, AP, 1990 (PD)
04-18-14	2-Berlin	*How to Acquire Understanding of the Spiritual World*, U.E.T. (HAUSW)
04-23-14	1-Cassel	*The Great School of Love in Life*, ANS, 9-8-46 (GSLL)
05-08-14	1-Cassel	*How does the Soul Discover its True Being?*, ANS, 7-8-45 (HSDTB)
05-27-14	1-Paris	*Progress in the Knowledge of the Christ*, U.E.T. (PKC)
06-01-14	1-Basel	*The Four Sacrifices of Christ*, AP, 1944 (FSC)
06-02-14	1-Basle	*A Defense Against Attacks*, ANS format (DAA)
06-07-14	5-Dornach	*Ways to a New Style in Architecture*, APC & AP, 1927 (WNSA)
07-12-14	4-Norrkoping	*Christ and the Human Soul*, 4th Ed., RSP, 1984 (CHS)
07-13-14	1-Norrkoping	*Anthroposophy and Christianity*, AP, 1985 (AC)
07-26-14	9-Various	*Colour*, RSP, 1992 (C)
08-13-14	3-Dornach	*Bandaging Course*, U.E.T. (BANDC)
09-01-14	14-Berlin	*The Destinies of Individuals and of Nations*, RSP & AP, 1987 (DIN)
09-19-14	1-Dornach	*Anniversary of the Laying of the Foundation Stone*, U.E.T. (ALFS)
10-13-14	4-Dornach	*Occult Reading and Occult Hearing*, RSP, 1975 (OROH)
10-25-14	1-Dornach	*The Building in Dornach*, U.E.T. (BD)
11-09-14	3-Dornach	*Concerning the Origin and Nature of the Finnish Nation*, ANS, 3-17-40 (CONFN)
11-20-14	3-Dornach	*The Balance in the World and Man/ Lucifer and Ahriman*, SBC, 1948 (BWM)
11-26-14	1-Berlin	*The Human Soul in Life and Death*, RSPC, no pub. date given (HSLD)
11-27-14	1-Berlin	*The Soul of the People, Considered in the Light of Spiritual Science*, RSPC, no pub. date given (SPLS)
12-12-14	4-Dornach	*How Does One Bring Reality of Being into the World of Ideas?/Mirror Images and Realities*, U.E.T. (HBRB)
12-28-14	8-Dornach	*Art as Seen in the Light of Mystery Wisdom*, RSP, 1984 (ALMW)
12-31-14	1-Dornach	*World New Year* ANS, 1-13-46 (WNY)

01-02-15	1-Dornach	*Of the Goetheanum and the Music of its Architecture*, U.E.T. (GMA)
01-03-15	1-Dornach	*The Future of Jupiter and Its Beings*, U.E.T. (FJAIB)
01-04-15	1-Dornach	*The Pythian, The Prophetic, and the Modern Clairvoyance*, U.E.T. (PPMC)
01-09-15	1-Dornach	*The Ego: its Manifestations in Speech and Song, in Creative Imagination, in Inner Experience*, U.E.T. (EMSS)
01-10-15	1-Dornach	*Perception of the Nature of Thought/ Sun Activity in Earthly Evolution*, U.E.T. (PNT)
01-15-15	1-Berlin	*Destiny* (Extract), ANS, #14 (DSTY)
01-15-15	1-Dusseldorf	*Preparing for the Sixth Epoch*, AP, 1957 (PSE)
01-30-15	1-Dornach	*Brunetto Latini*, AM, 12-2-28 (BLAT)
01-31-15	1-Zurich	*The Four Virtues*, AM, 5-17-25 (FV)
02-02-15	1-Dornach	*Prayers for Mothers and Children*, 3rd Ed., RSP, 1983 (PMC)
02-02-15	1-Dornach	*The Life Between Birth and Death as a Reflection of the Life Between Death and a New Birth*, U.E.T. (LBBD)
02-05-15	3-Dornach	*The Problem of Death*, U.E.T. (PRBD)
02-13-15	2-Stuttgart	*The Christ-Impulse as Bearer of the Union of the Spiritual and the Bodily*, U.E.T. (CIBU)
03-13-15	1-Nuremberg	*Spiritual Science, a Necessity for the Present Time*, ANS, 12-12-48 (SSNPT)
03-14-15	1-Nuremberg	*Moral Impulses and Clairvoyant Knowledge*, ANS, 1952 (MICK)
03-16-15	1-Berlin	*The Relation of Man to his Folk Spirit*, U.E.T. (RMFS)
03-27-15	3-Dornach	*Meditation and Concentration: Three Kinds of Clairvoyance/Brain-Thinking as Spiritual Activity/ Somnambulism or Consciously-Developed Clairvoyance/The Inner Culture of the Will*, U.E.T. (MCTKC)
04-20-15	1-Berlin	*The Etheric Being in the Physical Human Being*, ANS, 2-22-48 (EBPHB)
05-07-15	1-Vienna	*Effects of the Christ-Impulse upon the Historical Course of Human Evolution / The Occult Background of the Christmas Festival*, ANS, #14 (ECIH)
05-09-15	1-Vienna	*The Subconscious Forces*, ANS, 6-30-46 (SUBCF)
05-18-15	1-Linz	*Christ in Relation to Lucifer and Ahriman*, AP, 1978 (CRLA)
05-23-15	1-Dornach	*Whitsuntide in the Course of the Year*, U.E.T.(WCY)
05-29-15	1-Dornach	*Characteristics of Man's Occult Development*, ANS, 9-8-35 (CMOD)

05-30-15	1-Dornach	*Intervals of the Life on Earth*, Anthroposophy Today, Vol. 2 (ILE)
06-03-15	1-Dornach	*"Heaven and Earth shall Pass Away; but my Words shall not Pass Away"*, U.E.T. (HEPA)
06-13-15	1-Elberfeld	*The Etheric Body as a Reflection of the Universe*, ANS, 9-29-40 (EBRU)
07-17-15	2-Dornach	*The Realm of Language/The Lost Unison of Speaking and Thinking*, MP, 1984 (RL)
07-24-15	6-Dornach	*The Tree of Life and the Tree of Knowledge*, pub. data missing (TLTK)
08-16-15	1-Dornach	*The Realm of the Mothers*, AM, 10-12-30 (RMOTH)
08-23-15	8-Dornach	*Chance, Providence and Necessity*, AP & RSP, 1988 (CPN)
08-29-15	1-Dornach	*Twelve Moods*, MP, 1984 (TM)
09-05-15	1-Dornach	*How the Human Etheric Body is Related to the Whole World*, U.E.T. (HHEBR)
09-10-15	7-Dornach	*Community Life/Inner Development /Sexuality and the Spiritual Teacher*, AP, 1991 (CL)
09-11-15	1-Dornach	*The Life-Conditions of Our Society*, ANS, 3-19-39 (LCOS)
09-12-15	1-Dornach	*Swedenborg's Power of Vision*, ANS, 4-2-39 (SPV)
09-13-15	2-Dornach	*Psycho-Analysis*, U.E.T. (PSYC)
09-17-15	4-Dornach	*The Value of Thinking for a Knowledge Satisfying to Man*, U.E.T. (VTK)
10-10-15	10-Dornach	*The Occult Movement in the Nineteenth Century*, RSP, 1973 (OMN)
10-31-15	3-Dornach	*Outlooks for the Future* (From lectures, *Significant Facts Pertaining to the Spiritual Life of the Middle of the 19th Century*), ANS, 1-22-40 (OFSF)
11-16-15	6-Berlin	*The Forming of Destiny and Life After Death*, GBR, 1989 (FDLD)
11-22-15	1-Stuttgart	*The Mystery of Death*, U.E.T. (MYSTD)
11-23-15	1-Stuttgart	*The Birth of the Ego Consciousness after Death*, ANS, 9-26-37 (BECD)
11-24-15	1-Stuttgart	*Cosmic Considerations*, ANS, 10-31-37 (COSMC)
11-29-15	1-Munich	*The Riddle of Death*, ANS, 4-17-38 (RD)
12-16-15	1-Berlin	*The Spirit of Fichte Present in our Midst*, RSPC, no pub. date given (SFPM)
12-19-15	1-Berlin	*The Christmas Thought and the Mystery of the Ego/ The Tree of the Cross and the Golden Legend*, MP, 1986 (CTME)
12-27-15	1-Dornach	*Christmas Plays, Gnosis, A Book of Jehu*, ANS, 12-21-47 (CPGJ)

12-28-15	1-Dornach	*The Jesus and Christ Problem of Earlier Times*, ANS, 2-2-36 (JCPET)
1916	Book	*The Riddle of Man*, MP, 1990 (RM)
01-09-16	1-Berne	*The Spiritual Unity of Mankind through the Christ-Impulse* (aka "The Diversity of Human Nature"), AQ, 1968 (SUMC)
01-11-16	2-Various	*Approaches to Anthroposophy*, RSP, 1992 (AA)
01-12-16	5-Various	*Reincarnation and Immortality*, RSPB, 1970 (RI)
01-14-16	1-Basle	*The Harmony Between Spiritual Science and Natural Science/the Misunderstanding in Connection with SS and its Building at Dornach*, ANS, 10-29-39 (HBSNS)
01-15-16	1-Dornach	*From the Clairvoyant Concept, to the Rational Concept, and the Experienced Concept*, ANS, 12-5-37 (FCRE)
01-16-16	1-Dornach	*The Relationship Between the World of Concepts and the True World of Reality*, ANS, 12-12-37 (RBCT)
01-25-16	5-Berlin	*Necessity and Freedom*, AP & RSP, 1988 (NF)
02-03-16	1-Berlin	*Faust's World-Pilgrimage and His Rebirth out of the Spirit of German Life*, U.E.T. (FWPR)
02-04-16	1-Berlin	*A Sound Life of Soul and Sound Spiritual Research*, U.E.T. (SLSR)
02-13-16	12-Berlin	*Things in Past and Present in the Spirit of Man*, U.E.T. (TPPSM)
02-16-16	1-Hamburg	*Relationships Between the Living and the Dead*, ANS, SUPP #4/5 (RBLD)
02-18-16	1-Cassel	*Concerning the Life Between Death and a New Birth*, ANS, 5-21-39 (LBDNB)
02-22-16	1-Leipzig	*The Ego-Consciousness of the So-Called Dead*, ANS, 3-31-40 (ECSCD)
02-26-16	1-Berlin	*Why is Spiritual Investigation Misunderstood?*, RSPC, no pub. date given (WSIM)
03-20-16	1-Munich	*The Weaving and Living Activity of the Human Etheric Bodies*, ANS, #8 (WLA)
05-16-16	1-Berlin	*Value of Truth*, U.E.T. (VT)
06-06-16	7-Berlin	*Toward Imagination*, AP, 1990 (TI)
06-06-16	1-Berlin	*Whitsuntide: a Symbol of the Immortality of the Human Ego*, U.E.T. (WSIHE)
07-29-16	15-Dornach	*The Riddle of Humanity*, RSP, 1990 (RH)
08-19-16	1-Dornach	*Wisdom-Beauty-Goodness/Michael-Gabriel-Raphael*, U.E.T. (WBG)
08-20-16	1-Dornach	*The Historical Significance of "Faust"*, U.E.T. (HSF)
09-04-16	4-Dornach	*On the Second Part of Faust I-IV*, U.E.T. (OSPF-1 to OSPF-4)

09-18-16	2-Dornach	*Inner Impulses Working in the Evolution of Mankind* (Lects. 3 & 4 of 6), U.E.T. (IIWEM)
09-20-16	1-Dornach	*Architectural Forms Considered as the Thoughts of Culture and World-Perception,* RSPC, no pub. date given (AF)
09-30-16	1-Dornach	*The Problem of Faust,* Lect. 1 (of 12), U.E.T. (PF-1)
10-02-16	3-Dornach	*Goethe and the Crisis of the 19th Century,* U.E.T. (GCNC)
10-08-16	3-Dornach	*The History of Art,* U.E.T. (HART)
10-09-16	3-Various	*The Mystery of the Human Being/The Nature of Anthroposophy* (Lect. 3 is same as ASQ but diff. trans.), RSPB, 1964 (MHB)
10-15-16	1-Dornach	*The Main Impulse in Recent Times in the West and the East,* U.E.T. (MIWE)
10-21-16	1-Dornach	*Goethe's Approach to Metamorphosis,* U.E.T. (GAM)
10-24-16	1-Zurich	*The Problem of Destiny,* ANS, 8-22-37 (PRBDY)
10-26-16	1-St. Gallen	*The Opposition to Spiritual Science/ Lies of Modern Life and Masked Facts,* ANS, 6-1-41 (OPSS)
11-04-16	10-Dornach	*The Karma of Vocation,* 2d Ed., AP 1984 (KV)
11-06-16	1-Dornach	*Cyclic Movement of Sleeping and Waking,* AM, 10-30-27 (CMSW)
11-09-16	1-Bern	*On the Connection of the Living and the Dead,* AM, 11-4-28 (CLD)
12-03-16	1-Zurich	*Luciferic and Ahrimanic Influences/ Influences of the Dead,* AM, 5-22-27 (LAI)
12-04-16	13-Dornach	*The Karma of Untruthfulness,* Vol. 1, RSP & AP, 1988 (KU-1)
12-10-16	1-Dornach	*The Problem of Faust,* Lect. 2 (of 12), U.E.T. (PF-2)
1917	Extracts	*The Case for Anthroposophy* (from Steiner's "Von Seelenratseln"), RSP, 1970 (CASE)
1917	Article	*The Chymical Wedding of Christian Rosenkreutz,* RSPB, no pub. date given (CWCR)
01-01-17	12-Dornach	*The Karma of Untruthfulness,* Vol. 2, RSP & AP, 1992 (KU-1)
01-07-17	1-Dornach	*Introduction to the Performance of the Christmas Plays,* ANS, 12-31-34 (IPCP)
01-27-17	1-Dornach	*The Problem of Faust,* Lect 3 (of 12), U.E.T. (PF-3)
01-28-17	1-Dornach	*Man's Position in the Cosmic Whole/The Platonic World-Year,* ANS, 1-8-40 (MPCW)
01-30-17	1-Dornach	*Significance of Spiritual Science for the Present Time,* ANS, 9-10-39 (SSSPT)
02-06-17	7-Berlin	*Cosmic and Human Metamorphoses,* GBR, 1989 (CHM)

02-20-17	1-Berlin	*The Human Soul and the Universe*, SBC, 1982 (HSU)
03-15-17	2-Berlin	*The Human Soul and the Human Body/ Riddles of the Soul and Riddles of the Universe*, U.E.T. (HSBRSU)
03-27-17	10-Berlin	*Building Stones for an Understanding of the Mystery of Golgotha*, 2d Ed., RSP, 1972 (BSU)
05-19-17	1-Munich	*Laws of Human Evolution*, ANS, 6-27-43 (LHE)
05-29-17	8-Berlin	*Aspects of Human Evolution*, AP & RSP, 1987 (AHE)
06-10-17	1-Leipzig	*Characteristic Symptoms of the Pre-sent Time/ Alienation From Reality*, ANS, #17 (CSPT)
07-31-17	9-Berlin	*The Karma of Materialism*, AP & RSP, 1985 (KM)
09-10-17	Book	*Riddles of the Soul*, MP, 1996 (RS)
09-29-17	14-Dornach	*The Fall of the Spirits of Darkness*, RSP, 1993 (FSD)
Oct 1917	Essay	*The Chymical Wedding of Christian Rosenkreutz*, RSPB, no pub. date given (CWCR)
11-02-17	3-Dornach	*The Problem of Faust*, Lects. 4-6 (of 12), Lects. 4 & 6, U.E.T.; Lect. 5, AM, 11-9-30 (PF-4 to PF-6)
11-05-17	1-Zurich	*Anthroposophy and Psychology*, U.E.T. (AP)
11-06-17	2-Zurich	*Behind the Scenes of External Happenings*, RSPC & AP, 1947 (BSEH)
11-15-17	2-St. Gallen	*Geographic Medicine/The Secret of the Double*, MP, 1986 (GMSD)
11-18-17	3-Dornach	*The Wrong and Right Use of Esoteric Knowledge/ aka Secret Brotherhoods*, 2d Ed., RSP, 1966 (WRU)
11-29-17	1-Bern	*Imaginative Ground-Plan of the Life Between Death and a New Birth*, ANS, 10-12-52 (IGP)
12-02-17	7-Dornach	*Historical Necessity and Free Will*, ANS, 4-15-34 (HNFW)
12-23-17	1-Basel	*Et Incarnatus Est: The Time-Cycle in Historic Events*, MP, 1983 (EIE)
12-24-17	1-Dornach	*Pallas Athene/the Christmas Mystery/33 Year Cycle* (A Christmas Lecture), ANS, Supp #3 (PACM)
12-25-17	3-Dornach	*On the Mysteries of Ancient and Modern Times*, AM, 2-24-29 (MAMT)
12-30-17	1-Dornach	*The Zone of the Senses*, U.E.T. (ZS)
1918	Essay	*Supersensible Knowledge: Its Secrecy in the Past and Publication in our Time*, AQ, 1:3 (SKSPPT)
01-04-18	7-Dornach	*Ancient Myths/Their Meaning and Connection with Evolution*, SBC, 1971 (AM)

01-22-18	7-Berlin	*Earthly Death and Cosmic Life*, GBR, 1989 (EDCL)
02-10-18	1-Nuremberg	*The Dead Are With Us*, RSP, 1964 (DWU)
02-12-18	1-Nuremberg	*Manifestations of the Unconsciousness in the Life of the Soul*, ANS, #8 (MULS)
02-14-18	1-Munich	*Michael's Battle and Its Reflection on Earth*, Lect. 1 in 2-lect. cycle, *Signs of the Times*, no pub. data given (MBRE)
02-15-18	1-Munich	*The Physical-Superphysical: Its Realization Through Art*, U.E.T. (PSRTA)
02-23-18	1-Stuttgart	*The Alternating Conditions of Human Consciousness*, ANS, 8-6-44 (ACHC)
02-24-18	1-Stuttgart	*Michael, The Spirit of the Times*, ANS, 10-27-40 (MST)
02-25-18	1-Stuttgart	*Man as a Being of Spirit and Soul*, RSPB, 1964 (MBSS)
03-21-18	1-Berlin	*Manifestations of the Unconscious*, AQ, 1969 (MU)
03-30-18	1-Berlin	*Anthroposophical Life-Gifts*, U.E.T (ALG)
04-26-18	1-Stuttgart	*The Expectant Mood in Life*, ANS, #9 (EML)
04-30-18	1-Ulm-Donau	*The Requirement of our Time is to Give an Earth-Soul to the Earth-Body*, ANS, 7-16-39 (RTGE)
05-03-18	1-Munich	*Man and Mankind's Historical and Moral Life According to Results Obtained Through Spiritual Science*, ANS, 4-28-40 (MMHM)
05-05-18	1-Munich	*The Sources of Artistic Imagination/ Fantasy*, U.E.T. (SRIF)
05-06-18	1-Munich	*The Sources of Artistic Imagination and the Sources of Supersensible Knowledge*, U.E.T. (SAI)
06-14-18	1-Prague	*How is it Possible to Recognize the Human Soul's Supersensible Life and Nature?*, ANS, #14 ((HPR)
06-25-18	7-Berlin	*A Sound Outlook for Today and a Genuine Hope for the Future*, U.E.T. (SOFT)
08-17-18	3-Dornach	*Occult Psychology*, U.E.T. (OPSYCH)
08-24-18	3-Dornach	*Mysteries of the Sun and the Threefold Man*, U.E.T. (MSTM)
08-31-18	3-Dornach	*The Ruling Cosmic Intelligence/In Speech Formation/Aspects of Man's Life After Death in Connection with Phenomena of External Nature*, U.E.T. (RCI)
09-06-18	2-Dornach	*The Bridge Between the Ideal and the Real*, U.E.T. (BBIR)
09-13-18	1-Dornach	*On Hatred* (Extract), ANS, 11-17-46 (HATR)
09-14-18	1-Dornach	*On the Different Periods in Human Life*, ANS, #15 (DPHL)

09-20-18	3-Dornach	*The Cosmic Prehistoric Ages of Mankind/Space and Time/The Realm of Duration and the Realm of the Transitory*, U.E.T. (CPAM)
09-27-18	3-Dornach	*The Problem of Faust*, Lects. 7-9 (of 12), U.E.T. (PF-7 to PF-9)
10-04-18	6-Dornach	*Three Streams in the Evolution of Mankind*, RSP, 1965 (TSHE)
10-09-18	1-Zurich	*The Work of the Angels in Man's Astral Body*, 2d Ed., RSP, 1972 (WAMAB)
10-17-18	1-Zurich	*The History of Modern Times in the Light of Spiritual Scientific Investigation*, ANS, Supp #45, Michaelmas 1934 (HMT)
10-16-18	1-Zurich	*How Do I Find the Christ?*, AP & RSPC, 1941 (HDIFC)
10-18-18	9-Dornach	*From Symptom to Reality in Modern History*, RSP, 1976 (FSR)
10-26-18	1-Dornach	*Concerning Death and Evil*, U.E.T. (DE)
11-09-18	2-Dornach	*A Historical Background for the Formation of Judgment on the Social Question* (only Lects. 1 & 2 of 8), U.E.T. (JSQ)
11-29-18	6-Dornach	*The Challenge of the Times*, AP, 1941 (CT)
12-12-18	1-Bern	*Social and Antisocial Forces*, MP, 1982 (SAF)
12-13-18	5-Dornach	*The Fundamental Social Demand of our Time*, U.E.T. (FSDT)
12-22-18	1-Basle	*The Birth of Christ in the Human Soul*, AP & RSPB, 1940 (BCHS)
12-22-18	8-Dornach	*How Can Mankind Find the Christ Again?*, 2d Ed., AP, 1984 (HCMF)
12-31-18	1-Dornach	*Experiences of the Old Year and an Outlook for the New Year*, U.E.T. (EOONY)
1919	Articles	*The Renewal of the Social Organism*, AP & RSP, 1985 (RSO)
1919	Book	*Towards Social Renewal, Basic Issues*, 3rd Ed., RSP 1977 (TSR)
1919	Article	*Destiny*, ANS, #14 (DEST)
01-03-19	6-Dornach	*Goetheanism as an Impulse for Man's Transformation* (only lectures 5 & 6, dated 1-11-19 & 1-12-19, available at RS Library), AM, #10 GIMT)
01-17-19	3-Dornach	*The Problem of Faust*, Lects. 10-12 (of 12), U.E.T. (PF-10 to PF-12)
01-24-19	1-Dornach	*A Turning Point in Modern History*, GB, no pub. date given (TPMH)
01-26-19	1-Dornach	*Steiner's Address Before the Public Performance of Faust's "Classical Walpurgis-Night"*, U.E.T. (CWN)

01-26-19	1-Dornach	*The Migration of People in the Past and in the Present/The Social Homunculus*, ANS, 1-24-43 (MPPP)
01-31-19	1-Dornach	*What Form Can the Requirements of Social Life Take on at the Present Time?*, ANS, 3-7-43 (WFRSL)
02-04-19	3-Zurich	*The Inner Aspect of the Social Question*, RSP, 1974 (IASQ)
02-15-19	8-Dornach	*The Social Question as a Question of Consciousness*, U.E.T. (SQQC)
03-23-19	1-Dornach	*The New Youth* (Extract), ANS, #7 (NY)
03-28-19	2-Dornach	*The Social Question as a Problem of Soul Life/The Inner Experience of Language*, U.E.T. (SQPSL)
03-30-19	1-Dornach	*The Social Question*, AM, #7 (SQ)
Apr 1919	Book	*The Threefold Social Order*, 2d Ed., AP, 1972 (TSO)
04-01-19	5-Various	*Lucifer and Ahriman, The Influences of*, SBC, 1976 (LA)
04-05-19	16-Various	*An Introduction to Eurythmy*, AP, 1984 (INTE)
04-13-19	1-Dornach	*Spiritual Emptiness and Social Life*, GB, 1954 (SESL)
04-21-19	7-Stuttgart	*A Spiritual-Scientific Consideration of Social and Pedagogic Questions*, U.E.T. (SPQ)
05-11-19	3-Stuttgart	*A Social Basis for Primary and Secondary Education* (4th lect. not included), U.E.T. (SBPSE)
05-31-19	1-Stuttgart	*The Impulse Toward the Threefold Order: No Utopia, but the Practical Demand of the Hour*, U.E.T. (ITTO)
06-12-19	1-Heidenheim	*Some Characteristics of Today*, RSPC, no pub. date given (SCT)
06-22-19	1-Stuttgart	*Materialism and the Manifestation of the Spirit*, ANS, 8-18-40 (MMS)
07-11-19	1-Stuttgart	*The Supersensible Being of Man and the Evolution of Mankind*, AR, #2 (SBMEM)
07-22-19	1-Ulm	*The Knowledge of Man's Supersensible Being and the Tasks of the Present Time*, ANS, 8-24-47 (KMSBT)
08-09-19	6-Dornach	*Education as a Social Problem*, AP, 1969 (ESP)
08-21-19	14-Stuttgart	*Study of Man*, 2d Ed., RSP, 1966 (SM)
08-21-19	14-Stuttgart	*Practical Advice to Teachers*, 2d Ed., RSP & AP, 1976 (PAT)
08-21-19	15-Stuttgart	*Discussions with Teachers*, RSP, 1967 (DT)
08-24-19	6-Stuttgart	*The Spirit of the Waldorf School*, AP, 1995 (SWS)
09-06-19	2-Stuttgart	*Lectures on the Curriculum*, U.E.T. (CURR)

09-07-19	1-Stuttgart	*Waldorf School Opening, Address at the*, pub. data not given (WSO)
09-08-19	1-Stuttgart	*The Necessity for a Spiritual Deepening Through Freely Acquired Knowledge*, U.E.T. (NSD)
09-12-19	3-Berlin	*The Problems of Our Time*, RSPC, no pub. date given (POT)
09-15-19	1-Berlin	*New Aspects of the Social Question*, RSPC & AP, no pub. date given (NASQ)
09-28-19	1-Stuttgart	*The Arising of Cosmic Consciousness Out of Earth Consciousness*, U.E.T. (ACCOE)
10-04-19	1-Dornach	*Social Understanding Through Spiritual Scientific Knowledge*, AP, 1982 (SUSS)
10-05-19	1-Dornach	*Land-Consciousness, Earth-Consciousness, World-Consciousness*, ANS, #20 (LEWC)
10-11-19	1-Dornach	*A Different Way of Thinking is Needed for the Rescue of European Civilization*, ANS, 2-23-47 (DWTN)
10-12-19	1-Dornach	*Social Impulses for the Healing of Modern Civilization/Fundamental Impulses in History*, ANS, #15 (SIHMC)
10-17-19	1-Dornach	*Fundamentals of the Science of Initiation*, ANS, 1-30-38 (FSI)
10-23-19	1-?	*Spiritual-Scientific Knowledge and Social Understanding*, U.E.T. (SSKSU)
10-24-19	6-Zurich	*The Social Future*, 3rd Ed., AP, 1972 (SF)
10-27-19	1-Zurich	*The Ahrimanic Deception*, AP, 1985 (AD)
11-14-19	1-Dornach	*Incarnations of Lucifer and Ahriman*, (ILA)
11-22-19	1-Dornach	*"Faust" in Drama and Eurhythmy* (RS' Address Before the Public Representation in Drama and Eurhythmy of the Scene in the Study in Part I of *Faust*), U.E.T. (FDE)
11-27-19	1-Basle	*Spiritual Science and the Art of Education*, London, 1921, other pub. data stricken (SSAE)
12-06-19	2-Dornach	*The Michael Impulse*, U.E.T. (MI)
12-07-19	1-Dornach	*Man and the Environing World*, ANS, 3-21-37 (MEW)
12-12-19	7-Dornach	*Ideas for a New Europe/Crisis and Opportunity for the West*, RSP, 1992 (INE)
12-12-19	4-Dornach	*The Mysteries of Light, of Space, and of the Earth*, AP & RSP, 1945 (MLSE)
12-21-19	5-Stuttgart	*The Cosmic New Year*, RSPC, no pub. date given (CNY)
12-21-19	1-Stuttgart	*Stuttgart Lodge Lecture*, U.E.T. (SLL)
12-23-19	10-Stuttgart	*Light Course*, MP, no pub. date given (LC)
12-26-19	6-Stuttgart	*The Genius of Language*, AP, 1995 (GL)

ca. 1920	Article	*Spiritual Life in World Affairs,* TC, 2:1 (SLWA)
01-05-20	5-Dornach	*Social Issues,* AP, 1991 (SI)
01-18-20	1-Dornach	*Some Conditions for Understanding Supersensible Experiences,* GB, 1960 (SCUSC)
01-23-20	3-Dornach	*The Building at Dornach,* U.E.T. (BD-2)
02-01-20	1-Dornach	*Historical Characters and the Place in Evolution,* AM, #6 (HCPE)
02-06-20	1-Dornach	*Knowledge of Man and Social Reconstruction,* ANS, Feb 1941 (KMSR)
02-07-20	1-Dornach	*Practical Life and Spiritual Science,* ANS, #13 (PLSS)
02-08-20	1-Dornach	*Glances into the Evolution of Mankind,* ANS, #8 (GEM)
02-13-20	2-Dornach	*How the Higher Faculties of Man's Soul are Connected with the Spiritual World/The Metamorphoses of Man's Feeling, Desire and Will: How They are Related to Social Affairs,* U.E.T. (HHF)
02-20-20	3-Dornach	*Imperialism,* U.E.T. (IMP)
03-01-20	14-Stuttgart	*Warmth Course,* 2d Ed., MP, 1988 (WC)
03-05-20	11-Stuttgart	*Polarities in the Evolution of Mankind,* RSP & AP, 1987 (PEM)
03-10-20	1-Stuttgart	*The Peoples of the Earth in the Light of Anthroposophy,* AQ, #3, also in GB, 1980 (PELA)
03-12-20	1-Stuttgart	*The History of Man in the Light of Anthroposophy,* U.E.T. (HMLA)
03-20-20	2-Stuttgart	*Knowledge as a Source of Healing,* U.E.T. (KSH)
03-21-20	20-Dornach	*Spiritual Science and Medicine,* GBR, 1989 (SSM)
04-07-20	1-Dornach	*Health Care as a Social Issue* (an earlier trans. was published by MP as *Hygiene—a Social Problem*), MP, 1984 (HCSI)
04-09-20	16-Dornach	*Man: Hieroglyph of the Universe,* RSP, 1972 (MHU)
04-20-20	2-Basle	*The Renewal of Education Through the Science of the Spirit,* E. Sussex, U.K., Kolisko Archive Pub., for Steiner Schools Fellowship Pub. (RETSS)
05-22-20	3-Dornach	*The Redemption of Thinking,* AP, 1956 (RT)
05-30-20	3-Dornach	*Roman Catholicism,* U.E.T. (RCATH)
06-09-20	1-Stuttgart	*Stuttgart, Address at a Study Evening in,* U.E.T. (STUTT)
07-02-20	1-Dornach	*Oswald Spengler, Prophet of World Chaos,* AP, 1949 (OSPWC)
07-08-20	1-Bern	*The Philosophical Basis of Anthroposophy,* U.E.T. (PBA)

07-18-20	1-Dornach	*Man and Nature*, U.E.T. (MANAT)
07-24-20	1-Stuttgart	*Waldorf School, Address at the*, no pub. data given (WSA)
08-06-20	16-Dornach	*Spiritual Science as a Foundation for Social Forms*, AP & RSP, 1986 (SSFS)
09-03-20	1-Dornach	*East, West, and Middle in Relation to the Threefold Social Organism/ Ancient Ghosts and Modern Spectres/Eastern and Western World Contrasts*, AP, 1948 (EWM)
09-06-20	1-Dornach	*What is the Mission of the Small Intermediate Nations?*, ANS, #7 (WMSIN)
09-11-20	1-Dornach	*Changes in the Meaning of Speech*, ANS, 5-15-49 (CMS)
09-12-20	1-Dornach	*The Supersensible Origin of the Artistic*, no pub. data given (SOA)
09-15-20	4-Stuttgart	*Balance in Teaching*, MP, 1982 (BT)
09-27-20	8-Dornach	*The Boundaries of Natural Science*, AP, 1983 (BNS)
09-29-20	7-Various	*Poetry and the Art of Speech*, U.E.T. (PARTS)
10-07-20	4-Dornach	*Physiology and Therapeutics*, MP, 1986 (PT)
10-17-20	1-Dornach	*The Art of Eurythmy*, U.E.T. (AE)
10-17-20	7-Dornach	*The New Spirituality and the Christ Experience of the Twentieth Century*, RSP & AP, 1988 (NSP)
10-31-20	1-Dornach	*The Coming Experience of Christ*, GB, 1952 (CEC)
11-26-20	1-Dornach	*The Shaping of the Human Form out of Cosmic and Earthly Forces*, AQ, Spring, 1972 (SHF)
11-27-20	1-Dornach	*Three-Partition of the Human Organism, Concerning the*, ANS, #9 (TPHO)
11-28-20	1-Dornach	*Luciferic and Ahrimanic Influences in Human Evolution*, ANS, 1-1-52 (LAIHE)
12-12-20	1-Dornach	*Performance of Eurhythmy, Introductory Words at a*, U.E.T. (PE)
12-14-20	1-Bern	*The Soul's Progress Through Repeated Earth Lives/ The Historical Aspect of Social Life in its Reality*, AP & RSPC, 1944 (SPTREL)
12-17-20	3-Dornach	*The Bridge Between Universal Spirituality and the Physical Constitution of Man*, AP, 1958 (BBUS)
12-23-20	4-Dornach	*The Search for the New Isis, Divine Sophia*, MP, 1983 (SIS)
01-01-21	18-Stuttgart	*Astronomy: The Relation of the Diverse Branches of Natural Science to Astronomy*, U.E.T. (ARNS)
01-06-21	1-Stuttgart	*Past Incarnations of the Peoples of Today*, U.E.T. (PIPT)
01-09-21	1-Stuttgart	*Dangers Threatening the Spiritual Life of Today*, U.E.T. (DTSLT)

01-23-21	1-Dornach	*Spiritual Science in the Light of Today*, U.E.T. (SSLA)
01-29-21	4-Dornach	*The Responsibility of Man for World-Evolution through his Spiritual Connection with the Planet Earth and the World of the Stars*, U.E.T. (RMWE)
02-01-21	1-Basle	*The Threshold in Nature and in Man*, GB, 1949 (TNM)
02-05-21	2-Dornach	*East and West and the Roman Church / The Significance of Anthroposophy*, U.E.T. (EWRC)
02-15-21	1-Dornach	*Threefold Social Order* (Extracts), AM, 7-15-28 (TSOL)
02-23-21	9-Various	*Waldorf Education and Anthroposophy*, AP, 1995 (WEAN)
02-27-21	1-Hague	*It is a Necessity of our Times to Find Again the Path Leading to the Spirit*, ANS, 9-1-40 (NETFA)
03-16-21	8-Stuttgart	*Anthroposophy and Science*, MP, 1991 (AS)
03-28-21	1-Dornach	*Apollonius of Tyana*, AQ, Spring, 1958 (AOT)
Apr 1921	Article	*The Task of Spiritual Science*, TC, 5-14-21 (TSS)
04-02-21	17-Dornach	*Materialism and the Task of Anthroposophy*, AP & RSP, 1987 (MTA)
04-10-21	1-Dornach	*On Dramatic Art* (Questions & Answers), U.E.T. (DAQA)
04-11-21	9-Dornach	*Anthroposophical Spiritual Science and Medical Therapy*, MP, 1991 (ASSMT)
04-12-21	8-Dornach	*Curative Eurythmy*, RSP, 1983 (CEU)
05-05-21	1-Dornach	*Man, Offspring of the World of Stars*, AQ, Vol. 20, #4 (MOWS)
05-15-21	1-Dornach	*The Development of Thought From the Fourth to the Nineteenth Century*, AQ, #8 (DTFFN)
05-21-21	2-Stuttgart	*Natural Science and the Historical Development of Humanity*, AM Format (NSHDH)
06-12-21	8-Stuttgart	*Supplementary Course—The Upper School/Waldorf School for Adolescence*, U.E.T. (SUPP)
06-16-21	1-Stuttgart	*Hallucinations, Creations of our Fancy, and Imaginations*, ANS, #20 (HCFI)
06-24-21	5-Dornach	*Therapeutic Insights/Earthly and Cosmic Laws*, MP, 1984 (TIEC)
06-27-21	1-Dornach	*General Meeting of the Goetheanum Soc.*, Address Given by RS at, no pub. data given (GMGS)
06-28-21	1-Bern	*The Riddle of Man*, AM, #6 (RM-2)
06-29-21	1-Bern	*The Architectural Conception of the Goetheanum*, RSCP & AP, 1938 (ACG)
July 1921	Article	*Spiritual Life, Civil Rights, Industrial Economy*, AP, no pub. date given (SLCR)

07-01-21	1-Dornach	*The Inherent Nature of Hallucination,* ANS, 2-3-35 (INH)
07-08-21	3-Dornach	*Man in the Cosmos as a Being of Thought and Will,* U.E.T. (MCBTW)
07-15-21	1-Dornach	*Thinking and Willing as Two Poles,* AM, Vol. VIII, Supp #4 (TWTP)
07-16-21	1-Dornach	*Cosmic Formative Forces in the Animal Kingdom,* AM, #7 (CFFAK)
07-17-21	1-Dornach	*The Being of Man in Relation to the Spiritual Hierarchies,* AM, #8 (BMRSH)
07-22-21	3-Dornach	*Man as a Being of Sense and Perception,* SBC, 1981 (MBSP)
07-24-21	1-Dornach	*"Faust" in Drama and Eurhythmy—Prologue* (RS' Address Before the Public Representation in Drama and Eurythmy of the "prologue in Heaven" from part I of Goethe's *Faust*), U.E.T. (FDEP)
08-05-21	1-Dornach	*The Dual Form of Cognition During the Middle Ages and the Development of Knowledge in Modern Times,* ANS, Supp #1 (DFC)
08-06-21	1-Dornach	*The Remedy for Our Diseased Civilization,* ANS, Supp #s 2 & 3 (RDC)
08-12-21	5-Dornach	*The Ego as an Experience of Consciousness,* U.E.T. (EGOEXC)
08-15-21	1-Dornach	*Metamorphosis of Plants,* ANS, 9-22-35 (MPL)
08-23-21	1-Dornach	*Anthroposophy and Art,* AM, Vol. I, #s 7 & 8 (AART)
08-28-21	1-Dornach	*Goethe and the Present Time,* ANS, 3-7-49 (GPT)
08-29-21	8-Stuttgart	*Fruits of Anthroposophy,* RSP, 1986 (FA)
09-23-21	11-Dornach	*Cosmosophy,* Vol 1, AP, 1985 (CSMY-1)
10-09-21	Article	*Unemployment,* no pub. data given (UNEM)
10-11-21	6-Dornach	*The Art of Lecturing,* MP, 1984 (ALECT)
10-21-21	1-Dornach	*Outer and Inner Life,* ANS, 2-7-49 (OIL)
10-22-21	1-Dornach	*Sense-Perception, Thought—and the Working of Spiritual Beings,* AQ, Michaelmas, 1933 (SPTWSB)
10-23-21	1-Dornach	*On the Development of Consciousness From the Graeco-Latin Epoch to our own Time and the Intervention of Supersensible Beings,* AQ, #6 (DCFGLE)
10-28-21	5-Dornach	*Forming of Man Through Cosmic Influences,* U.E.T. (FMCI)
Nov 1921	Article	*A Frequent Point of Opposition to Anthroposophy,* AQ, July-Aug, 1923 (FPOA)

11-06-21	1-Dornach	*The Sun-Mystery in the Course of Human History*, RSP, 1955 (SMCHH)
11-12-21	2-Dornach	*The Configuration of Man's Moral-Spiritual Element in Sleep*, U.E.T. (CMMSES)
11-24-21	3-Oslo	*Cosmic Forces in Man*, no pub. data given (CFM)
11-24-21	10-Oslo	*Self-Consciousness*, GBR, 1986 (SCON)
11-25-21	1-Christiania	*On the Reality of Higher Worlds*, APC, 1947 (RHW)
11-26-21	1-Christiania	*Paths to Knowledge of Higher Worlds*, SBC, 1970 (PKHW)
11-28-21	3-Christiania	*Foundations of Anthroposophy*, ANS, 2-20-44 (FOA)
11-29-21	1-Christiania	*The Human Being in the Light of Anthroposophy*, ANS, 4-2-44 (HBLA)
11-29-21	1-Christiania	*Jesus or Christ*, ANS, 12-8-35 (JOC)
12-01-21	1-Christiania	*The World-Development in the Light of Anthroposophy*, ANS, 4-30-44 (WDLA)
12-02-21	1-Christiania	*The Renewal of Culture*, APC, 1947 (RCULT)
12-12-21	1-Dornach	*The Relation of Youth to Age*, AM, #6 (RYA)
12-18-21	1-Dornach	*The Alphabet*, MP, 1982 (ALPH)
12-23-21	1-Dornach	*Imaginative Cognition and Inspired Cognition*, U.E.T. (ICIC)
12-23-21	16-Dornach	*Soul Economy and Waldorf Education*, AP & RSP, 1986 (SEWE)
12-24-21	1-Dornach	*East and West in the Light of the Christmas Idea*, ANS, 12-29-46 (EWLCI)
12-25-21	1-Dornach	*Wisdom Working in Historical Evolution*, ANS, Supp #6, 1935 (WWHE)
12-31-21	1-Dornach	*The Rediscovery of Spiritual Reality in Nature and in Man*, U.E.T. (RSRNM)
01-01-22	14-Various	*Old and New Methods of Initiation*, RSP, 1991 (ONMI)
01-08-22	20-Dornach	*Economics/The World as One Economy*, Eng., New Economy Pub., 1993 (ECON)
01-21-22	Article	*The Question before the World*, TC, 1-21-22 (QW)
03-21-22	1-Bern	*Man's Soul-Life in Sleeping, Waking & Dreaming*, U.E.T. (MSLSWD)
03-24-22	1-Dornach	*The Mystery of Golgotha and its Relation to the Sleep of Man*, U.E.T. (MGRSM)
03-25-22	3-Dornach	*Changes in Human World Conception*, AM, 5-5-29 (CHWC)
Apr 1922	Article	*East and West*, no pub. data given (EW)
04-01-22	1-Dornach	*Pneumatosophy / Finding and Formulating the Cosmic Word in In-Breathing and Out-Breathing*, AP & RSPB, 1942 (PNEUM)

04-02-22   1-Dornach   *Exoteric and Esoteric Christianity*, SBC, no pub. date given (EEC)

04-08-22   1-Hague   *The Position of Anthroposophy among the Sciences*, GB, 1961 (PAS)

04-09-22   1-Hague   *Anthroposophy and the Visual Arts*, GB, 1961 (AVA)

04-13-22   1-Hague   *The Teachings of Christ, The Resurrected/ Reflections on the Mystery of Golgotha*, AP & RSPC, 1940 (TCR)

04-14-22   2-London   *Knowledge and Initiation/Cognition of the Christ Through Anthroposophy*, SBC, no pub. date given (KI)

04-24-22   6-London   *Planetary Spheres and their Influence on Man's Life on Earth and in Spiritual Worlds*, RSP, 1982 (PSI)

04-29-22   9-Dornach   *The Human Soul in Relation to World Evolution*, AP, ca. 1984 (HSRWE)

05-26-22   1-Dornach   *The Human Heart*, MP, 1985 (HUHT)

05-27-22   1-Dornach   *The Change in the Path to Supersensible Knowledge*, SBC, 1982 (CPSK)

06-01-22   10-Vienna   *The Tension between East and West*, AP, 1963 (TEW)

06-18-22   1-Dornach   *Vienna Congress/East-West Aphorisms/ et al.* (Extract), no pub. data given (VIEN)

06-21-22   1-Stuttgart   *Education for Adolescents*, JA, #29, Spring, 1979 (EFA)

06-22-22   1-Stuttgart   *The Artistic Element in Teaching*, U.E.T. (AET)

06-24-22   1-Dornach   *On the Dimensions of Space*, AM, #4 (DOS)

06-25-22   1-Dornach   *Human Questions and Cosmic Answers*, AM, 9-16-28 (HQCA)

06-30-22   1-Dornach   *Relationships Between Cosmic Events and the Periods of Civilization*, AQ, #19 (RBCEPC)

07-01-22   1-Dornach   *The Human Being in Relation to Planetary Life*, ANS, 7-12-36 (HBRPL)

07-09-22   1-Dornach   *Franz Brentano and Adolf Fick*, ANS, 7-9-22 (FBAF)

07-14-22   1-Dornach   *Franz Brentano and Friedrich Nietzsche*, ANS, 12-3-33 (FBFN)

07-16-22   1-Dornach   *Spiritual Wisdom in the Early Christian Centuries*, AQ, #5 (SWECC)

07-22-22   1-Dornach   *Cosmic Laws in Plant, Animal, Man*, U.E.T. (CLPAM)

07-23-22   8-Various   *The Mystery of the Trinity/The Mission of the Spirit*, AP, 1991 (MT)

07-24-22   14-Dornach   *World Economy*, 3rd Ed., RSP, 1972 (WE)

08-02-22   10-Dornach   *The Human Being in Body, Soul and Spirit/ Our Relationship to the Earth*, ANS, 10-29-39 (HBBSS)

08-05-22	1-Dornach	*Christ and the Evolution of Consciousness*, AQ, #4 (CEVC)
08-16-22	9-Oxford	*Spiritual Ground of Education*, GBR, 1989 (SGE)
08-28-22	2-London	*Threefolding—A Social Alternative*, RSP, 1980 (TSA)
08-30-22	2-London	*The Descent of the Spirit: Gaining a Relationship to the Dead through the Language of the Heart*, AP & RSP, 1946 (DSGRD)
Sept. 1922	Book	*The East in the Light of the West*, 2d Ed., RSPC & AP, 1940 (ELW)
09-06-22	10-Dornach	*Philosophy, Cosmology & Religion*, AP, 1984 (PCR)
09-17-22	1-Dornach	*Man's Place in the Universe*, U.E.T. (MPU)
09-20-22	4-Dornach	*Early Conditions of the Earth*, U.E.T. (ECE)
09-22-22	6-Dornach	*Supersensible Influences in the History of Mankind*, RSPC, 1956 (SIHM)
10-03-22	13-Stuttgart	*The Younger Generation*, AP, 1967 (YG)
10-09-22	1-Stuttgart	*The Experiences of Sleep and their Spiritual Background*, AM, #1 (ESSB)
10-14-22	1-Stuttgart	*The Soul and Spirit of Man Between Death and New Birth*, AM, #2 (SSMB)
10-19-22	9-Dornach	*Health and Illness*, Vol 1, AP, 1981 (HI-1)
10-20-22	3-Dornach	*Spiritual Relations in the Human Organism*, MP, 1984 (SRHO)
10-26-22	4-Stuttgart	*Fundamentals of Anthroposophical Medicine*, MP, 1986 (FAM)
10-31-22	1-Hague	*The Knowledge of Man's Spiritual Being*, ANS, 10-19-41 (KMSB)
11-01-22	1-Rotterdam	*The Supersensible in the Human Being and in the Universe*, ANS, 7-21-40 (SHBU)
11-03-22	1-Hague	*The Knowledge of the Spiritual Being of the Universe*, ANS, 11-30-41 (KSBU)
11-05-22	1-Hague	*The Concealed Aspects of Human Existence*, AP & RSPC, no pub. date given (CAHE)
11-17-22	2-London	*First Steps in Supersensible Perception/The Relation of Anthroposophy to Christianity*, APC, 1949 (FSSP)
11-19-22	1-London	*Problems of Education and Teaching*, U.E.T. (PET)
11-26-22	12-Dornach	*Man and the World of Stars*, AP, 1963 (MWS)
12-03-22	1-Dornach	*Life of Man in Sleep*, U.E.T. (LMS)
12-04-22	1-Stuttgart	*Memory and Love/Art in its Spiritual Nature*, GB, 1983 (ML)
12-07-22	1-Berlin	*Man's Experience in the Etheric Cosmos*, U.E.T. (MEEC)
12-24-22	9-Dornach	*The Origins of Natural Science*, AP & RSP, 1985 (ONS)

12-30-22	9-Dornach	*Health and Illness*, Vol 2, AP, 1983 (HI-2)
01-01-23	1-Dornach	*RS' Address on Morning After the Fire*, ANS, #10 (FIRE)
01-05-23	1-Dornach	*Man's New Need for the Christ*, U.E.T. (MNNFC)
01-06-23	1-Dornach	*Address to Members at Dornach*, AM, 1-4-31 (ATMD)
01-06-23	1-Dornach	*The Task of Academic Youth*, U.E.T. (TAY)
01-12-23	1-Dornach	*Giordano Bruno, Jacob Boehme, Francis Bacon*, pub. data unclear (BBB)
01-13-23	1-Dornach	*Salt, Mercury, Sulphur*, pub. data unclear (SALTMS)
01-14-23	1-Dornach	*The Search for the World in Man, for Man in the World*, ANS, #2 (SWM)
01-19-23	1-Dornach	*Truth, Beauty and Goodness*, APC & AP, 1927 (TBG)
01-20-23	1-Dornach	*Man and the Nature Spirits*, MP, 1983 (MNS)
01-21-23	1-Dornach	*The Intellectual Fall of Man*, ANS, #2 (IFM)
01-23-23	10-Dornach	*Awakening to Community*, AP, 1974 (ACOM)
01-23-23	1-Dornach	*Reflections After the Burning of the Goetheanum*, AQ, #19 (RABG)
01-26-23	1-Dornach	*Man's Fall and Redemption*, ANS, 5-20-34 (MFR)
01-27-23	1-Dornach	*Realism and Nominalism*, ANS, #2 (RN)
01-28-23	1-Dornach	*Concerning Electricity* (This is attached to front of MULS, 2-12-18), ANS, 6-9-40 (ELEC)
02-02-23	9-Dornach	*Earthly Knowledge and Heavenly Wisdom*, AP, 1991 (EKHW)
02-02-23	1-Dornach	*Self Knowledge and the Christ Experience*, RSP & AP, 1988 (SKCE)
02-03-23	9-Dornach	*Beekeeping*, GBR, 1988 (BEEK)
02-09-23	6-Dornach	*Cosmic Workings in Earth and Man*, RSPC, 1952 (CWEM)
02-10-23	1-Dornach	*The Connection of the Metals with the Planets and their Curative Effects*, U.E.T. (CMPCE)
02-11-23	1-Dornach	*The Invisible Man Within Us: The Pathology Underlying Therapy*, MP, 1987 (IMW)
02-21-23	2-Dornach	*The Nature of Color/Color and the Human Races*, Anthrop. Society, NY, no pub. date given (NC)
03-11-23	7-Dornach	*The Driving Force of Spiritual Powers in World History*, SBC, 1972 (DFSP)
03-25-23	2-Stuttgart	*Education and Art/Education and the Moral Life*, AM Format (EAML)
03-31-23	5-Dornach	*The Cycle of the Year as Breathing-Process of the Earth*, AP, 1984 (CY)

04-06-23	1-Berne	*The Forming of Destiny in Sleeping and Waking*, GB, 1973 (FDSW)
04-09-23	1-Basle	*What was the Purpose of the Goetheanum and What is the Task of Anthroposophy?*, U.E.T. (WPG)
04-13-23	1-Dornach	*The Recovery of the Living Source of Speech*, GB, 1973 (RLSS)
04-14-23	1-Dornach	*Of Thought, Feeling and Will in their Relation to Sleep*, U.E.T. (TFWRS)
04-15-23	1-Dornach	*On the Life of the Soul and its Evolution to Imagination and Inspiration*, U.E.T. (LSEII)
04-15-23	8-Dornach	*The Child's Changing Consciousness and Waldorf Education*, AP & RSP, 1988 (CCC)
04-20-23	3-Dornach	*The Spiritual Development of Man*, U.E.T. (SDM)
04-21-23	4-Dornach	*Concerning the Nature of Christianity/Sleeping and Waking/Life After Death/The Christ Being/The Two Jesus Boys*, U.E.T. (CNC)
04-28-23	2-Prague	*The Waking of the Human Soul and the Forming of Destiny/The Need for Understanding the Christ*, SBC, 1970 (WHSFD)
05-02-23	1-Stuttgart	*The Cosmic Word and Individual Man*, GB, 1951 (CWIM)
05-06-23	1-Dornach	*The Mystery of the Head*, U.E.T. (MH)
05-16-23	6-Christiana	*Man's Being, His Destiny, and World-Evolution*, 3rd Ed., AP, 1984 (MBD)
05-17-23	1-Christiana	*The Christ Mystery in Relation to the Secret of Pentecost*, RSPC, 1927 (CMRP)
05-27-23	8-Various	*The Arts and their Mission*, AP, 1964 (ARTM)
05-30-23	7-Dornach	*Light and Color Effects in Earthly Substances and Celestial Bodies/The Working of the Guardian Angel*, U.E.T. (LCEGA)
06-10-23	8-Dornach	*The Anthroposophic Movement*, RSSP, 1993 (ANMO)
06-21-23	1-Stuttgart	*Life After Death* (Extract), ANS, 1-7-34 (LAD-2)
06-24-23	1-Dornach	*St. John's Tide*, U.E.T. (SJT)
06-28-23	4-Dornach	*Learning to See into the Spiritual World*, AP, 1990 (LSIS)
06-30-23	2-Dornach	*Why an Anthroposophical Art of Education?*, AMLY, 1923 (WAAE)
07-06-23	3-Dornach	*A Review of the Century 1823-1923*, U.E.T. (RC)
07-15-23	1-Dornach	*The Mysteries of the Pleroma: the Corruption of their Influences in Europe and Asia Today*, AQ, #6 (MP)
07-20-23	3-Dornach	*Three Perspectives on Anthroposophy*, U.E.T. (TPA)

07-20-23	3-Dornach	*Rhythms in the Cosmos and in the Human Being,* U.E.T. (RCHB)
07-21-23	1-Dornach	*How Eurhythmy Arises out of Anthroposophy,* AM, 9-9-28 (HEAA)
07-27-23	1-Dornach	*The Spiritual Individualities of the Planets,* GB, 1966 & 1988 (SIP)
08-05-23	14-Ilkley	*A Modern Art of Education* (same cycle but different translation available entitled, *Education and Modern Spiritual Life*), GBR, 1989 (MAE)
08-19-23	13-Penmaen-mawr	*The Evolution of Consciousness* (this is the same cycle as *The Evolution of the World and of Humanity,* but different translation), GBR, 1989 (EVC)
08-22-24	1-Torquay	*Farewell Address—Torquay,* U.E.T. (FAT)
08-24-23	1-Penmaen-mawr	*Concerning Art and its Future Task,* ANS, 1-26-36 (AFT)
08-26-23	1-Penmaen-mawr	*A Lecture on Eurythmy,* 2d Ed., RSP, 1967 (LEUR)
08-28-23	1-Penmen-mawr	*Polarities in Health, Illness and Therapy,* MP, 1987 (PHIT)
09-02-23	1-London	*Man as a Picture of the Living Spirit,* 2d Ed., RSP, 1972 (MPLS)
09-02-23	2-London	*On Therapy and Method in the Manufacture of Medicines* (Two Lectures to Doctors), U.E.T. (TMMM)
09-10-23	1-Dornach	*The Sun-Initiation of the Druid Priest and his Moon-Science* (in MPPF, 9-14-23 below)
09-10-23	1-Dornach	*On the Origin and Meaning of Cults,* U.E.T. (OMC)
09-14-23	3-Stuttgart	*Man in the Past, the Present and the Future/The Evolution of Consciousness,* 2d Ed., RSP, 1982 (MPPF)
09-22-23	1-Dornach	*The World of Dreams as a Bridge Between the Physical World and the World of Moral Ideas,* U.E.T. (WDB)
09-23-23	1-Dornach	*Jacob Boehme, Paracelsus, Swedenborg,* U.E.T. (BPS)
09-27-23	2-Vienna	*Supersensible Knowledge: Anthroposophy as a Demand of the Age/Anthroposophy and the Ethical-Religious Conduct of Life,* AP & RSPC, 1943 (SKADA)
09-27-23	4-Vienna	*Michaelmas and the Soul-Forces of Man,* AP, 1946 (MSF)
Oct 1923	Essay	*On the Life of the Soul,* AP, 1985 (LS)

Oct 1923	Article	*A Fragment from my Visit to England*, AMLY, Oct, 1923 (FVE)
10-05-23	5-Dornach	*The Four Seasons and the Archangels*, 3rd Ed., RSP, 1984 (FSA)
10-08-23	1-Dornach	*On the Nature of Butterflies*, U.E.T. (NB)
10-13-23	1-Dornach	*Man and the Earth in Northern and Southern Regions*, U.E.T. (MENSR)
10-15-23	3-Stuttgart	*Deeper Insights into Education*, AP, 1983 (DIE)
10-19-23	12-Dornach	*Man as Symphony of the Creative Word*, RSP, 1991 (MSCW)
10-20-23	1-Dornach	*The Essential Nature of Hydrogen*, U.E.T. (ENH)
10-24-23	1-Dornach	*The Nature of the Comets*, U.E.T. (NCOM)
10-31-23	1-Dornach	*About the Causes of Infantile Paralysis/About Plant Growth*, U.E.T. (IPPG)
11-12-23	5-Hague	*Supersensible Man*, RSPC & AP, 1945 (SSMAN)
11-16-23	1-Hague	*Spiritual Knowledge: A Way of Life*, GB, #50 (SKWL)
11-23-23	14-Dornach	*Mystery Centers*, GBR, 1989 (MC)
11-25-23	Article	*A Foreboding of Our Time—Fifty Years Ago*, AMLY, Dec, 1923 (FOTF)
12-02-23	Article	*The Spiritual is "Forgotten" by the Ordinary Consciousness; It can be Remembered Again*, AMLY, Mar, 1924 (SFOC)
12-08-23	Periodical	*The Course of My Life*, AP, 1951 (CML)
12-24-23	*-Dornach	*The Christmas Conference*, AP, 1990 (CConf)
12-24-23	9-Dornach	*World History in the Light of Anthroposophy*, 2d Ed., RSP, 1977 (WH)
12-25-23	1-Dornach	*The Foundation of the Anthroposophical Society*, RSPC, 1942 (FAS)
12-31-23	3-Dornach	*Practicing Physicians, Three Lectures to*, U.E.T. (PP)
1924	*-Dornach	*The Constitution of the School of Spiritual Science*, London, Anthrop. Soc. in Gr. Br., 1964 (CSSS)
01-02-24	8-Dornach	*Christmas Course for Medical Students*, U.E.T. (CCMS)
01-04-24	6-Dornach	*Rosicrucianism and Modern Initiation*, RSP, 1982 (RMI)
01-13-24	18-Dornach	*The Life, Nature and Cultivation of Anthroposophy*, London, Anthrop. Soc. in Gr. Br., 1963 (LNCA)
01-17-24	1-Koberwitz	*Youth's Search in Nature*, MP, 1984 (YSN)
01-19-24	9-Dornach	*Anthroposophy and the Inner Life*, RSP, 1992 (AIL)
01-21-24	1-Dornach	*The Tasks of the 'Group at the Goetheanum'*, AM, 4-1-28 (TGG)

01-25-24	9-Various	*Karmic Relationships,* Vol 6, 2d Ed., RSP, 1989 (KR-6)
01-25-24	2-Berne	*Esoteric Studies—Karmic and Cosmic Connections/ The Gate of the Moon and the Gate of the Sun/ The Working of the Individuality Through the Evolution of History,* U.E.T. (KCC)
02-02-24	1-Dornach	*The Human Eye and Albinism,* U.E.T. (HEA)
02-06-24	1-Stuttgart	*The Significance of the Heavenly Bodies Around the Earth for the Life and Existence of Man,* U.E.T. (SHBAE)
02-09-24	1-Dornach	*The Circulation of Fluids in the Earth,* no pub. data given (CFE)
02-16-24	12-Dornach	*Karmic Relationships,* Vol 1, 2d Ed., RSP, 1972 (KR-1)
02-17-24	Letters	*Anthroposophical Leading Thoughts,* RSP, 1973 (ALT)
02-19-24	8-Dornach	*Eurythmy as Visible Song,* APC & AP, 1932 (EVSG)
03-01-24	3-Dornach	*Effects of the Atmosphere of Graveyards upon the Human Being/Views of Life among the Ancient Indians, Egyptians, Babylonians and Hebrews/ On the Forming of Scars/Excavation of Mummies/The Tree of the Sefirot,* U.E.T. (GSS)
03-05-24	1-Dornach	*The Birth of Christianity/ Christianity and the Mysteries of Antiquity,* RSPC, 1950 (BCCMA)
03-13-24	1-Dornach	*Star Wisdom, Moon Religion, Sun Religion/The Easter Festival and its Background,* RSPC, 1950 (SWMR)
03-15-24	3-Dornach	*The Spread of Christianity in Europe,* U.E.T. (SCE)
03-29-24	7-Various	*Karmic Relationships,* Vol 5, 2d Ed., RSP, 1984 (KR-5)
04-06-24	16-Dornach	*Karmic Relationships,* Vol 2, 2d Ed., RSP, 1974 (KR-2)
04-08-24	5-Stuttgart	*The Essentials of Education,* RSP, 1968 (EE)
04-13-24	5-Stuttgart	*The Roots of Education,* AP, 1978 (RED)
04-19-24	4-Dornach	*The Easter Festival in the Evolution of the Mysteries,* AP & RSP, 1988 (EFEM)
04-21-24	5-Dornach	*Easter Course for Medical Students,* U.E.T. (ECMS)
05-03-24	1-Dornach	*Edith Maryon's Death,* From a Lecture by R.S. on the Occasion of, AM, 3-11-28 (EMD)
05-14-24	1-Dornach	*The Starry Heavens and the Connection of Man with the Hierarchies* (*Philosophers of Recent Times,* Lect. 1), U.E.T. (SHCMH)

05-17-24	1-Dornach	*Concerning Comets and Solar-System, the Zodiac and the other Fixed Stars* (*Philosophers of Recent Times,* Lect 2), U.E.T. (CSSZ)
05-20-24	2-Dornach	*Asia and Europe/Ancient Knowledge and Cults,* U.E.T. (AEAKC)
05-25-24	1-Paris	*Address on the Occasion of the Annual Meeting of the Anthrop. Soc. in Paris,* U.E.T. (PARIS)
05-27-24	1-Paris	*Food Question,* Lecture on the, U.E.T. (FQ-2)
06-01-24	1-Stuttgart	*The Forming of Karma During the Life after Death/* (*Schiller, Goethe, Heine, Eliphas Levi*), U.E.T. (FKDLD)
06-07-24	9-Breslau	*Karmic Relationships,* Vol 7, RSP, 1973 (KR-7)
06-07-24	8-Koberwitz	*Agriculture, Spiritual Foundations for the Renewal of,* KBDF, 1993 (AGRIC)
06-09-24	1-Breslau	*Youth in an Age of Light,* GB, 1976 (YAL)
06-20-24	1-Dornach	Lecture—*Account of Conference at Koberwitz,* U.E.T. (KOB)
06-24-24	15-Dornach	*Eurythmy as Visible Speech,* APC & AP, 1932 (EVS)
06-25-24	12-Dornach	*Curative Education,* RSP, 1972 (CED)
06-25-24	1-Dornach	*Man and the Hierarchies/The Passing of the Old Knowledge/Concerning the "Philosophy of Spiritual Activity"* (*Philosophers of Recent Times,* Lect. 3), U.E.T. (MHPOK)
06-30-24	14-Dornach	*The Evolution of the Earth and Man,* AP & RSP, 1987 (EVEM)
07-01-24	11-Dornach	*Karmic Relationships,* Vol 3, 2d Ed., RSP, 1957 (KR-3)
07-17-24	9-Arnheim	*Human Values in Education,* RSP, 1971 (HVE)
07-17-24	3-Arnheim	*What Can the Art of Healing Learn Through Spiritual Science?,* MP, 1986 (WCAH)
07-20-24	1-Arnhem	*A Talk to Young People,* MP, 1992 (TYP)
07-31-24	2-Dornach	*Nutrition and Health,* AP & RSP, 1987 (NH)
08-11-24	11-Torquay	*True and False Paths in Spiritual Investigation,* 3rd Ed., RSP & AP, 1985 (TFP)
08-12-24	6-England	*Karmic Relationships,* Vol 8, RSP, 1975 (KR-8)
08-12-24	7-Torquay	*The Kingdom of Childhood,* 2d Ed., AP, 1988 (KC)
08-17-24	29-Weekly News Sheet	*The Michael Mystery,* Spring Valley, NY, St. George Pub., 1984 (MICHM)
08-28-24	1-London	*An Outline of Anthroposophical Medical Research,* London, Weleda Co. & Amer. Arlesheim Labs, no pub. date given (OAMR)
09-05-24	10-Dornach	*Karmic Relationships,* Vol 4, 2d Ed., RSP, 1983 (KR-4)

09-05-24	19-Dornach	*Speech and Drama*, AP & RSP, 1959 (SD)
09-05-24	18-Dornach	*The Apocalypse* (given privately to priests of The Christian Community), U.E.T. (APOC-CC)
09-08-24	11-Dornach	*Pastoral Medicine*, AP, 1987 (PM)
09-27-24	1-Dornach	*The Last Address*, RSP, 1967 (LAST)
1925	Book	*Fundamentals of Therapy*, 4th Ed., RSP, 1983 (FOT)

Anthologies

(AEL)   *Anthroposophy in Everyday Life*, AP, 1995

(ARCHM)   *The Archangel Michael/His Mission and Ours*, AP, 1994

(CD)   *Correspondence and Documents*, 1901-1925, RSP & AP, 1988

(CRA)   *A Christian Rosenkreutz Anthology*, GBR, 1981

(CRSP)   *Creative Speech*, RSP, 1978

(ESSS)   *The Essential Steiner*, NY, HarperCollins, Ed. McDermott, 1984

(NS)   *Nutrition and Stimulants*, KBDF, 1991

(RSVL)   *Rudolf Steiner's Vision of Love*, RSP, 1994

(RSWS)   *Rudolf Steiner in the Waldorf School*, AP, 1996

(SRMR)   *Spiritual Research: Methods and Results*, RSPB, 1981

(TWW)   *Truth-Wrought-Words*, AP, 1979

(VM)   *Verses and Meditations*, RSP, 1993

(WARK)   *A Western Approach to Reincarnation and Karma*, AP, Ed. Querido, 1997

(WEA)   *West-East Aphorisms* (from TEW), MP, no pub. date given

(WEDA)   *Waldorf Education and Anthroposophy*, AP, 1996

(WEEB)   *World Ether/Elemental Beings/Kingdoms of Nature*, MP, 1993

Steiner Biographies

Autobiographies are found in Steiner Writings above: especially *The Course of My Life* (CML).

Wachsmuth, *The Life and Work of Rudolf Steiner* (From the Turn of the Century Until His Death), GBR, 1989 (LWRS)

Easton, *Rudolf Steiner: Herald of a New Epoch*, AP, 1980 (RSHNE)

Shepherd, *Rudolf Steiner, Scientist of the Invisible*, Rochester, VT, Inner Traditions International, 1954 (RSSI)

Rittelmeyer, *Rudolf Steiner Enters My Life*, FB, 1963 (RSEL)

Lissau, *Rudolf Steiner; Life, Work, Inner Path and Social Initiatives*, Stroud, UK, Hawthorn Press, 1987 (RSLW)

Davy, *Rudolf Steiner, A Sketch of His Life and Work*, a four-page pamphlet available free from AP upon request (RSSLW)

Prokofieff, *Rudolf Steiner and the Founding of the New Mysteries*, RSP & AP, 1986 (RSFNM)

Kirchner-Bockholt, *Rudolf Steiner's Mission and Ita Wegman*, privately printed by RSP, 1977 for Members of the Anthroposophical Society (RSMW)

A Collection, *A Man Before Others, Rudolf Steiner Remembered*, RSP, 1993 (MBO)

Childs, *Rudolf Steiner: his Life and Work*, AP, 1995 (RSLW-2)

For the student more seriously interested in Steiner's biography, the Rudolf Steiner Library (RD 2, Box 215, Ghent, NY 12075), as one of its numerous catalogues, publishes one on Steiner's "Biographies, Work, Remembrances." From the one updated March 28, 1994, I prepared the following tabulation of listings thereunder, indicative of its scope:

	No. of Titles		
Category	German	English	Total
Biographies	19	8	27
Work	24	12	36
Remembrances, etc.	45	13	58
Total	88	33	121

The catalogue contains a total of fourteen pages, of which those in such tabulation occupy only the first seven pages. The last seven pages consist of "Articles (A Partial Listing)." Most of the biographical titles otherwise previously listed above are included in the above tabulation.

Other Anthroposophical Writers:

AAC   Leroi, *Anthroposophical Approach to Cancer*, MP, 1982

AAM-1   Husemann/Wolff, *The Anthroposophical Approach to Medicine, Vol. 1*, AP, 1982

AAM-2   Husemann/Wolff, *The Anthroposophical Approach to Medicine, Vol. 2*, AP, 1987

AAM-3   Husemann/Wolff, *The Anthroposophical Approach to Medicine, Vol. 3*, AP, 1989

AOMR   Wolff, *Anthroposophically-Oriented Medicine and its Remedies*, MP, 1991

ApSJn	Bock, *The Apocalypse of Saint John*, FB, 1957
ASAJ	Tomberg, *Anthroposophical Studies of the Apocalypse of Saint John*, 2d Ed., Spring Valley, NY, Candeur Manuscripts, 1985
ASOT	Tomberg, *Anthroposophical Studies of the Old Testament*, 2d Ed., Spring Valley, NY, Candeur Manuscripts, 1985
ASNT	Tomberg, *Anthroposophical Studies of the New Testament*, 2d Ed., Spring Valley, NY, Candeur Manuscripts, 1985
BATNC	Poppelbaum, *The Battle for a New Consciousness*, MP, 1993
BATSO	Lievegoed, *The Battle for the Soul*, Stroud, Glos., UK, Hawthorn Press, 1994
BC	Welburn, *The Beginnings of Christianity*, FB, 1991
BFS	Welburn, *The Book with Fourteen Seals*, RSP, 1991
BQ-1	Vreede/Frensch, *The Bodhisattva Question*, Monsey, NY, Candeur Manuscripts, 1989
BQ-2	Vreede/Meyer, *The Bodhisattva Question*, TLP 1993
BQ-3	Arenson, *Fruits of Earnest Study of the Lectures of Rudolf Steiner*, pub. data not available; contact Rudolf Steiner Library
BUL	Matthews, *The Bible/Unclaimed Legacy*, FB, 1981
CAFS	Powell, *Cosmic Aspects of the Foundation Stone*, Great Barrington, MA, Golden Stone Press, 1990
CaR	Frieling, *Christianity and Reincarnation*, FB, 1977
CHA	Powell, *Christian Hermetic Astrology*, Great Barrington, MA, Golden Stone Press, 1991
CLC	Powell, *Chronicle of the Living Christ*, AP, 1996
CMHm	Lorenz, *Cancer: A Mandate to Humanity*, MP, 1982
CoH	Tomberg, *Covenant of the Heart*, Rockport, MA, 1992
CONT	Capel/Dowuona, *Christ in the Old and New Testaments*, TLP, 1989
COSC	Sucher, *Cosmic Christianity / The Changing Countenance of Cosmology*, AP, 1985
CSC	Powell, *Christian Star Calendar*, North Vancouver, B.C., Suncross Press, pub. annually in Nov.
CYPI	Prokofieff, *The Cycle of the Year as a Path of Initiation*, TLP, 1991
DSHW	Powell (Anony.), *Divine Sophia, Holy Wisdom*, Nicasio, CA, Sophia Foundation of N. Amer., 1995
EB	Wolff, *The Etheric Body*, MP, 1990
EBWE	Querido, *The Esoteric Background of Waldorf Education*, Fair Oaks, CA, Rudolf Steiner College Press, 1995
EI	Prokofieff, *Eternal Individuality*, TLP, 1992
ELWAY	Prokofieff, *The East in the Light of the West, Part I: Agni Yoga*, TLP, 1993
ES	McDermott, *The Essential Steiner*, NY, HarperCollins, 1984
EUR	Seddon, *Europa, A Spiritual Biography*, TLP, 1995

EVM   Wachsmuth, *The Evolution of Mankind*, Dornach, Philosophic-
              Anthroposophic Press, 1961
FCC   Archiati, *From Christianity to Christ*, TLP, 1996
FSCace   Tomberg, *The Four Sacrifices of Christ and the Appearance of Christ
              in the Etheric*, Spring Valley, NY, Candeur Manuscripts, 1983
GAC   Querido, *The Golden Age of Chartres*, FB & AP, 1987
GNOS   Welburn, *Gnosis*, FB, 1994
GNSS   Bock, *Genesis*, FB, 1978
GWr   Adey, *G. S. Lewis' "Great War" with Owen Barfield*, University of
              Victoria, B.C., 1978
HA1   Powell, *Hermetic Astrology I*, Kinsau, W. Germany, Hermetika,
              1987
HA2   Powell, *Hermetic Astrology II*, Kinsau, W. Germany, Hermetika,
              1989
HNSS   Novalis, *Hymns to the Night/Spiritual Songs*, TLP, 1992
HoP   Powell, *History of the Planets*, San Diego, ACS Publications, 1988
HSBA   Prokofieff, *The Heavenly Sophia and the Being Anthroposophia*,
              TLP, 1996.
IB   Various, *The Image of Blood*, GB 48, 1996
IDEV   Tomberg, *Inner Development*, AP, 1992
IZOD   Julius, *The Imagery of the Zodiac*, FB, 1994
KPr   Bock, *Kings and Prophets*, FB, 1989
LWRS   Wachsmuth, *The Life and Work of Rudolf Steiner*, Garber, 1989
MAA   Poppelbaum, *Man and Animal*, London, Anthoposophical
              Publishing Co. & AP, 1931
MBO   Various, *A Man Before Others*, RSP, 1993
MEMY   Holtzaptel, *Medicine and Mysteries*, MP, 1994
MHG   Querido, *The Mystery of the Holy Grail*, Fair Oaks, CA, Rudolf
              Steiner College Publications, 1991
MHT   Powell, *Most Holy Trinosophia*, Great Barrington, MA, Golden
              Stone Press, 1994
MMBSS   Bock, *The Mystery of Mary—In Body, Soul and Spirit*, GB, date
              not available
MOS   Bock, *Moses*, NY, Inner Traditions International, 1986
MOT   Anonymous (V.T.), *Meditations on the Tarot*, Rockport, MA,
              Element, 1985
MSZ   Davidson, *Making Sense of the Zodiac*, NEWS, Winter, 1992
NEOA   Unger, *On Nuclear Energy and the Occult Atom*, AP, 1982
NEWS   Anthroposophical Society in America, *Newsletter*, Quarterly by
              the Society
OMW   Colum, *Orpheus, Myths of the World*, FB, 1991 (first pub. 1930 by
              McMillan, NY)
OSF   Prokofieff, *The Occult Significance of Forgiveness*, 2d Ed., TLP, 1992

PRE	Prokofieff, *Prophecy of the Russian Epic*, TLP, 1993
RCN	Rittelmeyer, *Reincarnation*, FB, 1988 (orig. 1933)
RMC	Harwood, *The Recovery of Man in Childhood*, NY, Myrin Institute 1958
RSEL	Rittelmeyer, *Rudolf Steiner Enters My Life*, FB, 1929
RSFNM	Prokofieff, *Rudolf Steiner and the Founding of the New Mysteries*, RSP & AP, 1986
RSHNE	Easton, *Rudolf Steiner: Herald of a New Epoch*, AP, 1980
RSIP-BA	"Rudolf Steiner's Ideas in Practice," Schilthuis, *Biodynamic Agriculture*, AP, 1994
RSIP-CSN	"Rudolf Steiner's Ideas in Practice," Luxford, *Children with Special Needs*, AP, 1994
RSIP-LA	"Rudolf Steiner's Ideas in Practice," Bayes, *Living Architecture*, AP 1994
RSIP-RC	"Rudolf Steiner's Ideas in Practice," Hindes, *Renewing Christianity*, AP, 1995
RSLW	Lissau, *Rudolf Steiner—Life, Work, Inner Path and Social Initiatives*, London, Hawthorn Press, 1987
RSLW-2	Childs, *Rudolf Steiner: his Life and Work*, AP, 1995
RSMW	Kirchner-Bockholt, *Rudolf Steiner's Mission and Ita Wegman*, RSP, 1977
RSRKMA	Prokofieff, *Rudolf Steiner's Research into Karma and the Mission of the Anthroposophical Society*, TLP, 1995
RSSI	Shepherd, *Rudolf Steiner: Scientist of the Invisible*, Rochester, VT, Inner Traditions International, 1983
RSSLW	Davy, *Rudolf Steiner, A Sketch of His Life and Work*, a four-page pamphlet available from AP upon request
SCH	Schwenk, *Sensitive Chaos*, RSP, 1965
SKY	Davidson, *Sky Phenomena*, Hudson, NY, Lindisfarne Press, 1993
SN	Stebbing, *The Secrets of Numbers*, Sussex, UK, New Knowledge Books, 1963
SOEE	Prokofieff, *The Spiritual Origins of Eastern Europe and the Future Mysteries of the Holy Grail*, TLP, 1993
SP	Bock, *Saint Paul*, FB, 1993
SZ	Powell, *The Sidereal Zodiac*, Tempe, AZ, American Federation of Astrologers, 1979
THNS	Prokofieff, *The Twelve Holy Nights and the Spiritual Hierarchies*, TLP, 1988
TY	Bock, *The Three Years*, FB, 1955
VL	Edwards, *The Vortex of Life*, FB, 1993
WHAS	Anthroposophical Society, *What is Happening in the Anthroposophical Society*, Bi-Monthly by the Society
WWIW	Emmichoven, *Who Was Ita Wegman; A Documentation, Vol. I— 1876 until 1925*, MP, 1995

Non-Anthroposophical Writers:

AAW   Donnelly, *Atlantis, The Antediluvian World*, NY, Gramercy Pub. Co., 1985
BOTR   M and L, *The Bridge Over the River*, AP, 1974
CcC   Fox, *The Coming of the Cosmic Christ*, NY, Harper & Row, 1988
CRIT   Plato, *Critias*, see 7 GB 442 under "Treatises and Other Reference Materials" below
DCOM   Dante, *Divine Comedy*, see 21 GB under "Treatises and Other Reference Materials" Below
EPOP   Girard, *Esotericism of the Popol Vuh*, Pasadena, Theosophical University Press, 1979
EWP   Frost & Prechter, *Elliott Wave Principle*, 6th Ed., Gainesville, GA, New Classics Library, 1990
FLd   Abbott, *Flatland*, Princeton, NJ, Princeton Univ. Press, 1991
FRAC   Lauwerier, *Fractals*, Princeton, NJ, Princeton Univ. Press, 1991
FWH   Courlander, *The Fourth World of the Hopis*, Albuquerque, University of New Mexico Press, 1971
FTSL   Goethe, *Fairy Tale of the Green Snake and the Beautiful Lily*, Garber, 1991
GI   Schuré, *The Great Initiates,* NY, Harper & Row, by authority of RSPB, 1961
GMR   Malina, *On the Genre and Message of Revelation: Star Visions and Sky Journeys*, Peabody, MA, Hendrickson, 1995
LAKM   Walker/Jahner, *Lakota Myth*, Lincoln, University of Nebraska Press, 1983
PHEN   de Chardin, *The Phenomenon of Man*, NY, Harper & Row, 1965
POP   Tedlock, *Popol Vuh*, NY, Simon & Schuster, Rev. Ed. 1996
RCM   Clement, *The Roots of Christian Mysticism*, NY, New York City Press, 1995
SCAL   Carolan, *The Spiral Calendar*, Gainesville, GA, New Classics Library, 1992
SHAD   Penrose, *Shadows of the Mind*, NY, Oxford Univ. Press, 1994
TEO   Schonfield, *The Essene Odyssey*, Rockport, MA, Element, 1984
TIM   Plato, *Timaeus*, see 7 GB 478 under "Treatises and Other Reference Materials" below

Treatises and Other Reference Materials:

AB   *Anchor Bible*, NY, Doubleday, dates for individual volumes vary
ABD   *Anchor Bible Dictionary*, NY, Doubleday, 1992
ABRL   *Anchor Bible Reference Library*, NY, Doubleday, dates for individual volumes vary
ALB   *Archaeology of the Land of the Bible*, NY, Doubleday, 1990 (part of ABRL)

AMPB   *Amplified Bible*, Grand Rapids, Zondervan Pub. Co., 1965
Barc   Barclay, Philadelphia, Westminster Press, N.T. volumes are rev. eds., dates vary for different volumes, N.T. being generally in 1975-1976
Brit   *Encyclopaedia Britannica*, Chicago, Encyclopaedia Britannica, 1992
CEV   *Contemporary English Version* (of the Bible), NY, American Bible Society, 1995
EBE   *The Ethiopic Book of Enoch*, Vol. 2, Michael A. Knibb, NY, Oxford Univ. Press, 1978
GB   *Britannica Great Books*, Chicago, Encyclopaedia Britannica, 1952
GEL   Liddell and Scott, *Greek-English Lexicon*, 9th Ed., Oxford Univ. Press, 1940, with rev. supp., 1996
HEL   Brown-Driver-Briggs, *Hebrew and English Lexicon*, Peabody, MA, Hendrickson, 1906
Interp   *Interpreter's Bible*, Nashville, Abingdon Press, 1951-1957
INTPN   *Interpretation*, A Bible Commentary for Teaching and Preaching, Atlanta, John Knox Press, dates for individual volumes vary
JDSS   Charlesworth, *Jesus and the Dead Sea Scrolls*, NY, Doubleday, 1993 (part of ABRL)
JOSEPHUS   *The Works of Josephus*, Complete and Unabridged, New Updated Ed., Peabody, MA, Hendrickson, 1987
KJV   *King James Version* (of the Bible), Nashville, Thomas Nelson Pub., 1984
KJV/NIV–INT   Marshall, *The Interlinear KJV-NIV Parallel New Testament in Greek and English*, Grand Rapids, Zondervan Pub. House, 1975
LB   *Living Bible*, Wheaton, IL, Tyndale House Pub., 1971
LJC   Anne Catherine Emmerich, *The Life of Jesus Christ and Biblical Revelations*, Rockford, IL, TAN Books, 1986
MWCD   *Merriam-Webster's Collegiate Dictionary*, 10th Ed., Springfield, MA, Merriam-Webster, Inc., 1996
NACB   *New American Catholic Bible*, Nashville, Thomas Nelson Pub., 1971
NEB   *New English Bible*, as contained in "The New Testament in Four Versions, NY, Iversen-Ford Associates, 1963
NGAW   *National Geographic Atlas of the World*, 5th Ed., Washington, D.C., National Geographic Society, 1981
NHL   Robinson, *The Nag Hammadi Library*, NY, Harper & Row, 1978
NIB   *The New Interpreter's Bible*, Nashville, Abingdon, dates for individual volumes vary from 1994 et seq
NICENE-1   *Ante-Nicene Fathers* (Vols 1-10), Peabody, MA, Hendrickson, 1994
NICENE-2   *Nicene and Post-Nicene Fathers*, Series 1 (Vols 1- 14), Peabody, MA, Hendrickson, 1994

NICENE-3   *Nicene and Post-Nicene Fathers*, Series 2 (Vols 1- 14), Peabody, MA, Hendrickson, 1994

NICNT   *New International Commentary on the New Testament*, Grand Rapids, William B. Eerdmans Pub. Co., dates for individual volumes vary

NIV   *The New NIV (New International Version) Study Bible*, Grand Rapids, Zondervan Pub. House, 1985

NJB   *New Jerusalem Bible*, NY, Doubleday, 1985

NKJV   *New King James Version* (of the Bible), Nashville, Thomas Nelson Pub., 1982

NRSV   *New Revised Standard Version* (of the Bible), Nashville, Thomas Nelson Pub. for Cokesbury, 1990

OAA   *The Oxford Annotated Apocrypha*, Expanded Ed. RSV, NY, Oxford Univ. Press, 1977

PHILO   *The Works of Philo*, Complete and Unabridged, New Updated Ed., Peabody, MA, Hendrickson, 1993

PMEB   *Phillips Modern English Bible*, as contained in "The New Testament in Four Versions," NY, Iversen-Ford Associates, 1963

PSEUD   Luibheid (Trans), *Pseudo-Dionysius*, Mahwah, NJ, Paulist Press, 1987

RoC   Frend, *The Rise of Christianity*, Philadelphia, Fortress Press, 1984

REVTD   Efird, *Revelation for Today*, Nashville, Abingdon, 1989

RHCD   *Random House College Dictionary*, Rev. Ed., NY, Random House, 1988

RSV   *Revised Standard Version* (of the Bible), Nashville, Thomas Nelson Pub., 1972

RSWE   *Rudolf Steiner's Works in English*, Jacques Goldman, Sydney, 1993

TORAH   *The JPS Torah Commentary*, Philadelphia, Jewish Publication Society, dates for individual volumes vary from 1989 to 1996

WNWD   *Webster's New World Dictionary*, 2d Coll. Ed., NY, Simon & Schuster, NY, 1982

ZC   *Zondervan NIV Bible Commentary*, Grand Rapids, Zondervan Pub. House, 1994

INDEX 1

Index of Scriptures Cited

6,9-13	20,35,182,216,336,362,398,511,653
6,10	256,298,299,310
6,11	245,354
6,11-12	356
6,11-13	182,196
6,12-13	343
6,13	291,292
7,14	66-67
8,6	442
8,19	65
9,2	427
9,2-7	69
9,6	154,207
9,17	389
10,2	389
10,17	285
11,1	451
11,1-4	207
11,1-9	676
11,6-9	207
11,4	279
11,6d	268
11,12	472
17,10	480
18,3	393,398
20,2-4	407
20,4	405
23,13	111
27,13	393
28,16	405
29,9-14	261
29,9-14,18	307
29,10	139
29,19	279
30,8	308
30,20-21	355
34,16	307
40-48	348
40-55	451,455
40-66	348
40,2b	271
40,3	136,270,271,274
40,4	207
40,6-8	112
40,31	518
41-52	260,261-265
41-66	261-266

	9,13	111
	11,1	533
Joel		613
	2,1,15	393
	2,10,31	193
	3,15	193
Amos		360,364,613
	1,3	364
	1,6	364
	1,9	359,364
	1,11	364
	1,13	364
	2,1	364
	2,2	393
	2,4	364
	2,6	364
	2,10	364
	2,11	364
	2,12	364
	2,16	408
	3,6	364,393
	3,7	365
Obad		613
	1,4	518
Jon		4,118,317,318,319,320,324,325,613
	3,3	312,324,445
Mic		613
	1,8	408,410
	1,11	410
	3,4	354
	3,4-7	356
	3,5-7	139
Nah		613
	3,5	410
Hab		613
	1,12	480
Zeph		613
	1,15-16	399,400
	1,16	393
	3,4	139
Hag		613
Zech		613
	6,10	451
	6,12	451
	7,10	390
	9,9	342
	9,14	393,399

INDEX 2

Index of Subjects from "Terms & Phrases"

three bodies, spiritual
   counterparts, 401
three states, 414
human body
   avatars' descents into, 94
   physical, etheric, astral, 9
   resurrected to Phantom form, 214
human consciousness, evolution the
   message of the Bible, 474
human creation, 332
human development
   guided by Mysteries, 334
   a new incarnation, 91
   preserved, 88
   zodiacal influence, 121
human intelligence, changes, 11
human memory, changes, 11
human procreative act, 45
human procreative act, embryonic
   consciousness, 46
human reproduction, ends, 190
human sexual development, 19
human sexuality, androgynous beings,
   467
human sexuality, division of sexes,
   334, 465
human state, final, atma, 414

I

I Am, 34
   connection to the burning bush,
     286
   dual aspect of name, 247
   Ego in transition, 246
   housed in the temple, 330
   in human Ego, 268
   identified as Christ, 246, 266
   in Isaiah, 255, 260
   the name of God, 276
   name for God, 252
   Oriental meditation, 268
   overcomes weaknesses of three
     bodies, 450
   reference to Christ, 246

   similarity to "here am I", 258
   synonymous with Yahweh, 270
   union of higher and lower, 284
incarnation
   of Christ, 283
   as unity, 284
Individuality, 130
   death, 131
   Elijah, 375
   and personality, 9, 146
   see Ego
Initiates
   Jacob, Moses, Jonah, 319
   two kinds, 318
initiation
   into the Mysteries, 329
   of Lazarus by Jesus, 315
   meaning to the Mysteries, 312
   new process in Christ, 315
   for perception into spiritual world,
     313
   procedure, 317
   process, 313
initiation, process of becoming
   fatherless, 368
   reorganization of astral body, 314
initiation, reorganization of astral
   body, death-like sleep, 314
initiation, paternal elements, 368
   spoken of as "hidden", 352
Isaac, 530
Isaiah, mandate quoted in Gospels, 2

J

Jacob, initiated into the Mysteries,
   319
Jacob, sons reflect signs of the Zodiac,
   527
James
   appearances with Peter and John,
     474
   brother of Jesus, 481
   uncertainty of identity, 480
Jereboam, son of a widow, 372